The Struggle

for

American Independence

By

Sydney George Fisher

Author of " The Making of Pennsylvania," " Men, Women, and Manners
in Colonial Times," " The True Benjamin
Franklin," etc.

ILLUSTRATED

Vol. I.

Philadelphia & London

J. B. Lippincott Company

1908

GENERAL

PREFACE

The present work is a continuation and enlargement of "The True History of the American Revolution," published some years ago in one volume. That work, while being a brief general account of the contest, dwelt more particularly on certain phases of the struggle which had been omitted or ignored by the historians. It soon became obvious that it did not go far enough, that the original plan should be extended and carried out in more detail, and that the whole mass of original evidence in libraries and historical societies should be made accessible, and revealed to the public in as complete a manner as possible. Our people have little or no conception of what the Revolution really was, no conception of the nature of the original evidence; and the unwillingness of our writers of general histories to cite that evidence keeps it a sealed book to the public.

Our national feeling is bound up in the Revolution, and the extreme importance of such an event, which was the foundation of our nationality and of the political and social principles by which we are still guided, seems to deserve all the light that it is possible to obtain. We naturally want to know the origin of our political existence and exactly why and how we broke away from that great empire which since then has never allowed another dependency to escape, which has reduced republics to colonies, and brought into subjection innumerable peoples and races, and whose rule, we are told, is an unmixed blessing, far preferable to independence.

Although our Revolution is said to have changed the thought of the world, like the epochs of Socrates, of Christ, of the Reformation, and of the French Revolution, yet no complete history of it has ever been written upon the plan of dealing frankly with all the contemporary evidence and withholding

v

nothing of importance that is found in the original records. Our histories are able rhetorical efforts, enlarged Fourth-of-July orations, or pleasing literary essays on selected phases of the contest. There has been no serious attempt to marshal all the original sources of information and reveal them to the reader, as has been done for the history of England, of France, and of other countries.

Our writers ignore the position of the loyalists and their terrible conflict with the patriots, whom they almost equalled in numbers. They have failed to describe the methods by which the loyalists were subdued, which amounted to another war in addition to that carried on by Washington against the British army. They ignore the controversy over General Howe's methods of carrying out his instructions from the British Ministry, the investigation of those methods by a Parliamentary inquiry, and Howe's defense of himself. They ignore the Clinton-Cornwallis controversy, without a knowledge of which it is impossible to understand the strategy of the last three years of the war, as it is impossible to understand the first three years without a knowledge of the Howe controversy.

There is no general history of the Revolution from which one can obtain an intelligent understanding of the Navigation and Trade Laws, and the part they played in the contest; of the smuggling in defiance of them, and the nature of the controversy over the writs of assistance that were issued to stop the smuggling. There is no history which tells us what became of the navigation and trade laws and the writs of assistance after our Revolution, whether they were continued in force among Great Britain's remaining colonies, or when they were repealed, and what were the reasons for the repeal.

Indeed, the effect of our Revolution on Great Britain's colonial policy never seems to have been honored with any serious investigation. We seek in vain to learn from the histories how England governed her colonies for half a century after our separation, what lessons she learned from our Revolution, and in what respects her present policy differs from or resembles the policy against which we rebelled.

PREFACE

I have never seen any attempt to describe, from the original records, England's exact position with regard to ourselves at the outbreak of the Revolution, except the usual assumption that the Tory statesmen who were in power were either ignorantly stupid, and blind to their own interests, or desperately corrupt and wicked, and that the Whig minority were angels of light who would have saved the colonies for the British empire.

According to this assumption, the contest was one of extreme virtue on one side against extreme vice of every sort on the other; and if the good Whigs had had their way we should still be innocent, loyal colonies, as Canada and Australia are supposed to be, happy in their lack of dangerous and tumultuous independence. Why this should be regarded by our historians as a desirable result of the Revolution, and why their attempts to show that we wanted to remain in the British empire should be considered patriotic I have never been able to understand.

There is no general history of the Revolution that gives any adequate description of the twelve or thirteen acts of Parliament the patriot colonists wished repealed; or a full explanation of why they wished them repealed. There is no account of the full meaning of their requirement that Great Britain should keep no troops and build no fortification in a colony, except by the consent of that colony.

All these subjects were very familiar ones to the people of those days; but, for want of adequate description, they are as unknown to modern readers of history as are the conciliatory measures Great Britain adopted, her gentle and mild efforts to persuade us to remain in the empire; and we must not obscure or ignore these measures because they do not show the British Government to have been stupid and tyrannical.

All these topics are of such interest and importance, that it is strange that they have always been left to persons who were unable or unwilling to reveal them. Our great masters of historic method and research, Prescott, Motley, and Parkman, never attempted to write the history of the Revolution.

They sought a field for their genius in describing the conquest and plunder of the native races of Mexico and Peru, the successful resistance of Protestant thrift and heroism in the Netherlands, the romantic adventures of Jesuit missionaries, and the French and Indian wars of Canada.

Why they considered the Revolution uninteresting, or unworthy of their genius, we shall perhaps never know. It may have been that they had the feeling, so common in their time among the educated classes, and by no means yet extinguished, that our annals were essentially dull and commonplace, incapable of any high order of literary use. They may have thought that the Revolution was too much involved with the rights of man and levelling principles of plebeian advancement, and too little connected with the splendor of monarchs and conquerors. It may have seemed to them too full of economic theories of trade, too dependent on legal and constitutional principles, leading too surely to the dead level of general prosperity, and a colorless triumph of the masses over princes and aristocracies.

Or, possibly, they may have inferred, from the histories published in their time, that no account of the Revolution would be acceptable that was not written in rhetorical or partisan language; that freedom of research and candid discussion were neither expected nor desired; and that events must be omitted or manipulated so as to subserve some definite moral purpose, as in the Reverend Mr. Weems' "Life of Washington."

The Weems lives of Washington, Franklin and Marion, beginning in 1800 and passing through over forty editions; Botta's history, a very complete partisan statement, the basis of many modern histories, of great popularity from 1809 to about 1850 and passing through ten editions in America and twenty in Europe, were in their way very valuable sources of information. But, like Bancroft's laborious pages and Hildreth's colorless chronicle, which succeeded them, they were not calculated to lead any one to suppose that the Revolution afforded an opportunity for the display of the high order of talents which Prescott, Motley, and Parkman possessed. Certain it is that no account of the greatest period in our political life has been written with the broad, thorough research, trained scholarship, dignified but fascinating style, and full intelligent inquiry which we find in "The Conquest of Mexico," "The Rise of the Dutch Republic," or "The Conspiracy of Pontiac."

Although we are a democratic country, our history of the event which largely created our democracy has been written in the most undemocratic method—a method which conceals the real condition; a method of paternalism which seeks to let the people know only such things as the writer supposes will be good for them; a method whose foundation principle appears to be that the people cannot be trusted with the original evidence.

We frequently hear the question, Who is an authority on the Revolution? or what is the "final and authoritative account" of some part of it. But there is no such authority, and never will be. There is no person whose statement on any point can be absolutely accepted; and any one who supposes that he can write a "final and authoritative account" of any historical event is likely to find himself disappointed. By authority or authorities is properly meant the original evidence of the persons concerned in the event, contained in letters, memoirs, and public documents. These must always be referred to when any question is raised. They are sometimes contradictory; but, nevertheless, they are the only authority we have. Any one has the right to draw his own inferences from them; but none of these inferences are authority. The original evidence in the records is the only real authority.

For example, the only authority for a battle like Long Island or Brandywine consists of the reports or letters of Washington, the report and defence of Howe, and the written experiences of the officers and men on both sides who saw the battle. They must be all read; no one of them is of much value by itself. After that we gain light by reading the criticisms on the conduct of the generals by contemporary writers, some of them military experts, some mere heated partisans, but all valuable as making up the history or picture of the times and of what actually occurred. Later military criticism from the modern point of view, as well as descriptions by modern historians are no authority at all, but merely more or less interesting, or confusing, comments on the original evidence.

Similarly in other episodes of the Revolution, whether battles, riots, arguments, or development and change of opinion, the only authority is the original testimony of the people of the time, the participants and witnesses, preserved for us in political pamphlets, letters, memoirs, and documents. In fact, it would be better in some respects if we could abandon the word authority and use instead the terms witnesses and evidence. In the case of the Battle of Long Island and some other events of the Revolution, the original evidence has nearly all been reprinted in accessible form, sometimes collected in a single volume, so that any person within reach of one of our better public libraries can read it for himself, and draw inferences just as good as those of any historian or so-called authority.

The historians of our Revolution made a great mistake in abandoning the good old-fashioned plan of referring to the original evidence by foot-note citations. Botta and Hildreth gave no citations. Bancroft, who is believed to have made a great study of the original evidence, has only a few citations and those rather unimportant, and he does not give the source of his quotations. Fiske, whose books are the most beautifully written and entertaining account of the Revolution that has ever appeared, gives no citations at all. The lesser lights, of course, follow these distinguished examples. Their readers are left entirely in the dark as to the nature of the original evidence. Instead of aiding investigation, so that subsequent writers could begin where they left off and accumulate evidence on all important points, they cut off this process altogether. Every subsequent investigator must begin over again the laborious process; and for the evidence on any point he must search in widely scattered sources, and hunt largely at random.

There is, of course, the excuse that foot-note citations give an air of learning and heaviness which alarm the general reader, and this is supposed to be a serious consideration in

PREFACE

American history, which, above all things, should be popular. It is perhaps unfair, therefore, to attach any blame to our historians for not using or citing the original evidence, when we consider that they were striving merely to popularize the Revolution and not to write works of research. But this feeling against research has been carried too far, and allowed altogether too much influence; and the practice of not citing the evidence leads one into very careless habits.

When no historians refer in any adequate way to the original evidence, the compilers of the popular histories, appearing almost every year, are tempted to become more and more perfunctory and inferior; for they cannot, of course, afford the time to search for the original evidence in its present widely scattered state. But there would be no reason why they should not read it, and write from it, if the greater part of it were cited under numerous topics in some general history.

It is not required, of course, that authorities should be cited for every statement, and in reading the original sources one acquires ideas and views which cannot be recorded in foot-note citations. But each chapter should in some way guide the reader to the more important parts of the evidence on which it is based. The writer should not only let the public know who the witnesses are, but if there are contradictions among them, controversies as to facts or the motives of public characters, or differences of opinion as to measures, he should not conceal these difficulties from the reader. He should not undertake to decide everything for him, and make things appear smooth which in reality are rough.

The disregard for the original evidence has been so universal that our most intelligent people do not know that there is this evidence, contained in innumerable letters, memoirs, and documents. In talking recently with a college professor of high reputation in his special branch, familiar with libraries, and of considerable knowledge of the world, he expressed surprise that there was any original evidence of the Revolution that was worth investigating or that would require much time to investigate. He supposed that there was nothing but certain

PREFACE

battles and dates, and that one could write a history only by reading secondary writers and commentators—Bancroft, Fiske, Botta—and essays and articles by various members of the Adams family, and from these preparing a re-statement of general views and principles.

That is, in truth, the process that has been going on; repeated rehashing of secondary opinions without ever recurring to the original evidence; and every re-statement, inspired often by a small money-making enterprise, carries us farther from the original reality.

Published lists and bibliographies of so-called authorities, instead of guiding us to the original evidence, contain for the most part mere secondary commentaries, which are of course more accessible and more easily collected. The secondary commentaries increase in numbers and make a goodly show. The original evidence is comparatively small in amount, but very difficult to bring together.

For these reasons I called the volume I wrote on the subject some years ago "The True History of the American Revolution"; for while I agree with certain objectors that there is no such thing as "absolute truth" except in the mind of God, yet the title, taken in the ordinary meaning of English, correctly describes my effort to lead our historical writing back to the original documentary evidence, which constitutes all the truth we ever have of a past event when the eye-witnesses are dead. The rising generation of Americans should be led to see that the dignity of history does not consist of rhetoric or pleasing literature, but of broad and candid investigation; and they should learn to admire truth and historic reality rather than mere popular or clever generalizations.

The present volumes have been given the title of "The Struggle for American Independence," because as supplementary to the original volume, which is to be retained in the series for which it was written, they bring out more clearly than ever that the Revolution was not the work of a war or of a decade, but of a long evolution of thought, experience, and events; that it was not a contest between a dragon

xii

PREFACE

and a fairy settled once and for all in favor of the fairy; that it was not a mere accidental mistake on the part of England, that she would not repeat, a contest mistakenly conducted through eleven years of argument and diplomacy and eight years of war by the King alone against the wishes of the English people; but that it was entered upon by the English nation as deliberately and intelligently as any other imperial expansion they have undertaken and upon principles which for them are still unchangeable; and that it was a long, uncertain struggle between the two opposing ideas of colonial empire and separate independence, both of which are still powerful in the world and preparing for future struggles.

There is all the more reason now for a free and open use of the original sources of the evidence of this struggle, because within the last sixty years they have been admirably collected and catalogued or reprinted by historical societies, university publication funds, and the efforts of public-spirited citizens. Drake's "Tea Leaves," reprinting the original letters, papers, and other authentic information relating to the destruction of the tea at Boston, is a good example. J. R. Bartlett's collection of all the evidence relating to the burning of the Gaspee reveals the true bearings of that incident in a way that cannot be found in any history, and at the same time throws light on other aspects of the Revolution. There is nothing so refreshing as to read original evidence of this sort after being surfeited with general statements and commentaries, cautiously written so as to make the Revolution seem smooth and easy.

Flick's "Loyalism" is another very satisfactory work, an admirable collection of real evidence; and in the same connection should be mentioned Van Tyne's "Loyalists." Then there is Judge Gray's exhaustive investigation of the subject of Writs of Assistance, in which he throws a flood of light on the whole subject of the smuggling trade and the working of the navigation laws; and in this same line of the navigation and trade laws some valuable researches have been published in the third volume of the Columbia University Studies in History.

There is Kidder's collection of original evidence relating

to the Boston Massacre, Striker's excellent work on the battles of Trenton and Princeton, Professor Bassett's thorough investigation of the battle of the Alamance, and Haywood's enlightening researches in the administration of Governor Tryon. The recent publication of the diary and letters of that very devoted loyalist, Governor Hutchinson, has opened for us a most important source of information, and there is also much to be learned from the writings of the more irascible and less accurate, but very sincere loyalist, Judge Jones.

These and the various researches in the French archives, letters, and diaries disclose how complicated the Revolution was, because it consisted of three wars waged at the same time, each one of which might fill a volume—our foreign war of the patriot party with England, our civil war of the patriots with the loyalists, and the European war which France, Spain and Holland waged on our behalf.

I have sometimes cited the more carefully prepared biographies, which reprint original letters and documents; and I have treated the accounts of the war by Harry Lee, by Gordon, and by Stedman as original evidence, not to be blindly followed, but to be considered along with the rest. Lee is a most intelligent eye-witness from the point of view of the successful partisan officer who was also a man of broad education and talents. Stedman was an officer with the British army in America all through the war; and his book, whether written solely by himself or with the assistance of Dr. William Thomson, is valuable evidence from the more moderate English point of view. Gordon, an English Congregationalist minister, lived in Massachusetts during the Revolution and afterwards returned to England. While in this country he took the patriot side, collected material for his book, visited battlefields, talked with generals and statesmen, and had access to their papers. That part of his work is a reprint of what had been published in the *Annual Register* is not, to my mind, a reason for excluding him as a witness, for the *Annual Register*, an English periodical of the time, written, it is supposed, by Burke, was generally admitted by both sides to have furnished the most reliable and impartial account of the events of the Revolution. A large part of the letters and documents which Gordon read in manuscript have since his day been published in the *American Archives,* and confirm his statements, notably in the important year 1775. But he is only one witness and tells only a part. I cite always from the first edition of his work published in London in 1788.[1]

It, of course, naturally follows from the position I have taken that I can see no good reason for the usual custom of rejecting entirely the point of view and the writings of the loyalists; and I accordingly accept them as relevant evidence to be weighed along with the rest.

It is also evident from this preface and the whole course of the narrative, that I reject, as too narrow and partisan, the English Whig point of view, on which both Fiske's and Trevelyan's charmingly written histories of the Revolution are based. The Whig point of view that the patriots were not seeking independence, that, if kindly treated and the troops withdrawn, they would voluntarily remain in the Empire, and that if the Whigs had been put in power the Anglo-Saxon race would never have been divided and America would still constitute part of the British empire, was, no doubt, a very proper platform for the Whig party as a minority trying to regain office. It was a source of endless minority eloquence as Burke, Fox, and Lord Chatham discovered. But it is entirely too restricted, as it seems to me, too unjust to the real patriots, and too much opposed to a great mass of evidence to be at all suitable for history.

Such modern English works as the 1894 edition of Todd's "Parliamentary Government in the British Colonies," Sir Henry Jenkyns' "British Rule and Jurisdiction Beyond the Seas," the edition of 1891 of Lewis's "Government of Dependencies," together with histories of Canada and Australia like

---

[1] See a rather extreme attack upon Gordon in Report Am. Hist. Assoc. 1899, vol. i, p. 365; *contra* Winsor, "Handbook of the American Revolution," p. 286.

those of Bourinot and Tregarthen, and works on India like those of Naoroji, Digby, Lilly, and Dutt, I have made considerable use of because they disclose the modern British colonial system and open a whole new domain of thought by comparison with the system against which our ancestors rebelled.

Besides all these sources of information, there are numerous articles and notes of general research in such periodicals as the *Pennsylvania Magazine of History*, the *American Historical Review*, the *Historical Magazine*, and in the reports of the American Historical Association. There are the thousands of pages in the huge volumes of Force's *American Archives*, besides various reprints of documents and letters too numerous to mention, as well as the vast field of investigation which opens before one when the old contemporary pamphlets are examined.

It is passing strange that so much scholarly and excellent work should have been done in collecting this material of the Revolution and that so little use of it should be made in writing general histories. It is strange that these isolated investigators should have been so genuine and sincere, so thorough-going and candid, and the general historians so much the reverse.

This excellent individual work is widely scattered, buried, and to all intents forgotten, in the libraries and historical societies. To bring together under proper topics, even in an approximate degree, all the instances of the original evidence, when it has never been done before, is a troublesome task; and to state the results briefly and without dulness is still more difficult. It is not likely that I have been able to do either to the satisfaction of everybody. It will be enough if the greater part of the evidence has been brought together so that the investigator of the future will not have to search for it at random.

CONTENTS

VOLUME I

CONTENTS

VOLUME II

CONTENTS

CONTENTS

LIST OF ILLUSTRATIONS

VOLUME I

LIST OF ILLUSTRATIONS

VOLUME II

MAPS

The Struggle
for
American Independence

I.

EARLY CONDITIONS AND CAUSE

If we look upon the Revolution merely as a war, or series of interesting battles, from 1775 to 1783, we shall fail to grasp its meaning. It was really a long continued political and economic movement, gradually creating among our people a political party which, against great odds and by persistent endeavor, established on this continent ideas and principles which are not yet entirely accepted in Europe.

To fix upon an exact date for the beginning of such a movement is, of course, impossible; but it was long before the year 1775. The eight years of battles from 1775 to 1783 were merely a conspicuous and violent outcropping of a range of human thought, which had been developing for many decades and continued to accomplish practical results long after Washington's work as a military commander was finished. "The late American war is over," said Dr. Rush in 1787, "but the Revolution is still going on." [1]

From its earliest beginning it was in every phase a process of evolution; and must be looked at in that light to be understood. The Revolutionary movement was still conspicuously altering our social and political conditions down to the time of the Civil War of 1861, and we have not yet passed out of the period of history which may be said to belong to its influence. We are struggling to-day to adapt its principles to new and unexpected conditions; and its ideas are slowly working their way not only in Europe, but in Japan, China, and Russia.

---

[1] Niles, "Principles and Acts of the Revolution," edition 1876, p. 234.

The great underlying conditions which brought about the Revolution were, first of all, the extremely liberal charters and governments which England gave her colonists in order to encourage the settlement of the American wilderness. The privileges thus allowed were increased by the semi-independence and disregard of laws and regulations which England could not prevent, partly because the English Government was not strongly organized, but principally because the increasing power of France in Canada occupied all England's attention in America up to 1763. She needed the help of the colonists to conquer France, and so long as that help was needed it was not advisable to discuss a stricter regulation of colonial affairs.

Canada having been conquered and the French power removed from the continent in 1763, the English Government at once began to regulate the American provinces, and reduce them to what she naturally considered a more orderly and colonial condition. If that were not done they would now, as the dread of France was removed, press for greater privileges and become entirely independent. This change to a severer regulation in 1764 was the beginning of the modern British empire. At that time the present methods and principles of that empire were first laid down and promulgated. But this change was regarded by a large part of our people as an infringement of long-established rights, and it brought about the outbreak, which began with ten years of argument, 1764-1774, and ended with eight years of war, 1775-1783.[2]

The liberality of some of the early charters was quite remarkable. No modern English colonies, not even Canada and the Australian provinces, have quite as much freedom as Connecticut and Rhode Island enjoyed all through our colonial period. They elected their own legislatures and governors, and did not even have to send their laws to England for approval. No modern British colony elects its own governor; and if it has a legislature elected by its people, the acts of that legislature can be vetoed by the home government. A community electing

[2] *American Archives*, 4th series, vol. ii, p. 1890.

its own governor and enacting whatever laws it pleases is not a colony in the modern English meaning of the word. Connecticut and Rhode Island could not make treaties with foreign nations, but in other respects they were, as we would now say, semi-independent commonwealths under the protectorate or suzerainty of England.

When the Ministry determined on reorganizing the colonies in 1764, one of the first subjects of discussion was how to abolish, with the least disturbance, the old charters which had been originally granted as mere "temporary means for settling the colonies," but which now, as Governor Bernard put it, "amount to an alienation of the dominions of Great Britain, and are, in effect, acts dismembering the British empire." The charters of Connecticut and Rhode Island were regarded as particularly bad examples, and utter absurdities in colonial government. In the beginning of the actual fighting, in 1776, when it was expected that the patriot colonists might compromise, or agree to some sort of peace or truce, Admiral Howe and General Howe were directed by their secret instructions to use every endeavor to obtain a surrender of the charters of Rhode Island and Connecticut.[*]

Neither Connecticut nor Rhode Island changed its form of government during the Revolution. The Connecticut charter was found to be liberal enough to serve as the constitution of an American State; and Connecticut lived under it until 1818. Rhode Island lived under her charter as a constitution until 1842.

Our ancestors in colonial times encouraged themselves to regard the old charters as so sacred that they were of higher authority than an act of Parliament. They had been granted, it was argued, not by Parliament, but by the old English kings, and were unalterable by Parliament, unless the colonists con-

---

[*] Bernard, "Select Letters on Government." See the charters in the collections of Poor or of Hazzard; also Palfrey, "History of New England," vol. ii, pp. 540–566; copy of the secret instructions of the Howes in the Historical Society of Pennsylvania; "Sagittarius's Letters," Boston, 1775, p. 20.

sented to the alteration. They stood in the way of all reorganization of the colonies by England; and after her experience with them in our Revolution, England never again granted such charters. In fact, she gave up granting colonial charters altogether; and her present relations, even with her most self-governing colonies, are usually regulated by a mere act or acts of Parliament, which no one questions may be altered at any time by any subsequent Parliament.

The first charter of Massachusetts was in effect as liberal as those of Connecticut and Rhode Island. It was probably intended that the governing body under this charter should remain in England; but the Puritans who had obtained it moved the whole governing body out to Massachusetts, elected their own legislature and governor, and did not submit their laws to England for approval. They assumed several of the attributes of sovereignty; coined their own money, and issued the famous pine-tree shilling; and established by law a form of religion, sometimes called Congregationalism, which was not recognized by the laws of England. They ceased to issue writs in the king's name; dropped the English oath of allegiance, and adopted a new oath in which public officers and the people swore allegiance, not to England, but to Massachusetts.

They debated what allegiance they owed to England, and concluded that they were independent in government, that no appeals could be taken to England, but that they were under an English protectorate. When some captains of vessels reminded them that no English flag was displayed in the colony, they debated whether the British flag should be allowed to fly on the fort at Castle Island, and conceded that it might be put there, as that particular fort was the king's property. But they had given so little attention to allegiance and the symbol of it that at the close of this debate no English flags could be found in Boston, and they had to borrow one from the captain of a ship.[4]

---

[4] Winthrop's Journal, published as the "History of New England," vol. i, pp. 187–188; vol. ii, pp. 279–282; Palfrey, "New England," vol. i, pp. 284, 375, 499, et passim.

FREEDOM IN VIRGINIA

Under this charter which allowed so much freedom Massachusetts existed from 1629 to 1685, when her disregard of British authority and the killing, whipping, and imprisoning of Quakers and Baptists had reached such a pass that the charter was annulled, and Massachusetts became a colony under a less liberal charter. She had a governor appointed by the king, and was controlled in a way which, after her previous freedom, was very galling.

These instances show why New England became so eager for independence the moment the French were driven from Canada. Virginia was also ardent, and there, too, we find that an extremely liberal government had been allowed to grow up. Virginia had, alone and single-handed, in 1676, rebelled against the whole authority of the British Government, because she thought her privileges were being impaired. Such an outbreak as this and a similar rebellion in Massachusetts in 1690 warned England to be as gentle as possible with the colonies, while France was becoming more and more of a power on the north and west.

The other colonies never had so much freedom. None of them elected their own governors; they had not had such a taste of independence as New England and Virginia, which from the English point of view were regarded as the leaders in rebellion. But they had all had a certain measure of their own way of doing things, and had struggled to have more of their own way, and had found that England was compelled at times to yield to them. It is not necessary to describe the details of this struggle, in all of its successes or failures. It is of more importance to describe a method of government which grew up in all the colonies that did not elect their own governors, a method which they regarded as the bulwark of their liberties, which in England was regarded as scandalous, but which nevertheless was allowed to go on and had an important influence on the Revolution.

This method arose out of the system by which the people of the colony elected the legislature, and the crown, or a proprietor under the crown, as in Pennsylvania and Maryland, appointed the governor. Under this system the legislature voted the governor his salary out of taxes which all these colonial legislatures had the power of levying. The governor had the power of absolute veto on all acts of the legislature, and, as representing the crown, he wanted certain laws passed to carry out the ideas or reforms of the home government.

The members of the legislature cared little or nothing for these reforms. As representing the people, they had their popular measures which they wished carried out. These measures the governor usually wanted to veto, either because he deemed them hostile to the interests of the crown, or because he wished to punish the legislature for failing to pass crown measures on which his reputation at home depended.

The governor and the legislature being thus dependent on each other, the question of salary threw the balance of power into the hands of the legislature; and they quickly learned the trick of withholding the governor's salary until he had assented to their measures. The system became practically one of bargain and sale, as Franklin called it. The people, through their legislators, bargained with the governor for such laws as they needed. The petty squabbles with the governor, necessary to carry on the system, were interminable in every colony where it prevailed. They fill the minute-books and records, making colonial history more tiresome than it might otherwise be, except in an instance, where Franklin, who often came in contact with the system, described it in his inimitable manner:

"Hence arose the custom of presents twice a year to the governors, at the close of each session in which laws were passed, given at the time of passing; they usually amounted to a thousand pounds per annum. But when the governors and assemblies disagreed, so that laws were not passed, the presents were withheld. When a disposition to agree ensued, there sometimes still remained some diffidence. The governors would not pass the laws that were wanted without being sure of the money, even all that they called their arrears; nor the assemblies give the money without being sure of the laws; Thence the necessity of some private conference, in which mutual assurances of good faith might be received and given, that the transaction should go hand in hand.

6

THE GOVERNOR'S SALARY

What name the impartial reader will give to this kind of commerce I cannot say. . . . Time established the custom and made it seem honest; so that our governors, even those of the most undoubted honor, have practised it. . . .

"When they came to resolve, on the report of the grand committee, to give the money, they guarded their resolves very cautiously, to wit: 'Resolved that on the passage of such bills as now lie before the governor (the naturalization bill and such other bills as may be presented to him during the sitting) there be paid him the sum of five hundred pounds.' . . .

"Do not, my courteous reader, take pet at our proprietary constitution for these our bargain and sale proceedings in legislation. It is a happy country where justice and what was your own before can be had for ready money. It is another addition to the value of money, and, of course, another spur to industry. Every land is not so blessed."—Works, Bigelow edition, vol. iii, pp. 311–316.

What was thought and said of this system depended entirely on one's point of view. Franklin ridiculed it when it worked against him. Afterwards, in the Revolution, when he saw that colonial self-government depended upon it, he became, like Dickinson and other patriot leaders, a stanch upholder of it.[a] In England it was regarded as corruption. There was plenty of corruption in England at that time; but outside corruption always seems the more heinous; and this so-called corruption blocked and thwarted nearly all the plans of the mother-country to regulate her colonies. It was believed to have seriously interfered with the raising of supplies and aids for the war against the French and Indians. If anything of the sort existed in our time, if a territory of the United States, or an island like Porto Rico, were governed in that way, we would denounce it; and in all probability put a stop to it very quickly. It was very natural that England, acting from her point of view, should start to abolish it as soon as France was driven from the continent, and this attempt was one of the fundamental causes of the Revolution.

[a] Franklin, Works, Bigelow edition, vol. iv, pp. 407–433; vol. v, p. 465. Dickinson, "Letters from a Farmer," letters ix, x; Wells, "Life of Samuel Adams," vol. i, pp. 485–486; Egerton, "Origin and Growth of English Colonies," ed. 1903, pp. 152–156; Report, American Historical Association, 1894, p. 148.

AMERICAN INDEPENDENCE

The colonists who had become Americanized, tinged with the soil, differentiated from English influence, or, as Englishmen said, rebelliously inclined, were all enthusiastic supporters of the system of withholding the governor's salary. They loved it and were ready to die for it, and resisted any change or reform in it. They would not hear of fixing regular salaries upon the governors, because they knew that the moment the governors ceased to be dependent on the legislatures for their salaries, the legislatures would be powerless to accomplish the popular will, and the colonies, except Connecticut and Rhode Island, would fall under complete control of Parliament and the King. So long as they controlled the governor the people felt themselves freemen; once lose that control and they were mere colonists, or, as they expressed it, political slaves. Each legislature was called and adjourned by the governor; and he would hardly take the trouble to call it, except to pass crown measures, unless he was dependent on it for his salary.

The system extended to the judges, who, though appointed by the crown or governor, were dependent for their salaries on the annual vote of the legislature. In New York the judiciary was believed to be notoriously dependent. A chief justice, it was said, gave a decision against a member of the legislature, who promptly, in retaliation, had the judge's salary reduced fifty pounds. The local magistrates in New York were controlled by the assemblymen. Some of these magistrates could not write, and had to affix their marks to warrants.[6]

The colonists insisted that they must retain control of the judges' salaries, because, if the crown both appointed the judges and paid them their salaries, the decisions would all be crown decisions. They were willing to compromise, however, and fix permanent salaries on the judges if the home government would agree that the judges should be appointed for life and good behavior instead of holding office at the pleasure of the crown. This apparently reasonable suggestion the English Govern-

---

[6] "Documents Relating to the Colonial History of New York," vol. vii, pp. 500, 705, 760, 774, 796–797, 906, 979.

8

ment would not adopt.[7] It seems to have feared that the judges holding office by that tenure would gradually drift to the side of the colonists, and make regulation and administration more difficult than ever. It was already extremely difficult to get a jury to decide in favor of the crown. The control of the colonies seemed to be slipping away, and the Ministry were anxious to retain as much of it as was possible.

Those acts of Parliament by which the money raised from taxes on the colonies was not to be cast generally into the English exchequer, but to be used for "defraying the expenses of government and the administration of justice in the colonies," and therefore would all be spent in the colonies, read innocently enough. What could be more fair and honorable towards you, Englishmen would say, than an act which takes no money out of your country? It is the same money which you now raise by taxing yourselves; it will be spent, in the same way as you apply it, to pay governors and judges, and on a fixed and regular system.

But the "fixed and regular system" destroyed what the Americans considered their fundamental, constitutional principle, by which executive salaries must be within popular control. That principle was vitally necessary to all the colonies, except to Connecticut and Rhode Island. It would become vital to Connecticut and Rhode Island if they should lose the right to elect their own governors, as was not improbable when England began her remodelling after the expulsion of France from Canada.

One effect of the system of withholding the governor's salary was to divide the upper classes of the colonists, and indeed all the people, into two parties—those who were interested in the governor and his family and following, and those who were interested in the legislature. Around every governor appointed from England there grew up a little aristocracy of powerful families and individuals, with their patronage, influence, and branches extending down through all classes. The people of this

---

[7] Franklin, Works, Bigelow edition, vol. v, pp. 463–464.

party who had means and education considered themselves social superiors, because they were so closely connected with England and the king, who was the source of all rank and nobility. They considered themselves the only American society that deserved recognition; and nearly all of them became loyalists in the Revolution.

Among the legislative party, as it may be called, there were individuals and families of as much means and as good education as any in the governor's party. But they formed a set by themselves, and were sometimes hardly on speaking terms with the executive party. In some of the colonies the two parties were on friendly terms; but in Pennsylvania, New York, and Massachusetts the contests and hatred between them were, at times, extremely bitter and violent.

Prominent men whose names have become household words among us—Hancock, Adams, and Warren, of Massachusetts; Schuyler, Hamilton, and Livingston, of New York; Reed, Morris, Dickinson, and Mifflin, of Pennsylvania; Paca and Chase, of Maryland; and Lee, Washington, Bland, and Harrison, of Virginia—were all of the Whig legislative set. They were more or less distinctly separated from the high society that basked in the regal sunlight, which, even when filtered through a colonial governor, was supposed to redeem America from vulgarity.

In the party which stood by the governors we find another set of family names, the names of the loyalist leaders, who believed that imperial restraint would be better for us than independence. If the Revolution had terminated differently their names instead of the others might have become household words in America. The Hunts, Galloways, Allens, and Hamiltons, of Pennsylvania; DeLancey, Van Schaack, and Jones, of New York; Leonard, Hutchinson, Sewall, Curwen, and Oliver, of Massachusetts, once filled a large place in the public vision, but their names are now meaningless to nearly every one.

The liberality of the early charters and governments was of course due to the desire of the crown to encourage emigration to America and get rid of troublesome people, rebels against either

10

the government or the established religion, like the Puritans, Baptists, Quakers, and Roman Catholics. The charters were not granted from any particular love of liberty; for the most liberal of them, those to Connecticut and Rhode Island, were granted by Charles II. Other liberal ones were granted by other Stuart kings, with the approval of their officials and courtiers, all of whom showed by every other act of their lives that they were the determined enemies of free parliaments and free representation of the people.[8]

For the sake of getting rid of Roman Catholics the crown gave Lord Baltimore a charter under which he and his colonists could set up any form of government they pleased not contrary to the laws of England; and for the sake of getting rid of Quakers, William Penn was allowed the same sort of charter for Pennsylvania. The Puritans were given great privileges in New England for the sake of getting them out of old England; and the royalists and churchmen of Virginia left England when the Puritans were in power under Cromwell.

It was difficult in those days to persuade people to go to America. They had to be driven out by persecution or coaxed out by offers of liberal government. There was no crowding and overflow of population in England. When the first colony was started, in 1607, England's population was only five millions, and one hundred and seventy-five years afterwards, at the time of the Revolution, it had increased to only eight millions, and large districts of country, especially in the northern part, were as primitive and uncultivated as the American wilderness.[9]

The policy of the Government was to have as many people as possible go to America, where they would encourage English trade and shipping by furnishing the mother-country with raw material and creating a demand for her manufactured goods. But people would not go for that reason; and if it had not

---

[8] The "Grievances of the American Colonies Candidly Examined," London, 1776, p. 10.

[9] See Macaulay's famous Third Chapter of his History, and numerous passages in Greene's "History of England."

been for the religious and political rebellions and persecutions of the seventeenth century, America would have remained for a long time uninhabited by white men.

When persecution ceased there was no migration of any importance to the colonies. Immigration to New England ceased after 1640; and in all the colonies the immigration was comparatively small. The people increased in the natural way by births, and increased with remarkable rapidity. The two million white colonists of 1776 were largely a native stock, whose ancestors had been on the soil for many generations; and they had grown out of an original stock of immigrants which had not numbered one hundred thousand. This native and natural growth is worth remembering when we are seeking to explain the desire for independence.[10]

After the reign of Queen Anne, Walpole when in power would not restrict the colonies in any way or even govern them with any attention. He wished his administration to have no trouble from them, and he thought it well to encourage their commerce by letting them alone, because the greater the prosperity of the colonies, the greater would be their demand for English goods.[11]

"Walpole was content with seeing that no trouble came from America. He left it to the Duke of New Castle, and the Duke left it so much to itself that he had a closet full of dispatches from American governors which had lain unopened for years. This was what Burke described as treating the colonies with salutary neglect; and what caused it to be said that George Grenville lost America because he was foolish enough to read the American dispatches."—Morley, "Life of Walpole," p. 169.

From other sources of information we learn how the colonial legislatures in this struggle with the governors increased their

---

[10] F. B. Dexter, "Estimates of Population in the American Colonies," p. 29, published by the American Antiquarian Society of Worcester, Mass.

[11] *Annual Register*, 1765, p. 25. As to departmental methods for governing the colonies before the Revolution, see Lewis, "Government of Dependencies," edition of 1891, pp. 149, 160–161; Pownall, "Administration of the Colonies."

privileges step by step. They gradually secured for themselves the appointment of all civil officers except the governors, judges, and court officers. Governor Shirley, writing in 1748, describes the steady encroachments which the colonial legislatures, especially in New York, had been making upon the authority of the home government. Since 1743 the legislatures, instead of voting the government supplies for five years, would vote them for only one year. They had usurped the nomination of officers. They were acquiring more and more control over the militia, the erection of fortifications, and the supplies of ammunition. They were gaining a stronger influence in regulating treaties and intercourse with the Indians; and in general "they have gone great lengths in getting the government, military as well as civil, in their hands."[12] In 1741 the governor of New York in rebuking the legislature for their aggressiveness warned them that for some years the people in England had been well aware of the inclination of the colonies to throw off their dependence on the crown.[13]

In short, as Sir George Cromwell Lewis says, "The early English colonies were in practice nearly independent of the mother-country except as to their external commercial relations." Instead of being like modern English colonies, they had become more like Greek colonies, which were communities sent forth to reproduce the mother-country, to become self-sustaining and independent, and to be assisted by the mother-country only when necessary in their wars.

To the Romans the word colony meant a conquered province, garrisoned and controlled by military authority, governed by officials sent out from Rome, and held as the property of the empire for the benefit and profit of the Roman people, very much as crown colonies are held by England. In England the term has usually meant an outlying community of people,

[12] "Documents Relating to New York Colonial History," vol. vi, pp. 432–437; Smith, "History of New York," edition 1814, p. 441; Egerton, "Origin and Growth of English Colonies," 1903, p. 158.

[13] Lewis, "Government of Dependencies," edition 1891, pp. xxix–xxx and 59–60.

completely under the authority of Parliament, with no self-government at all, or with a certain amount of representative or self-government, according to circumstances, but with no view to ultimate independence.

The old Greek colony of Corcyreans said that " they went out on the footing of equality with, not of political slavery to, those who were left behind." In a similar way the colonists in Barbadoes explained to Oliver Cromwell that they had the same rights as Englishmen living in England, and as Englishmen living in the Barbadoes did not interfere with Englishmen living in England, it was no business of the home-keeping Englishmen to rule the colonists. They were not a dependency, they said, but a second England.[14]

A striking illustration of the free condition of the colonies was the way in which their legislatures issued paper money, which in New England became very seriously depreciated. This paper currency the colonists considered absolutely necessary to supply the place of the gold and silver which were so rapidly drained from them into England to pay for the manufactured goods they bought. There seems to be no doubt but that they were right in this, and so long as the issues of paper money were kept within safe bounds, as in Pennsylvania, no harm resulted. But there were such disastrous results in some colonies that there was a great outcry in England. To many Englishmen this paper money seemed to be a mere dishonorable device to avoid paying the heavy debts which the colonists owed to the British merchants, who sold to them the axes with which they felled the forests, the plows with which they tilled the lands, and the utensils in which they cooked their dinners.[15]

At one time the independent spirit of the colonists had reached such a height that some of them attempted to pass stay laws to prevent English merchants from collecting debts by levy and sale of property in the colonies. This was going

---

[14] Lewis, " Government of Dependencies," edition 1891, pp. xxix-xxx and 59-60.

[15] Phillips, " Historical Sketches of Paper Currency in the American Colonies;" Franklin, Works, Bigelow edition, vol. v, p. 529.

too far even for that period, and an act of Parliament was passed in 1732 giving English merchants the same right to seize private property for debt in the colonies that they had in England. That such an act was necessary is in itself a striking commentary on the situation; and the act became a landmark in the constitutional relations between the colonies and the mother-country, and was frequently cited during the Revolution to show that Parliament had full jurisdiction in the colonies.[16]

No attempt, however, was made to restrain the paper money issues until 1751, when Parliament passed an act declaring the paper money of the New England colonies an illegal tender in payment of a debt. In 1764, when the French war was over and colonial reorganization begun, Parliament declared all future issues of paper money in the colonies illegal; and this was one of the acts which incited the outbreak of the Revolution.

When we look upon the situation candidly, after the lapse of nearly two hundred years, it seems quite natural that England, from her imperial point of view of a great obedient empire should conclude that the colonies were too independent and must be reorganized; and it was also natural that many of the colonists should look upon their semi-independence as their long-established privilege of doing as they pleased and, if they saw fit, governing themselves badly.

France having abandoned Canada by the treaty of 1763, the following year, 1764, was the beginning of the attempt to reorganize the colonies and the beginning of their resistance or Revolution. Nothing but her desire to conquer Canada had restrained England from starting that reorganization years before; and nothing but the fear of the French in Canada had kept the colonists from being still more independent in conduct. For a number of years the French power in the north had been increasing and was passing into the Ohio and Mississippi valleys, to cut off the colonies from westward expansion.

---

[16] "The Interest of the Merchants and Manufacturers of Great Britain in the Present Contest with the Colonies," p. 38, London, 1774.

Kalm, the Swedish botanist, who travelled in America in 1748, reported that the presence of the French in Canada was all that held the colonies in submission to England. He met both Americans and English who foretold that the colonies would be absolutely independent within thirty or fifty years.[17]

In fact, the English-speaking communities in America were not colonies in the modern meaning of the term. England had lost a large part of her sovereignty over them; and Dean Tucker shrewdly remarked that British sovereignty in the colonies was entirely gone as soon as the French were removed, and that the Revolution was a contest to recover it. Governor Bernard, writing in 1774, said that at the time of the passage of the Stamp Act, "there was no fixed idea of the relation between Great Britain and America."[18]

Englishmen were so well aware that as soon as the French power was removed from Canada the irregularities and independence of the colonies would increase, that at the close of the French war there was a strong feeling in favor of returning Canada to France to act as a check on the ambition of the New Englanders and Virginians. In place of Canada, it was proposed to take the rich sugar island of Guadaloupe, which, it was thought, would be fully as profitable as the Canadian wastes of snow.

Franklin, who was in London at that time, vigorously opposed this feeling and policy. He wanted the French entirely

---

[17] "Travels into North America," vol. i, p. 265.

[18] "The True Interest of Great Britain Set Forth," p. 12, London, 1774; Cartwright's "American Independence the Interest and Glory of Great Britain," pp. 90–91; "The Constitutional Right of the Legislature of Great Britain to Tax the British Colonies," p. 3, London, 1768. "Letters of James Murray, Loyalist," p. 154; Bernard, "Select Letters on Trade and Government." Speaking of smuggling in Rhode Island in 1761 Governor Bernard, of Massachusetts, said, "These practices will never be put an end to till Rhode Island is reduced to the subjection of the British Empire, of which at present it is no more a part than the Bahama Islands were when they were inhabited by the Buccaneers."— Quincy's Reports of Massachusetts Superior Court, 1761–1772, pp. 436–437.

removed from the continent, so that America might be free. But it remained the general opinion in England long after the Revolution that "had not the French been removed from Canada, the revolt of America never would have taken place."[19]

---

[19] Franklin, Works, Bigelow edition, vol. iii, pp. 62, 92, 111, 115; Eddis, " Letters from America," p. 54; Stedman, " American War," vol. i, p. 31.

The change in the situation by the conquest of Canada was quickly seen by the people of the time. " No sooner were the French kites and the Indian vultures scared away than they (the colonists) began to strut and to claim an independent property to the dunghill. Their fear and their natural affection forsook them at one and the same time."—" The Justice and Necessity of Taxing the American Colonies," p. 7, London, 1766.

" Ever since the reduction of Canada," wrote one of the ablest of the loyalist pamphleteers, " we have been bloated with a vain opinion of our own importance."—" A Friendly Address to all Reasonable Americans," p. 25, New York, 1774. See, also, " Strictures upon the Declaration of the Congress;" " Observations on the American Revolution," published by order of Congress, 1779. This document argues that the colonies were semi-independent states under a protectorate from Great Britain to save them from France.

II.

EFFECT OF THE REFORMATION AND THE RIGHTS OF MAN

BESIDES the semi-independent character of their political governments, there were other circumstances which tended to inspire a large part of the colonists with a strong passion for independence, and led them to resist with unusual energy the remodelling plans which England began in 1764.

Some of these characteristics were eloquently described by Burke in one of his famous speeches in Parliament. The Americans, he said, were not only Protestants, but protestants against Protestantism itself. They were dissenters from the Church of England; they were Puritans, Congregationalists, Presbyterians, Baptists, Quakers, whose ancestors had been persecuted in England and had fled to America from that persecution. They hated the English Church and the English Government. They had lost all that peculiar English reverence and deference for the church and the crown. In their religious beliefs and practices, they had advanced beyond all other Protestants in the liberty of the Reformation. They had rejected so many dogmas and sacraments that they were more free in their religion than most of the people of Europe. They had trained and accustomed themselves to the freest and most subtle debate of all religious questions, regardless of priests, councils, or creeds; and they had encouraged this individualism until even the women thought for themselves, and it was said that every one's hat was his church.

Such simple church organization as they had was democratic like that of the Congregationalists or republican like that of the Presbyterians. The people elected their own religious leaders, calling them ministers, pastors, elders or teachers, and dismissed them when their preaching ceased to please the majority. This religious liberty naturally led to equally extreme political liberalism. They had accepted the right of private judgment in religion and they recognized the same right in politics. They were the worst possible subjects for the formation of a great colonial empire.

This characteristic of strong Protestantism may be said to have applied more particularly to the New Englanders and the Scotch-Irish Presbyterians scattered along the frontiers of the other colonies. But, nevertheless, we find that the churchmen of Virginia descended from English royalists were as ardent for independence as the Puritans and Scotch-Irish. Washington and all the prominent leaders in Virginia had been brought up in the Church of England. The Rutledges, Laurens, Pinckney, Drayton, and Middleton, of South Carolina, and other patriots of the southern and middle colonies, were either of the Church of England or of lighter forms of religious belief than the Puritans and Presbyterians. The English established church had, in fact, been considerably transformed when transplanted to America. Many of the Roman Catholics of Maryland took part in the Revolution, and one of them, Charles Carroll, signed the Declaration of Independence. Dickinson and General Mifflin, of Pennsylvania, and General Greene, of Rhode Island, had been brought up in the Quaker faith.

The sturdy influences of Protestantism and American life had, however, not so great an effect on that large body of people called loyalists, whose numbers have been variously estimated at from one-third to over half the population. They remained loyal to England, and were so far from being inspired with a love of independence that they utterly detested the whole patriot cause and sacrificed their property and lives in the effort to stamp out its principles and put in their place the British empire method of alien control as the best form of government for America.

Patriot parties have existed in other countries without the aid of the particular influences which Burke described. The love of national independence is, in fact, the most difficult passion to eradicate, as the Irish, the Poles, and other broken nationalities bear witness. The desire for independence is natural to all vigorous communities, is generally regarded as more manlike and honorable than dependence, and usually springs up spontaneously whether in Holland, Switzerland, or America, in spite of the commercial and conservative influences of loyalism. But nevertheless the influences mentioned by Burke, and several that he did not mention, had no doubt considerable effect in creating the patriot party in America and inspiring it with enthusiasm and energy.

The self-confidence aroused in the colonists by their success in subduing the wilderness, felling the vast forests, hunting the wild game and still wilder red men, has often been given as a cause of the Revolution and the American love of independence. Eloquence is easily tempted to enlarge upon such causes, and to describe in romantic language the hunter and the woodsman, the farmer in the fresh soil of primeval forests, the fishermen of the Grand Banks, the merchants and sailors who traded with the whole world in defiance of the British navigation laws, and the crews of the whaling ships that pursued their dangerous game from the equator to the poles.

The American lawyers, according to Burke, were an important cause of the Revolution. They were very numerous in the colonies; law and theories of government were much read and studied, and the people were trained to discussion of political rights as well as of religious doctrine. Burke described in picturesque detail how, in the South, the ruling class lived scattered and remote from one another, maintaining themselves in self-reliant authority on plantations with hundreds of slaves; and slavery, he said, inspired in the white master a fierce love of independence for himself and an undying dread of any form of the bondage which his love of gain had inflicted on a weaker race.

The geographical position of the thirteen contiguous colonies, so situated that they could easily unite and act together, and having a population that was increasing so rapidly that it seemed likely in a few years to exceed the population of England, was possibly a more effective cause of the Revolution than any of those that have been named. The consciousness of

20

possessing such a vast fertile continent, which within a few generations would support more than double the population of little England, furnished a profound encouragement for theories of independence. People in England were well aware of this feeling in the colonies, and Joshua Gee, a popular writer on political economy in 1738, tried to quiet their fears. Some, he said, were objecting that "if we encourage the Plantations they will grow rich and set up for themselves and cast off the English government"; and he went on to show that this fear was groundless because the colonists nearly all lived on the navigable rivers and bays of America, where the British navy could easily reach and subdue them. He also attempted to argue away the advantage of the contiguous situation of the colonies and described them as split up into a dozen or more separate provinces, each with its own governor; and it was inconceivable, he said, that such diverse communities would be able to unite against England.[1]

English statesmen, however, saw the danger of union among the colonies long before the outbreak of the Revolution; and they shrewdly rejected the plan of union of the Albany conference of 1754; and in the Revolution itself a large part of England's diplomatic and military efforts were directed towards breaking up the easy communication among the colonies.

In modern times England's colonies have been widely separated from one another. There has been no large and rapidly increasing white population on contiguous territory with ability for union. The dark-skinned population of India is enormous in numbers, but incapable of the united action of the Americans of 1776, and India is not considered a colony but a territory continuously held by overwhelming military force. Instead of a colonial population which threatened in a short time to outnumber her own people, England's power and population have, in modern times, grown far beyond any power or population in her well-scattered white colonies.

---

[1] Joshua Gee, "Trade and Navigation of Great Britain," 6th ed., p. 71; Kidder, "History of the Boston Massacre," p. 121.

AMERICAN INDEPENDENCE

The colonists at the time of the Revolution have often been described as speaking of England as home and regarding the mother-country with no little degree of affection; and while there is no doubt some truth in this, especially as regards the people who were loyalists, yet a very large proportion of the colonists had become totally differentiated from the people of England. This was the inevitable result of having lived for over a hundred years in the American environment. They were no longer Englishmen. They had become completely Americanized. Certain classes kept up their connection with England, and many of the rich planters of the South sent their sons to England to be educated. But a very large part of the colonists, especially in the older settled provinces, like Massachusetts and Virginia, had forgotten England and were another people.

Instead of speaking, as novelists often describe them, in a formal, archaic way, using quaint phrases of old English life, the colonists spoke with mannerisms and colloquial slang which were peculiarly American. These peculiarities were ridiculed by Englishmen of the time and formed part of Grant's famous speech in Parliament, the burden of which appears to have been that the colonists had become entirely different from English people, and Grant is said to have given imitations of what he considered their strange speech and manners. Mrs. Knight, in her "Journal of Travel from Boston to New York," had, many years before the Revolution, given specimens of this difference; and the language of the New Englanders which she describes was certainly not like anything in England.

"Law for me—what in the world brings you here at this time of night? I never see a woman on the Rode so Dreadful late in all the days of my versall life. Who are you? Where are you going?"—Mrs. Knight's Journal, p. 23.

In 1775 some one wrote a set of humorous verses, said to have been the original Yankee Doodle song, to illustrate the colloquial Americanisms of the time. "Slapping" was used for "large," as in the phrase "a slapping stallion." "Nation"

22

was used for "a great deal," as in such a phrase as "only a nation louder." "Tarnal" was used for "very." "I see" was used for "I saw," "I come" for "I came," and "I hooked it off" in place of "I went away." [2]

Not only did the patriots feel themselves to be quite different from Englishmen, but they had a consciousness of ability and power, the result of having governed themselves so long in their towns, counties, and provinces, and of having carried on a commerce of their own in defiance of the English navigation laws. They felt that they, not Englishmen, had created the country; and they had a resolute intention to develop its future greatness in their own way without the advice of aliens across three thousand miles of ocean.

This high confidence, which was a conspicuous motive in the patriot party, was always ridiculed by the loyalists as mere bumptiousness and conceit. It was difficult for a loyalist to understand how any one could seriously put himself in opposition to the British empire or want any form of government except the British constitution. But the patriot estimate of their own ability was by no means an exaggeration. They could be overcome, of course, as the Boer republics and other peoples have been overcome, by the superior numbers or wealth of Great Britain. But the history of the Revolution disclosed qualities in which the Americans notoriously excelled Europeans as well as the Anglo-Saxon stock in England from which they were derived. They were of keener practical intelligence, more promptness in action, more untiring energy, more originality in enterprise, better courage and endurance, and more natural military skill among the rank and file. These distinctively American qualities, as we now call them, seem to have been much more in evidence among the patriot party than among the loyalists.

Every circumstance of their past and every consideration of their present convinced the patriots of the infinite pleasure

---

[2] Preble, "Flag of the United States," ed. 1880, 750; Harper's Cyclopædia of U. S. History, p. 1551.

and value of home rule and they had codified their opinions into a political philosophy which not only justified their semi-independence and disregard of acts of Parliament, but would also justify them in breaking off from England at the first opportunity and becoming absolutely independent. They had gathered this philosophy from the works of certain European writers—Grotius, Puffendorf, Locke, Burlamaqui, Beccaria. Montesquieu, and others—who had applied to politics and government the doctrines of religious liberty and the right of private judgment which had been developed by the Reformation. Being such extreme Protestants, and having carried so far the religious ideas of the Reformation, the colonists naturally accepted in their fullest meaning the political principles of the Reformation. If we are looking for profound influences in the Revolution, it would be difficult to find any that were stronger than two of the writers just mentioned, Locke and Burlamaqui, whose books had a vast effect in the break-up of the British empire which we are about to record.

Beginning with Grotius, who was born in 1583, and ending with Montesquieu, who died in 1755, the writers mentioned covered a period of about two hundred years of political investigation, thought, and experience. In fact, they covered the period since the Reformation. They represented the effect of the Reformation on political thought. They represented also all those nations whose opinions on such subjects were worth anything. Grotius was a Dutchman, Puffendorf a German, Locke an Englishman, Burlamaqui an Italian Swiss, and Montesquieu a Frenchman.

Hooker, who lived from 1553 to 1600, and whom Locke cites so freely, might be included in the number, and that would make the period quite two hundred years. Hooker, in his "Ecclesiastical Polity," declared very emphatically that governments could not be legitimate unless they rested on the consent of the governed; and this principle forms the foundation of Locke's famous essays.

There were, of course, other minor writers; and the colonists relied upon them all; but seldom troubled themselves to read the works of the earlier ones, or to read Hutchinson, Clarke, and other followers of that school, because Locke, Burlamaqui, and Beccaria had summarized them all and brought them down to date. To this day any one going to the Philadelphia Library, and asking for No. 77, can take in his hands the identical, well-worn volume by Burlamaqui which delegates to the Congress and many an unsettled Philadelphian read with earnest, anxious minds. It was among the first books that the library had obtained; and perhaps the most important and effective book it has ever owned.[3]

The rebellious colonists also read Locke's "Two Treatises on Government" with much profit and satisfaction to themselves. Locke was an extreme Whig, an English revolutionist of the school of 1688. Before that great event, he had been unendurable to the royalists, who were in power, and had been obliged to spend a large part of his time on the continent. In the preface to his "Two Treatises," he says that they will show how entirely legitimate is the title of William III to the throne, because it is established on the consent of the people. That is the burden of his whole argument—the consent of the people as the only true foundation of government. That principle sank so deep into the minds of the patriot colonists that it was the foundation of all their political thought, and became an essentially American idea.

Beccaria, who, like Burlamaqui, was an Italian, also exercised great influence on the colonists. His famous book, "Crimes and Punishments," was also a short, concise, but very eloquent volume. It caused a great stir in the world. The translation circulated in America had added to it a characteristic commentary by Voltaire. Beccaria, though not writing directly on the subject of liberty, necessarily included that

---

[3] The colonists were also fond of reading Montesquieu's "Spirit of the Laws," but more in after years when they were framing their constitutions. He dealt more with the details of governmental administration, the legislative, executive, and judicial departments. Burlamaqui confined himself exclusively to the fundamental principles of political liberty and independence.

subject, because he dealt with the administration of the criminal law. His plea for more humane and just punishments, and for punishments more in proportion to the offence, found a ready sympathy among the Americans, who had already revolted in disgust from the brutality and extravagant cruelty of the English criminal code.

But Beccaria also stated most beautifully and clearly the essential principles of liberty. His foundation doctrine, that "every act of authority of one man over another for which there is not absolute necessity is tyrannical," made a most profound impression in America. He laid down also the principle that "in every human society there is an effort continually tending to confer on one part the highest power and happiness, and to reduce the other to the extreme of weakness and misery." That sentence became the life-long guide of many Americans. It became a constituent part of the minds of Jefferson and Hamilton. It can be seen as the foundation, the connecting strand, running all through the essays of the *Federalist*. It was the inspiration of the "checks and balances" in the national Constitution. It can be traced in American thought and legislation down to the present time.

Burlamaqui's book, devoted exclusively to the subject of liberty and independence, is still one of the best expositions of the true doctrines of natural law, or the rights of man. At the time of the Revolution these rights of man were often spoken of as our rights as men, which is a very descriptive phrase, because the essence of those rights is political manhood, honorable self-reliance as opposed to degenerate dependence.

Burlamaqui belonged to a Protestant family that had once lived at Lucca, Italy; but had been compelled, like the family of Turretini, and many others, to take refuge in Switzerland. He became a professor at Geneva, which gave him the reputation of a learned man. He also became a counsellor of state and was noted for his practical sagacity. He had intended to write a great work in many volumes on the subject to which he had devoted so much of his life, "The Principles of Natural Law," as it was then called. Ill health preventing such a huge task, he prepared a single volume, which he said was only for beginners and students, because it dealt with the bare elements of the science in the simplest and plainest language.

This little book was translated into English in 1748, and contained only three hundred pages; but in that small space of large, clear type, Burlamaqui compressed everything that the patriot colonists wanted to know. He was remarkably clear and concise, and gave the Americans the qualities of the Italian mind at its best. He aroused them by his modern glowing thought and his enthusiasm for progress and liberty. His handy little volume was vastly more effective and far-reaching than would have been the blunderbuss he had intended to load to the muzzle.

If we examine the volumes of Burlamaqui's predecessors, Grotius, Puffendorf, and the others, we find their statements about natural law and our rights as men rather brief, vague, and general, as is usual with the old writers on any science. Burlamaqui brought them down to date, developed their principles, and swept in the results of all the thought and criticism since their day.

The term natural law, which all these writers used, has long since gone out of fashion. They used it because, inspired by the Reformation, they were struggling to get away from the arbitrary system, the artificial scholasticism, the despotism of the middle ages. They were seeking to obtain for law and government a foundation which should grow out of the nature of things, the common facts of life that everybody understood. They sought a system that, being natural, would become established and eternal like nature; a system that would displace that thing of the middle ages which they detested, and called "arbitrary institution."

Let us, they said, contemplate for a time man as he is in himself, the natural man, his wants and requirements.

"The only way," said Burlamaqui, "to attain to the knowledge of that natural law is to consider attentively the nature and constitution of man, the relations he has to the beings that surround him, and the states from thence resulting. In fact, the very term of natural law and the notion we have given of it, show that the principles of this science must be taken from the very nature and constitution of man."—"Principles of Natural Law," p. 156.

Men naturally, he said, draw together to form societies for mutual protection and advantage. Their natural state is a state of union and society, and these societies are merely for the common advantage of all of the members.

This was certainly a very simple proposition, but it had required centuries to bring men's minds back to it; and it was not altogether safe to put forth because it implied that each community existed for the benefit of itself, for the benefit of its members, and not for the benefit of a prince or another nation, or for the church, or for an empire.

It was a principle quickly seized upon by the Americans as soon as their difficulties began in 1764. In their early debates and discussions we hear a great deal about a "state of nature," which at first seems rather meaningless to us. But it was merely their attempt to apply to themselves the fundamental principles of the Reformation. Were the colonies by the exactions and remodelling of the mother-country thrown into that "state of nature," where they could reorganize society afresh, on the basis of their own advantage? How much severity or how much oppression or dissatisfaction would bring about this state of nature? Was there any positive rule by which you could decide? Patrick Henry, who was always very eloquent on the subject, declared that the boundary had been passed; that the colonies were in a state of nature.

Any one who is at all familiar with the trend of thought for the last hundred years can readily see how closely this idea of going back to natural causes and first conceptions for the discovery of political principles is allied to every kind of modern progress; to the modern study of natural history, the study of the plants and animals in their natural environment, instead of by preconceived scholastic theories; the study of the human body by dissection instead of by supposition; the study of heat, light, electricity, the soil, the rocks, the ocean, the stars by actual observation, without regard to what the Scriptures and learned commentators had to say.

A large part of the American colonists were very far advanced in all the ideas of the Reformation. Burlamaqui's book, applying to politics and government these free and wonderful principles, came to a large number of them as the most soul-stirring and mind-arousing message they had ever heard. It has all become trite enough to us; but to them it was fresh and marvellous. Their imaginations seized on it with the indomitable energy and passion which the climate inspired, and some who breathed the air of Virginia and Massachusetts were on fire with enthusiasm.

"This state of nature," argued Burlamaqui, "is not the work of man, but established by divine institution."

"Natural society is a state of equality and liberty; a state in which all men enjoy the same prerogatives, and an entire independence on any other power but God. For every man is naturally master of himself, and equal to his fellow-creatures so long as he does not subject himself to another person's authority by a particular convention."—"Principles of Natural Law," p. 38.

Here we find coupled with liberty that word equality which played such a tremendous part in history for the succeeding hundred years. And we must bear in mind that what the people of that time meant by it was political equality, equality of rights, equality before the law and the government; and not equality of ability, talents, fortune, or gifts, as some have fancied.

Burlamaqui not only found liberty, independence, and equality growing out of nature itself; but he argued that all this was part of the divine plan, the great order of nature and the universe. Indeed, that was what he and his Reformation predecessors had set out to discover, to unravel the system of humanity, to see if there really was a system that could be gathered from the actual plain facts; and to see also if there was a unity and completeness in this system.

"The human understanding," he says, "is naturally right, and has within itself a strength sufficient to arrive at the knowledge of truth, and to distinguish it from error." That he announces as the fundamental principle of his book, "the hinge whereon the whole system of humanity turns," and it was simply his way of restating the great doctrine of the Reformation, the right of private judgment.

But he goes on to enlarge on it in a way particularly pleasing to the patriot colonists, for he says we have this power to decide for ourselves, "especially in things wherein our respective duties are concerned."

"Yes," said the colonists, "we have often thought that we were the best judges of all our own affairs."

"Those who feel," said Franklin, in his examination before Parliament, "can best judge."

The daring Burlamaqui went on to show that liberty instead of being, as some supposed, a privilege to be graciously accorded, was in reality a universal right, inherent in the nature of things.

Then appears that idea common to the great leaders of thought in that age, that man's true purpose in the world is the pursuit of happiness. To this pursuit, they said, every human being has a complete right. It was part of liberty; a necessary consequence of liberty. This principle of the right to pursue happiness, which is merely another way of stating the right of self-development, has played as great a part in subsequent history as equality. It is one of the foundation principles of the Declaration of Independence. It is given there as the ground-work of the right of revolution, the right of a people to throw off or destroy a power which interferes with this great pursuit, "and to institute a new government, laying its foundation on such principles, and organizing its power in such form as to them shall seem most likely to effect their safety and happiness."

It has been interpreted in all sorts of ways—as the right to improve your condition, to develop your talents, to grow rich, or to rise into the class of society above you. It is now in its broadest meaning so axiomatic in this country that Americans can hardly realize that it was ever disputed.

THE PURSUIT OF HAPPINESS

But it was, and still is, disputed in England and on the continent. Even so liberal an Englishman as Kingsley resented with indignation the charge that he favored the aspiration of the lower classes to change their condition. Once a cobbler, remain a cobbler, and be content to be a good cobbler. In other words, the righteousness which he so loudly professed was intended to exalt certain fortunate individuals, and not to advance society.

This desire and pursuit of happiness being part of nature, or part of the system of Providence, and as essential to every man and as inseparable from him as his reason, it should be freely allowed him, and not repressed. This, Burlamaqui declares, is a great principle, "the key of the human system," opening to vast consequences for the world.

The consequences have certainly been vaster than he dreamed of. Millions of people now live their daily life in the sunshine of this doctrine. Millions have fled to us from Europe to seek its protection. Not only the whole American system of laws, but whole philosophies and codes of conduct have grown up under it. The abolitionists appealed to it, and freed six millions of slaves. The transcendental philosophy of New England, that extreme and beautiful attempt to develop conscience, nobility, and character from within; that call of the great writers like Lowell to every humble individual to stand by his own personality, fear it not, advance it by its own lines; even our education, the elective system of our colleges—all these things have followed under that "pursuit of happiness" which the patriot colonists seized upon so gladly in 1765 and enshrined in their Declaration of Independence in 1776.

They found in the principles of natural law how government, civil society, or "sovereignty," as those writers were apt to call it, was to be built up and regulated. Civil government did not destroy natural rights and the pursuit of happiness. On the contrary, it was intended to give these rights greater security and a fresh force and efficiency. That was the purpose men had in coming together to form a civil society for the benefit of all; that was the reason, as Burlamaqui put it, that "the sovereign became the depositary, as it were, of the will and strength of each individual."

This seemed very satisfactory to some of the colonists. You choose your sovereign, your government, for yourself, and make it your mere depositary or agent. Then as to the nature of government, the right to govern, they were very much pleased to find that the only right there was of this sort was the right of each community to govern itself. Government by outside power was absolutely indefensible, because the notion that there was a divine right in one set of people to rule over others was exploded nonsense, and the assertion that mere might or superior power necessarily gave such right was equally indefensible. There remained only one plausible reason, and that was that superior excellence, wisdom, or ability might possibly give such right.

As to this "superior excellence" theory, if you admitted it you denied man's inherent right to liberty, equality, and the pursuit of happiness; you denied his moral accountability and responsibility; you crippled his independent development, his self-development, his individual action; in a word, you destroyed the whole natural system.

Because a man is inferior to another is no reason why he should surrender his liberty, his accountability, his chance for self-development, to the superior. We do not surrender our property to the next man who is richer or an abler business manager. Our inferiority does not give him a right over us. On the contrary, the inferiority of the inferior man is an additional reason why he should cling to all those rights of nature which have been given to him, that he may have wherewithal to raise himself, and be alone accountable for himself. Or, as Burlamaqui briefly summarized it:

"The knowledge I have of the excellency of a superior does not alone afford me a motive sufficient to subject myself to him, and to induce me to abandon my own will in order to take his for my rule; . . . and without any reproach of conscience I may sincerely judge that the intelligent principle within me is sufficient to direct my conduct."— "Principles of Natural Law," p. 86.

Only the people, Burlamaqui explained, have inherent

inalienable rights; and they alone can confer the privilege of commanding. It had been supposed that the sovereign alone had rights, and the people only privileges. But here were Burlamaqui, Puffendorf, Montesquieu, Locke, and fully half the American colonists, undertaking to reverse this order and announcing that the people alone had rights, and the sovereign merely privileges.

These principles the Americans afterwards translated in their documents by the phrase, "a just government exists only by consent of the governed." All men being born politically equal, the colonies, as Dickinson and Hamilton explained, are equally with Great Britain entitled to happiness, equally entitled to govern themselves, equally entitled to freedom and independence.[4]

It is curious to see the cautious way in which some of the colonists applied these doctrines by mixing them up with loyalty arguments. This is very noticeable in the pamphlets written by Alexander Hamilton. He gives the stock arguments for redress of grievances, freedom from internal taxation, government by the king alone, and will not admit that he is anything but a loyal subject. At the same time there runs through all he says an undercurrent of strong rebellion which leads to his ultimate object. "The power," he says, "which one society bestows upon any man or body of men can never extend beyond its own limits." This he lays down as a universal truth, independently of charters and the wonderful British Constitution. It applied to the whole world. Parliament was elected by the people of England, therefore it had no authority outside of the British isle. That British isle and America were separate societies.

"Nature," said Hamilton, "has distributed an equality of rights to every man." How then, he asked, can the English people have any rights over life, liberty, or property in America? They can have authority only among themselves in England. We are separated from Great Britain, Hamilton

---

[4] " Dickinson's Works," vol. i, p. 202.

argued, not only by the ocean, by geography, but because we have no part or share in governing her. Therefore, as we have no share in governing her, she, by the law of nature, can have no share in governing us; she is a separate society.

The British, he said, were attempting to involve in the idea of a colony the idea of political slavery, and against that a man must fight with his life. To be controlled by the superior wisdom of another nation was ridiculous, unworthy of the consideration of manhood; and at this point he used that sentence which has so often been quoted—"Deplorable is the condition of that people who have nothing else than the wisdom and justice of another to depend upon."[5]

Charters and documents, he declared, must yield to natural laws and our rights as men.

> "The sacred rights of man are not to be rummaged for among old parchments or musty records. They are written as with a sunbeam in the whole volume of human nature by the hand of divinity itself and can never be erased by mortal power."

The Declaration of Independence was an epitome of these doctrines of natural law applied to the colonies. The Declaration of Independence originated in these doctrines, and not in the mind of Jefferson, as so many people have absurdly supposed. In order to see how directly the Declaration was an outcome of these teachings we have only to read its opening paragraphs:

> "When, in the course of human events, it becomes necessary for one people to dissolve the political bands which have connected them with another, and to assume, among the powers of the earth, the separate and equal station to which the laws of nature and of nature's God entitle them, a decent respect to the opinions of mankind requires that they should declare the causes which impel them to the separation.

> "We hold these truths to be self-evident, that all men are created equal; that they are endowed by their Creator with certain inalienable rights; that among these are life, liberty, and the pursuit of happiness. That, to secure these rights, governments are instituted among men, deriving their just powers from the consent of the governed; that, whenever any form of government becomes destructive of these ends, it is

---

[5] Works, Lodge edition, vol. i, p. 70.

the right of the people to alter or to abolish it, and to institute a new government, laying its foundation on such principles, and organizing its powers in such form as to them shall seem most likely to effect their safety and happiness. Prudence, indeed, will dictate that governments long established should not be changed for light and transient causes; and, accordingly, all experience hath shown, that mankind are more disposed to suffer, while evils are sufferable, than to right themselves by abolishing the forms to which they are accustomed."

By understanding the writings of Burlamaqui, Locke, and Beccaria, which the colonists were studying so intently, we know the origin of the Declaration, and need not flounder in the dark, as so many have done, wondering where it came from, or how it was that Jefferson could have invented it. Being unwilling to take the trouble of examining carefully the influences which preceded the Declaration, historical students are sometimes surprised to find a document like the Virginia Bill of Rights or the supposed Mecklenburg resolutions,⁶ issued before the Declaration and yet containing the same principles. They instantly jump to the conclusion that here is the real origin and author of the Declaration, and from this Jefferson stole his ideas.

Jefferson merely drafted the Declaration. Neither he, Adams, Franklin, Sherman, nor Livingston, who composed the committee which was responsible for it, ever claimed any originality for its principles. They were merely stating principles which were already familiar to the people, which had been debated over and over again in Congress; which were so familiar, in fact, that they stated them rather carelessly and took too much for granted. It would have been better, instead of saying, "all men are created equal," to have said that all men are created politically equal, which was what they meant, and what every one at that time understood. By leaving out the word "politically" they gave an opportunity to a generation unfamiliar with the doctrines of natural law to suppose that they meant that all men are created, or should be made, equal in conditions, opportunities or talents.

⁶ *Magazine of American History*, vol. xxi, pp. 31, 221; Niles, pp. 313–390.

III.

THE GREAT PROTECTIVE SYSTEM OF THE TRADE AND NAVIGATION LAWS

THE most conspicuous rejection of British authority was purposely omitted from the previous chapters because it deserves a distinct and separate treatment. It was the first irregularity that England attempted to remedy as soon as France was out of the way, and it shows more clearly than anything else the untamable spirit of the patriot colonists, and those aggressive independent qualities which Burke declared would be hard to subdue.

There were a number of laws on the English statute-books known as the navigation laws and the laws of trade. They constituted a great protective system of penalties, tariffs, and duties, designed to build up the shipping, the trade, the commerce, and the manufacturing interests of Great Britain and the colonies. They were to protect the colonies from foreign traders and foreign interference, and to unite them closely with the mother-country in bonds of wealth and prosperity against all the rest of the world.

In the commercial competition in which England was involved with Holland, France, and Spain, it was thought important to prevent those nations from trading with the British colonies. For if those nations were permitted to trade with her colonies, England's reason for protecting and governing them was defeated; it would be hardly worth while to have colonies.

Each nation at that time kept, or tried to keep, its colonial trade exclusively for itself. To accomplish this for England was one of the objects of the trade and navigation laws. Another guiding principle that ran th￼them was, that the profits of trade should be shared betw￼e colonies and the mother-country. The colonies must not monopolize any department of trade. Still another principle was that the colonies should confine themselves chiefly to the production of raw materials and buy their manufactured goods from England.

We find the beginning of these laws in the earliest period of the English colonies. The first important product from the colonies was tobacco from Virginia; and the King, who could *1621* at that time, without the aid of Parliament, impose duties and taxes, put a heavy duty on this tobacco. The Virginians accordingly sent all their tobacco to Holland.

This simple instance shows both the cause and the principle of all the navigation laws. If Holland, England's rival in commerce, was to reap all the advantage of Virginia's existence, of what value to England was Virginia? So the King ordered that no tobacco or other product of the colonies should be carried to a foreign port until it had been first landed in England and the duties paid.

This regulation was not merely for the revenue from the duties, but for the advantage of English tobacco merchants, and to prevent Holland trading with Virginia and establishing a connection there. Soon afterwards, in 1651, Cromwell's Parliament took the next step, and an obvious one, by prohibiting the ships of all foreign nations from trading with the colonies. This was part of Cromwell's vigorous and successful foreign policy, one of the methods he employed for building up the power of England. It was intended to keep for England all her colonial trade and encourage her ship-builders, ship-owners, merchants, and manufacturers by the same method other nations pursued.

Cromwell was of the same dissenting religion as a great many of the American colonists. He favored the colonists, and was generally regarded by them as a great prototype of liberty. But his Parliament passed the first navigation law; and the colonists were often reminded of this when, during the Revolution, some of them argued so strenuously against those laws.

In 1660, when the commonwealth period of Cromwell closed

and monarchy was restored in England, the famous navigation act was passed, carrying the protective system still farther:

1. No goods were to carried from the colonies except in English- or colonial-built ships of which the master and three-fourths of the sailors were English subjects.

2. Foreigners could not be merchants or factors in the colonies.

3. No goods of the growth, production, or manufacture of Africa, Asia, or America could be carried to England in any but English or colonial ships. And such goods must be brought direct from the places where they were usually produced.

4. Oil, whale-fins, etc., usually produced or caught by English subjects, must, when brought into England by foreigners, pay double alien customs.

5. The English coasting trade was confined exclusively to English ships.

The colonists never objected to these provisions, because most of them favored the colonists as much as they favored England. Such regulations encouraged colonial shipping. The provisions relating to the coasting trade we ourselves adopted as soon as we became a nation; and we still confine our coasting trade to our own vessels. We also, in 1816 and afterwards, passed navigation acts somewhat similar in their provisions to these clauses of the English act which have been cited. There is no question that these and similar protective regulations assisted in building up the greatness and power of England and the prosperity of the colonies.

But there was a clause in the navigation act of 1660 which did not please the colonists. It provided that no sugar, tobacco, cotton, indigo, ginger, fustic, or other dye-wood should be carried to any port on the continent of Europe. Such commodities must be carried only to England or to English colonies. The reason for this regulation was, that if the colonists sold these commodities on the continent of Europe they would reap all the profits of the sale and the mother-country would get nothing. It seemed fairer that these articles should be taken to England and sold to English merchants, who might then resell at a profit to continental merchants. Thus the profits of the colonial trade, instead of being monopolized by the colonies, would be shared between them and the mother-country.

These colonial commodities which could not be carried to continental Europe became known in history as the enumerated articles.[1] Judged from the point of view of the times, there was nothing harsh or tyrannical in this provision. But the colonists, having ships of their own, very naturally wanted to trade directly with the continent of Europe. They wanted all the profits for themselves. They wanted full control of all the natural advantages of the separate country in which they lived, and in this respect they were not unlike the rest of the world.

Accordingly this regulation about trading with the continent of Europe was disobeyed, or, if conformed to at all, it was to such a slight extent that it was practically a dead letter. The colonists repealed it as though they had had a parliament of their own for the purpose; and while France held Canada they could do so with impunity.

In 1663 another act was passed, to parts of which the colonists had no objection. They certainly approved of that clause which prohibited tobacco-planting in England, and complained that the weed was still cultivated there in spite of a previous act prohibiting its culture. The object of this act was to favor the Virginia and Maryland tobacco-planters. In consideration for sending all their tobacco to England they were to have the exclusive monopoly of tobacco-planting. The great object of the trade laws was to bind together by reciprocal favors the colonies and the mother-country as a unit against all of England's rivals.

But one of the clauses of the act of 1663 forbade any commodities of Europe to be taken to the colonies[2] except in English-

---

[1] In 1704 molasses and the rice of South Carolina were added to the enumerated articles. In 1730 rice was allowed to be carried to European ports south of Cape Finisterre.

[2] The act allowed certain exceptions—salt for the New England fisheries, wine from Madeira and the Azores, servants and horses from Scotland and Ireland.

built ships and from English ports. This was to compel the colonies to buy their manufactured goods and articles of luxury from England. Why should the colonists enrich the merchants of France, Holland, and Spain? Why not enrich the merchants of England?

This regulation naturally displeased enterprising colonists, and they disobeyed it. They carried the enumerated articles to Europe, and on the return voyage they brought back European products in their own ships and without obtaining them at English ports or from English merchants. Many a cargo of manufactured articles from France or Holland, and of wine, oil, and fruit from Portugal, and many a cargo of the famous cheap Holland tea, snugly packed in molasses hogsheads, did our vessels "run," as it was called, to the American coast, to the great damage and underselling of British merchants, and to the great profit of the natural enemies of Great Britain in France, Spain, and Holland.

If we could raise from the mud, into which she finally sank, any one of the curiously rigged ships of our ancestors, with her high-turreted stern, her queer little mast out on the bowsprit, her lateen sail, and all the contrivances which made her only a slight advance on the old "Mayflower," which brought such vast cargoes of ancestors and old china to Massachusetts, we would be tolerably safe in calling her a smuggler, for most of our ships were engaged in that profitable business.

The desire to share profits with England was not very ardent. In 1676 Edward Randolph was sent out to Massachusetts as an agent to look into its condition. He reported the navigation laws unexecuted and smuggling so universal that commerce was free; and the governor of Massachusetts "would make the world believe they were a free state."

In 1680 he returned to Massachusetts as collector of customs to enforce the navigation laws. The notice of his appointment was torn down, and the assembly created a custom-office of its own, so as to supersede him and administer the navigation laws in the Massachusetts manner. When he attempted to seize vessels he was overwhelmed with law-suits. The people were against him, and he returned to England disgusted.[3]

There was an act of 1696 requiring the trade between England and the colonies to be carried in English- or colonial-built ships; but to this the colonists of course had no objection.

In 1733 another trade act was passed, which levied duties on spirits, sugar, and molasses imported to the colonies from any of the French or Spanish West Indies. This, as the preamble of the act explained, was to protect the English sugar islands from competition with the French and Spanish sugar islands, as well as to give the mother-country a share in this trade. But the colonists found the trade so profitable that they preferred to have it for themselves without any tax or duties. They carried many of their products to the French and Spanish islands, making a good exchange for spirits and sugar, and bringing back gold and silver money which they needed in buying supplies from England and in decreasing the amount of paper money they were obliged to issue. The act of 1733, levying duties on this trade, was a subject of much discussion during the early stages of the Revolution, and was usually spoken of as the "old molasses act" to distinguish it from a sort of supplement to it passed in 1764, called the "sugar act." Our people made a dead letter of it, as they did of all the others that interfered with their purposes.

Modern writers have usually been inclined to dispose of all these trade laws with the brief statement that they were unnatural and absurd restraints. But we must look at them from the point of view of their times, and they were generally regarded by Adam Smith and other political writers as much less restrictive than similar laws of other countries.[4] The trade of all the Spanish colonies was confined by law to Spain; the trade of the Brazils to Portugal; the trade of Martinico and

---

[3] Palfrey, " New England," vol. iii, pp. 284, 375; Randolph's Report, Hutchinson Papers, published by Prince Society, vol. ii; Andros Tracts, vol. iii; Lossing, " Cyclopædia of United States History," pp. 957, 1182.

[4] See, also, " The Interests of the Merchants and Manufacturers of Great Britain in the Present Contest," London, 1774.

other French colonies to France; the trade of Curaçoa and Surinam to Holland. Until about the year 1750 the trade of the Spanish colonies was not only confined to Spain, but to one port of Spain, at first Seville, and afterwards Cadiz.[5]

There was, however, a famous exception to these stringent regulations of colonial commerce. The trade of the island of St. Eustatius was allowed by Holland to be free to all the world. England herself had free ports in Jamaica and Dominica, the French one in St. Domingo, and the Danes one in St. Thomas. The object of such free ports was to draw trade from a rival at some particular point, so as to reap the advantages of both free trade and protection and take profits both coming and going. The English considered Eustatius a great injury to their trade. A large part of the American smuggling was conducted there. It was used during the Revolution to obtain arms and supplies from France; its little rock-bound harbor was always crowded with vessels; there was no spot of earth more thoroughly hated for its free trade; and towards the close of our Revolution England seized it, capturing all the ships in its harbor and destroying its docks and warehouses.[6]

Adam Smith, while showing that England dealt more liberally than any other nation with her colonies in these matters of trade, was nevertheless opposed on principle to such restrictions. But the restrictions had as yet, he said, done no harm to the colonies.

"To prohibit a great people, however, from making all that they can of every part of their own produce, or from employing their stock and industry in the way that they judge most advantageous to themselves, is a manifest violation of the most sacred rights of mankind.

---

[5] Lewis, "Government of Dependencies," edition of 1891, p. 216. See the writings of Dr. Richard Price and Dean Tucker, as well as the works of Josiah Child, Joshua Gee, and John Ashley on the navigation and trade laws; chap. iii of Stokes' "Constitution of the British Colonies," and Stedman, "American War," edition 1794, vol. i, pp. 11–18.

[6] "Observations on North America," translated by J. G. Rosengarten, Phila., 1903; Joshua Gee, "Trade and Navigation of Great Britain," 6th ed., p. 111; "Prior Documents of the Revolution," p. 166; *American Archives*, 5th series, vol. ii, p. 165.

Unjust, however, as such prohibitions may be, they have not hitherto been very hurtful to the colonies. . . . In a more advanced state they might be really oppressive and insupportable."—"Wealth of Nations," Book iv, chap. vii, 5th ed., p. 261.

Adam Smith was a free-trader and believed that free trade would have been better for England than the attempt to monopolize the colonial trade. But it would have been a good deal to expect England to give up colonial monopoly when all other nations were practising it and watching their chance to absorb the trade of the English colonies. If they had all been willing to abandon restrictions, and trust to chance or the working of natural laws for their commercial advantage, there would have been a very pretty field in which Adam Smith and other political economists could have watched developments. But such an ideal condition of affairs was practically impossible.

From England's point of view the restrictive and protective system was of great importance. Even though the colonies violated such parts of the system as they disliked, there remained enough to add enormously to England's wealth. Sir Joshua Gee, writing in 1738, seems to have thought that the colonies had been the principal cause of England's growth and greatness. For nearly two hundred years many of the provisions of the navigation and trade laws had been of vast utility in accomplishing her purposes of trade and crippling her commercial rivals, Holland and France. The navigation acts have always been regarded in England as having, in effect, destroyed the Dutch commercial supremacy. English shipping and colonial shipping developed so rapidly under the first navigation act that old writers called it the Sea Magna Charta and the Charta Maratima. The trade and navigation laws are by no means to be despised and ridiculed, because, under changed conditions, their principle has been abandoned and England has seen greater advantage in free trade.[7]

---

[7] See Josiah Child's "New Course of Trade," published in 1698, as well Gee's "Trade and Navigation of Great Britain," published in 1738. The trade and navigation laws can be read in any edition of the British Statutes at Large. Eyre and Strahan's edition is good, and Stamp's Index to the Statutes at Large will be found convenient.

AMERICAN INDEPENDENCE

In the general European opinion of that time the restrictive system of the navigation and trade laws was believed to be particularly fair and liberal, because it was mutual; because, while the colonies were compelled to trade with the mother-country, the mother-country, besides protecting them with her army and fleet, was compelled to trade with the colonies. The British merchants were as closely bound to buy their raw material only from the colonies as the colonies were bound to buy manufactured goods only from the British merchants. The people of Great Britain, as we have seen, were not allowed to raise tobacco or buy it anywhere except in Maryland and Virginia.

The colonists were paid bounties on all the naval stores, hemp, flax, and lumber, which they produced; and the large sums thus paid to them were regarded by Englishmen as fully offsetting any inconveniences they might suffer from restrictions on their trade. South Carolina had a bounty on indigo, and could carry her rice to all European ports south of Cape Finisterre. The reason for this freedom south of the cape was that those parts of Europe were not manufacturing countries and the colony ships were not likely to carry home from them any manufactured articles that would interfere with English manufacturers.[3]

The laws which prohibited the colonies from importing directly from Europe were mitigated by a system of drawbacks on the duties. The great colonial staples of grain, lumber, salt provisions, fish, sugar, and rum the colonists were allowed to carry to any part of the world, provided they took them in their own or in British-built ships of which the owners and three-fourths of the crew were British subjects. The British West India colonies were compelled to buy their provisions and lumber from the American continental colonies. That colonies which had cost such a vast and long-continued expenditure of blood and treasure should be closely bound to the mother-

---

[3] Smith, "Wealth of Nations," 5th Edinburgh edition, 1859, Book iv, chap. viii, p. 260.

country in trade, and should take part in a system which would at the same time enrich the mother-country and themselves, seemed to most Europeans natural and right.

Montesquieu, who wrote just before the outbreak of our Revolution, and who was one of the liberal thinkers of that time, described the colonial monopoly system as well recognized by the law of nations, and he defends the system "because the design of the settlement was the extension of commerce and not the founding of a city or a new empire." What a colony loses by the restraint is, he says, "visibly compensated by the protection of the mother country, who defends it by her arms and supports it by her laws." [9]

Nor was colonial trade monopoly without its advocates even in America. Joseph Reed, of Philadelphia, who became a patriot general in the Revolution and an intimate friend of Washington, wrote an essay in 1766 in which he defended in the most enthusiastic manner the colonial monopoly as beneficial alike to both England and her colonies.[10]

The Americans were also restrained by acts of Parliament from manufacturing such articles as English merchants wished to furnish; and some of the acts on this subject were aimed not so much at manufacturing certain articles as at exporting them and injuring the foreign trade of the mother-country. The colonists could mine ore and turn it into iron, but they were not allowed to manufacture the iron into steel, tools, or weapons. Furs must be brought to England and not manufactured in the colonies. Hat-making was so successfully carried on that better hats were made in the colonies than in Europe, and many of them were exported to Spain, Portugal, the West Indies, and even to England. The English hat-makers thereupon petitioned Parliament, and in 1732 hat-making was restrained by forbidding the manufacture of hats in the colonies by any one who had not served an apprenticeship of seven years and allowing to a hatter only two apprentices. The object of this act was to

---

[9] "Spirit of the Laws," B. 21, c. xvii.
[10] Life of Joseph Reed, by W. B. Reed, vol. i, p. 409.

keep the industry within bounds, allowing the Americans to make only a few hats for themselves; and to attain this more effectually, the colonists were forbidden to export hats to Europe or from one colony to another. For the same reasons no wool and no article made of wool could be exported from the colonies; for the wool industry in England was of vast importance and must be encouraged by every means.[11]

The colonists seem to have violated these laws with impunity. They were not very strongly drawn to domestic manufacturing at that time, because they saw greater fields of profit in farming and on the ocean, in ship-building and the carrying trade, in whaling and in the fisheries of the Grand Banks. But they indulged themselves in a certain amount of manufacturing, both illicit and legitimate. They made steel, tools, anchors, scythes, and weapons of all sorts in spite of the prohibition. Rifles appear to have been made at Lancaster and Philadelphia long before the Revolution. Blacksmiths could forge muskets and smooth-bore barrels. Those who know the passion of the American for tools and machinery will smile at his being restrained by an act of a Parliament three thousand miles away.[12]

Such manufacturing as was carried on in America was confined almost exclusively to the northern colonies. It did not become large, and the products of it were not extensively exported. The colonists imported enormous quantities of manufactured goods from England. These importations were rapidly increasing in volume and appeared to be only slightly affected by the surreptitious colonial manufacturing. By reason of the enormous importations the profits of nearly every kind of busi-

---

[11] Acts 8 Geo. I, c. 15, sec. 24; 5 Geo. II, c. 22; 23 Geo. II, c. 29, sec. 9; 10 and 11 Wm. III, c. 10, sec. 19; 12 Geo. II, c. 21, sec. 11; Columbia Univ. Studies in History, &c., vol. iii, No. 2, p. 66.

[12] "The Interests of the Merchants and Manufacturers in the Present Contest," p. 22, et seq., London, 1774; *Pennsylvania Magazine of History*, vol. vii, p. 197; Achenwall, "Observations on North America," 1767, translated by J. G. Rosengarten, pp. 13–14; *American Archives*, 4th series, vol. i, p. 1002.

ness in the colonies tended to centre in England; specie was drained from the colonists; and they were forced to create an artificial paper money. In the matter of taking her manufactured goods, the colonies were certainly a source of wealth to England. Pownall thought that the English manufacturers would always be able to undersell American-made goods, and the colonists would always be dependent on England for such supplies.[13]

The policy of preventing a colony from establishing manufactures of its own and thus compelling it to buy goods from the mother-country was from earliest times considered an important and obviously necessary part of England's colonial system. It seemed absurd to allow a colony to develop an industry which could interfere with an industry of the mother-country, and sell to France or Spain products which the mother-country wished to sell. The Board of Trade and Plantations were, from their first constitution in 1696, instructed to watch for and report such dangers. For a hundred years before our Revolution the principal reason for holding and encouraging the colonies and sacrificing money and lives in their protection, was that they might afford a market, or give a vent as it was called, for English goods. After our Revolution this same method was successfully followed in British India, where England has largely suppressed the native industries, and reaped a vast revenue from the control of a population of 290,000,000.

"India, in the eighteenth century was a great manufacturing as well as a great agricultural country, and the products of Indian looms supplied the markets of Asia and of Europe. It is, unfortunately, true that the East Indian Company and the British Parliament, following the selfish commercial policy of a hundred years ago, discouraged Indian manufactures in the early years of British rule in order to encourage the rising manufactures of England. Their fixed policy, pursued during the last decades of the eighteenth century and the first decades of the nineteenth, was to make India subservient to the industries of Great Britain, and to make the Indian people grow raw produce only, in order to supply

---

[13] "Administration of the Colonies," 2d ed., p. 201.

material for the looms and manufactories of Great Britain. This policy
was pursued with unwavering resolution and with fatal success. . . .
It is a painful episode in the history of British rule in India; but it is a
story which has to be told to explain the economic condition of the
Indian people, and their present helpless dependence on agriculture."—
Dutt, " Economic History of India," p. viii. See also Digby, " Prosperous
British India," pp. 36, 85, 91, 145, 258–261.

Since 1879, however, the opposite policy has been pursued in
the case of Canada and Australia, whose populations have
always been comparatively small and whose ability and opportunities for manufacturing are so slight that they never could
become great and dangerous rivals like India or the United
States. The restraint of manufacturing in Canada and Australia was found to be depressing at a time when those colonies
needed the greatest encouragement. Even when England was
practising and advocating free trade most strongly it soon
became obvious that an exception must be made in the case of
Canada, whose manufacturing industries required encouragement; and accordingly after the year 1879 Canada was allowed
to enact a tariff "which was professedly based upon the principle of protection to native industries." [14]

---

[14] Johns Hopkins Univ. Studies in History, &c., vol. vii, " Federal
Government in Canada," p. 41; Achenwall, "Observations on North
America," 1767, pp. 15, 19; Todd, " Parliamentary Government in the
British Colonies," edition 1894, pp. 222–227, 231–232, 273.

IV.

THE WRITS OF ASSISTANCE

THE smuggling we indulged in so universally against the navigation laws was not a daring occupation. A vessel would enter her cargo as salt or ballast, or would pay duty on part, and "run" the rest. Popular opinion was so overwhelmingly in favor of smuggling that it was not regarded as a crime; and the customs officials wishing to live at peace with their neighbors and being well treated by captains and importers would take no notice of irregularities over which any sort of veil was drawn.

The law which required all tobacco to be taken to England was evaded by delivering the tobacco to the Dutch at sea, and this was supposed to be a loss of £10,000 a year to the English revenue. Great quantities of tobacco, however, went to England in accordance with the law. The southern colonies, especially South Carolina, were not so much inclined to indulge in illegal trade as their northern sisters, because the products of the South were more suited to the English market, while the northern commodities found a more natural and better exchange in the forbidden ports of the West Indies or continental Europe.

On the American coast, the creeks of the Delaware River and the inlets and sounds of the New Jersey shore gave ample opportunity for smuggling in the neighborhood of Philadelphia. Farther north we find that Long Island, with its sound and bays, became the natural and secure home of the smuggler; and goods were often landed at Cape Ann, and carried thence to Boston in wood boats. Under the pretence of trading in fish, the wild island of Newfoundland was much used by the smugglers, and was described as a "magazine of all sorts of goods brought thither directly from France, Holland, Scotland, Ireland, and other places." New England vessels carried on a large illicit trade with France, exchanging provisions and lumber for French manufactures and India goods. In the West Indies vessels obtained false clearances for casks supposed to contain sugar or molasses, but which, in fact, were empty; and the vessel then proceeded to the French Islands and loaded the forbidden articles.[1]

The issuing of false documents from the custom-houses and the general corruption of the customs officials seem to have been universal and taken as a matter of course. "If conniving at foreign sugar and molasses and Portugal wines and fruit," said Governor Bernard, of Massachusetts, in 1764, "is to be reckoned corruption, there was never, I believe, an uncorrupt custom officer in America till within twelve months." The governors themselves, it was said, shared in the profits of the smuggling, and a vessel engaged in the illicit trade in Rhode Island was owned by one of the judges of the Superior Court.[2]

Our people regarded the prohibitions of the navigation laws as contrary to their natural interests and therefore as wicked foreign legislation which it was no discredit to evade, and the tricks of evasion appear to have been openly discussed. I have been shown the diary of a member of a respectable Quaker family in which he describes one of these devices as if it were a regular part of business:

May 22, 1750. "Feathers may be shipped from Ireland paying a duty of 2/ per ct. provided the vesel be entered out from some forrain

---

[1] Hutchinson's letter to Richard Jackson, September, 1763; Ryerson's "Loyalists," vol. i, p. 276; Board of Trade Papers, Pennsylvania Historical Society, vol. ii, B. 34, 619; Rhode Island Colonial Records, vol. vi. 428–430; "Letters to the Ministry and Memorials to the Lords of the Treasury from Commissioners of Customs," pp. 115–120; Stedman, "American War," edition 1794, vol. i, p. 12; Columbia Univ. Studies in History, etc., vol. iii, chap. 2, pp. 39, 130, etc.; "Documents Relating to New York Colonial History," vol. iii, pp. 44–47; Quincy's Reports of Massachusetts Superior Court, 1761–1772, pp. 430, 436 *et passim;* "Letters to the Ministry from Gov. Bernard," &c., London, 1769, pp. 55, 115 *et passim;* "A Defence of the Letters from a Gentleman at Halifax," Providence, 1765, p. 22; *American Archives,* 4th series, vol. i, p. 1669.

[2] Quincy's Reports of the Massachusetts Superior Court, 1761–1772, pp. 423–424, 437.

port, such as the Dutch West Indies, Madeira, Jamaica, etc. The method would be to enter out for a forrain and the port designed for, take a particular cocket for the prohibited goods directed for a forrain port and when clear of the Kingdom destroy it and when arrived with us run the goods."

Smuggling was on so large a scale and so popular that it had become respectable. There had been for a hundred years and more a great deal of smuggling on the English coast, which has been vividly described by Macaulay as it existed, about the year 1700, when the people used to say that if a gallows were set up every quarter of a mile along the seacoast the trade would still go on briskly. Even after our Revolution, English smuggling seemed to be as bad as ever. It had been reduced, we are told, to regular system; forty thousand persons were engaged in it by sea and land; and gentlemen of rank and character in London were believed to furnish the capital required.[3]

The moral aspect of the situation was not allowed to pass unchallenged. We find a pamphlet[4] written as is supposed by John Drinker, of Philadelphia, implying that all merchants were habitual customs violators or corrupted others to break the laws, and that such a system was ruining the morals of the country. In our time a reform club would be organized to deal with the question. But the colonists usually regarded the trade laws as so contrary to their natural rights and opportunities that it was a sacred duty to break them.

In spite of the long series of trade and navigation laws filling so many pages of her statute-books, the revenue collected by England in America was only £1000 or £2000 per year, and it cost £7000 or £8000 to collect it. John Adams said that the duties on molasses alone, if collected, would have amounted to £25,000 per year. He asserted quite positively that the acts of trade "had never been executed as revenue laws, and there never had been a time when they would have been or could

[3] Stanhope, Life of Pitt, pp. 215–216.
[4] "Observations on the Late Popular Measures," Philadelphia, 1774.

have been obeyed as such."[5] He meant, of course, such parts of the trade and navigation laws as the colonists considered injurious to their interests.

On the other hand, the Reverend Cotton Mather, of Massachusetts, asserted with characteristic unction that it was a shameful slander on the colonists to say that they broke the acts of navigation. "The whole body of the people," he said, "would rejoice in the severest execution of those acts and lend their utmost help thereunto. There are but a few particular persons that have transgressed in the forbidden trade."[6]

Between these two extreme statements many others might be collected affirming or denying the universality of the smuggling. But the conclusion one draws is that it was universal; and was, as Lieutenant Governor Colden, of New York, said, "publickly espoused by numbers and more strenuously advocated than legal trade." There was no doubt occasional or partial conformity, and those parts of the trade and navigation laws which gave an advantage to colonial ships were, of course, faithfully and legally obeyed.

About the year 1755 writs of assistance began to be used in Massachusetts for authorizing custom-house officers to break into vessels, warehouses, and dwellings to search for contraband goods, and the controversy over these writs must be noticed. A writ of assistance, or assistants as it was often called in those days, was a writ issued by a court and directed to sheriffs, constables, naval and other officers, as well as to all subjects of the realm, commanding them to permit and aid the customs officers to enter vessels by day or night, and warehouses, cellars, and dwellings by day only, and break open chests, boxes, and packages of all sorts in the search for contraband goods. The writ was general and did not specify a particular house or particular goods. It did not have to be issued on sworn infor-

---

[5] Works, vol. x, pp. 246, 348. See also Colden's remarks, *American Archives*, 4th series, vol. i, p. 1030.

[6] Andros, Tracts ii, p. 57; see Beer, " Commercial Policy of England," Columbia Univ. Studies in History, &c., vol. iii, No. 2, p. 140; Quincy, Reports of Massachusetts Superior Court, 1761-1772, pp. 401-407.

mation. It was not limited, like most writs, to a short period of time, but endured in full power during the life of the king and for six months after his death. It was in fact a general authority to the custom-house officer of a particular place to search everywhere and violate the ancient maxim that a man's house is his castle.

A strong argument can, of course, be made against such writs as violating the general principle that a man's house should not be searched except by a writ issued for only a limited period and based on sworn information describing the particular house and giving a reason for the search. But in England writs of assistance had been held to be an exception to this principle ever since the time of Charles II. Every custom-house officer had one of them. They were used almost daily, and were continued in use in their full force in England down to the year 1817.[7]

They were established by an act of Parliament in the fourteenth year of the reign of Charles II, and another act in the eighth year of William III extended their use to the colonies. As this latter act named no particular courts in the colonies which should grant such writs, a doubt was raised as to their legality in America. But the courts of Massachusetts and of New Hampshire seem to have had no scruples about issuing them, because the Massachusetts court had been given by the assembly the same judicial powers as the Exchequer Court, which in England issued the writs.

When George II died, October 25, 1760, the writs of assistance that had been issued in New Hampshire and Massachusetts would expire in six months. The customs officers began to apply to the courts for new writs, and the application of Charles Paxton, Surveyor and Searcher of the Port of Boston, has been much noticed in our histories, because of the eloquent

---

[7] After that they seem to have been still issued by the courts, but the Board of Customs modified their use by an order that no officer should act under one unless he first took oath before a magistrate of his belief and grounds of belief that contraband goods were lodged in a certain house. Quincy's Reports *supra*, pp. 399, 452, 535.

but in some respects exaggerated description of it which John Adams has left us.[3]

Writs of assistance were of great importance to the government because, nearly the whole population being interested in smuggling, it was very easy to conceal goods in private stores and dwellings, and they never could be discovered unless the government had the largest liberty of search. Hutchinson, the lieutenant governor, a native of Massachusetts, but a strong loyalist and government man, said that about the only chance the customs officers had to detect contraband goods was after they were landed, and even then they could not discover them without a writ of assistance.

Hutchinson was also chief justice of the court that in February, 1761, heard the argument on Paxton's application for a new writ. Some patriot merchants, or illicit traders as the loyalists called them, had petitioned the court not to grant the writ; and they had retained as their counsel Thatcher and James Otis to convince the court that such tyrannical writs should not be issued in America. The government's side of the case was argued by Gridley. As counsel for the petitioners, Thatcher appears to have made a lawyer-like but unexciting speech against the technical legality of such writs. But Otis's argument has become famous from the enthusiastic description of it by Adams, who was then a young law student and sat at the trial taking notes.

The argument of the case drew an audience of all the members of the bar and probably some of the citizens of the town. Adams, in his confident and exuberant style, describes the scene in the council chamber of the old State House, which is still standing in Boston:

"That council chamber was as respectable an apartment as the House of Commons or the House of Lords in Great Britain, in proportion, or that in the State House in Philadelphia, in which the Declara-

---

[3] The whole subject has been exhaustively and admirably investigated by Judge Gray, of Massachusetts, afterwards one of the justices of the Supreme Court of the United States. See the Appendix to Quincy's Reports of Massachusetts Superior Court, 1761–1772, already cited.

tion of Independence was signed in 1776. In this chamber round a great fire were seated five judges, with Lieutenant Governor Hutchinson at their head as chief justice, all arrayed in their new, fresh, rich robes of scarlet English broadcloth, in their large cambric bands and immense judicial wigs. In this chamber were seated at a long table all the barristers at law of Boston, and of the neighboring county of Middlesex, in gowns, bands and tie wigs. They were not seated on ivory chairs, but their dress was more solemn and more pompous than that of the Roman Senate when the Gauls broke in upon them. . . .

" Two portraits at more than full length of King Charles the Second and of King James the Second, in splendid golden frames, were hung upon the most conspicuous sides of the apartment. If my young eyes or old memory have not deceived me, these were as fine pictures as I ever saw; the colors of the royal ermines and long flowing robes were the most glowing, the figures the most noble and graceful, the features the most distinct and characteristic, far superior to those of the King and Queen of France in the senate chamber of Congress—these were worthy of the pencils of Rubens and Vandyke. There was no painter in England capable of them at that time."—Works, vol. x, p. 245.

The speech by Otis, Adams said, was a "flame of fire." Judging from his account it was a most violent denunciation of the whole commercial system which was represented by the navigation and trade laws. Feeling no doubt that there was every probability that writs legal in England under acts of Parliament, and which had been so long used in the colonies, would be held legal by the Massachusetts court, Otis struck at the foundation and denied that Parliament had any authority whatever over the colonies. The acts extending the writs to America as well as the navigation and trade laws were, therefore, so far as the colonies were concerned, absolutely null and void, and writs issued in support of such acts ought to be held void and infamous.

Loyalists, and indeed some patriots, have ascribed Otis's violent denunciation to a personal hostility he felt towards Hutchinson, the chief justice of the court, as well as towards the British Government. Otis's father, usually known as Colonel Otis, had been twice promised that when a vacancy occurred he would be made one of the justices of the court. The promise had been twice broken, and on the last occasion Hutchinson had obtained the place and had been made chief justice. Before this last appointment had been made Otis had said, " If Governor Bernard does not appoint my father judge of the superior court I will kindle such a fire in the province as shall singe the governor, though I myself perish in the flames.''*

Up to that time the colonists were not in the habit of denying the whole authority of Parliament. They had not as yet decided to assail the authority of the numerous parliamentary statutes under which they had been living, in many cases without the slightest complaint, for more than a hundred years. Four years afterwards at the time of the stamp act we shall find them formally admitting the full authority of Parliament over them except in the one item of internal taxation; and it was not until some years after that, that they abandoned this distinction between internal and external taxation and rejected the whole authority of Parliament.

If, therefore, we can rely on the description by Adams of Otis's bold denial of all parliamentary authority, that denial was considerably in advance of the time. Such denial of authority had no doubt been discussed before 1761 among some of the radical colonists in private conversation; but there does not seem to have been anything in the nature of a general formal avowal of it.

Otis, aroused to what according to Adams was an extraordinary pitch of passion and eloquence, ridiculed and cast away the distinction between external and internal taxes and made the argument, often made publicly ten or fifteen years afterwards, that the colonies must necessarily be out of the jurisdiction of Parliament because they had been originally chartered by the Stuart kings without the assistance of an act of Parliament. Those kings hated parliaments and would not permit Parliament to share such a right with them. The whole system of English colonization was, Otis said, outside the realm, outside of parliamentary authority, and in the hands only of the King.

Not content with ridiculing the language and the provisions

---

* Gordon, " American Revolution," edition 1788, vol. i, p. 141.

of the acts of trade, Otis attacked those writers—political economists we would now call them—who had supported the propriety of controlling colonial trade. He began with Sir Josiah
Child, who wrote before the year 1700 and who was always
regarded as a great authority because of his practical experience. He was the ablest merchant of his time and controlled
almost the whole trade of England with the East. From him
Otis passed on to Sir Joshua Gee, and Ashley, and Davenant,
which brought the list down to his own time.

He had the books of these men in court and read quotations
from them. They upheld the necessity in those days of confining the trade of a colony to its mother-country, because other
nations did the same, and if the trade of a colony were not so
confined it would be absorbed by the Dutch and the colony
would become not only useless to its mother, but perhaps a
dangerous rival. They upheld the general principle that to
allow a colony unrestricted trade would necessarily be an
injury to the trade of the mother-country; and New England
would be a damage to old England, unless its trade were confined to England. Against these doctrines Otis poured forth
the whole venom and bitterness of New England hatred and
detestation. If the King of Great Britain in person, he
declared, were encamped on Boston Common at the head of
twenty thousand men, with all his navy on our coast, he would
not be able to execute those laws of navigation and trade.

His appeal was no doubt addressed to the audience which
filled the room as much as to the court; and to arouse hatred
for the whole British system, he read passages from the
writers mentioned in which they had sneered at the American colonists as outcasts and convicts who had left England for
England's good; "loose, vagrant people, vicious and destitute
of means," like the Virginians, who "could never have lived at
home, but must have come to be hanged or died untimely;" or
malcontents like the New Englanders, who "feared the re-estab-
lishment of the ecclesiastical laws," and "some of those people
called Quakers banished for meeting on pretence of religious
worship."

Otis also went over the whole ground of the laws regulating colonial manufacturing and Adams says "alternately laughed and raged against them all." A member of Parliament, it was said, had announced that not even a hobnail ought to be manufactured in America. Why then, said Otis, should not Parliament enact that the Americans must send their horses to England to be shod?

This defiant speech, in which British judges and governors were told to their faces that all England's laws were invalid in the colonies, and that those which were disliked never had been and never could be executed, produced, according to Adams, a tremendous impression.

It was not printed or published in any way except that the lawyers and others in the audience may have carried a very complete account of it out of doors. Adams in the excess of his admiration fifty-six years afterwards, describes it as the beginning of the Revolution; but that is of course an exaggeration. Allowing, however, for Adams's determination to have everything begin in Boston, we can understand that it was one of the events which encouraged the opponents of British rule in Massachusetts, encouraged the mercantile classes to evade the trade laws, and gratified the leaders of the little infant patriot party by bringing to their side a distinguished and able orator like Otis.

He was soon afterwards elected to the Massachusetts Assembly, and for the next ten years was accepted by the patriots as one of their leaders and advisers. We soon find him, however, stating milder views than he had urged upon the court. Indeed, he reversed his opinion and held that Parliament had complete and absolute power over the colonies in every particular, and that it was impossible to conceive of the colonial relation without that absolute power of Parliament. As a lawyer and a student of the British Constitution, he must have been well aware that such would be the final decision in England and that there was nothing for the Americans to do but accept that decision or break away from the mother-country by force.

He seems to have been a man of violent impulses, much

given to invective and abuse, full of egotism, absorbing every conversation and talking down opposition. His wife was a loyalist, and her curtain lectures, of which he bitterly and openly complained, seem to have aggravated his impulsive tendencies. He was disliked for his manners, but valued for his patriotic services, which were terminated in 1769 by an assault in the coffee-house by one of the customs commissioners, and his subsequent insanity.[10]

The court before which he made his famous speech reserved its decision as to issuing the writ of assistance until the judges could communicate with England and obtain further information. When that information was obtained the writ was issued, followed afterwards by the issuance of others in both Massachusetts and New Hampshire.

This decision seems to have been legally correct. Such general writs are contrary to American principles and would, with us, be now held unconstitutional. But Massachusetts was at that time an English colony under the jurisdiction of Parliament, which, by the act of the reign of William III, had expressly extended the English writs to the colonies; and the Massachusetts Assembly had given the superior court of the province the same powers as the Court of Exchequer in England, which issued such writs. The writs issued in Massachusetts and New Hampshire under that decision seem to have been of immediate service to the government in making seizures of illicit cargoes on the New England coast; and in 1764 the Ministry instituted repressive measures of a wider scope.[11]

---

[10] John Adams, Works, vol. ii, pp. 163, 219–220, 226–227.

[11] See Quincy's Reports, *supra*, p. 540.

James Cockle, the surveyor of customs for Salem, was also given a new writ, and under the custom-house advertisements of the Boston *Gazette* of May 20, 1762, an extreme patriot newspaper, is the following:

"Port of C—K—C—Borough

"Now riding at anchor and ready for sailing, the Idiot of full Freight with Ignorance, no commission, few Guns; any necessitious Person that wants daily sustenance may meet with suitable Encouragement by applying to J-s C-K-C the commander, at Kings Arms in S——."—Quincy's Reports, *supra*, pp. 422–423.

AMERICAN INDEPENDENCE

It was rather late, however, to begin to repress the American merchants and sailors, who had done pretty much as they pleased for over a hundred years. Their ships had sailed into every sea; the merchants were as daring in commercial enterprise as the crews were bold and skilful in navigation; and they laughed at the Parliament whose laws they had violated for generations. They were men who had won careers from rugged nature, and therefore believed in themselves; who were inventive, aggressive, self-confident, and unpleasant in English eyes; but the same men whom the eloquent Irishman, Burke, delighted to describe as pursuing the whales among the tumbling mountains of Arctic ice, or following the same dangerous game beneath the frozen serpent of the South.

What else had the colonists but their ships and their farms? Those were their two principal occupations. They ploughed either the sea or the land; and the farmers and the small traders were strongly inclined to wish success to the great merchants and the sailors because the shipping interest added value to the farms and the small trade.

When, therefore, the British Government, after the French war was over, resolved on more regular and systematic control, when revenue-cutters became more numerous, when the customs officials were stiffened for their duty and struck at what the colonists called "free trade," and what in England was called the infamous crime of smuggling, it seemed to many of the colonists a terrible thing, an interference with time-honored privilege, a suppression of their natural energies, and is not improperly described as an important cause of the Revolution.[12]

---

[12] " Prior Documents of the Revolution," p. 3.

V.

MORE STRINGENT NAVIGATION LAWS, ADMIRALTY COURTS AND CUSTOMS OFFICIALS

THE reform that irritated the colonial merchants and ship-owners most of all was aimed at their trade with the French and Spanish West Indies, the trade which, as we have seen, had been prohibited by the "old molasses act" of 1734. They had evaded that act for thirty years. But now, in this famous year 1764, with France driven from Canada, and the reorganization of the colonies resolved upon, the Ministry ordered men-of-war and revenue-cutters to enforce the law, and a supplementary act was passed, known among the colonists as the "Sugar Act."

This act reduced by one-half the duties which had been imposed on sugar and molasses by the "old molasses act" of 1734. This reduction, like so many other parts of the system, was intended as a favor to the colonists and a compensation for restrictions in other matters. But as the colonists, by wholesale smuggling, had been bringing in sugar and molasses free, they did not appreciate this favor of half-duties which were to be actually enforced.

The act also imposed duties on coffee, pimento, French and East India goods, and wines from Madeira and the Azores, which hitherto had been free. It also added iron and lumber to the "enumerated articles" which could be exported only to England; and it reinforced the powers of the admiralty courts, which could try the smuggling and law-breaking colonists without a jury.

But the worst part of the act was that it required the duties to be paid in specie into the treasury in London; and of this the colonial merchants bitterly complained, because it would drain the colonies of specie; and as Parliament was passing another act prohibiting future issues of paper money there would be nothing to supply the place of the specie.

AMERICAN INDEPENDENCE

From the English point of view the "old molasses act" and the Sugar Act were necessary to protect the English sugar islands from French and Spanish competition; were, in fact, part of the system of protection for all parts of the empire; the system of give and take, by which inconveniences suffered by one locality for the sake of another were compensated by bounties or special privileges in some other department of trade.[1]

This attempt to enforce the Sugar Act and the old trade laws aroused great opposition and indignation in America, and met with no real success. The loyalists afterwards said that the indignation was confined to the smuggling merchants and a few radical and restless people; but the indignant ones were able to make themselves very conspicuous, for they combined to protect and conceal smuggling, and at times they broke out into mob violence and outrage which made Englishmen stare. When the officials occasionally succeeded in seizing a smuggled cargo it was apt to be rescued by violence which was actual warfare, but into which the perpetrators entered not only without hesitation but with zeal, energy, and righteous indignation, as though they felt that the country was already their own and the Englishman a foreigner and invader.

After the new writs of assistance were issued, in 1761, there was possibly some little success in repressing smuggling until 1766, at which time the violence of the mobs in support of the illicit trading was so great in Massachusetts that the writs could not be used, and all attempts to seize cargoes or enforce the laws were abandoned as impracticable. In fact, at this time all authority in New England was in the hands of the populace.

This sudden defeat, in 1766, of all the Government's efforts against smuggling seems to have been the result of the repeal of

---

[1] The court of Madrid was opposed to the trade with the American colonies and the Sugar Act was regarded as in compliance with Spanish wishes and the treaties subsisting between Spain and England.—" Prior Documents of the Revolution," p. 4. See also pp. 163–167 for an interesting petition against the Sugar Act sent to the House of Commons by the merchants of New York. *Annual Register*, 1765, chap. vi.

the Stamp Act in that year, which inspired the patriot party with such confidence in themselves that they decided to abolish the trade and navigation laws altogether. Otis made a speech at this time in which he told the people that as Parliament had given up the Stamp Act it had given up the navigation laws, and that the merchants were great fools if they submitted any longer to laws restraining their trade, which ought to be free.[2]

In the hope of remedying this state of affairs, an act of Parliament was passed in 1767 creating a new Board of Commissioners of Customs, who were to reside in America instead of in England. There were five of these commissioners, and it was one of them, John Robinson, who quarrelled with and assaulted James Otis in the coffee-house.

The enumerated articles which the colonists were forbidden to carry to any country of Europe except Great Britain had now greatly increased in number. By the original navigation act of 1660 there had been only about seven of them—sugar, tobacco, cotton, indigo, ginger, fustic or other dyewood. But now there had been added molasses, hemp, copper ore, skins and furs, pitch, tar, turpentine, masts, yards, bowsprits, rice, coffee, pigment, cocoanuts, whale-fins, raw silk, pot and pearlashes. This tended to pass more trade through the hands of English people and make England the great market for the commerce of the world.

In 1766 Parliament also enacted that all non-enumerated articles should be subject to very much the same regulation as the enumerated articles, and not sent to any European country north of Cape Finisterre, except Great Britain and Ireland. These non-enumerated articles included for the most part grain of all sorts, salt provisions and fish. The colonies produced these in large quantities, and had heretofore been free to carry them to all the markets of the world. Their sale of them had not previously been confined to England, because it had been thought that forcing the whole colonial

---

[2] Quincy's Reports of Massachusetts Superior Court, 1761–1772, pp. 434, 445, 446.

supply of such products into England would interfere too much with English people who produced the same commodities.[3]

The British fleet on the American coast was instructed at this time to give every assistance to the customs officials. Each captain had to take the custom-house oaths, and be commissioned as a custom-house officer to assist in the good work. Admiral Colville, who commanded from the St. Lawrence to Florida, became in effect the head of a corps of revenue officers; and, to stimulate the zeal of his officers, they were to receive large rewards from all forfeited property. Some of the captains even went so far as to buy on their own account small vessels, which they sent, disguised as coasters, into the bays and shoal waters to collect evidence and make seizures; and one of the captains appears to have been given a writ of assistance.[4]

But to bring the colonists under the discipline of a more methodical government was an extremely difficult and slow process. The new commissioners of customs sent out more than twenty cutters and armed vessels to cruise for smugglers. But they rarely made a seizure; and the colonists laughed at the enormous exertion with small result, and said that it was like burning a barn to roast an egg.[5]

As a further check to smuggling, and in the hope of gaining more control of the colonies, the admiralty courts, which tried cases without juries, were made more numerous, and all the revenue cases brought within their jurisdiction. Such courts had been established in the colonies ever since 1696; but they were few, widely separated, and their jurisdiction it seems was

---

[3] Smith, "Wealth of Nations," supra, pp. 259-260. See also the printed instructions from the new commissioners of customs at Boston to their under-officials, giving full details of their duties, enumeration of articles and of the various acts of Parliament to be enforced. A copy of this very instructive and valuable document is preserved in the Carter-Brown collection at Providence, Rhode Island.

[4] "Observations on the Several Acts of Parliament," etc., p. 17, Boston, 1769; Quincy's Reports of the Massachusetts Superior Court, pp. 429-430; Annual Register, 1765, chap. v.

[5] Jared Ingersoll, "Letters Relating to the Stamp Act," New Haven, 1766.

limited. In 1765 the Stamp Act provided that not only the suits for penalties under that act, but all suits under the revenue laws, could be brought in admiralty. This act was repealed in 1766 and in 1768 another act was passed providing that revenue cases might be tried in any court of vice admiralty appointed or to be appointed. The intention of this act was to make the admiralty courts more numerous and convenient; and such courts were established at Halifax, Boston, Philadelphia, and Charleston.

This extension of admiralty seemed necessary to the British Government because it was difficult, if not impossible, to find a jury in America that would convict a smuggler or any one violating the Stamp Act of Parliament. The enforcement of such acts of Parliament in admiralty courts without juries seemed entirely justifiable to the Ministry because penalties under the revenue laws had long been recoverable in admiralty, and in England stamp duties were recoverable before two justices of the peace without a jury.[*]

But to many of the colonists it seemed as if these courts without juries would soon extend their power from their proper sphere of the seaports into the "body of the country," as it was called. They raised the alarm that Britain was depriving her colonies of the right of trial by jury; that she intended to cut off trial by jury more and more; and in the Declaration of Independence this is enumerated as one of the reasons for breaking up the empire.

It is interesting to remember in this connection that by act of Parliament the British Government can at any time with-

---

[*] Tucker, "True Interest of Great Britain Set Forth," London, 1774; "Correct Copies of Two Protests Against the Bill to Repeal the American Stamp Act," p. 17, London, 1766; "The Conduct of the Late Administration," etc., pp. 12–13, London, 1767; Columbia Univ. Studies in History, &c., vol. iii, No. 2, p. 129; "Strictures upon the Declaration of the Congress at Philadelphia," London, 1776, p. 24; "An Answer to the Declaration of the Congress," London, 1776, p. 71; Quincy, Massachusetts Reports, 1761–1772, p. 553 *et seq.;* "The Rights of the Colonies Examined," Providence, 1765, pp. 14–15.

draw trial by jury from Ireland, and in the year 1902 withdrew it by proclamation in nine Irish counties. Great Britain began the conquest and pacification of Ireland seven hundred years ago, but the Irish are not yet submissive and British sovereignty is not yet established. To Englishmen who reflected on the smuggling and illicit manufacturing, the thousands of convicts transported to the colonies, the thousands of fierce red Indians by whom the colonists were supposed to be influenced, and the million black slaves driven with whips—the withholding from such people of the right of trial by jury, as it still may be withheld from Ireland, or even of the right of self-government, seemed no doubt a small matter. It was the fashion among most Englishmen to despise the Americans, as it is indeed the fashion everywhere to despise a people who are in a dependent or colonial position.

The patriot colonists, however, rapidly learned to resent English contempt and revenge themselves. One of the first war-vessels which attempted to carry out the new policy of repressing smuggling was the schooner "St. John," which was stationed at Newport; and the colonists actually fitted out an armed sloop to destroy her, and when prevented by the presence of the man-of-war "Squirrel," they landed on Goat Island, seized the battery, and discharged its guns at the "Squirrel." [7]

During that same year the press-gangs of British war-vessels at Newport caused much irritation by taking sailors from colonial ships. In one instance the "Maidstone" pressed the whole crew of an American brig just arrived from Africa, and that night the Newport mob, finding one of the "Maidstone's" boats at the wharf, dragged it up to the common and burnt it amid shouts of applause from the people.

At the close of the year 1764, the first year of the attempt at reorganization and reform, the Ministry and Parliament had been inclined to congratulate themselves on having done a good deal towards remedying the disorders in America. At the opening of the next session of Parliament, in 1765, the King

---

[7] J. R. Bartlett, "Destruction of the Gaspee," p. 6.

reminded the Lords and Commons that the colonial question was simply "obedience to the laws and respect for the legislative authority of the kingdom," and Parliament, in reply, declared that they intended to proceed "with that temper and firmness which will best conciliate and insure due submission to the laws and reverence for the legislative authority of Great Britain."

But in the next two or three years they met with little or no success, and we find the pamphleteers in England recommending stronger measures, and a greater number of customs officers and war-vessels. The new Board of Commissioners of Customs had made its headquarters in Boston, a significant event, followed by a long train of the most important historical circumstances. Boston, Englishmen thought, was the worst place in America. It had always been so. It needed curbing. Massachusetts was, they said, the only colony which had persistently, from her foundation, shown a disloyal spirit to the English Government and the English Church.

The proceedings to stop smuggling were carried on for some years after 1764, and were contemporaneous with more conspicuous events, the Stamp Act and other taxing laws. It is somewhat difficult to tell how far the repression of smuggling was successful, because the colonists laughed at the revenue-cutters and men-of-war as failures, and at the same time complained that they were being ruined by the stoppage of their old "free trade." It seems to be true that the naval and customs officers made comparatively few seizures, and those they made were often rescued; but at the same time the fear of seizure and the presence of the men-of-war may at first have stopped a great deal of the smuggling. The island of Jamaica complained of much loss. Exactly what were the losses among ourselves cannot now be known.

The complete cessation, in 1766, of the Government's efforts against illicit trade in Massachusetts was apparently partially remedied by the creation of the new board of commissioners in the following year. But it seems probable that the efforts to check contraband trade for the next six or seven years met with very small success. When the year 1774 was reached, the mobs and tar-and-feather parties had driven so many British officials from office that all attempts to check smuggling and enforce the trade laws were necessarily abandoned until the army could restore authority.

Those old trade laws can still be read in their places in the English Statutes at Large. Some of their provisions undoubtedly built up and encouraged colonial prosperity, especially the shipping interests of New England and the middle colonies; but other provisions which the colonists disliked were from the beginning almost as dead as they are now. Those laws and the principles embodied in them were not, as many of us suppose, overthrown or abandoned as the result of our Revolution. England continued them in full force and the colonies that remained to her after our separation were ruled by those laws down to the year 1849, when changing conditions and the increasing power of the English liberal party had established free trade.

VI.

THE STAMP ACT

AFTER a great political movement or experiment has failed, it is easy enough to say that it should never have been undertaken, and to characterize it as an absurdity. After an event has happened we can all see its mistakes. The important and the difficult thing is to foresee what will happen; and in order to understand a historical episode we must take the point of view, not of the final critic, but of the men who undertook the enterprise and were obliged to use their foresight in an untried field.

There is no use in saying that the English Government and people should not have attempted to reorganize the colonies. They had to do it or abandon England's foundation principle of empire. It had never been her intention to create independent communities, or establish republics. It had never been her intention to recognize the doctrine that naturally separated peoples had a natural right to independence. But she would be recognizing that principle and would be encouraging her colonies to turn themselves into republics if she allowed the condition of affairs in America to continue.

The American colonists were multiplying so rapidly that they would soon equal in numbers the population of England. The colonial population doubled about every thirty years; but the population of England had not doubled in a hundred and fifty years. England now had 8,000,000 and the American colonies had 2,000,000 whites and about 1,000,000 slaves. If the respective rates of increase were maintained, the Americans would in 1810 be as numerous as Englishmen, and the colonial relation between them would cease; for that relation is hardly possible between equals, and impossible when the colony is the superior.[1]

Having resolved that a complete reorganization of the colonies was necessary, the British Government did not go about it in an ignorant or careless fashion, as has usually been taken for granted in our histories. As soon as the conquest of Canada was assured and before the treaty of peace was signed in 1763, the British Ministry, under the leadership of the Earl of Bute, took great pains to inform themselves of the exact state of affairs in the colonies, and learn what new regulations would be most suitable for "the grand plan of reforming the American governments." Agents were sent out to travel about and report, conciliate prominent persons and win them to the side of the ministerial measures.

There was no secrecy in the matter. The agents were introduced in their true character and the purpose of their coming explained. In fact, the British military officers in America and all British officials began to talk openly of the necessity of regulating and reforming the colonial governments, reducing the membership of the legislative assemblies, forming New Hampshire, Rhode Island, and Massachusetts into one colony, together with other changes that would give Great Britain better control.[2]

Besides the agents who were sent out, the home government had abundant sources of information in the colonial governors appointed by the Crown, so that it cannot be said that Great Britain went into this attempt to have what she considered

---

[1] Kidder, "History of the Boston Massacre," p. 121. In the year 1775 it was estimated that the American population would be 6,000,000 in the year 1800. As a matter of fact, it was only 5,500,000 in that year and England's population was 8,800,000. England's rate of increase unexpectedly improved after 1776, owing it is supposed to the great wealth drawn from India, so that the population of England and the United States were not equal until about 1837, and our population did not equal that of the United Kingdom until 1847.—*American Archives*, 4th series, vol. iii, pp. 9, 1557; Mulhall, "Dictionary of Statistics," review of 1898.

[2] Gordon, "American Revolution," edition of 1788, vol. i, pp. 142–147.

real colonies and consolidate her empire, without thorough investigation and discussion. Among the speeches, books, and pamphlets which enlarged upon the subject, Sir Francis Bernard's "Select Letters" and Thomas Pownall's "Administration of the Colonies" are of more than ordinary interest. Both of these men had had much experience in colonial affairs. Bernard's letters were written while he was a colonial governor to officials of the home government and afterwards published. He had been governor of New Jersey and of Massachusetts; and Pownall had been governor of Massachusetts, of New Jersey, and of South Carolina.

The policy and principles which Bernard recommended were the absolute sovereignty of Parliament over all British colonies, the right of Parliament at any time to change colonial governments and constitutions, the principle that colonial self-government is not a right but merely a privilege granted by Parliament and to be exercised in subordination to Parliament, the principle that salaries of governors must be fixed and permanent and not dependent on the annual vote of a colonial legislature. These ideas were all carried out in practice by Great Britain after our Revolution, as time and necessity showed that in no other way could colonies be retained and governed.

Pownall defined that ideal British empire which British statesmen have ever since been struggling to achieve. There is no substantial difference between his description and that which we read to-day in English newspapers and in the speeches of English statesmen.

England, he said, must not be a mere island, content with herself; nor must she be an island influencing in a vague way isolated colonies or provinces, disconnected fragments without a vital unity. The time had come for her to consolidate her colonies in a commercial empire. The conquest of Canada had given the opportunity, the "lead" as he calls it; and she must now make those "nascent powers" in America a part of herself. Their interest, he admits, may be "different and even distinct from the peculiar interests of the mother country;"

71

but they cannot become independent. They "will fall under the dominion of some of the potentates of Europe."

"It is therefore the duty of those who govern us to carry forward this state of things to the weaving of this land into our system, that Great Britain may be no more considered as the kingdom of this Isle only, with many appendages of provinces, colonies, settlements, and other extraneous parts, but as a grand marine dominion consisting of our possessions in the Atlantic and in America united into one empire, into one centre where the seat of government is."—"Administration of the Colonies," p. 9.

Pownall and Bernard urged their countrymen to immediate action. The old charters should be annulled, the forms of government should be all alike, and the colonies should be reduced in number and be given natural instead of artificial boundaries. Bernard pointed out that America would grow more and more difficult to subdue and reform. It would be well, Pownall said, to inquire whether the colonies were not already arrived "at an independency of the government of the mother country;" to learn also the measure of independency that they had built up "when the government of the mother country was so weak or distracted at home, or so deeply engaged abroad in Europe as not to be able to attend to or assert its right in America." [a]

Bernard did not agree with the Whig minority and their leaders, Burke and Chatham, that the colonies, if let alone, would come to themselves, see the advantage of membership in a great empire over an attempt at isolated independence, and become willing subjects of Britain's rule. From his long experience in the colonies Bernard was convinced that there was a powerful party which intended to break away from England if it could.

Everything in the relations between the colonies and the mother-country had, it was said, been left uncertain. It was not even determined whether the King or Parliament was the proper authority to govern the colonies and bring them into

---

[a] Pownall, "Administration of the Colonies," 2d edition, p. 29.

subjection. It was not settled whether the commander of military forces sent out from England could supersede the military authority of the colonial governors. It was disputed whether the Crown or the colonial legislatures could create courts of law. In England the colonies were regarded as mere corporations capable only of making by-laws, while in America the patriot party regarded them as independent states under a mere protectorate from the British crown.

These arguments of two of the most experienced of American governors show how the majority of Englishmen of that time looked upon the necessity of reorganizing the colonies. The trade of the colonies with England, in spite of all the smuggling, was now as large as England's trade with the whole world had been sixty years before; and must all this be lost? Must the colonists take it for themselves, divert it to Holland, France, and Spain, or dissipate it in attempting to control it exclusively for their own interests?

The recent long war had been fought to settle whether England or France should dominate on the North American continent, and England had won. But of what use would her victory be unless she could also conquer the Americans themselves and make them part of a united empire which would increase her own power and wealth?

So at the same time that the British Government started to suppress smuggling in 1764 it also prepared to enlarge the system of taxing the colonies and make it subserve the new plans for their better government and control. It is a great mistake to suppose that the stamp act which was now projected was the first instance of taxation of the colonies. They had been taxed in various ways ever since the reign of Charles II, and there were a number of old trade acts of Parliament levying duties on colonial exports and imports, as well as other acts regulating their domestic concerns and pursuits. These taxes on exports and imports were what the colonists called external taxes levied on their commerce for the purpose of regulating it and differed, they said, from the proposed stamp act, which they called an internal tax.

The proceeds of these old taxes had never equalled the cost of collecting them; so that although the people of England were enriched by colonial trade, the government itself was unable to meet its ordinary expenses in protecting and governing the colonies which produced this beneficial trade.

The colonies had also been taxed in another way. When England was engaged in a war for their benefit, as in the recent war with France, there was a regular system by which the British Secretary of State made a requisition on the colonies through the colonial governors, stating the quota of money or supplies required from each. Each colonial assembly thereupon began a long wrangle with its governor, and usually ended by voting the supply, or part of it, which was collected from the people by taxation.

This was a voluntary system, for sometimes a colony would grant no supply at all. It was, in short, the old feudal aid system, the system in which all taxation in England had originated. Taxation was originally not a self-acting system of compulsion. Taxes were gifts, grants, or aids, which the people, or their feudal lords, or Parliament as representing the people, granted to the King at irregular intervals to assist him in wars or other undertakings; or, as Mr. Stubbs puts it, "the people made a voluntary offering to relieve the wants of the ruler." [4]

This voluntary system had long since ceased in England, and the modern, annual, self-acting system prevailed both there and also in the local taxation of the colonies. The taxation proposed in 1764 was intended to be an extension of the modern system, to be applied in a regular and systematic way to the colonies in time of peace, so that they would pay all expenses of governing and securing them. This sort of taxation of a dependency is still enforced by England in her most important possession, India. It had often been discussed as applicable to the colonies in America. It had been suggested in 1713, when Harley was at the head of the treasury, and again at the opening

---

[4] Stubbs, "Constitutional History of England," edition of 1875, vol. i, p. 577. See Stedman, "American War," vol. i, p. 44.

of the Seven Years' War. It had also been advocated in the early part of the century by Governor Keith, of Pennsylvania, who was also one of those who foresaw the leaning of some of the colonists towards independence, and thought that such a spirit should be nipped in the bud. Other governors had recommended it, and Governor Shirley, of Massachusetts, had recommended a stamp tax. Spain, Holland, and France taxed their colonies to defray the expense of governing them. The taxation of America had for a long time been an obvious measure, and might have been tried much sooner if Canada had not belonged to France.

If the British Government could have foreseen what would happen, they would probably not have made the attempt. But there was no experience except the previous taxation of America and the taxation of their colonies by other nations, none of which had ever been seriously resisted. If it is allowable to have colonies and subject peoples, the mere legal right of the dominant country to tax them or do anything else with them is perfectly clear. But England has learned that certain colonies capable of making trouble must be left to their own methods of taxation. We ourselves discriminate against the Philippine Islands in our regulations of the protective tariff in a way that is in effect taxation. England no longer levies taxes on such dependencies as Canada and Australia, but on India, whose people constitute by far the most numerous and most profitable part of her empire, she levies taxes of the heaviest kind for the avowed purpose of defraying the expense of governing them. Indirect taxes are also levied by England on her crown colonies, and occasionally a direct tax, as in the case of colonial lighthouses. The taxation of dependencies seems to be a question of power and policy or color of skin rather than of right or equal justice.[5]

---

[5] Digby, " Prosperous British India; " Dutt, " Economic History of India; " Naoroji, " Poverty and Un-British Rule in India," pp. 49, 56, 58, 61, 248, 267, 279, 288, 298, 651, 558, 220. Jenkyns, " British Rule and Jurisdiction Beyond the Seas," pp. 10–11; Lewis, " Government of Dependencies," Lucas edition, 1891, pp. xlix, lvi; Lilly, " India and its Problems," p. 184.

AMERICAN INDEPENDENCE

In 1764 England was believed to be bankrupt, groaning under the vast debt of over £148,000,000 which had been incurred by the war she had just waged to save the colonies from the clutches of France. During that war she had granted to the colonists at different periods over £1,000,000 to encourage their exertions. Her present debt of £148,000,000 was a heavy one for a country of barely eight million people. The colonies had no taxes, except the very light ones which they levied on themselves by their own legislative assemblies. But the people in England suffered under very heavy and burdensome taxes on all sorts of articles, including the wheels on their wagons, the panes of glass in their houses, and other things which involved prying and irritating investigations. All this was to help pay for that great war, and why, asked Englishmen, should not the colonies be called upon to pay the expense of keeping them in the empire in time of peace? While the war was being carried on they had been taxed in the old voluntary way, and, on requisition from the home government, had voted in their legislative assemblies supplies of money, men, and provisions. Now that peace was declared, why should they not be taxed in a regular and orderly way to pay for their own government and military protection and relieve England of that expense?

This was the very plausible position taken by England. But the Americans argued that the advantage which Great Britain received from control of the colonial trade far exceeded any supposed colonial proportion of the expense for imperial defense. To this England answered that the colonists were such violators of the trade and navigation laws that England could not get her full share of the trade; and the colonists again replied that, nevertheless, she ought not to try to tax them and at the same time try to monopolize their trade. Let her abandon one or the other and not attempt to commit double extortion.

This had been one of the early phases of the dispute. There was no intention on the part of England that the proceeds of colonial taxation were to go into the English exchequer to enrich England or pay her debt at the expense of the colonies.

The plan of taxation that was actually formulated and intended to be enforced was to tax the colonies only for their own benefit; that is to say, the proceeds of the taxation were to be used to pay the expenses of colonial administration and government, the expenses of troops placed in the colonies for securing and protecting them, the salaries of governors, judges, and other officials, and what may be called the general administration expenses, to the end that the money raised in taxes should be all spent in the colonies and that the colonies should be more regularly and better governed.

The intention in the British mind was not merely to get money or revenue from the colonies, and above all not to get it in such a crude way that England could at once be charged with extortion and mere money-making. The intention was far deeper and more comprehensive, and had in view a general policy of bringing the colonies under better control by means of regular taxation which would take away from their popular assemblies the control of the salaries of the governors and other executive officials.

This sort of taxation, although not attempted in such colonies as Canada and Australia, has been carried out in the most complete manner in India, where England levies taxes to pay the salaries of the numerous English officials and other expenses of the vast system of the Indian civil and military administration. The results of the system in India seem to have been very much the same that our ancestors feared and predicted for America. They argued that if England were allowed to take an inch she would take an ell; the amount of the increased taxation would at first be of no importance, but the principle would be of the greatest importance. Once admit that Parliament had the right to increase taxation in the colonies or levy internal taxes, and taxation would be increased every year. Parliament would not stop at three pence per pound on tea. All the taxes on land, wagons, and window-panes which were endured in England would be transferred to America, and the English people would force this measure on the Lords and Commons or pull the parliament-house down about their ears.

AMERICAN INDEPENDENCE

"How would you like to pay four shillings a year, out of every pound your farms are worth, to be squandered (at least a great part of it) upon ministerial tools and court sycophants? What would you think of giving a tenth part of the yearly products of your lands to the clergy? Would you not think it very hard to pay ten shillings sterling, per annum, for every wheel of your wagons and other carriages; a shilling or two for every pane of glass in your houses; and two or three shillings for every one of your hearths? I might mention taxes upon your mares, cows, and many other things; but those I have already mentioned are sufficient. . . . Perhaps, before long, your tables, and chairs, and platters, and dishes, and knives, and forks, and everything else, would be taxed. Nay, I don't know but they would find means to tax you for every child you got, and for every kiss your daughters received from their sweethearts; and, God knows, that would soon ruin you."—Hamilton's Works, Lodge edition, vol. i, p. 35.

Hamilton and other patriots believed that the taxation of America would be used to create a vast patronage, an American civil service of salaried positions for younger sons and political dependents who would rule the colonies. Officialdom and taxes would mutually increase each other; and this, if we can believe the books by Digby, Dutt, Naoroji and others, has been the sad fate of British India.

It was commonly believed in America that the disposition to increase the taxation of the colonists had been strengthened by the reports of their gaiety and luxury which reached England through the officers and soldiers returning after the close of the French War. They described planters living like princes and all the people rich and even overgrown in fortune; in short, a sort of India to be despoiled for British profit. The colonists complained that these reports were very misleading, that they were based on observations made during the period of inflation at the time of the war with France, when large sums were spent for army supplies. The people were lavish in entertaining the officers who had helped them to conquer Canada; and it was somewhat contemptible, they said, when the officers returning to England denounced to the Ministry, as fit subjects for plunder, the Americans whose hospitality they had enjoyed.[8]

---

[8] Gordon, "American Revolution, edition 1788, vol. i, pp. 136–157.

THE VOLUNTARY SYSTEM

The colonists had no objection to continuing the old voluntary system, by which their legislatures sometimes voted supplies to the home government; for whenever a governor announced that he had been instructed to obtain a certain quota, the legislature had a chance to strike a bargain for his consent to some of their favorite measures. But the delays caused by these contests were very exasperating to generals in the field during the French War, and also to the home government.

The colonists, however, were fond of saying that the voluntary system must have been profitable enough to England. Did you not yourselves, they would say, think that in the last war we had been too complying and too generous in our devotion to the King, and did you not hand us back £133,333 6s. 8d., which you said we had paid over and above our share of the expense? Let the King·frankly tell us his necessities, and we will in the future, as in the past, of our own volition, assist him.

But public men in England thought that the refunding of the £133,000 was an argument against the old method, because the greater part of that sum had been returned only to Massachusetts and one or two other provinces, which had voted supplies in great excess over all the others. It was ridiculous, they said, for a great nation to have to conduct its finances by this sort of refunding. It would be better to have a simple self-acting method, like the stamp tax, that would bear equally on all.

Accordingly, on the 10th day of March, 1764, that famous year of colonial reorganization, and the same day on which the Sugar Act and the law for the further restraint of paper money in the colonies were passed, Mr. Grenville, Chancellor of the Exchequer, announced in Parliament the plan of a stamp tax for the colonies. He introduced and secured the passage of some resolutions on the right, equity, and policy of colonial taxation, which were intended to raise the whole question and have it discussed for a year before any particular measure was offered.

The Ministry went about this measure with that display of

considerate care and tenderness which England has so often shown to dependencies, a tenderness very much admired by some but very exasperating to a people who are fond of freedom. Mr. Grenville not only wanted the subject discussed for a year in England before final action was taken, but he wanted the colonists to discuss it and offer suggestions, or propose some better plan of taxation, or one that would be more agreeable to them. He was lavishly candid in saying that the Sugar Act just passed levied an external tax, the validity of which the colonists admitted; but the stamp tax might be an internal tax, the validity of which might be denied in America; and he wished that question fully discussed. He was also excessively liberal in hinting to the colonial agents in London that now was the opportunity for the colonies, by voluntarily agreeing to the Stamp Tax, or an equivalent, to establish a precedent for being consulted before any tax was imposed upon them by Parliament. He afterwards made a great point of selecting as stamp officials in America only such persons as were natives of the country.

But the patriot party in America was far too shrewd to accept the Stamp Act or offer an equivalent. They sent back some petitions and remonstrances against it, but for the most part were silent. A year went by. The proposed tax was drafted into the form of a law and debated in the House of Commons during the early spring of 1765. A few of the Whigs —Conway, Barré, and Alderman Beckford—made rather impressive speeches against it. But the debate was neither a long nor a great one, and the majority in favor of the act was overwhelming.

The expression "sons of liberty" which Barré used in the debate was taken up in America, and societies of these "sons" were organized in almost every colony. They were the first of the revolutionary committees and were composed of the most extreme patriots. They took the advanced position that Parliament not only had no right to tax the colonies, but no right to exercise authority over them in any case whatsoever. The colonies, they said, were under the King alone; and for the King the "Sons of Liberty" expressed the most extravagant loyalty. At the same time they stood ready to resist the Stamp Act with their lives, and those in New York and Connecticut bound themselves to "march with their whole force, if required, to the relief of those that may be in danger from the Stamp Act or its promoters." [7]

The Stamp Act provided for a stamp on newspapers and on most of the legal, official, and business documents used in the colonies. It was the sort of tax which we levied on ourselves during the Civil War and again at the time of the war with Spain. It is unquestionably the fairest, most equally distributed, and easiest to collect of all forms of taxes. Scarcely any one in England seems to have had any doubt as to the right of Parliament to levy such a tax, an internal one, so-called, on the colonies.

The penalties for infringement of the Stamp Act varied from £10 to £20 and could be collected in the admiralty courts, where there was no trial by jury; and to the great disgust and indignation of many of the colonists the act further provided that hereafter penalties and forfeitures under all of the revenue laws relating to the colonies could be collected through these same juryless courts of admiralty.

As it was a tax on documents used in the everyday affairs of life, the Stamp Act was expected to be self-acting; it could not be evaded by smuggling or by any of the other methods used against the molasses act and the navigation and trade laws. The colonists would enforce it themselves in carrying on their business; and this expectation would no doubt have been fulfilled in any country where governmental authority was in full force.

---

[7] Gordon, "American Revolution," edition 1788, vol. i, pp. 195, 197.

6

VII.

ARGUMENTS AGAINST THE STAMP ACT

MOST people in England and many in America appear to have thought that the colonists after a few protests would accept the Stamp Act and settle down to obedience. But this proved to be a mistake. All that was needed was for some one to start the opposition.

News of the passage of the act reached America in May, and soon afterwards, on May 29th, Patrick Henry, who had just been elected to the Virginia Assembly, introduced a set of resolutions which he appears to have drafted after consultation with two other members, George Johnston and John Fleming. The resolutions recited that the Virginians could be lawfully taxed only by their own assembly, that taxation by Parliament was illegal, unconstitutional, and unjust; that the Virginians were not bound to obey such laws, and that any person who spoke in favor of them should be deemed an enemy of Virginia.

Such resolutions, affecting to absolve colonists from obedience to acts of Parliament and denouncing as enemies all who inculcated such obedience, were regarded as criminal by many members of the Virginia assembly; and as Henry spoke,—"Cæsar had his Brutus, Charles I his Cromwell, and George III"—cries of " Treason! " " Treason! " were heard from every quarter,—" may profit by their example," cried Henry. " If *this* be treason make the most of it."

The resolutions were, nevertheless, adopted by the assembly sitting as committee of the whole; but when the committee reported them .the next day, the assembly amended them by striking out the parts which were deemed treasonable, so that the resolutions were changed to a mere argumentative protest against the right of Parliament to tax America, and in this changed form could cause no more excitement than previous protests before the Stamp Act passed.

But copies of the original unamended resolutions were sent in manuscript to Philadelphia and New York, where it is said they were handed about in secret among the "Sons of Liberty" and regarded as so extreme that no one would print them. Some one, however, took them to New England, and by the end of June they began to appear in their original form in the New England newspapers. It was the spark that was needed, and the universal testimony of the time was that these unamended resolutions started all the violent opposition and rioting which followed during the summer. Governor Bernard, of Massachusetts, said that he had thought that the Stamp Act would be accepted until those resolutions were published and acted like an "alarm bell to all the disaffected." General Gage, writing from New York, described them as "the signal for a general outcry over the continent."[1]

The assemblies of other colonies quickly followed with various forms of resolutions; and the argument contained in them was that Parliament had never before taxed the colonies in internal matters, and that internal taxation was, therefore, the exclusive province of the colonial legislatures. They admit that Parliament can tax them externally, or, as they put it, regulate their commerce by levying duties on it, and regulate them, as in fact it always had done, in all internal matters except this one of internal taxes.

This position was very weak, because it admitted the right to regulate all their internal affairs except one; and the distinction it raised between external and internal taxes was altogether absurd. There was no real or substantial difference between the supposed two kinds of taxes; between taxes levied at a seaport and taxes levied throughout the country. The colonists afterwards saw this weakness and changed their ground. But this supposed distinction between external and internal taxes was good enough to begin with; and the Revolu-

---

[1] Stedman, "American War," vol. i, p. 33; Gordon, "American Revolution," edition 1788, vol. i, pp. 167–171–175–200; Tyler, "Life of Patrick Henry," pp. 60–68–72–76. The unamended resolutions appeared in the Newport Mercury, June 27, and in the Boston Gazette, July 4.

tion, during the seventeen years of its active progress, was largely a question of the evolution of opinion.

During that summer of 1765, while the assemblies of the different colonies were passing resolutions of protest, the mobs of the patriot party, under the influence of Henry's unamended resolutions, were protesting in another way. It certainly amazed Englishmen to read that the mob in Boston, not content with hanging in effigy the proposed stamp distributors, levelled the office of one of them to the ground and smashed the windows and furniture of his private house; that they destroyed the papers and records of the court of admiralty, sacked the house of the comptroller of customs, and drank themselves drunk with his wines; and, finally, proceeded to the house of Lieutenant-Governor Hutchinson, who was compelled to flee to save his life. They completely gutted his house, stamped upon the chairs and mahogany tables until they were wrecked, smashed the large, gilt-framed pictures, tore up all the fruit-trees in his garden, and piled the wreckage with his clothes and linen in the street. Hutchinson was a native of the province, and with his library perished many invaluable historical manuscripts, which he had been thirty years collecting.[2]

That this outrage was said to have been incited the day before by the preaching of the Rev. Dr. Mayhew, a Puritan divine, did not lessen its atrocity in the eyes of Englishmen. He had preached on the text, "I would they were even cut off which trouble you;" and the mob came very near a complete compliance.

A great many respectable citizens were shocked, or appeared to be shocked, at this violence and excess. They held town meetings of abhorrence; Dr. Mayhew wrote a letter of regret to Hutchinson, disclaiming any intention of causing what had happened to him; a guard was organized to prevent such out-

---

[2] *New England Historical and Genealogical Register*, vol. xxxii, p. 268; Hutchinson, "Massachusetts," vol. iii, pp. 122–127; *Massachusetts Archives*, vol. xxvi, p. 143; Boston *Gazette*, August 19, September 2, 1765; Hutchinson's "Correspondence," vol. ii, p. 143; "Letters of James Murray, Loyalist," p. 258.

rages in the future, and rewards were offered for rioters. But it is quite significant that, although the rioters were well known, as the historians assure us, no one was punished. Two or three were arrested, but were rescued by their friends, and it was found impossible to proceed against them.[3]

In October a respectable body of colonists met in New York to deal with the Stamp Act question. This meeting, which has ever since been known as the Stamp Act Congress, originated at a consultation James Otis appears to have had with his father, Colonel Otis, and Dr. James Warren. They submitted their plan to the Massachusetts Assembly, which took measures to have the meeting called. Neither Virginia, North Carolina, New Hampshire, nor Georgia was represented in it. The assembly of New Hampshire is said to have favored the Congress, but was unwilling to send delegates. The other three received the call when their assemblies were not in session, and the assemblies were prevented from meeting until it was too late.[4]

The Stamp Act Congress passed resolutions of protest and sent a petition to the King and another to Parliament. The arguments in these documents are very much the same as those used in the previous remonstrances. They, of course, took the precaution of expressing great loyalty to Great Britain and admiration for the mighty British empire, to which, they said, it was a happiness to belong. They protested against the extension of the power of admiralty courts, and declared that they had the same rights as Englishmen born within the realm. But the groundwork of their position was that Parliament could not

---

[3] Elliott, " New England," vol. ii, pp. 254–255; Hildreth, vol. ii, chap. xxviii, p. 528; " Diary and Letters of Thomas Hutchinson," vol. ii, p. 228. Dr. Mayhew, who preached the inciting sermon, is said to have been the first of the Massachusetts ministers who became an outspoken advocate of the Unitarian movement which some years afterwards gained ground so rapidly in Massachusetts.—Cooke, " Unitarianism in America," p. 63.

[4] " Authentic Account of the Proceedings of the Congress held at New York, A. D. 1765; " Niles, " Principles and Acts of the Revolution," edition 1876, pp. 155–168; Stedman, " American War," vol. i, pp. 39, 40.

tax them internally unless they were represented in that body; from the nature of things, they could never be represented, and therefore Parliament could never tax them.

It is to be observed that they did not ask for representation in Parliament. They declared it to be impossible, and Englishmen were quick to notice and comment on this. Grenville, in his speech against the repeal of the Stamp Act, called forcible attention to it, and reminded his hearers of its significance.

It was the beginning of the rejection of all authority of Parliament. The colonists never changed their ground on this point. They always insisted that representation was impossible. The distance across the ocean, however, could hardly be said to render representation physically impossible. Each colony maintained one or more agents in London 'to look after its affairs and represent it at the executive departments of the government; and these agents sometimes appeared before Parliament as witnesses. Each colony could in a similar way have maintained representatives in Parliament. But representation was a political impossibility, because, as the colonists well knew, such representation would be a farce. The representatives would always be outvoted. England would never allow them to become numerous; she would never give a fair representation; never give representation in proportion to population, because, in a few generations, with the natural growth of America, the American members of Parliament would be more numerous than the English.

Governor Bernard, of Massachusetts, tells us, in his "Select Letters," that at first the colonists were willing to be represented in Parliament, and made their argument in the alternative that if they were to be taxed internally they must be represented; but fearing that representation might be allowed them, and that thus they would be irretrievably bound by any measure passed by Parliament, they quickly shifted to the position that representation was impossible, and therefore internal taxation was constitutionally impossible.

Hutchinson also said that the colonists saw the futility of

representation and changed their ground.[5] Bernard would have had Parliament voluntarily offer them representation for a time, until through their representatives they had assented to a settlement of the exact relations between America and England, and having been entrapped in that "refined stroke of policy" they would be helpless for the future.

This shrewd unwillingness to be represented was naturally regarded by many as a sure sign of the determination of the patriot party to break from England in the end. Raynal, the French writer, in his "Philosophical and Political History of the European Settlements in America," advised them never to yield on this impossibility of representation, for if once they were represented the rest of Parliament could easily outvote them, their liberties would be gone, and their fetters permanently forged upon them.[6]

The Stamp Act Congress also made the rather unfortunate admission that the colonies owed "all due subordination to that august body the Parliament of Great Britain." Parliament, therefore, had full authority over them, could tax their commerce by duties at the seaports, and levy this duty on exports as well as on imports—do everything, in short, except tax them internally.

But if the principle "no taxation without representation" was sound English constitutional law, why did the colonists admit that they could be taxed at their seaports without representation? A tax levied by Parliament on sugar, molasses, or other articles coming into the colonial seaports was paid by all the people of the province in the enhanced price of the goods. The duties on French and Spanish products, which had to be paid in specie, and drained specie out of the country, were a so-called external tax; but they drained specie out of the interior of the country as well as from the seaports. It was, as

---

[5] See his "Strictures upon the Declaration of the Congress at Philadelphia," London, 1776. See also Niles, "Principles and Acts of the Revolution," edition 1876, p. 156; "Prior Documents of the Revolution," p. 192.

[6] Extracts from Raynal's book were widely circulated in a pamphlet

Lord Mansfield said, like a pebble thrown into a pond—the circles from the splash would extend over the whole pond.

In fact, in the very nature of things there could be no tax that could properly be called an external one. Every tax was an internal tax, because any tax that could be conceived of had to be levied on people or property within the boundaries of the country. When once the tax-gatherer had entered the boundary, or taken private property for taxes just inside the boundary, at a seaport, it was as much internal taxation as though he were in the central town of the community.

"What a pother," said an Irish member of Parliament, "whether money is to be taken out of their coat-pocket or out of their waistcoat-pocket!"

The colonists tried to keep up the distinction by saying that the duties on imports and exports were external and allowable because they were to regulate the commerce of the empire; the regulation of the commerce was the main object, and the duties were merely incidental; but before long they gave up the whole distinction and took the ground that without representation Parliament had no right to tax them in any form or indeed to govern them in any form.

The principle of "no taxation without representation" had always been familiar to the colonists. It had been appealed to on several occasions in the past hundred and fifty years, notably in Virginia, and Massachusetts, against acts of the British Government. Its fairness was obvious to all who believed in representative government and republicanism, but not at all obvious to those who rejected such forms of government. It was part of the doctrine of government by consent which had been advocated by Locke and other political philosophers. The "consent of the governed" doctrine was often expressed by the phrase, "No laws can be made or abrogated without the consent

called " The Sentiments of a Foreigner on the Disputes of Great Britain with America." See, also, Cartwright's " American Independence, the Interest and Glory of Great Britain," p. 50. For a loyalist protest against the Stamp Act Congress, see Boston *Gazette*, May 5 and May 12, 1766.

of the people or their representatives." Therefore, taxing laws, like all other laws, must be by consent.

"No taxation without representation" was never a part of the British Constitution, and is not a part of it even now. It could not be adopted without at the same time accepting the doctrine of government by consent, and that doctrine no nation with colonies should adopt, because it is a flat denial of the lawfulness of the colonial relation. England governs millions of white colonists and over two hundred millions of East Indians without their consent, and will continue to do so as long as her present type of empire endures.[7]

"No taxation without representation" had often been advocated in England by liberals of different sorts, Puritans, Roundheads, and Whigs, who felt that they stood in need of it. The colonists thought that they had found two or three instances in which Parliament had partially recognized this doctrine. There were several old divisions of England, the counties Palatine of Chester, Durman, and Lancaster, and the marshes of Wales, which in feudal times had been semi-independent. They were for a long time not taxed by Parliament, and when at last Parliament determined to tax them they were, the colonists said, given representation. The colonists clung to these instances and kept repeating them in all their pamphlets; but the instances were certainly without avail in convincing Parliament and the vast majority of Englishmen.[8]

Englishmen easily replied that these two or three instances, even supposing them to be as the colonists stated, were accidental and amounted to nothing in the face of the long-continued practice and custom to the contrary. In the year 1765

---

[7] "The Conduct of the Late Administration Considered," p. 61, London, 1767; "The Constitutional Right of the Legislature of Great Britain to Tax the British Colonies," p. 51, London, 1768.

[8] See on this subject of taxation, "The Rights of Great Britain Asserted," p. 6. London, 1776; "Remarks on the Review of the Controversy between Great Britain and Her Colonies," p. 85; "The Controversy between Great Britain and Her Colonies Reviewed," London, 1769, p. 86; "An Enquiry Whether the Guilt of the Present Civil War Ought to be

scarcely any of the great towns in England had representatives in Parliament and yet they were taxed. London, Birmingham, Manchester, Liverpool, Leeds, and Halifax paid their taxes every year, and sent not a single member to Parliament. In fact, out of the eight million people in England there were not three hundred thousand represented.

In the early days of George III, 160,000 people elected all the members of parliament. At the close of his reign in 1820, 440,000 out of a population of 22,000,000 elected all the members of Parliament. Up to the year 1780 the members from the county of York, the largest and most influential of the counties, were elected in Lord Rockingham's dining-room. Parliament was made up largely from rotten boroughs or pocket-boroughs in the control of individuals or families. The Duke of Norfolk was represented by eleven members, who sat for places forming part of his estate. Lord Lonsdale was represented by nine, and Lord Darlington by seven. Old Sarum had not a single inhabitant, and yet sent two members to Parliament. Representative government as the colonists understood and practised it in their local assemblies, or as we now understand it, had at that time no existence in England.[9]

The American principle of equal representation, which requires that the representative must be a resident of the district he represents, in full sympathy with its people and a sharer in the benefit or evil of laws applicable to them, has never been accepted in England. We like our system and say that the English system has always been wrong and unequal. But however wrong we may consider it, and however wrong our ances-

---

Imputed to Great Britain or to America," London, 1776, p. 19, etc.; "A Letter to the Noble Gentlemen Who Have Addressed His Majesty," p. 5; Gibbes, "Documentary History of the American Revolution," 1764–1776, pp. 19–20; Todd, "Parliamentary Government in the British Colonies," edition 1894, p. 210; articles in Boston *Evening Post* for January, 1769, answered by Samuel Adams in the Boston *Gazette*. See also *Annual Register*, 1766, p. 40.

[9] "The Right of the British Legislature to Tax the American Colonies," London, 1774; "An Englishman's Answer to the Address from the Delegates to the People of Great Britain," etc., p. 8, New York,

tors may have considered it, there is no doubt that this unequal system was well established as part of the British Constitution at the time of our Revolution.

The representation in Parliament had slowly grown into that state from the old feudal customs; and that growth or that condition was the British Constitution of that day. There were a few, a very few, men in England who apparently wanted it changed and the principle of no taxation without representation adopted. Lord Camden argued to this effect during the Stamp Act debates in a most interesting speech in the House of Lords. William Pitt, in the Commons, also argued for no taxation without representation, and based his reasoning on natural law and natural right rather than on the British Constitution as it then existed. In short, he argued that the constitution should be changed. Lord Mansfield, the greatest lawyer of that time, argued on the other side; and the speeches of these powerful debaters, especially those of Camden and Mansfield, are well worth reading by any one who is interested in the details of the discussion.

Lord Mansfield's side was of course successful because he was arguing in favor of what had long been the established rule and practice of the British Constitution. It was not until nearly a hundred years after that time that any important enlargement was made in the parliamentary representation; and surely it could hardly be expected that Parliament would suddenly, in the year 1766, alter their whole system of representation and adopt government by consent at the suggestion of a patriotic party in the colonies. When the British Parliament announced by the Declaratory Act of the year 1766 that they had the constitutional right to govern and tax the colonies as they pleased, with or without representation, externally or internally, or in any other way, they were undoubtedly acting in

1775; Heaton, "The Three Reforms of Parliament," ch. 1-2; Paul, "History of Reform," ch. 1-6; Bright's "Essays on Parliamentary Reform," essay ii; Cox, "Ancient Parliamentary Elections;" Walpole, "The Electorate and the Legislature," ch. 4; Freeman, "Decayed Boroughs;" "Diary and Letters of Thomas Hutchinson," vol. i, p. 249.

accordance with the long-settled constitutional custom, and that decision has never been reversed.[10]

The sum of the matter in regard to no taxation without representation is, that America, having been settled by the liberal, radical, and in most instances minority element of English politics, adopted this much-discussed doctrine, and England, being usually under the influence of the Tory element, rejected it. Our patriot arguments were in effect an American interpretation of the British Constitution, an interpretation which Great Britain has rejected. We went our separate ways. Although we were of the same race as the people of England, the differences between us were far-reaching and radical, and the gulf was being steadily widened.

The rending and separation was a long process. Patriot and loyalist, Britisher and colonist, argued and struggled, each trying to force his theory on the other. The Englishman would sometimes leave his firm ground of pure constitutional right, and say to the colonists, You are already represented in Parliament, more amply and fully represented than you could be in one of your own, and better protected than if you sent your own people to the Parliament that sits in London. There are always members there who take a special interest in you and protect all the rights to which you are entitled. William Pitt and Lord Camden, as well as Fox, Barré, Conway, Pownall, Dowdeswill, and Edmund Burke, fight your battles for you with an eloquence far beyond any your ablest men possess; and it was by their defence of you that the Stamp Act and the paint, paper, and glass act were repealed.

There was a certain amount of plausibility in this argument, especially to a mind that was inclined to loyalism. But the

---

[10] Younge, "Constitutional History of England," p. 72. The British Parliament has to-day the right to tax any of its colonies without representation. Parliament is omnipotent in this as in every other respect. "American Historical Review," vol. i, p. 37; Proceedings of the American Antiquarian Society, vol. vii, p. 181; Jenkyns, "British Rule and Jurisdiction Beyond the Sea," p. 10; Todd, "Parliamentary Government in the British Colonies," edition 1894, pp. 241–245.

patriotic party replied that they wanted the protection of ascertained and fixed rights, so that they would not need the condescending protection of these so-called great men in Parliament, who would not live forever or who might change their opinions.

The Englishmen would then argue that the colonists were virtually represented in Parliament just as the vast majority of people in England were virtually represented. All the members of Parliament, although elected by an insignificant fraction of the people, were charged with the duty of legislating for those unrepresented, and of caring for their interests, and had always done so. The seven million people who had no direct representation were nevertheless virtually represented by all the members of Parliament, and in the same way the colonists were virtually represented.[11]

This was the only sort of representation which the majority of Englishmen recognized or understood, and they have maintained it down into our own time. The House of Lords represented all the nobility, the House of Commons represented all the commoners, and the colonists as commoners were therefore fully represented.

To this virtual representation the colonists replied that the unrepresented people in England were more or less intimately associated with the represented people, and the laws had to be the same for all. Those members of Parliament who laid taxes on unrepresented Leeds and Manchester taxed themselves and their constituents at the same time. But when they taxed America they could and did lay a tax entirely different from those they put on themselves and their constituents.[12]

---

[11] "Cursory Remarks on Dr. Price's Observations on the Nature of Civil Liberty," London, 1776, pp. 11–12. See also Eastwick's Letter to Tucker, p. 74.

[12] "Considerations on the Propriety of Imposing Taxes in the British Colonies," London, 1766. See, also, "Considerations on the Nature and Extent of the Legislative Authority of the British Parliament," Philadelphia; Niles, "Principles and Acts of the Revolution," edition 1876, p. 410.

Yes, the Englishman would reply, and the difference has been that they put far lighter taxes on you than they place on themselves. England is overwhelmed with taxes on wagons, furniture, and every article a man can have, even to the panes of glass in his house. The people of England pay twenty-five shillings per head in taxes. They ask from you only sixpence per head, although they have spent in support of your government and protection since 1690, without counting the cost of the war with France, £43,697,142, of which over £1,500,000 was paid in bounties on your products.[13]

Again the Americans replied that if taxation were once allowed England would make it what she pleased and rule America as she pleased; and so the interminable argument went on.

The loyalists were of course anxious to see the matter settled by allowing the colonies to send representatives to Parliament. This, they thought, would prevent rebellion and create an ideal British empire of overwhelming power, with the advantage in the end greatly in favor of America. They argued that the only fair and proper way by which the colonies could be represented would be by giving them representatives in proportion to their population, revenue, and growing power. As these were increasing every year, the representation would continually have to be enlarged; and, as America was greater in its size and resources than England, the colonies would before long have more representatives in Parliament than the British Isles; and the seat of power of the British empire would of necessity be removed to America.[14]

---

[13] "The Rights of Great Britain Asserted Against the Claims of America," p. 80, London, 1776. Cobbett, "Parliamentary History," vol. xviii, p. 222.

[14] The forecasts of the increase of population which those who used this argument made have been very nearly fulfilled. They estimated one hundred and twenty millions for the year 1924. We may not reach that number at the present rate of increase, but we shall not be very far behind it. Other estimates which they gave were twenty-four millions in sixty years from 1774 and ninety-six millions in one hundred years. They based their estimates on the rate of increase in their own time,

ENGLAND ABSORBED BY AMERICA

The solution of the dispute lay, they said, in closer union with the mother-country instead of drawing away from her. Many tried to win over the patriots by showing that equal rights with England and such a close union as would make the two countries identical would be for the greater glory of America. It was certainly a fond delusion to suppose that England would consent to a union that would absorb her, or that she had any idea of ever allowing any of her dependencies a political equality or commercial rivalry with herself. But it was characteristic of the loyalists to dream that London society, the aristocracy, the church, and all the other ornaments of English life, might be brought over to New York and Philadelphia.

"When the numbers, power, and revenues of America exceed those of Britain a revolution of the seat of empire will surely take place. . . . Should the Georges in regular succession wear the British diadem to a number ranking with the Louises of France, many a goodly prince of that royal line will have mingled his ashes with American dust, and not many generations may pass away before one of the first monarchs of the world on ascending his throne shall declare, with exulting joy, 'Born and educated amongst you, I glory in the name of American.' "—" A Few Political Reflections Submitted to the Consideration of the British Colonies," p. 49, Philadelphia, 1774.

The farther the discussion extended the more clearly it appeared that if Parliament had any power at all over the colonies it had the power to tax them. When one reflected that Parliament could enact the death penalty in the colonies, and take away a colonist's life by a law to which he had not consented, it seemed strange that it could not take from a colonist without his consent a shilling a year in taxes. Englishmen began collecting and publishing the numerous instances in which Parliament had long regulated colonial internal affairs, so as to show that it was hardly possible that there could be an exception in the one item of taxation inside of the seaports.

A notable instance of internal regulation was the colonial post-office system, which was begun by an act of Parliament in

when the population doubled within thirty years; but this rate was not kept up. ("A Few Political Reflections Submitted to the Consideration of the British Colonies," pp. 69–70.)

1692, and enlarged and extended by another act in 1710; and this same act fixed and regulated the rates of postage in all the colonies and exempted letter-carriers from paying ferriage over rivers. It was unquestionably an internal regulation, and seemed very much like a tax on the colonists for carrying their letters. It was an internal tax and a very heavy one, because the postage rates were high. In 1765, the same year as the Stamp Act, the postage rates in the colonies were again regulated by Parliament. But although the colonists complained of the Stamp Act they never complained of the postage regulations.

Loyalists could be very annoying on this point, for it was difficult to deny that there was a strong resemblance between demanding postage on letters and exacting a stamp duty on the legal or business document inside the wrapper. The real difference was that by paying the postage the colonists received in return an immediate and undeniable benefit in having their letters carried at the mother-country's expense by a general system which was uniform throughout the colonies, while in the case of the stamp tax, England seemed to be getting all the benefit. The general benefit of the post-office had been so great and obvious that in 1692, 1710, and 1765, when parliamentary post-office acts were passed, it had not occurred to the colonists to think of them as dangerous precedents of internal regulation.[15]

If the Stamp Act is unconstitutional, Englishmen would say, so also is the post-office act; but your arch patriot Franklin still remains postmaster of the colonies, enjoys the salary, and has done his utmost to increase the postal revenue, which is an internal tax.

If you want other instances, said the loyalists, of Parliament regulating the internal affairs of the colonies for the last century and more, they are innumerable. As far back as 1650, under the protectorate of Oliver Cromwell, that huge son of liberty, Parliament passed an act blocking up the ports of

---

[15] See " Considerations on the Propriety of Imposing Taxes in the British Colonies," etc., pp. 55–56, London, 1766; *American Archives*, 4th series, vol. i, p. 500.

Barbadoes, Virginia, Bermuda, and Antigua, and in that old act of Cromwell's time it is expressly declared that the colonies are subject to Parliament.

Going farther back than 1650, they found another instance in 1643, when Parliament passed an ordinance putting the whole government of the colonies in the hands of a governor-general and seventeen commissioners, with unlimited powers to "provide for, order, and dispose of all things which they shall think most fit and advantageous for the well-governing, securing, strengthening, and preserving of the said plantations." Was not Parliament then exercising power, and omnipotent power, in the colonies? And Oliver Cromwell himself was one of the commissioners.

Then, also, they said, there was the act in the second year of George II, levying duties out of the wages of all American seamen for the purpose of building up Greenwich Hospital. By the Parliament also were passed from time to time those acts restraining the colonies from manufacturing certain articles, notably hats, articles of iron and of steel; slitting mills were prohibited, and also the cutting of pine-trees; lands were made liable to the payment of debts; the statute of wills extended to the colonies; paper currency was restrained; indentured servants were empowered to enlist, troops raised in the colonies made subject to the articles of war, and so on. In fact, Parliament had over and over again walked about in the colonial internal organs, without arousing much, if any complaint, and without doing any harm.[16]

---

[16] "The Rights of Great Britain Asserted," pp. 27–39, London, 1776. "The Supremacy of the British Legislature Over the Colonies Candidly Discussed," London, 1775; "An Englishman's Answer to the Address from the Delegates to the People of Great Britain," p. 10, New York, 1775; "An Answer to the Declaration of the American Congress," London, 1776, pp. 65–70; Massachusettensis Letter VII; "The Controversy Between Great Britain and Her Colonies Reviewed," London, 1769, pp. 137–207; "The Rights of Great Britain Asserted Against the Claims of America;" "An Enquiry Whether the Guilt of the Present Civil War Ought to be Imputed to Great Britain or America," London, 1776; Todd, "Parliamentary Government in the British Colonies," ed. 1894,

Sometimes, it is true, said the loyalists, you have protested against some particular part of this regulation by Parliament when you happened not to like it. When Cromwell was handling Virginia rather roughly her people announced the doctrine that there must be no taxation without representation. But you never protested on principle against any internal regulation that was a convenience or a benefit to you. And what do the few isolated protests you may have made amount to against the fact of long-continued action by Parliament for over a hundred years?

As Parliament had done so much in colonial internal affairs without consent and without representation, and could impose a tax at the seaports, it seemed to loyalists and Englishmen very extraordinary that it could not tax generally or internally, when we consider that the power of general taxation is the most important part, and, indeed, the foundation, of legislative power, if legislative power is to exist at all.[17]

It was first claimed by the colonists that Parliament, in spite of all its internal regulating, had never actually assumed control of private property by a tax law to which the colonists had not consented; or, as the Stamp Act Congress put it, "Parliament could not grant to his Majesty the property of the colonists." But Parliament had taken away private property by so-called external taxes at the seaports, which the colonists admitted to be constitutional, and an act of Parliament was very soon found by which private property had been controlled by Parliament all over the colonies.

This was the famous Act of 1732, which made all lands,

---

p. 210; "Diary and Letters of Thomas Hutchinson," vol. i, pp. 4–7. See also Dulaney, " Considerations on the Propriety of Imposing Taxes in the British Colonies; Objections to the Taxation of Our American Colonies," London, 1775; "Right of the British Legislature to Tax the Colonies Vindicated," London, 1774; "Argument of the Exclusive Right of the Colonies to Tax Themselves," London, 1774.

[17] " Those who can tax will rule and those who can rule will tax."— *American Archives*, 4th series, vol. ii, p. 909.

slaves, and personal property in the colonies liable for the debts of British merchants. The English merchants had petitioned to have this act passed as a protection. They were obliged to give the colonists in America long credit for the goods they sold them. As this debtor class increased the English merchants feared that the colonial legislatures would be persuaded to pass stay laws to prevent the seizure of colonial property in payment of such debts. Jamaica had already passed a stay law of this sort. Accordingly, the act of Parliament of 1732 provided that all lands, goods, and negro slaves in America should at all times be liable to seizure and sale for debt just as if they were in England.[18]

An enormous trade and commerce sprang up, it was said, under the protection of this act. Without the act the English merchants would have refused to give the colonists long credit; and the colonists, having no specie and little money of any kind in circulation except depreciated paper, would have been unable to pay cash or pay on short time; would, in short, have been unable to trade. But under the protection of the act they reaped a greater harvest than the English merchants. Their wonderful prosperity in recent years, said the English, flowed from that act of Parliament; and accordingly they never protested or objected to it as exercising jurisdiction over private property. They never asked that they should first be represented in Parliament, and never complained of want of representation.

If, therefore, said the Englishman, Parliament can, without your consent, enact a law taking away your life by capital punishment, and can without your consent take away your private property by means of taxes levied on goods coming into your seaports; and can enact a law taking away your private property for debt, what do you mean by saying that Parliament cannot take away your private property by means of taxes

---

[18] " The Interest of the Merchants and Manufacturers of Great Britain in the Present Contest with the Colonies," p. 38, London, 1774.

levied in all your towns? Where is there any authority for such a distinction as that?

There was no authority; and the patriot party soon admitted that there was none by changing their ground and denying all the authority of Parliament, not only in taxes, but in every other matter. The truth was that Parliament had the right to rule, and had long ruled, the colonies without their consent. If a community is a colony in the English sense, it necessarily is ruled without its consent.

VIII.

THE STAMP ACT CANNOT BE ENFORCED AND IS REPEALED

THE American patriot argument meant in reality the extinguishment of the colonial relation; and the colonists now proceeded to extinguish that relation so far as the Stamp Act was concerned. Parliament no doubt had a clear legal right under the British Constitution to pass the Stamp Act, but it was very soon evident that fifty thousand troops should have been sent to America before any attempt was made to enforce it. Our people cared nothing about the legal right under a constitution on the other side of the Atlantic. They wanted to govern themselves by their own constitutions. They wanted to remain in the old semi-independent condition which they had enjoyed before the close of the French War in 1763. They did not want to be reorganized, remodelled, or reformed except by themselves.

Their opposition was very nearly unanimous. Thousands who afterwards became loyalists acted on this occasion as patriots, and the independent feeling of the people was as clearly displayed as in the opposition to the navigation and trade laws.

November 1, 1765, had been fixed upon as the day when the enforcement of the Stamp Act should begin; and the "Royal Charlotte" bringing the stamps and the stamped paper for Philadelphia arrived in the Delaware just below the city on the 5th of October. Flags were immediately displayed at half mast and the church bells were muffled and tolled for the rest of the day. The shops were closed and drums muffled in crape were beaten in the streets by very sable negroes. Several thousand citizens met at the State House, and it was decided to compel the stamp distributer, John Hughes, to resign. Robert Morris headed a committee which visited Hughes for this purpose, and

101

after warning him that the rioters were ready to tear down his house they secured his resignation.[1]

In Connecticut the stamp distributer, Jared Ingersoll, had been compelled to resign during the summer, long before the stamps arrived. Oliver, the Boston distributer, had been also compelled to resign; and the mob placarded the doors of public offices with the notice:

"Let him that shall first distribute or employ stamped paper look well to his house, his person, and his furniture.—Vox Populi."

The stamped paper that arrived in Boston was protected in the fort and the same precaution had to be taken in New York: but the New York mob forced the governor's stables, paraded his coach and his horses in the streets, hung him in effigy, and then burnt his carriage before his eyes on the Bowling Green. Proceeding to the house of Major James, who was reported to have said, "I will cram the stamps down the throats of the people with the point of my sword," they wrecked his house and rich furniture, destroying his fine library, pictures, and garden, as they had done with Hutchinson's house in Massachusetts. Emboldened by their success, they sent a deputation to the lieutenant-governor, and with threats of bloodshed and riot demanded the stamped paper. It was surrendered, and deposited in the City Hall. Another cargo of it, which afterwards arrived, was seized by the mob and burnt.[2]

In North Carolina the stamp-master was forced to resign, and when the stamped paper arrived at Brunswick in the twenty-gun sloop-of-war "Diligence," her captain was surprised to find his ship confronted by the militia, who forbade him to land the paper.[3]

---

[1] Oberholtzer, "Life of Robert Morris," p. 10; "Prior Documents of the Revolution," pp. 43–55; Boston *Gazette*, October 21, 1765; September 22, 1766; "The True Benjamin Franklin," p. 232.

[2] Gordon, "American Revolution," edition 1788, vol. i, pp. 175–190, 195; Botta, "American Revolution," 9th ed., 1839, vol. i, pp. 65–75; *Annual Register*, 1765, p. 49; "Prior Documents of the Revolution," pp. 7–37, 110; Boston *Gazette*, September 16 and November 18, 1765; Lamb, "American War," p. 11.

[3] Haywood, "Governor Tryon and His Administration," pp. 33, 37, 39, 44.

NO STAMPS IN THE COUNTRY

Less violent but equally effective measures were taken throughout the country and even in some of the West India islands; but Barbadoes and the Canadian provinces submitted to the act, and there appear to have been no disturbances in East Florida. In the other colonies, which afterwards formed the United States, the stamp-masters, with the examples in Pennsylvania, New York, and New England before their eyes, usually resigned voluntarily or retired to another locality. Such successful, widespread and thorough rioting has not often been known.

So general was the destruction of the stamped paper and the threats which prevented its use, that within a few weeks after the first of November, 1765, there was a condition of affairs which for a time puzzled the lawyers and judges. How could vessels legally proceed to sea without stamped papers? How could the people probate wills, execute deeds, leases, insurance policies, contracts, bills of lading, warrants for surveys, or any other legal document? The courts in many of the colonies refused to sit, because every paper used in their complicated proceedings and processes and every business document offered in evidence had to be stamped; and the stamps could not be obtained, or, if obtained, the attempt to use them would immediately bring on the mob.

John Adams relates how he was called upon on the 18th of December to join Gridley and Otis in an argument before Governor Bernard and his council to persuade them to open the courts. There seemed to these patriot lawyers two reasons why the courts should be opened—first, the invalidity of the Stamp Act; and second, the necessity of the case. Parliament had no authority to enforce internal taxes, and therefore the Stamp Act ought to be waived by the judges as against natural equity and the constitution. This argument would have pleased a patriot mass-meeting, but could not be accepted by officials or judges who were sworn to execute the laws of England and had no power to declare them void.[4]

---

[4] Adams, Works, vol. ii, pp. 157–163, 181; Boston *Gazette*, February 24, 1766.

The other reason, based upon the necessity of the situation, the impossibility of obtaining stamps or using them, and the importance of allowing the ordinary business of life to go on, finally prevailed all over the country. The governor and council of Massachusetts would do nothing; they would not take upon themselves to order the judges to open court; but the Massachusetts courts, custom-houses, and all public offices soon followed the example in other colonies and conducted business as if the Stamp Act had never been passed.

In Georgia a few vessels left the Savannah River with stamped clearance-papers; and there was an attempt to enforce the stamp law on vessels leaving North Carolina, but further compliance was soon prevented by the people of the province. The first ship that went to sea from Boston without stamped papers is said to have belonged to that daring patriot merchant John Hancock. The governor of South Carolina, compelled by the necessity of the case, opened the port of Charleston; and necessity accomplished the same result in New York and every port on the coast.[5]

The quiet determination of a very large proportion of the people, including apparently most of those who afterwards became loyalists, seems to have been irresistible and overwhelming. The Stamp Act never went into effect except in Canada and Barbadoes. The colonists, by a most remarkable unanimity of action, killed it more effectually than they had killed the clauses of the navigation and trade laws which did not suit them. The people were surprised at their own unanimity. John Adams said that there had never before been such an instance of unanimity, not even in the wars against the French and Indians; and it can hardly be said that there was such an instance of it again during the Revolution, for very soon the loyalists began to separate themselves into a distinct party.[6]

The business of the colonies went on as usual. Every one

[5] Haywood, " Governor Tryon and His Administration," pp. 41–43, 45.
[6] John Adams, Works, vol. ii, p. 173.

by common consent paid no attention to the stamp law in any of their dealings. The newspapers were published without a stamp or with a death's head where the stamp should have been; and no one would receive the Canadian newspapers which were printed on stamped paper.

It would be difficult to find in all history another instance of such complete and thorough disobedience to a law which one of the most powerful nations of the world had debated and enacted with the most careful consideration, and which was intended to be put in operation in the kindliest and gentlest manner. There had been no attempt to enforce the act with troops, or to send troops out beforehand and station them at important points in the modern manner. Grenville, fearing disorders and resistance, had brought in a bill to allow military officers in the colonies to quarter their troops in private houses; but there was so much opposition in Parliament to this method that it was dropped.

England had at that time some twelve regiments on the American continent; but most of them were holding the newly-acquired possessions of Florida and Canada, and guarding the Indian frontiers on the Ohio and the great lakes. General Gage, who was commander of the British forces in America, had some troops, possibly five hundred, at New York and Albany. which were the headquarters and strategic positions for the British. There was also part of a Scotch regiment in Philadelphia in the old barracks near Third and Green Streets. But most of the rebellious colonies were entirely without British troops. No attempt was made to use those in New York and Albany. In fact, the rioting, the burning of the governor's coach, the surrender of the stamped paper, and the burning of a cargo of the paper, took place directly under the eyes of the soldiers without the slightest attempt on their part to prevent it.

General Gage, while instructed to repel acts of outrage and violence, was also enjoined to act with great caution and delicacy. He also appears to have been under orders to reduce expenses in all the American military establishments; so that England was at this time attempting to establish her sovereignty in the colonies altogether by the conciliatory and persuasive plan and without the slightest use or even the threat of force.[7]

After the Ministry had heard of the rioting, the destruction of stamps, and forced resignations of stamp-masters, they wrote letters on the 24th of October to Gage and the governors, expressing great astonishment at what had happened. Gage was gently reprimanded for not having protected the stamps and stamp-master of New York; but at the same time the Ministry admitted that being on the ground he probably knew best what should have been done. Governor Bernard, of Massachusetts, was told that they had heard with the greatest surprise of the refusal of his council to call for military aid to help them support the law. All the governors were told that if there were any more disturbances they must call upon General Gage and Admiral Colvil for aid, and that troops could be obtained from Nova Scotia.[8]

It is of course now easy to see that before passing such a sweeping measure as the Stamp Act, England should have conquered the colonies into complete submission. It was almost like attempting to tax an independent nation. England collects stamp duties of three or four million pounds, as well as excise, salt tax and land taxes, in India; but she has thoroughly conquered the country and has there a very large standing army.[9]

The colonists were not content with disregarding the Stamp Act. They were determined to have it repealed, and to force the repeal by punishing England with what we would now call boycotting. They had already largely abstained from buying English goods because of the Sugar Act and the attempt to prevent smuggling. Their efforts and plans now became more elaborate and determined. Wholesale and retail merchants in New York and Philadelphia formed themselves into associations agreeing to cancel all their English orders. In Philadel-

---

[7] " Prior Documents of the Revolution," pp. 39, 124, 142.
[8] " Prior Documents of the Revolution," pp. 39–44.
[9] Lilly, " India and Her Problems," p. 187.

phia they even prohibited any lawyer from bringing suit to recover a debt due an inhabitant of England. These methods were followed in Boston and other towns, and societies were formed for encouraging domestic manufacturing.

Resolutions were passed to repress extravagance at funerals, and to abstain from eating lambs so that the supply of domestic wool for clothes might be increased. Butchers who offered lamb for sale were to be boycotted and driven from business; and so thoroughly were all these plans carried out that between November and January trade with England almost ceased.

Thousands of working people, manufacturers, laborers, and seamen in England were said to be thrown out of employment, and believed themselves threatened with starvation. Petitions began to pour into Parliament from London, Bristol, Lancaster, Liverpool, Hull, Glasgow, and, indeed, as the *Annual Register* of that date informs us, from most of the trading and manufacturing towns and boroughs of the kingdom. The trade with the colonies was between £2,000,000 and £3,000,000 per year. It was no light matter to cut down such an enormous sum. Worse still, the colonists were indebted to British merchants in some £2,000,000 or £3,000,000 on past sales, and when pressed for payment expressed great willingness, but declared that the recent acts of Parliament had so interrupted and disturbed their commerce, and thrown them into such confusion, that "the means of remittances and payments were utterly lost and taken from them." [10]

John Bull was apparently struck in his pocket, the most tender spot on his person. Meantime, during the previous summer the Grenville Ministry, which had secured the passage of the Stamp Act, quarrelled with the King and went out of power. A new Ministry was formed by Lord Rockingham out of a faction of the Whig party. This Ministry was very short-lived, and has usually been described as weak. But it secured some legislation which has been admired. It had to

---

[10] *Annual Register*, 1766, vol. ix, chap. vii, pp. 35, 36; Adam Smith, "Wealth of Nations," 5th ed., book 4, chap. 7, p. 272.

settle first of all the great question raised by the starving workmen, and the merchants and manufacturers with their petitions crowding the lobbies of Parliament. They asked to have the Stamp Act repealed. But general public opinion, both in Parliament and throughout the country, was exasperated at the resistance in America and was in favor of further coercive measures. [11]

The government was assailed for not having immediately employed troops and ships-of-war to enforce the Stamp Act "in such a manner as the outrageousness of the resistance required." Even the Whigs admitted that the situation was critical, and that there was an immediate necessity of enforcing the act by fire and sword or else of moving its immediate repeal. There was no doubt, the Whigs said, of the ability of England to crush or even extirpate the colonies, but in such action England would be using one of her arms to cut off the other.

The whole question of the taxation of the colonies was raised again; witnesses, experts on trade, all sorts of persons familiar with the colonies, including Franklin, were called to the bar of the House, examined, and cross-examined. The agents of the different colonies were constantly in attendance in the lobbies. No source of information was left unexplored. The ablest men of the country were pitted against each other in continual debates, and colonial taxation was the leading topic of conversation among all classes. It was investigated and discussed far more thoroughly and with more complete information and larger experience than at the time of the passage of the Stamp Act.

Aside from all eloquence and passionate feeling there were two great questions before Parliament. Was the Stamp Act constitutional? and if constitutional, was it expedient? England had the constitutional right to tax Ireland, but refrained. Should she also refrain in this instance from taxing America?

It was the innings of the radical section of the Whigs led

<hr>

[11] Lecky, " England in the Eighteenth Century," vol. iii, p. 100. See also *Annual Register*, 1766, pp. 31-48.

by Lord Rockingham. They were favorable to liberalism and the colonies; and there were enough Tories alarmed by the petitions of traders and merchants to give a majority which decided that the Stamp Act was not expedient. They accordingly repealed it within a year after its passage, with a minority of stanch Tories strenuously protesting and predicting the complete overthrow of British sovereignty in America.

The majority which repealed the Stamp Act because of its inexpediency felt quite sure, however, as did also the vast majority of Englishmen, that Parliament had a constitutional right to tax the colonies as it pleased, and so they passed a bill declaring null and void all acts of colonial legislatures which had denied the complete power of Parliament and they also passed what is known in history as the Declaratory Act, asserting the constitutional right of Parliament to bind the colonies "in all cases whatsoever;" and this is still the law of England.

The rejoicing over the repeal of the Stamp Act was displayed, we are told, in a most extraordinary manner, even in England. The ships in the Thames hoisted their colors and houses were illuminated. The colonists had apparently been able to hit a hard blow by the stoppage of trade. The rejoicing, however, as subsequent events showed, was not universal. It was the rejoicing of Whigs, or of the particular ship-owners, merchants, and workingmen who expected relief from the restoration of the American trade. It was noisy and conspicuous. There must have been some exaggeration in the account of the sufferings from loss of trade. It is not improbable that Parliament had been stampeded by a worked-up excitement in its lobbies; for very soon it appeared that the great mass of Englishmen were unchanged in their opinion of what should be England's colonial policy; and, as was discovered in later years, the stoppage of the American trade did not seriously injure the business or commercial interests of England.[12]

But in America the rejoicing was, of course, universal.

---

[12] "Letters of James Murray, Loyalist," p. 258.

There were letters and addresses, thanksgivings in churches, the boycotting associations were instantly dissolved, trade resumed, homespun given to the poor, and the people felt proud of themselves and more independent than ever because they could compel England to repeal laws.

The colonists were certainly lucky in having chanced upon a Whig administration for their great appeal against taxation. It has sometimes been said that both the Declaratory Act and the repeal of the Stamp Act were a combination of sound constitutional law and sound policy, and that if this same Whig line of conduct had been afterwards consistently followed, England would not have lost her American colonies. No doubt if such a Whig policy had been continued the colonies would have been retained in nominal dependence a few years longer. But such a policy would have left the colonies in their semi-independent condition without further remodelling, with British sovereignty unestablished in them, with a powerful party of the colonists elated by their victory over England, and they would have gone on demanding more independence until they snapped the last string.

In fact, the Whig repeal of the Stamp Act advanced the colonies on their road to independence. It gave the patriot party such confidence in themselves, that they at once put a stop by mob violence to all England's efforts to check smuggling. James Otis told the people that the government's abandonment of the Stamp Act could be construed into an abandonment of the navigation and trade laws. From the time of the repeal of the Stamp Act it does not appear that England ever succeeded in enforcing any laws which the patriot party did not like.[18]

Sir Francis Bernard, who was governor of Massachusetts at this time, said that the prestige of England was gone as soon as the colonists had successfully resisted the Stamp Act. The repeal of the Stamp Act was a declaration of independence. The nation that dared not or would not protect her chosen

[18] Quincy's Reports of Massachusetts Superior Court, 1761–1772, pp. 445, 446; Gordon, " American Revolution," edition 1788, vol. i, p. 234.

THE REPEAL

THE REPEAL, OR FUNERAL OF MISS AME STAMP

officials in the colonies, allowed them to be mobbed out of office, their private property destroyed and their lives endangered; the nation that would not even punish such rioting and resistance, but instead repealed a law at the demand of the rioters, was, he thought, trying the conciliatory policy to the verge of imbecility. The Tories condemned the repeal on this account, and in the course of the next ten or fifteen years ascribed to it the increasing coil of colonial entanglement.[14]

---

[14] The arguments against repealing the Stamp Act are well and briefly summarized in "Correct Copies of the Two Protests Against the Bill to Repeal the American Stamp Act," London, 1766. See, also, "The Constitutional Right of the Legislature of Great Britain to Tax the British Colonies," p. 25, London, 1768. "Prior Documents of the Revolution," pp. 81–89; Bernard, "Select Letters on Trade," &c., p. 54.

"If Great Britain can or will suffer such conduct to pass unpunished," said John Hughes, referring to the violence which had compelled his resignation as stamp distributor, "a man need not be a prophet or the son of a prophet to see that her empire in North America is at an end."—"Prior Documents," p. 49.

IX.

THE PAINT, PAPER AND GLASS ACT

DURING the year after the repeal of the Stamp Act politics were comparatively quiet in the colonies. The Assembly of Virginia voted a statue to the King and an obelisk to Pitt, and New York voted statues to both the King and Pitt. Maryland and Massachusetts passed acts indemnifying those who had suffered in the Stamp Act riots.[1]

There was, however, one cloud in the sky. A clause of the Mutiny Act, passed at the same time as the Stamp Act, required the colonial legislatures to provide the British soldiers quartered in America with barracks, fires, beds, candles, and other necessaries; and this provision was now enforced as part of the remodelling of the colonies. The officers in command at New York made a demand for these supplies, and the New York Assembly voted part of them, but failed to furnish vinegar, salt, and beer.

This disobedience on the part of a dependency was extremely irritating even to a Whig Ministry; and an act of Parliament was passed, and approved by the King on the 2nd of July, 1767, prohibiting the New York Assembly from enacting any law or performing any of its functions until it complied in every particular with the requisition for the soldiers. The assembly, however, had fully complied with the requisition on May 26, so that the act of Parliament was not really necessary; but it was nevertheless a startling revelation to the colonists of the power that could be exercised over them by Parliament. This was internal regulation with a vengeance, that Parliament and a Whig Ministry should actually suspend the power of a colo-

---

[1] " Prior Documents of the Revolution," pp. 103, 113, 116, 117, 123, 124, 134, 142. Gordon, " American Revolution," edition 1788, vol. i, pp. 210–212.

nial legislature. Yet the act seemed to be entirely constitutional, because the colonists themselves had admitted that Parliament had full control over them, except in the matter of internal taxation.[2]

The patriot leaders now began to realize that their distinction between internal and external taxation was impractical and would not stop the reorganizing plans of Parliament. They must go a great deal farther than that, and deny all the authority of Parliament. But at present nothing could be done because the New York Assembly had unfortunately yielded, and other opportunities must be awaited.

It has been sometimes argued that having escaped out of the Stamp Act difficulty, England's true course was to let the colonies alone, and not to raise another direct issue with them; and that if she had followed that course there would have been no war and everything would have been peaceable and happy down to our own time. If the advocates of this theory mean that the colonies would have gradually and peaceably become an independent nation we can readily agree with them. But apparently they mean that England would not have lost her colonies; and that there would have been some pleasant and ideal union between England and America which they do not definitely describe.

Such a union, indeed, cannot be definitely described except as part of political dreamland. The question at issue was one of colonies or no colonies, dependence or independence. If the colonies would not obey Parliament, or were not subject to its authority, then they were practically independent countries, and any so-called union with England would be the mere friendliness which sometimes exists between independent nations. A colony that can refuse obedience to the laws of the mother-country may be a colony in the old Greek sense of an independent community originally founded by the mother-

---

[2] " Prior Documents," pp. 92, 94, 95, 98, 99, 120, 125, 162; " Memorial History of the City of New York," vol. ii, 388; Lossing, " History of New York," chap. iii; Lamb, " History of New York," pp. 744–747.

country; but it is not a colony in the imperial sense, or in the English sense, and it is certainly not part of a consolidated empire which then as now was the object of England's ambition.

She accordingly not only punished and suspended the legislature of New York for its disobedience, and created the already described new Board of Commissioners of Customs to reside in America, but she devised a new taxing act which would it was hoped raise sufficient revenue to defray the cost of the military protection of the colonies, and at the same time fix permanent salaries on the governors, so that they would be no longer at the mercy of the legislatures.

A few months after the repeal of the Stamp Act the King and the Rockingham Ministry disagreed, and on the 7th of July, 1766, that Ministry went out of office. William Pitt formed a new one, made up of politicians from the various cliques and factions of the Whigs—a most impossible and impractical Ministry, and as short-lived as its predecessor.

Pitt was no longer the powerful statesman who had carried England through the great war with France and secured for her Canada and what seemed to be a world-wide empire. His ideas were no longer acceptable to the majority of Englishmen; for instead of appealing to their passion for conquest and empire, as he had done during the French War, he seemed to be asking them to allow the American empire, that they had saved from France, to slip away from them and become independent.

His health was broken and his nervous system shattered. He was afflicted with paroxysms of anger, could not bear the slightest noise, or even the presence of his children in the same house with him. He spent enormous sums of money in planting his country seat, "Hayes," and secluding himself within it. He sold the country-seat, but was so unhappy at parting with it that his wife bought it back for him. He required a constant succession of chickens to be kept cooking in his kitchens all day to satisfy his uncertain, but at times ravenous, appetite. Yet when he could summon sufficient health and strength to appear in Parliament and rise in his place to speak, the clearness and vigor of his intellect and the grandeur of his eloquence was still the admiration of his hearers.[3]

In forming the new Ministry he compelled the King to give him a title, and henceforth he is known as Lord Chatham. Within a few weeks after forming the Ministry his health failed so rapidly that he had to be taken to the continent. He never afterwards exercised any control in the Ministry of which he was supposed to be the head, and within little more than a year he retired from it altogether. But up to his death, in 1778, he would occasionally appear in the House of Lords to make those eloquent and pathetic appeals from which our school-boys used to recite passages, denouncing the government because it would not withdraw all the troops from America, and by peaceful discussion persuade the colonies to stay within the empire.

As for the Ministry he had formed, it was not his in any sense. On every question it pursued a course opposed to his policy; and after extraordinary confusion and divisions it soon ceased to bear even the semblance of a Whig Ministry, for by successive resignations Tories were admitted until it became all Tory. Lord Hillsborough and Lord North were admitted to it; and finally that extreme and thorough-going Tory, Lord George Germain. The Whigs went entirely out of power, and for the remainder of the Revolution we have a Tory government dealing with the colonies.[4]

The constant changing of ministries at this time had not a little to do with the development of the revolutionary spirit in America. A ministry had seldom lasted over a year. While there were the two great parties, Whig and Tory, they were strangely confused and split up into factions. Party lines were not distinctly drawn.[5] There could be no consistent and steady colonial policy. Whig ministries used Tory methods and

---

[3] Lecky, "England in the Eighteenth Century," edition of 1882, vol. iii, p. 121.

[4] *Ibid.*, pp. 123 *et seq.*

[5] Lecky, "England in the Eighteenth Century," edition of 1882, vol. iii, pp. 110-114.

Tory ministries used Whig methods. The uncertainty, the shifting back and forth from severity to liberality, passing taxing acts and repealing them, experimenting to see how the colonies could be consolidated, feeling their way towards the modern British empire, was a vast encouragement to the colonial patriots. As our Revolution advanced we find party lines and policies in England becoming clearer, until towards the end they are quite distinct; and after 1778 the ministry carried out a distinctly Tory policy.

As one reads in this period of English history how bankrupt and disturbed business had become; how violent the excitement and rioting over Wilkes; how incapable the government was to keep ordinary civil order even in London; how hostile to England were all the European nations, one cannot but see that it was a golden opportunity for the patriots. There was no period for nearly a hundred years when we could have broken away so easily. Good fortune and opportunity were an important factor in the Revolution, and attended us from the beginning to the end.

In the autumn of 1766 Parliament went to the country, and, as was naturally to be expected, the new election returned a body more determined than ever to remodel the colonies. It is difficult for any nation to endure a dependency where its sovereignty is not recognized. The colonists were still setting the trade laws at defiance. They had compelled England to repeal the Stamp Act, and had brought about this repeal by violence, by withholding trade, by starving English merchants and workingmen. Could this be endured? Could it be possible that a set of traders and farmers in a dependency had such power as that?

Observing the temper the House was in, Charles Townsend. Chancellor of the Exchequer, a Whig, and a most brilliant but uncertain member of the patch-work Chatham Ministry, announced, on the 26th of January, 1767, that the administration was prepared to solve the American problem. This solution would render the colonies self-sustaining, and relieve Great Britain of the expense of governing, defending, and protecting them. He knew, he said, a mode by which revenue could be drawn from America for this purpose without causing the heat and turmoil of the Stamp Act; and for this hopeful announcement he was vigorously applauded on all sides.

His plan was nothing more than taking the colonists at their word on the distinction between external and internal taxes. They had said that they were willing to pay external taxes, and accordingly a bill was introduced laying a duty on paint, paper, glass, and tea imported into the colonies; the duty to be paid at their seaports in the exact manner which they had said was lawful and constitutional.*

This measure was adopted by a Whig Ministry, which, besides Lord Chatham, contained Lord Camden, who two years before had made a brilliant argument to show that the colonies could not be taxed unless they were represented in Parliament. There were also in the same ministry Lord Shelburne and General Conway, both of them supposed to be warm friends and defenders of the colonies. But they all seem to have felt as strongly as the Tories the necessity for remodelling and consolidating the empire and preventing the colonies from escaping from control.

The Paint, Paper, and Glass Act was a great landmark in the Revolution, and wrought a great change of opinion. The colonists were fairly caught in their own argument. These new taxes were external, and, therefore, constitutional. At the same time they were laid on articles of such universal use, imported in such large quantities from England, that they would be paid in the enhanced price of the articles by all the people all over the country, and so were as much internal taxation as the stamp tax.

Besides being as internal in their effect as the stamp tax, it might very well happen that these new taxes could not be resisted as easily as the stamp tax had been resisted. The new

*This plan of taxation did not originate with Townsend. It had been discussed nearly a year before in the Boston *Gazette* of May 5, 1766, and was also a very obvious method.

taxes were to be collected at the seaports by the authority and force of the British army and navy and a host of new revenue officers who had recently been appointed. Paint, paper, and glass were imported in such quantities that it might be very difficult to evade the duties by any of the methods heretofore used. England seemed to be reaching out to secure control of the colonies in a most effective manner.

Petitions, resolves, and remonstrances were again sent across the water, and the associations for suspending importations were renewed; but it is noticeable that there was no rioting. In fact, the colonists seemed to be acting in a rather subdued manner. The patriot party had possibly become more conscious of its power, and relied on renewing the non-importation plan. But in any event the next step was a serious one. They must adopt new political principles. Their leaders were holding them in check. A town meeting was held in Boston to discountenance rioting, and Otis urged caution and advised that no opposition should be made to the new duties. On the 20th of November, 1767, when the taxes went into effect, the people were remarkably quiet, although two years before they had broken out with the utmost violence against the Stamp Act.'

Their petitions, letters, and public documents are full of the most elaborate expressions of loyalty and devotion. The petition which Massachusetts sent to the King in January, 1768, is apparently the perfection of unquestioning loyalty. With an intense love of independence in their hearts they, nevertheless, are compelled to use words of humble submissiveness. There is no bold arguing against the right to tax; no threats or denunciation which could be called treason like the resolutions and speech of Patrick Henry two years before. They merely beg and beseech to be relieved from these new taxes. If they cannot be relieved from them, they can only "regret their unhappy fate." They repeat the old unfortunate admission of the Stamp Act Congress that Parliament has superintending authority over them, but instead of adding the

' Barry, " History of Massachusetts," vol. ii, pp. 340, 341.

exception of internal taxation, they have a new exception, which they state by saying that this supreme authority extends to "all cases that can consist with the fundamental rights of nature and the constitution." Those words, "fundamental rights of nature," were a new way of limiting the authority of Parliament and significant of a change to complete reliance on the doctrines of the rights of man.

Glancing at the documents sent out by the other colonies, we find another idea obtruding itself. They ask for a return of the conditions and privileges they had enjoyed before the French War closed in 1763; the old days when the French in Canada prevented any remodelling or reorganization by England. This request for a return to that happy golden age became for some years a watchword in the patriot party, until the evolution of events brought them to declare absolute independence in 1776. After that the golden age seemed to be before them, and when England in 1778 offered in effect a return to the conditions before 1763 they rejected the offer with contempt.[8]

In February, 1768, the Massachusetts Assembly sent to all the other colonial assemblies a circular letter, very cautiously worded, and arguing the subject in a quiet way. There is nothing about external and internal taxes; but the recent duties on paint, paper, and glass are said to be infringements of their natural and constitutional rights, because such duties take away their property without their consent; which is simply a roundabout way of saying that no taxation without representation, and the doctrine of consent, must now be applied to external as well as internal taxes.

It is to be observed that they say that the new taxes are infringements of their natural and constitutional rights. A year or two before it was only their constitutional rights; now it is also their natural rights. Filled with a desperate determination to secure the freedom of national existence they are

---

[8] "To talk of replacing us in the situation of 1763 as we first asked," said George Mason in 1778, "is to the last degree absurd and impossible." —Niles, "Principles and Acts of the Revolution," edition 1876, p. 304.

broadening their arguments to meet England's broader and more determined efforts to control them. They are ceasing to rely upon their charters and the British constitution, and are building their hopes upon their rights as men and the right of naturally separated communities to national and independent existence.

The Massachusetts patriots said in the circular letter that the doctrine of government by consent of the governed was an "unalterable right in nature ingrafted into the British Constitution." This was altogether a new way of looking at the British Constitution, to "ingraft" upon it one of the rights-of-man doctrines. This sort of ingrafting would no doubt have improved the British constitution, but the English people would not accept the change, would not be Americanized to that extent.

The Massachusetts circular letter, of course, insists strongly that it is impossible that the colonies should ever be represented in Parliament. They evidently wish to keep Parliament at arm's length and have no connection with it whatever. The letter recites the petitions and arguments that had been sent to the Ministry, asks the various assemblies for their advice as to what else should be done, and declares in all seriousness that the colonists are not seeking "to make themselves independent of the mother-country." They meant that they were merely making themselves independent of Parliament, and still retained their allegiance to the King.

The British Government, however, regarded this letter as "of a most dangerous and factious tendency, calculated to inflame the minds of good subjects in the colonies." The chief object of the letter was obviously to promote union among the colonies, unite them in opposition, and encourage a reciprocal expression of feeling. The government quickly saw this, and directed the governor of Massachusetts to have the assembly rescind this letter; and at the same time a letter was sent to all the colonial assemblies requesting them to take no notice of the Massachusetts letter, "which will be treating it with the contempt it deserves."

This caused a great controversy and discussion, and became the subject of innumerable speeches, toasts, and humorous sallies both in England and America. The patriots bitterly complained that England was attempting to deny to the colonists the right to consult among themselves and even the right to petition. The Massachusetts legislature by a vote of 92 to 17 refused to rescind the letter and most of the colonial legislatures rejected the instructions of the Ministry and answered the Massachusetts letter with words of warm approval.[9]

There was great rejoicing in America over the Massachusetts refusal to rescind, and many Whigs in England celebrated the event as a famous occurrence in the cause of liberty. Paul Revere, a silversmith and engraver of Boston, celebrated the refusal by making a' handsome silver punch-bowl inscribed: "To the Memory of the Glorious Ninety-two Members of the Honorable House of Representatives of Massachusetts Bay, who on the 30th of June, 1768, voted not to rescind." The number 92, and also 45, the number of Wilkes' famous pamphlet, were constantly used at that time for indirect allusion to liberal or American ideas. The Whig society of Boston sent to a similar body in London two green turtles, one of which they said weighed 45 and the other 92 pounds. Colonel Barré presided at the dinner at which the turtles were served and other English Whigs were present. They drank a toast with three times three cheers to "The ninety-two patriots of Massachusetts Bay."[10]

The disobedience of the Massachusetts Assembly and of nearly all of the other colonial assemblies was another blow to British authority. It is easy now to see that the orders to one assembly to rescind and to the others to treat with contempt

---

[9] Most of the letters and documents in this controversy are printed in full in "Prior Documents of the Revolution," pp. 175–193, 202–222, 243. See also Ryerson's "Loyalists," vol. i, chap. xiv; Stedman, "American War," vol. i, pp. 53–63.

[10] Niles, "Principles and Acts of the Revolution," edition 1876, pp. 115, 116.

the circular letter were worse than useless, unless followed by sufficient military force to compel obedience or punish disobedience. It is easy to see that the Ministry should not have made the attempt unless prepared to enforce obedience. To allow the colonies to turn the tables so easily and treat the home government with contempt was turning British sovereignty into a laughing stock. England did not make such mistakes in her colonial system in later times. But in the year 1768 she was totally unaccustomed to enforcing her sovereignty in her colonies. No troops were sent out to compel obedience and she was again relying on mere letter-writing and paper proclamations for retaining control of America.

The Massachusetts circular letter was considered by the patriots as a petition and the government's attack upon it as an attempt to deny the sacred right of petition. Eloquent speeches on this subject fed the flame of patriotism, and as Franklin said, "warmed moderation into zeal and inflamed zeal into rage." The more the patriots examined the Paint, Paper, and Glass Act, the more their opposition was aroused. It expressly authorized writs of assistance to be issued in every colony. The colonists had objected to the Stamp Act because it was intended to "defray the expense of protecting, defending, and securing" them; which, they said, meant to keep a standing army among them. But the Paint, Paper, and Glass Act was not only to furnish revenue for the same purpose, but also for "defraying the charge of the administration of justice, and the support of civil government in such provinces where it shall be found necessary."

Further plans for the reorganization of the colonies were now disclosed. There was to be a colonial civil list, as it was called, and hereafter all governors, judges, and other colonial executive officials were to receive fixed salaries paid by the Crown out of the revenue raised by the duties on paint, paper, glass, and tea. The old system of the assemblies securing the passage of their favorite laws by withholding the governor's salary, and of controlling the judges in the same way, was to cease. There was to be no more withholding of a governor's salary until he consented to popular legislation, but in place of it orderly, methodical government, such as seemed proper for dependencies, and such as England had wanted to establish in the colonies ever since the reign of Charles II.

This struck at the root of what the colonists considered their system of freedom. If they could no longer control governors and executive officials through their salaries, they could no longer have their favorite laws. They would become mere colonies, compelled to take what was given to them, and to do as they were told.

The colonists had now three phases of British reorganization to resist—the new commissioners of customs, the suspension of the New York legislature, and the Paint, Paper, and Glass Act. In order to meet the last two they must invent a new argument and restrict still farther the authority of Parliament. They could no longer admit that Parliament had full authority over them except in internal taxation. Thus the Paint, Paper, and Glass Act brought them up to the inevitable position of denying all parliamentary authority; and the first man to take the important step of stating the new argument was John Dickinson, a Quaker lawyer of Philadelphia. He was about thirty-five years old, conspicuous in his profession and in Pennsylvania politics, and had been a member of the Stamp Act Congress, for which he had drafted several documents.

He stated the new argument in twelve "Letters from a Farmer," which were published in the *Pennsylvania Chronicle* between December 2, 1767, and February 15, 1768. They were quickly copied in most of the other colonial newspapers, reprinted in pamphlet form in numerous editions in America and England, and translated in France. They caused the greatest excitement in America. Town meetings, societies, and grand juries sent votes of thanks to the author. They toasted him at public dinners, and wrote poems and eulogies in his honor. At the same time these letters were also attacked as going entirely too far and "calculated to excite the passions of the unthinking." [11]

---

[11] " Life and Writings of Dickinson," vol. ii, p. 280.

They enlarged in detail on the danger of losing control of the salaries of the governors. They showed the full meaning of Parliament's suspension of the legislative power of New York. They showed that if Parliament could suspend the functions of a colonial legislature, it was omnipotent in its control of the colonies and could not be confined to mere external taxation. They were far more learned and comprehensive than any writings on the patriot side that had yet appeared, and were fortified by historical instances, clever anecdotes, and all the resources of a trained legal mind. Dickinson was bold enough to answer the argument that England was too powerful to be resisted. It is also significant that he describes as a warning to the colonists how Ireland had lost her liberties.

The old argument had admitted the full power of Parliament except in the one item of internal taxation. Dickinson denied that Parliament had any power or authority in the colonies at all; denied even its right of external taxation or taxation in any form; but conceded that Parliament could regulate the external or ocean commerce of the colonies by duties, which, however, must be solely for regulation and not for revenue, because if they were for revenue that would be a form of external taxation.

The argument, it will be observed, went just far enough to cut out the Paint, Paper, and Glass Act from allowable legislation. But the final admission that Parliament could regulate our commerce by duties, provided the duties did not rise to the dignity of taxes, was a very flimsy idea and seems to have rested on the old notion that England as head of the empire and mistress of the seas ought to be allowed in some way to regulate the general ocean commerce of the members of the empire. Dickinson worked out the theory with wonderful astuteness and ingenuity; but of course could not show how a duty on commerce could be kept from becoming a tax.

Indeed part of his own argument showed that almost any governmental command was in the end a tax. "An Act of Parliament," he said, "commanding us to do a certain thing, if it has any validity, is a tax upon us for the expense that accrues in complying with it." He also argued against the right of

Parliament to call on the legislature of New York for supplies
for the troops, because it was in effect a tax. He had said that
if Parliament could demand fire and candles, or vinegar, salt,
and pepper for the troops, it could also demand that any
colonial legislature supply the troops with arms and ammunition, or anything else they wanted, and was not that taxing?
And if the legislature refused to comply and Parliament punished them by suspending their powers, was not that forcing
them to pay a tax?

Any exercise of sovereignty, such as quartering troops in
public houses, impressing wagons or boats for transporting
them, their passage over ferries and toll-bridges, may be considered as taxes. Any exercise of governmental authority is
so intimately connected with taxation, that one cannot subsist
without the other. Dickinson's argument, although he would
not openly avow it, was really a denial of all the authority of
Parliament. His reasoning all led irresistibly to that end. He
was pushing Parliament completely out of all relations with
the colonies.[12]

But his cautious theories, his refusal to admit that he was
denying the whole authority of Parliament, served no doubt a
very useful purpose in checking too sudden an advance of the
American argument. He led on the moderate patriots step by
step, so that they could in the end see for themselves, from all
the discussion, that if they admitted any authority at all in
Parliament they would have to admit its authority in
everything.

There were many radicals who had for some time been
ready to reject all authority of Parliament, even its regulation
of commerce; but it was too soon to come out with such a
rejection in a formal and public manner. The moderate patriots
were not ready for it, and it shocked and annoyed loyalists who
might be persuaded to become patriots.

---

[12] Snow, "Administration of Dependencies," pp. 29–40; Critical
Review," xxvi; "Life and Writings of Dickinson," vol. ii, pp. 281, 282.
See also Snow, "Administration of Dependencies," p. 239, for an interesting account of the change wrought in Revolutionary thought by Dickinson's arguments.

X.

TROOPS SENT TO BOSTON, BUT THE PAINT, PAPER AND GLASS ACT IS REPEALED

MEANTIME the new commissioners of customs at Boston were calling upon the home government to send out troops to protect them in the performance of their duties. The governor and lieutenant-governor had made the same request; and it was said in a pamphlet of the time that even some citizens of Boston, presumably loyalists, had asked for troops.[1]

General Gage, at British army headquarters in New York, was accordingly instructed to send a regiment to Boston, and the admiral of the coast was directed to send a frigate, two sloops and two cutters. The fort, or castle as it was called, on an island in Boston harbor, was repaired and every arrangement made for a military and naval occupation.

The fifty-gun ship "Romney" arrived at Boston in May, and on the passage from Halifax had impressed several seamen from New England vessels. The press-gang was a recognized institution of that time, defended by arguments which somewhat resembled the arguments which defended slavery. It was regulated by acts of Parliament, and while its cruelties were shocking and its violation of the most sacred rights of human liberty infamous, it was nevertheless upheld by good people. because it was believed that in no other way could the British navy be sustained. England had always had great difficulty in recruiting her army and navy, and in all her wars had been obliged to hire troops from European princes. General Gage was at this time receiving recruits from Germany for one of his regiments.

In the state of feeling in which the colonists were, the work

---

[1] "The Conduct of the Late Administration Examined," p. 53 *et passim.*

of the press-gang was almost as irritating as an act of invasion by a foreign army. When the "Romney" reached Boston, the Massachusetts legislature asked her captain to allow no more impressment and to release those already taken. Possibly some terms might have been made with him, if one of the men whom he had taken had not been forcibly rescued by the people. He would release none, and stormed in true sea-dog fashion: "No man shall go out of this vessel. The town is a blackguard town, ruled by mobs. They have begun with me by rescuing a man whom I pressed this morning; and, by the eternal God, I will make their hearts ache before I leave it."[2]

Soon afterwards, on the 10th of June, the customs officers seized the sloop "Liberty," with a cargo of wine from Madeira, for violating the trade laws, and she was immediately rescued by the Boston mob. The cargo belonged to John Hancock, a patriot leader, and suits for penalties amounting to over £9000 were entered against him by the government.

The mob which rescued the cargo of the "Liberty" attacked the customs officers with bricks and stones, beat them with sticks, dragged the son of one of them by the hair, and broke the windows of their houses, until they were obliged to seek safety on board the war-ship "Romney." From there they were taken to Castle William, the government fort in the harbor, whence they wrote to General Gage and the admiral to hurry troops and war-vessels to Boston; and they remained at the castle until Boston was occupied by troops.[3]

This affair of the "Liberty" was an important event and brought the inevitable crisis a step nearer. The troops arrived

---

[2] " Prior Documents of the Revolution," p. 132; Wells, " Life of Samuel Adams," vol. i, p. 185. The press-gang acts of Parliament did not by their own wording, it is said, extend to America. Works of John Adams, vol ii, p. 163; vol. x, p. 204.)

[3] Gordon, " American Revolution," edition 1788, vol. i, pp. 231, 237, 240; Kidder, " History of the Boston Massacre," p. 115. Works of John Adams, vol. ii, p. 215. Adams said that the suits were pressed until ended by the battle of Lexington. Gordon says that they were dropped March 26, 1769.

from Halifax in September; and there were rumors that the patriots, who had already held a mass-meeting of protest, would not allow them to land. On the landing day, October 1, 1768, fourteen war-vessels lay with springs on their cables to haul their broadsides to the town. Under this protection Colonel Dalrymple landed his two Halifax regiments, the Fourteenth and Twenty-ninth, numbering, with the artillery, about 700 men, and with muskets loaded and fixed bayonets, marched them to Boston Common.

The army barracks were on Castle Island, in the harbor, but if the troops went there they could not overawe the patriots in Boston. The assembly and people would of course do nothing to provide quarters in Boston, and there was no law allowing troops to take possession of private houses. The governor and Colonel Dalrymple had no little difficulty in settling the question, but finally one regiment encamped on the common in tents, and the other, after spending the night in Faneuil Hall, was quartered in the State House. As cold weather came on both regiments were quartered in hired houses; but the main guard remained posted directly opposite the State House, with two field-pieces pointed at it. The commissioners of customs, who had fled to Castle Island in the harbor, now returned and resumed their duties.[4]

This was the first attempt on the part of Great Britain to enforce obedience in one of the colonies by military force. Some months before, troops had been spread out in New Jersey, Pennsylvania, Connecticut, and Georgia, as if the government was beginning to learn from the Stamp Act experiences that military force was becoming absolutely necessary.

Modern British colonists do not object to the presence of red-coats; but the Bostonians were not accustomed to them except as allies against the French; and the patriots among them were soon boiling with indignation against this alien

---

[4] Gordon, "American Revolution," edition 1788, vol. i, p. 248; Boston *Gazette*, November 3, 1768; Kidder, "History of the Boston Massacre," p. 115; "Prior Documents of the Revolution," pp. 129-132; Stedman, "American War," vol. i, p. 67.

occupation of their town, this overawing of the legislature, and this filling of the private houses of freemen with troops which had come to enforce a complete change in colonial government.

Nothing happened during the winter, but in the following June, when the Massachusetts Assembly met, they declined doing any business while surrounded by an armed force. They appear to have thought that by refusing to transact business they might compel the governor to remove the troops from the town. But the governor took the course of adjourning the assembly to meet in Cambridge, four miles away.[5] When assembled there, they passed resolutions protesting against the right of the governor to remove them and protesting against the establishment of a standing army in a colony in time of peace. These resolutions followed by similar resolves in other colonial assemblies, and a series of articles by Samuel Adams under the name "Vindex" in the Boston *Gazette,* seem to have started the opinion which afterwards grew into a formal doctrine and demand upon Great Britain, that in time of peace no regular troops should be kept in a colony and no fortification built there except by the consent of the colony.

As this right of a colony to receive or reject the troops of the mother-country has never been recognized by England, and as it in effect destroys the colonial relation as usually understood, it is of some interest to observe how Samuel Adams worked out the argument. A standing army was not allowed, he said, on the island of England without the consent of the people expressed through their representatives in Parliament. As the Americans were not and could not be represented in Parliament, a standing army could not be placed among them without the consent of the only legislative bodies in which they were represented, namely, their own assemblies. The argument was, of course, in effect, a declaration of independence; for when England had no longer the right to place an army in a colony to control it, the colony had become an independent state.

---

[5] "Diary and Letters of Thomas Hutchinson," vol. i, p. 526.

When asked by the governor at this time to provide supplies for the troops, the Massachusetts Assembly positively refused to supply them with anything; and the South Carolina Assembly also refused to furnish anything for the troops quartered in their colony; so that if Parliament followed the course which had been pursued in the case of New York, the functions of two more colonial assemblies would be suspended.

The year 1769 opened with Parliament declaring, in both speeches and resolutions that the colonies were in a state of disobedience to law and government, adopting measures subversive of the constitution, and disclosing an inclination to throw off all obedience to the mother-country. This was unquestionably a true description of the situation; and no good purpose is served by obscuring or denying it by means of those passages in the documents of the colonists in which they declare their "heartfelt loyalty" to the King, and disclaim all intention of independence. Those fulsome expressions deceived no one at that time, and why should they be used to deceive the guileless modern reader. They merely meant that the colonists were loyal as they understood loyalty, that they were willing to remain in the empire if they could remain in their own way, independent of Parliament and under a mere nominal headship of the English King.

There was, of course, a movement among the Whigs in Parliament to have the Paint, Paper, and Glass Act repealed, because the colonists had revived their non-importation societies, were refraining from buying English goods, and the Act seemed to be an inexpedient and imprudent measure like the Stamp Act. But Lord North, who had succeeded Townsend in the Ministry, decisively replied that "however prudence or policy may hereafter induce us to repeal the late paper and glass act, I hope we shall never think of it till we see America prostrate at our feet."

We find Parliament in this year directing that the governor of Massachusetts obtain "the fullest information touching all treason or misprision of treason within his government since the 30th day of December, 1767," in order, as the instructions went on to say, that his Majesty might have such offences tried within the realm of England, according to the statute passed in the thirty-fifth year of the reign of Henry VIII.

The meaning of this, in plain English, was that a colonist· suspected or accused of treason must not be tried in the colonies, where any jury that could be called would probably acquit him as a matter of course. It seemed better to take him to England, where juries would not be so hostile to the home government. This measure filled the patriotic party in the colonies with the most violent indignation. They denounced it in every form of language; and although no one was ever taken to England to be tried, it was enumerated in the Declaration of Independence as one of the causes of separation.

It was natural that our people, who had enjoyed so much liberty that they scarcely understood what a colony was, should be indignant at this suggestion of transporting them for trial. On the other hand, the Ministry wished to establish British authority in the so-called colonies; the law of Henry VIII was on the statute-book; it had been used several times; the Scotch rebels had been tried out of the country in which their crimes were committed; so also, the Sussex smugglers and the murderers of Mr. Park, the governor of the Windward Islands.[6]

The year 1769 wore away with various minor events which increased the irritation. The non-importation associations were renewed and force and intimidation used to compel merchants to join them. The people of Newport seized a revenue sloop, threw her armament overboard, cut away her mast, and burned her. James Otis, who had been assailing the government and the customs commissioners, was assaulted by one of the commissioners and badly wounded.[7] A British naval lieutenant at

----

[6] "An Answer to the Declaration of the American Congress," 1776, pp. 74–77; Gordon, "American Revolution," edition 1788, vol. i, p. 262; Stedman, "American War," vol. i, p. 70.

[7] J. B. Bartlett, "Destruction of the Gaspee," p. 7; Works of John Adams, vol. ii, p. 163; vol. x, p. 204; "Prior Documents of the Revolution," p. 132; Wells, "Life of Samuel Adams," vol. i, pp. 185, 275, 276; Tudor, "Life of Otis."

the head of a press-gang was killed by four sailors whom he attempted to drag from the forepeak of a Massachusetts merchant vessel. The sailors were not tried for murder because the government knew, it is said, that the press-gang acts of Parliament did not extend to America.

But in November the extraordinary and unexpected news was received that the Ministry, which had become largely Tory, had of their own accord decided to repeal the duties on paint, paper, and glass, and leave only the duty on tea. In the spring, they had been denouncing the colonial rebellion, preparing to punish traitors, and "bring America prostrate to their feet." In the autumn, they had eaten their own words, and in effect complied with the request of the patriots. The small duty on tea was left standing merely to show that the right to tax remained, just as the Declaratory Act had been passed when the Stamp Act was repealed. This duty on tea would also, it was believed, be a test of the real intentions of the colonists, and show whether or not they were bent on independence.[3]

During the following winter this promise of repeal was promptly fulfilled. An act repealing the duties on paint, paper, and glass was passed, and received the royal assent April 12, 1770; and the Ministry went still farther in conciliation, for no attempt was made to punish Massachusetts and South Carolina for refusing to furnish supplies to the regular troops stationed among them. The maintenance of such troops by the colonists was in effect abandoned unless the colonial legislatures voluntarily chose to maintain them. The patriot party was therefore more than ever encouraged to announce their new right that no troops should be stationed and no fortification erected in a colony in time of peace except by the colony's consent.

It would be difficult to imagine a colonial policy more conciliatory than the policy displayed by England at this time; and it is difficult to agree with those who hold that it was want of

---

[3] Ramsay, "American Revolution," Trenton edition, 1811, p. 119; Ryerson, "American Loyalists," vol. i, p. 361.

conciliation that lost Great Britain her American colonies. She lost her colonies simply because she wanted colonies and the colonies wanted independence. No amount of graciousness, friendliness, or kindness could make the colonial condition acceptable to the patriots of 1770.

We must remember that on this occasion Lord Hillsborough officially informed all the colonial governors that the Ministry "entertained no design to propose or consent to the laying of any further taxes on America for the purpose of raising a revenue." This was in strict compliance with the last American argument and with Dickinson's "Letters from a Farmer," that what America objected to was "taxation for the purpose of raising a revenue." The Ministry had abandoned the revenue and abandoned the compulsory maintenance of the army. They could hardly have done more, unless they had declared England the colony and America the mother-country. The colonies were put back very nearly into the old condition that prevailed before 1763.

Lord Hillsborough's promise that no more taxes should be laid on the colonies was faithfully kept. The British Parliament never passed another taxing act for America, and when, five lears later, actual warfare began, no one could say that the promise had been broken, for there had not been even an attempt to pass such an act.*

The reason for this sudden change on the part of the Tory Ministry was simply that they had found that the Paint, Paper, and Glass Act was a failure. The colonists were too strong for the mother-country. Their non-importation associations were successful and England's trade with her colonies was steadily decreasing. She could enforce neither the old trade and naviga-

---

* When the East India tea-ships were sent to Boston and other ports five years afterwards, it was said by many to be a violation of Lord Hillsborough's promise that no more taxes should be laid on the colonies. But the tea tax was in existence when he made his promise, which was that the Ministry would not ask Parliament to lay any further taxes on America.

tion laws nor the Paint, Paper, and Glass Act. The colonists were now buying their paint, paper, and glass in continental Europe, and the trade of England's colonies was being transferred to foreign nations. English merchants were complaining and had petitioned Parliament to repeal the Paint, Paper, and Glass Act, which, they said, brought no revenue to the government and was ruining English business in America.[10]

The Ministry therefore, after much hesitation and debate, decided to try again the conciliation plan. They may have been influenced in this by the fear of France assisting the American patriots, who had already threatened to appeal to her, and the Boston *Gazette* of the 20th of September, 1768, had openly urged such an appeal.[11]

Uneasiness as to what France would do was no doubt an underlying influence of all debates in Parliament and consultations of ministers at this period. England must avoid if possible the forcing of the dispute to that extremity. But whatever may have been the reasons and motives of the Ministry, the important fact remains that in this year 1770 Great Britain withdrew the two great colonial grievances—taxation for revenue, and compulsory support of a standing army; and this event should not be obscured or placed in the background of historical narratives merely because it does not show sufficient tyranny or oppression on the part of England.

One of the most serious results of this withdrawal and repeal was that among the patriot party England's prestige was gone forever. Keen observers had believed that her sovereignty was irretrievably lost when she repealed the Stamp Act at the dictation of that party; and now she had surely given the finishing stroke to her dominion.[12]

England, of course, lost very little prestige among the submissive people called loyalists, people un-Americanized, inclin-

---

[10] Stedman, " American War," vol. i, pp. 72, 73.

[11] Holmes, " Annals," vol. ii, pp. 177, 178.

[12] " Letters of James Murray, Loyalist," p. 170; Stedman, " American War," vol. i, pp. 77-79.

ing strongly towards England by taste and associations, and not inspired with the passion for ownership of the country in which they lived. These people accepted the repealing act in the spirit in which it was offered, as redressing grievances and tending to keep the colonies within the empire.

So very conciliatory was the repealing act and the promise of the Ministry, that it had a quieting effect on all parties and put an end to excitement and turmoil for three or four years. The moderates in the patriot party were willing to let well enough alone, and they were not disturbed by the small duty on the one item of tea any more than by the Declaratory Act. In truth, the extreme radicals of the Samuel Adams type had nothing with which to arouse the moderates.

In New York, in the autumn of 1769, the assembly under the leadership of James DeLancey seems to have gone completely into the control of the loyalists, and they promptly passed an act supplying the British troops with all that they required. The extreme patriots under the leadership of Isaac Sears, John Lamb, Alexander McDougall, and John Morin Scott, denounced this grant of supplies as a contemptible betrayal of the common cause of liberty. The New York Assembly, they said, should have stood by the assemblies of South Carolina and Massachusetts, which refused to grant the supplies.[13]

An inflammatory printed hand-bill assailing the New York Assembly was soon circulated. The assembly voted it libellous, and, having discovered through the printer that Alexander McDougall was the author of it, they had him arrested, and he was imprisoned for six months. He afterwards became a prominent patriot leader and officer in the Revolution, to the great disgust of many respectable loyalists who remembered him as a little boy helping his father to carry milk about the streets of New York. His imprisonment began his career of popularity among the patriots. He held receptions in prison every afternoon, and was overrun with visitors; all the Sons

---

[13] "Memorial History of New York," vol. ii, p. 401.

of Liberty and their wives and daughters vying with each other in showing him attentions. As a martyr to the cause of liberty he was compared to Wilkes in London, and the number forty-five was applied to him on every possible occasion.[14]

"Yesterday the forty-fifth day of the year, forty-five gentlemen, real enemies to internal taxation, by, or in obedience to, external authority, and cordial friends to Captain McDougall and the glorious cause of American liberty, went in decent procession to the New Gaol; and dined with him on forty-five pounds of beefsteaks, cut from a bullock forty-five months old."—Hudson, " Journalism in America," p. 112.

---

[14] "Memorial History," *supra;* Gordon, "American Revolution," edition 1788, vol. i, p. 303; Jones, "New York in the Revolution," vol. i, pp. 24–29, 431; McDougall's hand-bill was pasted on walls and fences by a device which is said to have been used in England in the time of the Pretender. A little boy was concealed in a box carried by a man who would place the box against a wall and sit down on it to rest. The boy would then draw back a slide, paste the hand-bill on the wall, shut himself in again, and the man would carry the box to another resting-place. (Jones, *supra*, pp. 426–436.)

XI.

THE FIRST BLOODSHED OF THE REVOLUTION IN NEW YORK AND BOSTON

AT this time there were British troops in New York, where in fact they had always been, for it had been the English military headquarters in America, and there were also in Boston the two regiments recently placed there, with probably a few small scattered commands in other parts of the country. Towards all these troops the patriot part of the population now displayed the greatest unfriendliness. Conflicts and quarrels were frequent; and nothing showed more clearly that the conciliatory policy of the Ministry would have no real effect. The patriot party was not satisfied with mere repeals of obnoxious statutes, and would never cease its endeavors until the last vestige and symbol of British authority was driven from the continent.

In New York the troops had cut down the liberty-pole every time the patriots replaced it, and at last in January, 1770, they not only cut it down but sawed it up and piled the pieces in front of the headquarters of the Sons of Liberty. An indignation meeting held by the patriots and insulting replies to the soldiers precipitated a riot and fight at Gordon Hill on Johns Street, the patriots using clubs and staves against the soldiers' cutlasses and bayonets. The officers succeeded in getting the soldiers back to their quarters; but several citizens were badly wounded and one killed with a bayonet. Michael Smith, a young apprentice, fighting with a chair-leg, compelled the surrender of a grenadier, and took from him his musket, which Smith afterwards carried on the patriot side throughout the war, the first trophy, it is said, of the Revolution.[1]

---

[1] "Memorial History of New York," vol. ii, p. 403; the *Historical Magazine*, 1860, vol. iv, p. 233.

AMERICAN INDEPENDENCE

New York historians have inclined to the opinion that this conflict should be regarded as the first battle of the Revolution; but two months afterwards there was a riot with the troops in Boston which attracted such widespread attention that it cast the New York disturbance entirely into the shade.

The Ministry had withdrawn a great deal of their reorganization plans; but they were still going through the form of trying to enforce the navigation laws, and troops were necessary in Boston to protect the customs officers. But to Boston patriots the presence of troops to enforce laws which Bostonians had disobeyed for a hundred years, and grown rich through disobedience, was unbearable. They regarded the troops as a foreign soldiery, and, inspired no doubt by what they had heard of the disturbances in New York, they were gradually working themselves into a mood for a pitched battle. Men and boys would call the soldiers "bloody backs," or "scoundrels in red;" and they would shout at them "Lobsters for sale." The soldiers in their turn had their insults for the Yankees, mohairs, or boogers, as they called the colonists, and every little circumstance of dispute was magnified.

On Friday, the second of March, 1770, a soldier going to John Gray's rope-walk was asked by one of the hands, "Soldier, will you work?" On his replying "Yes," he was told to go and employ himself at a very disgusting occupation. Angered at this jest, he continued talking at the windows of the rope-walk until a workman came out and knocked him down. The soldier then summoned his companions, who were driven off; and a larger number, coming to fight with clubs and cutlasses, were also driven off.

During the next two days, Saturday and Sunday, there was talk all over the town by both sides that blood would flow for the rope-walk affair, and on the night of Monday, the 5th of March, there was much disturbance in the streets; the soldiers and the people replying to each other in language extremely abusive; and many of the people had armed themselves with clubs. Several parties of soldiers appear to have sallied out from their barracks and passed through the streets cursing and threatening the people, striking at them with clubs, cutlasses, and bayonets and knocking down and injuring one or two citizens. At a few minutes after nine o'clock the church bells were rung as if for fire; but there was no fire; and the bells may have been rung to bring people out into the streets or as a signal for attacking the soldiers.

The sentinel before the custom-house knocked down a boy for upbraiding an officer for not paying his barber's bill; and soon afterwards a small crowd of boys and young men pressed upon the sentinel, snow-balling him, cursing him, and calling him a "lobster" and a "rascal." He retreated up the custom-house steps, loaded his gun, and called for the main guard to come and assist him.

Within a few moments Captain Preston, with eight men, arrived and formed a small semicircle with loaded guns and fixed bayonets at the sentry-box. Some of the crowd now appear to have moved off, leaving not more than seventy-five or a hundred pressing up close to the soldiers, who kept moving their extended guns from side to side and ordering the people to stand back. Some witnesses testified that the crowd did nothing to the soldiers but shout at them and dare them to fire: "Fire, fire, damn you; fire, you lobsters; you dare not fire!" Others swore that snowballs and ice were thrown; others that the guns of the soldiers were struck with sticks; others that one of the soldiers named Montgomery was struck with a stick or piece of ice, and immediately shot one of the crowd, Crispus Attucks, who was half Indian, half negro. Two witnesses testified that the blow which struck Montgomery knocked him down and knocked his gun out of his hand, and that he had to recover his gun before he shot Attucks. All the witnesses, however, agreed that immediately after the first shot the other soldiers began firing, killing two more citizens and wounding eight, of whom two afterwards died of their wounds.[2]

---

[2] "The trial of the British Soldiers of the Twenty-ninth Regiment of Foot for Murder," etc., Boston, 1807; "A Short Narrative of the Horrid Massacre in Boston," Boston, 1770; "Additional Observations to a Short Narrative," etc., Boston, 1770; Kidder's "History of the Boston

There was at once great excitement in the town. The bells rang again, the drums beat, the troops were all ordered under arms, and several companies of them were formed round the town-house in the half-kneeling position for street firing.

The cry was spread, "The soldiers are rising!" and the people began to arm themselves and pour into the streets. Many ran to the house of Thomas Hutchinson, who had lately become governor in place of Bernard, and besought him to come to King Street or the town would be all in blood. He immediately started, forcing his way through masses of furious people, clamoring for firearms, and he bore himself with a dignity and self-possession which belie the charges of cowardice and general malignity of character that have been thought necessary in order to uphold the patriot side.

The patriot cause needs no such unworthy assistance, and can easily stand on its own merits. Hutchinson quieted the people; he assured them that the law should have its course; he persuaded the officers to order the troops back to the barracks; he held a court of inquiry on the spot; and within three hours Captain Preston and the guard which had fired were arrested and turned over to the civil authorities to be tried for murder.

The next day a town meeting was called. A committee, of which Samuel Adams was chairman, urged Governor Hutchinson to remove all the soldiers from the town to preserve the peace and prevent an attack by the people, who would soon be swarming in from the country. After some hesitation Hutchinson agreed that the soldiers should be sent down the harbor to the castle. This was, from one point of view, a wise and creditable expedient to prevent violence. But we must also remember that the troops had been placed in Boston to protect

Massacre," contains a reprint of the foregoing. See also Niles, " Principles, and Acts of the Revolution," edition 1876, p. 15; Boston *Gazette*, March, 1770; Gordon, " American Revolution," edition 1788, vol. i, pp. 282, 298; John Adams, Works, vol. ii, p. 229; Ramsay, " Colonial History," vol. i, pp. 364, 365; Holmes, " Annals," vol ii, pp. 166, 167; Fortescue, " History of the British Army," vol. iii, pp. 35–45.

the commissioners of customs and other British officials from mob violence, and that the people had been demanding the removal of the troops and boasting that they would find means to force them out. Their removal was, therefore, an abandonment of the commissioners and a yielding to the demands of the patriots with the redoubtable Samuel Adams at their head.

As soon as the troops were removed the commissioners of customs, considering themselves no longer safe, abandoned their official duties. All of them but one left the town, seeking safety in different parts of the country, and the navigation and trade laws were more of a dead letter than ever. Before long one of them returned to England, apparently to inform the home government of the state of affairs and protest against the removal of the troops. The patriots believed that affidavits and depositions describing the street fight from the loyalist point of view had been taken in secret and sent with this commissioner, who would tell the home government that the customhouse had been attacked with intent to seize the revenue chest, and that the province was in a state of rebellion.

The patriots in a town meeting held on the 12th of March had appointed a committee to prepare their own account of the event. This committee reported on the 19th, and their report, entitled "A Short Narrative of the Horrid Massacre in Boston," was adopted and ordered to be sent to important persons in England. Annexed to this narrative were the depositions of nearly a hundred witnesses, and if their statements could be believed the soldiers had had no provocation to fire.

To the "Short Narrative" were afterwards added "'Additional Observations," complaining that the commissioners had been in no danger, that they need not have abandoned their posts, and that they had done so for the express purpose of making it appear that the province was riotous and rebellious, so that the home government would send out more troops. The soldiers, it was argued, had behaved in "so outrageous a manner" that they had "ceased to be the king's troops," they had "become traitors" and might "be resisted and expelled."

Captain Preston and his soldiers were tried in the following

141

November and ably defended by two of the patriot leaders, John Adams and Josiah Quincy. The greatest pains were taken by all the patriots to give these soldiers a fair trial. A town meeting voted that in order not to bias the minds of the jury the printed copies of the "Short Narrative" and accompanying depositions should be sent only to England and not allowed to circulate in Boston.

The evidence taken at the trial differed considerably from the evidence annexed to the "Short Narrative" and showed that the soldiers had received not a little provocation before they fired. Whether Captain Preston had given the order to fire was difficult to determine, because the crowd had been all the time shouting, "Fire, fire, if you dare!" and witnesses differed as to whether the order came from Preston. He was, however, acquitted of all guilt in this respect, and to the end of his life insisted that he had not given the order. Two of his men—Montgomery, who was seen to kill Attucks, and Killroy, who was seen to shoot a citizen named Gray—were brought in guilty of manslaughter, burnt on the hand in open court, and discharged. The remaining soldiers had fired and people had been killed and wounded; but as no witnesses could name any individual who had been killed by a particular soldier, the remaining soldiers were given the benefit of the doubt and all six of them acquitted.

The general opinion among leading patriots, and among the early commentators on the Revolution, seems to have been that the soldiers had received a great deal of provocation and were not seriously to blame for firing; and apparently the court and jury were somewhat inclined to this view.[*] But the masses of the patriot party would not accept this calm judicial conclusion. Filled with hatred for the British design of changing the condition of the colonies, they assigned the worst motives for the

---

[*] Among modern historians Bancroft, in the last edition of his "History of the United States," describes the firing as an unprovoked and murderous assault on peaceful citizens by a debased soldiery. Readers who are curious about the question are recommended to read all the evidence taken at the trial and judge for themselves.

conduct of the soldiers, and insisted on regarding them as the cruel and bloody agents of the Parliament and Ministry who wished to restrict the liberty of Americans.

The patriots of Massachusetts never wearied of using the events of the 5th of March to arouse the most passionate feelings. They would not make the mistake of the New York patriots and suffer their conflict to pass into oblivion. They called it the "Boston Massacre," and it has passed into history under that name. Paul Revere prepared a colored engraving of the scene, calling it the "Bloody Massacre." They exaggerated it into a ferocious and unprovoked assault by brutal soldiers upon a defenceless people, and the eagerness with which this exaggeration was encouraged showed whither events were tending.

The next year, 1771, the 5th of March was kept as the anniversary of the massacre, the church bells were tolled, and Paul Revere took an important part.

"In the Evening there was a very striking Exhibition at the Dwelling-House of Mr. Paul Revere, fronting the Old North Square.—At one of the Chamber-Windows was the appearance of the Ghost of the unfortunate young Seider, with one of his Fingers in the Wound, endeavoring to stop the Blood issuing therefrom; near him his Friends were weeping: And at a small distance, a monumental Obelisk, with his Bust in Front:—On the Front of the Pedestal, were the Names of those killed on the Fifth of March: Underneath the following Lines,

"Seider's pale Ghost fresh bleeding stands,
And Vengeance for his Death demands.

"In the next Window were represented the Soldiers drawn up, firing at the People assembled before them—the Dead on the Ground—and the Wounded falling, with the Blood running in Streams from their Wounds; Over which was wrote FOUL PLAY. In the third Window was the Figure of a Woman, representing AMERICA, sitting on the Stump of a Tree, with a Staff in her Hand, and the Cap of Liberty on the Top thereof,—one Foot on the Head of a Grenadier lying prostrate grasping a Serpent—Her Finger pointing to the Tragedy.

"The whole was so well executed, that the Spectators which amounted to many Thousands, were struck with solemn Silence, and their Countenances covered with a melancholy Gloom. At nine o'clock the Bells tolled a doleful Peal, until Ten; when the Exhibition was withdrawn, and the People retired to their respective Habitations."— Boston *Gazette*, March, 1771, and Hudson's "Journalism in America," p. 106.

Every year during the Revolution the anniversary of the 5th of March was solemnly kept in Boston as a day sacred to the cause of liberty, and an oration was delivered by some prominent citizen. These orations, printed and preserved with great veneration by the people of Boston, assailed standing armies by every argument that could be drawn from the whole history of the world, and repeated all the patriot arguments against alien control until they were worn threadbare.[4]

Governor Hutchinson and Colonel Dalrymple had certainly carried out the conciliatory policy of the Ministry in surrendering the guard to be tried by a jury of colonists and in removing the troops from Boston, so that the "massacre" could not at that time be worked up into rebellion. The removal of the troops, and the retirement of the commissioners of customs from their duties, quieted and satisfied the Bostonians. They had accomplished their purpose; the hateful commissioners and the hateful troops had been removed; and some months afterwards the assembly ceased to hold its sessions in Cambridge and returned to Boston, which for the next three years was a very peaceful town, because British sovereignty was practically extinct in Massachusetts.

No one could say that Great Britain had acted harshly. On the contrary, there had been so much yielding that the two regiments that had been sent out of Boston were ridiculed in England as the "Sam Adams regiments."

---

[4] After 1783 the ceremonies and oration of the 5th of March were transferred to the Fourth of July. John Adams, writing in his old age in 1816, said that he had heard or read forty-five of these 5th of March and Fourth of July orations, and was tired of having "young gentlemen of genius describing scenes they never saw and descanting on feelings they never felt and which great pains had been taken that they should not feel." Niles, "Principles and Acts of the Revolution," edition 1876, pp. 17, 490; John Adams, Works, vol. v, p. 203.

XII.

WITH the Stamp Act and the Paint, Paper, and Glass Act repealed, the British troops removed from Boston to harmless seclusion down the harbor, and the navigation and trade laws a dead letter, the colonies were in about the same semi-independent condition they had formerly enjoyed. The reorganization plans of the mother-country had completely failed; and for the next four years this condition continued, without any very serious attempt on the part of the Ministry to change it. They seemed to be at a loss what to do; and they allowed everything to drift as it was, while several minor events showed more clearly than ever the tendency of the times.

In 1771 there was a serious disturbance in North Carolina and an armed conflict known as the Battle of the Alamance, which has been sometimes incorrectly called the first battle of the Revolution; and people have wondered why it has not been given the importance and had not the effect of Lexington or Bunker Hill. But it was not a battle of the Revolution at all, and was only indirectly connected with the Revolutionary movement. It was a mere local outbreak or insurrection among the settlers of that part of North Carolina lying immediately west of Raleigh. These people were Baptists, Quakers, and Scotch-Irish Presbyterians, with a sprinkling of Germans and others. Many of them had come down from the frontiers of Pennsylvania; they were out of sympathy with the eastern part of North Carolina; they bought most of their supplies in Philadelphia, to which regular trading expeditions were made; and they felt that they were neglected and misunderstood by the eastern Carolinians.

Their chief grievance was the collection of illegal fees for recording deeds and land surveys. The clerks of court and the lawyers, they said, charged excessively, and the sheriffs collected excessive taxes. The officers who committed these extortions were usually appointed by the governor, who lived at New Berne, in the extreme eastern part of the colony, where there does not appear to have been much, if any, trouble from illegal fees. The governor admitted that "the sheriffs had embezzled more than one-half the public money ordered to be collected by them;" and in 1770 an official report showed that sheriffs of the province were £49,000 in arrears. The governor had attempted to check extortion by issuing proclamations directing all officials to charge no more than the fees allowed by law; but this, apparently, had no effect. The county governments were in the hands of official oligarchies, "full fledged office-holding birds of prey," and so firmly rooted was this system that a popular upheaval and revolution seemed necessary to bring any sort of redress to the western settlers.[1]

They undertook to have such a revolution; holding indignation meetings, stating their grievances, suggesting remedies; and they became known as the Regulators. The rough element among them resorted to riot and violence, rescued property seized by sheriffs, tied sheriffs to trees and beat them, and prevented the holding of an election. Soon they proceeded to worse measures, and in September, 1770, broke up the court at Hillsborough and beat the attorneys. No court could be held that year or the following spring; and they indulged in the same rough proceedings in Rowan County. They dragged Edmund Fanning out in the street, beat him, and destroyed his house and furniture. They took possession of the court-room, held a mock trial, scribbled profane and abusive comments in the docket, and burnt the house and barn of the judge.

The governor of the colony at that time was William Tryon, afterwards famous in the Revolution as the last colonial governor of New York. He was a very capable man, and at the eastern end of North Carolina he had succeeded in surrounding himself with that official magnificence and dignity which was

---

[1] Report, American Historical Association, 1894, pp. 150, 159, 171, 178, et seq.

not uncommon in the colonies and seems now in such strange contrast with their undeveloped and half-wilderness character. He had sufficient address to persuade the assembly to vote £15,000 for the erection at New Berne of a palace, which became the governor's residence, and contained the executive offices and a hall for the meetings of the assembly. There was a curious implication of ownership, as well as magnificence, in having the assembly conduct their business under his eye in his own house. Skilled artisans were brought from Philadelphia to construct the palace, which contained handsome chimney-pieces, Ionic statuary, columns of sienna, and richly ornamented marble tablets with medallions of the King and Queen. Balls and social functions could be given in this building with great effect; the governor insisted that Mrs. Tryon should always be called her excellency; and all these things were not without results in winning certain classes of people to the side of the imperial government.

But all this imperial dignity did not prevent Tryon's prompt advance upon the Regulators and his signal defeat of them on a small stream known as the Alamance. Six of the ring-leaders were hung, and a month was spent in marching through the rebellious counties, exhibiting prisoners in chains, devastating the homes of rioters, and exacting oaths of allegiance to the British crown. In all this Tryon was supported and assisted by the volunteer militia of the colony, the same men who, a few years before, had resisted the Stamp Act and prevented its enforcement in North Carolina. They afterwards fought on the patriot side against the British; but in suppressing the Regulators they seem to have regarded themselves as putting down mere rioters.

It was not in any sense a contest between the British and the patriots, although some Revolutionary histories describe it as such, and the monument erected on the Alamance recites that the battle had been fought "between the British and the Regulators." As a matter of fact, the Regulators were so far from being patriots that nearly all of them became loyalists. Their grievances, the excessive fees and taxes, as well as their defeat at the Alamance, they regarded as inflicted upon them by the patriot party in the province. Tryon had administered the British oath of allegiance to 6409 of them. They had sworn "never to bear arms against the king, but to take up arms for him if called upon." This became a great stumbling-block to many of them when the war began; and no ingenuity or argument, even by their own Presbyterian ministers, could relieve their consciences from that oath. Loyalists and neutrals were in consequence very numerous in North Carolina; and the patriot cause lost some able fighters when Tryon administered his oath to over 6000 Regulators.

It was natural, perhaps, that our histories should regard the contest as a struggle between patriot and British until modern researches in North Carolina brought the truth to light; for at the time of the Battle of the Alamance an attempt was made in Massachusetts to arouse patriot feeling by describing Tryon's hanging of his six prisoners as an act of British tyranny, accompanied by circumstances of deliberate cruelty and brutality, and articles to this effect appeared in the *Massachusetts Spy*. But the colonists of eastern North Carolina came to the rescue of their governor's reputation, and, in an indignation meeting, denounced the articles as calumnies and ordered the offending number of the *Spy* to be burned by the hangman.[2]

In June, 1772, an event occurred in New England which revealed both sides of the situation, the willingness of the Ministry to be extremely conciliatory and the willingness or rather determination of the patriots to take the government

---

[2] The publication in recent years of the Colonial Records of North Carolina has put the Battle of the Alamance in a new light. See Professor Bassett's article in Report of American Historical Association, 1894, pp. 141–212, and Haywood's " Governor Tryon and His Administration." Other sources of information are described in Foote, " Sketches of North Carolina; " Carruthers, " Life of Dr. Caldwell; " Husband, " Affairs of North Carolina; " Jones, " Defence of the Revolutionary History of North Carolina; " Martin's " History of North Carolina; " Revolutionary History of North Carolina in Three Lectures, by Hawks, Swan and Graham.

of the country entirely into their own hands and defy British authority.

An eight-gun British schooner, called the "Gaspee," under command of Lieutenant Dudingston, had for some time been very diligent in attempting to suppress smuggling, which for so long a time had been conducted with notorious success at Newport and at Providence, in Rhode Island. Dudingston was very much in earnest, searched all vessels systematically, and examined even the small market-boats. These thorough-going methods were extremely exasperating to people who, for a hundred years, had conducted their trade pretty much as they pleased, without any interference and were totally unaccustomed to the exercise of rigorous British authority within their boundaries. The Rhode Island colonists elected their governor, and the governor, though expressing the usual formal loyalty to the crown, could not be relied upon to assist either naval officers or customs officers in changing a condition of affairs which had given wealth and liberty to his people.

By the advice of the chief justice of the colony, the governor undertook to show that Dudingston was little less than a pirate, because he was acting "without applying to the governor, showing his warrant and being sworn to a due exercise of his office." The governor conducted an acrimonious correspondence not only with Dudingston, but with the admiral of the coast, under whom Dudingston acted, and admiral and governor mutually accused each other of insolence. The governor, the admiral said, must not interfere with naval officers, and must not attempt to send his sheriffs on board British war-vessels, and had no authority to demand a sight of an admiral's instructions to his officers. To which the governor replied, that he would send his sheriffs wherever he pleased within the limits of Rhode Island, and that he was not in the habit of receiving "instructions for the administration of his government from the king's admiral stationed in America."

Rhode Island was evidently a colony only in name. Her people denounced Dudingston and his crew as pirates and sons of Belial. The best citizens, merchants, vessel-owners, and captains appear to have regarded the lieutenant and his schooner as no more than the troublesome representatives of some foreign nation; and they proceeded to dispose of them by the violence that was suited to such intruders.

On the 9th of June, 1772, their opportunity occurred. Dudingston had sailed that day up Narragansett Bay to meet some sailors who were to come overland from Boston to Providence; but according to the patriot account, he was pursuing a suspected vessel. When within seven miles of Providence his schooner grounded on Namquit Point, and when the news of this accident reached Providence, Mr. John Brown, one of the most prominent merchants of the town, instructed one of his captains to have eight long-boats with muffled oars collected at Turner's wharf.

Soon after sunset a man went openly through the streets beating a drum and informing the people that the "Gaspee" was aground on Namquit Point, would not float until three o'clock the next morning, and those who wished to destroy her should meet at Mr. John Sabin's tavern. A considerable number of the most respectable citizens, merchants, and captains assembled at Sabin's, where they moulded bullets in the kitchen, loaded their guns, and about midnight, taking a surgeon with them, rowed down upon the "Gaspee," approaching her on the bows so that she could not use her guns.

It is probable that they intended to seize and burn her without shedding blood; but when Dudingston hailed them, fired his pistols and ordered his men to resist, he was shot down with a severe wound in the groin and his crew overpowered and sent ashore. Dudingston's wound was dressed by the surgeon; but otherwise he was treated with considerable severity. All his papers were taken, and his clothes and private property thrown overboard. He was put ashore on an island almost naked and left in charge of some of his men, who carried him in a blanket. The "Gaspee" was set on fire and burned to the water's edge.

The Governor was, of course, obliged to issue a proclamation offering a reward of £100 for the discovery of any of the persons concerned in this "atrocious crime," as he called it.

THE COMMISSION OF INQUIRY

The assembly, when it met, approved of all that he had done "to discover the perpetrators of that atrocious piece of villainy;" and the governor reported to Lord Hillsborough that "the conduct of those who committed this outrage was universally condemned" by the people of Rhode Island. But, although the "perpetrators" were among the most prominent merchants and captains of Providence, had been openly summoned by beat of drum, had assembled at a tavern, had started from a public wharf, and the next day one of them had paraded himself with Lieutenant Dudingston's gold-laced hat and described how he had obtained it, yet it was impossible to obtain any proof of their identity and guilt.[a]

The crime could be construed as either piracy or high treason, and might have been treason even under the modern American definition of that offense. But the Ministry and King took no measures of severity against this notorious defiance of British authority, this deliberately planned destruction of a British war-vessel. It is true they went through the form of appointing a commission, consisting of the governor of Rhode Island, the chief justices of New York, New Jersey, and Massachusetts, together with the judge of the vice admiralty court at Boston, to inquire into the affair and report to the Crown all the circumstances. Large rewards were offered for the discovery of the guilty. The commissioners were to call on General Gage at New York for any troops they might need to suppress riots. Any persons whom they should discover to have been concerned in burning the "Gaspee" were to be arrested by the civil magistrates of Rhode Island, and delivered to the admiral of the coast, to be by him sent to England for trial, together with the witnesses against them and also any witnesses they might need for their defence.

The commission might have been made up of persons sent out from England; but being made up of the governor of Rhode Island, elected by the people, and of the chief justices of neighboring colonies, it was in this respect fairly constituted and in

---

[a] J. R. Bartlett, " Destruction of the ' Gaspee,' " p. 139.

line with the conciliatory policy which had been adopted. The provision for taking to England for trial those who should be arrested was, of course, bitterly assailed by the patriot newspapers, and the commission was denounced as a star-chamber proceeding and "a court of inquisition more horrid than that of Spain."

The commissioners sat at Newport at various times during the following winter and the spring of 1773. It seems to have been intended that their coming and purpose should remain a secret; but the governor of Rhode Island, to whom all the documents were sent, felt bound to follow his usual rule of disclosing to the assembly all official papers from the home government. The purpose of the commission, therefore, became well known in Rhode Island and all the colonies. The commissioners heard a number of witnesses, but no evidence identifying any one who had assisted in destroying the "Gaspee" could be obtained from any inhabitant of the colony, except from a negro servant, who said he was with the attacking party and vaguely named persons whom he called Brown and Weeks, without giving their Christian names. He had sought refuge on the British war-vessel "Beaver;" and there was some evidence tending to show that any Rhode Islander who had had the hardihood to offer to identify the persons who burnt the "Gaspee" would probably have lost his life before he reached the presence of the commissioners.

When the commissioners submitted all the testimony they had taken to the superior court of Rhode Island, the judges of that court reported that there was no evidence on which any one could be arrested, and that ended the investigation. The home government took no further steps; and the Revolutionary movement was greatly encouraged, because the patriot party saw that they could not only defy the authority of the British Government, but commit acts of war and violence with impunity.[4]

---

[4] J. R. Bartlett, " Destruction of the ' Gaspee,' " pp. 81, 83; Gordon, "American Revolution," edition 1768, vol. i, p. 312. In consequence of the " Gaspee " affair Parliament passed an act making it a capital offence

THE QUESTION OF SALARIES

In one respect all this extraordinary mildness on the part of the Ministry may have seemed to be accomplishing the result which they expected. To a certain extent it took the wind out of the patriot sails. John Adams retired from politics and devoted himself to the practice of his profession. The Massachusetts legislature had a loyalist majority in 1771 and 1772, and, to the great disgust of Samuel Adams and other extreme patriots, acknowledged that the governor or crown had a right to remove the legislature from its usual place of holding sessions. Otis spoke in favor of this right of the governor; and John Hancock's exertions on the patriot side were so much reduced that the loyalists believed that they had captured him.[5]

The Ministry appear to have thought it a favorable time to try to bring the colonies under control by a mild but clever stroke of executive management, which would emancipate the governors and judges from the control of the colonial assemblies in the matter of their salaries. The attempt to accomplish this by parliamentary legislation had failed; but the end might perhaps be attained by a mere executive order of the Crown; and the experiment was now tried on Massachusetts in the form of a simple order from the King directing the salaries of the governor and judges to be paid by warrants drawn upon the revenue collected by the commissioners of customs.

It was, in one sense, a confession of weakness on the part of the home government; a confession that they could not govern the colonies by parliamentary legislation; and yet, under all the circumstances, it was a hopeful experiment and in line with more modern British methods, which since our Revolution have relied less on parliamentary legislation in colonial matters, and more on executive management. It was certainly taking advantage, in a shrewd, soft way, of the quiet and peace which the conciliatory policy had produced. It seemed well calculated to

---

to destroy any of his majesty's docks, magazines, ships, ammunition, or stores, and providing that any one arrested for committing this crime in the colonies could be brought to England for trial.

[5] Wells, "Life of Samuel Adams," vol. i, pp. 393, 397, 437, 358, 472, 473, 477, 478.

avoid all the difficulties and failures that had attended parliamentary legislation; it was taking the colonists at their word that they were at least loyal to the King and preferred his government to the government of Parliament.

But the patriots of Massachusetts saw the full meaning of this new device and offered a most vigorous resistance. They denounced it as a sudden and outrageous usurpation on the part of the Crown, because the salaries of the governor and judges of Massachusetts had been paid by the assembly, under the successive charters of the colony, for nearly a hundred and fifty years, and for the Crown to pay judicial salaries would be a continual bribe and expose the judges to a violation of their oaths.

Thomas Hutchinson, however, the governor of Massachusetts, accepted the crown salary and refused to take any salary from the assembly. The Crown had increased the salaries of the judges; and the assembly thereupon voted to all of them but the chief justice higher salaries for one year than the Crown offered, and demanded, with considerable peremptoriness, that they receive these salaries and reject the crown salaries. They yielded and accepted the assembly's salaries.

The increase of salary which the assembly voted to the chief justice did not, it appears, equal the increase the Crown offered, and he rejected the assembly's salary. He had served seventeen years, he said, with an inadequate salary and sunk £2000 in the service. If the assembly would reimburse him half his loss he would accept their salary and reject that of the Crown—if the King would allow him to do so. A storm of indignation was immediately raised against him among the patriots, and threats were made to drag him from the bench if he undertook to hold court. His friends warned him that his life was in danger, and the assembly sent him an order forbidding him to hold court. They drew up an impeachment of him as an enemy of his country, and made the King a defendant in the impeachment, for having offered the judge a bribe. This impeachment came up for decision during the winter of 1773–1774, and Governor Hutchinson disposed of it by adjourning the assembly.[6]

The plan of the home government was thus only partially successful in Massachusetts, and it also appears to have met with only partial success in New York. The Boston patriots worked hard against it; and it was made the occasion for organizing all the patriots of Massachusetts by means of committees of correspondence established in every town, with a central committee at Boston.

This system of committees was afterwards gradually adopted in all the other rebellious colonies, and by such committees the practical work of the Revolution—promulgation of arguments, encouragement of revolutionary ideas, party discipline, suppression or exile of loyalists—and a great deal of actual government of the country, were carried on. There seems to have been an immediate encouragement of revolutionary ideas in Massachusetts. We find the Boston *Gazette* of November 2, 1772, threatening that "unless their liberties are immediately restored" they will form "an independent commonwealth." The town committees busied themselves in drawing up lists of the acts of Parliament which England must repeal and the positions from which she must recede. She must withdraw even the right to tax; and they went on enumerating every objection, great and small, until their lists were, in effect, a complete denial of British sovereignty. They were ordering the British Government off the continent.

As this system of revolutionary committees spread to other colonies they were called by various names—committees of safety, committees of one hundred, or district committees—but their purpose and methods were always the same. They constituted an organization like that of an army, starting with a

---

[6] " Diary and Letters of Thomas Hutchinson," vol. i, pp. 138, 140, 142, 212; Wells, " Life of Samuel Adams," vol. i, pp. 479–493; J. R. Bartlett, " Destruction of the ' Gaspee,' " p. 163; Gordon, " American Revolution," edition 1788, vol. i, pp. 322, 345, 346; Stedman, " American War," vol. i, p. 81.

few men of character and brains, and spreading out, among innumerable subordinates, down to the privates in the ranks. It was a very compact and perfect party organization or "political engine," as John Adams called it.[1]

The Ministry's quiet little plan about the salaries, to be drawn in such a simple and natural way from the revenue collected in the custom-houses, not only failed of its purpose, but made matters a great deal worse for England by starting the organization of the committee system, which became the backbone of the Revolution. Another little experiment, to see if better control of the colonies could be gradually obtained without parliamentary legislation, was also tried by the Ministry. They undertook to ignore or suspend that provision in the Massachusetts charter which provided that all troops, even the regulars, should be under the control of the governor. It seemed better to place such troops under a military officer, who could more properly decide whether they should be moved here or there as "Sam Adams" or a patriot committee might direct.

A great deal has been written on this alteration of the charter of Massachusetts; but it is useless to debate the question over again at this late day. To the Americans a charter was a time-honored, solemn contract, which could never be altered except by the consent of the colonists. To the English the charters were mere conveniences of colonial government, which had been altered or annulled on several occasions in the past and must, of necessity, be altered from time to time in the future. If you are an Englishman and believe independence a crime and that the colonies should have been saved from independence, you will see in the alteration of the Massachusetts charter merely a military or British necessity. If you are a patriot, and believe independence and self-government to be natural rights, you will see in the alteration an atrocious crime.

---

[1] Gordon, "American Revolution," edition 1788, vol. i, pp. 313, 314: Report American Historical Association, 1901, p. 243; Van Tyne, "Loyalists," pp. 63, 90; John Adams, Works, vol. ii, pp. 162, 219; Winsor, "Handbook of the Revolution," p. 20.

XIII.

THE WHATELY LETTERS INCREASE THE ILL FEELING

ABOUT the same time that the question of the salaries was causing irritation and encouraging a better organization of the patriot party, another event occurred which brought the outbreak of hostilities a step nearer by irritating both Englishmen and colonists, and destroying their confidence in the conciliatory policy.

In the year 1768, when the mob in Boston rescued the sloop "Liberty," which had been seized for violating the revenue laws, and when the customs officers were mobbed and beaten and obliged to seek safety on a British man-of-war, several officials of the colony, notably Hutchinson and Oliver, as well as the commissioners of customs, wrote letters to important persons in England, suggesting that troops should be sent to Boston and some severe repressive measures taken, which, they said, were absolutely necessary to protect the lives of public officials, restore order, and pacify the country. Many of these letters were addressed to Mr. William Whately, a well-known Tory politician, and were handed about in London as part of the evidence of the condition of affairs in America.

Franklin, who was still in London as the agent of Pennsylvania, Georgia, and Massachusetts, was a strong advocate of the conciliatory policy, and wanted it carried still further. He always represented the colonies as most loyal and loving and without any desire for absolute independence; by which of course he meant that they were loyal to the King and willing to live under his headship if they could be entirely independent of Parliament. He argued that it was a mistake to send troops to Boston, and a mistake to keep them there. They were not necessary; they caused riots and tumults, like the "Boston Massacre," which irritated the colonists, created an unfortunate impression in England, and widened the breach with America.

AMERICAN INDEPENDENCE ·

When he was talking in this strain one day in the year 1772, a member of Parliament told him that he must be mistaken about the condition of affairs in America; the disorders and rebellion were much worse than he supposed; the troops had been absolutely necessary and had been asked for by the Massachusetts officials. When Franklin expressed surprise and doubt, the member said he would soon satisfy him; and in a few days placed in his hands the packet of letters written to Mr. William Whately by officials of the colonial government of Massachusetts.

The letters described the well-known situation in Boston in the year 1768; the riotous proceedings when John Hancock's sloop was seized for violating the revenue laws; how the custom officials were insulted and beaten, the windows of their houses broken, and they obliged to take refuge on the "Romney" man-of-war. Such proceedings the writers of the letters intimated were approved by a majority of the people, and they recommended that these turbulent colonists should, for their own good, be restrained by force, and the liberty they were misusing curtailed. "There must be an abridgement," said one of Hutchinson's letters, "of what are called English liberties."

Franklin immediately sent the letters to Massachusetts, where they aroused the greatest indignation among the patriots when it was discovered that the detested troops had been sent largely through the representations of Thomas Hutchinson, who had now become governor, and of Andrew Oliver, who had become lieutenant-governor.[1]

The member of Parliament had lent the letters to Franklin on condition that they should not be printed or copied, and after having been read in Massachusetts they were to be returned to London. Franklin, of course, mentioned this condition when he sent the letters to Cushing in Massachusetts;

---

[1] Franklin's Works, Bigelow edition, vol. v, pp. 378, 282, 284, 408; Gordon, "American Revolution," edition 1788, vol. i, p. 328; "Diary and Letters of Thomas Hutchinson," vol. i, pp. 82, 93.

but the state of feeling between England and America had become so violent that the condition was not respected. The letters were soon in print in London as well as in the colonies, causing a great scandal and setting all England wondering how the private letters of Mr. William Whately, who was now dead, could have got abroad and in print.

Mr. Whately's brother suspected that Mr. John Temple, who had lived in Massachusetts and was very hostile to Governor Hutchinson, had abstracted the letters from a bundle of the deceased Whately's papers which he had been allowed to examine. Temple denied this positively; but the suspicion against him getting into the newspapers, and Whately's brother not entirely exonerating him, the two fought a duel and Whately was badly wounded.

Franklin then came forward and announced that he was the person who had obtained the letters and sent them to Massachusetts. This partially exonerated Temple, but threw suspicion on Franklin, who was roundly accused of having obtained these private letters by fraud or theft. He had promised not to reveal the name of the member of Parliament who lent them to him, and was, therefore, compelled to keep silence.

Prominent people in London appear to have always believed that, in spite of his denials, Temple was the man who abstracted the Whately letters from the bundle he was allowed to examine, and gave them to Franklin for the purpose of making mischief. Many years after the Revolution John Adams said that Temple confessed to him in Holland that he had given the letters to Franklin, although he had not procured them, he said, in the manner represented. They were procured, it is supposed, by Dr. Hugh Williamson, a Philadelphia physician who was in London at the time raising money for the College of Philadelphia. He learned in some way of their existence and contents, and that they were deposited in a public office where they did not regularly belong. He went to the office, and finding the head of it out, demanded the letters in a bold tone, as if he were a person in authority. A subordinate handed them to him and he put them in a way to reach the hands of Franklin. He may have given them to Temple to give to Franklin, and John Adams believed that Temple employed Williamson to obtain the letters from the public office.[2]

In consequence of the revelations in the Whately letters the Massachusetts Assembly sent a petition to the Crown asking that Hutchinson and Oliver be removed from office because they had become abhorrent to the people, had plotted to intensify the quarrel of the colonies with the mother-country, had caused, by their false representations, a fleet and army to be brought to Massachusetts, and were, therefore, the cause of the confusion and bloodshed of the "Boston Massacre."

This petition reached the King in the summer of 1773. The whole affair of the Whately letters caused the greatest excitement and scandal on both sides of the Atlantic. London society kept talking about it for years afterwards, and never grew weary of denouncing Franklin for what they considered his fraud, theft, and most disgraceful and dishonorable conduct in obtaining possession of private correspondence. The letters, however, were of a decidedly public nature, and Whately, to whom they were addressed, was a politician who had held some subordinate public offices. There is no evidence that Franklin obtained them improperly; and having obtained them, it was his duty as an American and the agent of the patriot party in Massachusetts to send them to the leaders of his party in that province. It seems now as if everybody had made more fuss over the incident than it deserved; but the opinion of the time was that it had greatly intensified hostile feeling, visibly widened the breach; and it practically destroyed Franklin's influence in England.

He had been becoming more and more unpopular with the Tories because he took part so conspicuously with the Whigs,

---

[2] "Diary and Letters of Thomas Hutchinson," vol. i, pp. 82–93, 160, 163, 204, 205, 210, 221, 222, 232, 244, 279, 411; vol. ii, pp. 79, 118; Biographical Memoir of Hugh Williamson by Dr. David Hossack, pp. 30–41, 75–78.

and wrote Whig articles in the newspapers; and as his reputation seemed now to be smirched by his supposed discreditable connection with the Whately letters, he could do nothing more as an ambassador or a peacemaker. He had become *persona non grata*, too much disliked and even hated by the persons with whom he must make the peace. The Tories were watching their opportunity to assail him, drive him from office and from England, where, in their eyes, he had become only a mischief-maker.

All the recent occurrences—the salaries, the New York riot, the "Boston Massacre," the burning of the "Gaspee," the infringement of the Massachusetts charter, and the Whately letters—tended to widen the breach; and yet in spite of these events, some of which were actual hostilities, there was no formal break; and the condition of affairs was quite satisfactory to all the moderate patriots. England was gaining no advantage over them. They were holding their own, and better. If the conciliatory experiment were continued, America would drift gradually and peacefully towards absolute independence. Wedderburn is reported to have said in Parliament, at this time, that the colonists were already lost to the Crown.

The patriots learned that in place of the aggressive Lord Hillsborough they were to have as secretary of the colonies the good Lord Dartmouth, a gentle soul who said his prayers—"an insignificant character," if we can believe Arthur Lee, "with an affectation of piety and good intentions towards the public."[3] The patriots felt that they had either repealed or successfully defied all the new legislation and plans for remodelling the colonies. They were back again in the old semi-independent condition which they had enjoyed before the close of the French war. They were perhaps in an improved and more independent position, for had they not ordered the British troops out of Boston and, in effect, locked them up on an island in the harbor; and could they not do this again whenever the

---

[3] Wells, " Life of Samuel Adams," vol. i, p. 483.

mother-country's soldiery became troublesome? Therefore, they were willing to ignore, for the time, the attempt on salaries in Massachusetts and the "Boston Massacre," and they were indifferent about the slight tax on tea, because they continued to smuggle from Holland all the tea they needed.

The more radical patriots could not, however, look upon the situation so complacently. They made violent efforts to keep up the non-importation associations, but without success. One by one the Southern colonies, and then Pennsylvania and the New England colonies and New York, began importing all English commodities, except tea. The protest which the extreme patriots made against this is instructive, as showing the condition of parties. They declared that the spirit of liberty was dead. The students at Princeton, among whom was James Madison, put on black gowns, and Lynch, of South Carolina, is said to have shed tears over what he deemed the lost cause.

These extreme patriots feared that England by the conciliatory policy had cunningly trapped the people into remaining quiet until they should lose all desire for political manhood. They could be then enslaved when the government became more powerful. The leaders dreaded the weakening effects of conciliation. They longed for some severity, some outrage on the part of England, that would stimulate the patriot party to throw off every form of dependence. The savage Hillsborough had been infinitely better than the pious Dartmouth.

"If I am to have a master," said Samuel Adams, "let me have a severe one, that I may constantly have the mortifying sense of it. I shall then be constantly disposed to take the first fair opportunity of ridding myself of his tyranny. There is danger of the people being flattered with such partial relief as Lord Dartmouth may be able (if disposed) to obtain for them, and building upon vain hopes till their chains are riveted."—Wells, "Life of Samuel Adams," vol. i, p. 484.

The severity for which the radical patriots hoped and prayed was sure to come in time; for England could not remain indefinitely satisfied with a conciliatory policy which accomplished nothing towards consolidating the empire; which left the colonies more independent than they had been before the French War, and which encouraged them to strengthen their independent position. Gentle attempts to secure control, as in the matter of salaries, were sure to become less gentle; or some accident would happen which would enable the radical patriots to precipitate a conflict; and, in fact, the accident occurred in the very next gentle attempt, which was the very mild device, as it seemed to England, of sending to America cheap East India tea which would undersell the tea smuggled from Holland.

XIV.

THE TEA EPISODE

BEFORE the passage of the Paint, Paper, and Glass Act, tea had been taxed on its arrival in England at the high rate of a shilling per pound. This made the tea so expensive that the colonists usually smuggled cheaper tea from Holland. It was in the hope of breaking up this smuggling and encouraging the sale of English tea that Parliament, in the Paint, Paper, and Glass Act, struck off the shilling duty, and on all tea sent to the colonies placed a duty of only threepence per pound, to be paid in the colonial ports. Thus the colonists would pay ninepence per pound less tax, the sale of tea from English provinces in the far East, and especially the tea of the great East India Company, would be promoted, the smuggling of the Americans checked, and everybody made happy with good tea.

Some of this threepence-per-pound tea seems to have been imported; most of it, apparently, in Boston; and the duty paid. But because the duty was a tax, associations or clubs were formed whose members agreed not to drink this threepence tea. Merchants were applauded for not importing it, and encouraged to smuggle the Holland tea; and the smuggling, being very profitable, was extensively practised, especially in New York, Philadelphia, and other towns south of Massachusetts. In New York the smuggled Holland tea was openly carted about at noon-day.[1]

There was, therefore, every reason why the patriots should be content for the present; for they were successfully defeating England and the tea act by their old methods, and their

[1] Drake, " Tea Leaves," pp. 193, 194, 196, 201; Hutchinson, " History of Massachusetts," vol. iii, pp. 331, 332, 351, 422; " Free Thoughts on the Proceedings of the Continental Congress," p. 10, New York, 1774. Snow, "Administration of Dependencies," pp. 254–258; Life of Joseph Reed, by W. B. Reed, vol. i, p. 52.

merchants were growing rich by smuggling. The loyalists afterwards said that the trifling tea tax would soon have become obsolete, and some liberally inclined ministry would have repealed it. Colonial taxation had been abandoned, was dying a natural death, and harmony was returning, they said, if both England and the Americans would only be careful and forbearing.[2]

The Ministry might possibly have refrained for some time from trying another experiment to test their control of the colonies, if that great corporation, the East India Company, had not brought a pressure on the Government which could not be resisted. The company was at that time in a bad condition, and was generally supposed to be insolvent. Its stock was rapidly depreciating, and the fall of such a vast concern would precipitate a financial panic. The great company had already sunk so low that the panic was thought to have begun. Business firms were going bankrupt, and merchants, manufacturers, and traders suffering. It seemed quite absurd to Englishmen that the company could not sell its tea in colonies that belonged to England, while Holland sold in those colonies thousands of pounds of tea every year. There was, in fact, laid up in warehouses in England seventeen million pounds of the East India Company's tea, which might, it was thought, obtain a ready sale in America, were it not for the smuggling practices of those independence-loving colonists.

The East India Company and the Government were closely allied. The Government had already lent money to the Company, and was now asked to lend a million and a half more. The Company, besides paying into the exchequer £400,000 per year, was really a branch of the government for the control of India; and it afterwards became merged in a department of the government. Parliament accordingly in March, 1773, took into consideration the condition of the Company and, besides regulating its affairs in various ways, made what seemed to

---

[2] Ryerson, "American Loyalists," vol. i, p. 371; Hutchinson, "History of Massachusetts," vol. iii, p. 331.

Englishmen a very harmless and reasonable arrangement for sending the Company's tea to America.

The Company's tea had to pay duty on its arrival in England; but three-fifths of this duty was remitted or drawn back, as the expression was, when the tea was exported to the colonies. It was now proposed that all of this duty should be remitted on exportation to America, so that the East India Company could undersell the tea which the colonists smuggled from the Dutch. Accordingly an act of Parliament was passed, May 10, 1773, remitting the duty in England, but retaining the threepence tax to be paid in the colonies; and the East India Company freighted ships with tea for Boston, New York, Philadelphia, and Charleston.[*]

The East India Company had at first asked that the threepence tax to be paid in the colonies should be abolished, which would have given them still better opportunities to undersell the smuggled Dutch tea and would have still further conciliated the colonists by wiping out the last remnant of the new taxation to which they had so strenuously objected, leaving only the old taxes like those on sugar, molasses, and rum, to which they had grown accustomed. Such a course would no doubt have postponed the outbreak of the Revolution; it would have pleased the loyalists who considered it all that was necessary to keep the colonies within the empire; and it would have pleased the moderate patriots, like Cushing, who believed that American independence could be obtained gradually by growth of population and the natural course of events.

But as the threepence tax stood for the right of Parliament to tax the colonies—was, in short, a sort of badge and insignia of the slight sovereignty still remaining to Great Britain in America—the Ministry would not abolish it. Lord North dodged responsibility by saying that the King insisted on

---

[*] "History of Great Britain During the Administration of Lord North," p. 108; Stedman, "American War," vol. i, p. 85; Drake's "Tea Leaves," p. 218; Gordon, "American Revolution," edition 1788, vol. i, p. 324.

retaining the tax and was determined to try the issue with the Americans.

Looked at in cold blood the whole plan was a rather amusing and very English device for helping out the bankrupt company, coaxing the colonists to accept English taxed tea, and, if possible, stopping by ingenuity the smuggling that could not be stopped by revenue-cutters, boards of commissioners, troops, and men-of-war. It was so far from being tyrannous and cruel that it was pitiable; pitiable for a proud nation to be reduced to such straits for controlling its colonies.

The colonists had the whole summer and most of the autumn of 1773 to think over the matter, for the tea-ships did not begin to arrive until November. The patriots in all the colonies were well aware that not a little English taxed tea had been imported and the tax paid; but they were determined to resist this new plan of the Company and the Ministry. The tea must not be received; it must not be sold; the duty must not be paid. The best course was not to allow it to be landed; for if once landed some one might pay the duty; or the Government itself might surreptitiously pay the duty, and then the plan of the King and the Ministry would be successful. They could boast that the colonies had submitted.

There was now an opportunity for agitation, and the radical patriots bestirred themselves. The committees of correspondence worked upon the people all over the country. The tea was described as poison, a nauseous draft of slavery. Some of the newspapers openly advocated independence. The attacks upon the East India Company as a soulless corporation and an inhuman monopoly remind us of the language of our own times.

If such a company, it was said, once got a foothold in America, it would trade in other articles besides tea, and drive American merchants out of business. It would draw to itself all sorts of trade and the profits of American commerce. The gold and silver and the bills of exchange, would tend to centre in its hands. A printed handbill[4] was circulated in Pennsyl-

---

[4] It was addressed, "To the Tradesmen and Mechanics of Pennsyl-

vania describing the company's shocking deeds of plunder and cruelty in India, and arguing that it would overwhelm America with the same rapacity and slaughter that had been inflicted on the unfortunate East Indians. Franklin's old friend, the Bishop of St. Asaph, prepared a speech for the House of Lords, denouncing the Government for turning loose upon the Americans a corporation with such a record of bloodshed and tyranny.

It was at this time that Samuel Adams and the more ardent patriots took the next step in their plan, and suggested a union of all the colonies in a Congress. The Boston *Gazette* had been openly suggesting independence for over a year. It now demanded a "Congress of American States to frame a bill of rights," or to "form an independent state, an American commonwealth."[5] The boldness and impunity with which this was done show the effect of the conciliatory policy and the weakness of England.

Some of the patriots of the type of Cushing, of Massachusetts, or Reed and Dickinson, of Pennsylvania, advocated caution. We were not yet strong enough, not sufficiently united or sufficiently numerous, for a dash for independence. But the radical patriots of Boston would have no delay. They were for forcing a conflict; striking at once; for, said they, "when our liberty is gone, history and experience will teach us that an increase of inhabitants will be but an increase of slaves."[6]

The majority of the patriots were apparently for moderation, and had they had their way this episode would have been tided over. Their plan was quietly to prevent the landing and payment of duty on the tea; send it all back to England, and thus show that the Tea Act, the last remnant of the taxation

vania." Copies are now rare. The one I have examined is in the collection of Mr. Joseph Y. Jeanes, of Philadelphia. See also Drake, "Tea Leaves," pp. 216, 274.

[5] Hosmer, "Life of Samuel Adams," p. 238; Gordon, "American Revolution," Ed. 1788, vol. i, p. 331.

[6] Boston *Gazette*, Sept. 13, 1773, Essay signed A; Wells, "Life of Samuel Adams," vol. ii, pp. 87, 88.

system begun eight years before, was a failure. The act would then soon be repealed and taxation never again be attempted. It must be confessed that there were plausible reasons for supposing that this plan might have accomplished peaceful independence. "Our natural increase in wealth and population," said Cushing, "will in a course of years settle this dispute in our favor." [7]

On the other hand, Samuel Adams and the radicals had strong grounds for believing that the course of years would not necessarily bring independence without a war to settle it. England would not finally recognize the absolute independence of the colonies without fighting. No nation had ever done so. The inherent right of a naturally separated people to be independent according to their rights as men might be just and sound, but no nation had as yet recognized its justice. As there must be a fight, it was better, the radicals thought, to have it now at once while our people were hot and England was so weak. It would be an advantage to break from England before she recovered from the recent great war with France and the heavy debt it entailed. The longer she rested from that war the more capable she would become to attack the colonies and reduce them to absolute dependence on the will of Parliament. Her conciliatory policy was merely to gain time. She might settle the taxation question satisfactorily, and in the future settle the smuggling question, and be so conciliatory that the mass of the people, no matter how numerous they became, would forget the past and be content to live under an easy yoke, as mere dependencies.

For several years the argument had been insinuated that the weak, debt-ridden state of England had been ordained in the providence of God to give us a chance for independence. "It is now or never," wrote Joseph Hawley, one of the patriot leaders of the western part of Massachusetts. If the contest for independence were delayed, independence, he said, would be lost. If England succeeded in getting the control she

---

[7] Mass. Historical Soc. Collections, fourth series, vol. iv, pp. 360, 363.

wanted, the character of the independence-loving Americans would be changed, and after twenty years of such control the loyalists would be as numerous as the patriots.[8]

Most strenuous efforts were made by the extreme patriots to bring the moderates out of their contented state of mind and arouse them to the importance of an immediate contest for independence, instead of a reliance on mere lapse of time under the conciliatory policy which England had adopted. The patriot party in Boston was usually regarded as extreme enough; but so much English tea had been accepted there that the Southern patriots feared that the Bostonians would be too lenient and would allow the tea to be landed and the duty paid. Boston merchants had during the last five years imported nearly three thousand chests of English taxed tea, when New York and Philadelphia supplied the whole demand of their markets with smuggled tea from Holland. A part of this taxed tea imported to Boston was apparently stored and not sold, and John Hancock had lent one of his ships to carry some of it back to England. There appears to have been much conflict of opinion in Boston. There were associations pledging their members not to drink taxed tea, and a great deal of watching and threatening of merchants to prevent their importing and selling; and yet considerable taxed tea seems to have been imported. Thomas Mifflin, one of the patriot leaders of Philadelphia, appears to have gone to Boston to stiffen the patriots there, and he took a promise from them not to allow any tea to be landed, and he pledged Philadelphia to the same course.[9]

On the 18th of October, 1773, the Philadelphia patriots led off in formal opposition to the tea by adopting a very vigorous and complete set of resolutions going over the whole ground of the controversy; and these same resolutions were afterwards adopted in Boston. In fact, the Bostonians were so aroused

---

[8] Niles, " Principles and Acts of the Revolution," edition 1876, p. 107; Hosmer, Life of Samuel Adams, p. 134.

[9] Gordon, " American Revolution," edition 1788, vol. i, p. 331; Drake, " Tea Leaves," pp. 10, 15, 298, 304, 330.

that they resorted to more violent opposition than Mifflin and the Philadelphia patriots intended.

The first tea-ship to reach America was the "Dartmouth," which arrived in Boston harbor about the 26th of November, 1773, and was followed some days later by two others.[10] The consignees of the cargoes were five in number, including the two sons of Governor Hutchinson, who, like their father, were devoted loyalists, believing in the supremacy of the British empire, and regarding American independence as a delusion and a crime. They would not resign. Town meetings were held upon them, committees visited them, their lives were threatened in anonymous letters, they were called tigers and mad dogs, which, for the sake of public safety, should be destroyed; but they remained firm. They did not, however, attempt to land the cargoes. The patriots adopted the strong Philadelphia resolutions; expressed the greatest regret that they had ever allowed any of the taxed tea to be imported; placed a guard over the ships, and Hancock and Samuel Adams served on this guard. Six horsemen held themselves ready to alarm the country towns; and some of these towns collected all the taxed tea they could find among their people and burnt it on the public common. The radicals were determined to begin the active revolution at this point.

The moderate patriots and a strong loyalist minority protested. They foresaw violence; "the town and the colony would be drawn into a quarrel with Great Britain." Very likely, was the reply; but it must come to that sooner or later, and what better time than the present? Hundreds of years may pass away before the Parliament will make such a number of acts in violation of the British Constitution as it has done of late years, and by which it has excited so formidable an opposition. Besides, the longer the contest is delayed the more the Ministry will be strengthened.[11]

---

[10] There is said to have been a fourth tea-ship which was wrecked on Cape Cod and never reached Boston. (Gordon, " American Revolution," vol. i, p. 341.)

[11] Gordon, " American Revolution," edition 1788, vol. i, p. 335.

The owners and the captains of the ships were willing to take the tea back to England, but unfortunately no precautions had been taken by any one to stop the ships and send them back before they reached the wharves and entered their cargoes at the custom-house. The custom-house officers could not give the ships a clearance until the duty had been paid on the tea, and without a clearance the governor would not give a permit to pass the castle outward bound. Meanwhile, during these disputes the twenty days were passing, and at the end of that period the tea could be seized by the custom-house and sold for duty. The party of violence was in the ascendant; the town was placarded with liberty posters; riders were hurrying back and forth from the neighboring towns; and the country people were beginning to flock into Boston.

The common statements in some books of the Revolution that Governor Hutchinson was malignant, treacherous, or the vacillating and cowardly agent of tyranny, are utterly without foundation. He was a man of learning, ability, and refinement, a native of the colony, a graduate of Harvard College, a collector of historical material, and the author of an excellent history of Massachusetts; but like some other Americans, his tastes and feelings were with Europe and his intellect was overawed by English culture. He never could bring himself to see the slightest advantage in American nationality.

He was now sixty-two years old, and had been a useful public man in Massachusetts. He had had a long career as a member of the legislature, as a member of the council, as judge and as lieutenant-governor; and all the best citizens were grateful to him for his services. He had supported for years at the sacrifice of popularity a sound specie currency, had fought the land-banks and paper-money schemes, and largely contributed to save the province from bankruptcy. The charge that he opposed the patriot party in expectation of a high position in England as a reward for his loyalism does not seem to be sustained because he was offered a baronetcy and declined it.

His opinions were entirely sincere and honest, but they were not American. He seems to have really loved New England, but only as a subject province and dependency of Great Britain. In his letters to the British Government he explained that the tendency of Massachusetts to independence could never be overcome except by force, and he recommended the sending of troops and the use of the utmost severity. It was natural that the patriots should describe this as his contemptible treachery and meanness to his native province. He exasperated them by upholding the laws against the smugglers and discountenancing the odium in which those who informed upon smugglers were held. But looked at from the point of view of history he was doing what every colonial governor in an empire is bound to do. If the British system of empire was right, Hutchinson was right, and was an ideal governor. He found his duties congenial; for he was as completely devoted to colonialism by tastes, feelings, and convictions as any loyalist that ever lived.[12]

As for his conduct with the tea-ships, he was merely acting within the laws he had sworn to administer. There was no breach of legality in the English government reducing the tax on tea and a private corporation sending three cargoes to Boston to undersell smuggled tea. The ships had come up to the docks within custom-house jurisdiction, and no clearance could under the law be given to take the tea back to England until the duties had been paid. Hutchinson was perfectly justified in refusing to give a permit unless there was a clearance, and it was legally absurd to ask him for a permit before a clearance showed the payment of duties.

It is said that he stiffened the consignees in their resolution not to resign and that but for him they would have resigned. But their resignation would hardly have changed the situation, because the ships having come up to the wharves and within the jurisdiction of the custom-house the duties had to be paid

---

[12] Violent abuse of Hutchinson can be found in Bancroft's " History of the United States " and in Wells' " Life of Samuel Adams," vol. i, pp. 268, 269. See also John Adams' clever summary of him, Works, vol. ii, pp. 170, 189, 190.

and it was on the question of duties that the whole dispute hinged. The consignees of the tea that went to South Carolina resigned, but that did not prevent the custom-house finally seizing the tea and offering it for sale to pay the duty. If the Boston patriots had stopped the ships, as was done at Philadelphia, before they got within the jurisdiction of the custom-house, and persuaded the captains to go back to England, there would have been an end to all difficulties. Hutchinson suggested this course and advised the consignees to have the ships anchor below the castle, so that if it should appear to be unsafe to land the tea the ships might return to England. If this advice of Hutchinson had been followed we should probably never have heard of the "Boston tea party" and the Revolution would have been postponed for several years, or until some other accident or incident caused an outbreak.

The consignees were entirely willing, it is said, to follow Hutchinson's advice, and the first tea-ship that arrived anchored below the castle outside of the jurisdiction of the custom-house. But when the captain came up to town Hutchinson says that a committee composed of Samuel Adams and others prevailed upon him to bring his ship up to the wharves and land all of his cargo except the tea. This is Hutchinson's version, and he seems to mean that the radical patriots did not want a peaceful settlement, but were determined to bring the tea within the jurisdiction of the custom-house so that there could be a contest over the disposal of it.[12]

Governor Hutchinson followed the conciliatory policy of the home government. He abstained from any use of the men-of-war in the harbor or of the two "Sam Adams" regiments that were still down at the castle, except, it is said, to order them to see that no vessel, except a coaster, should go to sea without a permit. He left everything to the patriots. He even allowed them to guard the tea-ships. The war-ships or the soldiers could have taken possession of the tea-ships and

---

[12] Diary and Letters of Thomas Hutchinson, vol. i, pp. 100, 101, 103; Drake, " Tea Leaves," p. 42.

have prevented all that happened. But British sovereignty was on this occasion a mere spectator and visitor in what had been its American colonies.

The difficulty might have been settled as in South Carolina, by allowing the customs officials to seize the tea at the end of the twenty days and offer it for sale to pay the duties. No one would have had the temerity to buy it; the patriots of Boston could surely have prevented its sale as easily as a sale was prevented by the patriots of Charleston; and the tea would then have been stored till it rotted.

But the radical patriots would not take this conservative and moderate course, and their refusal to do so shows that they were planning an outbreak which would commit the patriot party all over the country to a more violent and radical position—an outbreak which would be self-restrained, and yet sufficiently violent to force both England and America to an open contest on the one great question which lay beneath all the past eight years of wrangling.

They prepared everything for action on the night of the 16th of December, because two days after that the twenty days' limit would expire on the "Dartmouth," which had been the first ship to arrive. Seven thousand people filled the Old South Meeting House on that afternoon, while Rotch, the Quaker owner of the "Dartmouth," drove out to Milton to Governor Hutchinson's country place, to ask him for a permit to pass the castle. Every one knew or felt confident that the permit would be refused; so that this meeting cannot be called a deliberative one.

Darkness came on, and still the meeting waited. At last Rotch returned, and made the formal announcement that the permit had been refused. Samuel Adams arose and gave the signal that had evidently been agreed upon: "This meeting can do nothing more to save the country."

Immediately, as has been so often related, the warwhoop was heard outside the door. Some forty or fifty men, painted and disguised as Indians, and with hatchets in their hands, suddenly appeared from some place where they had been waiting, and

175

hurried down to the tea-ships, directly encouraged by Adams, Hancock, and other patriots. The crowd formed around them as a protection, and posted guards about the wharf to prevent interference while the Indians worked with their hatchets. It is said that the vast crowd was perfectly silent, a most respectful Boston silence, and not a sound could be heard for three hours save the cracking of the hatchets on the chests of tea in all three ships.[14]

At the end of that time every pound of tea was in the water and a delicious aroma from it arose all along the wharves. There was not the slightest attempt by the governor, or the soldiers, to interfere with the work of the mob. The fleet which was lying within sight of the tea-ships did nothing. The admiral it is said was on shore and as the crowd returned he good naturedly joked with them, and said that having had their sport they might soon have to pay the piper.

All these proceedings, with their deliberateness and success, were certainly a violation of the rights of private property, for the tea belonged to the East India Company. They were conducted in a regular and systematic manner and yet they were rioting. The most comical part was that the Indians claimed particular credit for not having injured any other property on the ships, and declared that "all things were conducted with great order, decency, and perfect submission to government." Our ancestors had a fine sense of humor.

Seriously considered, the destruction of this private property can be justified only by the argument of the radical patriots who did it. They were unwilling to resort to the conservative method of allowing the tea to be seized and put up for sale to pay the duty because that "was too precarious a ground on which to risk the salvation of the country." Some loyalists might have bought the tea; and then the opposition to England would have been broken, the budding union of the colonies dissolved never to be restored, and all hopes of preventing British reorganization and curtailment of old privileges

---

[14] Mass. Hist. Soc. Proc., 1871-1873, pp. 177, 178; "The Origin of the American Contest with Great Britain," p. 39, New York, 1775.

shattered. Moreover, if, as many believed, the only real safety lay in independence, and if independence was the natural right of every naturally separated people, then the sooner an open breach occurred and independence was fought for the better. England would never willingly allow the old semi-independent condition to continue. She was determined to remodel and consolidate her empire and have America for a mere dependency. Her present conciliatory policy, the comparative mildness of sending over a few cargoes of tea, was mere insidiousness, a cunning way to gain time until she was strong enough for more effective measures of subjugation.[13]

From the point of view of the radicals there never was a piece of liberty or revolutionary rioting that was so sagaciously and accurately calculated to effect its purpose, and not go too far. If it had been very violent disorder, or brutality, it might have alienated moderate or doubtful patriots whom it was important to win over. It was intended to be violent enough to irritate England into abandoning smooth conciliation and beginning rugged severity. It was no doubt expected that it would be followed in other colonies, and thus bring on a general punishment that would arouse them all. But there seems to have been no disposition to follow Boston's example, except in the instance of the destruction of eighteen cases of tea in New York, of which the British Government took no notice.

The Philadelphians on the 24th of December heard of what had happened in Boston, and the next day learned that a tea-ship had arrived at Chester, fourteen miles below Philadelphia. Some weeks before printed circulars had been issued to all the pilots of the river, reminding them that tar and feathers and other unpleasant experiences would be the reward of any one of them who brought a tea-ship up from the capes. This threat and the 88 miles of difficult navigation up the Delaware would, it was supposed, protect the Quaker City from an invasion by the East India Company's ships. But here was one of them close at hand; and it was discovered that she had no pilot,

---

[13] Gordon, *supra*, vol. i, pp. 341, 342.

but had been able to follow close after another vessel with a pilot on board.

A mass meeting passed a resolution approving the conduct of the Boston patriots "in destroying the tea rather than suffer it to be landed," and a committee started for Chester to stop the further progress of the ship and keep her out of custom-house jurisdiction. But before they had gone half way her captain moved her up to within sight of Philadelphia at Gloucester Point, where crowds of people on the banks hailed her and asked the captain to come ashore. He landed, walked up through a lane formed by the crowd, and was escorted to the city, where he was soon convinced that the best thing he could do was to take his ship immediately back to England without touching a wharf or entering her at the custom-house. He was supplied with fresh provisions and on the 27th of December sailed down the river.[16]

The Charleston ship arrived on the 2nd of December. The consignees were induced to resign; but nothing more was done. When the twenty days expired the Carolinians had probably not heard of and were apparently uninfluenced by the Boston affair. The tea was seized by the customs officers to pay the duty; but no one dared to buy it; it could not be sold; and was stored in warehouses, where it remained for several years. From the point of view of the moderate patriots this was a proper way of solving the difficulty. It was perfectly lawful: there was no violence; the British Government could make no complaint, and yet the tea act, the duty, and the plan of the East India Company were killed as dead as Cæsar.[17]

The New York tea-ship "Nancy" was beaten off the coast

---

[16] *Pennsylvania Magazine of History*, vol. 15, p. 385. See also vol. 14, p. 78; Mrs. Drinker's Journal, 39; Niles, " Principles and Acts of the Revolution," edition 1826, p. 202; Drake, " Tea Leaves," p. 361.

[17] McCready, " History of South Carolina," vol. 1719–1776, p. 727; Drake, " Tea Leaves," pp. 339, 342. After the declaration of independence this tea was sold as property of the State of South Carolina and the money turned into the state treasury. (*American Archives*, fifth series, vol. iii, pp. 16, 20.)

by contrary winds and did not arrive until April, 1774, five months after the Boston affair. Some of the patriots, under the leadership of such men as Sears and McDougal, appear to have been wrought up into a very violent mood, and if opportunity had offered would have gone to any extremity. The governor, William Tryon, whose acquaintance we made when he was the ruler of North Carolina, tried like Hutchinson to have the tea-ships go back to England without coming within the jurisdiction of the New York custom-house. In this he was ably assisted by the consignees of the tea, who sent a letter to the captain of the tea-ship, at Sandy Hook, instructing him to return to England without attempting to enter New York harbor, and sending him newspapers and other evidences of the feeling of the people and of the fate which had befallen the other tea-ships. In a subsequent letter they assured him that if the tea were brought up to the town it would certainly be destroyed. He was wise enough to follow their advice, and thus prevented a violent outbreak in New York.

Another ship, called the "London," arrived at New York about the same time, having in her cargo eighteen cases of tea, belonging not to the East India Company, but to her captain. Observing the excited state of public feeling he kept very quiet about his tea; but at last it became known that he had it, and the vessel was boarded by a party of the Sons of Liberty, calling themselves Mohawks, who threw overboard the eighteen cases. The British Government, however, took no notice of this riot and attempted no punishment.[18]

In June, 1774, twenty-seven chests of tea arrived at Portsmouth, New Hampshire, and, by the skill of Governor Wentworth, who was a very judicious man and popular with both parties, it was all landed and the duty paid. But the patriot committee persuaded the consignee to send it away and it was re-shipped and sent to Halifax.[19]

---

[18] "Memorial History of New York," vol. ii, p. 432; Drake, "Tea Leaves," pp. 358, 360; *American Archives*, fourth series, vol. i, pp. 249, 250.

[19] *American Archives*, fourth series, vol. i, pp. 512, 783, 786, 964.

AMERICAN INDEPENDENCE

The most curious effect of the Boston example and the subsequent agitation occurred at Annapolis, Maryland. The brig "Peggy Stewart," with seventeen cases of tea among her cargo, arrived at that town in October, 1774, almost a year after the Boston affair. The captain had refused to take any tea and the seventeen cases had been smuggled on board concealed in blankets and without his knowledge. The tea was consigned to T. C. Williams and Company, merchants of Annapolis. Mr. Anthony Stewart, the owner of the brig, was anxious to have her discharged of her cargo as quickly as possible, because she was leaky and there were fifty-three indentured servants on board who had been confined to the ship for nearly three months. He at first tried to enter at the custom-house all the cargo except the tea; but the custom officials refused to accept such an entry. Then he entered all, and unwisely paid the duty on the tea, which instantly brought the mob upon him.

The patriots all over the country had by this time become more confident and their organization more complete. The Boston Port Bill had been passed, the Continental Congress had assembled, hostility to England had increased, and there had been serious violences committed upon loyalists during the summer. The Maryland patriots warned and threatened Mr. Stewart in a way which seems to have completely terrorized both him and his friends as well as the owners of the tea. He and the owners signed their names to a very repentant and humiliating paper, in which they offered to burn the tea in the presence of the multitude; but the patriots would not permit that, because in order to be burned the tea would have to be landed. It was bad enough that the duty had been paid, and if the tea itself was also landed the whole object of the Ministry would be accomplished. They must burn ship, cargo, and tea all together.

This seemed to entail such loss to Stewart and also to his captain, who owned a small interest in the ship, that many patriots objected and when put to vote in a meeting a large majority decided that Stewart need not burn his ship. But the minority gave such significant warnings about the rest of his property and his life that Mr. Stewart, whose wife was about to be delivered of a child, yielded to the advice of his friends, went down to the brig, set her on fire with his own hands, and in the presence of a large crowd of people watched her and the cargo burn to the water's edge.[20]

But neither this incident nor the incident of the eighteen cases destroyed in New York moved the British people or their government to make the punishment general or look beyond Boston for reparation. The destruction by a Boston mob of over £15,000 worth of tea, the private property of the East India Company, absorbed their whole attention and awoke both Whigs and Tories from their dream of conciliation. That the mob had been guided by respectable and wealthy men like Hancock, Molineaux, Warren, and Young, who prevented uproar and noise and enforced decency and order, made it all the worse in English eyes. Parliament and the Ministry resolved at all hazards and at any cost to establish British sovereignty in Massachusetts.

---

[20] *Pennsylvania Magazine of History*, vol. 25, p. 248; Eddis, "Letters from America," pp. 171–185; *American Archives*, fourth series, vol. ii, p. 310, vol. i. p. 885. Warfield, "Founders of Anne Arundel and Howard Counties," p. 445; Riley, "History of the General Assembly of Maryland," p. 302. Mr. Richard D. Fisher has collected some interesting documents relating to the burning of the "Peggy Stewart," which have been deposited with the Maryland Historical Society and were published in the Baltimore *News*. Stewart, who was an Englishman by birth and a merchant of wealth and prominence, afterwards became a loyalist, his property was confiscated and his life closed in great poverty in England.

XV.

THE Tory party, now thoroughly aroused, aimed their first blow at Franklin. The petition of the Massachusetts legislature asking for the removal from office of Governor Hutchinson and Lieutenant-Governor Oliver for writing the Whately letters had been pigeon-holed. It was now brought before the Privy Council for decision. Franklin appeared as the representative of Massachusetts, and was assailed by the Solicitor General, Alexander Wedderburn, in a speech of unexampled denunciation. He was charged as the arch plotter and traitor who, while living in England as a peacemaker, had secretly fomented the rebellion in the colonies, and had been guilty of the most contemptible of all petty crimes, the stealing of private letters.

The petition of the Massachusetts Assembly was rejected, Franklin summarily deprived of his office of post-master general of the colonies, and his influence in England as a representative of the colonies destroyed.[1] But with characteristic persistence and courage he remained in England for another year and even when finally leaving for America entertained the hope that the controversy would be amicably settled.[1]

As to Boston, that town, Englishmen said, must be fined and pay damages for allowing private property to be destroyed by a mob within its limits. This fine could not very well be enforced through the courts of Massachusetts, and there were not sufficient troops there to collect it; but there was a considerable force of British warships in those waters; and an act of Parliament was accordingly passed, known as the Boston Port Bill, which closed the harbor of the town by the blockade of a fleet. No trading vessels or commerce of any sort could pass in or out.

---

[1] *American Archives*, fourth series, vol. i, p. 235.

THE BOSTON PORT BILL

The custom-house officials, "who were now not safe in Boston or safe no longer than while they neglected their duty," were moved to Salem. This closing of the port of Boston was to continue until Boston, by her own official act, paid for the £15,000 worth of tea she had allowed to be destroyed, and reimbursed the customs officials for damage done by the mobs. When the governor should certify that this had been done, and that the colony was peaceable and orderly, the blockade should be removed and the port opened.

There was some slight opposition to this measure in Parliament; but the bill was quite generally approved by both parties. Even extreme Whigs like Colonel Barré were in favor of it as a just and proper punishment, in the interests of good order, for the unpardonable mob violence in destroying the cargoes of peaceful British merchant-vessels. "I like it," said Barré, "adopt and embrace it for its moderation." [2]

Englishmen argued that if such acts as destroying the tea were allowed to go unpunished, British commerce would not be safe. The Boston people, they said, can easily escape from any hardships they suffer from the closing of their port by simply paying for the tea. The punishment is not tyranny, because it is not intended to be perpetual. It will not last an hour after they make reparation. It all rests with themselves.

The Port Bill was the first strong, forceful measure undertaken by Great Britain, and yet it left open a door by which a return could be made to the conciliatory policy. If the tea were paid for the colonies would apparently be again under the let-alone policy by which the moderate patriots believed full freedom would be eventually attained. There was a strong feeling in the patriot party throughout the country in favor of paying for the tea as an act of good policy in the interests of peace. Franklin was in favor of this course to the last, and the feeling showed itself even in Boston, where the loyalists

---

[2] *American Archives*, fourth series, vol. i, pp. 40, 514; *Annual Register*, 1774, chap. vi.

and moderates tried to carry a town meeting in favor of payment.[3]

But the extreme patriots declared that they would never pay for the tea. They might just as well, they said, pay for the powder and ball with which the regulars shot down Boston citizens four years before on the 5th of March. They exerted themselves to the utmost to prevent payment. They argued that the town had no legal power to pay for the tea or pay any damages to any one. Only the assembly could authorize such payment. Some of them quieted the scruples of the moderates by admitting the justice of payment, but at the same time pointing out that the question had become one which might affect all the colonies; and there would in all probability soon be a meeting of a continental congress. It would be better to wait till then and take the sense of the continent. The congress would very likely recommend payment and then each colony would willingly pay its share; whereas if Boston or the Massachusetts Assembly should immediately order payment the other colonies might resent it as submitting to the tax on tea, and thus the union and harmony among the colonies would be destroyed.[4]

Thus payment was prevented; there was no return to the conciliatory policy, and the Revolution moved on. The Massachusetts patriots stirred the whole continent into a state of resentment against the punishment of Boston. It was a punishment, they said, which included the innocent with the guilty, and punished the whole town for the acts of a few. It was absurd, they said, to ask Boston to pay for the tea, for by closing her port the town within a few weeks lost far more than the

---

[3] Niles, " Principles and Acts of the Revolution," edition 1876, p. 206; Wells, " Life of Samuel Adams," vol. ii, pp. 175, 185, 186; Franklin's Works, Bigelow edition, vol. v, pp. 452, 454; vol. vii, p. 3. The Virginia patriots seem to have been opposed to payment. (Niles, *supra*, p. 273.)

[4] "Observations on the Act of Parliament Commonly Called the Boston Port Bill," Boston, 1774; " The Two Congresses Cut Up," Boston, 1774 (Carter Brown collection); *American Archives*, fourth series, vol. i, p. 487.

value of the tea. Instead of such wholesale punishment, the Government should proceed in the regular way in the courts of law and obtain any damages that were due. It would certainly have been rare sport for the patriots to watch the Government trying to obtain verdicts from Boston juries.

No attempt was made to punish any of the disguised persons who had destroyed the tea. Their names were known to many; and in modern times have been published.[5]

The closing of the port was intended to be severe, and it was severe. Within a few weeks thousands of people were out of work and threatened with starvation. Would Boston be able to hold out indefinitely, or must she at last pay for the tea and the other damage in order to have her port and means of livelihood restored?

The people of the country districts rallied to her assistance and began sending in supplies of food. Soon this system spread to the other colonies; provisions and subscriptions in money began streaming along all the colonial roads, even from far down in the Southern colonies. If this could be kept up England was beaten again; for the patriot party in Boston would hold out against paying for the tea as long as it was possible.[6]

The supplies were continued for over a year. But such a contest could not be kept up indefinitely. A break would have to come, and what that break should be depended on how much rebellion and independence Massachusetts could arouse in the other colonies.

The second measure of punishment for Boston was an act of Parliament accomplishing a long-threatened change in the Massachusetts charter, so that the colony could be held under

---

[5] Drake, " Tea Leaves," pp. 84, 85.

[6] The loyalists, who were now beginning to be heard from, objected to these supplies. Boston, they said, was becoming too important. Let her take care of herself. One of them complained that it seemed as if " God had made Boston for Himself, and all the rest of the world for Boston." (" The Congress Canvassed," p. 17, New York, 1777.)

control and prevented from rushing at its will to independence. The change provided that the governor's counsel, heretofore elected by the legislative assembly, should be appointed by the Crown; that the governor should appoint and remove at pleasure judges, sheriffs, and all executive officers; that the judges' salaries should be paid by the Crown instead of by the legislature; that town meetings should be prohibited, except by permit from the governor; that juries, instead of being elected by the inhabitants, should be selected by the sheriffs.

This change from the election of jurors by the people to the selection of them by the sheriffs does not now seem a serious change, because the modern method is to have all jurors selected by the sheriffs. It was a change, however, which Parliament thought very important because the election of jurors by the people of Massachusetts was believed to be an aid to riot and rebellion.

" Juries were packed. They were nominated at the town meetings by the heads of a party. A jury, for instance, was summoned to inquire into riots. Among these impartial and respectable jurors one was returned who was a principal in the very riot into which it was the business of the very jury to inquire. Can any man entertain a moment's doubt whether this part of their constitution stood in need of reformation? "—" An Answer to the Declaration of the American Congress," London, 1776, p. 69. See also *Annual Register*, 1774, chap. vii.

All these alterations in the charter were as fiercely denounced as the Boston Port Bill, and the echoes of that denunciation are still repeating themselves in our history. But when impartially examined, and compared with other instances of colonial regulation, they did not go so far as England has often gone in regulating dependencies. There are to-day dependencies of Great Britain which have no better government than that which the alteration in the Massachusetts charter provided, and many that have less self-government than was left to Massachusetts. But compared with the semi-independence Massachusetts had once known, and the absolute independence she was seeking, this alteration was a punishment which set her patriot party furious with indignation.

AN UNPOPULAR LAW

As to the constitutional right to alter or suspend a colonial charter there were numerous precedents. William III, that great founder of liberty, once withdrew all self-government from both Maryland and Pennsylvania without even an act of Parliament; and George I took the government of South Carolina into his own hands. The Crown had always considered itself at liberty to grant new charters, alter old ones, or take part of the land included in an old charter, and give it to another colony. New charters had been granted and rescinded for Virginia until she was left without any charter; part of her territory had been given to Maryland; New Jersey charters had been granted and rescinded; Massachusetts' first charter cancelled and a new one granted; and all this without the consent of the colonies concerned.[7]

Two minor measures of regulation were adopted: a law providing that persons indicted in the colonies for murder in suppressing riots might be taken for trial to another county, or to England; and a law legalizing the quartering of troops on the inhabitants in the town of Boston. All these measures of punishment became laws before the first of April, and were to go into force in June, 1774.

The law for preventing the colonists from trying for murder British officials who should take life in suppressing riots was severely denounced as contrary to all the principles of English liberty, and Barré was very much opposed to it as unfair and unnecessary. He pointed out that Captain Preston and his soldiers who were tried by the colonists for shooting citizens in the streets of Boston, in March, 1770, had been fairly tried by a colonial jury and most of them acquitted. But the supporters of the new measure, although they never enforced it, rested its rightfulness on the reasons recited in the preamble, namely, that the colonists had denied the authority and validity of certain acts of Parliament and it was reasonable to suppose

---

[7] "The Address of the People of Great Britain to the Inhabitants of America," p. 49, London, 1775; "An Answer to the Declaration of the American Congress," p. 81, London, 1776.

that their juries would find any official guilty of murder who took life in enforcing those acts.[8]

Thoroughly aroused, at last, to the necessity of the most strenuous endeavors, Parliament at this same time passed the famous Quebec Act. Canada had been in an unsettled condition ever since it had been conquered from France in 1763. It was ruled by military governors, with the French population clamoring for their old French rights, and the less numerous English settlers clamoring against the French. There was supposed to be danger that the French population might join the union that was forming to the south of them. Massachusetts and the patriot party had as yet done nothing to secure the Canadians. It would be well, therefore, to cut off all chance of such action; and accordingly we find the Quebec Act giving to those French people their Roman Catholic religion established by law, the French code of laws in civil matters, and the English law in crimes.

Having thus secured the loyalty of the Canadian French the Act went on and established what was considered in America an extremely arbitrary crown-colony government, of a governor and council appointed by the Crown, without any legislature or representation of the people, and without trial by jury; and the boundaries of Canada were extended southward to the Ohio River so as to include the present states of Ohio, Indiana, Illinois, Michigan, Wisconsin, and Minnesota, a region which the patriot party hoped to have for their own Protestant expansion.[9]

---

[8] *American Archives*, fourth series, vol. i, pp. 112, 128, 129.

[9] "The Other Side of the Question; or, a Defence of the Liberties of North America," p. 23, New York, 1774; Hamilton's Works, Lodge edition, vol. i, p. 173; *Annual Register*, 1774, chap. vii; Achenwall, "Observations on North America," 1767 (translated by J. G. Rosengarten), Philadelphia, 1903; "Reflections on the Present Combination of the American Colonies," p. 40, London, 1777; De Courcy, "Catholic Church in the United States" (translated by Shea), pp. 209, 210; Bourinot, "Story of Canada," pp. 276–279, 304; Gordon, "American Revolution," edition 1788, vol. i, pp. 357, 359; *American Archives*, fourth series, vol. ii, p. 519.

A CONGRESS DEMANDED

The establishment of Roman Catholicism and despotic government and the extending of these institutions to the westward of the colonists in the fertile valley of the Mississippi naturally aroused the patriot party to still greater hostility against the mother-country. But from England's point of view the Quebec Act was the only successful measure passed by Parliament that year. It was a bold and sagacious piece of statecraft and saved Canada for the British empire. After the passage of that Act all our efforts to win over the Canadians were in vain.

The weak point about the other measures, the Boston Port Bill and the alterations in the Massachusetts charter, was that they would not necessarily prevent Massachusetts from forming a confederacy of all the colonies; and it was this tendency to united action and a confederacy that was the real danger to the British empire. The Massachusetts patriots saw this very clearly, and they called aloud for assistance and united support. They demanded a congress of delegates from all of the colonies to consider the Massachusetts difficulty, as a national question concerning them all. But the word national was as yet too strong to be used; so continental was used, and the congress is still known as the continental congress.[10]

---

[10] *American Archives*, fourth series, vol. i, pp. 55, 412.

XVI.

THE CULMINATION OF THE PATRIOT ARGUMENT

THE Revolution was on in earnest, and all over the country preparations were made for electing the continental congress, the most daring act of union that had yet been attempted. In every colony there were groups of patriots or, as they seemed to the English, secret knots of conspirators, who met, like Jefferson and his Virginia friends, at the Raleigh Tavern in Williamsburg; or like Reed, Dickinson, Thomson, and Mifflin in Philadelphia; or Sears, Lamb, McDougal, and Scott in New York. In Boston the North End Caucus which met at William Campbell's house and at the Green Dragon Tavern had been established by Dr. Joseph Warren. "We were so careful," says Paul Revere, "that our meetings should be kept secret, that every time we met every person swore upon the Bible not to discover any of our transactions but to Hancock, Warren, or Church and one or two more leaders." [1]

A similar organization, called the Long Room Club, prepared paragraphs and articles for the Boston *Gazette*, which in the advocacy of extreme opinions far outstripped all the other patriot newspapers. Cushing, Wells, Otis, Pemberton, Gray, Austin, Waldo, Inches, were prominent in this work, as well as Quincy, Mayhew, Cooper, Paine, Molineaux, Dexter, Thatcher, Avery, Crafts, Barr, Chase, and Eddis, with the indefatigable Samuel Adams. John Adams describes an evening spent with some of these choice spirits " in preparing for the next day's newspaper—a curious employment, cooking up paragraphs, articles and occurrences, &c., working the political engine." [2]

---

[1] Drake, " Tea Leaves," p. 23.
[2] John Adams, Works, vol. ii, pp. 162, 219; Hudson, " Journalism in America," pp. 102, 105.

ADAMS AND HANCOCK

All the clubs and groups seem to have been a part of the general organization of the Sons of Liberty which was found in every colony. It managed the details of the revolutionary movement, was very secret in its councils, with private passwords and other precautions against the investigations of loyalists or British government agents. As it grew in importance it rivalled in authority the regular government; it had its headquarters in New York, with a system of correspondence all over the country and means of obtaining exact information from England. In its early days in Boston in January, 1766, John Adams describes it as occupying a very small room in Chase and Speakman's distillery in Hanover Square.[3]

Of the numerous names of the Boston patriot workers all are now meaningless to most of us except Adams, Hancock, Warren, and Otis; and of these Samuel Adams and John Hancock are now best known, and were in their day also the most conspicuous. They were regarded as typical of all the rest, and more persistent and effective. In the offers of pardon, which the British Government soon began to make, John Hancock and Samuel Adams were always excepted. Their conduct was regarded as absolutely unpardonable; and if Great Britain had been able to use a little more power, or to use it more quickly, as she has done at times in Ireland or in India or in the Canadian rebellion of 1837, there is very little doubt that these two worthy patriots would have ended their careers on a gallows in London and their ghastly heads would have ornamented London Bridge or Temple Bar.

It is not altogether clear why the ministry regarded Hancock as such a particularly dangerous patriot. One would suppose that Otis, or Warren, or the publishers of the Boston *Gazette* had been far more effective in developing the revolutionary movement. Hancock had none of the arts of the orator or the writer; he had framed no remarkable arguments on the patriot

---

[3] Drake, "Tea Leaves," p. 24; *Pennsylvania Magazine of History*, vol. 25, p. 438.

side; nor does he appear to have been more active in party management than many of the others.

He was a young man, thirty-six years old, fond of dress; somewhat vain and sensitive, his critics said; and it afterwards appeared that he fancied he could command armies. He was more conspicuous for his wealth than for any personal quality. He had recently inherited his uncle's fortune and business as a merchant and the wealth and position may have aided the patriot cause in ways which were well known at the time. He risked a great deal by becoming a patriot, and his devotion to that cause must have grown out of a strong and honest conviction of its merits. His uncle had been a loyalist; and one would suppose that regard for the safety of the inherited wealth would have led the nephew to loyalism. But he was, on the contrary, ready to sacrifice his whole fortune for independence. Most of his property consisted of houses in Boston, and when the question arose whether Boston should be burned to prevent its occupation by the British, he urged Washington not to hesitate on his account.

His uncle's fortune was reputed to have been amassed by the methods which violated the laws of navigation and trade. He himself was believed to have continued those methods and it was his sloop "Liberty" and her cargo which were rescued by the mob in the riot that caused the troops to be sent to control Boston. The Ministry perhaps connected him with this disorder, and believed that a young man of such wealth and position who associated himself with smuggling, rioting, and revolutionary ideas, should be made a conspicuous example by the severest punishment that could be inflicted.

As for Samuel Adams, it is not difficult to see why he was honored as the other unpardonable American. He gradually became less conspicuous after the tea episode; and in the later stages of the Revolution, though continuing a member of the Congress, he adopted very narrow-minded views, was always opposed to Washington, feared his becoming a dictator, and suspected France of ulterior purposes on our liberties and territory. But up to the battle of Lexington, if we can judge from contemporary comment, no one of the patriot leaders was so well known or so thoroughly detested by both Englishmen and loyalists.

He was a man of good education, a graduate of Harvard College; the public documents he prepared show considerable ability; and his patriot arguments in the Boston *Gazette* are quite remarkable for dialectical skill and cautious sagacity in leading up to his very advanced opinions.

The portrait we have of him, which has often been reproduced, represents what would seem to be a stout, handsomely dressed, prosperous merchant, with a very firm chin and jaw, proud of his wealth and success, and proud of his long-tested ability in business. Unfortunately, the only part of this portrait which is true to life is that iron-like jaw. Samuel Adams was not a merchant, was seldom well dressed, was not at all proud, and never rich. He was always poor. He failed in his malting business, was unthrifty and careless with money, and had, in fact, no liking for, or ability in, any business except politics. He lived with his family in a dilapidated house on Purchase Street, and when in 1774 he was elected a delegate to the Continental Congress at Philadelphia, his admirers had to furnish the money to make him look presentable.

However some may despise him, he has certainly very many friends. For not long since, some persons (their names unknown) sent and asked his permission to build him a new barn, the old one being decayed, which was executed in a few days. A second sent to ask leave to repair his house, which was thoroughly effected soon. A third sent to beg the favor of him to call at a tailor's shop, and be measured for a suit of clothes, and choose his cloth, which were finished and sent home for his acceptance. A fourth presented him with a new wig, a fifth with a new hat, a sixth with six pairs of the best silk hose, a seventh with six pairs of fine thread ditto, an eighth with six pairs of shoes, and a ninth modestly inquired of him whether his finances were not rather low than otherwise. He replied it was true that was the case, but he was very indifferent about these matters, so that his poor abilities were of any service to the public; upon which the gentleman obliged him to accept a purse containing about fifteen or twenty Johannes. I mention this to show you how much he is esteemed here. They value him for his good sense, great abilities, amazing fortitude, noble resolution, and undaunted courage;

13   193

being firm and unmoved at all the various reports that were propagated in regard to his being taken up and sent home, notwithstanding he had repeated letters from his friends, both in England as well as here, to keep out of the way.—Wells, " Life of Samuel Adams," vol. ii, p. 209.

All this assistance Adams was not too proud to accept. A year afterwards, when he quitted Boston at the time of the battle of Lexington, these new clothes were left in his house and he could not return for them with the British troops occupying the town under orders to capture him and send him to England. He required good clothes in which to attend the congress of May, 1775, in Philadelphia; but was so poor that he felt justified in charging the expense of a new outfit on the public funds of Massachusetts.[4]

He had long been engaged in small local politics. His father had been so successful in organizing the ship-calkers for political purposes that the modern word caucus is supposed to be a corruption of his "Calker's Club." The son displayed even greater talent in political management, and the small salaries furnished the means which, with the aid of a thrifty New England wife, gave him some of the comforts of home in the old house on Purchase Street.

He had been made one of the tax collectors of Boston shortly before the time of the Stamp Act, and had failed to collect and turn over such a large part of the taxes committed to him, that suit was brought against him by the city treasurer, and judgment obtained for a sum which would have ruined him and sent him to prison if a town meeting and the legislature had not come to his rescue.[5]

" Samuel Adams had great virtue, but he was not a good collector of taxes. He was not even a good man of business. Neither in the Provincial Assembly nor in the Continental Congress did he shine as a practical legislator. His crude notions as to maintaining the army and conducting

---

[4] Hosmer, " Life of Samuel Adams," pp. 37–47, 240.
[5] Wells, " Life of Samuel Adams," vol. i, pp. 3, 273, 37–40 note; vol. ii, p. 301; Gordon, " American Revolution," edition 1788, vol. i, pp. 348, 365; Hutchinson, " History of Massachusetts," vol. iii, pp. 274, 275; Mass. Hist. Soc. Proc., 1882–1883, vol. 20, pp. 213–226.

the war gave Washington infinite trouble; and when he became governor, he did not administer his office particularly well.

"That anybody should ever have thought to make Samuel Adams a collector of taxes is a marvel. His hatred of taxes was not so much a conviction as an instinct. Apart from his unbusiness-like habits, he was about as well fitted to collect taxes as Garrison to personally conduct a coffle, or Andrew to work a guillotine."—Massachusetts Historical Society Proceedings, 1882–1883, vol. 20, pp. 224, 225.

The patriots easily forgave Adams this lapse, which was not repeated in his subsequent career; and his political influence and importance rapidly increased. But among loyalists and Englishmen his misfortune in the tax office, coupled with his poverty and shiftlessness, and a constitutional tremulousness of his head and hands, naturally intensified the disgust with which those opponents of the revolutionary movement regarded him. No epithets of abuse were too strong for this patriot who, they said, had deluded the youthful and wealthy Hancock.

"With his oily tongue he duped a man whose brains were shallow and pockets deep, and ushered him to the public as a patriot, too. He filled his head with importance and emptied his pockets, and as a reward kicked him up the ladder, where he now presides over the "Twelve United Provinces," and where they both are at present plunging you, my countrymen, into the depths of distress."—Wells, "Adams," vol. ii, p. 431.

"Mr. Adams's character may be defined in a few words. He is a hypocrite in religion—a republican in politics—of sufficient cunning to form a consummate knave—possessed of as much learning as is necessary to disguise the truth with sophistry, and so complete a moralist that' it is one of his favorite maxims that "the end will justify the means." When to such accomplished talents and principles we add an empty pocket, an unbounded ambition, and a violent disaffection to Great Britain, we shall be able to form some idea of Mr. Samuel Adams."— "Independency the Object of the Congress," pp. 15, 16; Wells, "Adams," vol. ii, p. 426.

Adams's capacity for inspiring all this British hatred lay in his unusual skill and indefatigable persistence in party management. Incompetent in money matters and business, and unable to grasp the larger and more complicated questions of statecraft which arose later in the Revolution, he was nevertheless of infinite value in the early stages as an organizer of agitation and a master of the small details. He watched the growth of every promising young man in Massachusetts, won his interest and affection, and drew him to the side of patriotism and independence. He understood the temper of the people from the bottom, and knew how to draw them into the movement of the Revolution. An account of his language and advice to such people, to fight England, to "destroy every soldier that dare put his foot on shore," and that "we shall have it in our power to give laws to England," was reported to the home government as a basis of an indictment for treason.[*]

He was assailed or lauded as Sam the Malster, Sam the Publican, the Father of America, the Palinurus of the Revolution, the Grand Incendiary, the American Cato. He was one of those men whom we call a devoted and enlightened patriot, or scoundrel, conspirator, and fanatic, according as we are on the side of the government or of the rebellion. He was unquestionably one of England's most dangerous enemies; and if the expansion of the British empire is as right and beneficent as Englishmen believe it, Adams was the worst political criminal that has ever lived.

The clear-sighted consistency and determination of purpose with which he labored to shape the first arguments of the Revolution were more than mere political agitation. He saw that there was only one issue. He spurned all compromises. All modifications of colonial rule to make it easier or better were to him mere delusions. The liberality of the Whigs or the conciliatory policy of the Tories, their affectation of broadmindedness and friendliness, those methods which in modern times we have learned to call pacific penetration, were to him mere cunning means of inducing a weaker people to hew wood and draw water for the stronger, or imperceptibly to surrender their national rights. Colonialism in itself was wrong; any form of it was to him despicable and contemptible beyond expression; and to its utter destruction he devoted all the powers of his being.

---

[*] Hosmer, "Life of Samuel Adams," p. 117.

ADVANCEMENT OF ARGUMENT

Among all the millions of patriots who in almost every climate of the world have resisted the British empire and her methods, and who for their resistance have perished in battle, on the scaffold, or in exile, it is not likely that there have been any who were more sincere and earnest in their hatred of alien rule than Samuel Adams; and most wonderful of all, he escaped all changes and chances, lived to see the full measure of his passion gratified, his most extreme ideas adopted, and the new nation of his fondest hopes created out of the ruins of colonialism.

His extreme views of abolishing altogether the British connection were shared, of course, by many who did not openly avow them. But now, in 1774, the patriot party had educated itself up to these radical opinions and was on the eve of formally adopting them. All acts of Parliament that had been disliked had now been either repealed, disregarded, or defeated by force. The only acts that were enforced were old ones like the Post-office Act, which had always been regarded as great conveniences. Even these might soon be disposed of; for in July, 1774, the Maryland *Journal,* a patriot newspaper, was so enterprising that it started an American post-office to carry the Southern mails and take the place of the British Colonial post-office established by Parliament.[7]

The patriot argument had now advanced to the position of denying all authority of Parliament. The old notion that Parliament had full power over the colonies except in the one item of internal taxes, and Dickinson's distinction that Parliament had no authority except to regulate their external ocean commerce, were both thrown to the winds as rubbish; and a new ground was taken that only the king, the original creator of the colonies, had any authority over them. All acts of Parliament, even those like the Post-office Act, that the colonists had accepted and lived under for generations, were mere usurpations, accepted perhaps without protest, because, as the Continental Congress afterwards put it, the colonists "were

---

[7] *American Archives,* fourth series, vol. i, p. 500.

too sensible of their weakness to be fully sensible of their rights.''

The argument in support of this new position was largely based upon the charters. Those charters, the patriots said, contained words which cut off Parliament entirely from any control of those much-discussed internal affairs, or vital organs, of the colonies. Some of the charters, they said, might at first appear non-committal, or seem to say nothing directly about the authority of Parliament. But these non-committal ones often contained general expressions giving a great deal of vague authority to the colony or to its legislature; and such authority, given in such a broad and general way, must be exclusive and imply an extinguishment of any rights of Parliament.

Queen Elizabeth's charter to Sir Walter Raleigh gave him such vast prerogatives and privileges in America, was so sweeping and general, that it must have been intended to exclude the authority of Parliament. The first Virginia charter provided that the colony was to be ruled by such laws as the king should make, which necessarily excluded, it was said, the making of laws by Parliament. There was a clause which said that the colonists should have the same liberties in other British dominions '' as if they had been abiding and born within our realm of England,'' which showed that the colony was a territory outside of the realm, and therefore, inferentially, outside of all authority of Parliament. The second Virginia charter declared that all the colony's privileges were to be held of the king, which again excluded all authority of Parliament. Indeed, such charters as those of Connecticut and Rhode Island, which gave such large privileges to the colonists, and spoke only of the colonists and the king without any mention of Parliament, seemed to exclude the authority of Parliament.

Diligent students also found instances where the action of British officials, and even of Parliament itself, looked in the same direction. In April, 1621, a bill had been introduced in Parliament for indulging British subjects with the privilege of fishing on the coast of America; but the House was informed through the Secretary of State, by order of his Majesty, King James, that "America was not annexed to the realm, and that it was not fitting that Parliament should make laws for these countries."

This was certainly strong evidence, and supported all that had been said. The evidence became stronger still when they found that some years afterwards, in the reign of Charles I, the same bill had been again proposed in Parliament, and the same answer made that "it was unnecessary; that the colonies were without the realm and the jurisdiction of Parliament." [*]

These charters and the action of high officials seemed to show that in the early days Parliament had no authority whatever over the colonies; could not tax them, and could not regulate their internal affairs in any way whatsoever. The colonies were, in short, outside the realm and to be controlled only by the king.

There was one charter, however, that of Pennsylvania, granted in 1681, which looked the other way. It provided in unmistakable language that the king could never levy any custom or tax on the inhabitants of the province except "with the consent of the proprietors, or chief governor or assembly, or by *act of Parliament in England.*" That was a flat contradiction of the doctrine drawn from the other charters, and what could be done with it? Pennsylvania could surely be taxed by Parliament as much as Parliament pleased; and her people, said the loyalists, had no possible excuse for their rebellion except to call it by its name and fight it out. But the patriot writers replied that such a reservation of the right to tax showed that there could be no such right without express reservation.

The king, the patriots went on to say, had originally granted the charters to the colonies because in the early times Parliament had no power to charter corporations. He had

---

[*] "The Farmer Refuted," p. 27; Hamilton, Works, Lodge edition, vol. i, pp. 53, 89; "An Address on Public Liberty in General and American Affairs in Particular," p. 17, London, 1774; *American Archives,* fourth series, vol. i, pp. 338, 448.

also given the colonists the title to the land they were to occupy in America, for Parliament had not then the right to grant away the public domain. He had also given the colonists permission to leave the realm, a permission which at that time could be granted only by the king. These facts showed, it was said, that the colonies were exclusively the king's property, because he and not Parliament had created them. They were completely outside of parliamentary jurisdiction, and were to be ruled by the king alone.

This meant no rule at all, because the king had now lost nearly all his old powers, which had been absorbed by Parliament; and this thread of attachment to the king was, of course, much ridiculed by the loyalists as well as by people in England.[*]

"Here we have a full view of the plan of the delegates of North America, which, when examined, appears to be that of absolute independence on the mother-state. But conscious that a scheme which has so great a tendency to the forfeiture of her rights, and so destructive to her safety and happiness, could not meet with the approbation and support of the colonists in general, unless in some measure disguised, they have endeavored to throw a veil over it, by graciously conceding to the mother-state a whimsical authority, useless and impractical, in the nature."—"A Candid Examination of the Mutual Claims of Great Britain and the Colonies," p. 27, New York, 1775.

The argument was, in effect, that the colonies were independent in government and merely under the protecting influence of the king who would keep foreign nations from interfering with them, a condition which in international law is called a protectorate. They could not be brought into subjection to Parliament, because the king, as Edward Bancroft put it, "had a right to constitute distinct states in America," and had so constituted the colonies. No power could unite them to the realm or to the authority of Parliament without the consent of the king and their own consent, given as formally and as solemnly as Scotland gave her consent to the union

* Niles, "Principles and Acts of the Revolution," edition 1876, p. 204; Snow, "Administration of Dependencies," pp. 223, 294; "The Association," by "Bob Jingle," being some political verses of the period.

with England. Such consent, so far as the colonies were concerned, had never been given.[10]

This argument Englishmen might admit to be entirely sound up to a certain point. The colonies as originally constituted had been perhaps the creations of the Crown, and Parliament had had little or nothing to do with them. But had not that condition changed and had not Parliament since the year 1700 gradually acquired an authority in the colonies?

All those instances of the exclusion of the authority of Parliament from the colonies occurred previous to the year 1700; not a single instance could be found after that date. In fact, a totally reverse condition could be found; for it was since that time that Parliament had been habitually regulating the internal affairs of the colonies; and until quite recently the colonists had submitted to it.

Those charters containing clauses impliedly excluding Parliament from the government of the colonies, and those admissions by British officials to the same effect, were previous to the revolution of 1688, by which any power there might have been in the crown to dispense with or abrogate laws or rights of Parliament was abolished. If the king, in granting those early charters, intended to abrogate or dispense with the taxing power or any other legislative power of Parliament in the colonies, those charters were to that extent now void, because the dispensing power of the English kings had been abolished by the revolution of 1688, which put William III on the throne. In other words, the dispensing power had been abolished for nearly a hundred years; and the colonists, as good Whigs and lovers of liberty, would surely not uphold the wicked dispensing power of the Stuart kings against whom their Puritan ancestors had fought.[11]

---

[10] " Remarks on the Review of the Controversy between Great Britain and her Colonies," pp. 48, 49; Jenkyns, " British Rule and Jurisdiction beyond the Seas," p. 165.

[11] It was and still is the unbroken opinion of English lawyers that all charters which kings had granted were since 1689 subordinate to the will of Parliament. Indeed, any one who has made the slightest attempt

AMERICAN INDEPENDENCE

Moreover, said Englishmen, the present King George III, whom the colonists pretend to be so anxious to have govern them, to the exclusion of Parliament, is king by the act of Parliament which placed the house of Hanover on the throne. The colonists are, therefore, compelled to acknowledge that Parliament can give them a king, which is, of all other things, the highest act of sovereignty and legislative power. If Parliament has the right to give them a king, it surely has the right to tax them or rule them in every other way. Since the revolution of 1688 Parliament has become omnipotent. One hundred years ago it may have been the law that Parliament had no authority in the colonies, but within the last hundred years the law has evidently changed, for Parliament has been exercising in them a great deal of authority, which the colonists cannot deny.

The colonists were, therefore, asking for independence of Parliament under an ancient form of the British Constitution,—a form which had been abolished in the previous century by their friends the Whigs and William III. In the time of those old Virginia charters Parliament was of little importance and small authority. Sometimes many years passed without a Parliament being held. The king was then necessarily the important power in the government. He both created and governed the colonies. But Parliament had now become vastly more powerful. It was in session part of every year. The revolution of 1688, the steady development of ideas, the needs of a nation that was rapidly increasing its trade and commerce and adding new conquests and territories to its domain, compelled a very different, a more powerful, far-

to understand the development of English history knows that for a century previous to 1689, under the Stuart kings, the great contest was whether Parliament had any power at all. That was the problem with which Cromwell struggled, and the problem which William III solved in favor of Parliament in 1689. (See Bernard's "Select Letters on the Trade and Government of America," London, 1774.)

202

reaching Parliament than that of the time of Charles I, who hated parliaments and tried to rule without them.[12]

Parliament had abolished the former powers of the king and extended itself to every part of the empire, just as to-day the power of Parliament is sovereign and unlimited over all the British colonies. To suppose that there was any part of the empire to which the whole power of Parliament did not extend was as absurd to an Englishman in 1774 as it is to-day. It had the same authority over the people in America that it had over the people in London.

" It is a contradiction, in the nature of things," said one of the ablest loyalists, " and as absurd as that a part should be greater than the whole, to suppose that the supreme legislative power of any kingdom does not extend to the utmost bounds of that kingdom. If these colonies, which originally belonged to England, are not now to be regulated and governed by authority of Great Britain, then the consequences are plain. They are not dependent upon Great Britain; they are not included within its territories; they are not part of its dominion; the inhabitants are not English, they can have no claim to the privileges of Englishmen; they are, with regard to England, foreigners and aliens; nay, worse, as they have never been legally discharged from the duty they owe it, they are rebels and apostates."—"A Friendly Address to all Reasonable Americans," p. 3, 1774.

Thus, in the year 1774, all the reasoning and argument of the last ten years was brought to one direct and simple issue: Was Parliament omnipotent in the colonies? It was either omnipotent there or it had no power at all there. The English people, both Whigs and Tories, Burke, Chatham, and Barré, as well as North, Germain and Mansfield, were entirely agreed that Parliament was supreme in the colonies. The American patriot pamphleters denied that supremacy in toto; and faced the ridicule of Englishmen and loyalists, who took great pleasure

---

[12] " The Right of the British Legislature to Tax the American Colonies," pp. 18, 19, London, 1774; " The Address of the People of Great Britain to the Inhabitants of America; " " The Supremacy of the British Legislature over the Colonies candidly discussed," London, 1775. See, also, " The Claim of the Colonies to an Exemption from Internal Taxes examined," London, 1766; *American Historical Review*, vol. i, p. 37.)

in pointing out that if Parliament had no authority whatever in the colonies then the colonists during the last hundred years had been accepting and living under invalid acts of Parliament like the Post-office Act and numerous others, of which they never had complained: and all the numerous colonists who had been fined, imprisoned, or hung under acts of Parliament, had been illegally punished, and those now in jail should be set free.[13]

But to the patriots it seemed that a stand must be made against the whole idea of parliamentary supremacy, which England was now enlarging into a consolidation of empire contrary to the natural rights of man. It was this consolidation under the doctrine of the absolute supremacy of Parliament that the patriots dreaded as they saw it steadily developed to form the legal basis of the modern British empire. The complete supremacy of Parliament is absolutely essential to a colonial empire like that of England, and it is now never questioned in the British colonies. But the American patriots, with the longing for self rule and nationality firing their blood, revolted with the most passionate indignation from this prospect of modern colonialism. They would do anything, they would tear the British empire to pieces, to escape from it. They saw in it nothing but infamy, repression of their energies and ambition, dwarfing of their political manhood, and political degradation for themselves and their children. They described it as slavery; their leaders denounced it in every term of abuse that the language would supply and appealed to every sentiment of honor, unselfishness and high courage among the people.[14]

Honor, justice, and humanity call upon us to hold, and to transmit to our posterity, that liberty which we receive from our ancestors. It is not our duty to leave wealth to our children; but it is our duty to leave liberty to them. No infamy, iniquity, or cruelty, can exceed our own, if we, born

---

[13] See an article quoted from some London Journal in the Boston *Gazette*, for April 28, 1766.

[14] See " Address to the Pennsylvania Assembly," in 1774; Niles, " Principles and Acts of the Revolution," edition 1876, p. 204; " Diary and Letters of Thomas Hutchinson," vol. i, pp. 234, 266.

THE DREAD OF PARLIAMENT

and educated in a country of freedom, entitled to its blessings, and knowing their value, pusillanimously deserting the post assigned us by Divine Providence, surrender succeeding generations to a condition of wretchedness, from which no human efforts, in all probability, will be sufficient to extricate them; the experience of all states mournfully demonstrating to us, that when arbitrary power has been established over them even the wisest and bravest nations, that ever flourished, have, in a few years, degenerated into abject and wretched vassals.—Niles, "Principles and Acts of the Revolution," edition 1876, p. 204.)

So alarming, said the patriots, was the development of this absolute authority of Parliament, with such artful and incessant vigilance was it supported, so cunning was its creeping process when carried on by conciliation and kindness, to such apathy and contented indifference did it reduce a people, and to such a height had it attained in the year 1774, that unless they could interrupt it at once, their children, debilitated by its grasp, would never be able to overthrow it when completed; and as a matter of fact, it has never since then been over-thrown in any of the other British colonies.[15]

---

[15] See on this subject, "Diary and Letters of Thomas Hutchinson," vol. i, pp. 202, 266, 272, 388, 389; vol. ii, pp. 93, 141, 163, 164; Wells, "Life of Samuel Adams," vol. ii, pp. 29, 46. The pamphlet containing Hutchinson's famous argument, with Answers of the Massachusetts Assembly, is entitled, "The Speeches of His Excellency Governor Hutchinson to the General Assembly of Massachusetts Bay, etc., with the Answers of his Majesty's Council and the House of Representatives," Boston, 1773. The contents of the pamphlet will also be found in "Speeches of the Governor of Massachusetts from 1765 to 1775," Boston, 1818, pp. 336–396, which is a volume more easily obtained. Jefferson's argument that all acts of Parliament, even those that the colonists had accepted without complaint, were usurpations and void, is well worth reading. It was called, "A Summary of the Rights of British America," and is in the Ford edition of his works, vol. i, p. 434. See also Lewis, "Government of Dependencies," p. 331; Todd, "Parliamentary Government in the British Colonies," edition 1894, pp. 241, 242, 244, 245; and James Wilson's pamphlet, "Considerations on the Nature and Extent of the Legislative Authority of the British Parliament." Many of the chapters in Snow's "Administration of Dependencies" are very interesting in this connection.

XVII.

THE PASSION FOR INDEPENDENCE RESTRAINED OR CONCEALED

THAT a large and growing party in America wanted absolute independence and had been working to that end for a long time admits of no doubt, was well known in England, and can be shown from various sources. Sometimes the intention, though partially veiled, was notorious, as in the case of Samuel Adams; sometimes it was openly expressed, as in the Boston *Gazette;* and very often it was nourished in secret, or the individuals who entertained it were scarcely conscious of how far they were going, or hesitated about the risks to be run.

In the first chapter of this volume a passage has been cited from the Swedish botanist, Kalm, who travelled in the colonies in 1748, and described the movement for independence as so advanced that the people were foretelling a total separation within thirty or fifty years, which forecast was literally fulfilled. Franklin himself, in 1766, two years after he went to England, had received a letter from Joseph Galloway describing the plans for independence:

"A certain sect of people, if I may judge from their late conduct, seem to look on this as a favorable opportunity of establishing their republican principles, and of throwing off all connection with their mother-country. Many of their publications justify the thought. Besides, I have other reasons to think that they are not only forming a private union among themselves from one end of the continent to the other, but endeavoring also to bring into this union the Quakers and all other dissenters, if possible."—Sparks, " Franklin," vol. vii, p. 303. (See also " Diary of Thomas Hutchinson," vol. i, p. 12.)

John Wesley, in one of his pamphlets, says that his brother visited the colonies in 1737, and reported "the most serious people and men of consequence almost continually crying out,

EARLY IDEAS OF INDEPENDENCE

'We must be independent; we shall never be well until we shake off the English yoke.' '' [1]

"You may depend upon it," says a loyalist, writing from Philadelphia August, 1775, "that the present breach with England is not the device of a day and has not arisen with the question about taxation (though that has been a favourable plea) but is part of a system which has been forming here even before the late war."—*American Archives*, seventh series, vol. iii, p. 30. (See also Jones, "New York in the Revolution," vol. i, p. 24.)

Galloway, in his examination before the House of Commons, testified that there had been a considerable number of persons who advocated independence in the principal towns of the colonies as early as 1754. Dr. Eliot, writing to England, in 1767, says, "We are not ripe for disunion; but our growth is so great that in a few years Great Britain will not be able to compel our submission." [2]

That very plain-spoken Englishman, Dean Tucker, writing in 1774, took a common-sense view when he said,—

---

[1] "A Calm Address to the Inhabitants of England," pp. 6, 9, London, 1777.

[2] Massachusetts Historical Society, 4th series, vol. iv, p. 240; "Kalm's Travels," vol. i, p. 265. A pamphlet called "The Conduct of the Late Administration examined," pp. 22, 31, 37, 43, 44, 45, London, 1767, refers to the plans for independence in numerous passages. People were saying that their children would "live to see a duty laid by Americans on some things imported from Great Britain." The ministry, it was said, had been repeatedly informed of the plans for independence (p. 37). In "Reflections on the Present Combination of the American Colonies," p. 5, London, 1777, the author says he has been personally acquainted with the colonies for forty years, and that they had been talking independence all that time. "The principles they suck in with milk," he says, "naturally lead to rebellion." On page 35 he gives the patriot toast to the mother-country as "Damn the old B——." See, also, Bancroft, "History of the United States," edition of 1883, vol. iii, pp. 406, 427; Boston *Evening Post*, May 27, June 24, October 28, 1765; Boston *Gazette*, January 6 and 27, March 2, August 17 and 24, November 1 and 2, 1772; January 11, March 15, 1773; *American Whig*, April 11, 1768; "Americans against Liberty," p. 39, London, 1776; "The Constitutional Right of the Legislature of Great Britain to tax the British Colonies," pp. 27, 28, *et passim*, London, 1768.

It is the nature of them all (*i.e.*, colonies) to aspire after independence, and to set up for themselves as soon as ever they find they are
able to subsist without being beholden to the mother-country, and if
our Americans have expressed themselves sooner on this head than others
have done, or in a more direct and daring manner, this ought not to be
imputed to any greater malignity.—"The True Interest of Great Britain
set forth," p. 12. (See, also, Stedman, "American War," vol. i, p. 1,
London, 1794.)

Of course, it is true that all the patriot documents are full
of profuse expressions of the most devoted loyalty, and the
leaders were constantly putting forth these profuse expressions.
If such assertions are proof, it is easy enough to accumulate
great numbers of them. In fact, judged by their documents,
the nearer the patriots approached to the year 1776, the more
devoted, loving, and loyal they became, and the more they
detested the thought of independence.

There are many letters of John Jay, Jefferson and others
regretting separation or "looking with fondness towards reconciliation," and some patriot documents like the first Constitution of New Hampshire professed to provide mere temporary
arrangements until reconciliation could be effected. But what
did they mean by reconciliation? They meant reconciliation
on their own terms, which England would not grant and never
has granted to any of her colonies; that is, entire freedom from
any sort of control by Parliament, which was in effect independence, or so slightly removed from it that absolute
independence could soon be assumed. When they insisted that
they were loyal they meant that they were loyal to this idea of
the government of the king without Parliament. Their idea of
reconciliation was that England should accept their plan and
restore friendly feelings as between two independent nations,
the sort of reconciliation which we now have with England.

When Franklin in England in August, 1774, assured Lord
Chatham that he had never heard in America "from any
person drunk or sober, the least expression of a wish for
separation,"[3] he must have meant separation from the king as

---

[3] Franklin, Works, Bigelow edition, vol. v, pp. 345, 446; The statement of Washington, October 9, 1774, that it was not the wish or inter-

general head or protector of the empire. He had then been in England for ten years and could, of course, say that he had not heard any of the independence talk in America in that time, although in 1766 he had received the letter from Galloway already quoted describing the independence movement.

That bluff and vigorous patriot, John Adams, writing long after the Revolution, said that there never was a time during the contest when he would not have given everything he possessed "for a restoration to the state of things before the contest began, provided we could have had a sufficient security for its continuance." He saves his statement by the proviso that there must be "sufficient security" for the continuance of the old times. That is to say, he would be loyal if allowed to give his own definition of loyalty and have things his own way. There was the rub. England would not give that security; the only security as Adams well knew was independence; and in the same letter he throws light on the way in which the subject was regarded:

There is great ambiguity in the expression, there existed in the Colonies a desire of Independence. It is true there always existed in the Colonies a desire of Independence of Parliament in the articles of internal Taxation, and internal Policy; and a very general if not a universal opinion, that they were constitutionally entitled to it, and as general a determination if possible to maintain, and defend it; but there never existed a desire of Independence of the Crown, or of general regulations of Commerce, for the equal and impartial benefit of all parts of the Empire. It is true there might be times and circumstances in which an Individual, or a few Individuals, might entertain and express a wish that America was Independent in all respects, but these were "Rari nantes in gurgite vasto." For example, in one thousand seven hundred and fifty-six, seven and eight, the conduct of the British Generals Shirley, Braddock, Loudon, Webb and Abercromby was so absurd, disastrous, and destructive, that a very general opinion prevailed that the War was conducted by a mixture of Ignorance, Treachery, and Cowardice,

---

est of any of the colony governments to set up for independence was of course true at the time he wrote it. A year or two afterwards those governments were captured by the patriots and one after another declared for independence; but in October, 1774, they were not ready for it. (Washington, Writings, Ford edition of 1889, vol. ii, p. 443.)

14

and some persons wished we had nothing to do with Great Britain for ever. Of this number I distinctly remember, I was myself, one, fully believing that we were able to defend ourselves against the French and Indians, without any assistance or embarrassment from Great Britain.—*New England Historical and Genealogical Register*, 1876, vol. 30, p. 329.

After that, he says, he would have been willing to be loyal again "had not the King and Parliament committed high treason and rebellion against America" in attempting to reorganize the colonies. In other words, the patriot party always wanted independence of Parliament. When they said that they did not want independence they meant independence of the King, whom, however, they stood ready to cast off at any moment if he did not fulfil their wishes.

Another reason for the rather confusing statements on the subject of independence, was that the patriot leaders felt that an open advocacy of absolute independence would lose them the support of the English Whigs, whose stock argument was that the colonies if leniently treated would voluntarily remain within the empire. The open advocacy of absolute independence would also shock many timid patriots and alienate loyalists who might become patriots. To refrain from advocating absolute independence was, therefore, a policy which would tend to unite America and divide England; and so convinced were the patriots of the importance of this policy that in several instances the revolutionary committees prosecuted and punished those who asserted that the colonies were aiming at independence.[4]

Jefferson and Elbridge Gerry have described the great care that had to be taken to lead the masses of the patriot party step by step and slowly accustom them to the thought of absolute separation. "Some timid minds," said Gerry, "are terrified at the word independence * * * the fruit must have time to ripen." "Regrets" and "distress" at separation had to

---

[4] *American Archives*, fourth series, vol. iii, pp. 21, 158, 644. See, also, title "Independence" in the index of vol. iii, fourth series, and other volumes of the *American Archives*.

be expressed, and all sorts of phrases used about the King and loyalty by men who in their hearts entirely agreed with John Adams that "there is something very unnatural and odious in a government a thousand leagues off;" and that it is a kindly or liberal government does not materially lessen its odiousness to men of spirit, ability, and ambition.[5]

To many of the patriot party such an inspiring idea as independence seemed at first too much like a beautiful dream. Thousands of them were in terrible uncertainty. At the thought of independence they trembled about the future which they could not see or fathom; on which was no landmark or familiar ground; and which their imaginations peopled with monsters and dragons like those with which the old geographers before Columbus filled the Western Ocean. We laugh at their fears, because that future has now become the past. But their fears were largely justified by the history of the world up to that time.

They felt that the old argument with which the loyalists continually plied them might very well be true. The colonies, if left to themselves, would fight one another about their boundaries. They had been quarrelling about boundaries for a century, with England for their final arbiter. What would they do when they had no arbiter but the might of the strongest? Would not Pennsylvania combine with the South to conquer New England? or, more likely still, New England would combine with New York to conquer all the South,— New York, for the sake of her old Dutch idea of trade, and New England, for the sake of improving the fox-hunting, Sabbath-breaking Southerner and freeing his slaves; for the estrangement between North and South on the slavery question was already quite obvious at the time of the Revolution. Then there would be rebellions and struggles to reform the map and straighten the lines and boundaries. If in the confusion France or Spain did not conquer them, or England reduce

---

[5] Hudson, "Journalism in the United States," p. 114; *American Archives*, fourth series, vol. vi, p. 488; vol. i, p. 690 note; vol. v, p. 507.

them again to colonies, they would likely enough try to form a confederacy among themselves for protection against Europe. Then there would be one war to decide which section should have the commercial advantage of the seat of government in this confederacy, and another war to decide what should be the form of government of the confederacy,—monarchical, aristocratic, or republican,—and probably a third war to establish securely the form of government finally adopted.[*]

We must remember that in South America there has been much confusion and misgovernment as the result of independence, and out of it only two or three stable governments,—like Chili and Brazil,—have as yet arisen. The monsters that the timid ones saw were unquestionably possibilities; and the loyalist prophecies of sectional war have been largely fulfilled. We have not had quite as many sectional wars as they foretold. But we have had one great war between the North and the South, very much as they foretold; and in costliness, slaughter, and fierceness of contest far exceeding their warnings.

They foretold also that even if, with the assistance of France, a sort of independence was won, it would be an independence only on the land. Great Britain would still retain sovereignty on the sea; and there would be another war or series of wars over this question. This happened exactly as they foretold, and thirty years after the Revolution we fought the war of 1812, often called at the time of its occurrence the Second War for Independence.

So the suggestion that they could abolish Parliament and yet remain entirely loyal by submitting themselves to the king

---

[*] "A Candid Examination of the Mutual Claims of Great Britain and the Colonies," p. 47, New York, 1775; "What think ye of the Congress now?" p. 25, New York, 1775; Works of John Adams, vol. ii, p. 351; "The Origin of the American Contest with Great Britain," New York, 1775; Bancroft, "History of the United States," edition of 1886, vol. v, p. 406. The patriots put forth some very interesting arguments to show that there would be no danger of sectionalism, and that independence once attained would be the greatest blessing, which could never be interfered with by the European nations.—*American Archives*, fourth series, vol. iii, p. 1013; vol. iv, p. 1143; vol. v, p. 96.

alone was a great help to the timid ones. By a slender thread connecting them in a romantic sort of way with the king they would remain a part of the British empire, and always have the advantage of its steadying hand, with Parliament merely an object of outside historic interest. They would always pray for the king, as some one in New England suggested, and would kindly vote him from time to time little presents of money to help him in his wars, he in return to protect them from the ravages of the great powers, France and Spain, and possibly from their own disunion and anarchy.[7]

---

[7] It is interesting to observe that when in modern times imperial rule presses a little severely on a British colony the patriot party in that colony will repeat the plan of our patriot party and suggest the rule of the king alone as a substitute or step towards the desired end. In the autumn of 1903, when there was much dissatisfaction in Canada over England's settlement of the Alaska boundary, the Halifax *Chronicle*, after declaring that the subordinate condition of Canada was no longer endurable, was reported to have said that "there are now only two courses open to Canada—complete legislative independence within the empire, acknowledging the sovereignty of the king of England alone, or the status of an independent nation;" and that there was much to commend the latter step.—Philadelphia *Record* and other American journals of October 29 and 30, 1903.

XVIII.

THE BOSTON PORT BILL IS ENFORCED

GOVERNOR HUTCHINSON of Massachusetts had obtained leave to visit England to recuperate his health and attend to private business, as well as to give the Ministry information on public affairs. General Thomas Gage was meantime sent out to enforce the Port Bill and have the province reduced to good order and loyalty by the time Hutchinson should return.

General Gage arrived in Boston the 13th May, 1774, with four regiments, which with the assistance of the fleet, would close the harbor and put the Port Bill in force on the first day of June. On the morning of that pleasant June day, when Gage took command, Governor Hutchinson left his country place at Milton and walked along the road bidding his neighbors good-by. When near Dorchester Neck he got into his carriage, which had followed him, and drove to Dorchester Point, where a boat took him on board the "Minerva," bound for England.[1]

It was significant of the change that was taking place in affairs and forming the loyalists into a distinct party, that over one hundred and twenty merchants and gentlemen met together in Boston and presented Hutchinson with a farewell address, extolling his conduct, and regretting his departure. About the same time twenty-four members of the Boston Bar presented him with a similar address, and he also received addresses from the merchants of Marblehead and the magistrates of Middlesex County. There were patriot protests against this laudation of the governor. Those who signed the addresses became marked men, and some of them suffered severe treatment at the hands of the pariots.[2]

---

[1] Diary and Letters, vol. pp. 104, 152; Gordon, "American Revolution," edition 1788, vol. i, p. 359, 360.

[2] American Archives, fourth series, vol. i, pp. 358–364.

HUTCHINSON IN ENGLAND

Hutchinson was so thoroughly detested by the patriots that they always tried to persuade themselves that his conduct was disapproved even in England, and statements to this effect have crept into many of our histories. But the recent publication of his journal and letters shows that he was received in England with every mark of approval and distinction. The London newspapers reported that his services were "held in so capital a light that a Patent of English Peerage is talked of for him." He was offered a baronetcy, but declined it on account of his small estate and declining years; and he was also offered a seat in Parliament. During the remainder of his life he was always treated in England with the greatest consideration, and he certainly deserved all that the Government and English society could do for him. He had held the most difficult governorship in the most rebellious colony, among the most determined, energetic, and independence-loving people in America. He had argued with them and resisted them with most remarkable persistence and ability; and the extent of his service to the crown is shown by the contempt and infamy in which his name has been held in Massachusetts down even to our own time.

He was a native of the province; his family had lived there for four generations; they had accumulated wealth; his father was a rich man; he himself owned houses and valuable wharves in Boston, a valuable estate in Rhode Island, and another in Maine, besides considerable personal property. All this the patriots confiscated and reduced him from affluence to penury. He was the target for as much vindictive abuse and misrepresentation as has ever been heaped on a human being; his children and their families suffered with him, and he was turned adrift in his old age to live in a foreign land among strangers.

The English government gave him a pension which enabled him to live in London as became his station in life; and he rented a house where he entertained prominent people, and all the respectable refugee loyalists that arrived from America. He rode in his own coach with a footman, took part in all the social functions of the Court and town and was a frequent visitor at the country seats of Lord Hardwicke and Wilbore Ellis. Oxford University gave him the degree of D.C.L., and he was frequently consulted by the Tory ministers.

But although he suited London life, that life did not suit him; and it is very touching to read of his longing to return to Massachusetts when she should be reduced by conquest to her proper sphere of usefulness in the empire which he worshipped. His strangely perverted and artificial nature loved his native country only when conquered, and he clung to this hope of conquest until the surrender of Burgoyne in 1777, when he lost all confidence in a restoration of order, and saw nothing in store for America but tumultuous independence with all the horrors of paper money, sectional wars, mob rule, and democracy which the loyalists foretold and dreaded.[1]

He, of course, never returned to America, and died in London in 1780 at the age of sixty-nine. About the same time that he went to England, Governor Tryon of New York and Carleton from Canada also returned there and consulted with the Government. Like Hutchinson, they believed that force and spirited measures were absolutely necessary. Hutchinson thought that the colonists would not fight. Carleton said that 10,000 troops would subdue them. But Tryon believed that large armies and long effort would be needed.

On the first of June General Gage with the troops and warships closed Boston harbor and put the Port Bill into effect. He had received numerous addresses of welcome from loyalists in different parts of the province. But the patriots printed copies of the Port Bill with a wide black border of mourning, posted them on walls, and spat on them as they passed by. They were obliged, however, to submit to all that the Bill required. Warehouses were closed, ships lay dismantled at the wharves, the harbor was deserted, work in all occupations gradually ceased, and rents fell to nothing, while Gage built

---

[1] " Diary and Letters of Thomas Hutchinson," vol. ii, pp. 75, 77, 216, 291, 292, 335, 365, 367; vol. i, pp. 283, 387, 389, 542, 543.

his camps and barracks, quartered his troops and threw up fortifications to make Boston a British stronghold.[4]

On the 13th of May, the day of Gage's arrival, the patriots had held a public meeting and passed resolutions denouncing the Port Bill and calling on the other colonies to adopt a strict system of non-importation of British goods until the bill was repealed. Copies of these resolutions were sent all over the country. Paul Revere carried them to Philadelphia and consulted with the patriot leaders, Mifflin, Thomson, and Reed. They called a meeting of prominent Philadelphians, and in spite of a strong feeling of conservatism among the loyalists and Quakers, a committee was appointed which sent a letter of sympathy to Boston. Copies of this letter were sent to other colonies; and a month afterwards, the 28th of June, a mass meeting was held which came out strongly in favor of Boston, recommended a general congress of all the colonies and appointed a committee to organize the patriot movement in Pennsylvania.[5]

This action influenced the patriots in other colonies; and that summer was a tumultuous one. Patriot conventions and meetings all over the country passed resolutions of sympathy with Boston, suffering in the common cause; the objectionable acts of Parliament printed on mourning paper were burnt on village commons; subscription papers were passed about to assist starving Boston; droves of cattle and wagons and ships loaded with wheat, corn, rice and provisions from as far south as the Carolinas, were moving northwards to Boston all summer.

" All America is in a flame! I hear strange language every day. The colonists are ripe for any measure that will tend to the preservation of what they call their natural liberty. I enclose you the resolves of *our* citizens; they have caught the general contagion. Expresses are flying from province to province."—Eddis, " Letters from America," p. 158.

---

[4] *American Archives*, fourth series, vol. i, pp. 333, 398, 401, 402, 424, 515; Elliot, " History of New England," vol. ii, p. 284; Gordon, " American Revolution," edition 1788, vol. i, p. 361.

[5] H. W. Smith, " Life of Rev. W. Smith," vol. i, p. 491; Harley, " Life of Charles Thomson," p. 68.

But the people were by no means unanimous; for a few days afterwards Eddis describes a loyalist meeting protesting by resolutions against the patriot methods.

The Massachusetts patriots were collecting guns and knapsacks and casting bullets. Gage was receiving reinforcements at Boston from Ireland and New York; he strengthened the British control of Boston by fortifying the narrow neck or isthmus which at that time joined Boston to the mainland, and he seized the powder in the arsenal at Charlestown. The patriots steadily annoyed him by burning his straw and upsetting the wagons that hauled wood and supplies for his men.

He was required by his instructions to make his headquarters at Salem; and Boston he left in charge of a very capable officer, Earl Percy, who had a vigorous Tory contempt for Americans. ''The people here,'' says Percy, ''are a set of sly artful hypocritical rascals, cruel, and cowards. I must own I cannot but despise them completely.''[6] Meantime, he and Gage found the greatest difficulty in carrying on the government of the province. The patriots easily eluded that part of the act of Parliament forbidding town meetings. They held adjourned meetings, meetings without formal notice, and often county meetings which, they said, were not mentioned or prohibited in the act.[7] The loyalists who held office were compelled by the threats of the patriots to resign, and patriot officials blocked and thwarted Gage at every step. When he seized the powder at Charlestown, the 1st of September, a rumor was spread that the fleet and troops were firing upon Boston. The patriots all over New England were aroused, and from thirty to fifty thousand armed men are said to have started from their homes in various parts of New England and had marched twenty or thirty miles towards Boston before they were undeceived.[8]

[6] ''Letters of Earl Percy,'' edited by C. K. Bolton, pp. 28, 31, 40, 44.

[7] ''Letters of Earl Percy,'' p. 35; *American Archives*, fourth series, vol. i, pp. 743, 767.

[8] *American Archives*, fourth series, vol. i, pp. 793, 804, 942; vol. ii, p. 157; Gordon, '' American Revolution,'' edition 1788, vol. i, p. 388.

ATTACKS UPON LOYALISTS

The number must have been greatly exaggerated. There could not have been as many as thirty thousand; and there were probably not five thousand. But the incident was a warning. Gage immediately abandoned his headquarters at Salem, concentrated all his force inside of Boston, and was never again able to seize any military supplies. The patriots began to drill more diligently and hunted down loyalists more mercilessly. The officials and members of the governor's council whom Gage had appointed were obliged to fly for their lives and take refuge with the army in Boston; and in this summer of 1774 the severe methods of dealing with the loyalists began.[*]

"Out with him! Out with him!" shouted the mob, as they rushed after Francis Green into the inn at Norwich, Connecticut, where he was taking refuge. He had already been driven out of Windham. They tumbled him into his carriage, lashed his horses, and, shouting and yelling, chased him out of Norwich. What was his crime? He had signed the farewell address to Governor Hutchinson, of Massachusetts.

In Berkshire, Massachusetts, in that same summer of 1774, the mob forced the judges from their seats and shut up the court-house, drove David Ingersoll from his house, and laid his lands and fences waste; they riddled the house of Daniel Leonard with bullets, and drove him to Boston; they attacked Colonel Gilbert, of Freetown, in the night, but he fought them off. That same night Brigadier Ruggles fought off a mob, but they revenged themselves by painting his horse and cutting off its mane and tail. They robbed his house of all the weapons in it and poisoned his other horse. They stopped the judges in the highway, insulted them, and hissed them as they entered court. The house of Sewell, attorney-general of Massachusetts, was wrecked; Oliver, president of the council, was mobbed and compelled to resign; an armed mob of five thousand at Worcester compelled the judges, sheriffs, and gentlemen of the bar to march up and down before them, cap in hand, and read

---

[*] Gordon, " American Revolution," edition 1788, vol. i, pp. 384, 388, 389, 411–414; " Letters of Earl Percy," p. 37; *American Archives*, fourth series, vol. i, pp. 744, 767.

thirty times their disavowal of holding court under Parliament.

In a similar way the courts at Taunton, Springfield, Plymouth, and Great Barrington were mobbed. Loyalists everywhere were driven from their houses and families, some being obliged to take to the woods, where they nearly lost their lives. One Dunbar, who had bought fat cattle from a loyalist, was, for that offence, put into the belly of one of the oxen that had been dressed, carted four miles, and deprived of four head of cattle and a horse. For the three months of July, August, and September of this year, 1774, one can find in the *American Archives* alone some thirty descriptions of attacks of this sort upon loyalists in New England.[10]

---

[10] *American Archives*, fourth series, vol. i, p. 1261.

XIX.

THE Connecticut Assembly, being entirely in control of patriots, took the lead in sending delegates to the Congress and on the 13th of June, 1774, authorized the patriot committee of correspondence to choose suitable persons. In other colonies similar methods were adopted, and by the middle of August delegates were chosen in all the colonies except Canada, Georgia, and Florida.[1]

The loyalists afterwards complained that the Congress was created in an irregular, one-sided manner, and could not be called representative. They ridiculed and denounced most unsparingly the methods that were used. It was certainly not representative in the sense in which the word is usually understood. It was not chosen by a vote of the people at large. The delegates sent by Connecticut, by the New York counties, by New Jersey, and by Maryland, were chosen by the patriot committees of correspondence without any vote of the people at large. These delegates were, therefore, merely the representatives of the patriot movement in those colonies. The loyalists, who were now beginning to increase in numbers, had no voice whatever. In Massachusetts, Rhode Island, Pennsylvania, and apparently also in Delaware, the delegates were chosen by the legislative assemblies, which in those provinces happened to be more or less in control of the patriot party.

In Massachusetts, with the British army in control of Boston and General Gage acting as military governor, one would suppose that the patriot committees would have chosen the delegates. But Samuel Adams was equal to the occasion.

---

[1] The certificates showing the dates and manner of election of each delegation can be found in "Journals of the American Congress," vol. i, pp. 2–7. See, also, as to South Carolina delegates, *American Archives*, fourth series, vol. i, pp. 525, 534.

The plans were all secretly prepared, a majority of the assembly very adroitly won over in a private way, and at the next meeting the doorkeeper was ordered to let no one enter or leave after the meeting began. As he seemed to hesitate, Samuel Adams locked the door and put the key in his pocket. One of the minority pleaded sickness and was allowed to go out. He ran to Gage, informed him of what was intended, and the general instantly drew a proclamation dissolving the assembly. But the messenger who carried the proclamation found the door locked and was obliged to read the document from the steps. Meanwhile, the assembly had chosen as delegates Thomas Cushing, Samuel and John Adams, Robert Treat Paine, and James Bowdoin.[2]

South Carolina appears to have sent her delegates by a general convention of the white people of the province. These delegates were as stanch for patriotism as any that appeared. Either the loyalists were very few, or they were absent or passive. A few years afterwards they were very numerous, and seem to have constituted fully half the population of the province.

In New Hampshire, the towns appear to have appointed deputies who met on the 2nd of July, and chose the delegates to the Congress. The only instance besides South Carolina where there seems to have been a chance for a perfectly free vote was in the town of New York, where a vote was taken generally among the people. The loyalists on this occasion voted with the patriots and for reasons which have been quite clearly set forth by one of their number:

> They were chosen by the people at large with little or no opposition all parties, denominations, and religions apprehending at the time that the colonies labored under grievances which wanted redressing. To redress which and to form a happy, perpetual, and lasting alliance, between Great Britain and America, were the reasons which induced the New York loyalists so readily to agree to the delegation. The republicans wanted members chosen out of their own faction. This the loyalists

---

[2] Hosmer, "Life of Samuel Adams," pp. 290, 297; Gordon, "American Revolution," edition 1788, vol. i, p. 365.

opposed and a kind of compromise took place. . . . With such a delegation the New York loyalists thought themselves safe. A redress of grievances and a firm union between Great Britain and America upon constitutional principles was their only aim. This they hoped for, this they
wished for, this they expected. To this purport they also verbally
instructed their delegates.—Jones, " New York in the Revolution," vol. i,
pp. 34, 35; also pp. 449–467.

The people who at that time inclined to loyalism appear to
have been willing in all the colonies to let the patriot party
have its own way in electing the Congress. This passivity was
a loyalist trait. They were never as aggressive as the patriots,
and lacked the patriot genius for organization. They believed
that the Congress would be conservative and adopt some plan
of reconciliation or compromise. The majority of the members
would restrain the hot-heads from Massachusetts; and in any
event it would take the controversy out of the hands of the
rabble. The Congress was avowedly for the redress of grievances; and the loyalists relied, they said, on this purpose being
fulfilled. They professed to be very much surprised when they
found it taking decided steps towards independence.[3]

As the assembling of such a body was a serious menace to
English sovereignty, the question naturally arises, why did not
the home government break up the Congress, prevent the election of delegates in the different colonies, or disperse with
troops the Congress itself when it assembled? Its meeting was
fraught with more danger to the empire than any other project
of the patriots; for it united nearly the whole continent in
opposition.

---

[3] " An Alarm to the Legislature of the Province of New York," p. 4,
New York, 1774; " The Congress Canvassed," p. 10, New York, 1774;
" A View of the Controversy between Great Britain and her Colonies,"
etc., pp. 7, 8, New York, 1774; " Galloway's Examination before Parlia-
ment," p. 11. See, also, Flick, " Loyalism in New York," pp. 23, 24;
Van Tyne, " Loyalist of the American Revolution," pp. 87, 88, 116;
Political Science Quarterly, vol. xviii, pp. 44, 45; *American Historical
Review*, vol. ix, pp. 60, 66; New York Historical Society Collections, 1877,
p. 360; Gordon, " American Revolution," edition 1788, vol. i, pp. 365; 372;
American Archives, fourth series, vol. i, p. 819.

But it was impossible to foresee in the year 1774 what the Congress would do, and England had never before had such an experience. The subject was discussed, however, in some interesting correspondence between Lord Dartmouth and Lieutenant-Governor Colden of New York.

"An attempt by the power of the civil magistrates," said Colden, "would only show their weakness, and it is not easy to say upon what foundation a military aid should be called in; such a measure would involve us in troubles, which it is thought much more prudent to avoid; and to shun all extremes, while it is yet possible things may take a more favorable turn."—*American Archives*, fourth series, vol. i, p. 517; also Jones, "New York in the Revolution," vol. i, pp. 468–475.

The truth was that England was so hopelessly weak in military force in America that it would have been extremely difficult for those of her statesmen who feared the effects of the Congress to take any strong measures. The Revolution had already progressed so far that no governor, except in Canada, had sufficient power to prevent the election or assembling of the delegates. Some people thought the Congress should be suppressed; but most Englishmen saw no danger in it. "Nobody," says Hutchinson, writing from London, "seems to give themselves the least concern about the consequences of the projected Congress, supposing it can do no hurt to the kingdom."[4]

After the election Governor Colden congratulated himself and the Ministry that no attempt at repression had been made. "If the government had interfered," he said, "the most violent men would have gained great advantage, and would have prevented the acquiescence in the nomination of moderate men, which has now taken place."[5]

The only governor who succeeded in checking for a time the election of delegates was Wentworth of New Hampshire. Learning that the committee of correspondence was about to meet and hold the election, he appeared before them accompanied by his council and the sheriff; rebuked them in a set

---

[4] "Diary and Letters of Thomas Hutchinson," vol. i, pp. 221, 415, 419.
[5] *American Archives*, fourth series, vol. i, pp. 669, 782, 783.

speech, and the sheriff ordered them to disperse. But soon afterwards the patriots in the different parishes secretly chose persons to meet at Exeter and appoint the delegates; and this plan the governor found himself unable to obstruct.

In Canada the governor would have been strong enough to stop the delegates; but the patriot party was so few in numbers and so weak that they made no attempt to send any. In Georgia there were some patriots, but they were not yet organized; and in Florida, which had recently come from under Spanish rule, there were practically no patriots.

As for breaking up the Congress when it assembled, that could no doubt have been done with a comparatively small force. But as the Congress had been avowedly called for a redress of grievances, and there was a great difference of opinion among the patriots as to paying for the tea, it was supposed that the Congress might as likely as not turn out to be a conservative body that would favor the empire rather than independence, take the controversy out of the passions of local politics, and advise Boston to comply with the Port Bill and pay for the tea.[6]

---

[6] *American Archives*, fourth series, vol. i, pp. 516, 517, 536, 669, 742, 782, 783, 880, 1062.

XX.

THE CONGRESS GIVES ENGLAND AN ULTIMATUM

THE Congress held its sessions in Philadelphia in a neat brick building used by a sort of guild called the Carpenters' Company, and both the building and the guild are still in existence. The session lasted from the 5th of September until the 26th of October, a delightful time of year to be in the metropolis of the colonies and discuss great questions of state.

Fifty-two delegates finally assembled. Most of them were able and some became very conspicuous men. Whatever intentions they may have had as to ultimate independence, most of them seem to have thought that it would be well to act as conservatively as possible. But John and Samuel Adams, Cushing, and Paine, were inclined to break through all restraint. Coming from Boston, crippled and suffering under the exactions of the Port Bill, these Massachusetts delegates were very violent. They were known to be so hot for extreme measures that some of the patriots rode out to them before they reached Philadlphia, and warned them to be careful and not to utter the word independence.[1]

From Virginia came Randolph, Washington, Henry, Bland, Harrison, and Pendleton, the best delegates of all, calm, judicious, earnest patriots with a very broad range of ability. From South Carolina came Middleton, John Rutledge, Gadsden, Lynch, and Edward Rutledge, who were almost if not quite the equals of the Virginians. Pennsylvania sent a very conservative but not a very strong delegation. Galloway was the only eminent man in it. A few weeks later Dickinson was added; and a year or two later the addition of Robert Morris, Franklin, and Dr. Rush made a considerable change both in

---

[1] John Adams, Works, vol. ii, p. 512.

its ability and conservatism. The little community of Delaware sent three good men,—McKean, Rodney, and Read. From New York John Jay was the only delegate who afterwards attained much prominence.

The delegates and the townsfolk seem to have enjoyed most thoroughly the excitement of that session of nearly two months. The early steps of a rebellion are easy and fascinating. The golden October days and the bracing change to the cool air of autumn were a delightful medium in which to discuss great questions; see and hear the ablest and most attractive men from the colonies; and dine at country places and the best inns. It was a mental enlargement and an experience which must have been long remembered by every one.

Every form of festivity and pleasure-going increased. Many who afterwards were loyalists, or neutrals, could as yet be on friendly terms with patriots; for was not the avowed intention merely to accomplish redress of grievances? No one had ever seen the streets so crowded with the bright and gay colors of the time. We read in Adams's diary that one of the delegates from New Jersey was very much condemned because he "wore black clothes and his own hair." Everybody saw all the delegates, and there were few who could not boast of having had a word with some of them in the streets, shops, or market-place.

Philadelphia was at that time a pretty place on the water-side. The houses, wharves, warehouses, and inns were scattered in picturesque confusion along the river front from Vine Street to South Street, a distance of exactly one mile. Westward, the town reached back from the river about half a mile—to the present Fifth Street. The chime of bells in the steeple of Christ Church was an object of great interest. These bells played tunes on market days, as well as Sundays, for the edification of the country people, who had come in with their great wagon-loads of poultry and vegetables.

John Adams relates how he and some of the delegates climbed up into the steeple of Christ Church and looked over all the roofs of the town, and saw the country with its villas and woods beyond. It was their first bird's-eye view of the metropolis of the colonies of which they had so often heard; and they thought it a wonderful sight.

The Philadelphia Library, founded by Franklin and James Logan, had its rooms in the Carpenters' Hall. The directors of the library passed a vote giving the Congress free use of all the books. No doubt some of them worked hard among the volumes, burying themselves in Grotius, Puffendorf, Burlamaqui, and Locke. It was their duty to understand the state of nature and the natural rights of man; those arguments which showed that rebellion was sometimes not treason. They must have read with hard, uneasy faces the recent heroic struggles, but sad fate, of Corsica, of Poland, and of Sweden.

Both John and Samuel Adams and all of the Massachusetts delegates pressed hard for resolutions which would commit all the colonies to the cause of Boston, as Boston had chosen to make her cause. She would not yield, would not pay for the tea, would not pay damages of any sort. The British troops must be withdrawn, the Boston Port Bill must be repealed, the act altering the government of Massachusetts must be repealed, and also the ten or twelve other acts which were not acceptable in America. The Congress sat with closed doors, and nothing, as a rule, was known of their proceedings except the results which took the shape of certain documents, which shall be discussed in their place. There was, however, one act of the Congress known as the approval of the Suffolk resolutions, which became known at the time of its occurrence, which committed the Congress irrevocably to the cause of Boston and marked a turning-point in the Revolution.

Paul Revere, deserting his silversmith shop and his engraving tools, rode to and fro from Boston to Philadelphia on horseback, carrying documents and letters in his saddle-bags. He had already, it appears, on several occasions during the Massachusetts disturbances, voluntarily acted as messenger in this way. He was evidently fond of horses. He had been shut up for so many years hammering out silverware, tea-pots and sugar-bowls, and wearing out his eyesight with engraving-tools, that he no doubt found himself delighted with this excuse for riding over the wild woodland roads of the colonies.

Town meetings having been prohibited in Massachusetts by act of Parliament, the patriots of Suffolk County, in which Boston was situated, held a county meeting, which was not prohibited in the act, and this meeting passed the famous Suffolk resolutions and sent them by Paul Revere to the Congress. The purpose of these resolutions was to create a new government for Massachusetts, independent of the government under the charter as modified by Parliament and now administered by General Gage. To that end the Suffolk resolutions declared that no obedience was due from the people to either the Boston Port Bill or to the act altering the charter; that no regard should be paid to the present judges of the courts, and that sheriffs, deputies, constables, and jurors must refuse to carry into execution any orders of the courts. Creditors, debtors, and litigants were advised to settle their disputes amicably or by arbitration. This had the effect desired and abolished the administration of the law for a long period in Massachusetts,—a period extremely interesting to political students for the ease with which the people, by tacit consent, got on without the aid of courts or juries.

The resolutions further recommended that collectors of taxes and other officials having public money in their hands should retain those funds and not pay them over to the government under Gage until all disputes were settled. The persons who had accepted seats on the council board under the Gage government were bluntly told that they were wicked persons and enemies of the country, which was in effect to turn the mob upon them at the first opportunity. The patriot inhabitants of each town were instructed to form a militia, to learn the art of war as speedily as possible, but for the present to act only on the defensive. If any patriots were seized or were arrested, officials of the Gage government must be seized and held as hostages. All this was rather vigorous rebellion, which could not be leniently regarded in England; and, finally, it was recommended that all the towns of the colony should choose delegates to a provincial congress to act in place of the assembly under the Gage government.

This provincial congress suggested by the Suffolk resolutions was elected and became the government of Massachusetts for a long period during the Revolution. It is quite obvious that the resolutions were in effect a declaration of independence by the patriots of Massachusetts, although the word independence was not used. If Congress approved of them, approved of a government set up by the patriots in hostility to the British government, it was certainly committing the rest of the colonies to an open rebellion and war unless England was willing to back down completely, as she had done in the case of the Stamp Act and in the case of the Paint, Paper, and Glass Act.

Besides creating a new government for Massachusetts the Suffolk resolutions contained some strong expressions not likely to assist the cause of peace. England was described as a parricide aiming a dagger at "our bosoms." The continent was described as "swarming with millions" who would not yield to slavery or robbery or allow the streets of Boston to be "thronged with military executioners." The people were described as originally driven from England by persecution and injustice, and they would never allow the desert they had redeemed and cultivated to be transmitted to their innocent offspring, clogged and fettered with foreign rule and tyranny.

Violent as were the Suffolk resolutions, the Congress approved of them in a resolution justifying the Massachusetts patriots in all they had done. If it had ever been a Congress for mere redress of grievances, it was now certainly changed and had become a Congress for making a new nation. The veil, as the loyalists said, was now drawn aside and independence stood revealed. From that moment the numbers of the loyalists rapidly increased. This new step separated them more and more from the patriots with whom many of them had heretofore been acting.[2]

There was an important and far-reaching measure of reconciliation proposed in the Congress, but it utterly failed. Galloway offered a plan which would in effect have been a constitutional union between the colonies and the mother-country. There was to be a Parliament or Congress elected by all the colonies and to hold its sessions at Philadelphia. It should be a branch of the Parliament in England, and no act relating to the colonies should be valid unless it was accepted by both the Parliament in Philadelphia and the Parliament in England. This would, it was said, settle all difficulties in the future; for it would be a practical method of obtaining the "consent of America," which the patriots were saying was necessary to the validity of an act of Parliament which was to be applied to the colonies.

The plan represented loyalist opinion, and would in their view have prevented all taxation or internal regulation, and have amply safeguarded all the liberties for which the patriots were contending. There was sufficient conservatism in the Congress to approve of it so far as to refer it under their rule for further consideration. But soon all proceedings connected with it were ordered to be expunged from the minutes so that they could never be read. As the meetings were secret, it may have been supposed that no news of it would get abroad. But the loyalists took pains to spread the history of it. They charged that the Congress had expunged the proceedings because they feared that the mass of the people might hear of the plan and be willing to have a reconciliation effected on such a basis without an attempt at independence. They circulated printed copies of the plan and declared that the attempt to

---

[2] " A Friendly Address to all Reasonable Americans, p. 32, New York, 1774; "The Congress Canvassed," p. 5, New York, 1774; "An Alarm to the Legislature of the Province of New York," New York, 1775; "Free Thoughts on the Proceedings of the Congress," New York, 1774; Jones, "New York on the Revolution," vol. i, p. 36.

suppress it by expunging showed a clear intention to secretly kill all efforts at reconciliation.[3]

The Congress closed its session, and Wednesday, the 26th of October, was the last day. Many of the members appear to have lingered for a day or two longer. But on Friday there was a general exodus. It was raining hard, John Adams tells us in his diary, as he took his departure from Philadelphia, which he described as "the happy, the peaceful, the elegant, the hospitable, and the polite." There was perhaps a covert sneer in the words. He had found it too peaceful, too elegant, too polite and happy to be as enthusiastic for independence as himself and his colleagues.[4]

It was not likely, he said, that he would ever see Philadelphia again, by which he may have meant that the British lion would surrender to the requirements of the patriots, and there would be no occasion for calling another meeting of the Congress. The Congress, however, had taken the precaution to provide for another meeting in the following May, "unless the redress of grievances, which we have desired, be obtained before that time"; and John Adams himself writing in his old age, more than forty years afterwards, said that in that autumn of 1774 he had told Patrick Henry that all the documents of the Congress, though "necessary to cement the union of the colonies, would be but waste water in England."[5]

In the minds of many the documents of the Congress were more for the purpose of uniting the colonies and strengthening the cause of independence than for effecting any sort of possible reconciliation with England. Henry, it seems, agreed with Adams that the action of the Congress would never be accepted in England, and there were others who held the same view. Joseph Hawley summed up the situation by saying: "After all, we must fight." But some, like Richard Henry

---

[3] John Adams, Works, vol. ii, p. 387; *American Archives*, fourth series, vol. i, p. 1234.

[4] John Adams, Works, vol. ii, p. 402.

[5] Niles, *Register*, vol. xiv, p. 258.

Lee, professed to believe that the Congress would carry all its points; all the objectionable acts of Parliament would be repealed, and the fleet and army would be recalled from Boston.

The documents which were to produce this result had been carefully prepared by the Congress and sent to England; and they were soon made public to all the world in newspapers and pamphlets.

The first of them was called "The Declaration of Rights," and is profoundly interesting as displaying the patriot reasoning against the colonial relationship. It was the ultimatum which the patriots offered to the mother country to accept or reject. It required that England should repeal thirteen acts of Parliament, the Boston Port Bill, the act changing the government of Massachusetts, the Quebec Act, all the old acts for imposing duties on molasses, wine, and other articles, and extending the powers of the admiralty courts, together with the acts for keeping troops in America without the consent of the colonies, and for carrying to England for trial persons accused of certain offences. No colonies before or since, have ever been in a position to demand such a sweeping change. It must be confessed that it was a rather stiff demand, and hard for England to accept, because it in effect abolished her colonial system.

The rest of the document argued out the question very much as we have already described it as argued in the pamphlets of the time, except that the Congress stopped just short of the most extreme views of the pamphlets. There had been great difference of opinion in the Congress as to whether they should deny that Parliament had any authority at all in the colonies. Dickinson repeated his argument of the "Farmer's Letters" that Parliament should have no power whatever in the colonies, but might be allowed to regulate the external commerce of the empire provided it could be done without duties and taxation for revenue. But others like the Adamses and Gadsden would allow Parliament no power of any kind. America and England, so far as their legislatures were concerned, must be independent communities. But they might recognize perhaps a common king.*

The vote was for a long time about evenly divided; and every phase of the subject was debated. In the end Dickinson's view prevailed. The king was to retain his power of vetoing the laws of the colonial assemblies; and the power of Parliament over the colonies was to be abolished except as regards "our external commerce for the purpose of securing the commercial advantages of the whole empire." But this regulation of external commerce must not be accomplished by taxation of any kind for raising a revenue.

This small scrap of impossible power left to Parliament was no doubt a wise concession which quieted many timid patriots. It meant nothing; for how could Parliament regulate colonial commerce without duties and penalties which would in effect be taxes and raise revenue; and would not England resent the cutting down of her imperial power to this insignificant and impossible privilege just as much as if they had decided to cut off Parliament's authority altogether?

The next document, "The Association," as it was called, was quite a remarkable and curious paper, signed by all the delegates on behalf of themselves and of those whom they represented, and was intended to be the most complete non-importation, non-exportation, and non-consumption agreement that had yet been attempted. The previous measures of this sort which had been so effective had been voluntary and tacit understandings carried out in a general way. But this association of the Congress was intended to be systematic, thorough, and compulsory. The whole British trade was interdicted, and punishments were most ingeniously provided for those merchants who would not obey.

Although it was in form only an agreement, yet it was worded as if it were a law passed by a legislative body. In some paragraphs we find it speaking as a mere agreement, as,

---

* John Adams, Works, vol. ii, pp. 374, 379, 393, 397; Snow, "Administration of Dependencies," pp. 284, 286, 290; *American Archives*, fourth series, vol. i, p. 541.

for example, "we will use our utmost endeavors to improve the breed of sheep;" or "we will, in our several States, encourage frugality, economy," etc. In other paragraphs it speaks in the language of a legislature:

"That a committee be chosen in every county, city, and town by those who are qualified to vote for representatives in the legislature, whose business it shall be attentively to observe the conduct of all persons touching this association."

A large part of the document is taken up with these positive commands, directing the committees of correspondence to inspect the entries in "their custom-houses"; directing owners of vessels to give positive orders to their captains, and directing that all manufactures be sold at reasonable prices.

The Congress, it must be remembered, had no law-making power. It was a mere convention, without the authority of law. Yet here it was adroitly assuming for itself legislative functions. From our point of view, it was a most interesting beginning of the instinctive feeling of nationality and union, the determination, consciously or unconsciously, to form a nation out of a convention that had been called merely for "a redress of grievances."

But the loyalists were unable to see it in this light. They attacked it at once as an usurpation; and they called on all the legislative assemblies of the colonies to protect themselves against this monster of a Congress, which would soon take away from them all their power. From a legal point of view the loyalist position was unquestionably sound, for the assemblies in each colony were the only bodies that had any law-making power. The Congress seemed to the loyalists to threaten an American republic, and their premonition was certainly justified by events:

"Are you sure," asks a loyalist, "that while you are supporting the authority of the Congress, and exalting it over your own legislature, that you are not nourishing and bringing to maturity a grand American Republic, which shall after a while rise to power and grandeur, upon the ruins of our present constitution. To me the danger appears more than possible. The outlines of it seem already to be drawn. We have had a grand Continental Congress at Philadelphia. Another is to meet in May next. There has been a Provincial Congress held in Boston government. And as all the colonies seem fond of imitating Boston politics, it is very probable that the scheme will spread and increase; and in a little time the *Commonwealth* be completely formed."—"The Congress Canvassed," p. 24, New York, 1774.

There was a considerable body of people at that time who assumed, as a matter of course, that an American republic would be anything but a blessing. They were still more shocked when they read in the association how the Congress intended to have its attempted laws and commands enforced. Those who would not obey the rules of the association against importing and exporting were to have their names published as enemies of the country, and no one was to buy of them or sell to them; they were to be cut off from intercourse with their fellows; to be ostracized and outlawed. In short, they were to be boycotted, as we would now say, and turned over to the mob.

In this arrangement and in the committees that were to pry about and act as informers, the loyalists saw a most atrocious violation of personal liberty. These county committees, who were given the judicial power to publish, denounce, and ruin people merely of their own motion, without any of the usual safeguards of courts, evidence, proof, or trial, would, they said, be worse than the Inquisition. How could the patriots, they said, consistently object to admiralty courts when they were setting up these extraordinary tribunals that could condemn men unseen and unheard? They looked forward to a long reign of anarchy; and their expectations were largely fulfilled. Men like John Adams admitted the injustice often inflicted by patriot committees, and dreaded the effect of it on American morals and character.[7]

The tenth article of the association provided that if any goods arrived for a merchant they were to be seized; if he would not reship them, they were to be sold, his necessary

---

[7] "The Congress Canvassed," pp. 14-20, New York, 1774; Adams, Works, vol. iii, p. 34; "The Two Congresses Cut Up," Boston, 1774, pp. 8, 9; Van Tyne, "Loyalists," pp. 63, 69. For the injustice of forcing the paper money upon the people at its par value, see Phillips, "Sketches of American Paper Currency," vol. ii, pp. 63, 65, 67, 79, 154, 158.

charges repaid, and the profits to go to the poor of Boston. In other words, said the loyalists, a man's private property is to be taken from him, without his consent, by the "recommendation" of a Congress that has no legal power; and the same Congress is sending petitions to England arguing that Parliament cannot tax us because it would be taking our property without our consent.

It would be easy to multiply these inconsistencies; and the more the loyalists called attention to them the more the patriots felt compelled to violate personal liberty in suppressing the loyalists, until free speech was extinguished and thousands of loyalists driven from the country. On a smaller scale, and with less wholesale atrocity, it was like the French Revolution, in which we are told that "the revolutionary party felt themselves obliged to take stringent measures; that is, the party which asserted the rights of man felt themselves obliged to refuse to those who opposed them the exercise of those rights." [8]

Every provision in the association shows a people who were uniting in a struggle for nationality, and therefore cared little for their inconsistencies or violation of rights. Struggles for independence are not apt to be tame or necessarily legal. There is nothing so elementary and natural as the nation-forming instinct; its efforts are always violent; and in such a contest the laws are thrust aside.

For the milder forms of this struggle, as shown in the association, we find them agreeing to kill as few lambs as possible, to start domestic manufactures, and encourage agriculture, especially wool, so as to be independent of England in the matter of clothing. And they were trying to be economical, to discourage horse-racing, gaming, cock-fighting, shows, and plays, to discontinue the slave trade, and to give up the extravagant mourning-garments and funerals which were so excessive and expensive at that time.

Another document put forth by the Congress was "The Address to the People of Great Britain." It claimed for the

---

[8] Ropes, " Napoleon," p. 8.

Americans all the privileges of British subjects, the right of disposing of their own property and of ruling themselves. Why should "English subjects, who live three thousand miles from the royal palace, enjoy less liberty than those who are three hundred miles distant from it?" Like all the other documents, it had much to say about the wickedness of the Quebec Act, which had established Roman Catholicism in Canada; and it restated all the patriot arguments against control by Parliament.

The most striking part of it was an argument that if the ministry were allowed to tax and rule America as they pleased, the enormous streams of wealth to be gathered from such a vast continent, together with the Roman Catholic inhabitants of Canada, would be used to inflict the most atrocious persecution and tyranny on the masses of the people in England. This attempt to excite the English masses against Parliament and the ministry was very much resented in England, and was not likely to bring a favorable compromise any more than was a similar attempt to arouse rebellion in Ireland, which was tried the next year.

Another document, called "An Address to the Inhabitants of Canada," was much ridiculed by both the loyalists and the English, because it seemed so very inconsistent with "The Address to the People of Great Britain." In addressing the people of Great Britain the Congress vilified and abused the religion of the Canadians as despotism, murder, persecution, and rebellion. Yet they asked those same Canadians to join the rebellious colonies against England; and they sent to them a long document instructing them in their rights, and quoting Montesquieu and other Frenchmen, to show what a mistake they were making by submitting to the tyranny of Great Britain. The Canadians, said the loyalists, would, of course, see both documents and laugh at the Congress.[*]

The last paper put forth by the Congress was "The Peti-

---

[*] Codman, "Arnold's Expedition to Quebec," p. 9. All the documents put forth by the Congress and also the Suffolk Resolution can be read in full in "Journals of the American Congress," 1774–1788, vol. i.

tion to the King," drawn by Dickinson and intended to soften the denial of the authority of Parliament by showing that, although Parliament was rejected and no allegiance to it admitted, yet the colonists were willing to accept the King as general head of the British empire. He was implored to protect them from the usurpations of Parliament and the Ministry; to obtain for them a repeal of the Boston Port Bill, the Quebec Act and all the other objectionable legislation of recent years; and to remedy all their other grievances, which were again recited in full. The Congress was therefore not rebellious or disloyal; for were they not showing the greatest loyalty and the most unquestioning devotion to the King?

In line with this petition was a banquet given in the State House to the members of the Congress about the middle of September by some of the prominent citizens of Philadelphia. It was evidently one of those magnificent colonial entertainments, frequent in Philadelphia in those days, with tables loaded down with every imaginable form of food, drink, and delicacy. There were thirty-two formal toasts carefully prepared to support ardent patriotism and at the same time to favor "A happy reconciliation between Great Britain and her colonies on constitutional ground." Every toast was accompanied by a discharge of cannon followed by music, cheers, and shouts from the five hundred guests.[10]

All these demonstrations and dinners being finished, the documents having been sent forth and the Congress adjourned, the people settled down to comparative quietude for the whole of the following winter. There was nothing more to be said, because what had been done had been done, and there was no help for it. The result must be calmly awaited during four or five months while the vessels that communicated with England should beat their way over and back against the winter gales of the Atlantic.

---

[10] Jones, "New York in the Revolution," vol. i, pp. 475, 476; John Adams, Works, vol. ii, pp. 379, 387, 374, 393, 397, 423, 539; Niles, *Register*, vol. xiv, p. 258, No. 16, July 13, 1818; Snow, "Administration of Dependencies," pp. 284, 286, 290, etc.

XXI.

THE RISE AND NUMBERS OF THE LOYALISTS

As it is from the year 1774 that we date the rise of the loyalists as a distinct and powerful party, it will contribute to a clearer understanding of the Revolution to give the main features of their history at this point in our narrative. As the patriot position became more pronounced and leaned more towards independence, it naturally developed the feeling and opposition of the loyalists. They were compelled to take a distinct, outspoken position of their own, and their numbers were greatly increased.

In their origin and principles they were a party which is apt to appear whenever the question of independence arises, whenever a country or a party within a country wishes complete self-government and separation from an empire or an alien control. In all the histories of struggles for independence, in Poland, Greece, Switzerland, the South American republics, Mexico, Cuba, and in the South African difficulties of Cape Colony, the Transvaal, and the Orange Free State, we find a loyalist party arguing in favor of alien control as necessary to peace and order; or as more beneficial to business stability, prosperity, morals, and progress; and such loyalists often have a passionate belief in their creed which they are ready to seal with their blood.

The loyalists of the American Revolution were in some respects more sincere and more in earnest than the mother-country. They were less willing to quit the game; they believed that England gave up too easily and made peace when the patriots were on the verge of exhaustion. They seemed more anxious to have America conquered and reduced to complete dependence under the empire than the English generals or the Tory Ministry that carried on the war. They were thorough believers in empire as against independence.

240

CONTEMPT FOR LOYALISTS

The fatal defect in the loyalist position was its unnaturalness. They gave their devotion not to the land they lived in, and the government and social system that would naturally grow from that soil. They loved and worshipped a country and a government three thousand miles away. They had vaguely magnificent ideas that the colonists should support and encourage the superiority of England, join her in vast schemes of conquest, and reap some enormous reward in the plunder of inferior peoples in Asia, Africa, and India. The desire of the patriot party to own America as their own country was, the loyalists said a mere "sentiment of self importance," too ridiculous to be mentioned in the presence of the "power and splendor of Great Britain." All the loyalist writings and arguments are filled with this awe-struck admiration for the wonderful British constitution and the glorious British empire. Such devotion to a distant excellence, an excellence not of our own creation and environment, is both political and spiritual degeneration. In the long run nothing but contempt awaits the men who will not stand by their own, who weakly wish to be ruled by a foreign power for the sake of what they suppose to be a superior refinement or civilization.[1]

Previous to the year 1774 most of the people who afterwards became loyalists had supported the measures for resisting taxation and had been in favor of not importing English goods, and of cutting off all trade with England in order to bring her to terms. Such measures they regarded as a legal and constitutional means for redressing grievances in which loyal colonists could with perfect propriety take a part. Some of them went a little farther, and held that a mild show of force against Great Britain would be allowable; and those who held this view continued to act with the patriots until the adoption of the Declaration of Independence, which they regarded as going altogether too far.

There had been, however, even in the times before 1774, a small but socially powerful loyalist party under the leadership

---

[1] See for example Eddis, "Letters from America," pp. 139, 145, 149.

of the government officials and some of the Anglican clergy who defended taxation by the mother-country, approved of the stamp tax, and denounced the Stamp Act Congress as unconstitutional and unlawful. These early loyalists were extremely consistent, and foreseeing; for they believed that they saw in the proceedings of the patriots the beginning of open rebellion.[2]

It is a mistake, however, to infer, as most of us have done, that the loyalism which finally developed was altogether an affair of the Episcopal clergy and their people and government officials, or that it was an affair merely of the upper classes. The loyalist pamphleteers and leaders were, it is true, usually lawyers, clergymen, doctors, or officials, like Leonard, Sewall, Hutchinson or Oliver of Massachusetts; or Isaac Hunt, Galloway, Kearsley, or the Allen family of Philadelphia; or the Rev. Dr. Cooper and Isaac Wilkins of New York; or such Anglican clergymen as Seabury, Chandler, Inglis, and Vardhill. But the rank and file of the party was composed of all faiths—Presbyterians, Lutherans, Roman Catholics, Methodists, and Quakers; of all races and nationalities—English, Dutch, German, French, Irish, Scotch, Indians, and Negroes; and of all classes of society from cobblers, blacksmiths, and farmers up to rich merchants, lawyers, and gentlemen.[3]

At the time of the Revolution a large part of the lower classes of our people were more or less on the loyalist side, because of the habit of dependence on England, fear of change or lack of conviction of any material advantage in Americanism. As William Wirt long ago pointed out in his "Life of Patrick Henry," the Revolution originated among the upper classes of Americans, among rich planters, merchants, and lawyers, who led the masses into the movement often very much against their will. The whole fabric and foundation of the

---

[2] New York *Mercury*, May 20, 1765, No. 708; June 17, 1765, No. 712; New York Assembly Journal, vol. ii, p. 787; New York Historical Society Collection, 1877, pp. 35, 61; Jones, "New York in the Revolution," vol. i, p. 34; Dawson, "Westchester County," p. 11.

[3] Flick, "Loyalism in New York," p. 35; *American Archives*, fourth series, vol. vi, p. 1157.

Revolution, those long years of argumentation from 1764 to 1775, that basis of constitutional and legal reasoning, that application of the Reformation doctrines of the rights of man, could never have been wrought out in their perfection and finally expressed in effective language and drafted into state constitutions and governmental documents except by men of the highest education and training. No ignorant or untrained man, no upstart or mere popular demagogue can be found among the great leaders of the patriot party. It was the work of a Hamilton, a Jefferson, a Dickinson, the Adamses, the Lees, and the Rutledges, a Bland, a Mason, a Drayton, a Cushing, or a Laurens.

After the Revolution was over, however, all feeling of mental or moral dependence on England passed completely away from the masses of our people, who became American to the core as soon as they really tasted national independence. They saw their advantage in the rights of man, equality and all the other doctrines of the Revolution. But among many of our modern people of wealth and of fashion, among the collegiate and educated or over-educated classes, the feeling of mental and moral dependence on England is still often as strong as it was among the loyalists of the Revolution.

In New York the loyalist party was no doubt considerably dominated by the Anglican Church. In New England, also, the Anglican Church and loyalism were more or less closely associated, although the most notorious New England loyalist, Governor Hutchinson, was of the faith of the old Puritans. The masses of the patriot party in New England were encouraged by their Congregationalist preachers to favor independence as a means of escaping from English bishops, who, it was said, were to be sent over as part of the reorganization of the colonies. The bishops were magnified into monsters, and described as "biting beasts and whelps of the Roman litter," that would renew all the persecutions of Archbishop Laud.

But south of New York it can hardly be said that the Church of England was distinctly associated with loyalism. We must remember that Washington was an Anglican Churchman, and that most of the Virginia patriots, as well as a large proportion of the members of the Continental Congress, were of the same faith. In South Carolina the patriots were usually of the Church of England and only five out of twenty of the clergy were loyalists. The Rev. William White of Philadelphia, afterwards Bishop of Pennsylvania, was an ardent patriot; and loyalism in the neighborhood of Philadelphia was largely supported by the Quakers.

As time went on all sorts of influences contributed to the increase of the loyalists. Persons inclined to patriotism became wearied with the length of the war, its cruelties and atrocities; they were disheartened by the long interruption to business and money-making, and they lost hope of any final success. Such people gradually drifted to the loyalist party, until it was composed of many shades of opinion and under the influence of a variety of motives.

As to the actual numbers of the loyalists, there has been great diversity of opinion. No census was taken, and there is no collection of statistics by which we can learn the relative numbers of loyalists and patriots. It is all estimating and guessing; and in this respect the men who took part in the Revolution were not much better off than we are.

The loyalists themselves always believed that they were a majority. Twenty-five thousand of them, and according to some accounts fifty thousand, are said to have enlisted in the British army; and their writers have been fond of citing a letter of Germain's in which he said that in 1781 there were more of them in the British army than there were soldiers in the patriot armies of the Congress. But these estimates were exaggerations. Clinton denied Germain's estimate, and showed that the loyalists in the British army at that time were only 8,168, while the Continental patriot troops numbered 9,400.[4]

----

[4] "In nearly every loyalists's letter," says Sabine, "or paper which I have examined, and in which the subject is mentioned, it is either assumed or stated in terms that the loyalists were the majority."— "American Loyalists," edition of 1847, p. 65; Ryerson, "Loyalists of America," vol. ii, pp. 57, 123; Niles, "Principles and Acts," p. 504;

NUMBERS OF LOYALISTS

When we examine all the various estimates which were made of their numbers by their contemporaries, we find the most extraordinary disagreement. Harry Lee estimated them at one tenth of the whole population. John Adams, writing in 1780, estimated them at not more than a twentieth. In 1815 he estimated them at a little more than a third. Galloway, in his examination before Parliament, and in one of his pamphlets, estimated them at nine-tenths and at four-fifths. General Robertson, in his testimony before the committee on the conduct of the war, estimated them at two-thirds. He described the population as one-third for the Congress, one-third neutral, and one-third loyal, which he thought gave two-thirds which could be called loyal.

These discrepancies may possibly be reconciled by defining what is meant by the term loyalist. There were, in a general way, four classes of persons to whom the name could be applied. The first class was composed of people who were thoroughly English, untouched by the American environment and not only uninfluenced by the rights-of-man and Whig principles, but loathing and detesting everything of that kind. Most of these people finally left the country and went to live in England, Canada, or the West Indies. That very muscular Christian, Rev. Dr. Boucher, of Maryland, was of this class; and perhaps Jonathan Sewall and Daniel Leonard might be included in it.

The second class were somewhat more Americanized. They were anxious to remain; but they wished the country to be ruled by England. They had no confidence in any other rule. They were willing to argue and struggle in a "legal and constitutional manner," as they called it, for greater privileges, or for "redress of grievances"; but if England decided against

B. F. Stevens, Clinton–Cornwallis Controversy, vol. i, p. 335; vol. ii, p. 83; Van Tyne, "Loyalists of the American Revolution," pp. 172, 183; Stedman, American War, vol. ii, pp. 168, 448; Johnson, Life of General Greene, vol. i, pp. 257–260. In the preface to the correspondence of German published in 1784 it is very positively asserted "that the American loyalists alone were superior in numbers to the rebels," B. F. Stevens, *supra*, vol. ii, p. 308.

them that would end the matter. These were the people who were willing to accept British rule without "guarantees of liberty," having full confidence that in the long run that rule would be satisfactory, and that the "guarantees" which the patriots demanded were unnecessary. They were strong believers in the empire, and wished to live in colonies which were part of the empire. Curwen, of Massachusetts, and Van Schaack, of New York, who have left us such interesting memoirs, seem to have been of this class; so also were some of the De Lancey family of New York, and Joseph Galloway and the Allen family, of Pennsylvania.

The great stumbling-block with these people was the Declaration of Independence. In the early stages of the Revolution they had acted with the patriots and prevented any distinct line of demarcation between the parties. But when the movement for independence showed itself strongly, as in the approval by the Congress of the Suffolk resolutions, they began to drop out of the patriot ranks; and when it became evident that there was to be an open declaration of independence, they went out in greater numbers. They were often treated with contempt by British officers, and called "whitewashed rebels"; and the well-to-do among them were sometimes informed that by their former association with the rebels they had forfeited their right to be treated as gentlemen. A very large proportion of this second class left the country before the war was over and never returned.

These two classes included all that could be strictly called loyalists. But the term was often applied to the neutrals and those who, for want of a better name, may be called the hesitating class. The neutrals would have nothing to do with the contest either one way or the other. Most of the Quakers of Pennsylvania, and many of the Pennsylvania Germans, who held the same religious belief as the Quakers, were neutrals. There were also all sorts of persons scattered over the country who held entirely aloof, and are properly described as neutral.

The hesitating class have sometimes been described as the people who were wondering on which side their bread was buttered. Some of them would at times enlist for a few weeks with the patriots; but a patriot disaster would scatter them; and many of them deserted to the British or took the British oath of allegiance, which they not infrequently broke at the first opportunity.

Most of them, however, never enlisted at all. They were more or less willing that the patriots should win; but they were waiting for that event to happen. All through the Revolution we hear of the prominent ones among them, especially in New York, going over to the British side, having made up their minds that at last the current had set that way. In the dark days of 1780 a great many of them went over, and these defections were particularly numerous in the Southern colonies.

When these classes were counted together, there was a certain amount of plausibility in General Robertson's saying that the loyalists were two-thirds of the people; and when Galloway says that they were four-fifths or nine-tenths, he was evidently counting, with considerable exaggeration, all the people that could be in any way relied upon, positively or negatively, to assist the British cause.[*]

When Adams said that the loyalists were only one-twentieth of the people, he was interested in making their numbers seem as small as possible, and we may assume that he was speaking only of the extreme loyalists, possibly only of the class first mentioned. He was then in Amsterdam trying to persuade the Dutch to take the side of the American patriots with loans of money, if not by actual war. He was answering a request of the famous Dutch lawyer, Calkoen, who had asked him "to prove by striking facts that an implacable hatred of England reigns throughout America," and, "to show that this is gen-

---

[*] Since the first edition of this work appeared the analysis made by Dr. Rush in 1777 has been published and agrees substantially with mine. (*Pennsylvania Magazine of History*, vol. xxvii, pp. 143–145. See, also, Van Tyne, "Loyalists of the American Revolution," p. 158.) Washington speaks of "half tories," as he calls them, who could under certain circumstances be employed as spies. (Writings of Washington, Ford edition, vol. vii, p. 345.)

eral, that the Tories are in so small a number and of such little force that they are counted as nothing.''

Adams complied to the best of his ability, and did not think it necessary to count the neutrals and hesitating class, or to exaggerate at all the numbers of the extreme loyalists. Many years after the Revolution, in 1813, he said that the loyalists had been about a third, and he was then evidently counting the first and second classes. In 1815 he said substantially the same, and gives an interesting estimate which is very like that of General Robertson.[*]

"I should say that full one-third were averse to the Revolution. These, retaining that overweening fondness, in which they had been educated, for the English, could not cordially like the French; indeed, they most heartily detested them. An opposite third conceived a hatred for the English, and gave themselves up to an enthusiastic gratitude to France. The middle third, composed principally of the yeomanry, the soundest part of the nation, and always averse to war, were rather lukewarm to both England and France; and sometimes stragglers from them, and sometimes the whole body, united with the first or last third, according to circumstances."—Adams, Works, vol. x, p. 110 .

The violence, the tar and feathers, and the restricted freedom of speech must, as Sabine points out, have turned many patriots into loyalists. Many who sympathized with patriot principles tried to check what they considered the patriot disorders and the violation of the rights of person and property. But failing in this, and being treated with suspicion, abuse, and contempt, they were forced in self-defence into the ranks of the loyalists.

After hostilities began and the Revolution was well under way, the loyalists were a minority in Virginia and in New England, but probably a majority in New York and in Georgia. In South Carolina they are said to have been a minority in the eastern part of the State and a majority in the western. In

[*]Adams, Works, vol. vii, p. 270; vol. x, pp. 63, 110, 193; *American Historical Review*, vol. i, p. 27; "View of the Evidence, etc., on Conduct of General Howe," pp. 46, 50; Lee, Memoirs, vol. i, p. 212, note. See, also, Egerton, "Origin and Growth of English Colonies," edition 1903, p. 160.

Pennsylvania, Maryland, and New Jersey, they are supposed to have been evenly balanced, each side claiming the majority. Even in New England and Virginia the loyalists were more numerous than is generally supposed.

General Reed thought that the loyalists might be a majority in Pennsylvania. In 1781 he said that the majority of people from New York southward were in the British interest; and he probably included in this description all classes of loyalists including possibly the hesitating class just described. General Greene, writing from South Carolina, described the people as at first about "equally divided between the King's interest and ours"; but afterwards the loyalists were in the majority because many patriots had left the country. In North Carolina he said the loyalists were more numerous than the patriots.[7]

There would probably not have been so many loyalists if the patriots had not been under the necessity of seeking an alliance with France. It was generally admitted on all sides that independence was impossible without French assistance; and many of the colonists could not endure the thought of begging assistance from the great Roman Catholic power, the hereditary enemy of the English race, that had been fought for generations in Canada, and that being devoted to despotism would never really give independence, but would use the opportunity to inflict on America the worst form of colonialism and destroy the protestant religion.

In a carefully prepared letter which in October, 1776, was sent to France by the secret committee of Congress, the loyalists are described as so numerous that they were more dangerous than the British army:

"The only source of uneasiness amongst us arises from the number of Tories we find in every State. They are more numerous than formerly and speak openly; but Tories are now of various kinds and various principles. Some are so from real attachment to Britain, some from interested views, many, very many, from fear of the British force; some because they are dissatisfied with the general measures of Congress, more

---

[7] "Life of Joseph Reed," by W. B. Reed, vol. ii, pp. 351, 352, 358, 372; Johnson, Life of General Greene, vol. i, pp. 257–260.

because they disapprove of the men in power and the measures in their respective States; . . . and if America falls, it will be owing to such divisions more than the force of our enemies." (*American Archives*, fifth series, vol. ii, p. 821.)

An example of the way in which the large hesitating class could be worked upon and kept in the British interest is seen in the mischief which was believed to have been done by the captured British officers. They were paroled and put to board with families in villages throughout the country where they talked with the characteristic confidence of the true Briton.

"I am convinced," said Washington, "that more mischief has been done by the British officers who have been prisoners, than by any other set of people. During their captivity in the country they have confirmed the disaffected, converted many ignorant people, and frightened the lukewarm and timid by their stories of the power of Britain." (W. B. Reed, "Life of Joseph Reed," vol. ii, p. 27, note.)

We may also form some idea of the numbers of the loyalists when we learn that all through the Revolution they were leaving the country by thousands. Eddis describes them as beginning to leave Maryland as early as 1775; and after that we read of three thousand leaving here, four thousand there, twelve thousand at another place, up even to one hundred thousand, that are said to have left when Sir Guy Carleton evacuated New York.[8]

In spite of all these migrations the patriots found it necessary, all through the Revolution, to banish, confiscate, lessen their numbers, and break their spirit in every possible way. Some of the severest measures were taken against them after peace was declared, and this is said to have caused the great migration with Sir Guy Carleton. Many of them became convinced that there would be no use in trying to live in the country even in peaceful times. There was quite a strong opinion among the patriots that if the extreme loyalists re-

[8] De Lancey's note to Jones' "New York in the Revolution," vol. ii, p. 504; Elizabeth Johnston, "Recollections of a Georgia Loyalist;" Eddis, "Letters from America," pp. 226, 230, 231, 232, 235, 272; Van Tyne, "Loyalists of the American Revolution," p. 293.

mained they would form a dangerous political party which would check the growth of nationality and watch every opportunity to assist England to recover some sort of suzerainty or control over America; and no doubt England had hopes of this for many years.

The province of New Brunswick in Canada was settled by loyalists, and cut off from Nova Scotia for their satisfaction and accommodation. They became also the founders of Upper Canada. They appear to have held extreme Tory opinions and were opposed to free institutions. They infused a strong English strain among the Canadian French and prevented that country becoming altogether French. Between forty and fifty thousand of them are believed to have entered Canada by the year 1786. Sir George Bourinot has described them as the founders of the present Dominion of Canada and imbued with the loftiest principles of self sacrifice. Animated with a feeling of intense animosity against the United States, both they and their descendants have shown this feeling in later times whenever questions of difference have arisen between ourselves and England.*

The serious effect which the neutrals and hesitating class had in increasing the strength of the loyalists and in weakening the patriots is seen in the number of Washington's forces. One of the most intelligent estimates of the number of the patriot population puts them at two-thirds, or, say, 1,400,000 out of the 2,200,000 white population. But if there were really 1,400,000 patriots, a great number of them were lukewarm or they would surely have furnished more than the ten or fifteen thousand men which Washington usually had for his battles. He should have had at least 50,000 out of a patriot population of 1,400,000; and, indeed, 50,000 is the number which the Congress always expected to have, but never obtained. They could never obtain 25,000 all told. For particular occasions considerable numbers could sometimes be raised, as, for example, the 20,000 at the time of the Battle of

---

* Bourinot, " Story of Canada," pp. 280, 292, 297.

Long Island, or the 11,000 at Brandywine. But between 5,000 and 10,000 were all that could be raised and maintained continuously.[10]

There was supposed to be quite a considerable patriot force composed of those who would not join Washington or any of the patriot armies, but who professed a willingness to consider themselves as militia to protect their own province from invasion, watch the loyalists or guard particular points. These troops may have been numerous on paper, but when called on for active service very few of them would appear. In May, 1776, the number of possible patriot troops was estimated at 80,000 in addition to which there were supposed to be 140,000 minute men. Pennsylvania, New Jersey, and New York would alone furnish, it was said, 35,000. But two months later, when these troops were called upon to prevent General Howe from taking New York, it was with the greatest difficulty and by drawing on all the New England, Middle, and Southern colonies that 20,000 ragged, half-armed militia could be collected, and of these only 14,000 were effectives.[11]

During the winter of 1777–78 the patriots must have been very few in number in Pennsylvania; for during that winter

---

[10] Writings of Washington, Ford edition, vol. i, p. 242; vol. viii, p. 235.

In the Boer War, in South Africa in the year 1900, the Boers of the Transvaal and Orange Free State did not number 300,000 and yet they put into the field an army of over 40,000. Their greater unanimity is, of course, easily explained, because they already had independence, which they were fighting to retain, while we were colonies rebelling to obtain independence.

An error has crept into some standard books of statistics, to the effect that the number of patriot troops in the Revolution was 231,959. These astonishing figures, so irreconcilable with Washington's returns and the reports of battles, grew out of some incomplete and random statements of General Knox, not at all intended to produce the inferences that were drawn from them. (See Massachusetts Historical Society Proceedings, second series, vol. ii, p. 204, where Mr. Justin Winsor deals with the subject.)

[11] Niles, " Principles and Acts of the Revolution," edition of 1826, p. 493. Jones, " New York in the Revolution," vol. i, p. 599.

PENNSYLVANIA LOYALISTS

Washington's small force of less than nine thousand men almost starved to death at Valley Forge. They were surrounded in every direction by a rich farming country. The British army of twenty thousand shut up in Philadelphia relied chiefly on ships which brought supplies up the river. But the farmers of the surrounding country voluntarily brought and sold their supplies to the British in Philadelphia, leaving the patriot army to starve. The few provisions Washington had were obtained by raiding these loyalist supply wagons on their way to Philadelphia and by sending far to the south in Virginia and the Carolinas.[12]

The country round Philadelphia was indeed overwhelmingly loyalist, as Washington found to his sorrow at the time of the Battle of the Brandywine; and we find much evidence to the same effect in the biography of General Reed.[13]

Many who believed in independence, and wished the patriot cause success, were very lukewarm in giving it assistance or enlisting in the army except perhaps for a few weeks. The pay was small and they could see no use, they said, in exerting themselves over much in a cause from which others would reap as much benefit as themselves.

After the first emotions are over, a soldier reasoned with upon the goodness of the cause he is engaged in, and the inestimable rights he is contending for, hears you with patience, and acknowledges the truth of your observation, but adds, that it is of no more importance to him than others. The officer makes you the same reply, with this further remark, that his pay will not support him, and he cannot ruin himself and family to serve his country when every member of the community is equally interested and benefitted by his labors.—Washington to Hancock, September 24, 1776.

---

[12] Sargent, " Life of André," p. 159; Galloway, " Letter to Right Honorable Lord Viscount Howe," p. 27, London, 1779; Cobbett, " Parliamentary History," vol. xx, p. 346; Parliamentary Register, vol. xiii, p. 464.

[13] Baker, " Itinerary of Washington," p. 92; " Life of Joseph Reed," by W. B. Reed, vol. i, pp. 305, 308, 313, 380. See, also, Niles, " Principles and Acts of the Revolution," edition of 1876, p. 227; Graydon, " Memoirs," edition 1846, pp. 34, 37.

The truth is that those who were really willing to risk themselves or their property in the cause of independence, and die in the last ditch, were comparatively few. There is every reason to suppose that they were less than a million. They were the heroic element, deeply inspired by the desire for a country of their own. Then there were those only a little inspired, who were willing that the heroes should perform the miracle of succeeding. But they could not see any advantage in risking their own necks, health, property, or comfort in the performance of something, which, after all, might be super-human. They were waiting and watching. If the rebellion were crushed they would be sorry, but they would also be safe.

After the Revolution had proved itself successful this class threw up their caps and shouted for independence. They were heroic at Fourth of July celebrations and in politics; they governed the country; and were inclined to ignore the old soldiers of the war.[14]

---

[14] W. B. Reed, "Life of Joseph Reed," vol. ii, pp. 372, 373; Johnson, Life of Greene, vol. ii, p. 453; also Graydon's Memoirs, where in several passages he complains that the majority which ruled the country after the Revolution was principally composed of the neutrals and hesitators who had stood aloof during the contest.

XXII.

THE METHODS OF SUPPRESSING THE LOYALISTS

THE loyalists were so numerous that the patriots had to resort to measures of the utmost severity for suppressing them. These measures amounted to another war, which if described in detail, would fill as much space in history as is usually given to the war with the British Army. But the details of the loyalist war are so shocking and unpleasant that they have usually been entirely omitted.

The loyalists were far more numerous than the British Army ever became. They were to be found in every county and village and in such places often in a decided majority. In some parts of the country it was necessary for the patriot militia to stay at home to overawe the loyalists and prevent them gaining control. In parts of Maryland and Delaware, in Monmouth County, New Jersey, and in various parts of New York, as in Westchester County, Long Island, and the region around Albany, they at times were in control; and in the Carolinas and Georgia they were still more numerous, materially assisted the British in subjugation, and were most murderous in their dealings with the patriots.[1]

In every part of the country they knew of all the doings of the patriots, all the movements of the patriot forces, and rendered the British spy system and secret service far-reaching and complete. Powder was stolen from the magazines of the patriots, stores of salt broken open, and horses and cattle driven to the British lines and sold. They supplied the British army with provisions as well as information; and were particularly useful in depreciating the value of the Continental paper-

---

[1] *American Archives,* fourth series, vol. vi, pp. 808, 83; fifth series, vol. i, p. 9; Gordon, " American Revolution," edition 1788, vol, ii, p. 426, 474; " Life of George Read," by W. T. Read, pp. 212, 213; Van Tyne, " Loyalists," pp. 162, 167.

money. The British army had presses for counterfeiting and printing this paper money, which was given in large quantities to the loyalists, and the more they circulated it the more it weakened the patriot cause. They would enlist in the patriot service, draw the bounty money, and then desert to the British. Washington often found his whole army, by reason of these methods, largely disaffected, and it was wonderful that he was able to hold it together.[2]

In Northern New York, near the Canada line, loyalist bands conducted savage raids, often in company with Indians, and inflicted barbarous cruelties on the patriots; and the massacres by loyalists and Indians in the Wyoming Valley of Pennsylvania, and in Cherry Valley, in New York, were the most merciless raiding of the war.

The loyalists enlisted in British regiments and were permitted to a certain extent to form military organizations of their own. In 1779 the British Government allowed them to commission privateers, which were fitted out in New York and had their station at Lloyd's Neck. Of the separate loyalist regiments, Tarleton's command was active in the southern campaigns, and the troops defeated at the battle of King's Mountain were Ferguson's loyalists. That battle was the only important engagement of the war in which the force on the British side was entirely loyalist. There was also a very active and in their own estimation very efficient regiment of loyalists known as the Queen's Rangers, commanded by Colonel Simcoe, who was afterwards governor of Canada. Robert Rogers, of New Hampshire, who had been a distinguished Indian fighter and partisan officer in the war against the French, joined the British and raised a regiment of loyalists who fought in the battles round New York in 1776. One of the DeLancey family of New York commanded another well-known loyalist regiment. There was the Royal Highland Regiment, composed of Scotch loyalists; the "Royal Invincible Americans," the "Royal Greens,"

[2] *American Archives*, fifth series, vol. ii, p. 821; also vol. i, p. 1492; also fourth series, vol. vi, p. 1072; Flick, "Loyalism in New York," p. 100.

Jessup's Battalion, Pieter's Corps, the "King's American Regiment," the New Jersey Volunteers, and others of which little can now be known. In Pennsylvania a loyalist regiment was raised among the Pennsylvania Germans, and another among the Irish, called "Rawdon's Volunteers of Ireland."[3]

Besides these and the ordinary enlistments in the regular British army, there were numerous temporary loyalist bands which preyed upon the patriots and inflicted serious loss and damage. During the British occupation of New York these bands raided in Connecticut and New Jersey, destroying property, pillaging and burning. This petty marauding warfare made the name of loyalist more detested than ever among the patriots.

Besides the damage to property, the loyalist bands were often active in seizing prominent patriots and bringing them prisoners to New York. Richard Stockton, a signer of the Declaration of Independence and a man of wealth and influence, was seized by a band of loyalists on the night of the 30th of November, 1776, while staying with John Covenhoven at Monmouth, New Jersey, and both he and Covenhoven carried to New York, where Stockton was imprisoned until his health was broken and his usefulness to the patriot cause destroyed. Prominent patriots in some places near the British army had to keep constantly on the move and dared not remain at home more than one day at a time.[4] If the loyalists had been encouraged to carry out this system more thoroughly, it might have been very disastrous to the patriots, for a little energy and enterprise might have captured the whole Continental Congress.

Joseph Galloway, a very prominent loyalist, who actively assisted the British army with information and advice, planned some daring enterprises which might have been terrible blows to the patriots had General Howe allowed them to be executed.

---

[3] David Fanning, Narrative, p. 79; Orderly Book of C. Jones, edited by R. L. Ford, in Brooklyn Historical Print Club; American Catholic Historical Researches, vol. 14, pp. 65–80; Caulkins, "History of New London," p. 546; Stedman, American War, vol. ii, p. 168.

[4] "Life of Joseph Reed," by W. B. Reed, vol. i, p. 359.

One of Galloway's plans was to seize the patriot governor, council and assembly of New Jersey; and he also prepared a plan for capturing the Continental Congress. Governor Tryon, of New York, had a similar plan to capture the New York Assembly, and there were several plans for seizing Washington, any one of which might by chance have been as successful and as effective as the capture of Richard Stockton, or General Funston's capture of the insurgent leader, Aguinaldo, in the Philippine Islands.

There was also the Hickey plot among the loyalists in New York, in June, 1776, to assassinate Washington and his staff officers and to blow up the patriot magazine. But fortunately for us, these staggering blows, which in other lands have changed dynasties or ended rebellions for liberty, were never delivered.[5]

It was evident that in the end England would have to rely upon the loyalists. Without their assistance, as Germain put it, "an attempt to subdue and retain dominion of the country will be fruitless." If the patriot party and its army had been conquered, Great Britain would have had to depend solely upon the loyalists to take possession of the various state governments and hold them in the interests of the empire.[6]

Nothing but the promptness of the patriot party in attacking the loyalists, disarming them, and breaking up their organization, saved American independence. The disarming was one of the first measures, and probably had more effect on the final result of the Revolution than any other method that was adopted. Disarming parties went from house to house and took away all loyalist weapons. This broke up their union and organization and prevented them taking advantage of their

---

[5] Van Tyne, "Loyalists," p. 161; Flick, "Loyalism in New York," pp. 100–115; Diary and Letters of Thomas Hutchinson, vol. ii, 259; Jones, "New York in the Revolution," vol. i, pp. 237, 238; David Fanning, Narrative, p. 79; *American Archives*, fourth series, vol. vi, pp. 1054, 1058, 1101, 1116, 1118, 1120.

[6] B. F. Stevens, Clinton-Cornwallis Controversy, vol. i, p. 461; vol. ii, pp. 85, 121, 179, 180; Van Tyne, "Loyalists," pp. 165, 167.

numbers. It was the foundation of all other measures. Without it all other measures might have been in vain, because the loyalists might have been able to resist them.

It was a method which the British Government had thought of using against the patriots; and they inquired of General Gage as to the feasibility of disarming all the people of certain provinces. But he replied that it would first be necessary to be in complete possession of the country, and for that he had not sufficient force. That was the great difficulty. The British army was not strong enough to protect the loyalists, and the loyalists were not prompt enough to protect themselves. They were always waiting for the British army to help them. They looked to the King and Parliament for protection. If they had been as full of the American atmosphere of energy and organization as were the patriots, they might have got the start with the disarming, and worked it to the suppression of independence.[7]

But loyalism seldom inspires as much aggressiveness and courage as patriotism. A few patriots are usually a match for almost twice their number of loyalists. Men do not throw their whole soul into the contest and fight with such desperate energy and intelligence for alien government as for separateness and nationality. In such wars the advantage at first is nearly always with the patriots, and loyalism, if it wins, usually conquers by overwhelming numbers, and great wealth and resources applied steadily and persistently for a long period.

The energy and promptness of the disarming parties soon collected in the revolutionary committee-rooms piles of curious and beautiful weapons, which would now be the delight of collectors. Duelling pistols, brass-barrelled pistols, holster pistols, blunderbusses, hangers, cutlasses, silver-hilted swords, morning swords, muskets, guns, belts, cartouch-boxes, powderhorns, and ammunition of all sorts, were brought in, labelled, listed, and appraised, so that they might be returned or paid for

---

[7] *American Archives*, fourth series, vol. i, p. 1046; vol. ii, p. 451; Van Tyne, "Loyalists," pp. 125, 128, 163.

after the war. In the spring of 1776 the Continental Congress became anxious that the measure should be more completely carried out, and recommended to all the colonies that all persons "notoriously disaffected to the cause of America" should be disarmed.[a]

But other systematic measures besides disarming were necessary, and these had to be kept up all through the Revolution; for there never was a day or an hour from 1774 to 1783 in which the patriots could relax their vigilance. There were two classes of measures, the regular procedure of district committees and State legislatures using imprisonment, banishment, and confiscation, and the violent, irregular procedure of mobs which used tar and feathers or other methods of terror and cruelty.

The committees of correspondence, which originated in Massachusetts and were adopted in all the colonies for encouraging and organizing the patriot party in its resistance to acts of Parliament, soon had a natural development into revolutionary committees of a more active character. These committees were known by various names, as Committees of Safety, Committees of Sixty, Committees of One Hundred. Town Committees, Precinct Committees, Committees of Inspection, Committees of Observation. There was often a District Committee, representing the patriots of a small locality like a township, and a County Committee, which acted in a larger field and had a certain controlling influence over the district committees. Above this was a general body for the whole province, elected by the patriots and usually called a convention, but in Massachusetts and New York it was called a provincial congress. It was in effect the patriot legislature of the province, and acted as such until as the Revolution progressed State constitutions and modern legislatures were adopted.

The investigation, trial, and punishment of loyalists was the principal work of the district and county committees; and as

_____
[a] *American Archives*, fourth series, vol. v, pp. 215, 873, 1638; vol. vi, p. 984.

To the T O R I E S.

MIND how ye fight your *Lies* Tomorrow, Gentlemen. As we know ye can't go on without *some*, we'll give ye Leave to use a *few*; but let them be harmless ones. A *funny Lie*, or a *merry Lie*, we don't care about; but don't *lie* out of our Reach. None of your *cursed Lies*, that is, none of your Catonian Lies, your Canadian Lies, your religious Lies, nor your commercial Lies; none of *your old Lies* about foreign Troops and English Ambassadors; none of *your new Lies* about Property and Division of Property. In short, let's have none of your red-hot ones; none of your two and forty Pounders.——No-thing higher, Gentlemen, than small Arms and Swan-shot; for by Heavens you'll be in a Hobble if you do! And hark ye, old Friends, don't put in two for one any more——remember the Admiralty Juggle.

As I love to see every Thing go on fair and above board, I have drawn up an Advertisement for ye, which, being a true State of your Case, I recommend to you for a Handbill.

To the E L E C T O R S.

WE, the King's Judges, King's Attornies, and King's Custom-House Officers, having had a long Run in this City, grown rich from *nothing at all*, and *engrossed* every Thing to ourselves, would now most willingly *keep* every Thing to ourselves. Wherefore, we earnestly intreat your Support at the State-House Tomorrow, then and there to secure our Places and Perquisites, by electing some of us for Burgesses, in Return for which Favor, we do promise and engage, that when our most gracious Master the King of Great-Britain, shall be reinstated in the Government of these provinces, that WE, agree to the Laws of our Duty, as *Custom-House Officers, Attornies, Judges*, &c. will take your Property for Smuggling, fit ye for Treason, condemn ye for Treason, and hang ye up for Rebels, without charging ye a Farthing.

O L D   M A L L O R Y

we read of their doings and steady, continuous efforts in every part of the country, and through every week, month, and year of the Revolution—supplemented by the efforts of the legislatures in confiscation of loyalist property—we gradually reach the conclusion that the patriot organization for holding in check and destroying loyalism was fully as systematic, elaborate, and far-reaching as the military establishment which Washington and his generals directed against the British regular army.

The proceedings of these committees were entirely arbitrary. They called such witnesses as they pleased; they made secret investigations; they often condemned their victim in his absence, without anything like a regular trial; and in Albany they do not appear to have allowed loyalists to employ counsel. They were not in any sense trial courts; but rather investigating, inquisitorial, and executive bodies. Great injustice and unfairness must necessarily have been sometimes committed.[9]

The various offences which were usually included under the general term "loyalism" were very numerous.

" Loyalists were arrested for arming to support the British or aiding the enemy in any way; for harboring or associating with Tories; recruiting soldiers; refusing to muster; corresponding with loyalists or with British; refusing to sign the association, or violating its provisions; denouncing or refusing to obey congresses and committees; writing or speaking against the American cause; rejecting continental money; refusing to give up arms; drinking the King's health; inciting or taking part in Tory plots and riots; being royal officers; and even for endeavoring to remain neutral. Mere suspicion was sufficient to cause seizure, and this meant at least imprisonment. On this wide definition of loyalism, hundreds were arrested, and soon all the jails were overflowing."—Flick, " Loyalism in New York," p. 83.

The committees were usually deluged with business. They were kept busy fining, imprisoning, dismissing on parole, releasing under bond, banishing, disarming, sometimes inflicting the

---

[9] *American Archives*, fifth series, vol. i, pp. 361, 381; Flick, " Loyalism in New York," pp. 82, 122; *American Archives*, fourth series, vol. vi, p. 1273; " Life of John Jay," pp. 41, 42, 49, 50.

penalty of death, and adopting every imaginable form of punishment and repression to suit individual cases, and wear out, convert, or destroy the loyalists. It was quite a wonderful system in its way, beginning with the Continental Congress and passing down through provincial congresses, and conventions, to the county, district, and precinct committees, without any legal basis and resting entirely on the voluntary consent and action of the patriot party and their earnestness in the cause of independence.

"A loyalist," said the patriots, "is a thing whose head is in England, whose body is in America, and its neck ought to be stretched." In the elections which took place under the new revolutionary state constitutions, no loyalist was allowed to vote. He could hold no office of trust or profit. In some of the states he could make no use of the courts of law. He could bring no suit to recover money that was due him or to recover damages for trespass, assault, or slander. He could not act as executor, administrator, guardian, juryman, or attorney, or convey or receive a valid title to land. Even some mercantile callings, like that of apothecary, were denied him. He became, in fact, a political and legal outcast, and was obliged to content himself with drinking silent healths to royalty. It was not often that he could join openly with his companions in singing what they called their "grand and animating song, 'God Save great George our King.'"

His position, however, varied in the different states. Some of them did not deprive him of as many rights as were taken from him by others; nor were the restrictions always enforced, unless an emergency arose. But he considered his position from his own point of view well described by a writer who said: "There is more liberty in Turkey than in the dominions of the Congress."

When a full account of all the restrictions and disabilities, together with incidents of tarring and feathering and other mob violence, was stated, it unquestionably looked like very arbitrary, tyrannous conduct on the part of people who were at the same time clamoring for more liberty for themselves. The complaints of the loyalists remind us somewhat of the complaints in the French Revolution that the revolutionary committees which were overthrowing the tyranny of kings "had perpetrated more atrocities in twelve months than all the kings of France had in twelve centuries." The proclamations issued by British generals or royal governors usually described the British Government and its army as coming to America "to deliver his Majesty's people from the intolerable yoke of arbitrary power, which his Majesty with indignation sees imposed by the tyranny of the rebel congress."[10]

The patriot party believed that these severities to the loyalists were necessary, a mere temporary violation of individual liberty for the sake of securing national independence and larger liberty for all in the future. But the English Tory party and the majority of Englishmen, on their part, believed that the patriots were the most frightful and lawless anarchists that the world had ever seen, and that England was doing no more than her duty to law and civilization by repressing them.

The Revolution was, in short, the very worst kind of a civil war. It was more of a civil war than the conflict between the states in 1861, because that was essentially a war between two sections of the country, while the Revolution was a war between two parties, each of which was numerous in every part of the country.[11]

All through the Revolution the loyalists, disarmed and disorganized, were the prey of the rough element among the patriots. Everywhere they were seized unexpectedly, at the humor of the mob; tarred and feathered, paraded through the towns, or left tied to trees in the woods. Any accidental circumstance would cause these visitations, and often the victim was not as politically guilty as some of his neighbors, who, by prudence or accident, remained unharmed to the end of the war.

Men were ridden and tossed on fence-rails; were gagged and bound for days at a time; pelted with stones; fastened in rooms

[10] Niles, " Principles and Acts of the Revolution," edition 1876, p. 317.
[11] Lee, Memoirs, vol. l, p. 212, note.

where there was a fire with the chimney stopped on top; advertised as public enemies, so that they would be cut off from all dealing with their neighbors. They had bullets shot into their bedrooms; money or valuable plate extorted to save them from violence and on pretence of taking security for their good behavior. Their houses and ships were burnt; they were compelled to pay the guards who watched them in their houses; and when carted about for the mob to stare at and abuse, they were compelled to pay something at every town.

The expenses put upon loyalists of means were sometimes very heavy. Mr. James Christie, a merchant of Baltimore, after narrowly escaping with his life, had to pay nine shillings per day to each of the men who guarded his house, and was ordered to pay five hundred pounds to the revolutionary convention, "to be expended occasionally towards his proportion of all charges and expenses, incurred or to be incurred, for the defence of America during the present contest." [12]

Sometimes the loyalists were put to work like criminals in a chain-gang. In Vermont, in January, 1778, the overseer of the imprisoned loyalists was ordered to take them for three days into the Green Mountains to "march and tread the snow in said road of suitable width for a sleigh and span of horses." After the battle of Bennington loyalists were tied in pairs and attached by traces to horses, which were, in some cases, driven by negroes. All this was considered necessary in order to repress these enemies of independence and punish them for assisting the British. But hatred for loyalism and the excitement of the times carried the patriots to deeds of which afterwards they often repented. "One Tory with his left eye shot out," says a patriot, " was led by me mounted on a horse who had also lost his left eye. It seems to me cruel now—it did not then." [13]

Some of us, perhaps, have read of the treatment of the Rev. Samuel Seabury, afterwards the first bishop of the Protestant

---

[12] Bolton, " A Private Soldier under Washington," pp. 214, 215.
[13] *American Archives*, fourth series, vol. iii, pp. 105, 125, 129.

Episcopal Church in the United States. His house was invaded by the mob, his daughters insulted, their lives threatened, bayonets thrust through their caps, and all the money and silverware in the house taken. Seabury himself was paraded through New Haven and imprisoned for a month. Afterwards he and some other loyalists fled for their lives, and lived in a secret room, behind the chimney, in a private house, where they were fed by their friends through a trap-door.

In South Carolina the mob, in one instance, after applying the tar and feathers, displayed their Southern generosity and politeness by scraping their victim clean, instead of turning him adrift, as was usually done, to go home to his wife and family in his horrible condition or seek a pitiable refuge at the house of a friend, if he could find one.

" Of the few who objected (to the Charleston Association) there were only two who were hardy enough to ridicule or treat it with contempt,—viz., Laughlin Martin and John Dealey, on which account . . . Yesterday they were carted through the principal streets of the town in complete suits of tar and feathers. The very indecent and daring behaviours of the two culprits in several instances occasioned their being made public spectacles of. After having been exhibited for about half an hour, and having made many acknowledgments of their crime, they were conducted home, cleaned, and quietly put on board of Captain Lasley's ship."—*American Archives*, fourth series, ii, p. 922.

From a letter written at Charleston, in August, 1775, we gain another glimpse of such proceedings:

" Yesterday evening the gunner of Fort Johnson (one Walker) had a decent tarring and feathering, for some insolent speech he had made. There is hardly a street through which he was not paraded—nor a tory house where they did not halt—particularly Innes's, Simpson's, Wragg's, Milligan's, Irving's, &c., &c., &c. At Gen. Bull's they stopped; called for grog; had it—made Walker drink d——n to Bull, threw a bag of feathers into his balcony—desired he would take care of it till his turn came, and that he would charge the grog to the account of Lord North. Finally the wretch was discharged at Milligan's door. The people were in such a humor, that I believe there was scarce a non-subscriber who did not tremble and Wells had his shop close shut."—Gibbs, " Documentary History of the American Revolution," 1764–1776, p. 139.

The South Carolina patriots had a secret committee of which William Henry Drayton, Arthur Middleton, and Charles Cotesworth Pinckney were the leading members. It was bold and prompt in its action, and its secret orders to the patriot populace were instantly obeyed. If the Revolution had been overthrown, the loyalists would have no doubt demanded from Great Britain some very summary vengeance upon the men who composed this committee.[14]

Instances of severity to loyalists at every stage of the Revolution might possibly be collected in great numbers from the records. But we would not then have them all; for there must have been countless instances of violence which were not recorded in print. Like the other instances, they played their part; were well known by common report; contributed towards forming opinion and action in the great problem; and now, being unpleasant or inconvenient to remember, have passed out of human recollection as though they had never happened.[15]

Many saved themselves by yielding, by resigning the offices they held under British authority, or by writing out a humiliating apology and reading it aloud, or letting it be published in the newspapers. When this system of terrorism was once well under way, there was a crop of these recantations everywhere. But we do not always know from the records the severity by which these recantations were forced.

Loyalists would often resist for a time before subjecting themselves to the ignominy of a recantation. In one instance twenty-nine loyalists were carried about by a party of militia for several days from town to town. They were told that they

---

[14] *American Archives*, fourth series, vol. ii, p. 923.

[15] *American Archives*, fourth series, i, pp. 630, 663, 716, 724, 731, 732, 745, 763, 787, 806, 885, 965, 970, 974, 1009, 1042, 1061, 1070, 1105, 1106, 1178, 1236, 1243, 1253, 1260; fourth series, ii, pp. 33, 34, 91, 131, 174, 176, 318, 337, 340, 466, 507, 545, 552, 622, 725, 875, 920, 922, 1652, 1688, 1697; fourth series, iii, pp. 52, 59, 105, 119, 127, 145, 151, 170, 326, 462, 682, 823, 1072, 1254, 1266; fourth series, iv, pp. 19, 29, 203, 247, 288, 475, 564, 679, 719, 847, 884, 887, 941, 1043, 1228, 1237, 1241, 1284, 1288, 1571, 1580, 1585, 1590, 1692, 1717. See also title " Tories " in the indices of the volumes of the *American Archives*.

were to be put in the Simsbury mines, which were damp, underground passages for mining copper in Connecticut, not far from Hartford. These mines were often used for terrorizing loyalists. The twenty-nine were exhibited and tormented until, before they reached the mines, the last one had humbled himself by a public confession and apology.

As time went on there were comparatively few who, when visited by the mob, did not finally make a public apology, because, although that was bad enough, they knew that in the end there was the far worse infamy and torture of the tar and feathers. There were few men of any position or respectability —and it was such men that were usually attacked—who could bear the thought or survive the infliction of that process, unless they afterwards left the country altogether. To be stripped naked, smeared all over with disgusting black pitch, the contents of two or three pillows rubbed into it, and in that condition to be paraded through the streets of the town for neighbors and acquaintances to stare at, was enough to break down very daring spirits.

One could never tell when an angry mob might rush to this last resource. On the 24th of August, 1774, a mob at New London were carrying off Colonel Willard, when he agreed to apologize and resign his office. But the account goes on to say:

> One Captain Davis, of Brimfield, was present, who showing resentment and treating the people with bad language, was stripped and honoured with the new-fashion dress of tar and feathers; a proof this that the act of tarring and feathering is not repealed.—*American Archives*, fourth series, i, 731.

In the raids to break up the loyalists on Long Island they were hunted, says Judge Jones, like wolves and bears from swamp to swamp and from hill to hill. When we consider that this mob rule was steadily practised for a period of nearly ten years, it is not surprising that it left an almost indelible mark on our people. They may have acquired from it that fixed habit now called lynch law, which is still practised among us in many parts of the country in a most regular and systematic manner, and participated in by respectable people. The term lynch law originated in the method of handling the loyalists in the Revolution, and perhaps derived its name from the brother of the man who founded Lynchburg, in Virginia.[16]

By the year 1775 the patriot portion of the people had grown so accustomed to dealing with the loyalists by means of the mob, that they regarded it as a sort of established and legalized procedure. In New Jersey we find an account of tar and feathers inflicted on a loyalist closing with the words, "The whole was conducted with that regularity and decorum that ought to be observed in all public punishments.[17]

As for the liberty of the press, the mobs had pretty much extinguished it by the year 1775; and after that some of the legislatures, under the revolutionary constitutions, formally abolished it as a necessary war measure. Evil speaking against the Congress or the patriot cause was prohibited even in prayer, for some did under "that guise wish for the success of the King's arms, and that he might vanquish and overcome all his enemies."

James Rivington, of New York, who printed and published many of the loyalist pamphlets, was boycotted and assailed by town and village committees and his printing presses seized by a party of patriots from Connecticut under command of Isaac Sears of New York. Rivington apologized and humbled himself, but narrowly escaped with his life, and finally took refuge on a British man-of-war.[18]

Such severity in extinguishing free speech was deemed necessary, because the loyalists were unremitting in their arguments, their ridicule of Continental paper money, and everything patriotic. The stars and stripes of the patriot flag, they said, had originated in Mrs. Washington's mottled tom-cat, with

---

[16] Jones, "New York in the Revolution," vol. i, pp. 68, 69, 71, 109, 568; *Atlantic Monthly*, vol. lxxxviii, p. 731; *The Nation*, vol. lxv, p. 439; Cutler, "Lynch Law," p. 23.

[17] *American Archives*, fourth series, iv, p. 203.

[18] *American Archives*, fourth series, vol. iii, p. 1707; vol. iv, pp. 185, 186, 393, 400, 401; vol. v, p. 439; Jones, "Revolution in New York," vol. i, pp. 64, 66, 561.

thirteen yellow rings round his tail, which he waved so often that it suggested the rebel flag to the Congress. [19]

People engaged in a revolution must necessarily take measures which may afterwards seem extreme. Their minds are wrought up to a state of excitement in which trifles seem important; and it need not surprise us when we find a patriot committee calling an Episcopal clergyman before them to answer the charge of having baptized a child by "the opprobrious name Thomas Gage," which the committee described as a "religious manœuvre" to insult the cause of liberty. [20]

Patriots were often moved to protest against some of the shocking scenes they were compelled to witness. The carting of Dr. Kearsley wounded and bleeding through the streets of Philadelphia was more than Captain Graydon could endure in silence. John Adams protested against the treatment of Richard King, whose store was broken open by the mob and his property laid waste as early in the difficulties with England as 1766. Seven or eight years afterward, in 1774, the mob assailed him again because one of his cargoes of lumber, without any fault of his, had been purchased by the British army in Boston. Forty men visited him on this occasion, and, by threatening his life, compelled him to disavow his loyalist opinions. He shortly afterwards went insane and died.

"The terror and distress, the distraction and horror of his family," writes John Adams to his wife, "cannot be described in words or painted upon canvas. It is enough to move a statue, to melt a heart of stone, to read the story. A mind susceptible of the feelings of humanity, a heart which can be touched with sensibility for human misery and wretchedness must relent, must burn with resentment and indignation at such outrageous injuries. These private mobs I do and will detest. . . . But

---

[19] Van Tyne, "Loyalists," p. 200.

[20] *American Archives*, fourth series, vol. v, pp. 405, 406. For other curious and noteworthy instances, see *ibid.*, vol. iv, pp. 1630, 1631; vol. v, p. 951; vol. vi, p. 626; vol. ii, pp. 35, 466, 467; vol. iii, pp. 170, 176, 986; Niles, "Principles and Acts of the Revolution," edition 1876, pp. 247, 262, 263; "Life and Correspondence of George Read," p. 137; Graydon's Memoirs, edition of 1846, p. 127; Ryerson, "Loyalists,' vol. ii, pp. 123-144; "Life of Peter Van Schaack," pp. 109, 110, 112, 113, 126, 127.

these tarrings and featherings, this breaking open houses by rude and insolent rabble in resentment for private wrongs or in pursuance of private prejudices and passions, must be discountenanced. It cannot be even excused upon any principle which can be entertained by a good citizen, a worthy member of society."—" Familiar Letters of John Adams to His Wife," p. 20.

The disorder and confusion wrought by the mobs in business and in every department of life caused torturing doubts to many enthusiastic souls who had been reading about the rights of man. Many were no doubt driven from the patriot cause by it and joined the loyalists, and it sometimes almost unnerved John Adams. A man in Massachusetts one day congratulated him on the anarchy, the mob violence, the insults to judges, the closing of the courts, and the tar and feathers, which the patriots and their Congress were producing.

" Oh, Mr. Adams, what great things have you and your colleagues done for us. We can never be grateful enough to you. There are no courts of justice now in this province, and I hope there never will be another."

" Is this the object for which I have been contending, said I to myself, for I rode along without any answer to this wretch; are these the sentiments of such people, and how many of them are there in the country? Half the nation, for what I know; for half the nation are debtors, if not more; and these have been in all countries the sentiments of debtors. If the power of the country should get into such hands, and there is a great danger that it will, to what purpose have we sacrificed our time, health and everything else? "—Works of John Adams, vol. ii, p. 420.

There appears to have been some difference of opinion among the patriot leaders as to how far mob violence should be encouraged. In the town of New York one of the favorite methods of the mob in dealing with loyalists was to ride them astride of a rail carried on the shoulders of two tall men, with a man on each side to keep the victim straight and fixed in his seat. General Putnam accidentally meeting one of these processions in the street, attempted to put a stop to it, and both he and General Mifflin appealed to the Provincial Congress of New York to put an end to what they thought unnecessary severity. But the Congress would do nothing definite to stop the work of the mobs, except to pass a resolution saying that they disapproved of such riots, but they had no doubt they "proceeded from a real regard to liberty and a detestation of those persons who by their language and conduct have discovered themselves to be inimical to the cause of America." [21]

As a matter of fact the work of the mobs could not be stopped, for no one had any control of the patriot masses. Thoughtful patriots who deplored the confusion, the turmoil and the mobs, nevertheless felt satisfied that it was a phase through which we must pass, a price which we must pay for independence. The long years of anarchy were trying, terrible, and digusting; but to remain the political slaves of England was, they said, infinitely worse.[22]

The claim of the loyalists that they should at least be allowed to talk and write in vindication of their opinions could not be allowed. The majority of patriots took the very natural view that a talking influential loyalist making converts was just as dangerous to the cause of independence as the invading soldier from Great Britain. These civilian unarmed enemies must be terrorized, punished with suffering in body and mind, and driven out of the country.

" Why should persons," said Washington, " who are preying on the vitals of the country, be suffered to stalk at large, whilst we know that they will do us every mischief in their power." [23]—Sparks, "Writings of Washington," vol. iii, p. 263.

Patriot ministers of the Gospel declared that the loyalists should be silenced. The situation, said the Rev. Dr. Witherspoon in his sermon of the 11th of May, 1776, was like that of a leaking ship at sea. After the proper course has been resolved

---

[21] "Memorial History of New York City," vol. ii, p. 495; Lamb's "History of New York City," vol. ii, pp. 77-78; Jones, "History of New York," vol. i, pp. 101-103, 596; Flick, "Loyalism in New York." pp. 74, 75; Journal New York Provincial Congress, vol. i, p. 232.

[22] Journals of Congress, vol. i, pp. 222, 224, 225, 285; Niles, "Principles and Acts of the Revolution," edition 1876, p. 221.

[23] For other expressions by Washington on the subject of the loyalists, see Ford's edition of his Writings, vol. iii, p. 506; vol. iv, p. 6.

upon those who object or complain or discourage others should "be thrown overboard in less time than I have taken to state the case." Patriot lawyers announced that civil rights, free speech, and a free press must be temporarily suspended until independence was secure.[24]

The contest was one of fundamental principles. It was a question between the right of empire and the right of national independence. It was war to the knife; and the day of argument had passed. It was idle to talk of civil rights, free speech, and the ways of peace. The loyalists were by no means free from severity and cruelty when they got the upper hand, and if they had gained anything like permanent control they would have adopted measures of unparalleled rigor to exterminate or exile most of the patriots and hold down the remnant. Only by relentless severity could the American provinces be turned into colonies, and only by similar means could they be saved for independence.

So the mobs and the revolutionary committees and the state legislatures went on with their terrible work. At first there was no attempt to confiscate loyalist property. In fact, orders were often issued for the careful protection and preservation of the property of loyalists who were arrested or punished. But after independence was declared and violent feelings and active warfare increased, the patriots adopted confiscation as a necessary measure. The British Government had already ordered American ships and cargoes on the high seas to be confiscated; and General Howe confiscated patriot property in New York. The loyalists expected to be rewarded for their fidelity by gifts of rebel estates. This method had been adopted in the subjugation of the Irish and has been the foundation of a large part of the subsequent troubles and degradation in Ireland, and would undoubtedly have produced a worse state of confusion and misery in America, if the loyalist cause had been successful.

By the year 1777 the confiscation of the personal property

[24] Gibbs, "Documentary History of the American Revolution," 1764-1776, pp. 12, 13; American Archives, fifth series, vol. i, p. 403.

and land of such loyalists as had left the country was well under way, and was carried out systematically during the rest of the Revolution and even long after the treaty of peace of 1783. Forfeitures were made after the year 1800, and some sales of forfeited lands were not complete until 1819. More than half the landed property in New York is said to have belonged to loyalists, and it has been estimated that New York received $3,160,000 from the forfeited land and $3,600,000 from forfeited personal property. There were also large forfeitures in Pennsylvania from the estates of rich loyalists like Joseph Galloway.

The treaty of peace of 1783 provided that the Congress should recommend to the states the restoration of the rights and possessions of real British subjects and of loyalists who had not borne arms against the patriots, and that other loyalists should be allowed to go into any state within a year to adjust their affairs and recover their confiscated property on paying the sale price. But the Continental Congress, with which the treaty was made, had no power to compel the states to carry out any of these measures, and the states refused to carry them out. Loyalists who returned to New York to settle their affairs after the treaty of peace were insulted, and tarred and feathered. About a thousand of the richest of them were indicted by the grand jury for treason.[25]

Every effort was made to drive them out of the country and keep them out. Some who had been banished were forbidden to return under pain of death. A year after the treaty of peace most of the loyalists in New York were disfranchised and disqualified from holding office. They were taxed, and debts due them were cancelled on condition that one-fortieth was paid into the state treasury.

Men like Alexander Hamilton protested against such treatment, and tried to check it, but with very little result. Hatred and love of vengeance were too strong among the masses of

---

[*] Flick, "Loyalism in New York," 158; Jones, "New York in the Revolution," vol. i, pp. xii, xvii, 150.

the patriot party, and there was a feeling that if the loyalists were allowed to remain in the country they might still be able to thwart the continuance of independence. It was no doubt well to be rid of them, for they were not Americans. But at the same time it must be confessed that their exodus deprived the country of a fine stock of people who could ill be spared.

The British Government made great efforts to lighten their sufferings, supported thousands of them with food, money, clothing, employment, pensions, and offices, as well as liberal grants of land in Canada. They were supplied with rations, tools, and seeds to start life afresh, and the wealthy ones were partially reimbursed for the fortunes they had lost. England spent altogether over $30,000,000 in maintaining and rehabilitating the loyalists, and that sum was fully the equivalent of $100,000,000 to-day.[26]

---

[26] Flick, " Loyalism in New York," p. 213.

XXIII.

THE ships which had sailed in the autumn with the documents of the American Congress, when scarcely ten days out, were driven back by a gale. They returned to port, and several weeks were lost before they were again on their way. But at last, about the middle of December, they began arriving at different ports, and the petition, the declaration of rights, the articles of association, and all the papers, with their duplicates, travelled by various means to London.

Soon they were published, and everybody was reading them. But it was so near Christmas time that nothing could be done. Parliament adjourned over the holidays, and members, ministers, and officials rushed off to the country to enjoy the pleasures of the winter sports, house-parties, and family gatherings.

The impression produced by the documents of the Congress was at first, Franklin said, rather favorable. By this he seems to have meant that the Whigs were pleased because the rebellion party were making a good fight and not yielding in their demands, and the Tory administration was rather staggered at the uncompromising nature of the demands, and a little inclined to grant some of them.

During the Christmas holidays, every one in town and country discussed the documents. Dr. Johnson began his vigorous refutation of them in his pamphlet, "Taxation no Tyranny." Lord Chatham read them with delight and admiration. They gave him a strong interest and roused the mighty energies of the mind that had saved the colonies from France and won a whole empire for England. Burke and Fox admired them, and so also did all the Whigs, as a matter of course.

But that was not enough, because the Whigs were already

on the side of the colonies, and willing to grant any favors short of absolute independence and withdrawal of the supremacy of Parliament. The object of the documents, if they were to accomplish peace, was to win over the doubting Tories in such numbers that they would turn the Whig minority into a majority, which would compromise with the colonies. In that they utterly failed, exactly as the loyalists foretold, and as such men as Samuel Adams hoped and prayed they might.

In fact, these documents, instead of accomplishing reconciliation, made reconciliation impossible. When the Tories recovered from their first surprise at the boldness of the demands their indignation and resentment mounted higher and higher every day. If the members of the Congress could have passed December in Tory households, they would not have eaten their Christmas dinners with much complacency. Their statements of American rights, which are still so much admired by us and which were admired by Lord Chatham and the Whigs, seemed ridiculous to the Tories. The documents were admirable only to those who already believed their sentiments, and they were exasperating and hateful to others in exact proportion as they were admirable to us. It would be difficult to find in any previous period of English history more vigorous denunciation than was soon poured forth by Tory writers and orators.

The Tories saw independence in every line. Why, they would say, their very first resolution says that they have never ceded to any power the disposal of their life, liberty, and property. They assume, in other words, that they have a right to cede it if they wish. They believe that they are already independent of us. They deny that they are British subjects. They deny that they are subject to the British constitution, by which alone the life, liberty, and property of every Englishman is held.

The inconsistency of asking in one document for a repeal of the Quebec Act, because it established in Canada the bigotry and ignorance of the Roman Catholic religion, mingled with the absurd customs of Paris, and in another document appealing to these same French Roman Catholics, in flattering phrases, to join the Congress at Philadelphia, was quickly seen, and formed one of the stock jokes at every Tory gathering.

"They complain of transubstantiation in Canada," said Dean Tucker, "but they have no objection to their own kind of transubstantiation, by which they turn bits of paper, worth nothing at all, into legal tender for the payment of debts to British merchants."

Dr. Johnson's "Taxation no Tyranny," with its whole-souled Toryism, is capital reading. No doubt he and many another Tory were expressing the same sentiments in conversation. At his Friday evening club, surrounded by Sir Joshua Reynolds, the ever-faithful Boswell, Charles Fox, Gibbon, Burke, and others, we can almost hear the doctor pant and roar against the Americans like an infuriated old lion.

"Sir, do they suppose that when this nation sent out a colony it established an independent power? They went out into those wildernesses because we protected them, and they would not otherwise have ventured there. They have been incorporatd by English charters; they have been governed by English laws, regulated by English counsels, protected by English arms, and it seems to follow, by a consequence not easily avoided, that they are subject to English government and chargeable by English taxation."

And if Samuel Adams had been there, he might have said, "You are entirely right, and that is the reason we are so anxious to have our independence." But he was not there, and so the doctor roared on, while his listeners cautiously smoked their long pipes.

"When by our indulgence and favor the colonists have become rich, shall they not help to pay for their own defence, If they accept protection, do they not stipulate obedience? Parliament may enact a law for capital punishment in America, and may it not enact a law for taxation? If it can take away a colonist's life by law, can it not take away his property by law?"

And again Samuel Adams would have said, "Why, yes, certainly; that is the cause of the whole trouble."

"Sir, your people are a race of convicts," the doctor would have replied; "a race of cowardly convicts. Has not America always been our penal colony? Are they not smugglers? I am willing to love all mankind except an American. How is it, sir, that we hear the loudest yelps for liberty from these people, who are themselves the drivers of negroes?"

We can easily imagine what a telling hit that must have been among the Tories, for most of the members of the Continental Congress owned slaves, and all of them could have owned them. Lord Mansfield had recently decided that a slave who set foot on the soil of England was by that act set free while he remained in England. For Americans or colonials to talk about liberty, and drive their slaves like cattle, seemed very absurd to Englishmen.[1]

The doctor made many telling hits, and it would be easy to go on summarizing or paraphrasing them.

"One minute," he would say, "the Whigs are telling us, 'Oh, the poor Americans! have you not oppressed them enough already? You have forbidden them to manufacture their own goods, or to carry their raw materials to any but English ports.' The next minute they tell us you can never conquer them; they are too powerful. 'Think of their fertile land, their splendid towns, their wonderful prosperity, which enables their population to double itself every twenty years.' But I say, if the rascals are so prosperous, oppression has agreed with them, or else there has been no oppression. You cannot escape one or the other of those dilemmas."

An English pamphlet called "Considerations on the American War,"[2] published during this period, is interesting for its forecasts. It describes America's unbounded extent of lands, such vast length of coast, such harbors, such fertility, such

---

[1] See, also, "Americans against Liberty," p. 23, London, 1776. The Boston *Gazette* of July 22, 1776, contained the Declaration of Independence in full and also an advertisement of a slave for sale.

[2] "Considerations on the American War addressed to the People of England," London. See, also, "The Honor of Parliament and the Justice of the Nation vindicated," London, 1776.

prospect of provisions for ages to come, such certainty of vast increase of population, that unless subdued and controlled she would before long overwhelm the mother-country with her riches and power. As America rises in independence England will as gradually decay, and therefore the lawless colonists in America should be subdued. No minister of discernment and honesty, it was said, could see the increasing power and opulence of the colonies without marking them with a jealous eye.

Fears were expressed that the patriot colonists, having the whole big continent to hide in, might get off into the Western wilderness and live there as free as they pleased. Doctor Johnson ridiculed this idea most savagely. If the Americans were such fools as that, they would be leaving good houses to be enjoyed by wiser men. Others cited Ireland to show how easily the Americans could be conquered. When the great rebellion, it was said, began in Ireland there were nearly as many inhabitants there as there are in America, yet in nine years five hundred thousand Irish were destroyed by the sword and by famine, and Cromwell, with but a small body of troops, could easily have made a desert of the whole island.[3] That was many years ago, when England's power was weak. England had only recently hunted the French out of North America and conquered the Indians. How could the colonists escape?

The Tory pamphleteers complained bitterly of the Whigs, who by their sympathy and talk about freedom encouraged the riot and rebellion of the Americans. If the Whigs in England would cease to support the disorderly colonists, they would soon quiet down. It was afterwards charged that the Whigs regularly furnished the patriots with information and encouraged the rebellion in the hope that its success would put them again in office and power.[4]

---

[3] " The Right of the British Legislature to tax the American Colonies," p. 44, London, 1774.

[4] " A View of the Evidence Relative to the Conduct of the American War under Sir William Howe," etc., p. 97; Galloway, " A Letter from Cicero to Right Hon. Lord Viscount Howe," p. 33, London, 1781; Lecky, " England in the Eighteenth Century," edition of 1882, vol. iii, p. 545;

The author of the pamphlet already cited uses Ireland as an instance and a warning for the Americans. The sole cause of Ireland's long years of disaster, devastation, and failure, he says, has been because she would never give up her love of independence. If she would only just give up that one "teasing thought," how happy and prosperous she might be. What long terrors and misery the Americans were preparing for themselves.[5]

As England had then been six hundred years in crushing the independent spirit of Ireland, and is still engaged in that noble occupation, this Englishman's argument is a strange piece of pathetic British intelligence.

Dean Tucker was the most interesting of the political writers. He was a Tory, and yet took the ground that the colonies should be given complete independence. His reasons for this were that to conquer them would be very expensive, and that as independent communities, supposing they remained independent, they would trade with Great Britain more than they had traded as colonies. But they would not remain independent, he said. They would either lapse into a frightful state of sectional wars and confusion, or they would petition for a reunion with England. In short, independence would be a cheap and excellent punishment for them.

The Tories who were so indignant at the suggestion of allowing America independence could quote the French philosopher Raynal. He had written in favor of the colonists, encouraged them in rebellion, warned them not to allow themselves to be represented in Parliament, which would rivet their chains and fetters. But he had said that it would be absurd to give them independence. They could not govern themselves. They would burst the bonds of religion and of laws. They would become a dangerous, tumultuous military power; they would menace the peace of Europe. They would try to seize the

Galloway, "Reply to the Observations of Lieutenant-General Sir W. Howe." Gordon, "American War," vol. i, p. 435; Stedman, "American War," vol. i, p. 162.

[5] "The Right of the British Legislature to tax," etc., p. 23.

French and Spanish possessions in the West Indies. The moment the laws of Britain were withdrawn both continents of America would tremble under such unscrupulous tyrants.[*]

The Christmas house-parties soon broke up and Parliament resumed its sessions. January and February dragged along and March came while the mightly assembly of the Anglo-Saxon race tossed and struggled with the great question, whether universal liberty was consistent with the universal empire.

The Tory majority was overwhelming, and everything that occurred, all the information that arrived, even the arguments of the Whigs, convinced that majority more and more that they were in the right. Letter after letter was read from General Gage and from the provincial governors describing the situation in the colonies. Civil government in Massachusetts had ceased; the courts of justice in every county were expiring. British officials were driven out of the country by terrorism and mob violence; and the rebels had organized a government of their own independent of General Gage and the charter. They were drilling a militia of their own, seizing arms, ammunition, and artillery, casting cannon-balls, and looking for blacksmiths who could forge musket-barrels. They upset the carts that hauled firewood for the British army and sank the vessels that brought provisions. In New Hampshire they seized the fort at Portsmouth and carried away the powder, cannon, and muskets; and in Rhode Island they were equally daring and aggressive.

They proposed getting all the women and children out of Boston and then burning it to ashes over the heads of Gage and his soldiers. They were ready to attack him; and on a false rumor that his ships were about to fire on Boston the whole patriot party in New England were in arms, and the patriots in Connecticut made a two days' march to give their assistance to Massachusetts.

---

[*] "The Sentiments of a Foreigner on the Disputes of Great Britain with America," p. 24, Philadelphia, 1775; translated from his "Philosophical and Political History of the European Settlements in America."

AMERICAN INDEPENDENCE

As the Whigs admitted that Massachusetts was in rebellion, the Tories said that the rebellion must be put down. How can we endure such insubordination unless we are willing to give them independence outright? If we are to have colonies at all they must be subordinate in some slight degree.

"You have raised the rebellion yourselves," said the Whigs, "by your excessive severity and intermeddling."

"No," said the Tories, "not at all; we raised it eight years ago by repealing the Stamp Act; by yielding for a time to whiggery and weakness. We taught the colonists to think that they could get anything they wanted if they threatened us."

Then Burke would break forth in impassioned eloquence. England could not conquer the Americans without ruining herself. Remember the archer, he said, who was drawing his bow to send an arrow to his enemy's heart, when he saw his own child folded in the enemy's arms. America holds in her arms our commerce, our trade, our most valuable child. Even now the tradesmen and merchants of the whole kingdom are thronging to the doors of this house and calling on you to stay your cruel hand.

During these debates General Howe rose to be recognized by the chair. His constituents at Nottingham, he said, had asked him to present a petition, and it was handed to the clerk, who read it. Nottingham would be ruined, the petitioners said, unless Parliament found some honorable means of conciliating the Americans. Already the trade of the town was ceasing, useless goods were piling up in the warehouses; laboring men would soon be out of employment.

Petitions from London, Bristol, and other towns told the same story, and Howe must have been amused in watching the effect of them. The effect was the reverse of what the petitioners intended; for, said the Tories, can it be endured that those colonists shall have this handle over us? Shall they be able, every time they are dissatisfied, to raise a rebellion among the commercial classes here in England, and flood our tables with petitions, and fill our lobbies with stamping, impatient traders?

So they investigated, to see if it were really true that the

REBELLION MUST BE SUBDUED

Americans were starving England into obedience, and making her the dependency and America the ruler; and they aroused an army of counter-petitioners, who swarmed to Parliament, declaring that British trade could not be injured by anything America could do. Thus the appeal to the commercial classes in England, which had been so successful in bringing about the repeal of the Stamp Act, utterly failed in this second attempt; for the Tories were prepared to counteract it.[7]

The Tory position that America was attacking the supremacy of Parliament, the sovereignty of the empire, was a strong appeal to most Englishmen, and could not be successfully answered, when letters and documents showed that the rebellion was spreading from New England to all of the colonies. But it would be easily subdued, the Tories said; and General Grant, who had served in the French war, assured them that the Americans would not fight; they were a people of absurd manners and speech and disgusting habits; they had none of the qualifications of soldiers, and a small force would overcome them.

When Wilkes tried to prove at great length that the rebellion might become successful, he merely increased the determination of Englishmen to put it down at all hazards. When Burke, in a torrent of eloquence, declared that it was not Boston alone, but all America, with which England must now deal, the Tories thanked him for having made their duty clearer.

Could they allow such a rebellion to go unpunished? They would lose all their other possessions. Canada, Jamaica, Barbadoes, India, even Ireland, must be allowed to do as they please, rebel whenever they were dissatisfied, and get what they wanted by blustering and threatening to fight.

Our school-boys still recite extracts from the speeches of Burke and Barré. We shall always admire them. They will always seem to us incomparably and immortally eloquent for the beautiful and romantic aptness of language in which they expressed for us our sincerest thoughts and aspirations. But

---

[7] "Letters of James Murray, Loyalist," p. 172; "Diary and Letters of Thomas Hutchinson," vol. i, p. 432.

they never had the slightest chance of accomplishing the smallest result in England. They were mere useless protests. Burke, Barré, and their followers were not Englishmen. They were totally out of sympathy with the principles and tone of thought which had ruled England for centuries.

Burke, you may say, was at this time an American, a man with American ideas accidentally living in England. He was, in fact, an Irishman. He had come to London, in 1750, as a penniless Irish adventurer, and risen to distinction by his talents and brilliant Irish mind. When he pleaded in Parliament for the utmost liberty to the Americans, was he not showing the Irish side and influence of his character, the Irishman's natural sympathy with home rule and independence?

He foretold great things for us, and flattered us in the most glowing language. He described us as daring sailors following the whales among the "tumbling mountains" of Arctic ice, or crossing the equator and the tropics to "pursue the same dangerous game in the Antarctic Circle, under the frozen serpent of the South. No sea was unvexed by the American fisheries; no climate that was not a witness to their toils. Neither the perseverance of Holland, nor the activity of France, nor the dexterous and firm sagacity of the English was equal to the enterprise of this recent people still in the gristle and not hardened into the bone of manhood."

In glowing terms this Irish-Englishman went on to describe the rapid growth of our population. It was impossible to exaggerate it, he said, for while you were discussing whether they were two million, they had grown to three. Their trade with England was prodigious, and was now almost equal to England's trade with the whole world in 1704. Should not people of such numbers, such energy, and such prosperity be handled cautiously and gently?

Conscious of the weakness of this argument, conscious of the absurdity of such an appeal to the typical Englishman, he went on to say that he knew that his descriptions of the greatness of America made her seem a more noble prize to the Tories, an object well worth the fighting for; and to overcome this

Tory feeling he went on arguing in a way that made it a great deal worse. He was obliged to say in effect that British valor was not equal to the conquest of the Americans. Even if you should conquer them at first, can you go on conquering them, can you keep such a people subdued through the years and centuries that are to come?

Having enlarged on this point until he had drawn against himself the whole national pride of England, and lost every vote that might be wavering, he went on to ask eloquently, beautifully, but ineffectually, how are you to subdue this stubborn spirit of your colonies? You cannot stop the rapid increase of their population; you would not wish to cut off their commerce, for that would be to impoverish yourselves; you cannot stop their internal prosperity which is spreading over the continent. And here again his fervid imagination pictured a wonderful scene of the colonists driven by British conquest from the seaboard to dwell in the vaster and more fertile interior plains of boundless America; how they would become myriads of raiding Tartars, and pour down a fierce and irresistible cavalry upon the narrow strip of sea-coast, sweeping before them "your governors, your counsellors, your collectors and comptrollers, and all the slaves that adhere to them." [3]

His argument was a good one for independence, and possibly in his heart he was in favor of independence; but he would not admit it. He clung to the impossible dream that the colonies could be retained as colonies without coercion and conquest. His remedy was to give the colonists what they asked, to comply with the American spirit; "or, if you please," he said, "submit to it as a necessary evil."

A very simple and easy method, laughed the Tories. It would certainly dispose of the question completely.

Barré, our other great friend in Parliament, who was more dreaded than any other orator of the opposition, was descended

---

[3] This retreat into the interior beyond the Alleghany Mountains was the plan which Washington and the other patriot leaders intended to adopt if hard pressed, and the Congress also announced it in 1775, in their Declaration of the Causes for taking up Arms.

from a French Protestant family of Rochelle and had been born and educated in Ireland. He had served with Wolfe in the French and Indian War, was a favorite of that officer, and shared his liberal opinions. With his Irish education, his French blood, and the bias towards liberty of his Huguenot religion, he was not an Englishman at all. He was an American in all but migration, and we accordingly read his eloquence with great delight.

As for the rank and file of that hopeless minority called the Whig party, they were largely made up of those people who, for centuries, had been maintaining doctrines of liberty not accepted by the mass of Englishmen. In the previous century the majority had persecuted them so terribly that they had fled to America by thousands as Quakers and Puritans.

At intervals this minority has achieved success and made great and permanent changes in the English Constitution. They had a day and an innings in Cromwell's time; a long day in Gladstone's time, accomplishing wonderful changes and reforms in England; but perhaps their greatest triumph was in the revolution of 1688, when they dethroned the Stuart line, established religious liberty, destroyed the power of the Crown to set aside acts of Parliament, and created representative government in England. For the most of their existence, however, they would have been able to live in America more consistently with their professed principles than in England.

On the present occasion, in the year 1775, after they had expended all of their eloquence and stated all of their ideas, and shown themselves in the eyes of the majority of Englishmen absolutely incompetent to settle the American question, except by giving the colonies independence, the Tory majority proceeded to its duty of preserving the integrity of the empire in the only way in which it could be preserved.

They introduced five measures, well-matured and comprehensive plans, which would be unpleasant for our people, but proper enough if we once admit that it is a good thing to preserve and enlarge the British empire. They declared Massachusetts in a state of rebellion, and promised to give the ministry every assistance in subduing her. They voted six thousand additional men to the land and naval forces. They passed an act, usually known as the Fisheries Bill, by which all the trade of the New England colonies was to be confined by force to Great Britain and the British West Indies. This cutting off of the New England colonies from the outside world was a serious matter, but it was not the most important part of the act. The important part was that it prohibited the New England colonies from trading with one another. They must be cut off from every source of supply except the mother-country; and if this could be enforced they would be starved into submission and dependence, their self-reliance broken, and their budding unity and nationality destroyed.

The surest way to break up a rebellion is to prevent the rebels from uniting, to cut off not only their outward supplies, but their internal self-reliance. Having to deal with colonists whom they knew were aiming at independence, this act was a wise one for England. It is easy and cheap to criticise it now after its execution has been forcibly prevented by France, Spain, and Holland turning in to the assistance of the Americans. But at the time of its passage it was well calculated to achieve its purpose.

The Whigs attacked it for its cruelty. Burke rose to such heights of eloquence and denunciation that he had to be called to order. They proposed an amendment to it which would allow the colonists to carry fuel and provisions from one colony to another, but it was voted down by the three to one majority.

The last part of the act was still more severe. It prohibited the New England colonies from fishing on the Newfoundland banks, and allowed that privilege only to Canada and the middle and southern colonies. These prohibitions on fishing and trade were to last only until the rebellious colonies returned to their obedience.

Up rose the Whig orators to protest in pathetic strains against such hardship. The New Englanders were dependent for their livelihood on the fishery of the banks. Witnesses were called to the bar to show that over six hundred vessels and over six thousand men were employed in that fishery, that it was the foundation of nearly all the other occupations in New England, and that its prohibition would ruin or starve one-half the population.

"We are glad to hear that," said the Tories, "for then they will return the sooner to obedience. They would have returned to their obedience long ago if they had not been encouraged in rebellion by Whig oratory and eloquence in England."

When information arrived that the rebellion was spreading, the Tory ministry introduced another bill extending the prohibitions of the Fisheries Act to all the colonies except loyal New York, North Carolina, and Georgia. They intended, they said, as far as possible to separate the innocent from the guilty. Only the guilty should be punished.

We do not wish to oppress them, argued Lord North. As soon as they return to their duty, acknowledge our supreme authority, and obey the laws of the realm, their real grievances shall be redressed. We must bring them to obedience or abandon them. There is no middle ground.

Bills to settle the American difficulties were introduced on the Whig side by Lord Chatham, by Burke, and by David Hartley, who were for repealing the Boston Port Bill and all the other acts of Parliament as the colonists demanded, and allowing them to tax themselves for the purpose of granting aids and subsidies to the Crown, very much as they had done before the close of the French War. But Parliament was to have complete sovereignty over them, which they must fully recognize and formally acknowledge, and the right they claimed of having no standing army kept among them without their consent was firmly denied.[9]

These bills were of course rejected by the Tory majority; and on the 20th of February, 1775, Lord North presented the last measure of the Ministry's policy in a bill which at first surprised everybody by being a conciliatory measure. It was, however,

---

[9] See an interesting discussion of these bills in Snow, " Administration of Dependencies," pp. 299, 311, 315.

partly intended to destroy the last argument of the Whigs by adopting many of the ideas contained in the three bills which Chatham, Burke, and Hartley had offered. It provided that if any colony would make such voluntary contribution to the common defence of the empire and establish such fixed provision for the support of its own civil government as met the approval of Parliament, that colony should be exempted from all taxation except duties for the regulation of commerce, and the net proceeds of such duties should be turned over to the colony.

This measure seemed to concede a good deal, for while it did not offer to repeal the obnoxious laws, it required no acknowledgment of the supremacy of Parliament and left unsettled many other matters. North's own party were at first aghast at so much concession; but in the end they accepted the bill as an admirable plan to break up the union of the colonies by holding out a bait which might capture two or three of them.

The bill is supposed to have been framed with a special view of enticing New York to break away from the union. Her assembly had refused to elect delegates to another congress and they had to be elected by the patriot committees. There was believed to be every prospect that the loyalist element of her population would be strong enough to bring about an open and formal disavowal of the proceedings of the congress, and considerable sums of money were, it is said, sent over by the Ministry to encourage the disaffection. If New York made a separate treaty and compromise with England, North Carolina might do the same and the united front of American patriotism would be broken.[10]

After the Revolution, when all these measures of the Ministry and Parliament had failed, it became the fashion to represent them as a mere foolish scheme of the King, who forced his ideas on Lord North. But the contemporary evidence shows

---

[10] *American Archives*, fourth series, vol. ii, pp. 1, 28, 449, 453, 511, 535, 594, 600, 1727, 1728; vol. iii, p. 1729. Gordon, " American Revolution," edition 1788, vol. i, pp. 432, 436, 437, 464, 471; Journals of Continental Congress, Ford edition, 1905, vol. ii, p. 62; *Annual Register*, 1775, chaps. vi, vii, viii.

that the measures had the full approval of the majority of Englishmen both in and out of Parliament. The attempt to show that the English nation at large had no wish or intention to make war on America, but was deluded into it by some one person, is an easy and cheap way of shifting the responsibility for measures that failed, but it is a perversion of the facts of history.

"I am fully persuaded," wrote Governor Hutchinson from England in August, 1774, "that there never has been a time when the nation in general was so united against the colonies." The subjugation of the colonies, the reducing them to the condition of mere dependencies, was a popular measure in England from the beginning to the end. "The war was a popular war," said General Reed, writing from London in 1784, "and only ceased to be so when all hope of final success ceased." The King, Lord North, and the Ministry were guiding themselves by what they knew to be the overwhelming sentiment of the nation, which had the same desire to maintain dominion over as many countries as possible that it has to-day.[11]

Dominion of every kind, even slender control, draws trade to England and to English ships, and gives a market for English manufactures. Trade is the real purpose of imperialism, even of Whig imperialism; and before the documents of the Congress arrived some prominent Whigs, seeing that a dangerous crisis was impending, entered into secret negotiations with Franklin to bring about a reconciliation. When the documents came the danger of a bad civil war was more evident than ever, and they increased their efforts.

[11] "Diary and Letters of Thomas Hutchinson," vol. i, pp. 212, 230, 268, 293, 298, 410, 425, 431, 441. "Life of Joseph Reed," by W. B. Reed, vol. ii, p. 403. See also Lecky, "England in the Eighteenth Century," edition of 1882, vol. iii, p. 528; Stedman, "American War," vol. i, chap. xi, p. 258, London, 1789; *American Archives*, fourth series, vol. i, pp. 709, 1680.

The debates and proceedings in Parliament are best read in Cobbett's Parliamentary Debates, sometimes called Cobbett's Parliamentary History; also in the Parliamentary Register and in the "Votes of the House of Commons."

NEGOTIATION WITH FRANKLIN

The persons chiefly concerned in this undertaking were David Barclay, a Quaker member of Parliament; Dr. Fothergill, the leading physician of London, also a Quaker, and Admiral Howe, a Whig, very favorably inclined towards the colonies and very ambitious to win the distinction of settling the great question. He hoped to be sent out to America at the head of a great peace commission which would settle all difficulties.

The plan of these negotiations was, by means of private interviews with Franklin, to obtain from him the final terms on which the patriot colonists would compromise; and by acting as friendly messengers of these terms to the Ministry the negotiators hoped to prevent a war of conquest. Secrecy was necessary, because ordinary Englishmen might look upon such negotiations as somewhat treasonable, and the charge of treason was made when afterwards the negotiations were known.[12] Franklin was led into the plan by being asked to play chess, of which he was very fond, with Admiral Howe's sister, and his description of her fascination and the gradual opening of the plan are written in his best vein.[13]

The ultimate terms of these negotiations were worked down to as mild a basis as possible, and Franklin was willing to be much easier and more complying than the patriot party in America. He was willing, for example, to pay for the tea. But even when reduced to their mildest form one cannot read them without seeing that they would now be regarded as most extraordinary terms for colonies to be suggesting. They show in what a weak grasp England had held her colonies. They are absolutely incompatible with any modern idea of the colonial relation. It would be utterly impossible for any British colony of our time to get itself, for the fraction of a moment, into a position where it could think of suggesting such terms; for the military and naval power of England over her colonies is now overwhelming and complete.

---

[12] Works, Bigelow edition, vol. v, p. 440; Galloway, "A Letter from Cicero to Right Hon. Lord Viscount Howe," London, 1781.

[13] Works, Bigelow edition, vol. v, p. 440.

Most of the terms were, of course, concerned with the repeal of laws which the colonists disliked, and certainly the amount of repealing demanded seemed very large to Englishmen. But some of the other terms may be mentioned as showing the situation. England was not to keep troops in time of peace or to build a fortification in any colony, except by that colony's consent. England must also withdraw all right to regulate colonial internal affairs by act of Parliament; and the colonies must continue to control the salaries of their governors. If Parliament's authority and the right to keep troops had been surrendered those concessions alone would have destroyed the colonial relation, and the American communities would have become independent. But Franklin knew he could not yield on these points, and he even suggested to Lord Chatham that the Congress be recognized as a permanent body.

These terms were too stiff even for Whigs. The friendly negotiators could only politely withdraw and say that they were very sorry; and the delightful games of chess came to an end. The Ministry were amused, and believed that they saw the situation more clearly than ever. Admiral Howe was deeply disappointed. He had expected to take Franklin out with him as one of the members of his peace commission; and, to make the terms easier and everything smooth, Franklin was offered any important reward he chose to name. As a beginning, he was to be paid the arrears of his salary which the colonies, whose agent he was, had for some years neglected to send to him. But they were entirely mistaken in supposing that he would yield to any of these temptations.

XXIV.

PREPARING FOR THE BREAK

MEANWHILE during that winter and spring of 1775 in which Parliament was considering the documents of the Congress and passing the Fisheries Bill and other repressive acts, General Gage was having a curious experience in Massachusetts. He issued writs, summoning the Massachusetts Assembly to meet at Salem, on the 5th of October, 1774. But soon after he issued this call the Congress at Philadelphia approved of the Suffolk resolutions, and he immediately issued a proclamation suspending the meeting of the Assembly. The new members, however, met in spite of the proclamation, and no governor appearing to swear them in they seized the opportunity to create a patriot government for the province, as recommended in the Suffolk resolutions. By the passage of a mere resolution they turned themselves into an independent government, which they called the Provincial Congress of Massachusetts, and it assumed to itself the supreme authority of the province, which Gage had been unable to exercise. Massachusetts became de facto independent and never again passed under British authority. A British colony had become an independent American State.[1]

This had occurred before Parliament had received the documents of the Congress. In America both sides prepared for war as if they took for granted that the ultimatum of the Congress would be rejected. The patriots moved their private supplies of arms and ammunition from Boston. They protested against Gage fortifying the narrow neck which at that time connected Boston with the mainland. It was an act, they said, unfriendly in appearance and entirely unnecessary, for no one intended to hurt him; and Gage smilingly replied that neither had he any

---

[1] *American Archives*, fourth series, vol. i, pp. 829–853, 880; Stedman, "American War," vol. i, pp. 107, 108; *Annual Register*, 1775, chap. i.

intention of hurting anybody. Each side understood the other quite thoroughly.

In Virginia the governor reported in December, 1774, that the patriots were arming and drilling in every county, the courts of justice were abolished, and the royal government "entirely disregarded if not wholly overturned." The other colonies had not gone so far as Massachusetts and Virginia, but contented themselves with passing county resolutions protesting against Parliament and the Ministry and professing the most unbounded devotion to the King, whose ministers they said were leading him astray.[2]

Gage was buying up all the blankets, canvas, and camp equipment he could find, and the patriots were persuading the merchants not to sell. The patriots were purchasing arms and ammunition in all parts of Europe, and when the Ministry forbade the exportation of powder and firearms to America, the patriots in Rhode Island seized all the cannon belonging to the Crown; and in New Hampshire they surprised Fort William and Mary and removed from it all the arms and military stores. An account of their proceedings formed part of the evidence of rebellion laid before Parliament.[3]

France and Spain refused England's request to prohibit their people from selling powder to the Americans. The Dutch agreed to the prohibition, but their merchants sold us powder in large glass bottles under the appearance of spirits.[4]

Gage had only 4000 troops and was unable to hold any place

---

[2] Niles, " Principles and Acts of the Revolution," edition 1876, pp. 99, 100, 246; Gordon, " American War," edition 1788, vol. i, p. 396; *American Archives*, fourth series, vol. i, pp. 780, 806, 939, 954, 1078; vol. ii, pp. 1062, 1694. For the county resolutions see volumes i and ii of *American Archives*, fourth series; Gordon, " American Revolution," vol. ii, p. 74.

[3] Stedman, " American War," edition 1794, vol. i, pp. 110, 111; *American Archives*, fourth series, vol. i, pp. 1041, 1042, 1053, 1069; vol. iii, pp. 1199, 1200, 1630.

[4] *American Archives*, fourth series, vol. i, pp. 953, 979, 1065, 1066; vol. ii, p. 463; Gordon, " American Revolution," edition 1788, vol. i, p. 498.

but Boston, for the patriots could put 10,000 militia in the field. He, however, sent 300 muskets to the loyalists at Marshfield, New Hampshire; and in the end of February, 1775, he sent an expedition to seize some brass cannon at Salem. This excursion to Salem under Colonel Leslie came very near beginning the war. The patriots had dragged off the cannon by the time the British troops arrived and the draw of the bridge across the river was up. There was a chance for a few moments that the troops and the townsmen would fight at the bridge. In fact, Leslie gave the order to fire, but it was not obeyed, and one of the townsmen dissuaded him from repeating it. Thus a slight circumstance postponed the war from February to April.[5]

About the same time Gage sent out two young officers, Captain Brown and Ensign Bernicre, to travel in disguise as far as Worcester and report on roads and the nature of the country. They were passed on from one loyalist family to another, and Bernicre's journal gives an amusing account of the adventures of these two lambs which the wolves allowed to play in the forest. Their disguise was quickly discovered, and Bernicre tries to leave the impression that they were every moment in danger. But they were safe as mice in a church. The patriots watched them narrowly in a fatherly way and saw that they returned safely to Boston; for it would have been contrary to the policy that had been adopted to allow a British officer to suffer ill usage at the hands of the rougher element.[6]

There was naturally much curiosity on both sides to see what would happen on the 5th of March, the anniversary of the Boston Massacre, which for four years had been celebrated by a patriotic oration against standing armies. The oration of the previous year had been delivered by John Hancock; and as there were no British troops then in Boston, there was no danger in his describing such armies as composed of outcasts

---

[5] Stedman, " American War," edition 1794, vol. i, pp. 113, 114; " Life of Timothy Pickering," p. 60; Hale " One Hundred Years Ago," p. 6.

[6] *American Archives*, fourth series, vol. i, p. 1268; Hale, " One Hundred Years Ago," p. 7.

unfit to live in civil society. But now Dr. Warren had to deliver the oration surrounded by the troops, and with officers and privates composing a large part of his audience. The officers had threatened vengeance to any orator who should dare repeat Hancock's contemptuous slurs on regular soldiers. They went armed to hear the oration in the Old South Church; and Captain Chapman is said to have sat on the pulpit stairs ostentatiously playing with three pistol bullets and watching the orator.

It was a trying and delicate position for Warren. He must not flinch from the patriot position; and yet he could have no wish to precipitate a conflict among women and children in the church. It is easy to see that by a few hasty words he might have begun the Revolution in the Old South instead of a month later at Lexington. But he was equal to the occasion. He went over the whole patriot argument in a most able and enlightened manner. He described how the contest had already raised an almost universal inquiry into the rights of mankind in general which would advance the cause of liberalism in the world. He touched upon the actual scenes of the massacre. He made those powerful appeals to passion and feeling for which these orations were intended. He called upon the widow and the mother to weep over their dead.

> "And to complete the pompous show of wretchedness, bring in each hand thy infant children to bewail their father's fate. Take heed, ye orphan babes, lest whilst your streaming eyes are fixed upon the ghastly corpse your feet slide on the stones bespotted with your father's brains."

But he gave no direct affront to the soldiers until he began to speak of the standing army which was now again quartered upon Boston, and said that it must not be allowed to destroy our liberty.

> "Our streets are again filled with armed men; our harbor is crowded with ships of war, but these cannot intimidate us; our liberty must be preserved; it is far dearer than life; we hold it even dear as our allegiance; we must defend it against the attacks of friends as well as enemies; we cannot suffer even Britons to ravish it from us."

That was as near as he went to the danger point; and according to one account Captain Chapman shouted that curious English exclamation, "Fie, Fie!" and some thought there was a fire. But the old Town Clerk, William Cooper, arose and said, "There was no fire, but the fire of envy burning in the hearts of our enemies, which he hoped soon to see extinguished."

According to another account, the soldiers waited till the oration was completed, and when a motion was made to appoint an orator for the next year, they hissed and made such an uproar that some of the women in alarm jumped out of the windows.

Another tradition has it that when Captain Chapman became particularly conspicuous in exhibiting his pistol-bullets the orator dropped a white handkerchief over them; and there are also other versions. We shall never know exactly what happened. But it was really wonderful that there was no riot. It was an instance of great self-restraint on both sides, and we cannot imagine such an incident passing off so peaceably in a revolution among Frenchmen.[7]

Indeed, it had become quite obvious to every one that the strained relations and affectation of friendliness could not be continued much longer. Cannon-balls and half barrels of gunpowder were now carried out of Boston concealed in wagonloads of manure or in butcher's carts, and paper cartridges of powder were concealed in candle-boxes. The troops finally, on the 18th of March, seized 13,425 musket cartridges and 300 pounds of ball which were passing out in this way. They were private property, but their destination was so obvious that Gage felt compelled to confiscate them in spite of the form of friendliness that was being observed.[8]

The ammunition which was passed out of Boston, however,

---

[7] Niles, "Principles and Acts of the American Revolution," edition 1876, p. 113; *American Archives*, fourth series, vol. ii, pp. 38, 120, 177; E. E. Hale, "One Hundred Years Ago," pp. 8, 9; "Diary and Letters of Thomas Hutchinson," vol. i, p. 529.

[8] Gordon, "American Revolution," edition 1788, vol. i, p. 473; *American Archives*, fourth series, vol. ii, p. 211.

was nothing compared to the warlike material, spades, pick-axes, camp-pots and kettles, knapsacks, bullets, powder, and arms which were being collected at Worcester and Concord. The question was becoming more and more important whether it was not the duty of Gage to seize these supplies and arrest Hancock, Adams, and Cushing. The patriots had already collected such a force that it was doubtful whether Gage could seize either the military supplies or the leaders, and lapse of time appeared to be making the situation worse for him.

An attempt had been made by Gage to win over Samuel Adams. Colonel Fenton was sent to him with an intimation that it would be greatly to his profit and safety should he withdraw from the rebellion. The exact nature of the reward he was to receive is not known; but, no doubt, it was considerable, and most tactfully and delicately offered. But they had again mistaken their man, and Adams continued to be as busy as a bee with his plans for independence.[9]

From a letter written in London on the 18th of March, it appears that Gage may have received instructions some time in February to seize Cushing, Adams, and Hancock, and send them to England for trial; and subsequently he is supposed to have received orders to hang them in Boston without waiting to send them to England. Gage was unwilling to execute these orders, although he apparently had a good opportunity to execute the first one at the celebration on the 5th of March. He feared an open conflict with the patriots, who were supposed to have over ten thousand militia ready for the outbreak whenever it should come. He asked for reinforcements and meanwhile hoped for favorable circumstances.[10]

It was now the end of March, and no one in America had heard about the Fisheries Act or anything else that Parliament and the Ministry had decided upon. But on the 2nd of April,

[9] Stedman, "American War," edition 1794, vol. i, pp. 113, 114; "Life of Timothy Pickering," p. 60; Hosmer, "Life of Samuel Adams," p. 302.

[10] Wells, "Life of Samuel Adams," vol. ii, pp. 289, 290; *American Archives*, fourth series, vol. ii, pp. 336, 386; vol. v, p. 41; "Diary and Letters of Thomas Hutchinson," vol. i, pp. 183, 203, 219, 416.

1775, a vessel called the " Hawke " reached Marblehead and brought the news of what Parliament had been doing in February. The vessel had left Falmouth, England, February 17, and brought a London newspaper of February 11, which described the Fisheries Bill which Lord North the day before had obtained leave to introduce.[11]

The arrival of that vessel marks a great turning-point in the Revolution. Both Gordon and Earl Percy describe the change which they saw take place almost instantly. It was now known in America that the ultimatum had been rejected; that England would no longer repeal acts of Parliament and yield to colonial demands; an end had come to one stage of the controversy; one act of the great drama was closed. From that moment both patriot and Englishman were compelled to look at the situation in a new light.

---

[11] Gordon, "American Revolution," edition 1788, vol. i, p. 474; Boston *Gazette*, April 3, 1775. "Letters of Hugh, Earl Percy," p. 48; *American Archives*, fourth series, vol. i, pp. 1566, 1570, 1622. See also Boston *Gazette*, April 17, 1775. The news of the final passage of the Fisheries Bill on March 30 reached Philadelphia, June 7. (Gordon, *supra*, vol. ii, p. 63.)

XXV.

THE BATTLE OF LEXINGTON

THE principal places for the accumulation of patriot military supplies were Concord and Worcester. Concord was only twenty miles from Boston, and from the 8th of March to the 14th of April wagons had been hauling into it casks of balls, hogsheads of flints, beef, rice, and tow cloth. The Massachusetts Provincial Congress was also holding its session there; and, influenced no doubt by the recent news from England, Gage resolved to seize Hancock and Samuel Adams while attending the Congress and at the same time capture the military supplies.

That this enterprise failed is not surprising. It would have required more than double Gage's whole force to have gone supply-hunting such a distance with any chance of safety or success. As for capturing Hancock or Adams, that might have been done by a quick and well-concealed movement of a small force; but the English are always notoriously deficient in such enterprises; and were now so carefully watched by such a large patriot population that it would have required a secret expedition composed of only two or three men to reach the patriot leaders.

Gage tried hard to conceal his purpose and defeat the watchfulness of the patriots. He sent out five regiments one morning with all the appearance of marching on the Provincial Congress at Concord; but they returned within a few hours; and this and other countermarching were regarded by the patriots as feints to put them off their guard. They were thoroughly convinced that a secret or sudden expedition of some sort was preparing. Paul Revere and his fellow-watchers patrolled the streets of Boston every night noting the smallest indications of preparation among the troops. Adams and Hancock were warned, and the patriot Committee of Safety ordered the military supplies at Concord and Worcester to be scattered among nine towns, so that Gage's expedition was half defeated before it started.[1]

Meanwhile the meeting of the Provincial Congress at Concord had adjourned. But Adams and Hancock had not returned to Boston, and were staying at the house of the Rev. Jonas Clark, at Lexington. This was exactly what Gage wanted; for. the seizure of the two patriots could be made much more quietly. at Clark's than at a meeting of the Congress. Accordingly on the 18th of April a number of British officers went out to Cambridge, where they dined, and towards night stationed themselves along the roads to Lexington and Concord so as to intercept patriot messengers going to alarm the country.

At eleven o'clock that night eight hundred British troops, under command of Lieutenant-Colonel Smith, with Major Pitcairn, of the marines, in the advance, crossed in boats to the Charlestown shore and took the road to Concord. They had hoped that their starting was sudden and unexpected, but the secret had leaked out. Paul Revere had arranged for signal lanterns in the North Church steeple which would show to certain people on the mainland the moment the British started, and the alarm could then be carried by swift messengers. Dr. Warren sent William Davies early in the evening to ride express to Lexington. Revere himself started a little later, crossing over to Charlestown and borrowing a horse. But this elaborate system of messengers was scarcely necessary. The marching of eight hundred infantry along the roads at night, passing by farmhouses and setting every dog to barking, was in itself a sufficient alarm. Scores of active young farmers could run or ride ahead of the troops and warn the whole countryside. It would seem as if Gage might have better accomplished his purpose by a sudden dash of cavalry. But he was probably

---

[1] *American Archives*, fourth series, vol. ii, pp. 253, 362, 626; Gordon, " American Revolution," edition 1788, vol. i, p. 476; Massachusetts Historical Society Collections, vol. v, p. 106; Bolton, " Private Soldier under Washington," p. 10.

not well supplied with that arm; and it now made no difference, because most of the supplies had been removed.

Gordon says that some of the messengers were intercepted by the mounted officers who had gone out on the roads. Revere was nearly caught by three of them soon after he started, but he had a good horse and escaped. He describes the night as very pleasant, and with his love of horsemanship we can readily believe that he had a grand ride. He reached Lexington, where he stirred Adams and Hancock out of their beds, and was pressing on to Concord through the exhilarating night air when he was suddenly surrounded by four of the British officers and taken prisoner. They turned back to Lexington with him, plied him with questions, and having deprived him of his horse let him go.[2]

It was afterwards discovered that the British officers who went out on the roads gave the alarm more effectively than the messengers; for everybody they met was seized and treated in such a rough and bullying manner that people quickly inferred that some important British expedition had started. In a community that was expecting something of that kind, the alarm once given spread with great rapidity by the ringing of bells and firing of signal guns. Within three hours after the troops started the alarm had reached their destination, before they had travelled half the distance. Their commander, hearing the ringing of bells and the signal-guns, sent a messenger back to Boston for reinforcements.

At two o'clock in the morning a company of about one hundred and thirty militia assembled on the green in front of the Congregational church at Lexington. They appear to have got the alarm by being told that British officers were seizing and stopping people on the road. They waited for some time, but seeing no enemy and the night being cold, they were dismissed, some going to their homes and others to the tavern to

---

[2] Revere's account of his ride can be read in Massachusetts Historical Collections, vol. v, p. 106. See, also, *American Archives*, fourth series, vol. ii, pp. 359, 362, 487, 489, 626; Stedman, "American War," edition 1794, vol. i, p. 119.

wait further orders. At five o'clock they were called and told that the regulars were coming, and about seventy of them assembled in rather irregular order under the command of a veteran of the French War, Captain Parker, the grandfather of the famous Unitarian preacher, Theodore Parker. The advance guard of the British, under Major Pitcairn, approached just after sunrise, and it became a question which side should begin; for every one felt that this was the break with England that had long been expected.

In any large-minded view of such a situation it made no difference who fired the first shot. Every one knew that there was to be war, and that it would begin at some locality and at some hour that year. As a matter of fact, the first shots had been fired and the first blood had been shed when the British troops five years before killed patriot citizens in New York and in Boston. But in the public mind those events were not counted as a beginning; for neither side had been ready for actual war. Now, however, organized troops of each party faced the other in anger; and in popular estimation it is a matter of much sentimental importance which side strikes the first blow.

In modern imperial operations it is usually considered advisable to take sufficient time to irritate the people to be annexed into some act of pronounced aggression. The war of conquest can then be given a stronger moral basis; can be called a war of self-defence, and more easily upheld among liberals and lovers of peace. All this is usually easy to accomplish, because the weaker people, or patriots, are apt to be uneasy, indignant, and excitable, while the imperial power is already well-armed, cool, and unimpulsive.

If England had had her modern experience she would have taken such cautious action that there would have been no question as to which side began the attack, and such an aggressive expedition as this one to Concord would probably not have been made. Colonel Smith, however, gave repeated instructions to the regulars to wait till they were fired upon. The patriots on their side had been equally cautious, and for months it had been the watchword among them to act entirely on the defensive and let England begin.

Under these circumstances it very naturally became a subject of much dispute as to which side began the war by firing the first shot. Captain Parker and some of his men gave their version of the story under oath within a week after the battle. The British, they said, came up with three officers riding ahead, and one of these officers waving his sword shouted, "Disperse, you rebels, immediately!" or according to another witness, "Throw down your arms, ye villians!"

The militia were then ordered by Parker, their captain, to disperse, and immediately began to retire. This seems to have been in accordance with the policy agreed upon among the patriots, to do nothing whatever to withstand the British or resist by organized force the authority of the King until the King's soldiers fired the first shot. In all their arguments against the authority of Parliament they had repeatedly admitted that they owed a certain allegiance to the King as head of the empire and they had described their devotion to him in the most glowing language. They would not, therefore, assume formal independence or make war upon the King, until some act had been done by him, or by his servants, which would snap the last thread of allegiance and leave them free to do as they chose.

Parker's men retired in accordance with this principle; but they had not gone far, they said, when one or two pistol-shots were fired by the British officers, and immediately afterwards an officer ordered the soldiers to fire, which they did with good effect, killing eight and wounding ten militiamen, who, the witnesses said, had not yet fired a shot.

On the British side Major Pitcairn gave a very different story, which Gage reported to the British Government and also published in the colonies. Two miles outside of Lexington, Major Pitcairn had met, he said, a large body of armed patriots, one of whom advanced and attempted to shoot, but his musket flashed in the pan. On this the Major gave instructions to the troops to move forward, but on no account to fire without orders. When they arrived at the edge of the village, they observed about two hundred armed men drawn up on the green, and when the regulars came within one hundred yards of them, they began to file off towards some stone walls on their right flank. The Light Infantry, observing this, ran after them. The Major instantly called to the soldiers not to fire, but to surround and disarm them. Some of the patriots who had jumped over a wall then fired four or five shots at the troops, wounding a man of the Tenth Regiment and the Major's horse, and at the same time several shots were fired from a meeting-house on the left. Upon this, without any order or regularity, the Light Infantry began a scattering fire and killed several of the country people, but the fire was silenced by the authority of the officers.[8]

Meanwhile Samuel Adams and Hancock had quietly waited at the house of the Rev. Jonas Clark until the British reached Lexington, and then made their escape across the fields. As the reports of the muskets reached their ears Adams knew that the crowning day of his life had come, the formal break which would put an end to plans of reconciliation and compromise. The deepest wish of his heart was gratified, and he is said to have exclaimed, "What a glorious morning is this!"

So the first part of the British expedition had failed. The two patriots who were to be taken to England to be hung had escaped. But the chance still remained of securing the patriot military stores at Concord; and Colonel Smith coming up with the main body, he and Pitcairn pressed on to accomplish this purpose. The six miles to Concord were soon covered, and at seven o'clock the militia drawn up before the town were easily

---

[8] The testimony of Parker and his men can be read in *American Archives*, fourth series, vol. ii, pp. 489-496. One of the wounded regulars made prisoner by the militia testified that the British fired the first shot; another one testified that he could not tell which side fired the first shot. *Id.*, pp. 496, 501. See, also, pp. 197, 742, 627, 434-436, 440, 945, 947, vol. iii, p. 1729; Jones, "New York in the Revolution," vol. i, p. 552; "Letters of Earl Percy," p. 55; Stedman, "American War," edition 1794, vol. i, pp. 116, 117.

driven back over the north bridge, and the bridge secured by a force of one hundred light infantry. The main body at once entered the town and seized the remains of the patriot military supplies—two cannon, which they disabled; 500 pounds of ball, which they threw into the river and wells, and sixty barrels of flour, which they broke up and scattered.

This small plunder was all that was accomplished, and to do this they had advanced into a dangerous position. The militia of the country were assembling and were already, it is supposed, three hundred in number. They approached the British force at the bridge, waited, as they afterwards testified, until they were fired upon, and then attacked the regulars, driving them across the bridge into the town. If the militia had followed up this advantage and held the bridge they might possibly have kept Colonel Smith and his men on the other side of the river. But they drew off, and Smith took his whole force out of the town, crossed the bridge, and began to retreat towards Lexington.[4]

It was now noon, and why Smith had remained five hours in the town has never been explained. The delay was nearly fatal to his command, for the militia had collected in larger numbers. They pressed on both sides of him and in his rear, shooting down his men from behind trees and the low stone walls which divide New England fields. His retreat was rapidly becoming a rout and disaster, and long before he could reach Boston his force would be annihilated.

Fortunately for him General Gage had kept himself well informed of the situation and responded to his call for reinforcements. By eight or nine o'clock in the morning he had started Earl Percy and nine hundred men to the rescue. They marched out playing the new tune, "Yankee Doodle," which had been composed in derision of the New Englanders. Percy's name suggested memories of an old English ballad, and as he marched through Brookline a bright patriot boy is said to have shouted at him that he would soon have to dance to Chevy

---

[4] *American Archives*, fourth series, vol. ii, pp. 497-501, 630, 674.

Chase. He reached Lexington at two o'clock, just as Colonel Smith's men were passing through it in full flight, their ammunition all spent, and their "tongues hanging out of their mouths," says Stedman, "like dogs after a chase."[5]

Percy had now the task of getting the whole force, rescuers and fugitives, back to Boston with only thirty-six rounds of ammunition. It was a mental enlargement for him, and he was very much surprised to find that his seventeen hundred light infantry and grenadiers, the flower of the British army, were on the eve of being destroyed by the people whom he had described as psalm-singing, cowardly hypocrites. He was ever afterwards very proud of the rescue and of the skilful and lucky manner in which he retreated for fifteen miles to Boston.

He put the fugitives in front of him, covering them with his own brigade, and sending out strong flanking parties, for "there was not a stone wall or house, though before in appearance evacuated, from whence the rebels did not fire upon us."

"As soon as they saw us begin to retire, they pressed very much upon our rear guard, which for that reason I relieved every now and then. In this manner we retired for fifteen miles under an incessant fire all round us till we arrived at Charlestown, between seven and eight in the even, very much fatigued with a march of about thirty miles and having expended almost all our ammunition."—Letters, p. 50.

He was impressed with the bushwhacking method of the American attack, which was obviously the best one for them. He saw that they evidently knew what they were about, and were led by old rangers and Indian fighters. Their desperate courage astonished him, for many of them concealed themselves in houses and advanced within ten yards to fire "at me and other officers, tho' they were morally certain of being put to death themselves in an instant."

---

[5] Stedman, "American War," vol. i, p. 118. Gordon, "American Revolution," edition 1788, vol. i, p. 481. Mr. Bolton in his edition of Earl Percy's Letters (p. 49) notes that Horace Walpole on hearing of the battle of Lexington was struck with the suggestiveness of Percy's name. "So here is this fatal war commenced. 'The child that is unborn shall rue the hunting of that day.'"

The numbers against him have not been ascertained. They may have equalled or exceeded his own. His troops plundered and destroyed as many houses as possible upon the road, and considerable injury of this sort had been done in Lexington and Concord. Aged and sick persons and women who had just given birth to children are said to have been shot in the houses or driven out into the fields; and these atrocities, whether true or false, were quickly used by the patriots to make the British name detestable in America.

Percy reached Bunker Hill, just across the water from Boston, a little after sunset, formed his men in a strong position which the militia could not successfully attack, and the next morning took his force into the town. He had lost 273 and the patriots only 88.*

---

* Contemporary estimates or guesses of the numbers of the minute men and militia that drove the British back to Boston vary from 250 to 20,000. The last number of 20,000 is, of course, impossible. According to an estimate of the militia in the neighboring towns kindly prepared for me by Mr. David M. Matteson from town histories and the Lexington alarm rolls, not over 4000 lived near enough to reach the scene of action in time to take part. We can hardly assume that all who were near enough obeyed the call, and that recorded numbers are always the same as actual numbers. After making this allowance a thousand seems like a liberal estimate, and I am inclined to have some faith in that contemporary estimate which says that " there never was more than 250 men engaged," although others may have been coming on and trying to get into the fight. (*American Archives*, vol. ii, pp. 362, 440, 444, 472, 509: " Letters of Hugh, Earl Percy," p. 54 note; " Life of Timothy Pickering," pp. 69–75.)

XXVI.

THE PATRIOTS BESIEGE BOSTON AND
TAKE TICONDEROGA

THE news of the battle of Lexington was carried through
New England and southward to the Carolinas by express-riders,
as they were called, employed by the patriot committees. The
riders passed from committee to committee and had each committee attest by signature the document they carried. The
news was sent in this systematic way to arouse the patriot party
in other provinces to rally to the support of Boston; and it
was followed up by letters and appeals calling for militia to
come to Boston and render it impossible for Gage to send out
another expedition. They even went farther and urged the
collection of an army that would compel the British to evacuate
Boston and sail away in their ships.[1]

Immediately after the battle the patriot leaders had taken
the sworn testimony of Captain Parker and his men as to what
had happened at Lexington and who had fired the first shot.
A statement was made up from this evidence and sent out to
all the colonies to draw them into sympathy and alliance; and
the same statement was sent to England to strengthen the
hands of the Whigs, and throw the odium of the first shot on
England. Gage in a similar way circulated his account of
the battle. Each side was anxious to justify its conduct in an
affair which obviously marked a momentous and terrible change
in the conflict.

Gage's side of the story was sent to England in a ship called
the " Sukey; " and four days afterwards, on the 29th of April,

---

[1] Bolton, " Private Soldier under Washington," *Pennsylvania Magazine of History*, vol. 27, p. 257. *American Archives*, fourth series, vol. ii,
pp. 446, 447, 472–474, 482, 506, 507, 780, 786, 787; J. J. Boudinot,
" Life of Boudinot," vol. i, pp. 7, 8.

the Committee of Safety started their version in a fast ship commanded by Captain John Darby, who was instructed to "conceal his mission from every person on earth" and drive his vessel to her utmost speed. Darby "cracked on," as the sailors say, outstripped everything on the sea, and reached England the 28th of May, eleven days before the "Sukey;" so that the American version of the first shot had the advantages of nearly two weeks' circulation before the British version was heard of.[2]

The appeal of Massachusetts for troops was promptly responded to in New England. Many of us used to read in our school-books a very dramatic account of how Israel Putnam, the rough and ready old soldier of the French and Indian Wars, was ploughing on his farm at Pomfret, Connecticut, when a messenger told him of the fight at Lexington. He instantly mounted his horse—some say he seized one of the horses from the plough—left word for the militia to follow him, and rode one hundred miles in eighteen hours to Cambridge.

What actually happened is still a matter of dispute. But the most probable story is that he heard the news at eleven in the morning while building a stone wall on his land, where he had a tavern and a farm. He went to the house, got his horse, and rode about to the neighboring towns to consult with the militia officers. On his return he found several hundred militia assembled, who informed him that they had elected him their general and that they wanted to march immediately. He said he was not ready and had no money. They supplied him from among themselves; and then it was that, after giving directions for them to follow him, he started on the same horse, reached Concord the next morning at sunrise, and soon after was with the troops that were collecting at Cambridge just outside of Boston.[3]

---

[2] E. E. Hale, "One Hundred Years Ago," p. 21; "Diary and Letters of Thomas Hutchinson," vol. i, pp. 455, 456, 461, 464, 465; vol. ii, p. 118; Gordon, "American Revolution," edition 1788, vol. i, p. 503.

[3] Tarbox, "Life of Putnam," pp. 83, 86; Gordon, "American Revolution," edition 1788, vol. ii, p. 2.

News of the Battle of Lexington.

MILITIA MARCH TO BOSTON

John Stark, a New Hampshire hunter and popular leader, had been equally prompt and reached Cambridge before Putnam. Benedict Arnold, a trader and shipmaster of New Haven, had been chosen captain of a militia company. When the news of Lexington arrived his company expressed their willingness to march the next morning, and he paraded them before the tavern in which the Committee of Safety were sitting and demanded a supply of ammunition. The committee refused it on the ground that he was not duly authorized. Whereupon, with characteristic impulse, he got the consent of his men to reply that he would take the ammunition by force. The committee yielded and he marched for Cambridge.

But his little company did not reach Cambridge until the 29th of April, more than a week after the battle, and during that time and for some days afterwards it is probable that there were very few militia collected, and Gage might have sent a force out to attack them with some prospect of success.

The day after the battle the Massachusetts Provincial Congress had placed General Artemas Ward in command of all the militia; but he was a very inactive officer in bad health. Possibly during that first week it had not been definitely decided what should be done. Some thought that there was no danger of Gage's attempting to send out another expedition.

The assembly and governor of Connecticut had assumed a sort of leadership and began to enter into negotiations with Gage for a cessation of hostilities and an agreement as to future conduct; but this course was strongly disapproved by the Massachusetts Committee of Safety. They denounced it as a serious blunder which would be encouraged by Gage in order to gain time and check patriot measures until his reinforcements should arrive from England. They professed to have information that Gage intended speedily to sally out and wreak vengeance for his defeat. They felt it their duty to protect their people from such an attack and take aggressive action in the war which had evidently begun.

The first militia began to arrive in the neighborhood of

311

Boston about ten days after the battle, and all through the month of May they continued to arrive—rough, ungainly men, fresh from farm labor, without much order or discipline, joking with their leaders and trailing every variety of old musket and shot-gun, until by the 10th of June they were 7644 strong and had established themselves on the mainland west of Boston, where at first they were half-starved and shivered in the cold nights without blankets. They kept on increasing until by midsummer they numbered about 14,500 effectives rank and file, which, with the officers added, made about 17,000.[4]

A strong force was placed directly in front of the narrow neck of land leading to Boston, so as to prevent Gage breaking out at that point. This precaution had at first been neglected and caused much anxiety. The rest of the motley patriots were distributed in a large half-circle on the west side of Boston from the Mystic River on the north, through Cambridge, which became the patriot headquarters, round to Roxbury and Dorchester on the south, shutting in Gage and his four or five thousand men, who, the patriots said, must now take ship and leave Boston free.

Members of this volunteer force were constantly going home to attend to their affairs or obtain necessaries. Some of them returned or others came to take their place. It was a question whether such a strange sort of army could be kept in sufficient numbers for any length of time.

Outside of New England no troops were at first sent; but resolutions of sympathy were adopted, declaring that the cause of Boston was the cause of the whole continent. In New York

---

[4] The sick and absent were very numerous and, if added, ran the numbers up to 20,000. Gordon, "American Revolution," edition of 1788, vol. ii, pp. 27, 65; *American Archives*, fourth series, vol. ii, pp. 1623, 1636, 1735, 1736; Journal Provincial Congress of Massachusetts, p. 482; Sparks, "Writings of Washington," vol. iii, pp. 488, 493; *American Historical Review*, vol. i, p. 292; *American Archives*, fourth series, vol. iii, pp. 254, 853, 1165, 1404, 1611; vol. iv, p. 491.

the patriots were strong enough to seize the custom-house, arm themselves from the city arsenal, and stop all vessels going to the British in Boston, and also vessels going to Canada and Georgia, which had not sent representatives to the Congress.

The same plan of stopping vessels was carried out in Pennsylvania and Maryland, and recommended by the Congress to all the colonies. The New Jersey patriots seized the treasury of their colony and secured £20,000. In Maryland they seized the arsenal containing 1500 stand of arms; and in South Carolina the arsenal was seized.[5]

In Virginia the royal governor, Lord Dunmore, saved some of the powder in the arsenal and had it taken on board a British war-vessel. The patriots never forgave him for this clever trick, and if county resolutions of denunciation are of any avail the soul of Dunmore is not yet at rest. Patrick Henry, at the head of one hundred and fifty militia, marched on Williamsburg to seize the treasury. But messengers from the receiver-general of the colony met him and offered £330 as a compensation to the patriots for the powder that had been taken from the arsenal. This compromise was accepted, and the militia dispersed. But Dunmore shut himself up in his house, which he turned into a garrison surrounded with artillery, and talked of destroying the town, setting the negroes free and arming them against their masters, with other threats not calculated to soothe the minds of Southerners.[6]

The Massachusetts Provincial Congress kept pushing the most extreme measures, and on the 16th of May they sent a letter to Philadelphia offering to turn over to the Congress, just assembled, the army before Boston "for the general defence of the rights of America;" and the Congress was urged to form

[5] *American Archives*, fourth series, vol. ii, pp. 154, 229, 1829, 1834; Gordon, "American Revolution," edition 1788, vol. ii, p. 81.

[6] Gordon, "American Revolution," edition 1788, vol. ii, pp. 3–9, 85; *American Archives*, fourth series, vol. ii, pp. 380, 441–444, 449, 460, 464, 465, 477, 516, 525, 539–541, 578, 641, 681, 711, 1023, 1209; Jones, "New York in the Revolution," vol. i, pp. 39, 40.

a civil government for the whole country to which, it was assured, Massachusetts would gladly submit.[7]

Gage was helpless in Boston. He could hold the town, but not venture out of it, and his proclamations offering pardon to all rebels except Hancock and Adams, if they would lay down their arms, were rather ridiculous. But the patriots were almost as helpless. They could keep Gage in the town, but they had not enough cannon or powder to attack him. Boston was at that time surrounded by water except at the narrow neck which Gage had strongly fortified. The two opposing forces were in a deadlock position, in which they remained nine months.

They exchanged shots, however, quite frequently. The patriots welcomed to their ranks deserters from the British; and made use of the wind at night to blow into the British lines hand-bills encouraging desertion and describing the righteousness and advantage of the patriot cause. The patriots shut up in the town signalled information to their friends outside by means of gunpowder at night and during the day from the church steeples. There were numerous skirmishes for the possession of the hay and cattle on the islands in Boston harbor; and for this work and their scouting and reconnoitring the patriots collected from the neighboring coast large numbers of whale-boats, which easily outrowed any boats of the British.[8]

As the summer wore on the patriots ran intrenchments close to some of the British lines, and used their few small cannon. At the narrow neck of land leading into Boston, the opposing lines were very close. The British dug across the neck and let the water through. The patriots intrenched close up to them, burnt their outer guard-house, and drove the guard back into the lines.

---

[7] Gordon, " American Revolution," edition 1788, vol. ii, pp. 22, 58; *American Archives*, fourth series, vol. ii, pp. 378, 610, 611, 620, 621, 714, 936, 937, 1842.

[8] *American Archives*, fourth series, vol. ii, pp. 516, 786, 969, 1636, 1638, 1659, 1651, 1696, 1722, 1727, 1755; Gordon, " American Revolution," edition 1788, vol. ii, pp. 127, 143, 147.

PUTNAM'S AMBUSCADE

This close investment had been decided upon in opposition to a suggestion to draw off a little way and leave a space or neutral zone round the town. The close investment presented a bolder front and would prevent the British getting a start in breaking out from the town. The British, with abundant supplies of ammunition, were continually firing, and indulged in some very heavy cannonading, but with infinitesimal results. The patriots became so indifferent to the shot and shell that they would not take the trouble to build bomb-proofs.

At Gloucester the militia successfully protected the town from the British war-ship "Falcon." At Noddle's Island, now East Boston, the attempt of the patriots to carry off the cattle brought on a somewhat notable engagement. The British came to save the cattle with a schooner, sloop and boats. The patriots were led by Putnam, eager for his first fight in this new war, and with characteristic shrewdness at ambuscading he placed his men in a ditch up to their waists in water and covered by the bank to their necks. They poured a destructive fire into the unsuspecting schooner when she passed within sixty yards of them, but were obliged to continue the fight all night before they had the satisfaction of burning her. Putnam returned to camp covered with mud and delighted. '' I wish we could have something of this kind,'' he said, ''every day. It would teach our men how little danger there is from cannon balls.'' [*]

But these slight skirmishes used up nearly all the patriot supply of powder. They were scouring the country and the world for it. Men who understood its manufacture were eagerly sought; the loam in the floors of Virginia tobacco-houses was dug up to make saltpetre; Franklin was consulted; the small amount in other colonies was hurried to Cambridge by men who travelled by night and concealed themselves by day. Vessels visited the west coast of Africa and had procured powder from the British forts in exchange for rum before the

American Archives, fourth series, vol. ii, pp. 719, 720, 874; vol. iii, p. 99. Tarbox, " Life of Putnam," p. 96; *American Archives*, fourth series, vol. ii, p. 516.

Ministry could stop the traffic. Two daring American captains landed at Bermuda and abstracted a hundred barrels of powder from the government magazine. Twelve men from South Carolina surprised a British vessel at St. Augustine, Florida, and took from it 15,000 pounds of powder, which they carried safely to Charleston.[10]

The loyalists laughed at what they called the powderless militia mob who fancied they could win independence from the British empire; and loyalist and patriot began to accuse each other of lying, treachery, and every imaginable outrage of the blackest dye. Parents made frantic appeals to prevent their sons joining the rebels, who, they said, were "more savage and cruel than heathens" and worse than devils; [11] and the patriots in their turn denounced the cowardice, the treachery to kith and kin, and native land, or the hopeless degradation of spirit, which led a neighbor or friend to declare his acceptance of alien British rule.

Strange stories were circulated in England about the cruelties committed by the farmers on the dead and wounded regulars at Concord. They had not forgotten, it was said, their habits in the French and Indian War. They scalped some of the wounded British soldiers, leaving them to drag themselves about in torture with their bleeding, skinless skulls; and they gouged out the eyes of others in true Virginia fashion. Lord Percy, in his report to General Gage, had complained of the "barbarity of the rebels, who scalped and cut off the ears of some of the wounded men who fell into their hands." But Gordon, who made a careful investigation immediately after the battle, refused to credit any of these stories and explained that they originated in one wanton act by a boy at Concord, who,

---

[10] *American Archives*, fourth series, vol. ii, pp. 908, 1035, 1037, 1062, 1084, 1085, 1120, 1621, 1714, 1724; vol. iii, pp. 36, 37, 38, 137, 180, 653, 654, 682, 703, 1181; vol. iv, pp. 370, 723, 1253, 1456, 1488, 1491; Gordon, " American Revolution," edition 1788, vol. ii, pp. 84, 128.

[11] *American Archives*, fourth series, vol. ii, p. 508.

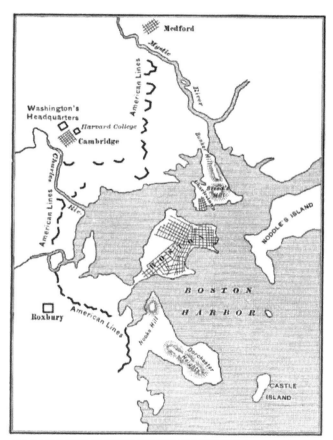

MAP OF THE SIEGE OF BOSTON, SHOWING THE IMPORTANCE OF BREED'S HILL,
DORCHESTER HEIGHTS, AND NOOK'S HILL

following after the militia, attacked a wounded regular trying to rise, and broke open his skull with a hatchet.[12]

Not satisfied with shutting up the British army in Boston, which they regarded as merely defensive warfare, the patriots planned a bolder movement. The vital strategic position at that time in America was generally believed to be the line of the Hudson River extended to Lakes George and Champlain and passing northward by the Richelieu River to Canada. This magnificent chain of water highways cut the colonies in half and would be of vast importance to Great Britain. If controlled it would stop communication between New England and the Middle States, and also afford an easy route for bringing into the rebellious colonies reinforcements from Canada, which might become a base of supplies for attacking the patriot movement to the southward.

The province of New York consisted at that time of nothing more than the settlements scattered along the banks of the Hudson and its tributary, the Mohawk. The interior of the province, as we now see it on the map, was totally unsettled. The important water highway of the Hudson and the lakes therefore controlled the whole province of New York, besides separating New England from the middle and southern colonies. It had always been the bone of contention in the war with France; and it had been taken for granted that the control of that highway would be equivalent to the conquest of New England, New Jersey, and Pennsylvania. The British had always established their military headquarters in the town of New York, so as to control the southern end of the line, and a great deal of the fighting in the French War had been for the control of Ticonderoga, near the northern end of the line.

---

[12] " Letters of Hugh, Earl Percy," p. 51; " An Answer to the Declaration of the American Congress," London, 1776, p. 102. " The Rights of Great Britain Asserted," p. 57, London, 1776. " View of the Evidence Relative to the Conduct of the War under Sir William Howe, with Fugitive Pieces," etc., p. 72, London, 1779; Gordon, " American Revolution," edition 1788, vol. i, p. 480; *American Archives*, fourth series, vol. ii, pp. 436, 440, 517, 630, 674, 862, 863.

Fort Ticonderoga, or "Fort Ty," as the colonists sometimes called it, was situated on a point of land where the waters of Lake George join the waters of Lake Champlain. The water highway was very narrow at this point; the guns of the fort commanded the water in every direction, and Ticonderoga could dominate the navigation between Lake George and Canada.

The seizure of Ticonderoga and the subsidiary fortresses to the north of it, Crown Point, Chamblee, and St. Johns, very naturally came into the minds of the patriots as a capital stroke against the mother-country. There was a strong feeling among them that the British would collect in Canada a great army of regulars, Canadians, and Indians, to invade New York and New England and hold the Hudson valley. But if the northern forts were secured before this expedition started its purpose would be defeated and the patriots could use the forts as a base for invading Canada, which might thus be persuaded to join in the Revolution.[13]

This idea of seizing Ticonderoga had some months before been suggested to the Massachusetts Committee of Safety by their secret agent in Montreal; and Benedict Arnold the day after he arrived in Cambridge made the same suggestion to them. In the country at large there was some opposition to such a plan, because it was too aggressive and would be a break in the policy of acting entirely on the defensive. This feeling afterwards found expression in the Congress. But the Massachusetts Committee of Safety did not share it. They were already engaged with patriots in Connecticut in maturing a plan for taking Ticonderoga; and without, it seems, telling Arnold of this, they gave him a colonel's commission on the 3rd of May, with instructions to raise 400 men in the western part of Massachusetts and attack Ticonderoga.[14]

He set out immediately, and on the 9th of May, before he had succeeded in recruiting any force, he was at Castleton, in

---

[13] *American Archives*, fourth series, vol. ii, pp. 624, 668, 669, 706, 733, 736, 892, 902, 944, 1042, 1066, 1539, 1540.

[14] *American Archives*, fourth series, vol. ii, pp. 450, 485.

what is now Vermont. Here he found Ethan Allen in command of 150 men of the Connecticut expedition, which was a private enterprise started by some members of the Connecticut legislature, Parsons, Deane, Wooster, and Wyllys. Parsons had obtained the money from the Connecticut treasury by simply giving a receipt signed by himself and four associates, and there was no formal or legal authority from the Connecticut government.

There is some evidence that Arnold in passing through Hartford on his way to Boston had suggested the enterprise to Parsons; for Parsons afterwards said that Arnold gave him a description of Ticonderoga, its cannon and defenses. But Arnold now found himself compelled to take a subordinate position under Allen, who was a rough frontiersman, with an education sufficient to induce him to write a book called "Reason the Only Oracle of Man," a very tiresome work inculcating deistical doctrines. He was able to assemble his men quickly because he was the chief leader of the Green Mountain Boys, who occupied the region now called Vermont, but then usually known as the New Hampshire Grants, and claimed by New York. Allen's followers had resisted by force the New York claim of sovereignty, and were inclined to have a little revolution of their own and become an independent state.[15]

Accounts differ as to the manner in which Allen and Arnold took Ticonderoga on the 10th of May. According to the British account Allen borrowed twenty of the garrison for the pretended peaceful purpose of helping to transport goods across the lake, and having thus weakened the fort easily took it by surprise in the night. By the American account Allen and Arnold marched directly towards the fort, landing alongside of

---

[15] *American Archives*, fourth series, vol. ii, pp. 507, 550, 557, 558, 707, 849; "Life of Arnold," p. 42; Gordon, "American Revolution," edition 1788, vol. ii, p. 40; Appleton, National Cyclopædia of Biography, vol. iv, p. 663. The Connecticut assembly afterwards approved of the transaction and discharged Parsons and his associates from liability on their receipt. (Conn. His. Soc., vol. i, pp. 182-185.)

it at night with only eighty-three of their men. Arnold arrogantly claimed the right to lead and be the first to enter the fort, which Allen was not the sort of man to allow, and they settled it by marching side by side at the head of their men. They accomplished a complete surprise of the garrison, walking quickly into one of the entrances, where a sentry snapped his gun at Allen and retreated. The next moment the Americans were all inside, and the forty-nine British surrendered.

The commander, De la Place, is said to have been surprised in his bed, and asked by what authority he must surrender. It was a rather puzzling question to answer. The expedition was a private enterprise originating among Connecticut people, without any sort of governmental authority, and had taken a fort within the boundaries of New York. But Allen was equal to the occasion and in grandiloquent style confidently replied, "In the name of the Great Jehovah and the Continental Congress."

It was a magnificent capture for the patriots, for there were over a hundred large cannon of the kind that were so sorely needed at Cambridge, besides smaller pieces, swivels, mortars, ten tons of musket-balls, three cart-loads of flints, shells, small arms, powder, and provisions.

Arnold was at once sent to capture Crown Point, which he easily accomplished, because it was garrisoned by a sergeant and only twelve men. He then was given command of an armed schooner, which, accompanied by Allen in charge of a fleet of bateaux, started to capture a British sloop-of-war, lying at St. Johns, at the lower end of the lake. The wind being fresh, Arnold's schooner out-sailed the bateaux; and he easily captured the sloop and returned. He was left in charge of Ticonderoga, and this interesting little expedition which destroyed the British power on Lake Champlain, was completed.

In order to make the enterprise a part of the general patriot cause, the forts, with all the captured cannon and supplies, were turned over to the Continental Congress at Philadelphia.

That body accepted the responsibility and committed the custody of Ticonderoga to the province of New York.[16]

The expedition was a great surprise, and alarmed the British, for it left Montreal unprotected. General Carleton quickly sent two regiments from Canada which retook St. Johns, at the foot of Lake Champlain, and strongly fortified it to protect Montreal, which was only twelve miles distant. Gage sent two ships with troops from Boston to Canada, and Guy Johnson, the British agent to the Six Nations of Indians in New York, went to the assistance of Carleton with five hundred warriors, and offered to retake both Ticonderoga and Crown Point. But nothing was done except to garrison St. Johns, which was supposed to be sufficient to protect the entrance to Canada.[17]

England was never again able to secure a permanent foothold as far south as Ticonderoga. It is true Burgoyne retook Ticonderoga in 1777; but the patriots got it back again within a few weeks; and from the time Allen and Arnold captured it the Americans may be said to have held it throughout the rest of the war. This was a great gain, and the importance of it can hardly be overestimated, for it gave the patriots control of the upper portion of the strategic line on which it was generally believed all military operations depended. They afterwards secured the lower portion of the line by holding West Point on the Hudson.

---

[16] *American Archives*, fourth series, vol. ii, pp. 556, 584, 585, 606, 618, 623, 624, 639, 645, 646, 668, 676, 686, 693, 698, 699, 705, 707, 715, 716, 719, 722, 731–737, 808, 839, 840, 847, 1086; Stedman, "American War," edition 1794, vol. i, p. 131; Arnold, "Life of Arnold," p. 37; Jones, "New York in the Revolution," vol. i, pp. 543–551.

[17] Stedman, "American War," edition 1794, vol. i, p. 133.

XXVII.

THE SECOND CONTINENTAL CONGRESS

THE Continental Congress assembled for the second time in Philadelphia on the 10th of May, the very day that Allen and Arnold took Ticonderoga. Thomas Jefferson now appeared as a new delegate from Virginia. Franklin had just returned from England and had been immediately elected to the Congress. He had sailed almost on the day the Fisheries Bill had passed, wondering whether he would be seized before he could start and locked up in the Tower; and the British Government, it seems, had serious thoughts of this measure, which might have considerably altered some interesting episodes in history.[1] He had steadily declared his belief in the possibility of a compromise, and expected to go back to England in a few months charged with the mission of finally settling all difficulties. But when he reached Philadelphia and heard of Lexington he quickly abandoned every thought of a peaceful settlement and took his place among the extreme patriots.

Lexington, the unorganized army besieging Boston, the final passage of the Fisheries Bill, the prompt and blunt refusal of all colonial suggestions of liberty, and fresh troops and armaments sailing for America, were now the great and deplorable facts of the day. What was to be done?

The business of the Congress became heavy and laborious. Those who engage in an open rebellion against the British empire have no time to lose. Franklin describes how, in spite of his seventy years, he toiled in debates and committee work from early morning until far into the night. John Adams' diary contains no descriptions of the wondrous dinner-parties that had surprised and delighted him the year before, when

---

[1] "Diary and Letters of Thomas Hutchinson," vol. i, pp. 405, 414, 421; vol. ii, p. 238.

hope was high and buoyant. Such entertainments were not, we may suppose, entirely abandoned; but in the darkened and serious circumstances they had become comparatively few.[2]

There was great difference of opinion between the moderate and the extreme patriots as to what course should be pursued and how far we should separate ourselves from Great Britain. John Adams, for example, was advocating most extreme measures in both public and private. He was proposing to recommend to each colony to seize all the crown officers and officials within its limits, and hold them as hostages for the safety of the patriots shut up with the British army in Boston. That done, the colonies were to be declared free and independent states, and then Great Britain could be informed that they would negotiate for a settlement of all difficulties on permanent principles. If she refused to negotiate, and insisted on war, she was to be informed that the colonies, now independent states, would seek the alliance of France, Spain, or any European country that would assist them. Finally, the Congress was to adopt the unorganized farmers at Cambridge as its army, and appoint a general to command them.[3]

Equally extreme with John Adams were the people of Mecklenburg County, North Carolina. They were largely Scotch-Irish in origin, and delegates from them assembled at Charlotte, on the 31st of May, and passed certain resolutions which had been carefully prepared. Having denied all authority of Parliament and having admitted only an allegiance to the King, the patriots all over the country were very anxious for the King to do something which would legally break the allegiance to him and leave America independent. The Mecklenburgers believed that they had found such an act[4] by the

[2] "Life of George Read," p. 108.

[3] Adams, Works, vol. iii, p. 407.

[4] Individuals were constantly looking for some act which in their minds would break the allegiance. Johnson, of Maryland, said, "The first Hessian soldier that puts foot on the American shore will absolve me from all allegiance to Great Britain."—Scharf, "History of Maryland," vol. ii, p. 218 note.

King in his address to Parliament on the 1st of February, declaring the American colonies in a state of rebellion.

That declaration of rebellion, said the Mecklenburg resolutions, necessarily annulled all British laws in America and suspended for the present all civil government derived from Great Britain. The people of each colony were therefore thrown back on their natural right of self-government; and for the sake of preserving good order, at least in Mecklenburg County, it was necessary to establish in place of the suspended or annulled British authority certain rules and regulations, which were set forth at length in the resolutions.

These resolutions were in effect a declaration of independence, although they do not contain a formal statement of such purpose. They were sent to the Congress by a special messenger, but attracted very little attention there or in the rest of the country, probably for the reason that they were merely another instance of that extreme patriot opinion which, for the present, the Congress was striving to keep in the background. Many years after the Revolution, however, it was asserted that these resolutions were not passed. They were prepared for passage, it was said, at a meeting on the 19th of May when word was received of the battle of Lexington, and amid great excitement among the delegates and assembled multitude and shouts of "Let us be independent! Let us declare independence!" another set of resolutions were adopted, in which it was announced that "We, the citizens of Mecklenburg County, do hereby declare ourselves a free and independent people; . . . to the maintenance of which independence we solemnly pledge to each other our mutual coöperation, our lives, our fortunes, and our most sacred honor."

This would certainly have been a very remarkable outbreak of extreme patriot opinion, using some of the same phrases which more than a year afterwards appeared in the Declaration of Independence made by the Congress. It was a great surprise to Jefferson and Adams when it was first brought to their attention in 1819, and they declared that they had never before heard of this Mecklenburg document. It is probably spurious, a mere mistake in the recollection of aged men. But the North Carolinians will not give it up and the controversy shows no signs of abating.[5]

The Congress were so anxious to be conservative that at the time these Mecklenburg resolutions were brought to them they were preparing the second petition to the King expressing the greatest attachment and devotion to his "Majesty's person, family and government," and imploring him to deliver them from the wicked designs of the ministry. After the fall of Ticonderoga was announced, they had voted, on the 18th of May, that an exact inventory be taken of the captured cannon and supplies in order that they might be safely returned, "when the restoration of the former harmony between Great Britain and these colonies, so ardently wished for by the latter, shall render it prudent and consistent." Three days before that the Congress had recommended to the New York patriots that if British troops arrived among them, they should act strictly on the defensive, so long as consistent with safety; that the troops should be permitted to occupy the barracks so long as they behaved peaceably, but not suffered to erect fortifications or cut off the communication between town and country, as Gage had done in Boston.[6]

These instructions for a peaceful reception of a British army in New York, while an American and British army were in a deadlock and death-struggle at Boston, were certainly a curious, but under the circumstances a very necessary, arrangement. When Washington arrived in New York on his way to the army at Cambridge, he was received with cheering and

[5] Hoyt, " The Mecklenburg Declaration of Independence; " Graham, "The Mecklenburg Declaration of Independence," *American Archives*, fourth series, vol. ii, pp. 855, 1683. *American Historical Review*, vol. xi, p. 548; *Magazine of American History*, vol. 21, pp. 31, 221; Niles, " Principles and Acts of the Revolution," edition 1876, pp. 313, 390; Bibliographical Contributions of Library of Harvard University, No. 48, pp. 34ff.

[6] Journals of Continental Congress, Ford edition, 1905, vol. ii, pp. 52, 56.

hearty welcome by the same people who, a few hours afterwards, gave a similar welcome to Tryon, the royal governor.[']

It was all in the line of policy that had been adopted by the patriots. They were willing to go only as far as circumstances had gone. They recognized a state of war as existing only in Massachusetts. They were loth to quit the defensive policy too suddenly, in spite of the aggressiveness of the Ticonderoga expedition. A great deal of their action for the next year was based on this feeling, and on the assumption of a possible reconciliation with England or restoration of harmony, which would stop the war. Many instances could be cited besides the notable one of the New Hampshire constitution, adopted in January, 1776, which declared that it was to continue only "during the present unhappy and unnatural contest with Great Britain."

These instances have been sometimes used in both America and England to show that our people were always perfectly willing to remain colonies "if well treated by the mother-country," and might still to this day be part of the British empire. But the only reconciliation which the patriot party would have accepted was that which they had already defined many times, namely, that Parliament should abandon all authority over the American provinces, which should be independent states, recognizing the British King as head of an empire not united or held together by any sort of compulsion, and that the King should have no authority to erect fortifications or keep troops in any province except by the consent of that province. That was their idea of a "restoration of harmony;" and under such a plan of reconciliation they might have been called colonies in the old Greek meaning of the word; but they would certainly not have been colonies in any meaning of the word as used in England in either ancient or modern times.

The expressions about loyalty and reconciliation were merely those legal fictions which Anglo-Saxon lawyers and

---

[']Jones, "New York in the Revolution," vol. i, pp. 55-58, 555, 556.

statesmen always adopt to keep the record technically correct. The technical fiction adopted by the Congress this year was that they were rebelling not against England or the King, but against a ministry that had deceived Parliament into extending its authority to the colonies. The British troops were spoken of by the patriots not as his Majesty's army or the English army, but as "the ministerial troops." Under this theory the Congress were compelled to speak of the King as the good man and their friend whom the wicked Ministry had deceived into approving of evil and tyrannical measures. They lived in hope, they said, that "he will at length be undeceived, and forbid a licentious ministry any longer to riot in the ruins of the rights of mankind." [a]

It was the same fiction or principle that the Cromwellian party had adopted more than a hundred years before. They too were rebelling, they said, not against the king or against England, but against a wicked ministry. Under this same principle the Congress adopted and sent to the King that second "humble and dutiful petition" in the regulation language of "loyal devotion," throwing all the blame upon the Ministry.

Every one knew, of course, that the King was not in the least deceived and that he, the Ministry, the whole Tory party —in short, the large majority of Englishmen—were all agreed that the colonies must be compelled to remain in the empire under the full authority of Parliament. The statements so common in documents and letters at this time expressing the hope of "a happy and honorable accommodation between Great Britain and her colonies," meant that the colonies as independent communities should negotiate a treaty or a compromise with Great Britain. But when a nation is at war with her colonies and has a colonial rebellion to put down, compromise means defeat, because a compromise or accommodation would in itself be an admission on the part of the mother-country that the supposed colonies had ceased to be colonies

---

[a] *American Archives*, fourth series, vol. ii, pp. 1839, 1882.

and had become so far independent as to make a treaty or agreement of accommodation like an independent nation.[*]

The conservatism of the Congress and the patriot party, their gradual development of revolutionary principles step by step, their clinging to old terms and old forms, and old ideas and arguments, and their postponement of the first blow and all aggressive action as long as possible, was unquestionably commendable, and won respect for their cause both at home and abroad.

With all their careful conservatism, they had already adopted enough radical and daring measures to shock that numerous class who mistrust popular rights and revolutions. The loyalists shrank from all the patriot proceedings with horror. They were amazed and almost dumb with indignation to hear that the Congress was proposing to ask assistance of France and Spain, old England's bitterest enemies. They could hardly believe the news that Ethan Allen and Benedict Arnold had had the temerity to take the two British forts on Lake Champlain, Ticonderoga and Crown Point, and send the captured British flags to the Congress, which had used them to decorate the walls of the halls in which they sat. Would not England's vengeance for this be swift and terrible? [10]

But as the summer wore on the Congress not only made more vigorous preparations for war, but began to create a national government for the whole country. They established a general post-office system; they created a Department of Indian Affairs; they organized a regular army, adopted articles of war, and inaugurated a hospital service, with doctors and nurses. These beginnings of nationality are now profoundly interesting to us, but they were marks of Satan to the loyalist and the Englishman.

The British intercepted two letters written by John Adams, in which he abused Dickinson for his conservative views and

---

[*] *American Archives,* fourth series, vol. ii, pp. 1836, 1882; vol. iv, p. 467.

[10] Jones, " New York in the Revolution," vol. i, p. 47.

complained with self-conscious pride of his own heavy labors in the Congress in creating a new nation. He had a constitution to form, "millions to arm and train, a naval power to an extensive commerce to negotiate with, a standing army of 27,000 men to raise, pay, victual, and officer." These letters were published by the British in order to show the real purpose of the Congress and the emptiness of all its loyal phrases about reconciliation and allegiance to the King.[11]

Adams, however, as an extreme patriot was delighted with the publication of the letters as tending to force a breach with England and encourage the idea of independence among Americans. In this respect he characteristically believed that they had had more effect than Paine's famous pamphlet, "Common Sense."

" They thought them a great prize. The idea of independence, to be sure, was glaring enough, and they thought they should produce quarrels among the members of Congress and a division of the Colonies. Me, they expected utterly to ruin, because, as they had represented, I had explicitly avowed my designs of independence. I cared nothing for this. I had made no secret, in or out of Congress, of my opinion that independence was become indispensable, and I was perfectly sure that in a little time the whole continent would be of my mind. I rather rejoiced in this as a fortunate circumstance, that the idea was held up to the whole world, and that the people could not avoid contemplating it and reasoning about it. Accordingly, from this time at least, if not earlier, and not from the publication of " Common Sense," did the people in all parts of the continent turn their attention to this subject. It was, I know, considered in the same light by others. I met Colonel Reed, soon afterwards, who was then General Washington's secretary, who mentioned those letters to me, and said that Providence seemed to have thrown those letters before the public for our good; for independence was certainly inevitable, and it was happy that the whole country had been compelled to turn their thoughts upon it, that it might not come upon them presently by surprise."—Works, vol. ii, p. 412.

The Congress denounced England's methods in all parts of her empire. They denounced her rule in India, which they

---

[11] John Adams, Works, vol. ii, pp. 410–414, 423; *American Archives*, fourth series, vol. ii, p. 1717.

described as the sacrifice of millions of lives to gratify her "insatiable avarice and lust of power." They encouraged the colony of Jamaica to rebel. They sent an address to the people of Ireland, telling them that they were well aware that "the labors and manufactures of Ireland were of little moment to herself, but served only to give luxury to those who neither toil nor spin." They enlarged on the wrongs of Ireland, in whose rich pastures "many hungry parricides have fed and grown strong to labor in its destruction;" and they offered the whole region of America as a safe asylum for the Irish people.

There could be no peace with a Tory ministry after such language as that. The Ministry also, it is said, intercepted a letter from Benjamin Harrison, one of the Virginia delegates, in which the purpose of the petition to the King is described as merely to enable the English Whigs to keep up their opposition in Parliament by showing that the Americans were not bent on independence, but ready for reconciliation and compromise.[12]

The Congress published a Declaration of the Causes for Taking up Arms, in which, to the astonishment of loyalists, they defied the British navy and the destruction it could work on the American coast.

"Admit that your fleets could destroy our towns, and ravage our sea coasts; these are inconsiderable objects, things of no moment to men whose bosoms glow with the ardor of liberty. We can retire beyond the reach of your navy, and without any sensible diminution of the necessaries of life, enjoy a luxury, which from that period you will want, the luxury of being free. . . . Of this at least, we are assured, that our struggle will be glorious, our success certain; since even in death we shall find that freedom which in life you forbid us to enjoy."—*American Archives*, fourth series, vol. ii, pp. 1874, 1876.

Rebellion was then a more serious thing than it has since become. "The naked poles on Temple Bar," said a London newspaper, "will soon be decorated with some of the patriotic

---

[12] "Diary and Letters of Thomas Hutchinson," vol. i, p. 557.

noddles of the Boston saints."[13]   Loyalists lived in full expectation of witnessing a great exiling, hanging, and confiscation of estates; and they sent to England lists of those who should suffer.   Samuel Adams was well aware of his own danger, as well as of the danger in which he had involved others; and his cousin, John Adams, has described him in his lodgings at Philadelphia, carefully destroying the evidence contained in letters, which would, doubtless, throw a flood of light on the Revolution if they had been preserved.

"I have seen him at Mrs. Yard's in Philadelphia, when he was about to leave Congress, cut up with his scissors whole bundles of letters in atoms that could never be reunited, and threw them out of the window to be scattered by the winds.   This was in summer, when he had no fire.   As we were on terms of perfect intimacy, I have joked him, perhaps rudely, upon his anxious caution.   His answer was, 'Whatever becomes of me, my friends shall never suffer by my negligence.'"—Wells, "Life of Samuel Adams," vol. ii, p. 391.   See, also, p. 250.

The recent struggles of small states in Europe to secure their independence were not encouraging.   Sweden had been very unfortunate, and the liberties of the free towns of Germany had been curtailed.   Within the last two or three years Austria, Russia, and Prussia had joined forces in conquering and making the first division of Poland's territory.   In fact, this first attempt on Poland had been so successful that many expected soon to see a division of Switzerland and of the United Provinces.

The Corsicans had won a temporary independence by the heroism and intelligence of their leader, General Paoli, who was popular in America, where a famous inn on the western road from Philadelphia was named after him.   "Pascal Paoli and his brave Corsicans" was a popular toast among the patriots. But in 1769 France had completely crushed Corsican independence.

"Behold your fate when you appeal to France," said the

---

[13] Boston *Gazette*, October, 1774.

loyalists. "Do you suppose that the power which destroyed the independence of Corsica will give you independence?"[14]

The patriots nerved themselves with strong appeals. They would risk everything. They would "die or be free." Death was far preferable to political slavery.[15]

" I will tell you what I have done," writes a patriot woman to an Englishman. " My only brother I have sent to the camp with my prayers and blessings; I hope he will not disgrace me; I am confident he will behave with honor, and emulate the great examples he has before him; and had I twenty sons and brothers they should go. I have retrenched every superfluous expense in my table and family; tea I have not drank since last Christmas, nor bought a new cap or gown since your defeat at Lexington, and what I never did before, have learnt to knit, and am now making stockings of American wool for my servants, and this way do I throw in my mite to the public good. I know this, that as free I can die but once, but as a slave I shall not be worthy of life."—Niles, " Principles and Acts of the Revolution," edition of 1876, p. 117.

---

[14] " A Letter to the People of America," p. 29, London, 1768. See, also, Lecky, " England in the Eighteenth Century," edition of 1882, vol. iii, p. 223; " The Political Family; or, a Discourse," &c., by Isaac Hunt, Philadelphia, 1773, pp. 15–27; Wells, " Life of Samuel Adams," vol. i, p. 203; Gordon, " American Revolution," edition 1788, vol. i, p. 492; Curwen, Journal and Letters, pp. 207, 339, 344; " Life of Van Schaack," p. 272; *American Archives*, fourth series, vol. i, p. 1184.

[15] Niles, " Principles and Acts of the Revolution," edition of 1876, pp. 104, 106, 171, 193, 210, 305, 307; Gordon, " American Revolution," edition 1788, vol. ii, p. 82.

XXVIII.

BUNKER HILL

During the month of May, 1775, while the Congress was debating whether it would adopt the extreme measures which such men as John Adams were advocating, General Howe was on the ocean bound for America, to serve in a subordinate capacity for a few months and then supersede Gage as commander-in-chief to put down the rebellion. He was accompanied by Burgoyne and Clinton, with several thousand men, and on the 25th of May they sailed into Boston harbor.

The patriots greeted them with derisive congratulations, and night after night their houses were placarded with mock proclamations of British power and vengeance.[1] The troops they brought raised Gage's force to about 10,000, so that it seemed comparatively easy for him to face the 16,000 farmers who shut him in on the land side. The British troops were camped on that hill where we now follow the streets called Beacon and Tremont. From the hill one could then look over the houses in the lower part of the town, see far out in the harbor, and watch the approaching ships rise up out of the horizon.

The English soldiers, Lieutenant Clarke tells us, seemed shorter in stature than the Americans. There were regiments of veterans, famous organizations, such as the Forty-seventh, "Wolfe's Own," the Thirty-eighth, and the Welsh Fusileers, who had distinguished themselves at the battle of Minden. There were Irishmen in the ranks, and a regiment called "The

---

[1] One of the pasquinades was clever enough:
  " Behold the Cerberus the Atlantic plough,
    Her precious cargo, Burgoyne, Clinton, Howe.
       Bow, wow, wow! "
          —Fonblanque, Life of Burgoyne, pp. 135 note, 136.

Royal Irish." It was rather curious that Irishmen should be fighting to destroy the ideas and principles which in the next century saved thousands of their race from death in the Irish famine, and gave millions more a refuge and a home, a liberty and prosperity unattainable for them under Britain's rule.

In Boston, however, at this time, Britain's soldiery, boisterous and boastful, were living merrily enough. They took the Old South Church for the cavalry, or, as an officer described it, "a meeting-house where sedition has been often preached, is clearing out to be a riding-school for the dragoons."[2]

It was a strange position for ten thousand regulars to be shut up in a town with so many of their enemies, the patriots. Sentinels were perpetually challenging the people, and quarrels were frequent because of the strained relations. The people were ready to believe any evil of the soldiery, and the soldiery were anxious to find evil among the people. The people insisted that they had caught Captain Wilson, of the Fifty-ninth, inciting the negro slaves of the town to attack their masters, and the army believed that it had complete evidence of a plot among the townsfolk to massacre all the British officers who were quartered in dwelling-houses.[3]

Most of the patriot townsfolk, especially the prominent ones, had gone away. Hancock's handsome residence was closed. No one would have answered a knock at Samuel Adams's rickety dwelling. But many of the ordinary people, who could not very well be tried for treason, remained. Loyalists were numerous, and Gage had a citizens' patrol of three hundred of them, whom he made very proud by giving them badges. No doubt they ridiculed the farmers' army, gave plenty of suggestions for suppressing the wicked rebellion as quickly as possible, and were happy in their confidence that the beneficence of British rule would soon be reëstablished.

Soon, however, there came a day, a Saturday afternoon, of

---

[2] Carter, "Genuine Detail of the Blockade of Boston," p. 8.
[3] Clarke, "Impartial and Authentic Narrative of the Battle of Bunker Hill," p. 25.

the greatest possible excitement, when all the inhabitants then in the town, loyalists, patriots, and soldiers, could stand on the hill or climb on the roofs of the houses, or on the masts of ships, and, looking across towards Charlestown, see redcoats mowed down, whole ranks at a time, by old fowling-pieces and Queen Anne muskets in the hands of farmers; see the blood staining the bright June grass, and wounded men rising on their elbows to vomit, than which, after a bull-fight, what could be a grander or more ennobling sight!

It is not often that a battle is seen with perfect distinctness by non-combatant spectators who outnumber by thousands the forces engaged on both sides of the fight. But Gage, military governor and commander-in-chief of Massachusetts, insisted on giving his people this spectacle.

It had been for a long time quite obvious to him that the hill north of Boston across a narrow strip of water should be occupied as an outpost, because if the farmers seized it they could cannonade the town. So now, being greatly reinforced by the new arrivals, he made preparations for occupying and fortifying that hill, when lo! one morning, the 17th of June, 1775, he beheld the farmers in full possession of it. They had worked like beavers all night, making a redoubt of earth, and they kept working away all morning, adding other breastworks of earth, hay, fence-rails, and stones, in spite of the guns fired at them from the men-of-war.

The hill which the farmers had seized was Breed's Hill, on a peninsula connected with the mainland by a very narrow passage. The patriot army, which at this time was commanded by General Ward, assisted by Putnam, Stark, Prescott, and others, had learned of the probability of the British seizing the hill, and had determined to forestall them. In the judgment of military critics it was a rather desperate undertaking, because they were going out on a peninsula where the British, by seizing the narrow passage at the mainland, might catch them like sheep in a pen.

It is probable that they were led to take this risk by the feeling that, if they remained inactive and avoided fighting, the patriot cause would be injured and discouraged. This explanation applies to several battles during the first three years of the Revolution which were fought under great disadvantages, and in which defeat for the Americans was certain. But certain defeat was far less injurious than a refusal to fight.

The first intention had been to occupy Bunker Hill; but the party of about a thousand men, that went out under Prescott in the night to seize and fortify it, found Breed's Hill easier to fortify and nearer Boston. After they had built the earth redoubt on it they extended a breastwork of earth on their left part way towards the Mystic River. In the morning more troops came out, Connecticut regiments under Putnam and the New Hampshire regiments under Stark. Prescott took command in the redoubt; the Connecticut troops, under Captain Knowlton, were on the left of the redoubt, and extended the earth breastwork more towards the river by taking up two rail fences, putting them together and heaping on them the hay which had recently been cut and was lying in windrows on the ground. Still farther to the left Stark stationed the New Hampshire men and extended the defences to the river by a breastwork of loose stones. The extreme right of the line was protected by some troops placed in the houses of Charlestown.

There are said to have been about fifteen hundred men behind the defences. Nearly as many more were in the rear on Bunker Hill, and never took part in the fight. Putnam rode and walked up and down the whole line, encouraging the men, telling them to shoot officers, to wait till they could see the whites of the enemy's eyes, and left the command of the Connecticut troops to Knowlton. But in the controversy that afterwards arose, some of the survivors of the battle testified that Putnam was not on the fighting line at all but remained on Bunker Hill with the reserves, whom he could not persuade to enter the fight.

The patriot troops had for the most part been supplied on setting out with powder for their horns, some buckshot and about fifteen bullets apiece, which they put into their pockets or pouches. The Connecticut men had each a pound of powder

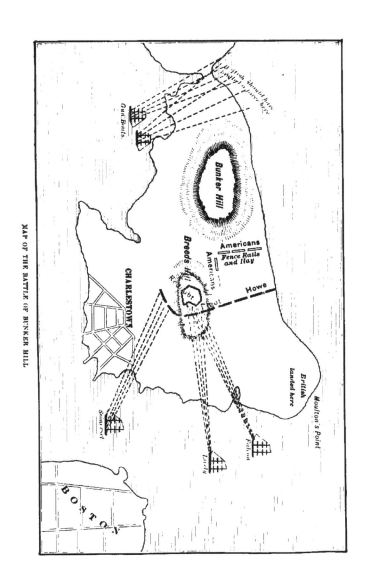

MAP OF THE BATTLE OF BUNKER HILL.

and forty or fifty bullets. Some made up their ammunition into paper cartridges and others loaded it loose. As their shotguns and smooth-bore muskets were their own weapons and of various bores, many of the bullets had to be hammered or cut to fit the muzzles.

Gage declined to take the obvious course of sending a force behind the patriots at the neck of the peninsula. He said he would be placing such a force in a dangerous position between the patriots on Breed's Hill and their reinforcements near Cambridge. There was no necessity, he thought, for taking so much risk as that, because two or three thousand of his Majesty's troops could easily send these peasants flying by attacking them in front in British fashion. This force he placed in command of Howe, with General Pigot to assist him.

It was a strange position for Howe to lead such an attack on the New England farmers, who had fought under both him and his brother in the French and Indian War. One wonders also why he did not make one of those flanking and rear movements with which afterwards, whenever compelled to fight, he was invariably successful against Washington without a great loss of life. But possibly he felt himself under instructions to make a front attack, or considered it too late for a flank movement.

In all the controversy over Howe's conduct in the Revolution, his courage was never questioned. In fact, his reputation for rather remarkable courage had long before this been well established. Sending Pigot up against the redoubt, Howe led his own division against the line of fence-rails and hay which had been completed to the waterside in time to prevent the British passing round to the rear of the Americans.

Howe is said to have made a speech to his men, which was, in substance, "You must drive these farmers from the hill, or it will be impossible for us to remain in Boston. But I shall not desire any of you to advance a single step beyond where I am at the head of your line." [4]

[4] Clarke, "Impartial and Authentic Narrative of the Battle of Bunker Hill," p. 3.

Howe was always very precise on the battlefield. When within one hundred yards of the hay he compelled his troops to deploy into line. For this he was afterwards severely criticised. He should have taken them up, it was said, in columns. But in columns they would have been just as much of a target. He usually knew what he was doing, especially in sparing the lives of his men. They moved up, about twelve feet apart in front, but very close after one another, in deep, long files. They were beautiful, brilliant, their red coats, white knee-breeches, and shining musket-barrels glittering in the sun. At the distance of about a hundred yards they began firing at the hay, from which there was an occasional shot from some patriot who could not be restrained.

No doubt they joked and encouraged one another, and shouted at the mohairs and dunghill tribe, as they called the colonists. "Let us take the bull by the horns," some of them are reported to have said; and they may have sung snatches from their favorite song, "Hot Stuff:"

> "From such rascals as these may we fear a rebuff?
> Advance, grenadiers, and let fly your hot stuff."

They moved up to within fifty steps of the hay, amazed that there was so little reply to their volleys. Fifty steps seem now a very short range, but all the battles of that time were fought at about that distance, because the smooth-bore muskets and shot-guns that were used were inaccurate beyond fifty yards, and practically useless at a hundred.

Suddenly, when the front line of the regulars had moved a few steps nearer, the faces of the farmers rose above the barrier and the sweep of the farmers' scythe, those dreadful volleys of miscellaneous missiles that had been crammed into the old guns, made a terrible day for British soldiers.[5] Whole ranks were cut down to a man. The survivors hesitated, and

---

[5] A bullet and from three to nine buckshot was a common load for a musket, and this practice of using buckshot in addition to the bullet prevailed down to the time of the Mexican War.—Codman, "Arnold's Expedition to Quebec," p. 241.

then turned down the hill like frightened sheep, to halt at the bottom and stare back at their comrades, struggling and dying on the grass.

Pigot's division was in a similar plight.

The men-of-war in the harbor now renewed their cannonade. The balls ricochetted up the hill-side, and the shells burst savagely overhead, but the farmers were again entirely silent.

Howe rallied his men. He had been with some of these regiments in Canada in the French War, and no doubt addressed to them stirring words which have not been recorded. He led them up again, up to within that same fifty paces, without a shot in reply. They moved nearer. Could it be that they could reach the breastwork and spring over it unharmed? They moved on, drew closer; they were within thirty yards of the hay, which suddenly, at a word from the old trapper, Stark, turned into a spitting flame and smoke, and Howe must have believed that this was the last fight of his career. They stayed a little longer this time; they had come so far that they tried to move up closer; they saw the American face as no Englishmen had ever seen it before.

"Colonel Abercrombie, are the Yankees cowards?" a farmer would shout, as he rested his piece on the breastwork. No doubt also terrible curses and fierce denunciations of British rakehells, tyrants, and brutes were poured over with the bullets. It was something new for a British officer to see an old farmer let a young redcoat come up close and then, levelling his rusty duck-gun of vast bore, draw on the boy the deadly aim that tore him to pieces with buckshot and slugs.

The English, as in all subsequent battles of the Revolution, aimed too high and overshot their enemy. An apple-tree in the rear of the breastworks had its limbs cut to pieces and not a bullet in its trunk. But every American was using the gun he had hunted with for years and was allowed to load and fire in the way to which he was long accustomed.

"There, there!" they would cry; "see that officer! Shoot him!" And two or three would cover him with their guns, terrible old pieces, loaded with all manner of missiles. They had been told to aim for the belt, and nearly every soldier was hit in the thighs or abdomen. When he had received there the discharge from an old duck-gun he was a horrible sight for the surgeon.

But Howe, though resolved, if necessary, to make that day his last, could not hold his men up there by the hay. They fled panic-stricken. Some even rushed into their boats at the shore; and Howe soon found himself at the bottom of the hill, no doubt very much surprised to be yet alive. His white silk knee-breeches and long white stockings were soaked with blood; but it was the blood of his men among whom he had trampled. He had not a single subordinate officer remaining; they were all lying on the hill-side.

A long time elapsed while he consulted with Pigot and his officers, who were for giving it up and going back. But Howe had a reputation to support, and was determined to see it out.

The village of Charlestown, along the right of the patriot line, was now on fire. The thick, black smoke that comes from burning dwelling-houses was rolled out by the wind in a vast cloud, clear-cut against the brilliant, sunny sky of that June day. Beneath that terrible gloomy canopy that was moving through the glittering sunlight crouched the silent Americans, looking down at a thousand dead and dying Englishmen on the hill-side, while all around, almost as close as in a theatre, the thousands of spectators in windows, and perched on the tops of houses and chimneys and ship-masts, watched this wondrous close of the second act.

No such battle with such a large audience close at hand can ever be fought again, unless we go back to fire-arms that are useless at one hundred yards. The curtain rose on the third act in this theatre, this drama of history that has become a sign and a monument to the world, the sneer and sarcasm of monarchs, conquerors, and lovers of dominion, the hope of the enthusiastic and the oppressed. Was it the design that it should be enacted like a gladiator's show in a little natural arena with overwhelming clouds of witnesses that it might become a

View of the ATTACK on BUNKER'S HILL, with the Burning of CHARLES TOWN, June 17, 1775

BOSTON

symbol, an example to keep alive the endless struggle, the unsolvable problem of the world?

Howe sent Pigot up again, and he went up himself. He ordered the men to free themselves of their heavy knapsacks. He concentrated the whole British force on the redoubt, and used the artillery more effectively. Even with this advantage the first volley his men received was very destructive. But the ammunition of the patriots was exhausted. They were hurling stones over the breastwork and retreating. The regulars sprang up upon the redoubt. They saw barefooted countrymen with trousers rolled up to their knees walking away; and there were scarcely any dead or wounded in the trenches. But only a few of those regulars who first mounted the redoubt lived to tell what they saw, for they were shot down almost to a man with the remains of the ammunition.

Then the whole British force swarmed over the breastwork, and for a time there was confusion and hand-to-hand conflicts as the Americans retreated. The British were finally able to deliver a cross-fire, which caused most of the loss of the patriots that day.

But they moved off in good order. A few yards' retreat easily put them beyond the effective range of the muskets. Howe ordered no pursuit, although Clinton urged him to do it, and the helplessness of the farmers was obvious. He had been ordered to take the hill; he would do no more. But the loyalists always believed that he could have inflicted a terrible disaster, could have slaughtered or captured three-fourths of the patriots, and seriously crippled the rebellion.

This was the first specimen of his line of policy, and also the beginning of the serious criticism upon him. From that time, though invariably successful in any battle he personally directed, he never pursued, never followed up the advantage of a victory or allowed it to be followed up by others.

The farmers, grouped in an irregular mass, a most miscellaneous, strangely clad, disorganized body to soldiers' eyes, withdrew from the arena on which they had played their part while the black smoke of the burning town was still rolling high overhead. They had represented their new idea, and they returned somewhat leisurely along Charlestown neck, pelted, as their only applause, by spent and random balls and cannonaded to no purpose from two gunboats or floating batteries.

There had been about 1500 or 1700 of them, and they had lost in dead and wounded 449. Howe took out from Boston between 2500 and 3000 regulars, and he left 1054, more than a third, on the hill-side.[*]

---

[*] Coffin's "History of the Battle of Breed's Hill," reprinted in Fellows' "The Veil Removed," 113–138; *American Historical Review*, vol. i, p. 401; *American Archives*, fourth series, vol. ii, pp. 1018, 1101, 1373, 1628; Lieutenant Clark's "Narrative of the Battle of Bunker Hill;" *Historical Magazine*, vol. vi, pp. 321–442; Swett, "History of Bunker Hill," with notes, containing testimony of survivors; Swett, "Historical and Topographical Sketch of Bunker Hill;" Swett, "Who Was the Commander at Bunker Hill?"; Parker, "Colonel William Prescott the Commander at Bunker Hill;" Dearborn, "Account of the Battle of Bunker Hill;" Daniel Putnam's "Letter to Major-General Dearborn;" "An Enquiry into the Conduct of General Putnam;" Richard Frothingham, "Battle Field of Bunker Hill;" Jones, "New York in the Revolution," vol. i, p. 51; Ashbel Woodward, "Memoir of Colonel Thomas Knowlton;" Stedman, "American War," vol. i, pp. 125–129.

XXIX.

INCIDENTS AND RESULTS OF BUNKER HILL

FOR the rest of the afternoon and far into the night carriages and chaises, furnished by loyalists, were streaming back and forth from the waterside in Boston, dragging the wounded British soldiers into the city as fast as they could be brought from the battle-field in boats. It was Sunday morning before the task was finished.[1]

When the British finally rushed over the breastwork at the redoubt, Major Pitcairn, who had led the advance at Lexington, was killed, and his body carried from the field by his son. At the same time Dr. Joseph Warren, hesitating to retreat, was shot down in the trenches. He had drawn the famous Suffolk resolutions, and in the absence of Hancock at the Congress of Philadelphia, had become temporary president of the Massachusetts Provincial Congress. In the absence of both Hancock and Samuel Adams at Philadelphia, he may be said to have been the chief political manager of the patriot party, as well as the executive head of the patriot government of Massachusetts. He had been given a complimentary commission as major-general, and when he appeared on the field both Putnam and Prescott offered to take orders from him. But he declined to give directions to veterans of the French War and insisted on serving as a volunteer in the redoubt. His loss was serious, for his broad ability and popularity gave promise of a valuable career. The British officers boasted that his death was "better to them than five hundred men."[2]

The most pathetic incident of the battle was the appearance in the patriot lines of James Otis, who for several years had

---

[1] Clark, "Narrative of the Battle of Bunker Hill."

[2] *American Archives*, fourth series, vol. ii, p. 1551; Fonblanque, "Life of Burgoyne," p. 154.

343

been insane and living quietly with his sister, Mercy Warren, at Watertown. Hearing of the preparations, he left the house to follow the patriot troops and is supposed to have borrowed a musket and fought in the trenches, from which he returned to his sister's faint and weary at midnight.

Burgoyne, in his description of the battle, said that the British officers were heroic, but were ill seconded by the rank and file, whom he accused of cowardice and lax discipline. Some of them were so excited and unskilled in shooting that they shot their own officers who were leading them; and this, Burgoyne said, partly accounted for the large number of officers killed and wounded.[3]

He labors hard to prove that the Americans are not as heroic as might be supposed from this battle. They are good shots, it is true, like Tartars, Croats, and other wild people. But it is as preposterous, he says, to compare them in point of courage to the Spartans and Athenians as it is to suppose them inspired by the real spirit of liberty which animated those ancient peoples.[4]

Many years after the battle, when it had ceased to be regarded as an American defeat and retrospect increased its importance, a great controversy arose in New England as to whether Putnam or Prescott was in command of the patriot troops. Massachusetts writers naturally favored their own citizen, Colonel Prescott, who had served with merit in the French War, and was the grandfather of Prescott, the historian; while the Connecticut people naturally favored Putnam. The controversy took on a political bearing and raged with such intensity that some people succeeded in convincing themselves that Putnam was a coward, a "swaggerer and blusterer," who was not in the fight at all, and inclined to play traitor and go over to the British.

Prescott was a colonel who never rose to any important rank during the Revolution. He undoubtedly took the troops from

---

[3] Fonblanque, "Life of Burgoyne," p. 47.
[4] Fonblanque, "Life of Burgoyne," pp. 155, 159, 192, 193, 194.

By an Express arrived at Philadelphia *on Saturday evening,* *we have the following account of the battle at* Charlestown, *on Saturday the 18th of* June, Instant.

ON Friday night, the 17th Instant, fifteen hundred of the Provincials went to *Bunker's-Hill,* in order to intrench there, and continued intrenching till Saturday ten o'clock, when 2000 Regulars marched out of *Boston,* landed in *Charlestown,* and plundering it of all its valuable effects, set fire to it in ten different places at once ; then dividing their army, part of it marched up in the front of the Provincial intrenchment, and began to attack the Provincials at long shot ; the other part of their army marched round the town of *Charlestown,* under cover of the smoke occasioned by the fire of the town. The Provincial centries discovered the Regulars marching upon their left wing. Upon notice of this given by the centry to the *Connecticut* forces posted upon that wing, Captain *Nolton,* of *Ashford,* with 400 of said forces, immediately repaired to, and pulled up a post and rail-fence, and carried the posts and rails to another fence, put them together for a breast work. Captain *Nolton* gave orders to the men not to fire until the enemy were got within fifteen rods, and then not till the word was given. At the words being given, the enemy fell surprisingly ; it was thought by spectators who stood at a distance, that our men did great execution.

The action continued about two hours, when the Regulars on the right wing were put in confusion and gave way ;---the *Connecticut* troops closely pursued them, and were on the point of pushing their bayonets, when orders were received from General *Pomeroy,* for those who had been in action for two hours to fall back, and their places to be supplied by fresh troops.---These orders being mistaken for a direction to retreat, our troops on the right wing began a general retreat, which was handed to the left, the principal place of action, where Captains *Nolton, Chester, Clark* and *Putnam,* had forced the enemy to give way, and were before them for some considerable distance, and being warmly persuing the enemy, were, with difficulty, persuaded to retire ; but the right wing, by mistaking the orders, having already retreated, the left, to avoid being encirculed, were obliged to retreat also with the main body. They retreated with precipitation across the causeway to *Winter's-Hill,* in which they were exposed to the fire of the enemy, from their shipping and floating batteries.---We sustained our principal loss in passing the causeway. The enemy pursued our troops to *Winter's-Hill,* where the Provincials being reinforced by General *Putnam,* renewed the battle with great spirit, repulsed the enemy with great slaughter, and pursued them until they got under cover of their cannon from the shipping. When the enemy returned to *Bunker's-Hill,* and the Provincials to *Winter's-Hill,* where after intrenching and erecting batteries, they on Monday began to fire upon the Regulars on *Bunker's-Hill,* and on the ships and floating batteries in the harbour when the Express came away. The number of Provincials killed is between 40 and 70 ; 140 are wounded, of the *Connecticut* troops 16 were killed.---No officer among them was either killed or wounded, excepting Lieutenant *Grosvenor,* who was wounded in the hand. A Colonel, or Lieutenant Colonel of the *New-Hampshire* forces, is among the dead. It is also said that Doctor *Warren* is undoubtedly among the slain.

Cambridge out to Bunker Hill on the night they made the intrenchments, and during the battle he undoubtedly had command of the redoubt. From these facts the inference is drawn that he must necessarily be considered as commander of the whole field during the battle. But he appears to have confined his exertions to the redoubt, and from his own letter describing the battle one would suppose that there had been but little fighting anywhere except at the redoubt.

Some of the British appear to have thought that Warren was in general command; but most of them spoke of Putnam as the commander; and one of his biographers has shown that for many years after the battle he was represented as the commander in pictures and descriptions.[5]

He was a more popular and better-known character than Prescott, very bustling and active; and on the day of the battle moved about a good deal. But the controversy will never be settled, for neither Connecticut nor Massachusetts will give up their hero, although the truth is that the patriot military organization was so loose and irregular that no one was in general command. Wilkinson, who went over the field with Stark a year after the battle was fought, says "there was no general command exercised on the field," and this is in agreement with all the circumstances. The troops were volunteers fighting with a common purpose, each regiment acting on its own responsibility, and they got on very well without a general commander.[6]

Historians and Fourth of July orators have described the thrill of exultation which they say passed like a wave southward through the colonies with the news of the battle of Bunker Hill. The patriots were defeated, lost their hill and 449 in killed and wounded, but they had laid low 1054 British regulars in resplendent uniforms, of which 89 were commis-

---

[5] Tarbox, "Life of Putnam," p. 216. For authorities on both sides of the controversy see Winsor, "Handbook of the American Revolution," pp. 48–53.

[6] Coffin, "History of Battle of Breed's Hill," p. 14.

sioned officers. They were encouraged; they could afford to sell
the English many hills at the same price; and all manner of
inferences have been drawn as to the inspiring effect of this
battle upon the patriot colonists.

This, however, is largely modern rhetoric and supposition.
Contemporary patriot opinion expressed no elation; but, on
the contrary, disappointment, indignation, and severe censure
for an expedition which was said to have been rash in conception, discreditable in execution, and narrowly escaped overwhelming disaster. The patriots abused their troops for going
into a trap on the peninsula as loudly as the loyalists abused the
regulars for not closing the trap, and not pursuing when they
had the opportunity. Colonel Gerrish, who remained in the
rear, was court-martialed for cowardice and cashiered. Washington considered the troops in the battle badly officered, and
the failure of the reserves to assist them a grave error.

In contemporary opinion, Bunker Hill was regarded as
having given neither side any particular advantage. Looking
back through the long perspective, it of course seems most
dramatic and interesting; but the patriots wanted no more
Bunker Hills. They knew that something very different was
required.[7]

From a military point of view, both sides learned a lesson.
It was the first notable instance of the American use of
intrenching which since then has become a national trait. The
quickness with which the patriots had intrenched themselves
on Bunker Hill was a surprise to the British, and the advantage of this intrenching was a still greater surprise. European
soldiers of that time seem to have placed little or no value on
this method of defence, which the American troops of the
Revolution used so readily and at which they became so skilful
and successful. Burgoyne reported to the British Government
in 1777 that the Americans were expert at defence by intrench-

[7] Frothingham, "Siege of Boston," p. 154; *American Historical
Review*, vol. i, p. 404; Writings of Washington, Ford edition, vol. 14.
p. 313; Coffin, "History of the Battle of Breed's Hill," pp. 13, 22, 26-30.

ment beyond any other nation. They would throw up high intrenchments of earth and logs sometimes in a few moments; and this method was universally practised by both sides in our Civil War of 1861. But in Europe it was very little used for a hundred years after the Revolution; and American officers who were spectators of the battles of the Franco-Prussian War of 1870 were surprised that the French neither used it nor appreciated its value.[*]

At the time of the Revolution, such intrenching on every possible occasion was supposed by some to weaken the courage of the soldier and give him habits of timidity. General Putnam used to argue against this superstition in his rough way by saying that it had the contrary effect. What the raw militia-man is afraid of, he said, is his shins. Give him a low ridge of earth to hide his shins and he will fight to the death.

One reason that intrenching was of such value to the Americans, and of less value to the British, seems to have been that it gave the Americans a chance to use their unerring aim with full effect. When their bodies were protected until the enemy got within fair range, every bullet from the American guns found its mark. It became an axiom of American revolutionary tactics that they must avoid level regions and fight among the hills, where they could intrench above their enemy. They sometimes carried this system out in great perfection, intrenching themselves from hill to hill, as in the retreat from Harlem to White Plains.

But the British soldier always shot wide, no matter how close he was or how well protected. Trenches were no advantage to him, because he would miss the enemy and they would then rush over the trenches. At the battle of Bennington, which was almost the only occasion in the Revolution when the British intrenched in American fashion, the patriot militia

---

[*] Burgoyne, " State of the Expedition from Canada; " Gordon, " American Revolution," edition 1788, vol. ii, p. 553; *American Historical Review*, vol. i, pp. 411, 412; Bolton, " Private Soldier under Washington," p. 234.

rushed on their trenches and carried them with comparatively little loss. But the frightful loss which was inflicted on the British at Bunker Hill made them shy of American trenches for all the rest of the war.

British manœuvres were always directed towards getting the Americans in level, open country and rushing upon them with the bayonet after their first fire and before they had time to reload. Howe never made another front attack like that at Bunker Hill. Ever after that his front attack was always a feint and his real attack was delivered on the flank or rear; and in this method he was eminently successful in both of his battles with Washington.

The British officers in Boston comforted themselves as well as they could with the thought that in spite of their heavy loss they had won an important hill; and they proceeded to fortify it as an outpost in such a manner that the patriots never attempted to take it. Besieged and besiegers settled down to comparative quiet, which was to last nearly a year. British soldiers were quartered at Samuel Adams' abandoned house, where they painted caricatures upon the walls, and cut upon the window panes coarse witticisms ridiculing the owner and his religion.[9]

---

[9] Wells, Samuel Adams, vol. ii, p. 380; Writings of Washington, Ford edition, vol. 14, p. 313.

XXX.

WASHINGTON IS APPOINTED COMMANDER-IN-CHIEF

On the 16th of June, the day before the battle of Bunker Hill, the Congress, having accepted Massachusetts' gift of the army before Boston, gave the command of it to Colonel George Washington, of Virginia, and made him a general and commander-in-chief of all the forces of the patriot cause.

Hancock, it is said, had ambitions in that direction, and was somewhat disappointed at the choice. But the fitness of Washington for the office was generally admitted as soon as John Adams urged his appointment. He would conciliate the moderate patriots, for he had clung to the old arguments as long as possible, and refrained from forcing events. If substantial independence of Parliament and the Ministry could be secured, he was willing to allow the King a vague or imaginary headship until in the course of years that excrescence should slough away.[1]

Many were inclined to think that a New England general should command the New England army that was gathered before Boston; but they were obliged to admit that the appointment of a general from Virginia, the most populous and prosperous of the colonies, would tend to draw the Southern interest to the patriot cause.

Washington was forty-three years old, which was the right age for entering upon the supreme command in what might be a long war. He had distinguished himself by helping to rescue Braddock's defeated army in 1755, and he had taken a more or less prominent part in the subsequent campaigns which ended in driving the French out of Canada. This military education and experience seemed slight and not equal to that of the

---

[1] John Adams' Works, vol. ii, pp. 415–418; Writings of Washington, Sparks edition, vol. iii, pp. 479–486.

British officers who would be opposed to him. But it was American experience, no colonist was any better equipped, and he was of a larger intelligence than Putnam, Ward, and other Americans who had served in the French War.

His strong character and personality had impressed themselves upon his fellow delegates in the Congress. It was this impressive personality which made his career and brought to him grave responsibility without effort on his part to seek office or position. When he was only twenty-one the governor of Virginia had sent him through the wilderness to interview the French commander near Lake Erie, a mission which required the hardihood of the hunter and some of the shrewd intelligence of the diplomat.

But much to the surprise of travellers and visitors, Washington never appeared to be a brilliant man. He was always a trifle reserved, and this habit grew on him with years. His methods of work were homely and painstaking, reminding us somewhat of Lincoln; and the laborious carefulness of his military plans seemed to European critics to imply a lack of genius.

But it was difficult to judge him by European standards, because the conditions of the warfare he conducted were totally unlike anything in Europe. He never commanded a real army with well-organized departments and good equipment. His troops were usually barefooted, half-starved, and for several years incapable of performing the simplest parade manœuvre. Brilliant movements, except on a small scale as at Princeton, were rarely within his reach; and large complicated movements were impossible because he had not the equipment of officers and organization for handling large bodies of men spread out over a great extent of country. He was obliged to adopt the principle of concentration and avoid making detachments or isolated movements that could be cut off by the British. To some of his contemporaries it therefore seemed that his most striking ability lay in conciliating local habits and prejudices, harmonizing discordant opinions, and holding together an army which seemed to the British always on the eve of disbanding.

LABORIOUS METHODS

He reasoned out, however, in his own way the peculiar needs of every military position, and how he did this will appear more clearly as our narrative progresses. He often spoke of his own lack of military experience, as well as of the lack of it in the officers about him; and this seems to have led him to study every situation like a beginner, with exhaustive care, consulting with everybody, calling councils of war on every possible occasion, and reasoning out his plans with minute carefulness. This method, which his best friends sometimes ridiculed, was in striking contrast to the method of one of his own officers, General Greene, and also to the method of Grant in the Civil War. Both Greene and Grant dispensed altogether with laborious consultations and councils of war.

But the laborious method was well suited to Washington, whose mind was never satisfied unless it could strike a balance among a great mass of arguments and details which must be obtained from others and not through his own imagination. He liked to reserve his decision until the last moment, and this trait was sometimes mistaken for weakness. His preparedness and devotion to details remind us of Napoleon. His cautious, balancing, weighing habit, developed by lifelong practice, runs through all his letters and every act of his life, appearing in some of the great events of his career as a superb and masterful equipoise. It became very impressive even to those who ridiculed it; it could inspire confidence through years of disaster and defeat; and it enabled him to grasp the general strategy of the war so thoroughly that no military critic has ever detected him in a mistake.

As a soldier he fought against distinguished British officers four pitched battles—Long Island, Brandywine, Germantown, and Monmouth; in the first three of which he was defeated and the last was a draw. He conducted two sieges—Boston and Yorktown—in both of which he was successful; and he destroyed two outposts—Trenton and Princeton—in a manner generally regarded as so brilliant and effective that he saved the patriot cause from its first period of depression. His characteristics as a soldier were farseeing judgment and circumspection, a certain long-headedness, as it might be called, and astonishing ability to recover from and ignore a defeat. In his pitched battles, like Long Island and Brandywine, he knew that defeat was probable and he prepared for it.

"Limiting by his foresight the extent of his loss, guarding by his disposition security of retreat, and repairing with celerity the injury sustained, his relative condition was often meliorated although victory adorned the brow of his adversary."—Lee, Memoirs, vol. i, p. 237.

He was compelled to act so much on the defensive, and the British methods were so slow, that his activities in the field were not numerous when we consider that he was in command for seven years. The greater part of his time and energy were employed in building up the cause by mild, balanced, but wonderfully effective arguments; reconciling animosities by tactful precautions; and by the confidence his personality inspired preventing the army from disbanding. A large part of this labor was put forth in writing letters of wonderful beauty and perfection in the literary art, when we consider the end they were to accomplish. Complete editions of his writings of this sort usually fill a dozen or more large volumes; and there have been few if any great generals of the world who have accomplished so much by writing or who have been such consummate masters of language.

Sufficient care has not always been taken to distinguish between the different periods of his life. He aged rapidly at the close of the Revolution; his reserved manner and a certain "asperity of temper." as Hamilton called it, greatly increased[1]; and some years afterwards, when President, he had become a very silent and stiffly formal man, far different from the young soldier who in the prime of life drew his sword beneath the old elm at Cambridge to take command of the patriot army.

The Virginians of his time appear to have had occupations and social intercourse which educated them in a way we are unable to imitate. Washington in his prime was a social and convivial man, fond of cards, fine horses, and fox-hunting.

---

[1] Writings of Washington, Ford edition, vol. 10, p. 167 note.

EFFECT OF PLANTATION LIFE

Although not usually credited with book learning, his letters and conduct in the Revolution show that he was quite familiar with the politics of foreign countries and the general information of his time. We have not yet learned to appreciate the full force of his intellect and culture.

He had always kept open house at his plantation. That plantation, with its three hundred slaves, its coopers, bricklayers, carpenters, and shoemaker, its flour mill and its schooner for carrying products to market, was one of the large enterprises of that age, in which our organized industries were unknown. The Southern planter and the Northern ship-owning merchant, Washington and Robert Morris, for example, were the men of the time whose occupations gave them the broadest training and experience.[3]

Washington was a product of conditions in Virginia life which have long since passed away. A man of such exactness and thoroughness in all details of business, of such wide information, of such faultless tact, such comprehension of everybody's point of view, such good taste in all matters of courtesy and ceremony, capable of French delicacy with a D'Estaing or a DeGrasse, and of British bluntness with a Howe or a Clinton, a man of this versatile culture we now usually associate with large cities or universities, because for three or four generations our lives have been completely absorbed in those modern instrumentalities.

But there were no cities or universities in Virginia in Washington's time. He never saw a town until he grew up and travelled nearly a week's journey on horseback to Philadelphia. His mind and character and the minds and characters of Jefferson, Mason, Patrick Henry, the Lees, the Blands, and the Harrisons, were developed on large, isolated plantations and in country life which is now believed capable of producing nothing but awkwardness, vulgarity, and ignorance.

---

[3] For an account of Washington's plantation, habits of life, and personal characteristics as shown by contemporary evidence, see Ford's "True George Washington."

AMERICAN INDEPENDENCE

How the Virginians created such a world of high practical intelligence and culture out of country life that is now the subject of newspaper ridicule and contempt, is a great mystery to modern minds. Our city-bred men of education ride along the roads near Mount Vernon, visit the neighboring region, and read the dozen volumes of Washington's letters in amazement that such a country should produce such a man. They forget that although the soil, the grass, and the trees are the same, the old life which he lived is as completely gone as the snow of the year in which he was born; and they also forget that the standard of intelligence and culture which our hot-bed system strives to attain was created long before our modern instrumentalities were heard of. The men who set the pace we can scarcely imitate had none of our supposed advantages.

To give up his pleasant and prosperous life, to deliver his beloved Mount Vernon to the chances of British confiscation, and to take the chances that his head might be exhibited to the London populace, was no light sacrifice for Washington. It would have been easier to be a loyalist, easier to rely upon the British Government to uphold the position of a Southern country gentleman, easier to accept the ready-made civilization of England than to forge one of his own, and easier to apply for the high rewards that an empire could bestow on such ability as his.

When his appointment was announced in Congress he rose in his place and accepted the honor with a certain reluctance which we have every reason to believe was sincere; for he knew the difficulties of open war with Great Britain and the terrible sacrifice he was making of his happy private life.

"But, lest some unlucky event should happen, unfavorable to my reputation, I beg it may be remembered, by every gentleman in the room, that I this day declare, with the utmost sincerity, I do not think myself equal to the command I am honored with."—*American Archives*, fourth series, vol. ii, p. 1848.

In keeping with the high tone of the Southern planter, and the spirit of the patriot party, he would accept no pay. "I will keep," he said, "an exact account of my expenses. These, I doubt not, you will discharge, and that is all I desire."

SUBORDINATE OFFICERS

Upon the same day that he accepted the command, the Congress established a full set of subordinate officers, two major-generals, eight brigadiers, adjutant-general, commissary, paymaster, quartermaster, a chief engineer, and a secretary to the commander-in-chief. General Artemas Ward, who commanded the army before Boston, was made the first major-general, second in rank to Washington, and his successor in case of accident. It was a complimentary appointment, for Ward's ill health soon took him from active duties, and the officer next in rank to Washington was General Charles Lee, like Gates and Montgomery, an Englishman who had seen service in the British army.

For his military secretary Washington appointed Joseph Reed, a prosperous young patriot lawyer of Philadelphia; and this choice was another instance of those cautious, painstaking methods which afterwards caused so much comment. Reed was to be his confidential adviser on the phases of public opinion, give the arguments of all sides, and disclose the intricacies of party politics.

XXXI.

CHARACTER AND CONDITION OF THE PATRIOT ARMY

WASHINGTON reached Cambridge on the 2nd of July, and spent the rest of the year trying to persuade the mob of disconnected militia to become an army. It was a curious collection of volunteer fighting men, with but little order or discipline; and throughout the war our forces were always so irregular and destitute that English statesmen and generals expected that every campaign would surely be the last.

Our pictures of handsome Revolutionary uniforms are very misleading. It is pleasant, of course, to think of the Revolution as a great spontaneous uprising of all the people, without doubt, hesitation, or misgiving, and that each hero put on his beautiful buff-and-blue uniform, brought to him presumably by a fairy, and marched, with a few picturesque hardships, to glorious victory. But the actual conditions were very different from what most of us have been led to believe. Some companies and regiments tried at the start to have uniforms. We find uniforms mentioned here and there, and the Congress directed the adoption of very beautiful uniforms, of which colored fashion plates have been published. But there is many a slip between a fashion-plate and getting the beautiful garments on a patriot's back. Those who actually saw the patriot troops in the field describe them as without uniforms, very ragged, many of them bare-footed, and at the best clothed in home-made hunting-shirts. Many regiments stained their hunting-shirts with butternut, which was used for a similar purpose by the Confederates of the Civil War. The hunting-shirts were light colored, and butternut gave at once the color that the linen cloth would assume after a few weeks of dirt and smoke in camp.

Washington, in an order of the 24th of July, 1776, recommended the hunting-shirt for all the troops; [1] and Lafayette has described in his memoirs the patriot army he found on his arrival in the summer of 1777:

"About eleven thousand men ill-armed and still worse clothed, presented a strange spectacle. Their clothes were parti-colored and many of them were almost naked. The best clad wore hunting-shirts, large gray linen coats which were much used in Carolina. As to their military tactics, it will be sufficient to say that, for a regiment ranged in battle order to move forward on the right of its line it was necessary for the left to make a continued counter-march. They were always arranged in two lines, the smallest men in the first line."—Vol. i, p. 19, London, 1837.

Great efforts were made to import clothes from France. Lafayette interested himself to obtain supplies of cloth from which clothes could be manufactured. Some of these may have arrived. The Congress appointed a clothier-general, and numerous resolutions and letters on the subject can be found, leading one at first to infer that the troops must have been well supplied. But it seems they were not; for the contemporary evidence of the actual condition of the troops shows that they were almost destitute of shoes and clothes all through the contest; and Washington in his letters constantly complains of the uselessness of the clothier-general's office. In 1778 he reported "a great many men entirely destitute of shirts and breeches, and I suppose not less than a fourth or fifth of the whole are without shoes." [2] He at times had difficulty in keeping his own bodyguard and servants decently clad.

"I cannot get as much cloth as will make clothes for my servants, notwithstanding one of them that attends my person and table is indecently and most shamefully naked."—Writings of Washington, Ford's edition, vol. ii, p. 469. See, also, American Archives, fourth series, vol. v, p. 207.

---

[1] American Archives, fifth series, vol. i, pp. 676, 677; Writings of Washington, Ford edition, vol. 4, p. 297; See also Saffell, Records of the Revolution, p. 325; American Archives, fourth series, vol. ii, pp. 1738–1739; Pontgibaud, p. 125. Niles, "Principles and Acts of the Revolution," edition 1776, p. 250; Wilkinson's Memoirs, vol. i, pp. 19, 20.

[2] Writings of Washington, Ford's edition, vol. vii, p. 143; see also vol. vi, p. 288 and note.

AMERICAN INDEPENDENCE

When Sullivan's men returned from the expedition against the Six Nations of New York, in 1779, the remains of their clothes were "hanging in streamers behind them." Yet they insisted on putting sprigs of evergreen in their hats and powdering their hair with flour. The patriot troops, it seems, always clung to that custom of long hair done into a queue and powdered. They would give great attention to their hair and shaving, even when they were barefooted and in rags; and everybody, including their own officers and chaplain, was laughing at the incongruity of their appearance.[8]

The ragged condition of the troops prevailed down to the siege of Yorktown, in 1781, when the French soldiers cracked their jokes over the nakedness of the Continentals. Everywhere the evidence is the same. Barefooted, coatless, and blanketless, shirts hanging in strings, standing in their bare feet as sentinels in the snow of the northern winter, walking barefooted on the snow at Quebec, selling their blankets and shirts when sick in order to get bread, begging for food along the roads, lying on straw or the cold ground while dying of pleurisy, pneumonia, and the small-pox, "no nation," said a British officer, "ever saw such a set of tatterdemalions." They often deserted to the British to get a suit of clothes and then deserted back to the patriot army.

The so-called hospitals in which patient after patient lay on the unchanged straw, became the terror of every neighborhood in which they were placed, especially when the discharged invalids emerged from them penniless, starving, and began begging from house to house. The misery of all these conditions undoubtedly affected enlistments, and partially explains the unexpectedly small numbers of the patriot armies. We can easily understand that there were many people who wished the Revolution every success, but who would not themselves endure such privations and misery in order to make it successful.[4]

[8] Bolton, "Private Soldier under Washington," p. 237.

[4] Bolton, *Id.*, 51–54, 103, 182, 183; *American Archives*, fourth series, vol. iii, p. 1006; Codman, "Arnold's Expedition to Quebec," p. 168.

GOOD UNIFORMS IN PICTURES

Dr. Benjamin Rush explained the amazing endurance of the patriot soldiers by saying that they were upheld by the passion for independence. Their terrible hardships could not have been endured by Europeans. To the loyalist the disease, rags, and dirt of the patriot troops was another proof of the absurdity of the patriot cause. But the patriot officers learned to love "those dear, ragged Continentals," whose patience, said young Colonel Laurens, " will be the admiration of future ages, and I glory in bleeding with them." [5]

In 1781 Claude Blanchard describes the absence of uniforms in almost the same language that Lafayette used in 1777. There were in 1781, he says, children of twelve or thirteen years old serving in the ranks, and the men were thin and worn. [6] In the southern campaigns at the close of the Revolution, General Greene's troops could be tracked along the roads of North Carolina by the blood from their naked feet, and had only one blanket for every four men.

Many of us have, of course, seen scores of portraits of Revolutionary officers in very good uniforms, which do away with all appearance of rebellion. Those were uniforms for a picture in order that our officers and men might appear as smart-looking as European troops; but they were not the garments worn by our ancestors in the war. Good uniforms could always be painted in a picture. Who would have an ancestor painted in a butternut rifle-shirt and labelled "Rebel," when an artist could paint a portrait clothed in a uniform from the fashion-plate of the Board of War—such a uniform as our ancestors would have worn had they had the time and money to buy one.

There has for a long time been a general impression that the regulation uniform of all the Continental troops was buff-and-blue, and people frequently speak of their ancestors who wore the buff-and-blue. But that uniform was seldom seen during the Revolution. It was designed for the New York and

[5] Bolton, "Private Soldier under Washington," p. 126.

[6] Bolton, "Private Soldier under Washington," p. 237; Claude Blanchard's Journal, p. 115; New York Historical Collections, 1873, vol. iii, p. 186.

New Jersey troops in the autumn of 1779, when Washington, under direction of the Congress, went through the form of adopting a regular system of uniforms. Blue was adopted as the color for the coats of all the patriot infantry; the New England troops to be distinguished by white facings, New York and New Jersey by buff facings, Pennsylvania, Delaware, Maryland, and Virginia by red facings, and the Carolinas and Georgia by button-holes edged with white.[7]

It is from the descriptions in this general regulation that the portraits of revolutionary characters obtain their uniforms. The buff-and-blue was the most beautiful and striking of all. Art and literature have seized upon it for their purposes; and it has been seen on canvas and in the theatre in modern times more than it was ever seen during the war for independence. The New York and New Jersey troops could seldom get the colored cloth of which to make it even for parade; and when they were in the field they were lucky if they had a whole shirt or a coat of any color.

There were many muskets and other smooth-bore guns in the country before the war began, and some cannon. The various iron furnaces could at times cast cannon. But cast-iron cannon were not liked by military men. The best artillery was made of brass, shooting balls of from three up to twenty-four pounds. They seldom burst, and even if that accident happened, very little damage was done, and the gun could be cast over again. Probably most of these brass pieces were imported from Europe or captured from the British.

There were numerous blacksmiths and other mechanics who could make the barrels and stocks for the sort of musket used in those days, and also some who could make the locks. These men were put to work wherever they could be found; and here and there in country districts a smith would every few months turn out some muskets for the neighboring militia. Particularly good guns were said to be made in New Jersey. A Maryland workman in Harford County describes himself as strug-

---

[7] Bolton, " Private Soldier under Washington," pp. 91, 95, 96.

gling to produce a couple of dozen guns in spite of the interference of harvesting duties, bursting barrels, and sickness. He tested the barrels by firing them with a load of two ounces of powder and a ball. As Washington's army became better organized, an armorer's shop for repairing and making guns became part of its regular equipment, and at least one soldier of the Revolution prided himself upon fighting with a gun he had made with his own hands.[8]

But not enough muskets could be obtained in this way. There was a great lack of them during the first year or two; and a portion of the troops was frequently described as unarmed or armed with weapons that were almost useless. Our main supply came from France, and the first shipment arrived in 1777.[9]

The powder for the patriot muskets was usually put up in paper cartridges, which the troops made in their leisure time in camp. When loading his gun the soldier bit off the end of one of these cartridges, shook a little of the powder into the pan of the lock, and poured the rest down the barrel, ramming the paper down on it as a wad, and afterwards ramming down the bullet and buckshot. It was a slow process, and later in the war the British learned to take advantage of its slowness. They would purposely draw the fire of the patriot militia at short range and then rush upon them with the bayonet before they could reload.[10]

[8] *American Archives*, fourth series, vol. vi, pp. 608, 758, 817, 1068, 1147; *Id.*, fifth series, vol. i, pp. 363, 365, 400; Writings of Washington, Ford edition, vol. v, p. 27. There seems to have been a gun-lock factory in Philadelphia and another at Fredericktown, Maryland; two lockmakers were discharged from jail on their agreeing to work in the Philadelphia factory. *American Archives*, fifth series, vol. ii, pp. 27, 678, 778, 833; vol. iii, pp. 100, 1147; Journals of Congress, vol. i, p. 270.

[9] Writings of Washington, Ford edition, vol. v, p. 262 note. Gordon, "American Revolution," edition 1788, vol. ii, p. 424.

[10] Bolton, "Private Soldier under Washington," pp. 108, 121, 122; *American Archives*, fourth series, vol. v, p. 1177; fifth series, vol. ii, p. 1385; vol. iii, p. 532; Codman, "Arnold's Expedition to Quebec," p. 241; *American Archives*, fifth series, vol. iii, pp. 473, 532.

AMERICAN INDEPENDENCE

The patriot army consisted for the most part of mere squads of militia. The officers were elected by the men and commissioned as a reward for recruiting a certain number of privates. Any one who raised a company of fifty-nine privates was commissioned captain, and one who procured ten companies to accept him and serve under him was commissioned colonel. The system encouraged rapid recruiting; but made regular discipline extremely difficult. Washington and even their own chosen officers had very little authority over the men, except that of enthusiasm and persuasion. The army often melted away before their eyes without any power on their part to stop the disbanding. In 1777 the Continental line was formed of men who enlisted for three years or for the war, and they constituted a small but somewhat steady nucleus round which the militia squads could rally. The militia served for six or three months, or a few weeks. It was a "come-and-go" army; and Graydon tells us that the officers as well as the men felt that they could leave with impunity when they were dissatisfied.[11]

The army besieging Boston had at first been composed exclusively of New Englanders; but it was joined during the summer by a few troops from the frontiers of Pennsylvania and Virginia, who aroused much interest, because they were expected to make deadly use of the rifle at three hundred yards instead of using the smooth-bore musket, which was useless at only half that distance.

Shortly before the battle of Bunker Hill the Congress passed a resolution for raising six companies of riflemen in Pennsylvania, two in Maryland, and two in Virginia. Subsequently, on the 22nd of June, they increased the number of Pennsylvania rifle companies to eight, which were to be formed into a battalion and join the patriot army at Boston.[12]

---

[11] Writings of Washington, Ford edition, vol. iii, p. 487; vol. v, p. 2 note; Graydon, " Memoirs," edition of 1846, pp. 181, 184.

[12] The rifle is supposed to have been introduced in the colonies previously to the year 1730 from the Austrian Tyrol. We find it manufactured at Philadelphia and at Lancaster, Pennsylvania, about that time. Its use spread rapidly on the western frontiers of Pennsylvania, Mary-

REVOLUTIONARY WEAPONS AND AMMUNITION

THE FRONTIER RIFLEMEN

During July these eight companies were rapidly recruited in the interior of the colony among the Scotch-Irish frontiersmen and hunters. No money had to be appropriated to buy their weapons, for, like the Boer of South Africa, each one of them procured his rifle by taking it down from the pegs on which it rested above his fireplace. He slung his own powder-horn across his shoulder and strapped his bullet-pouch around his waist.

As for his uniform, it consisted of a round hat, which could be bought for a trifle at any country store, and the hunting-shirt, already described, which was merely a shirt worn like a coat, belted round the waist instead of being tucked into the trousers, and was sometimes ornamented by a cape with fringe. It could be made at home by any man's wife, and was of the coarse linen manufactured from the flax which the colonists raised on their farms and plantations.

The rifle companies were rapidly recruited in Pennsylvania and Virginia during July, and as each company got ready it started for Boston, and for several weeks these hardy fellows were scattered along the beautiful route through the mountainous region of Pennsylvania and New York, crossing the Hudson above West Point, thence through another mountainous region by Litchfield, Connecticut, and on through Massachusetts. Their first destination was Reading, in Pennsylvania, where they received their blankets, knapsacks, and ammunition. These supplies were all they required from the patriot government, and when these were furnished they immediately sought the enemy.

The expectations from the long range of their weapons were fully realized. The rifle companies did good service, their numbers were increased, and we hear of them in almost every

land, Virginia, and the Carolinas, which we may call the rifle districts at the time of the Revolution, the only regions where riflemen could be recruited. The weapon was but little known or used in New England. *Magazine of American History*, vol. xxiv, p. 179; *Harper's Magazine*, vol. 50, p. 961; *The Pennsylvania German Magazine*, vol, 7, p. 355.

battle. Besides those already mentioned, there was a corps of them under McCall, another under Wills, and there were numerous temporary organizations. The British also had a few riflemen, and the Hessian Yagers, as they were called, carried a short rifle, used with very little skill.

The rifle was not generally adopted by the military profession until about one hundred years afterwards, when the breech-loader came into use. As a muzzle-loader it was too slow in reloading, and required more care and skill than could be had from the ordinary recruit. To insure accurate and long range, the bullet had to be carefully wrapped in a leather patch and forced with difficulty into the muzzle, often aided by a little mallet. The weapon was easily fouled by repeated firing. It would then lose its range and accuracy, and become almost useless.[13]

At Boston the riflemen seem to have done little or nothing except to pick off an occasional regular who incautiously showed himself above the line of fortifications round Bunker Hill. For the rest of the time they were inactive with the others. One day they picked off an officer in his handsome uniform, and the report quickly spread that this man's income had been £10,000 a year. On the 4th of August they were reported to have shot three captains. On another occasion William Simpson, who had accompanied the rifleman as a gentleman volunteer, was shot in the foot and died of his wound. They had a grand funeral over him, and eulogized and mourned for him as though he had been a statesman. Incidents were few in that long summer and autumn, and they had to make the most of anything that happened.

It must have been a rare sight to see that patriot army living in huts made of field stones and turf, or twisted green boughs, some in improvised tents made of sail-cloth or any stuff they could stretch over poles; some quartered in friendly houses; some sleeping in Massachusetts Hall of Harvard

---

[13] *American Archives*, fifth series, vol. ii, p. 1247; Draper, "King's Mountain," p. 392.

College; and all the sixteen thousand scattered in this manner through Cambridge and half round Boston, with the patient Washington and the humorous Greene trying to coax them to submit to discipline.[14]

There was cannonading almost every day from the British. Thousands of balls and shells were fired during the summer with the most trifling result. The ground was ploughed up, the apples came rattling down in the orchards as the big missiles thumped the trees and the shells spluttered among the limbs. Occasionally a ball would pass through a house, filling every room and the plates and dishes with a cloud of plaster-dust.

McCurtin tells us of a loyalist who, being, one evening, the only man in company with a number of young patriot women, began to abuse the Congress. The girls seized him, tore off his coat and shirt, and, instead of tar, covered him to the waist with molasses, and for feathers took the downy tops of flags that grew in the garden.

Patriots deserted to the British, and regulars deserted from the army in Boston and came into the Cambridge camp in twos or threes. Sometimes they had to swim the water which surrounded Boston, and were not infrequently drowned in the attempt. McCurtin kept a steady record of their arrivals, and they were heartily welcomed to the patriot ranks, which were believed to be growing to such stupendous numbers that they would soon be able to overwhelm all the armies that could be sent from England.[15]

---

[14] W. G. Greene, "Life of General Greene;" McCurtin, Journal in Papers Relating to the Maryland line, Seventy-six Society, 1857; Records of the Pennsylvania Riflemen in *Pennsylvania Archives*, vol. x; *American Archives*, fourth series, vol. iii, p. 28; vol. ii, p. 1764.

[15] Some of the patriot pamphleteers, for the sake of encouraging their party, made most extraordinary statements of the number of troops that could be raised. In "The Farmer Refuted" (Hamilton, Works, Lodge edition, vol. i, p. 158) it is said that America would have at least 500,000 soldiers, while England could send only 15,000. Another writer places the number at 300,000 to 400,000.—"Considerations on the Measures carrying on with Respect to the British Colonies," etc., fifth

There seems to have been a systematic exaggeration of numbers at this time, as well as later on, in the Revolution. It could not be very well prevented, because the officers were quite willing to have it so. There was much coming and going, and consequently an apparent increase. Some of the men were returning to their farms, and others were coming to take their places.

It was an army in which, in most instances, you could not distinguish the captain or the colonel from his men; an army in which there were applications every day for leave to go home to help get in the hay, or to see how the wife was getting on; and, if leave were granted, the fellow always took his allotment of powder with him to shoot squirrels, and he seldom brought any of the powder back. Shaving was more universal than now, and great importance was attached to it. It was believed that it could be made a good starting-point for regular discipline, and a captain was sometimes seen shaving one of his own men.

The New Englanders of that time, and more especially the lower classes, were full of what the colonists farther south called "the levelling spirit." Their manners were very shocking to the educated and conservative people of that day, and are described by Mrs. Knight in her diary of 1704, and at a much later date in Mrs. Grant's "Memoirs of an American Lady." The rank, crude, and unpleasant side of democracy seems to have had its first foothold in New England.

Mrs. Grant describes the disgust of the old New York aristocracy about Albany when they were first invaded by enterprising Yankees who came to take up the wild land. The rural New Englander of that time abounded in uncouth

edition, p. 25, London, 1774. See also Niles, " Principles and Acts of the Revolution," edition 1876, pp. 212, 501; *American Archives*, fourth series, vol. iii, pp. 1740, 1742. The famous loyalist pamphlet, " Plain Truth," says that, after deducting Quakers, Anabaptists, and loyalists, the patriots might have 60,000 to 70,000 capable of bearing arms. As it turned out, the British government sent Howe over 50,000 men, and Washington never had 25,000.

phrases and slang, abused rank and titles with amazing audacity, and had the nasal drawling voice which afterwards became notorious and now fortunately has largely passed away. One of these Yankees was certainly a terrible fellow when he fastened himself upon you, pressing you with drawling questions about your most private affairs, railing in the meantime against aristocrats and haranguing on liberty and the "eternal rights of man."

They were the beginning of a class which, becoming inflated by the success of independence, spread over the country to the horror of all well-educated people and in fulfilment of loyalist prophecies. They gave Grant the material for his famous speech in Parliament, and many years afterwards they furnished the stock material for Dickens and other Englishmen who found profit in ridiculing the Americans.

The extraordinary prevalence of "levelling" reveals to us how widespread among all classes had been the discussion of the rights of man and equality as set forth in the works of Burlamaqui, Beccaria, and Locke, described in a previous chapter. In the army before Boston "levelling" was so necessary that the officers, instead of cultivating the usual severity and dignity of manner, were obliged to cultivate the most extreme and absurd humility. It was their only way of controlling their men, who were almost out of their minds on the subject of equality. Graydon gives us some amusing glimpses of this. He was not with the army before Boston, but he saw the New Englanders and all classes of patriot troops the next year at New York, when levelling and equality were so rife among them that Adjutant-General Reed resigned his office in disgust.[16]

---

[16] "Life of Joseph Reed," by W. B. Reed, vol. i, p. 243; *American Archives*, fourth series, vol. ii, p. 905. See, also, Wilkinson's "Memoirs," vol. i, p. 16; Bolton, "Private Soldier under Washington," pp. 127–135; Writings of Washington, Ford edition, vol. v, p. 189. See, also, for conditions in the camp before Boston, Thacher, Military Journal; Proceedings of Massachusetts Historical Society, June, 1858, and November, 1863.

"The irregularity, want of discipline, bad arms, and defective equipment in all respects, of this multitudinous assemblage, gave no favorable impression of its prowess. The materials of which the eastern battalions were composed were apparently the same as those of which I had seen so unpromising a specimen at Lake George. I speak particularly of the officers who were in no single respect distinguishable from the men, other than in the colored cockades, which for this very purpose had been prescribed in general orders; a different color being assigned to the officers of each grade. So far from aiming at a deportment which might raise them above their privates and thence prompt them to due respect and obedience to their commands, the object was, by humility to preserve the existing blessing of equality, an illustrious instance of which was given by Colonel Putnam, the chief engineer of the army, and no less a personage than the nephew of the major-general of that name. "What!" says a person meeting him one day with a piece of meat in his hand, "carrying home your rations yourself, colonel?" "Yes," says he, "and I do it to set the officers a good example."—"Memoirs," edition of 1846, p. 147. See, also, Stedman, "American War," edition of 1794, p. 206.

A colonel often made drummers and fifers of his sons for the sake of the small additional revenue to his family chest; and a captain was known to have made money by stealing blankets. Small money-making, pettiness, and pilfering of every kind were so rife as to cause Washington and many others the greatest discouragement and anxiety. The first outburst of the rights of man was by no means promising or in good taste. Many of the New England regiments had negroes mixed promiscuously among the white troops, which, to a person like Graydon, coming from farther south, had a very disagreeable and degrading effect.[17]

He also noticed that none of the subordinate officers belonged to the upper classes of colonial society. Accustomed to a totally different state of things farther south, he inquired the cause, and was curtly told that the sons of such people had all been sent to Europe to be educated and to keep them out

---

[17] In the Congress at Philadelphia, Edward Rutledge, supported by many of the Southern delegates, moved that all negroes, bond or free, be discharged from the patriot army. *American Historical Review*, vol. i, page 292; also, Bolton, "Private Soldier under Washington," pp. 21, 22.

of harm's way. Probably the real reason was that such men could not have controlled the troops gone mad with levelling.

Taken all in all, that army must have been one of the most interesting military exhibitions that the world has ever seen. Neither extreme age nor extreme youth was a bar to service, and, as in the Boer army of independence in South Africa in 1900, there were grandfathers serving with their grandsons.

Mingled with the small money-making, the "dirty mercenary spirit," as Washington called it, and the disorder which nearly drove him distracted, there was the Puritan fondness for long sermons and elaborate discussions of religion which to British and loyalist observers, and even to some Southern patriots, was very bad taste, if not offensive hypocrisy. But, nevertheless, there was behind it that New England moral purpose which has accomplished wonderful results; and all this with the negroes freely associating in the white regiments was a strange sight for a Southerner. "Such sermons," exclaimed one of the riflemen, "such negroes, such colonels, such boys, such great-great-grandfathers!" [13]

It is always very easy, however, to ridicule a patriot army. No army of freedom or independence was ever well dressed. There was more in these troublesome fellows than mere "levelling" or disorder. They had come of their own free will to accomplish a political purpose, and many of them afterwards proved the faith that was in them by years of suffering, poverty, and hardships. They may have been opinionated, self-willed, intolerant of discipline and order; but they could fight more intelligently and persistently than the English, shoot truer, march farther and survive disease, exposure, nakedness, and hunger that would have annihilated the whole British army.

There was plenty of good material at Cambridge. Greene, Sullivan, and Gates, names afterwards well known in the war, were there. Daniel Morgan, the commander of the Virginia

---

[13] Bolton, "Private Soldier under Washington," p. 43.

riflemen, was one of those frontier characters of superb manhood and intelligence, of which we have, fortunately, had many specimens down into our own time; but with another generation they will have all passed away. He became a remarkably good officer in the Revolution, and although unappreciated, and in a measure suppressed, by the Congress, he was the victor in a very important battle.

He had been born in New Jersey, of Welsh parents from Pennsylvania, but began life as a common laborer on the Virginia frontier, where he rose to be a waggoner, which was a profitable occupation. He hauled supplies for Braddock's army in the French War and was lucky enough to escape at the time of that general's defeat. Soon he plunged into a wild career of gambling, drinking, and fighting; but his enormous strength and courage and legitimate fighting with the Indians made him a leader among frontiersmen. He reformed, married, and became a farmer. But the first news of war brought him to Boston with ninety-six riflemen, who covered the distance of six hundred miles on foot in twenty-one days."[19]

General Putnam, or "Old Put," as they called him, the hero of the French War, was the life of the camps. In his shirt-sleeves, which was his usual summer garb, with an old hanger slung by a broad strap across his brawny shoulders, he was to be seen everywhere, encouraging, regulating, talking. People listened by the hour to the tales of his cutting-out expeditions and adventures. The troops who believed in levelling could have no objection to him as an officer, for he was a plain, jovial farmer. When the Boston Port Bill went into effect he started from his farm in Connecticut with one hundred and thirty sheep, driving them before him to Boston, to relieve the suffering of the people.[20]

He was well acquainted with many of the British officers from his old association with them in the French War. They

---

[19] G. W. Greene, " Life of General Greene," vol. iii, p. 94.
[20] Tarbox, " Life of Putnam," p. 118.

now made several friendly efforts to persuade him to take the safer and more profitable side, and the loyalists were in the habit of saying that he was at first inclined to accept their overtures.

In the French War the regulars had usually snubbed and ignored the provincial officers; but they had found great difficulty in suppressing Putnam, whose natural audacity and exuberant physique walked over all conventional distinctions. He was one of those popular characters about whom many anecdotes, true and false, accumulate. He had a dispute with a British officer, was told he must fight a duel, and was given the choice of weapons. He chose two kegs of gunpowder with lighted slow-matches in them, each man to sit on a keg until one of them exploded. The matches burned slowly, and the Englishman, unable to endure the mental strain, got up. The kegs were then opened and found to contain nothing but onions.[21]

---

[21] See, also, on the general subject of this chapter, Frothingham, "Siege of Boston," p. 118; "Life of Joseph Reed," by W. B. Reed, vol. i, p 140; Humphrey, "Life of Putnam;" Bolton, "Private Soldier under Washington," p. 140; *American Archives*, fourth series, vol. iv, pp. 468, 469; vol. v, p. 471; vol. vi, p. 420.

XXXII.

BRITISH SOVEREIGNTY EXTINGUISHED IN 1775

WHEN General Howe brought 5000 troops to reinforce Gage in Boston in May, 1775, it was all England could do for the present in the way of sending an army to America. The Ministry contemplated sending out a great force of thirty or forty thousand, but at least a year must elapse before this force could be collected and transported across the Atlantic.

England had not a large standing army, and the troops she had were very much scattered. She had always been obliged to hire troops from other nations, and she must now negotiate for a considerable number of these hirelings from Germany, and, if possible, from Russia and Holland. To gather together all these forces and transport them in sailing vessels with adequate supplies across three thousand miles of ocean, which was often a voyage of two months and sometimes of three or four months, and have them arrive in sufficient numbers and with sufficient provisions to conquer the thousand miles of sea coast from Maine to Florida, was a stupendous task.

We can now hardly realize the difficulties with which England had to contend in the mere matter of sending fresh provisions to her American army in those days of sailing vessels. Her troops could not rely on living on the country, because they were often surrounded and cut off from supplies by the patriot forces. The Ministry were, therefore, at the great disadvantage of keeping their forces close to some harbor which they controlled from the sea; and even then the expense and hazard of sending the supplies was enormous.

For supplying their small force shut up in Boston, they had collected 5000 cattle, 14,000 sheep, vast numbers of hogs, 10,000 butts of beer, and large quantities of hay, oats, and beans, for the cavalry. They undertook to carry out the animals alive; but the ships were beaten back and forth by bad weather until most of the live stock perished almost within sight of England, and the channel was everywhere strewn with their floating carcasses.[1]

During the year from June, 1775, to June, 1776, in which the great army of invasion was preparing, nothing was done in America except to hold Boston; and Gage was informed that no reinforcements need be expected until the following spring.[2] This delay seems to have been unavoidable, but it was very disastrous to England; for outside of the town of Boston there was no force of any kind to protect British sovereignty from Maine to Florida. That sovereignty was now represented only by the governors; for the patriots had captured the legislatures in all the provinces or had a provincial congress or other body which rendered the legislature powerless. The governors were the only symbol of authority that stood between the patriots and independence; and during the year 1775 the patriots proceeded to rid themselves of the governors in a way which was very characteristic and successful.

The governors had no troops, nothing to protect them except their dignity and the respect with which their office had always been regarded. They could have been made the easy victims of assassination, but nothing of that sort was attempted. In Massachusetts Gage was the governor; but he was already disposed of by being locked up with his British troops in Boston; and the patriots had already organized an independent American government in the rest of the province. In Connecticut the governor was elected by the people, and the incumbent of the office was Jonathan Trumbull, a staunch patriot. There was practically no revolution in Connecticut. The people continued to live and govern themselves as they had done for over a hundred years and as they have done ever since.

In Rhode Island, where the governor was also elected by the people, there was some little trouble with the incumbent,

---

[1] Gordon, " American Revolution," edition 1788, vol. ii, p. 221.
[2] *American Archives*, fourth series, vol. iii, pp. 6, 8, 15, 94; vol. v, p. 526.

Joseph Wanton, who, though a vigorous patriot in the early stages of the contest, now suddenly began to show symptoms of loyalism. But the legislature forbade him to exercise his functions and directed the lieutenant-governor, Nicholas Cooke, to act in his place.[3]

In Virginia the energetic and irascible governor, Lord Dunmore, removed the locks from all the muskets in the arsenal, buried the powder where it was injured by the rain, set a spring-gun in the building, and when the patriot assembly demanded admission, gave them the keys. When one of their servants had been wounded by the spring-gun, and they had discovered that the muskets and ammunition were ruined, such a large assemblage of armed patriots began gathering in Williamsburg that Dunmore and his family took refuge on board a British man-of-war at Yorktown. He demanded that the assembly attend him on board the ship to finish their business, which they, of course, refused to do. When they adjourned, they never met again. The people elected a convention, which became the revolutionary government of the province, and British authority was completely extinct. Dunmore had to remain out on the water, and Virginia was an independent state.

Dunmore had written to the Ministry in May that with a supply of arms and ammunition which he might be able to collect from negroes and Indians, he hoped to hold Virginia for the crown. This was certainly a pathetic commentary on the weakness of England in America, that the governor of her largest and most prosperous colony had no hope of defending it except with weapons borrowed from slaves and Indians.[4]

Sir James Wright, the governor of Georgia, might have been expected to hold his own because the patriot party was so weak in that province. But what the patriots lacked in

---

[3] *American Archives*, fourth series, vol. ii, p. 662, 667, 967.

[4] *American Archives*, fourth series, vol. v, or iii, p. 6; Gordon, "American Revolution," edition 1788, vol. ii, pp. 85-91; Stedman, "American War," vol. i, p. 145.

numbers they made up in energy; and when British men-of-war arrived on the coast in June, 1775, Joseph Habersham entered Wright's house and took him prisoner to prevent him communicating with the men-of-war. Wright, however, quickly escaped and fled to the war-ship, "Scarborough," from which he addressed a letter to his council and planned an attack on Savannah, but soon afterwards sailed for England.

Dunmore and Wright were the first governors to be ejected; and Governor Martin, of North Carolina, met the same fate in July. He attempted to fortify himself in his house, as Dunmore had done; but when he began to move some cannon for that purpose the committee of safety interfered and seized them. He fled to Fort Johnson, on the Cape Fear River, where he declared himself ready to arm the slaves; and he would probably have secured himself in the fort if Colonel Ashe had not quickly collected a body of patriots to march against him. He fled again, taking with him the cannon and stores of the fort, and retired like Dunmore and Wright to the safety of the water and a British man-of-war. He went through the form of attempting to govern from the water; but his proclamations were so magnificent in language and impotent in effect that British sovereignty became more than ever a laughing-stock in America.[5]

Lord William Campbell had only just been appointed governor of South Carolina, where he was received with all the usual demonstrations of loyalty. But finding the assembly opposed to him he dissolved it, and never called another. He began to organize the numerous loyalists of the province so secretly and effectively, and was so successful in convincing them that it was useless to resist the power of Great Britain, that some of the patriots were for seizing and confining him in jail. The majority disapproved of the plan; but there were enough in favor of it to alarm the governor, and in September he also fled to the water and a British man-of-war. The province passed into the control of the patriots; but the loyal-

---

[5] *American Archives*, fourth series, vol. iii, pp. 8, 9, 61, 75, 713, 773.

ists were so numerous and powerful that the patriot rule was very precarious.[6]

Governor Wentworth, of New Hampshire, was a tactful and judicious man for whom the patriots had much respect; but his influence waned so rapidly during the summer that he was obliged to take refuge in Fort William and Mary.

In New York, Governor Tryon, of North Carolina fame at the battle of the Alamance, had returned in June from a long visit to England to consult with the ministry.[7] The strong loyalist feeling in the colony and his own prudent determination to take no very positive action for the present, preserved him from trouble during the summer. But he was so obviously strengthening and organizing the loyalists, that it was proposed in the Continental Congress to seize and imprison him. The motion failed. But afterwards a general resolution was passed recommending the patriot conventions and committees in every colony to imprison any person who endangered the public safety. Tryon was warned by a swift messenger from a friend in the Congress that this resolution was intended to accomplish his arrest, and before the New York provincial congress could act he also fled out on the water, and from the refuge of the ship "Halifax" attempted in vain to conduct the government of his province.[8]

In New Jersey, Franklin's wayward son, William, an ardent loyalist, was the governor. He made no effort to conceal his opinions or to escape, and kept up appearances during the greater part of the year 1775. But his authority was steadily undermined and a patriot provincial congress was gradually assuming control of the province. In January, 1776, we find him placed under guard at Perth Amboy, and compelled to

---

[6] *American Archives*, fourth series, iii, pp. 1606, 1607.

[7] *American Archives*, fourth series, vol. ii, pp. 508, 677; Gordon, "American Revolution," edition 1788, vol. ii, p. 94; *American Archives*, fourth series, vol. iii, pp. 834–838. "Diary and Letters of Thomas Hutchinson," vol. i, p. 433.

[8] *American Archives*, fourth series, vol. iii, pp. 1052, 1054; vol. v, p. 44; Jones, "New York in the Revolution," vol. i, pp. 61, 559.

give his parole not to leave the province.   But in the following
June he had the courage, or obstinacy, to issue a proclamation
calling a meeting of the defunct legislature.   He was then
arrested, imprisoned in Burlington, and afterwards in East
Windsor, Connecticut, until exchanged in November, 1778.   He
was well pensioned and rewarded on his return to England.
But his unpleasant and useless experience in trying to hold
his post shows the wisdom of those governors who saw that
their dignity could be more comfortably maintained on the
water than on the land.[9]

Pennsylvania's governor was John Penn, one of the proprietary family, who had owned the whole province and still
owned a large part of it, collecting quit-rents from the inhabitants.   He seemed more than half inclined to sympathize with
the patriots and never attempted to check any of their proceedings.[10]   They never disturbed or annoyed him, and as the
Revolution advanced, he gradually dropped out of office; but
remained quietly in the province.   In the summer of 1777, when
General Howe's army was expected in Philadelphia, it seemed
so incongruous to have a regularly-constituted British governor
at large, that Penn was put under arrest and sent to Connecticut until Howe's army was about to evacuate Philadelphia
in May, 1778.   The people appreciated his position and difficulties, and after the Revolution made a most liberal allowance
to his family for the confiscation of their estates.

Maryland was also a proprietary province, owned by the
family of Lord Baltimore, and the governor was Robert Eden,
who also found himself in a position of conflicting duties.   He
represented the interest and estates of the proprietary family,
and also the interests of the British Government, and his wife
was one of the proprietary family.   It was quite difficult to
balance among these responsibilities and know exactly what to

---

[9] Title " Franklin " in *Index of American Archives*, fourth series,
vol. vi.

[10] One of his letters indicates strong sympathy with the patriot cause.
(*American Archives*, fourth series, vol. vi, p. 1116.)

do as the patriot convention usurped more and more the functions of the colonial legislature.

Eden made no serious resistance to the encroachments. He expressed moderate views, advocated the repeal of the tea tax, and when the patriot militia demanded the arms and ammunition in the arsenal, he gave them up without protest or question. His authority was steadily undermined, and by the autumn of 1775 the patriot convention and the committees of safety were governing the province.

Eden, however, remained at Annapolis all the following winter and spring, performing some of the social functions of the governor's office, and apparently a few routine executive duties. He held meetings of his council and as the assembly would not support the British cause, he kept it perpetually prorogued.[11] His letters were all examined before he was allowed to receive them; but otherwise he was treated by everybody with the greatest respect and consideration.

He appears to have understood the Maryland character and was evidently a very convivial man, fond of entertaining and well suited to that picturesque and jovial high living which was so characteristic of Annapolis. Before the Revolution Washington, it is said, frequently rode up from Mount Vernon to dine with this very genial Maryland governor and share "the hour of social and sentimental discourse."[12]

Those were the closing days of the grand old times in the Maryland capital, and it is possible that Eden might have remained as an inhabitant of Maryland throughout the Revolution. But in April, 1776, one of General Charles Lee's officers intercepted a letter to him from the British Ministry, thanking him for certain confidential information and directing him to assist Lord Dunmore in his operations against Virginia. General Lee thereupon requested the Maryland committee of safety to arrest Eden and the Continental Congress made the same

---

[11] *American Archives*, fourth series, vol. iii, p. 1570.
[12] Eddis, " Letters from America," pp. 236, 266.

request. The committee, however, would go no farther than to take Eden's parole, and this very liberal treatment aroused much indignation in Virginia. The Marylanders were accused of playing into the hands of the enemy and betraying the common cause. But a considerable number, if not a majority of the Maryland patriots, seem to have heartily approved of this generosity to Eden. They wanted Eden to stay as long as possible. They apparently thought that his remaining would have a conservative influence, and prevent anarchy and confusion, while the province gradually became patriotic and independent.[13]

There was a strong minority in favor of very violent measures, and one of them, young Samuel Purviance, undertook to arrest Eden and being unsuccessful was brought before the patriot convention and reprimanded for his disrespect to the governor of the province.

These two attempts by individuals to arrest a governor, one in Maryland and the other in Georgia, would in many countries have been attempts at assassination. We were unable to finish the Civil War of 1861 without an official assassination, and since then we have had two Presidents assassinated; but there were no political assassinations of high officials in the Revolution in spite of the intense bitterness of the struggle and the violent feelings between patriot and loyalist.

Eden remained quietly in Annapolis under his parole, but was told that he had better arrange to have a British war-ship come for him. The frigate "Forney" was allowed to come up to the town under a flag of truce, and on the 23rd of June, 1776, the patriot committee of safety took an affectionate leave of Governor Eden, conducting him to the barge with every mark of respect. It was a rather curious incident in the midst of a Revolution, an unusual but a very good-natured way of abolishing British sovereignty, very kindly, very American, and

---

[13] *American Archives*, fourth series, vol. v, pp. 954, 960, 964, 970, 983, 1222; vol. vi, pp. 732, 739.

very like the typical Marylander and the good old days of Annapolis.[14]

His departure was none too soon, for the more violent patriots were losing patience. Like the other ejected governors, he was well rewarded in England and given a baronetcy. He returned to Annapolis after the Revolution to look after his wife's estate, and died there in 1784.

Thus the royal governors were adroitly removed during that lull in the Revolution while Great Britain was preparing for a heavy blow. The colonies had become independent states; and the Revolution had become more than ever what Dean Tucker always had said it was, a war on the part of England to recover a lost sovereignty.[15]

To render their condition as independent states more complete, the Congress in November of this same year, 1775, took measures to clear away the colonial forms of government and the old charters, round which lingered a certain amount of sentiment which encouraged loyalism. The patriots of New Hampshire, South Carolina, and Virginia were advised to "establish such a form of government as in their judgment will best produce the happiness of the people and most effectually secure peace and good order during the continuance of the present dispute between Great Britain and the colonies."

The language of the recommendation was purposely made very moderate, and the assumption that there would be a reconciliation with England was put in to satisfy the timid and those who hesitated as to the advisability of the step to be taken. But it was intended that each of the provinces should openly adopt a new government independent of all authority of Great Britain. In a word, they were to become independent "during the present dispute."

---

[14] *American Archives*, fourth series, vol. vi, p. 629; Scharf, "History of Maryland," vol. ii, pp. 216, 219; Eddis, "Letters from America," pp. 207, 215, 234, 238, 241, 251, 266, 279, 283, 285, 290, 292, 303, 304, 311; *American Archives*, fourth series, vol. iii, pp. 704, 1570; vol. v, index title "Samuel Purviance;" vol. vi, pp. 682, 1044, 1046, 1505; vol. vii, p. 629.

[15] "Diary and Letters of Thomas Hutchinson," vol. ii, pp. 55, 56.

Out of this very cautious recommendation have grown all our modern state constitutions. The New Hampshire patriots were the first to adopt the suggestion. They elected a convention, calling it a congress, which sat from the 21st of December, 1775, to the 5th of January, 1776, and framed the first American Constitution, with a legislature of two branches but no governor. The recommendation of the Congress was strictly complied with, and this constitution was to continue in force only "during the present unhappy and unnatural contest with Great Britain."

In the following March the South Carolina patriots followed suit and prepared a very complete constitution for their province, provided for a governor, whom they called "President and Commander in Chief," and gave him a veto on all laws passed by the legislature. There was no declaration of independence in this or in the New Hampshire constitution, and the word itself was not used, because, as Chief Justice Drayton said, that was a matter which must be left to the Congress. It would require the united strength of all the colonies to give stability to the independence of any one of them.[16]

The patriots of Virginia adopted their new constitution in June, 1776; and under further recommendation from the Congress constitutions for New Jersey, Delaware, Pennsylvania, Maryland, and North Carolina were adopted during that year. Constitutions for Georgia, Vermont, and New York were prepared in 1777. The Massachusetts patriots had adopted an independent government in the autumn of 1774; but framed no written constitution until 1780. Rhode Island and Connecticut, having always elected their own governors and never submitted their laws to England for approval, were already independent enough for all practical purposes and continued to live under their old charters for several generations after the Revolution.[17]

---

[16] *American Archives*, fifth series, vol. ii, p. 1047.
[17] Fisher, " Evolution of the Constitution," chapter iii.

XXXIII.

DESTRUCTION OF PORTLAND AND NORFOLK

THE British war-ships, which seem to have been rather numerous along the whole coast, had afforded a welcome refuge for the governors; and every one wondered why they had not done more. A loyalist writing from Philadelphia complains that they made no attempt to seize the armed galleys which the patriots were building before their eyes, or to stop the importation of French arms and ammunition; and they certainly did nothing to uphold the authority of the governors on shore.[1]

The patriots dreaded the British navy because most of their towns and a very large proportion of their farms and plantations were on navigable water, and they expected terrible devastation from the war-ships and the small boats which could follow up the creeks and shoal rivers. The probability, and to some minds the certainty, of this destruction was one of the strongest arguments used by the loyalists when they were enlarging on the hopelessness of a contest with Great Britain. Many patriots were so impressed that they loaded their furniture on wagons and moved inland; but in the end they were agreeably disappointed, for the British navy was strangely unaggressive during the war.

In this year, 1775, however, when the governors were being pushed off the continent, the navy displayed not a little activity. But it was ill-directed and had no effect in upholding the authority of the governors. Stonington, in Connecticut, was shelled, houses shattered, two citizens killed, and a schooner taken. Sailors and marines landed on Canonicutt Island, in Narragansett Bay, and destroyed houses and barns. In New York, when the patriots undertook to remove the cannon from the city battery at night, the "Asia" man-

---

[1] *American Archives*, fourth series, vol. iii, p. 3.

of-war fired upon them. On the 12th of October a British fleet of sixteen vessels ranged themselves in line before the town of Bristol, Rhode Island, and bombarded it with shells and fire-carcasses for an hour and a half. Colonel Potter in the hottest of the fire went out on the end of the wharf, hailed the frigate "Rose" and went on aboard of her to expostulate. Captain Wallace agreed to spare the town if it would supply him with two thousand sheep and thirty fat cattle; but as the people had driven off nearly all their stock, he finally compromised on forty sheep, which was surely a glorious victory for the British navy.[2]

In fact, several of these minor naval aggressions seem to have been inspired by the mere desire to obtain fresh provisions and save the crews from the scurvy. There were, however, two very serious aggressions, the burning of Portland and of Norfolk. The people of Portland (then Falmouth), Maine, had obstructed the loading of one of the vessels which habitually came to that coast for white-pine trees to make masts and spars for the British navy. The admiral, after consultation with General Gage, sent the "Canceau" and three other vessels in command of Captain Mowat, who some time before had been seized and detained by the patriots when he landed in the town. The expedition was intended to accomplish the destruction of Cape Ann as well as Portland; but the attack on Cape Ann was abandoned. On the 18th of October Mowat wreaked his vengeance on Portland by firing into the town, from nine in the morning until sunset, some three thousand round shot, besides shells, bombs, fire-carcasses, grape-shot, and musket-balls. The people fled to the woods; but five hundred houses, constituting three-fourths of the town, every store and warehouse, the

---

[2] Gordon, "American Revolution," edition 1788, vol. ii, pp. 122, 124; American Archives, fourth series, vol. iii, pp. 250, 261, 990, 1106, 1145; vol. iv, p. 230. Apparently other towns on the coast dreading bombardment supplied the British war-vessels with fresh provisions. Some refused. (American Archives, fourth series, vol. iv, pp. 99, 175, 248, 367, 592, 798, 799, 1128, 948, 980, 1227, 1237, 1256, 1279, 1287; vol. v, pp. 347, 796.)

church, the new court-house, the public library, and fourteen vessels were completely destroyed, and the people left homeless for the winter.

The destruction of Norfolk, in Virginia, was accomplished by Lord Dunmore, who, after he had been driven from the governorship, had established himself on a flotilla of three war-ships and some smaller vessels which he kept close to Norfolk. He offered freedom to the slaves and recruited a large number of them together with loyalists, who were numerous in the town. He conducted some notable and successful raids on the land; but in attempting to prevent a patriot force from entering Norfolk he was defeated at the Great Bridge and obliged to retire to his ships.

No longer able to maintain a force on shore, or obtain supplies from Norfolk, and being much annoyed by the fire of the patriots from that part of the town which lay nearest the water, he determined to dislodge them by destroying the town. He first sent a flag ashore with a demand that the people should regularly supply his Majesty's ships with water and provisions. This being refused, he gave notice of bombardment and warned the inhabitants to seek safety in flight. On the 1st of January, 1776, he opened a cannonade on the houses and landed parties of sailors and marines, who set fire to the nearest buildings, and the whole town was reduced to ashes.[3]

This destruction of Norfolk, coupled with the destruction of Portland in the previous October, were never forgotten or forgiven by the patriot party. For years afterwards they were

---

[3] *American Archives*, fourth series, vol. iii, pp. 923, 1067, 1103, 1137, 1138, 1188, 1190, 1193, 1385, 1616, 1669, 1670, 1716, 1714, 1717; vol. iv, pp. 224, 228 note, 233, 292, 293, 344, 349, 352, 461, 540, 575, 335, 350, 357, 465, 476, 538–541, 577, 579, 794, 819, 827, 819, 827, 830, 946, 947, 1477; Gordon, "American Revolution," edition 1788, vol. ii, pp. 112, 206, 207; "Life, Correspondence and Speeches of Patrick Henry," by W. W. Henry, vol. i, p. 321; Stedman, "American War," vol. i, pp. 146–151; Eddis, "Letters from America," pp. 250, 255, 257, 309, 326. Dunmore's account of the fight at Great Bridge is entirely at variance with other descriptions. (*American Archives, id.*, vol. iii, p. 1714.)

used to inflame the patriot imagination and rouse the desire for war and vengeance. They furnished much-needed material for breaking up a certain sentimental attachment to the old order of things, and the hope of compromise. They were described as acts of wanton barbarity and atrocious cruelty at a time when the patriots were abstaining from severe acts of warfare in the hope that England might still be able to see her way to accept the ultimatum which the Congress had offered.

Pictures of these two towns in flames, shelled by the ships, and the women and children flying from them, were among the scenes which Franklin intended to have engraved in France so that they could be put in children's books and burn into the American mind an undying hatred of England and her government. Those two acts of devastation undoubtedly strengthened the American position, and won over to the idea of absolute independence many hesitating patriots.

It is extremely probable that the Ministry never intended that either Portland or Norfolk should be destroyed. It was contrary to the policy they had adopted of beginning the war with moderation; and for the next three years they permitted no more of this sweeping devastation.[4]

Dunmore had shown great energy and persistence. Washington regarded him as a formidable enemy and urged the Virginians to suppress him. Before he was defeated at Great Bridge he had evidently hoped to occupy Norfolk and hold it as Howe was holding Boston. Meanwhile through John Connelly, a Pennsylvania loyalist, he was preparing a grand plan for enlisting all the loyalists of the Virginia and Maryland frontiers, with the Indians of Ohio. Connelly visited Gage in Boston, who approved of the undertaking; and the plans were extended so as to include the Indians of Canada as far west as Detroit and Illinois. The whole of this vast force was to

---

[4] *American Archives,* fourth series, vol. iii, p. 1927; vol. iv, p. 577; vol. v, pp. 187, 961, 962, 1232; Writings of Washington, Ford edition, vol. v, p. 294; "Diary and Letters of Thomas Hutchinson," vol. i, p. 583; Stanhope, "History of England," vol. vi, p. 75.

march through Virginia in the following April and meet Dunmore, who, by that time, would have collected a British fleet in the Potomac. This design was carefully matured during the summer and autumn of 1775. But late in November, when Connelly and two associates, with all the plans in their pockets, were on their way to Detroit, they were suspected and seized at Hagerstown, Maryland, by one of those watchful patriot committees of safety without which the Revolution would never have been successful.[5]

Dunmore maintained his floating colony of negroes and loyalists until the summer of 1776. A printing press, which he had seized in Norfolk, he used on his ship for printing a little newspaper called the *Virginia Gazette*, which he seems to have succeeded in distributing on shore among the loyalists. But the hot weather of the summer and the crowding and dirt in his colony carried off most of his negroes with malignant fevers. There was not a ship in his fleet that did not throw overboard two or three dead every night. He effected a landing on Given's Island and built some intrenchments; but in a short time the ground was covered with the graves of his dead, and on the 8th of July, the patriots attacked the place and compelled him to escape in his ships after a heavy loss. In August he abandoned all hope of regaining authority over Virginia; and his ships, some forty or fifty in number, sailed away and scattered, conquered at last by the climate and natural conditions, and he himself, with about a hundred of his followers, joined the fleet of Admiral Howe at New York.[6]

---

[5] *American Archives*, fourth series, vol. iii, pp. 847, 923, 1047, 1543, 1660; vol. iv, pp. 201, 250, 342, 458, 508, 615, 616, 822, 781, 950; vol. vi. pp. 433–436; and the title "Connelly" in Index; Scharf, "History of Maryland," vol. ii, p. 190; Journals of Congress, vol. i, pp. 300, 361; Gordon, "American Revolution," edition 1788, vol. ii, p. 114; *Ohio Arch. and Hist. Quar.*, vol. ii, pp. 167–197.

[6] Eddis, "Letters from America," p. 326; Gordon, "American Revolution," edition 1788, vol. ii, pp. 298, 299; "Diary and Letters of Thomas Hutchinson," vol. ii, pp. 87, 93; *American Archives*, fifth series, vol. i, pp. 949, 963, 1064; vol. ii, pp. 158–166.

XXXIV.

THE AMERICAN NAVY AND PRIVATEERING

IN that same autumn of 1775, when the British navy destroyed Portland, the patriots began to create a navy of their own. Washington from the camp at Cambridge encouraged the New Englanders to fit out private armed schooners to capture the supply vessels of the British army. One of the first of these, the "Lee," of Marblehead, took the English ordnance-ship "Nancy," carrying brass cannon and a mortar, besides a large cargo of arms, ammunition, and camp equipment. When this spoil was brought to Cambridge, there was great rejoicing General Putnam, without regard to dignity, stood on the great mortar, with a bottle of rum in his hand, and General Mifflin stood by as godfather to christen it—"The Congress."

Other prizes were soon taken and before Christmas there were half a dozen privateersmen cruising off the New England coast. Their success was largely due, it was said, to the incompetence and timidity of Admiral Graves, who, instead of sending his ships to cruise outside, kept them at anchor in Boston harbor surrounded with booms to prevent their being boarded by the patriot whale-boats. The patriots did what they pleased in the harbor, burnt the light-house, took prizes almost under the guns of Graves's ships, and supplied themselves with cattle from the islands, while the admiral lay protected by his booms and unwilling even to furnish Gage with ships for communicating with other parts of the coast. He was finally superseded on the 30th of December, 1775, by Admiral Shuldham, who, however, was only a trifle more active than Graves.[1]

---

[1] *American Archives*, fourth series, vol. iv, pp. 376, 587; Gordon, "American Revolution," edition 1788, vol. ii, p. 168; "Diary and Letters of Thomas Hutchinson," vol. i, pp. 499, 571, 581, 583; vol. ii, pp. 3, 40, 85, 136, 139; Fonblanque, "Life of Burgoyne," p. 197.

The American privateers were instructed to avoid any contest with men-of-war and to confine their captures to transports and provision ships. Ordinary traders were to be allowed to pass in peace; for the patriots, in conformity with their conservative policy, were not yet willing to admit that there was war with Great Britain in the full sense of the word. The privateers were not turned loose on all British commerce until the spring of 1776.[2]

A privateer could be fitted out very quickly and cheaply. Any of the numerous American schooners, with a reputation for speed, could within a few weeks have from four to eight of the small cannon of those days put on her deck and be supplied with a crew of from eight to twenty men with muskets and cutlasses. A few more guns and men would put her very nearly on an equality with the smaller class of British war-ships.

The profits to the owners, and even to the crews of privateers, were enormous; and the hint having been given in this autumn of 1775, privateersmen were fitted out all down the coast, especially in Chesapeake Bay, and there were soon requests for the establishment of prize courts. The privateering service became so popular that it seriously interfered with recruiting for the army. Those who enlisted in the army became dissatisfied. They longed for the expiration of their time that they might join in the spoils of England's ocean commerce. General Greene lamented that he could not share that golden harvest so as to provide a fortune for his family. At the close of 1776, Dr. Rush estimated that there were at least 10,000 New Englanders on board the privateers.[3]

The soldier of the Revolution was usually a melancholy figure of suffering and poverty, who, even if he escaped disease, bullets, and the horrors of a British prison, found in the end

---

[2] *American Archives*, fourth series, vol. v, pp. 472, 474, 1642, 1650; Journals of Congress, Ford edition, vol. iv, p. 229.

[3] *American Archives*, fifth series, vol. iii, pp. 1072, 1513; G. W. Greene, "Life of Nathanael Greene," vol. i, pp. 226, 227.

that he had sacrificed everything for his country. But the privateersman served his country and at the same time grew fat and rich; and so lucrative was his calling that French, Spanish, and Dutch merchants sent out money to Baltimore to buy shares in privateering ventures.

When all British commerce was thrown open to their depredations, the privateersmen swarmed from every port.

"Thousands of schemes for privateering," wrote John Adams, "are afloat in American imaginations. Some are for taking the Hull ships with Woolens for Amsterdam, and Rotterdam; some are for the tin ships; some for the Irish linen ships; some for outward bound and others for inward bound East Indiamen; some for the Hudson's Bay ships; and many for West India sugar ships."—*American Archives*, fifth series, vol. i, p. 908.

There is no occupation that appeals so strongly to the primitive instinct of adventure, plunder, and fight; and we shall never become so civilized that we shall not like to read about privateering. It was the prosperous side of the Revolution; and not a few solid and permanent fortunes in America were begun by those low rakish schooners from the Chesapeake that could outsail anything on the sea. During the six years from April, 1777, to March, 1783, 285 of them are said to have sailed from the Chesapeake alone, carrying in all 1810 guns and 640 swivels.[4]

Complete lists of all the captures during the Revolution do not seem to be obtainable; but there are a few during certain periods which throw considerable light on this species of warfare. Up to the spring of 1777, according to one list, the American privateers had captured 342 British vessels, of which 44 were retaken. During the same period the British fleet had taken only 140 American vessels, of which 26 were recaptured.[5]

The British war-vessels and privateers were slow at starting on their work; but once fairly under way, they are generally believed to have done more damage to our merchant marine

---

[4] Scharf, "History of Maryland," vol. ii, pp. 201, 210.
[5] *American Archives*, fifth series, vol. iii, pp. 1523–1530.

than we did to theirs. In an estimate made in 1778 the honors were rather even, with the advantage just beginning to turn in favor of England. But a modern estimate made by the Secretary of Lloyd's seems to show that during the whole war our privateers took over 3000 English merchant ships, while barely 1200 American vessels were taken by the British. England, however, could stand her loss, because she had many vessels left, while our loss was nearly the whole of our merchant marine.[*]

As the contest progressed this disastrous side of the ocean warfare became very serious for us, and assisted in bringing the patriot cause to a very low ebb in the years 1779 and 1780. The British cruisers were unable to restrict the operations of our privateersmen; but our resources were being exhausted and in the long run England's superior naval power would tell against us.

Although our privateersmen were out for booty rather than fighting, and avoided the men-of-war, there must nevertheless have been many fierce encounters as well as strange adventures, which have not been recorded. One of the most desperate fights was between the Yankee "Hero" and the British frigate "Milford," in June, 1776, just outside of Boston harbor. The "Hero" mistook the frigate for a merchantman and learned her mistake too late. The war-ship overhauled the "Hero," punishing her terribly with her bow chasers; but when alongside and overtopping the little privateersman, she found an unexpected resistance. For several hours, Captain Tracy, of the "Hero," kept up the unequal contest, lying side by side and not a hundred feet from the frigate, while they poured broadsides into each other and emptied their muskets and pistols. He seems to have actually silenced some of the frigate's forward guns, and at last broke away from her only to find his sails cut

---

[*] *American Archives*, fourth series, vol. v, p. 1082; vol. ii, pp. 717, 979; Hansard's Debates, vol. 19, pp. 709, 717; "The Remembrancer," vol. iv, p. 312; vol. v, pp. 108, 405, 513; vol. vi, p. 39; Gordon, "American Revolution," vol. iii, pp. 103, 104; Clowes, "Royal Navy," vol. iii, p. 396.

to rags and his yards flying about without braces. While repairing his shattered rigging in the hope of escaping, in the darkness, the frigate bore down on him again and renewed the fight.

In this second attack Tracy was badly wounded; and tried to keep command by laying himself across the armchest. He fainted and was taken below; but as soon as he recovered, he insisted on being carried on deck in a chair. He became again so faint that his voice failed him; and seeing the utter hopelessness of the situation, he allowed his men to surrender.

The British are said to have exulted over this fight as a great victory; and the Americans were indignant because thirty American prisoners that happened to be on the "Milford" were forced at the forfeit of their lives to fight against their countrymen on the "Hero." [1]

The stratagems of the privateersmen were innumerable and ingenious. At dusk one evening the "Hancock" came up with a merchantman whose captain mistook the American for a British man-of-war, was delighted to fall in with her, and kept along in company all night.

"At daylight the next morning, the vessels being near together, the captain of the ship invited the captain of the 'Hancock' to come on board and take breakfast; who replied, his hands were so few and sick, that he had not enough to man his boat and work the vessel, and in his turn invited the captain of the ship to come aboard him, which he readily complied with, by ordering his boat out, when he and about a dozen of his hands went on board the 'Hancock,' and were taken as good care of as men in such circumstances could allow. The 'Hancock' then sent an equal number of her own hands on board the ship, when she fell into the hands of the United States of America."—*American Archives*, fifth series, vol. i, p. 874.

Paul Jones, in his little sloop, the "Providence," was pursued and overtaken by a British frigate, both vessels beating to windward. He prepared all his light sails so that he could set them quickly, and run before the wind before the frigate could alter her canvas for that course.

---

[1] *American Archives*, fourth series, vol. vi, p. 746.

"As they continued firing at us from the first without showing colors, I now ordered ours to be hoisted and began to fire at them. Upon this they also hoisted American colors and fired guns to leeward. But the bait would not take; for having everything prepared, I bore away before the wind and set all our light sail at once, so that before her sails could be trimmed and steering sails set, I was almost out of reach of grape and soon after out of reach of cannon-shot. Our hair breadth escape and saucy manner of making it must have mortified him not a little. Had he foreseen this motion, and been prepared to counteract it he might have fired several broadsides of double headed and grape shot which would have done us very material damage. But he was a bad marksman, and though within pistol shot, did not touch the 'Providence' with one of the many shot he fired."—*American Archives*, fifth series, vol. ii, p. 171.

The prisoners taken out of prizes not infrequently rose on their captors and took the ship. The British offered high rewards to crews who should retake their own vessel or their captor's vessel, and these rewards were very much complained of in America as encouraging mutiny, and assassination of officers.[8]

At the same time that privateering began in the autumn of 1775, the Congress at Philadelphia ordered thirteen war vessels to be built, six in New England, two in New York, four in Pennsylvania, and one in Maryland. They also chartered several vessels for immediate service, appointed officers, and placed Ezekiel Hopkins at the head of this first American navy. But privateering was so successful, and the profits so high for the crews, that it was difficult to obtain recruits for the regular Continental navy, which gave only a small share of prize money. Some of the ships voted by the Congress were never built; and there was great delay caused by the want of sea coal for the smiths who forged the anchors, and also by the difficulty in having cannon cast at the iron furnaces. It was of course impossible that we should in a short time build up a navy that could contend on anything like an equal footing with the long-

---

[8] *American Archives*, fifth series, vol. ii, pp. 811, 812. "Memoirs and Correspondence of Lafayette," London edition, 1837, vol. i, p. 66; *American Archives*, fifth series, vol. i, p. 754.

established and powerful English navy. For that part of the warfare we must rely on the fleets that France would send to our aid. So far as our own efforts were concerned, the privateers were our most effective navy in the Revolution. The regular navy created by the Congress accomplished very little, and Hopkins was dismissed from his command in 1777. It has been usual to blame the inefficiency of the Congress navy on the committees and boards that undertook to manage it; but the real cause seems to have been the want of money and resources and the superior attractions and evident efficiency of privateering. The ships ordered by the Congress were equal in force only to the small British cruisers, and were hardly superior to the better class of privateers. The Congress went bankrupt in trying to support the army. Why then should it have attempted to support a navy when it could encourage privateering without expense and rely on France for fleets which were rapidly becoming a match for those of England? [9]

* Clowes, "Royal Navy," vol. iii, p. 396; Gordon, "American Revolution," edition 1788, vol. ii, p. 155; *American Archives*, fourth series, vol. iii, pp. 1075, 1076, 1125, 1126, 1402, 1407, 1515, 1529–1540, 1687, 1722, 1927; vol. iv, pp. 180, 237, 256, 334, 379, 796, 964, 987; fifth series, vol. ii, pp. 282, 599, 1105; vol. iii, pp. 609, 872, 1335; and title "Vessels" in index of the various volumes of the *Archives;* Bolton, "Private Soldier under Washington," pp. 45, 46, 163, 164; "Diary and Letters of Thomas Hutchinson," vol. ii, pp. 111, 129; Cooper, "History of the American Navy," pp. 47–54.

XXXV.

THE ATTACK UPON CANADA

DURING the whole summer of 1775 while the patriot army kept up its inactive siege of Boston, Washington and the patriot leaders had in mind the importance of following up the taking of Ticonderoga by an invasion of Canada. Information was constantly received which led the patriots to think that General Guy Carleton, the Canadian governor and military commander, was planning some heavy invasion into the Hudson Valley. He would set out as soon as he could receive reinforcements from England to assist the horde of Indians and Canadians he might be able to raise. A daring and sudden attack upon him would, it was thought, break up these plans and possibly bring Canada into the union. Reports were constantly received which seemed to show that the Canadians, if given a chance, would join the patriot cause.[1]

The importance of Canada to which ever side should hold it seemed to be obvious, because it would help to control the upper part of the great strategic line of water communication through Lake Champlain and down into the Hudson River valley. If Canada were secured for the patriots, it would be more difficult than ever for England to control the line of the Hudson, cut the colonies in half, isolate New England from the less rebellious communities to the south, and prevent her from influencing them and receiving supplies from them.

The attempt to take Canada was the most aggressive and daring effort that the patriots made during the war, and was characteristic of this year 1775, when they felt that everything was going in their favor. It was an invasion of British territory, an invasion of a colony that had not rebelled or joined

---

[1] *American Archives*, fourth series, vol. ii, pp. 1676, 1702, 1704, 1833, 1855, 1868, 1892, 1026, 1027.

them, and in that respect was inconsistent with the position they had assumed of acting merely on the defensive, and might be thought to justify England in acts of the severest retaliation. It was made at a time when, as the loyalists pointed out, the documents of the Congress and the patriot party were declaring that they were still loyal subjects of the crown, and wished to remain in the empire. Under such circumstances, said the loyalists, every invader of Canada taken prisoner would be doubly liable to be hanged "as a traiter to his king, to his country, and to the constitution of old England." [2]

But the assertions of loyalty in the patriot documents were well known to be mere forms and political fictions of conservatism. Every child knew that the two countries were at war, and had broken the colonial relationship, although the breach had not yet been officially announced. As war had begun, the patriots naturally felt that the more vigorous war they waged, the better would be their chances of success. They had captured one by one so many of the colony governments, they had been so successful in locking up the British army in Boston, that it seemed as if they would be able to drive British authority completely off the continent, make Canada an American state, and punish the British nation for passing the Quebec Act establishing Romanism and despotic government in such close proximity to New England. [3]

Two expeditions were planned. One, in command of General Schuyler, was to proceed directly to Montreal by way of Lake Champlain, and the other, to be commanded by Benedict Arnold, was to pass through the wilderness of Maine and take

---

[2] Jones, " New York in the Revolution," vol. i, pp. 310, 311.

[3] Nova Scotia was not included in the invasion of Canada. Washington disapproved of any attack on Nova Scotia, which it was hoped would of its own accord join the American union. If Quebec and Montreal could be secured, the reduction of Nova Scotia would easily follow. *American Archives*, fourth series, vol. iii, pp. 90, 619, 1127, 1184. As to the state of feeling in Nova Scotia during the Revolution see *American Historical Review*, October, 1904, vol. 10, p. 52; *American Archives*, fourth series, vol. v, pp. 522–524, 936–939; vol. vi, p. 484.

Quebec. This method of two expeditions, one to take Quebec and the other to take Montreal, was the natural way to attack Canada, and had been successful when the British conquered the country in the French War. In the present instance it was expected that General Carleton, whose force was not sufficient to defend both Montreal and Quebec, would have to abandon either one or the other. He was now occupied in holding St. Johns, on Lake Champlain, as a defence to Montreal. If he continued to defend St. Johns and Montreal, Arnold might take Quebec. If, on the other hand, Carleton rushed to the defence of Quebec, Montreal would be easily taken by Schuyler. Montreal was without fortifications and untenable. But Quebec, with its famous citadel, was the Gibraltar of America. On the river side the steep cliff was over 300 feet high, and on the land side the bastions and curtains were twenty feet thick and thirty feet high. It was the stronghold of Canada, and full of valuable military supplies. If it could not be taken the conquest of Montreal would be of little or no avail. If, however, the patriots secured it, the conquest of the rest of the country would be comparatively easy, provided a British fleet did not retake Quebec.

The important point in the whole plan was to have Carleton remain with his whole force defending Montreal until Arnold should have taken Quebec. Carleton would then be placed between the forces of Schuyler and Arnold, his refuge would be cut off, and his surrender could be compelled. But to bring this delicately turned plan to a conclusion, with badly organized forces of militia and inadequate means of communication, through vast tracts of wilderness, was a great deal to expect: and the patriots were seriously handicapped for want of war-vessels to prevent the British reinforcing Quebec from the sea with troops and supplies of provisions.[4]

Schuyler spent the summer at Ticonderoga, collecting troops and supplies and contending with the overwhelming difficulties

---

[4] *American Archives*, fourth series, vol. iii, pp. 926, 927, 945, 947, 1609, 1633, 1638, 1639, 1664.

of a total lack of organization and preparedness. He was given as a second in command, General Richard Montgomery, a British soldier of Irish birth and education, who had served with distinction in America during the French War, and had settled in New York, where he married Miss Janet Livingston.

In September Schuyler and Montgomery started with about 1000 men to move upon St. Johns, which, with its outpost, Chamblee, blocked the road to Montreal, only twelve miles away. Washington had thought that they might have passed round St. Johns and leaving it in their rear have gone direct to Montreal. There might, possibly, have been an advantage in this plan. Montreal had no defenses, could easily have been taken, and if they had captured Carleton there he could not have reached Quebec before Arnold took it by surprise, and St. Johns could have been reduced at their leisure. But Schuyler and Montgomery were unwilling to leave a strong fortified place like St. Johns in their rear to cut off their retreat or attack their line of communication. They began a regular siege of it which lasted all the rest of September and all of October; and so far as the ability of Arnold's expedition to take Quebec was concerned, it would have been well if the siege of St. Johns had lasted longer.[5]

Soon after the siege began, Schuyler's health failed and he returned to Ticonderoga, where he remained for the rest of the autumn, suffering greatly from a complication of disorders, but working with unremitting fidelity to organize the base of supplies and keep open the lines of communication with Montgomery.

Schuyler, who had served in the French war, was one of the great landed proprietors of New York, owning vast estates near Albany, which were worked to some extent by negro slaves like a southern plantation. The patriarchical life on his great domain where his family, after the manner of those times, had created a little world of intelligence, culture, and refinement,

---

[5] *American Archives*, fourth series, vol. iii, pp. 1197, 1374; Jones, " New York in the Revolution," vol. i, p. 58.

independent of city life, has been admirably described by Mrs. Grant in her "Memoirs of an American Lady." Schuyler was a devoted patriot and a man of good executive ability, with broad ideas of philanthropy; but he was much disliked by the levelling New Englanders for what they considered his offensive aristocratic tendencies.

The invasion of Canada had now devolved on Montgomery; and on the 1st of November St. Johns surrendered. Besides the cannon and small arms, the spoil was not great; for the ammunition and provisions were almost exhausted. But the way was now open to Montreal, which Montgomery entered on the 13th of November, without meeting with any resistance. Carleton and his whole force had abandoned the town the day before, and tried to escape in their ships to Quebec; but Montgomery had sent Colonel Easton with some troops to Sorel on the St. Lawrence, forty miles below Montreal, where they intercepted Carleton's fleet and compelled its surrender.[6]

It was huge spoil of flour, beef, muskets, cartridges, and powder for the patriots; and the ships could be used for transporting Montgomery's force to join Arnold at Quebec. But the most important person escaped. Carleton the night before had disguised himself as a Canadian, fled down the river, and reached Quebec. His escape was probably the fatal accident which lost Canada for the patriots; for he was the life of the resistance; there was no one to take his place, and if he could have been captured or detained, Montgomery and Arnold might have taken Quebec.

There is, of course, the open question whether the Canadians were sufficiently in our favor to enable the small patriot force to take possession of the country and hold it against subsequent attacks of the British army and fleet; and on this point the evidence is somewhat conflicting. The letters of Schuyler and

---

[6] The original letters of Schuyler and Montgomery, describing the invasion of Canada, can be found in *American Archives*, fourth series, vol. iii, and fifth series, vol. i, by reference to their names in the index. See also Gordon, "American Revolution," edition 1788, vol. ii, pp. 157, 164.

gomery had for months been expressing the greatest confidence in the Canadians. Arnold experienced the most kindly
assistance from them when he emerged into their country from
Maine wilderness. More than two hundred of them assisted
gomery to take St. Johns; and after he took Montreal he
seems to have found his hopes of the friendliness of the people
realized, for he writes from there on the 19th of November,

inhabitants are our friends on both sides of the river to
see; our expresses go without interruption backwards and
wards."

But the French priests were for the most part against us, and
influencing the people by withholding absolution. Such a
like influence was serious; and the nobility took the same
as the priests; for both had been won to the English side
the Quebec Act, which upheld the nobility, gave the priests
governmental authority for their religion and more privileges
than they could hope for from a union with the extreme
protestantism of the rebellious colonies on the south.

Apparently, however, it was all a question of success in
arms; and if the patriot force had been larger and its conquest
of British authority assured, there would have been no difficulty
with the majority of the people; for there was no strong sentiment attaching them to England, which only a few years before
had conquered them from France. Thus far Montgomery had
been very successful, and numerous Canadians were joining him
and learning to say "Liberty and Bostonian;" and numerous
Indians were coming in who would smite their breasts and say,
"Je Yankee."[7]

The Continental Congress also caught the spirit of success
and it is curious now to read of their preparations to organize
the Canadians into regiments, establish American forms of
civil government, and deal with the serious question of liberty
of conscience among French Roman Catholics.[8]

---

[7] *American Archives*, fourth series, vol. iii, pp. 973–74.
[8] *American Archives*, fourth series, vol. iii, pp. 1012, 1098, 1695; vol.
iv, p. 220.

XXXVI.

ARNOLD'S MARCH TO QUEBEC

ON the success of Arnold everything depended. If he failed to take Quebec, Montgomery's success at Montreal was use' and the situation was so critical and delicate that a very s: change of circumstances might alter the course of history

Arnold had visited Quebec, traded there in horses merchandise, and was supposed to be familiar with the for tions. His acquaintance with the people was not altogeth advantage, for it led him to send some confidential letters had better not have been written.

His dash through the wilderness was desperate, rom and very American in its character. He was to lead his through more than a hundred miles of unknown fo swamps, mountains, lakes, and rivers, impenetrable by military methods of Europe, and to emerge suddenly from fastnesses into the heart of the enemy's country, and by prise and strategy attack his great citadel. He was to pr from the coast of Maine up the Kennebec as far as its w: would carry him and then cross the water-shed as bea could to the Chaudière, which would bear him to the Lawrence.

He took with him about 1100 men, most of them ordi New England musketmen from the army at Cambridge; to complete his force he was given three companies of the r. men, selected by lot. The companies on which the lot fell w Daniel Morgan's Virginians and Matthew Smith's and 1! drick's Pennsylvanians. A great many of Arnold's men journals of their experiences, and several of them, not those by Henry and Morrison, are most graphic and vivid their descriptions.[1]

---

[1] A list of these journals is annexed to "Wild's Diary," Cambridge, 1886, and also to Mr. Codman's admirable book, "Arnold's Expedition to Quebec."

BOATING UP STREAM

Towards the end of September Arnold's troops marched from Cambridge to Newburyport, where sloops and schooners took them across the Gulf of Maine to the Kennebec, and very sea-sick they were before they entered the river. At Fort Western, where Augusta now stands, their boats were ready for them, rough bateaux, built of common boards, two hundred and twenty of them, very badly constructed and leaky.

They started up the stream, rowing and poling, in four divisions, a considerable distance apart, with the indefatigable Daniel Morgan and his Virginians at the head. But soon they could neither pole nor row in the rocky stream. The men jumped overboard and dragged the boats, wading in the cold water all day, often sinking to their necks or over their heads in the deep pools, upsetting the leaky boats, losing provisions and often guns. They reached carrying places where they had to transport the heavy bateaux and cargoes round falls and rapids. The black soil was soaked with rain, and they sank knee-deep, stumbling over stones and roots and fallen logs. With the heavy bateau grinding into their shoulders, or almost dragging their arms from their sockets, as they carried it on handspikes, a misstep of one man in the mud would bring the whole party, bateau and all, to the ground. They would rise, covered with black mud, cursing and laughing, and laugh still louder to see the next boat crew in a similar plight.

The glory and enthusiasm of the rights of man was heard on every side. They were no coerced soldiery, they said, and the officers were given to understand that they must know their place and keep it. The men had taken charge of the expedition and tolerated the officers as assistants. They bluntly let it be understood that for any officer to attempt compulsion would be fatal, for the men were going through to Quebec of themselves.

Soon they were amazed at the sights they saw. The swamps, thickets, and hill-sides were covered with a vast network of the fallen trees of centuries, through which a man could climb and crawl at scarcely a mile an hour. Their most violent efforts with the bateaux could move them at only about six miles a day. The character of the country through which they passed has been greatly changed by lumbering operations and fires. The woods are less encumbered and dense; there is less water, and the Chaudière has become a less important stream.

They saw in the black mud the great hoof-marks of the moose. Almost every day they would rouse some of these magnificent, wild creatures from their lairs to see them disappear with a crash into thickets that seemed impenetrable to a squirrel. There seem to have been few if any deer; and the riflemen killed scarcely any game. They were apparently working so hard with the boats that their weapons were seldom ready; and the necessity of pressing forward prevented any delay for hunting. It would have required a great deal of hunting and consequent delay to kill enough moose to feed a thousand men.

Aaron Burr, the son of the president of Princeton College, a mere lad, and an adventurous one, accompanied the expedition in the capacity of what was called a gentleman volunteer, uncommissioned and unenlisted. He found a pretty Indian maiden, Jacataqua, of a romantic disposition, whom, with her dog, he persuaded to accompany him and help hunt. He took her all the way to Canada, where it is supposed the nuns near Quebec befriended her and her child that was born there.

They reached Dead River, which was to connect them with the head-waters of the Chaudière. It was deep, black, and still; but they had so few paddles or oars that they could take but little advantage of the lack of current, and it was too deep for their setting poles. Famine had set in; provisions, guns, ammunition, and the money for wages had been lost from the leaky, overturning boats. Colonel Enos and three companies of musketmen in the rear, appalled at the difficulties, had abandoned the expedition and returned to Massachusetts. It was the end of October, cold and snowing. Torrents of rain had swollen the streams, overflowed the shores, and made nearly the whole country a black morass.

To send the sick back with a guard and press on was the order agreed upon. Arnold and a small party started ahead to reach the Canadian settlements and send back provisions.

FAMINE AND EXHAUSTION

The romance was fading, and even the rights of man and equality seemed less glorious.

They had reached the Chaudière and decided to abandon their boats with the exception of one or two to carry some of the crippled and sick who would not give up. It was down hill to the St. Lawrence on the rushing Chaudière. But the river was too swift. The boats narrowly escaped being dashed over falls, and all took to the land along the shore.

The situation had become alarming. Jesting and good nature had ceased. When a rifleman fell headlong in the mud no gay voice sang out, "Come here and I'll pick you up." Some of them killed and ate a pet dog—flesh, skin, and entrails, and then boiled the bones. They dug roots out of the half-frozen mud with bleeding hands. They boiled and ate their extra moose-skin moccasins. Some six hundred men, strung out in a long line by the Chaudière, a line that reeled, stumbled, and fell, and bent up and down over the high wooded hills; were these the conquerors of Quebec?

Dazed, delirious, half-blinded by famine and exhaustion, they would look back as they ascended a hill to see others falling over one another and rolling down the opposite slope. On the top of the hill they would halt as if calculating whether their strength would take them down; then they would start, falling over logs and stones and sending their guns flying into the muddy snow. Then up the next slope they would wearily go, pulling themselves by any twig and bush that offered assistance.

"Every man for himself," was the word now passed along the line; and there were loud protests against it. But stern necessity compelled it. The strong were convinced of it, and they stopped their ears as they left a companion who had taken his last fall over a log and could rise no more.

On the 2nd of November, the day Montgomery took St. Johns, Morrison emptied the bullets out of his leather pouch and boiled it; and soon all of his comrades were boiling bullet-pouches. Then the leather breeches were cut up. A mere twig across the way would now bring the strongest man to the ground. And still it was on and on, while from every hill they could see a thousand more monotonous wooded hill-tops stretching away forever and ever like a bad dream, with the rushing Chaudière always winding in and out among them, as if it too could never escape.

The men at the head of the line saw cattle driven towards them, and men leading horses with great sacks laid across their backs, and they sat down and stared at one another as if this was part of the bad dream. But it was true; Arnold had returned from the Canadian settlements with provisions; and soon great fires were built and the beef and potatoes were cooking, and the men with the horses were going back along the line to restore the dying. Arnold himself arrived, strong, enthusiastic, and jovial. The French Canadians were on their side, he said, and would give provisions; and Montgomery had already beaten the British in Canada and taken many prisoners.

So, after those who would not listen to reason had killed themselves with overeating, all that was left of the expedition marched down among the French Canadians; and truly those simple-minded people looked with blank amazement at the pale ghosts and spectres with muskets in their shadowy hands, coming out of the impenetrable winter forest to drive the English from the continent.

They reached the shore of the St. Lawrence at Point Levi. The British had removed all the small boats, and the Americans saw the strongly fortified Quebec, twelve hundred yards away across the water, guarded by armed merchantmen and two men-of-war. They caught a little midshipman, fifteen years old, who, imprudently venturing ashore, was deserted by his boat's crew; and his good-natured and plucky refusal to give information amused the grim hunters.

They had set out with 1100 men. Three hundred had gone back with Colonel Enos. The sick that returned and their guards had been 200. The wolves were gnawing the bones of eighty or ninety in the woods. Those who stood looking at Quebec half-armed and in rags were about 510.

The expedition had already failed. The dash through the Maine wilderness had produced nothing but a tale of disaster and some interesting diaries and reminiscences. The 1100 men would have been as efficiently used if they had been sent with Montgomery by way of Lake Champlain. They were now too late to take Quebec by surprise, as they might have done a few days earlier. Letters sent forward by Arnold, as he supposed to friends, and by trusty messengers, had fallen into the hands of Guy Carleton, who a few days afterwards was able to escape from Montgomery and reach the garrison of Quebec.

But Arnold and his men were as hopeful as ever. They collected canoes and dugouts from great distances, and on the night of the day Montreal was taken, the 13th of November, by the skilful still paddling of the hunters, they dodged the merchant vessels and men-of-war and landed before Quebec on the Plains of Abraham. Arnold soon after sent to the town a summons of surrender, but his flags were fired upon and the summons never received. Many of his men believed that they could now take the town by assault. But conservative counsels prevailed; and they waited to be joined by Montgomery.

If they had arrived ten days sooner it has been supposed that they could easily have taken the town. But meantime General Carleton had entered Quebec and his forces were soon raised to some 1800 men. He felt confident of holding the town and making it a base from which to save Canada.[2]

Sir Guy Carleton, afterwards Lord Dorchester, was an accomplished and rather interesting man. He is said to have suggested the Quebec Act; and in his defence of Canada he certainly rendered good service to England. He is described as firm, humane, and of the most unvarying courtesy under all circumstances. He was troubled with no Whig principles or doctrines of the rights of man, although he had been Wolfe's quartermaster-general. He believed in subduing the colonies by the most overwhelming severity and force; but that all rebel prisoners, after a short confinement, should be allowed to return to their homes on parole, to be afterwards, if necessary, exchanged.

---

[2] *American Archives*, fourth series, vol. iii, p. 1696.

Montgomery soon joined Arnold, and they began a mild siege of Quebec. They built breastworks of snow and poured water on them to freeze them solid, for scarcely any earth could be scraped from the frozen soil. Such protections were easily shattered by the enemy's cannon; and the American artillery was of such small caliber and so ineffective that the women came out on the ramparts of Quebec to ridicule it. But the riflemen were very effective. Creeping close to the walls and sheltering themselves behind houses, or any object that presented itself, they dealt destruction with their tiny bullets to any incautious soldier in the town.

The addition of Montgomery's troops raised the American force to about eight hundred men, hardly enough to take such a stronghold as Quebec. To take it by siege seemed impossible. An assault must be tried, and they grimly waited for their opportunity, while the winter snows fell deeper and deeper. The signal finally agreed upon was to come from nature—a snow-storm at midnight.

The evening of the 31st of December, 1775, was an intensely cold one; the men were scattered among the farms and tippling-houses enjoying themselves and keeping warm. But as they started to return to their huts the snow-storm began. Soon it was a stinging blast carried horizontally along the ground and cutting the face. By two o'clock in the morning they were hurrying through it, every man holding the lapel of his coat wrapped over the flint-lock of his gun, stumbling and falling in the snow-drifts. Montgomery, with his aide, McPherson, of Philadelphia, and also, it is said, accompanied by Aaron Burr,[3] led the attack on one side of the lower town, and Arnold on the other.

Arnold's command was a long column, almost in single file, with Daniel Morgan and his Virginians in front and the Pennsylvanians closely following. Presently were heard the sharp reports of their rifles at the first barrier. The riflemen sent

---

[3] Codman, "Arnold's Expedition to Quebec," p. 232; with which compare *Magazine of American History*, vol. xi, p. 294, note.

their little bullets through the port-holes with such unerring aim that the gunners were killed or driven from their posts. Morgan was the first to spring upon the barrier and throw himself down among the enemy. The rest of the column followed and swept the English before them. Those who were not riflemen quickly seized the excellent English muskets from the dead and wounded in place of their own inferior weapons. Arnold was wounded in the leg before the barrier was taken and had to be supported back to the American camp.

The taking of the first barrier let them into the lower town, and they rushed through it up a street to another barrier, from which the cannon and the muskets of the Englishmen were spitting flame through the dim light of the driving snow. The riflemen again tried their device of shooting carefully into the port-holes, but it failed. The cannoneers and musketmen were too well settled at their work. Pennsylvanians and Virginians were falling on every side. It was strange that they were not all killed, for the British had them hemmed within the narrow street. As the wounded rolled over into the deep snow they quickly died of the intense cold which stiffened their limbs into the last frantic or fantastic attitude of their death agony.

There was confused fighting in the streets and houses for a long time. Some of the Americans rushed up close against the barrier; they crowded under it in a mass; the cannon could not be sufficiently depressed to reach them, and they could inflict instant death on a musketman who showed himself at a port-hole. In the lull they called out to the English to come out and fight in the open.

"Come out and buy our rifles," they shouted; "they are for sale cheap."

The tall, powerful figures of Morgan and Hendricks were conspicuous in every part of the fight encouraging the men. The stentorian voice of Morgan could be heard above all the din. He fought like an ancient knight, a Cœur de Lion, killing Englishmen with his own hands, and in one of the intervals disguising himself and penetrating into the town to learn its condition.

The rear of Arnold's column arrived with scaling-ladders, which they threw against the barrier. But the neighboring houses were filled with English, and volleys of musketry were poured upon the assailants. They could no longer crouch under the barrier or man the ladders.

The barrier could not be carried, and the Americans were ordered into the houses. They battered down the doors with butts of guns and rushed up to the windows in the full belief that they could shoot all the gunners in the barrier. Pennsylvanians and Virginians were aiming their rifles through every opening. It was at one of these windows that the gallant Hendricks was shot. He staggered back into the room and fell across a bed in the corner.

There was now a short time when the Americans, thoroughly convinced of the hopelessness of their task, might have drawn out and escaped. Some of them did so, especially the few Indians and Canadians who had joined them. These hurried down to St. Charles Bay and started across the two miles of ice heaped up by the tide and full of air-holes deceptively covered by the snow. The rest were presently caught in the streets and houses as in a trap. General Carleton sent Captain Laws on a sortie out of the Palace gate, and he came in behind the Americans in the street.

On the other side of the town Montgomery broke through the palisades by the aid of his carpenters, and rushing in, shouted to his men, "Push on, brave boys; Quebec is ours." He was met by the discharge of a cannon from a barrier which stretched him and his aide, McPherson, lifeless on the snow. It was subsequently learned that the British were so demoralized by the onset that they were retreating from the barrier, which could easily have been carried and the town entered. But Colonel Campbell, who succeeded Montgomery in command, ordered a retreat.

The attack on Quebec, whatever may have been its possibilities, had failed. The American loss has been variously estimated; but was probably 300 prisoners and 70 killed and wounded. It was a sad fate for so many of Arnold's column to have to surrender after such a gallant struggle, and be ridiculed for the piece of paper pinned on their hats on which was written "Liberty or Death." Morgan, weeping with vexation, at first refused to surrender, and, placing his back against a wall, with his drawn sword in his hand, defied the enemy to take it from him; but he finally consented to hand it to a priest whom he saw in the crowd.

The officers were confined in what was called the seminary, and the privates given a less comfortable jail. The English, as afterwards often happened, were much amused at finding the officers to be men of no social position. "You can have no conception," wrote Major Caldwell, "what kind of men composed their officers. Of those we took one major was a blacksmith, another a hatter; of their captains, there was a butcher, a tanner, a shoemaker, a tavern-keeper, etc.; yet they pretended to be gentlemen." [4]

Henry, who was among the prisoners, relates the extraordinary appearance of the dead whom he saw hauled through the streets in carts. They were frozen as stiff as marble statues in every imaginable attitude of agony or horror. They were tossed into the carts like rigid boards, with outstretched arms, pointing fingers, and contorted legs and necks.

Among the privates who were prisoners, those who admitted that they had been born in England, Scotland, or Ireland were told that they had their choice of enlisting in the British army or going to England to be tried for treason. Under the advice of their comrades, and in the belief that the oath of allegiance under those circumstances would not be binding on any conscience, about ninety-five of these men enlisted, and took their chances of an opportunity to desert.

Two of them, Conners and Cavanaugh, soon made an opportunity for themselves. They walked up to a sentinel guarding the edge of the high precipice that surrounded part of Quebec, and offered the man a bottle of rum. While the sentinel hesitated they wrenched his gun from him, knocked him down with

---

[4] Codman, " Arnold's Expedition to Quebec," p. 265.

the butt of it, and then ran to the precipice and leaped over. It was a daring leap, but in some respects a safe one, for the snow was drifted twenty feet deep at the bottom. They nearly suffocated in the drift, but managed to scramble out while the British were shooting at them from above. Cannon-balls and grape-shot were fired at them as they ran over the snowy roads; but they escaped out into the country where the remains of Montgomery's and Arnold's commands still maintained an unconquered and sullen siege of Quebec.

The privates that remained in the jail planned a most ingenious method of escape, which failed by a mere accident. Most of them were heavily ironed and looked forward to a hard fate, from which, however, they were unexpectedly released the following summer. Carleton, with the greatest kindness, set them all free on parole, and a year or so afterwards they were regularly exchanged. This treatment was in striking contrast to the cruelty and suffering usually inflicted on the patriots in English prisons. It released Morgan and saved his health to win the battle of the Cowpens. The prisoners were taken in a ship to New York Bay, in the summer of 1776, and turned loose on the Jersey shore at midnight. Morgan threw himself flat on the ground and kissed it. They then all ran a race to Elizabeth, where they danced, sang, and gave the Indian war-whoop for the rest of the night.

There was great consternation in the American camp when it was known that the assault had failed with such heavy loss. and that Montgomery was dead. About one hundred of the troops fled to Montreal. Some of the invalid soldiers in the hospital were panic-stricken, and in attempting to spring from their beds and escape fell helpless on the floor. But Arnold, stretched on his bed with a painful wound, was as resolute as ever. When told that the enemy were sallying he would not allow himself to be carried to a place of safety, but ordered his pistols and sword to be placed beside him so that he could fight to the last. He coolly issued orders reorganizing the shattered forces, which now numbered only 700 men; and he wrote letters to the South calling loudly for reinforcements. He resigned the command in favor of Colonel Campbell; but the officers would not permit it. In spite of his protests and wound, and although he was beginning to have personal quarrels with them, they unanimously elected him commander; and Congress soon made him a brigadier-general.

"I have no thought of leaving this proud town," he wrote, "until I first enter it in triumph. My wound has been exceedingly painful, but it is now easy, and the surgeon assures me that it will be well in eight weeks. Providence, which has carried me through so many dangers, is still my protector. I am in the way of my duty, and know no fear." (Codman, "Arnold's Expedition to Quebec," p. 256.)

But heroism alone will not win wars or revolutions. Washington's opinion of the assault on Quebec was that it was a rash, useless piece of heroism, and that Montgomery had been misled into making it by the feeling that he might soon be left without any troops and that before they disappeared some stroke must be attempted.[5]

---

[5] Writings of Washington, Ford edition, vol. 8, p. 504. The numerous diaries of the survivors, Codman's "Arnold's Expedition to Quebec," Justin H. Smith's "Arnold's March from Cambridge to Quebec," and *American Archives*, fourth series, vols. iii, iv, contain very full and reliable information as to Arnold's expedition and the assault on Quebec. The number of troops which Arnold and Montgomery had for the assault has sometimes been stated at 1200, but letters from Arnold and Montgomery show it to have been less than 900. See *American Archives*, fourth series, vol. iv, pp. 190, 309; Codman, "Arnold's Expedition," p. 182. The letters of Arnold, Colonel Campbell, and Carleton describing the assault can be read in *American Archives*, fourth series, vol. iv, pp. 480, 481, 589, 656, 670, 836, 1652. The original letters of Arnold and Montgomery can be found under their names in the index of the *Archives*. See also Jones, "New York in the Revolution," vol. i, p. 729; Graham, "Life of General Morgan." Mr. Justin H. Smith's recent work, "Our Struggle for the Fourteenth Colony," contains in footnotes a mass of valuable citations of the original evidence.

XXXVII.

THE RETREAT FROM CANADA

ALTHOUGH the assault on Quebec had failed, the Americans still held Canada all the way from the Quebec ramparts back to Montreal, where General Wooster was now in command of a few patriot troops. The Canadian population was not hostile; they were inclined to be passively friendly; but they were not enthusiastic and were watching events to see if the Americans could really win and get possession of the country.

Arnold had no idea of retreating. He clung to his position in the snow before Quebec all the rest of the winter, keeping up a feeble and ineffective blockade of the old town, which regularly received its most important supply, firewood, in spite of all he could do to prevent it. The garrison of the town outnumbered his forces three to one; but they made no attempt to sally out and attack him. They were content to wait quietly until spring, when, after the ice had melted, British war-vessels and transports could reach them with reinforcements, which they felt sure would drive the Americans out of Canada.

It was quite clear that if Canada was to be retained Quebec must be taken during the winter before navigation opened. Washington urged Arnold to action, assured him that success would crown his efforts and that he would enter Quebec in triumph with his brave followers. Washington even went so far as to say that the whole success of the patriot cause depended on the capture of Quebec, the stronghold of America. Arnold replied with equal zeal and hopefulness, but asked for a reinforcement of 5000 men, which, of course, could not be sent.[1]

Every effort, however, was made in New England; and during the winter a few scattered troops worked their way

---

[1] *American Archives,* fourth series, vol. iv, p. 1513.

northward on snow-shoes through New Hampshire and Vermont. One company cut a road for forty miles across the Green Mountains to the Otter River, and descended that stream on rafts. Arnold supplemented these endeavors by trying to recruit Canadians, pledging his own credit and the credit of the Congress. But the Canadians were very suspicious of paper money and credit. The heroic Arnold could accomplish very little during that terrible northern winter of continuous snowstorms, and severe cold, while gloom, bad food, and the smallpox were decimating his men.

In comparing this campaign with the one which was its model conducted by Wolfe and Amherst, in the old French War, one cannot but notice an important point in which Arnold and Montgomery failed to follow the original. In the attack upon Canada in the French War, England had complete command of the sea, and the heaviest forces were massed against Quebec. Wolfe moved upon Quebec with a fleet and 12,000 men and the rest of the forces, consisting of about 11,000, were given to Amherst to assail Montreal by way of Lake Champlain. Amherst's slow advance on Montreal merely served to hold Bourlamaque's 3000 troops in that place, and prevent their going to the rescue of Quebec. Wolfe was successful in taking Quebec, which really ended the war, and the taking of Montreal afterwards was a mere formal matter.[2]

But in the campaign of Arnold and Montgomery the patriots had no control of the sea. They hoped to make up for this disadvantage by attacking Quebec quickly in the autumn, before the British navy could arrive in force; and they relied on the ice to prevent the arrival of the warships until the following spring. Moreover, instead of the heaviest force being massed on Quebec, the weakest force was massed on it. After his hardship in the Maine wilderness and the loss of Enos's men, Arnold arrived before Quebec with only five hundred badly-armed and ragged troops, instead of with a thousand, as was hoped. Even a thousand would have been little enough. But

---

[2] Wood, "The Fight for Canada," chap. vii, pp. 147, 165, 166.

it was expected that this defect would be made up by his arriving soon and suddenly when the garrison was weak and unprepared. But he arrived ten days too late, all his plans had been discovered, and Carleton escaped from Montgomery and got into Quebec to reorganize and animate its garrison.

In March, 1776, the efforts to send troops to Arnold began to give him some slight assistance. A regiment of three hundred and forty men had started from Pennsylvania in January. These troops are said to have had regular uniforms, brown with buff facings, and knapsacks of Russian duck. They had to make a march of over six hundred miles in the dead of winter. The patriots in the country through which they passed assisted them at times with sleds, but a large part of their march was made on foot. They travelled the length of Lake George and of Lake Chaplain on the ice; and from Ticonderoga to Montreal, having no sleds, they were obliged to carry all their provisions on their backs through that wilderness country. They reached their destination almost as exhausted as Arnold's men had been when they emerged from the forests of Maine.

Other small bodies of troops from New York, New England, and New Jersey, reached Arnold; but at first these accessions merely made up for the losses by small-pox and hardships. In April General Wooster came down from Montreal bringing cannon and ammunition, and superseded Arnold, who retired to Montreal in disgust. Wooster had now about two thousand men, and he began to bombard the fortifications of Quebec, but to the great surprise of the patriots the shot made not the slightest impression, and the return fire of the garrison was so continuous and accurate that the bombardment had to be abandoned.

Meanwhile, however, patriot reinforcements were moving up through New York, hurried on by the untiring labors of General Schuyler, who was still in command of the transportation and supplies on Lake Champlain. The British evacuated Boston, which set free the army before Cambridge, and regiment after regiment started on the route through Lake Champlain. At the same time the British Ministry started a large force on transports under General Burgoyne to enter Quebec as soon as the opening spring melted the ice of the St. Lawrence.

It was to be a race for the Gibraltar of America; but unfortunately nature fought against the Americans. The ice on Lake Champlain was so rotten that the troops could not march on it, but it was strong enough to prevent the passage of boats. The trails and roads through the wilderness on either side were impassable with slush and mud, so that patriot troops were blocked and held inactive at Ticonderoga and Crown Point. Nothing shows more clearly how the possession of Quebec and Canada depended on the control of the sea; for during the first week of May the British war-ships sailed through the floating ice of the St. Lawrence and poured a reinforcement into Carleton's garrison.[2]

The first vessel to arrive in the mouth of the St. Lawrence was the "Isis," a fifty-gun ship, which had sailed from England on the 11th of March and spent a month in reaching St. Peters Island. From there nearly another month was spent in driving the ship with great labor and hardship scarcely two hundred miles through fields of thick ice to Anticostie Island. When well within the river the "Isis" was joined by two other British vessels, which had likewise spent nearly two months in making their way from England. They reached Quebec on the 6th of May, followed within a few days by the rest of the fleet, bringing about 10,000 men.

General John Thomas, of Massachusetts, had been appointed by the Congress to the command in Canada to supersede General Wooster, who was throwing everything into confusion. Thomas was a physician by profession, and had served in the French War. In the recent siege of Boston he had had charge of that part of the line which faced Boston Neck, and had commanded the troops which seized Dorchester Heights in March, 1776. When he reached the patriot forces before Quebec, on the 1st of May, he found there 1900 men, of whom 900 were invalids with

---

[2] Writings of Washington, Ford edition, vol. 4, pp. 8, 14.

the small-pox, which in the beginning had been caught from a girl who came out from Quebec as a nurse. The disease spread with frightful rapidity, not only by natural contagion, but by the inoculation which the troops, and every fresh company of reinforcements, secretly practised to save themselves from the disease itself.[4]

The thousand effectives had to support scattered forts, some of them on the other side of the river. The enlistments of three hundred of them were about expiring, and all were anxious to return home. Thomas began preparations for removing the invalids and the supplies further up the river to a place of safety. He was in the midst of these preparations when the first division of the British force arrived, on the 6th of May. He immediately ordered a retreat, and his decision was none too soon, for the troops were landed and a sally made from the city at one o'clock with scarcely a moment's delay. Thomas's force was so weak and demoralized by small-pox and hardships that his retreat might have been a very disastrous rout if the British had had the courage to press him more vigorously. The desperate character of Arnold's and Montgomery's assault on the city seems to have inspired Carleton with most conservative caution.

Thomas was obliged to leave behind him two hundred sick and several detached parties, which, with his cannon, provisions, powder, and five hundred stand of arms, fell into the hands of the enemy. It was a hurried retreat and a mortifying one to the patriot party; for Thomas's men hardly had time to carry off anything with them except the ragged clothes on their backs. Many of the sick who had the small-pox out thick on them got out of their beds and followed the retreat, exposed to wet and cold without blankets or anything to cover them.[5]

There was danger that the British ships would pass up the river and cut off their retreat; and after halting for a time at

---

[4] Gordon, "American Revolution," edition 1788, vol. ii, p. 251; Writings of Washington, Ford edition, vol. 4, pp. 2 note, 120 note.

[5] *American Archives*, fifth series, vol. i, p. 129.

Deschambault and again at Three Rivers, the main body crossed to the southern side of the St. Lawrence and entrenched themselves at Sorel, which was the beginning of their line of communication back to New York, and the route by which they obtained supplies and reinforcements.[6]

Arnold now left Montreal and joined the army at Sorel with the intention of repossessing Deschambault and checking the British advance; for to remain at Sorel was to abandon Canada. Scattering reinforcements were coming on through Lake Champlain now that the ice was disappearing; and there was hope that Canada might yet be saved for the patriots. But just at this moment a blow was struck from the westward which showed the essential weakness of our hold on Canada.

The British in Canada had outposts and forts far to the westward along the Great Lakes, even so far as Detroit. There had been some thought among the patriots of securing these in the beginning, but the force under Schuyler and Montgomery had not been sufficient. One post, called the Cedars, forty-five miles southwest of Montreal, was, however, occupied by a patriot force of nearly four hundred men under Colonel Bedel. This post was now attacked by about six hundred Indians and Canadians and fifty regulars, under Captain Foster, its surrender forced, and a rescuing party of patriots from Montreal cut to pieces by the Indians. The expedition had been cleverly planned by Carleton to strike the patriots on the west at about the same time that Burgoyne's force from Quebec attacked them on the east.

Arnold with his usual promptness and intrepidity collected eight hundred patriots and by a bold advance stopped the further progress of this movement from the west. After long negotiations he obtained a release of the prisoners who had fallen into the hands of the Indians, had been stripped naked and treated with great barbarity. It must have been some satis-

---

[6] *American Archives,* fourth series, vol. vi, pp. 398, 430, 438, 448, 452, 454, 458, 1089; Codman, "Arnold's Expedition to Quebec," p. 300; Gordon, "American Revolution," edition 1788, vol. ii, pp. 212, 251, 252.

faction to them to reflect that many of the Indians contracted the small-pox from stripping the prisoners who had it.[7]

When General Thomas had retreated from Quebec not a few of the men of his outlying detachments, unable to join him, had become scattered in the swamps and woods, in which they were still hiding and were making their way out with difficulty. On the 20th of May Carleton issued a remarkable proclamation addressed to these dispersed Americans. They were perishing. he heard, from hunger and cold; "and, lest a consciousness of past offences should deter such miserable wretches from receiving that assistance which their distressed condition might require," he promised that, if they would surrender, they should be cared for in the hospitals, and, when restored, should be free to return to the rebel colonies.[8]

This policy was much admired by some of the loyalists, who said that if it had been universally carried out by all British commanders it would quickly have ended the rebellion, because there would soon not have been a rebel willing to fight an empire of such generous liberality. There was no officer in the British army, it was said, so dangerous to the cause of independence as Carleton.[9] But it is not reported that any patriots took advantage of his proclamation. Prisoners whom he released, of course, spoke highly of him. But the independence movement was beyond the reach of kindness and conciliation, as the Ministry soon discovered.

---

[7] *American Archives*, fourth series, vol. vi, pp. 458, 469, 479, 480, 481, 482, 560, 566, 576, 578, 579, 588, 589, 590, 596, 598, 600, 647, 838, 1083; fifth series vol. i, pp. 158, 169, 1571; vol. ii, pp. 891, 893, 919; Gordon, "American Revolution," edition 1788, vol. ii, p. 375; Jones, "New York in the Revolution," vol. i, pp. 93, 94; Writings of Washington, Ford edition, vol. iv, p. 357 note; Wilkinson, Memoirs, vol. i, pp. 41–47; Stedman, "American War," vol. i, p. 171.

[8] *American Archives*, fourth series, vol. vi, p. 418; "Diary and Letters of Thomas Hutchinson," vol. ii, p. 115; Fonblanque, "Life of Burgoyne," p. 222; Lamb, "American War,' p. 89.

[9] Jones, "New York in the Revolution," vol. i, pp. 89, 90, 133, 181, 182; vol. ii, pp. 469, 470; *Pennsylvania Magazine of History*, vol. xx, p. 513; Wilkinson, Memoirs, vol. i, p. 55 note.

COMMISSIONERS TO CANADA

In March, 1776, a committee of the Congress, composed of Franklin, Samuel Chase, and Charles Carroll, of Maryland, went to Canada to help win it to the side of the revolted colonies. John Carroll, a Roman Catholic priest, accompanied them in the hope of influencing the French Canadian clergy. It was a terrible journey for them in the month of March, and nearly cost Franklin his life. They found only defeat and disaster and large debts contracted by Montgomery's army with the Canadians, which could not be paid.

Franklin and John Carroll, the priest, had now returned to New York; but Chase and Charles Carroll were still in Montreal. After the retreat of Thomas from Quebec they lost all hope of retaining Canada, and their letters and reports reveal the deplorable condition of our troops, who were heartily tired of the service and believed themselves neglected and abandoned by Congress. The commissioners regretted that reinforcements were arriving, because there was no food for them except what they could get by plundering our supposed friends, the Canadians, and there was no way of protecting them from the small-pox.[10]

"We cannot find words strong enough to describe our miserable situation. You will have a faint idea of it if you figure to yourself an army broken and disheartened, half of it under inoculation or under other diseases; soldiers without pay, without discipline, and altogether reduced to live from hand to mouth, depending on the scanty and precarious supplies of a few half-starved cattle and trifling quantities of flour, which have hitherto been picked up in different parts of the country." (*American Archives*, fourth series, vol. vi, p. 590; see also pp. 592, 649.)

The small-pox was at all times a most serious problem in the patriot army and in almost every part of the country. In Canada it seems to have got entirely beyond control. It was difficult to tell which was worse, the disease itself or the remedy of inoculation. The officers were in favor of inoculation, provided it was done under their supervision and with a limited

---

[10] *American Archives*, fourth series, vol. v, pp. 412, 1166, 1167, 1237, 1643-1645; vol. vi, pp. 610, 649, 740.

number. But the men so dreaded the disease that, wishing to become immune, they would inoculate themselves, or bribe the surgeons to do it, and in this way whole regiments would sometimes become invalided and put out of service.[11]

General Thomas was stricken with the small-pox about two weeks after his retreat and retired to Chamblee, where he died. General Wooster, being unequal to the situation, was recalled. General Thompson arrived with a few reinforcements and took command at Sorel. Arnold returned to Montreal, of which he remained in command; and General Sullivan was rapidly coming up Lake Champlain with several thousand reinforcements.[12]

General Schuyler, in spite of his illness, was still at his post at Fort George, in the neighborhood of Ticonderoga, where he had been all winter, engaged in the arduous task of managing the transportation and supplies through the lakes and controlling the New York Indians and loyalists. He was still working untiringly; but seemed to be pursued by ill fortune; for in spite of his devotion to the patriot cause, all the misfortunes in Canada, the smallness of the army, the shortness of supplies, the retreat from Quebec, and the disaster at the Cedars, were blamed on him, and the charges set forth in a formal document prepared by some of the patriots of Western Massachusetts. He was accused of loyalism, of purposely sending provisions to Canada so that they would fall into the hands of the enemy; and a party of patriots were said to be plotting to seize him. It is hard to account for these unfounded suspicions against a man of such integrity and devotion, unless it was that his reserved manners and great landed interest made him unpopular with certain extreme enthusiasts for the rights of man.[13]

As General Sullivan came on with the reinforcements he

---

[11] *American Archives*, fourth series, vol. vi, pp. 589, 594, 635 *et passim;* fifth series, vol. i, p. 129.

[12] *American Archives*, fourth series, vol. vi, pp. 679, 684, 740.

[13] *American Archives*, fourth series, vol. vi, pp. 610, 640, 641, 744, 746, 758, 768.

was shocked and indignant at the state of affairs which he found. Our troops, he said, were demoralized, and retreating from a phantom; for Carleton had as yet made no serious advance with either ships or men from Quebec.

"I am extremely sorry to inform you that from the officers whose business it was to give Congress the true state of matters, Congress has not, as I believe, received anything like it. This I conclude from the repeated letters sent to General Washington giving the most favorable accounts and promising a speedy reduction of Quebec; when there was not even a probability of it, and the army with which this was to be done had dwindled into a mob, without even the form of order and regularity—the consequences of which we have experienced by the infamous retreat from Quebec and the still more scandalous surrender of the fort at the Cedars." (*American Archives*, fourth series, vol. vi, p. 679.)

Being now in command, Sullivan sent General Thompson and a strong force to stop Carleton's army, which was coming from Quebec up the left bank of the St. Lawrence. So much energy did Sullivan display in all his dispositions that the Canadians thought that the patriots might succeed, and they came flocking in with offers of assistance and provisions. Full of enthusiasm and confidence, Sullivan wrote to the Congress that he hoped to drive Carleton back below Deschambault, which, being the key to the situation, should be strongly fortified by the patriots, and after that Quebec might be taken if Congress continued to send reinforcements and money.

General William Thompson, whom Sullivan had sent forward, had commanded the rifle companies which went from Pennsylvania to the siege of Boston. On the 8th of June he attempted to surprise Carleton's army at Three Rivers by a sudden attack at daybreak. But his Canadian guides were teacherous; it was broad daylight when he reached his enemy; his little army was defeated and scattered and he himself taken prisoner.

Sullivan's high hopes were now shattered. Carleton's army was moving towards him, and there was nothing for him to do but abandon Canada and retreat southward through Lake Champlain. He left Sorel only two days before Carleton arrived there. Arnold's force was very nearly taken in Montreal, but was warned in time, and joined Sullivan in the general American retreat to Chamblee, St. Johns, and Ticonderoga.[14]

Burgoyne conducted the pursuit and followed so close that he entered Chamblee at one end when the American rear guard quitted it at the other. Sullivan finally halted at Isle Aux Noix. on the 18th of June, and Burgoyne gave up the pursuit.

But Isle Aux Noix was low and damp, and crowding the troops on it added dysentery to the small-pox. The retreat began again, and halted at Crown Point to recruit and restore the men, who, as Sullivan said, were "daily dropping off like the Israelites of old before the destroying angel." St. Clair describes them as a mob rather than an army, "devoid of discipline or subordination, the officers as well as men of one colony insulting and quarrelling with those of another."[15]

Meantime the Congress had recalled Sullivan and put in his place General Horatio Gates, who was very much disgusted to find himself in command of a small-pox hospital and pesthouse, with no opportunity to win honor or glory. He and Schuyler agreed upon a further retreat to Ticonderoga, which they fortified, and believed it would stop all further advance of the British to the southward.[16]

[14] *American Archives*, fourth series, vol. vi, pp. 640, 684, 758, 770, 795, 796, 826, 839, 921, 923, 937, 977, 1002, 1036, 1103, 1251; fifth series, vol. i, p. 1069. Gordon, " American Revolution," edition 1788, vol. ii, p. 256; St. Clair Papers, vol. i, p. 21.

[15] *American Archives*, fourth series, vol. vi, pp. 925–30; 937–948, 975, 997, 1002, 1009, 1028, 1035, 1038–1040, 1052, 1053, 1057, 1069, 1101–1103, 1121, 1201, 1217, 1219, 1222; fifth series, vol. i, p. 131. Wilkinson, Memoirs, vol. i, pp. 49, 55, 57. St. Clair Papers, vol. ii, p. 24; Gordon, "American Revolution," edition 1788, vol. ii, pp. 177, 178, 259–263.

[16] *American Archives*, fourth series, vol. vi, p. 1232; fifth series, vol. i, pp. 234, 232, 375, 389, 390, 445, 450, 259, 237, 260, 559, 747, 933, 1032, 604, 606, 637, 649, 650, 651, 716, 826, 899, 1119, 1123, 1127; Gordon, "American Revolution," edition 1788, vol. ii, pp. 318, 319, 276; Writings of Washington, Ford edition, vol. iv, p. 209 note; Wilkinson, Memoirs, vol. i, pp. 61, 63.

CANADIANS PASSIVE

Thus the enthusiastic attack on Canada came to an ignominious end. The small-pox, the terrible winter, and inferior organization, had reduced our force to only about four thousand effectives, while Carleton had some twelve thousand regulars and Canadians. Canada was lost to the American union. Its population had given us only passive assistance. They were friendly in a way; they furnished provisions; they wished us well, and would accept us if we won. But they had not the heart to fight losing battles; and to fight such a power as England seemed to them madness. They were altogether lacking in what Graydon called revolutionary nerves.[17]

> "The Canadians," said Montgomery, "will be our friends as long as we are able to maintain our ground; but they must not be depended upon, especially for defensive operations." (*American Archives*, fourth series, vol. iv, pp. 189, 310.)
> "They are not persevering in adversity," said General Wooster; "they are not to be depended upon; but like the savages are extremely fond of choosing the strongest party." (*American Archives*, fourth series, vol. iv, p. 588; see, also, p. 1114, and vol. v, pp. 752–754, 869.)

But even after our defeat and retreat from Canada the desire to secure that country for our union remained; and the Congress kept looking about for ways and means to organize another invasion. When the French allied themselves with us, their generals always had an eye on Canada and issued seductive proclamations to the French Canadians. In January, 1778, Lafayette was commissioned by the Congress to take command of such a Canadian expedition, and he went to Albany, to collect supplies and recruit men. The plan was apparently part of the cabal against Washington, and was intended to detach from him the support of Lafayette. The

---

[17] Niles, "Principles and Acts of the Revolution," edition 1876, p. 461; "Quebec and the American Revolution," Bulletin of University of Wisconsin, vol. i, pp. 21, 22, 23; Codman, "Arnold's Expedition to Quebec," pp. 8, 296; Bourdinot, "The Story of Canada," p. 281; Writings of Washington, Ford edition, vol. 4, p. 29 note; Wilkinson, Memoirs, vol. i, p. 41; *American Archives*, fifth series, vol. ii, p. 532.

difficulties were soon seen to be insuperable, and at Lafayette's advice the Congress abandoned the attempt.

But twelve months afterwards they were again considering the advisability of "the emancipation of Canada in coöperation with an armament from France," and Washington was called to Philadelphia for consultation. Again the plan was abandoned, not only from the inherent difficulties of it, but also, it is supposed, because if successful France might be tempted to claim the Lady of the Snows as her share of the spoil and thus become so powerful in North America that she could dictate to the United States. It would be safer to leave Canada with the British.[18]

---

[18] Memoirs and Correspondence of Lafayette, London edition, 1837, vol. i, pp. 38–44; Pontgibaud, "A French Volunteer of the War of Independence," p. 47; Washington's Writings, Ford edition, vol. vi, pp. 298 note, 361, 410, 432, 437 note; vol. 8, p. 142 note; Gordon, "American Revolution," edition 1788, vol. iii, pp. 179, 209, 210; Smith, "Our Struggle for the Fourteenth Colony," vol. ii, chap. 36.

XXXVIII.

THE EVACUATION OF BOSTON

In October, 1775, when Arnold's expedition was on its perilous march through the Maine woods, General Gage retired, and General William Howe took the supreme command of all the British military operations south of Canada to the Gulf of Mexico. Carleton's command in Canada was a separate department.

General Howe succeeded no better at Boston than Gage; and a candid survey of all the circumstances would seem to indicate that Gage had done all that could reasonably be expected with his small force opposed to a whole continent. He understood the situation as well as anybody, and told the Ministry from the beginning that there was no hope in the conciliatory policy, that the patriots were bent on independence, and that nothing but large reinforcements and complete subjugation would save the colonies to the empire. His ideas of the proper strategy and methods to be pursued, the occupation of New York and the Hudson Valley as a base of operations, were accepted by Howe as correct and do not appear to have been disputed or doubted by any of the military authorities of that time. Burgoyne very properly said of him, that few characters in the world would have been fit for his task, for he was in a situation in which a Cæsar might have failed.[1]

During that same autumn of 1775, that rather colorless character, Lord Dartmouth, ceased to be colonial secretary, and Lord George Germain for the rest of the war became the Min-

---

[1] "Diary and Letters of Thomas Hutchinson," vol. i, p. 497; Gage's letters to the ministry can be read indexed under his name in the first three volumes of the fourth series of the *American Archives; American Archives*, fourth series, vol. iii, pp. 927, 991, 1069; Fonblanque, " Life of Burgoyne," pp. 129, 140, 144, 145, 149, 196.

istry's means of communication with the commanders in America. Germain was an extreme Tory, a duellist, a man of fashion and a soldier, who some years before had been dismissed from the army and, as was supposed, forever disgraced for refusal to charge when ordered at the battle of Minden. The King, it was said, wanted him to be court-martialed and shot for cowardice; but family influence saved his life, and the court found him guilty only of disobedience of orders. He was incapacitated from military but not from civil employments. He was described by his contemporaries as having many contemptible traits of character; but there seems to have been no question of his ability and talents. In spite of his heavy load of disgrace he had succeeded in politics and had now raised himself to a very important position in the Cabinet.[2]

In America a very capable young officer of the Massachusetts militia was becoming prominent. Early in the autumn he had appeared before Washington, offered to go to Ticonderoga as soon as snow covered the ground, and bring down on sleds the large cannon which Allen and Arnold had captured there in May. This was Henry Knox, who had kept a little book-store in Boston, read all the works he could collect on artillery practice, joined the patriot militia, and married, against the wishes of her parents, a young lady who often came to buy books. She was the daughter of an extreme loyalist, Thomas Flucker, secretary of the colony. Knox had recently escaped from Boston in disguise, accompanied by his wife, who had quilted his sword into the lining of her cloak.

Washington was a good judge of character. Knox was given a party of men, and he returned in December dragging on sleds thirteen brass cannon, twenty-six iron cannon, fourteen mortars, two howitzers, 2300 pounds of lead, and a barrel of flints. There was great rejoicing in the camp at Cambridge, and the Congress made young Knox a brigadier-general of artillery.[3]

[2] "Diary and Letters of Thomas Hutchinson," vol. i, pp. 556, 557, 575; vol. ii, p. 11; Fonblanque, "Life of Burgoyne," p. 493.

[3] Drake, "Life of Henry Knox;" *American Archives*, fourth series, vol. v, p. 169.

Unfortunately there was no powder to use in these cannon. For months together they had not thirty rounds per man; and at one time in August only nine rounds per man. Gage, it is said, refused to believe that his enemy was so destitute. But it is difficult to believe that Howe did not know of all this weakness with the frequent intercourse through the lines, the numerous desertions, the loyalists, and his spies. "Our situation," wrote Washington in November, "is truly alarming; and of this General Howe is well apprized, it being the common topic of conversation when the people left Boston last Friday."[4]

The patriot force of 16,000 in the summer had dwindled as soon as winter came to 10,000, but Howe had evidently made up his mind to do nothing. The Ministry had suggested that he abandon Boston and take his army to Long Island, a loyalist community, where he could easily obtain supplies and be ready to take New York the following summer when reinforcements arrived. But he declined to do this because he had not sufficient transports to carry his army, and he remained locked up in Boston by an undisciplined force which had scarcely ammunition enough for a skirmish. He was "cooped up," his officers complained, "by a set of dirty ragamuffins."[5] He allowed his enemy's force to be disbanded under his eyes and sent to their homes while others came to take their places.

"Search the volumes of history through and I much question whether a case similar to ours is to be found—namely, to maintain a post against the flower of the British troops for six months together, without

---

[4] Stedman, "American War," edition 1794, p. 190; *American Archives*, fourth series, vol. iii, pp. 558, 1672, 1698; vol. iv, pp. 458, 1203; vol. v, p. 499; Carter, "General Detail of the Blockade of Boston," pp. 8, 14–16, 22, 23; J. J. Boudinot, "Life of Boudinot," vol. i, p. 11. The British spy system was very thorough and complete. (Ford, Writings of Washington, vol. iii, pp. 319, 413; "Life of Joseph Reed," by W. B. Reed, vol. i, p. 157; Gordon, "American Revolution," edition 1788, vol. ii, p. 68; *American Archives*, fourth series, vol. iii, pp. 36, 37, 38, 137; "Diary and Letters of Thomas Hutchinson, vol. ii, p. 64.)

[5] *American Archives*, fourth series, vol. iii, p. 169.

—— and then to have one army disbanded and another to be raised within the same distance of a reinforced enemy." (Ford, Writings of Washington, vol. iii, p. 318.)

But Howe's answer to all criticisms was that the Americans were too numerous and strongly fortified to be attacked with any chance of permanent advantage; and from the point of view of a man like Howe, there was much to be said in favor of this position. Boston was to be evacuated in the spring, in any event; it was admitted that the colonies could never be conquered by holding Boston; so what would be the use of a raid into the country, which might be as disastrous to his Majesty's arms as Lexington had been, and even if not disastrous, could accomplish no permanent advantage, because there was not force enough to occupy and permanently hold any point outside of Boston.[6]

In Boston that winter General Howe began a romantic attachment for a loyalist lady, Mrs. Loring, who accompanied his army through the three years of his campaigning, and was often spoken of by the officers as the sultana. She encouraged the general in his favorite amusement, for she was passionately devoted to cards and capable of losing three hundred guineas at a sitting. Her influence secured satisfactory arrangements for her husband, who was given the office of commissary of prisoners, which was an opportunity for making a fortune.[7]

Being thus provided with a congenial companion, and abundant leisure for card-playing, it is difficult to tell how long

---

[6] Fonblanque, "Life of Burgoyne," p. 148. *American Archives*, fourth series, vol. iii, p. 1672. General Wilkinson thought that the patriot besieging line was so widely extended and scattered that Howe could have beaten it in detail, by concentrating on any one point. (Wilkinson's Memoirs, vol. i, pp. 19, 20.)

[7] Jones, "History of the Revolution in New York," vol. i, pp. 171, 189, 253, 351; vol. ii, pp. 57, 89, 423; "A View of the Evidence Relative to the Conduct of the American War under Sir W. Howe," p. 77; Appleton's "Cyclopædia of American Biography," vol. iv, p. 28. In Hopkinson's "Battle of the Kegs" there was a verse about Mrs. Loring which is often omitted in modern editions.

DORCHESTER HEIGHTS

Howe might have remained in Boston. In March he showed no signs of moving; and he would probably, if left to himself, have remained until June, when his reinforcements were expected to arrive.

Washington had always been anxious to make an assault on Boston. The Congress had urged it in the autumn of 1775. It might have involved the burning and destruction of the town; but John Hancock, whose large fortune was invested there, wrote that he was willing to sacrifice every penny and become a pauper. Washington's officers were opposed to it as hazardous. In February, when the water had frozen between Roxborough and Boston Common, Washington thought that in spite of his deficiency in powder he would like to try an assault by a rush across the ice; but his officers again advised against it. His anxiety to risk such a hazardous enterprise arose from his knowledge of the weak condition of his army, which he felt might melt away during the winter, and the ease with which Howe might at any moment break up the patriot besieging line. He had not yet learned how completely he could trust to Howe's inactivity; and he abandoned the dash across the ice with great reluctance in exchange for a more cautious plan well suited to the British general's temperament, and which was crowned with success.[3]

Dorchester Heights and Nook's Hill commanded Boston on the south as effectually as did Bunker Hill and Breed's Hill on the north; and these southern hills at Dorchester had the advantage of commanding the shipping in the harbor. Howe could have occupied Dorchester at any time during the winter and fortified it with a force similar to that with which he held Bunker and Breed's Hills. In fact, when Gage in June, 1775, decided to take and fortify Bunker Hill, he also contemplated the occupation of Dorchester Heights; but this part of his plan was abandoned.

---

[3] *American Archives*, fourth series, vol. iii, pp. 6, 848, 927, 956, 991; vol. iv, pp. 1203, 1502, 1503, 1515; vol. v, p. 91; Wilkinson's Memoirs, vol. i, pp. 21, 22, 24, 26, 28.

Having received a sufficient supply of powder to use in the cannon which Knox had brought down from Ticonderoga, Washington decided to occupy Dorchester Heights, and when everything was ready, on the night of the 4th of March, 1776. the patriots began to expend their precious powder in a heavy cannonade all round their lines, to which the British promptly replied. "It's impossible," said Curtin, "I could describe the situation. This night you could see shells, sometimes seven at a time, in the air, and as to cannon, the continual shaking of the earth by cannonading dried up our wells."

Unfortunately this firing burst three of the heaviest patriot mortars which they had hoped to use in bombarding Boston from Dorchester Heights. But the noise and excitement accomplished the purpose intended; for under cover of it, General Thomas and a couple of thousand men with wagons, cannon, and bales of hay, made a détour far inland behind the hills, where the rumble of the wheels on the frozen ground could not be heard, and suddenly descended upon Dorchester Heights.

The earth was frozen so hard that they could not dig intrenchments; but they made breastworks of the bales of hay. Howe directed Lord Percy, with a force of 2400 men, to attack Dorchester; but a wind and rainstorm coming on just after the expedition started, it returned, and nothing more was attempted.

If this attack had been made Washington intended to make a counter assault on Boston, and had 4000 picked men ready under Putnam, assisted by Sullivan, Greene, and Gates, who on a given signal were to enter boats, row across the water, and make a dash at Beacon Hill. Washington had great confidence in this plan, for the defences of Boston would be weakened by the troops drawn out to attack Dorchester. If the plan had been carried out there would have been some desperate fighting and what is conventionally called a brilliant episode in the Revolution.

One can readily understand that Howe might not want to furnish such an episode, and his unwillingness to attack Dorchester was now, no doubt, the part of prudence. But when we find by one of his letters to the Ministry that he knew as early as the 13th of February that the patriots intended to take Dorchester, his utter apathy in not attempting to occupy it, so as to prevent them, is most extraordinary.[9]

Washington had no confidence in a bombardment of Boston, and was hoping every day that the British would come out to attack him. But as they showed no signs of it, he kept up a bombardment, which was continued intermittently by both sides for two weeks, without much effect. Washington settled down to wait results and sent to several iron furnaces to have heavy thirteen-inch mortars cast. On the 16th of March he occupied Nook's Hill, somewhat nearer the town. But meanwhile, the unambitious and apathetic Howe relieved him from all further anxiety by announcing that he would evacuate the town immediately without firing another shot.

His reasons, in his letter to the Ministry, for this not very glorious move, were that he could gain nothing by remaining; he could not attack the rebels with any prospect of permanent success; and they might soon be able to annoy him. He feared, it is said, that they might occupy Noddle's Island, on the other side of Boston, and cannonade the town from two sides. He also said that his provisions and supplies of all sorts were running very low; and probably another of his reasons was that in any event he would have to leave the town within two or three months to go to New York.[10]

He made a very peculiar sort of informal agreement with Washington, that if the Americans would not fire on the British, the British would evacuate the town without doing it any injury. With this understanding, Howe withdrew his whole

---

[9] *American Archives*, fourth series, vol. v, p. 458; Heath, Mem., pp. 31, 33.

[10] *American Archives*, fourth series, vol. v, pp. 458, 484, 499, 507, 559. (See generally *American Archives*, id., pp. 91, 106, 110, 165, 166, 177, 200, 201, 205, 223, 224, 232, 233, 374, 399, 419, 420, 423-27, 458, 483, 499, 500; "Diary and Letters of Thomas Hutchinson," vol. ii, pp. 253, 292; Frothingham, "Siege of Boston," Stevens, "Fac-similes," vol. 9, p. 855; Gordon, "American Revolution," edition 1788, vol. ii, pp. 189, 196, 199.

army on the 17th of March, accompanied by some two thousand loyalists.

There had been not a little discomfort and suffering among the troops and loyalists in Boston for want of fuel, as well as of fresh meat and vegetables. As the winter advanced the buildings that remained from the fire in Charleston had been demolished. Garden fences, old houses, even the steeples of some of the churches, were taken for fire-wood, and the famous patriot liberty-tree yielded fourteen cords. To keep up the spirits of the army, amusements of all sorts were encouraged, and the bells were not allowed to be tolled for the dead.

In spite of all their suffering, however, neither soldier nor loyalist cared to be turned out of the town and crowded into transports in the month of March for a dangerous voyage up the coast. But the order was given, and for a week all was uproar and confusion. "Carts, trucks, wheelbarrows, hand-barrows, coaches, chaises, driving as if the very devil was after them" to and from the waterside to load the vessels. Criminals took the opportunity to plunder right and left. The loyalists, frantic with fear of being left behind to the vengeance of the patriots, corrupted the sailors to load merchandise and all the property they could scrape together on the transports. There were one hundred and seventy sail of transports, mostly small schooners, crowded to their utmost capacity with goods, soldiers, and loyalists, "men, women and children, servants, masters and mistresses, obliged to pig together on the floor, there being no berths." If a great storm had caught the overloaded fleet it would have been one of the most shocking disasters in history.[11]

Among the loyalists who departed with Howe were the son, daughter and grandchildren of Governor Hutchinson, accompanied by Chief Justice Oliver, who had incurred so much odium among the patriots by accepting a salary from the

[11] Van Tyne, "Loyalists of the American Revolution," pp. 53–59; *American Archives*, fourth series, vol. iv, p. 266; vol. vi, pp. 362, 372; Gordon, "American Revolution," edition 1788, vol. ii, pp. 180, 204.

crown. The chief justice left an interesting description of the evacuation as well as of the voyage, and his farewell to America had the true loyalist ring:[12]

> "And here I bid A Dieu to that shore which I never wish to tread again till that greatest of social blessings, a firm established British Government accompanies me thither."

Before starting the British blew up and burnt Castle William in the harbor, and then lay for over a week in Nantasket Road, arranging their cargoes and preparing for sea, the patriots meanwhile anxiously suspecting them of intending a sudden return to attack Boston.

Finally, on the 27th of March, they sailed out into the ocean. Washington thought that they might be going to New York, and he sent the riflemen and other troops to that town. But when Howe put to sea he abandoned the rebellious colonies entirely and took his whole fleet and army to Halifax, Nova Scotia. There he awaited the arrival of the supplies and the enormous army of reinforcements which had been promised him by the Ministry for the coming summer's campaign.[13]

His conduct was approved by the Ministry. But however advisable it may have been under all the circumstances, it was in the eyes of the public a British defeat. It was a retreat from an enemy that had scarcely any ammunition. It was an abandonment of the patriot country, and to some it seemed like an abandonment of all attempt to crush the rebellion.

Loyalists in America and Tories in England were disgusted. Howe's own officers felt the disgrace and had to exert themselves to keep up appearances, while the enlisted men were with difficulty restrained from plunder and drink. Were not the British regulars to drive the Yankees, the cowardly American poltroons, the fanatic, praying, psalm-singing provincials all through their country like a flock of geese? But instead

---

[12] "Diary and Letters of Thomas Hutchinson," vol. ii, pp. 41, 42, 46–53.

[13] *American Archives*, fourth series, vol. v, pp. 458, 459, 485, 498, 500, 522, 541, 785, 1081, 1086.

of that the conquerors had been "cooped up like inoffensive poultry," and were retreating to Halifax, which was as bad as a surrender or a retreat back to England.[14]

What greater encouragement, it was said, could Howe have given to the rebellion! His Whig friends in Parliament were delighted. It was another piece of strong evidence to show that the war was impracticable; and the thunders of Whig eloquence again resounded.

In evacuating Boston Howe took little or no pains to follow the usual military rule of destroying the ammunition and supplies which he was compelled to leave behind. The amount destroyed was very trifling compared with the ships, cannon, and muskets, the large quantities of powder, lead, and miscellaneous military stores which he left in Boston in such a way that it seemed as if he were making a present to the patriots. His arrangements for protecting the supply-ships which would soon arrive were very inadequate; for, although he left Commodore Banks with two or three war-ships for this purpose, Howe was hardly clear of the coast when a patriot privateersman captured a large powder-ship which was just arriving. From that time the favorite toast in the patriot camps was "General Howe." [15]

To the patriot party the evacuation of Boston was, of course, a glorious event. It was Washington's first victory, and it was a long time before he had another. The people and patriot troops flocked into the town and wandered through it, full of curiosity to note the desolation and ruin. The common was disfigured with the ditches and cellars of the camps. The great trees had been cut down for fuel. Dirt and squalor were to be seen on every hand. The pulpit and pews of the Old South Church had been carried out and burnt, a grog-shop erected

---

[14] "The Critical Moment," London, 1776, pp. 46, 47; *American Archives*, fourth series, vol. v, p. 485.

[15] *American Archives*, fourth series, vol. v, pp. 523, 792, 934, 935; vol. vi, p. 495; Gordon, "American Revolution," edition 1788, vol. ii. pp. 200, 201; Niles, "Principles and Acts of the Revolution," edition 1876, p. 486; Stedman, "American War," vol. i, p. 167.

in the gallery, and cart-loads of earth and gravel spread on the floor for the cavalry training-school. But these remnants of an enemy's occupation could soon be obliterated, and they were not allowed to check the rejoicing. The new patriot legislature thanked and congratulated Washington on his success, which they declared to have exceeded the most sanguine expectations, and the President and Overseers of Harvard College voted him the degree of Doctor of Laws.[16]

---

[16] Niles, " Principles and Acts of the Revolution," edition 1876, pp. 128, 130, 131.

XXXIX.

INDEPENDENCE OPENLY DISCUSSED

DURING the winter and spring of 1776, there was a decided change in the methods of the patriot leaders. They openly discussed the question of absolute independence, and advocated it in letters, documents, and pamphlets. The events of the last six months were all in their favor. Their ideas were gaining ground. The doubting ones were being converted. Had not all the royal governors been driven from the country? Was not British authority extinct in every colony? Was not each colony governing itself by committees of safety and a convention or other body acting without any dependence on British authority? Had not Howe and his army been driven from Boston and every British soldier expelled from the colonies between Canada and Florida?

Was there not also a general government for all the colonies, called the Continental Congress, which showed no sign of dependence on Great Britain? This Continental Congress had an army of its own, and also had a navy. The little navy of two brigs, two ships, and a sloop, under command of Commodore Hopkins, had made its first cruise in February and March, 1776, and, in spite of the smallpox on board four of the vessels and defective equipment and organization, had already achieved a striking success. They had visited the Bahama Islands, and finding New Providence unprotected had seized the fort there and carried off the military supplies as well as the governor, lieutenant governor, and other officials. Returning to the New England coast they had fought an indecisive action with the British frigate "Glasgow," and, though they were blamed for not destroying her, they were expected to atone for this failure in the future.[1]

---

[1] *American Archives*, fourth series, vol. v, pp. 823, 846, 932, 1082, 1156, 1168; vol. vi, p. 765; Gordon, "American Revolution," edition

EVIDENCES OF NATIONALITY

The patriot party were enthusiastic over their navy, and at Philadelphia, where new frigates were building, many patriots who were prosperous citizens went voluntarily to the shipyards to carry heavy deck-beams and assist the shipwrights by every means in their power At Cape Henlopen, at the entrance of Delaware Bay, a patriot schooner bringing in powder, was run on the beach to escape the tender of a British man-of-war. The militia of the neighborhood, with muskets and swivels, fought off the tender for two hours, while they unloaded the schooner. Soon afterwards the British frigates "Liverpool" and "Roebuck" sailed up the Delaware as far as Newcastle, where they were driven back by armed row-galleys manned by the militia of the neighborhood.[2]

The Continental Congress was issuing paper money and creating a national debt like a sovereign state. It had sent agents across the Atlantic to establish diplomatic relations with European nations. It was prepared to make treaties of commerce and alliance. In many of the colonies the king's name was now omitted from writs and all legal processes, and these colonies were adopting new forms of oaths by which officials swore allegiance to the colony instead of to the king.

All these circumstances were surely the evidences of independent national existence; and John Adams declared that he was well content with the situation.[3] The other leaders were also elated. It had been supposed, they said, that the British would have the advantage in the beginning of the war; but now in the very beginning they were worsted and driven from the country. The Swiss had fought sixty battles to defend the independence of their little state, which was not larger than Massachusetts, but the independence of the great continent of America seemed already secure.[4]

1788, vol. ii, pp. 214–217; Writings of Washington, Ford edition, vol. iv, pp. 15, 16 note.

[2] *American Archives*, fourth series, vol. v, pp. 838–39, 965, 1145; "Life of George Read, pp. 158–59; vol. vi, pp. 408, 429, 810, 954, 1006.

[3] *American Archives*, fourth series, vol. v, p. 931.

[4] Niles, " Principles and Acts of the Revolution," edition 1876, p. 133.

Why then should the word itself be avoided for the sake of the timid and doubting? When the country was independent as a matter of fact, had been independent for six months, and was organizing fleets, armies, and diplomacy, and making war as an independent nation, what was the use of keeping up any longer the old conservatism about reconciliation with England, or loyalty to the king, or remaining part of the empire? Would we now accept reconciliation if it was offered us? Would we not spurn it as the most contemptible subserviency?

" Some people among us seem alarmed at the name Independence while they support measures and propose plans that comprehend all the spirit of it. Have we not made laws, erected courts of judicature, established magistrates, made money, levied war and regulated commerce, not only without his Majesty's intervention, but absolutely against his will? Are we not as criminal in the eye of Britain for what we have done, as for what we can yet do? If we institute any government at all, for God's sake let it be the best we can; we shall as certainly be hanged for a bad as a good one." (*American Archives*, fourth series, vol. iv, p. 1210.)

The situation had been made still more favorable for the patriots by the passage in Parliament of a new bill, which became a law on the 21st of December, 1775, and was known as the Prohibitory Act. It was intended by the Ministry to meet the increasing difficulties of the situation, and establish a legal and legislative basis for the coercion and subjugation of the colonies.

The Prohibitory Act repealed the Port Bill, closing the harbor of Boston, because that bill was of no further use, as all the colonial harbors were now to be closed. The Prohibitory Act also repealed the Fisheries Acts prohibiting the colonies from fishing on the Grand Banks and prohibiting them from trading with one another and with the rest of the world. These special prohibitions were no longer necessary, because they were now included in the general provisions of the Prohibitory Act, which in due formality declared war against the colonies and established a general blockade.

THE PROHIBITORY ACT

All nations were prohibited from trading with the revolted colonies; and all ships belonging to the inhabitants of the colonies, or belonging to the inhabitants of other nations which should be found trading with the colonies, would be forfeited with their cargoes and become lawful prize for the officers and crews of the British navy. But if any colony, county, town, port or district, should return to loyalty and obedience it would be lawful for any of the persons appointed by his Majesty to grant pardons in America, to declare such colony, county, or town to be in the peace of the King and exempt from the provisions of the act.[5]

The Ministry had, of course, thought that it was necessary to pass some such act legalizing the warfare which was to be waged against the colonies and notifying all nations that a state of war existed. But they were hardly prepared for the construction which the patriots put upon it, or for the delight with which it was received by the whole patriot party. It was the very thing they wanted. Parliament and the King by thus declaring war upon the colonies were voluntarily giving them the legal status of a foreign nation, and declaring them independent. If war had to be formally declared against them they must be already independent, and were not rebels. It is not usual to declare war against a rebellion; for if it is a rebellion it can be put down as a violation of existing law and allegiance.

Never before or since has the British Parliament passed an act which has been more thoroughly satisfactory in every respect to all true Americans. They hailed it as the first recognition of their independence, and it supplied them with an invaluable argument. It was almost as valuable to them as

---

[5] The act can be read in the British statutes at large and is reprinted in *American Archives*, fourth series, vol. v, p. 1667. See, also, vol. vi, p. 1, for the address from the throne and debate on the Prohibitory Act; also pp. 186, 191, 237; Gordon, " American Revolution," edition 1788, vol. ii, pp. 235–237; *Annual Register*, 1776, chap. vi.

the treaty of peace of 1783 which formally acknowledged independence.

> "I know not," said John Adams, "whether you have seen the act of Parliament called the Restraining Act, or Prohibitory Act, or Piratical Act, or Plundering Act, or Act of Independency—for by all these titles is it called. I think the most apposite is the Act of Independency; for King, Lords, and Commons, have united in sundering this country from that, I think, forever. It is a complete dismemberment of the British Empire. It throws thirteen Colonies out of the Royal protection, levels all distinctions, and makes us independent in spite of our supplications and entreaties.
>
> "It may be fortunate that the Act of Independency should come from the British Parliament rather than the American Congress; but it is very odd that Americans should hesitate at accepting such a gift from them." (*American Archives*, fourth series, vol. v, p. 472.)

We have already seen how the patriots denied all allegiance to Parliament, but admitted a slight allegiance to the King, and we have seen how eagerly and patiently they waited for acts by the British King or his agents which would absolve them from that slight allegiance. For this reason they had waited for the British to fire the first shot at Lexington and at Concord. For this reason the patriots of Mecklenburg County in North Carolina had in May, 1775, put forth the idea that Parliament having declared the colonies in rebellion, and the King having accepted that declaration and acted upon it, all British charters and laws in America were annulled and the colonists left free to govern themselves as they pleased.

But the Prohibitory Act gave the best excuse of all. It had been preceded by the address from the throne on the opening of Parliament, in which the King formally announced that the colonies were in rebellion and that it was his purpose to conquer and subdue them; and this followed by his assent to the passage of the Prohibitory Act, necessarily, said the patriots, put the colonies out of the protection of the Crown. Protection and allegiance were reciprocal. There could be no allegiance where there was no protection. The allegiance to the King had been given in exchange for his protection; and when his protection was withdrawn by a declaration of war, the allegiance was annulled.

" It is," said Chief Justice Drayton, of South Carolina, " the voluntary and joint act of the whole British Legislature . . . releasing the faith, allegiance and subjection of America to the British crown by solemnly declaring the former out of the protection of the latter; and thereby, agreeable to every principle of law, actually dissolving the original contract between king and people." (*American Archives*, fifth series, vol. ii, p. 1049.)

" By an Act of Parliament," said John Adams, " we are put out of the royal protection and consequently discharged from our allegiance and it has become necessary to assume government for our immediate security." (*American Archives*, fourth series, vol. iv, p. 1138. See, also, " Diary and Letters of Thomas Hutchinson," vol. i, pp. 265, 266.)

Elias Boudinot tells us that, having at one time as a colonial official taken the British oath of allegiance, he hardly knew what course to pursue in the Revolution until the Prohibitory Act relieved him of all scruples of conscience. Doubtless there were hundreds of others who, seeing protection and allegiance destroyed by act of Parliament, reasoned that there could be no binding oath to support an allegiance which no longer existed. For these timid ones the date of the Prohibitory Act, the 21st of December, 1775, was independence day; and accordingly as soon as the news of the address from the throne, and the probable passage of the Act, reached America, the open discussion of independence began.[6]

The argument so common the year before that America was waging war merely for the sake of returning to the old semi-independent condition that prevailed before the year 1763, was now abandoned. The utmost contempt was expressed for those who preached the old doctrine, and the condition of affairs before 1763, instead of being looked back

---

[6] Elias Boudinot's Journal, pp. 22, 23. The Whigs in Parliament foresaw very clearly the effect of the Prohibitory Act in America and foretold that it would have a " direct tendency to effect an entire and permanent separation." *American Archives*, fourth series, vol. vi, p. 225; fifth series, vol. iii, p. 996; fourth series, vol. v, p. 804; vol. iv, pp. 1210, 1220.

upon as the golden age, was described as abject slavery, to which it would be madness to return.[1]

All this feeling was greatly encouraged and intensified by the appearance of a remarkable pamphlet called "Common Sense," which circulated in thousands of copies from one end of the country to the other and the phrases of which became household words on the lips of every man in the patriot party. The author of this firebrand, Thomas Paine, was a young Englishman, a stay-maker by trade, with something of an education, and inclined to write essays and take an interest in the popular and democratic side of public questions. He had, of course, never prospered in England, and had come out to Philadelphia upon the recommendation of Franklin.

We owe Paine a debt of gratitude for his services to our cause and our people have always wished to think well of him. He had little or no respect for conventional forms of religion, and his habits and manners were not, it seems, all that could be desired. But he had undoubted talent in writing, and there must have been a certain amount of attraction or promise in him.[2]

He had the boldness to assail in unmeasured terms of ridicule the lingering sentiment about England, and that conservatism among hesitating patriots which had led them to masquerade under schemes of reconciliation. He appeared at the psychological moment, as we would now say, when a literary man of desperate fortunes was needed who rather enjoyed violating all the proprieties and conventionalities of the age. The patriots had persisted for so many years in their cautious plan of disavowing the real passion of their

[1] *American Archives*, fourth series, vol. iv, p. 1508; vol. v, pp. 88, 226. See, also, *id.*, vol. iv, pp. 377, 368, 472, 529, 839, 1204, 1478, 1496; vol. v, pp. 48, 50, 96, 129, 130, 187, 188, 786, 972, 959, 992, 1011–1015, 1020, 1078, 1133, 1163, 1168, 1169, 1180, 1215; vol. vi, p. 488, and title " Independence " in the index of the *American Archives;* Gordon, " American Revolution," edition 1788, vol. ii, p. 269.

[2] Conway, " Life of Paine; " " Life of John Jay," p. 97; Gordon, " American Revolution," edition of 1788, vol. ii, p. 275.

hearts, that they had got into a rut from which they had to be jostled by very rough and plain language from a man of the people whose low estate in the world brought him closer to real democracy than the Adamses, the Jeffersons, or the Hamiltons.

" But Britain is the parent country, say some. Then the more shame upon her conduct. Even brutes do not devour their young, nor savages make war upon their families; wherefore the assertion if true turns to her reproach."

In this way, at every opportunity, Paine sneered at this artificial relation which had been assumed to be that of mother and daughter; and also at that habit among many of the colonists which led them to speak of England as home. It certainly was a rather curious habit when we consider that they had been born in America, were identified with American interests, had never seen England, and were unfitted for any form of English life.

This opened to him a large field for satire which he worked to perfection. The provincial sentimentality about "tender and brotherly affection for our fellow subjects at home" had always been a great absurdity to any one who knew the real Englishman with his arrogant contempt for. the colonists as social inferiors, convicts, and cowards. The sentimentality had now become a still more extraordinary spectacle when Americans were talking about reconciliation and union with a nation that was burning their towns over the heads of women and children, and torturing prisoners. America must strike for something higher and nobler than mere compromise or she was a ruined land. A return to the conditions before 1763 was impossible, for the old feeling which held the relations of that time sacred was gone and could never be restored.

Paine had much to say about the "Royal Brute of Great Britain," as he called the King; and this was a lucky, catching phrase for the times. It ran through the country and expressed with the utmost exactness the feelings of thousands of patriots, who were furious at the treatment of the prisoners, the irons on the limbs of their hero Allen, and the sufferings of women and children . when Portland and Norfolk were shelled by the British ships.

"In England a king hath little more to do than to make war and give away places, which in plain terms is to impoverish the nation and set it together by the ears. A pretty business indeed for a man to be allowed eight hundred thousand sterling a year for, and worshipped into the bargain! Of more worth is one honest man to society and in the sight of God, than all the crowned ruffians that ever lived."

It has been sometimes supposed that Paine had peculiar or original theories of government. But a close examination of his first pamphlet, and the rest of the series which he kept going for several years, shows that his political philosophy was merely a restatement or application in a very popular and modern manner of the doctrines of the rights of man, which had already had such influence on the colonists. He was a student of Locke, Burlamaqui, Beccaria, and Montesquieu, amplified their ideas, applied them in unexpected ways, and expressed them with homely vividness. Burlamaqui had stated those ideas in the most attractive form for the comprehension of Americans of education and position. Paine expressed them for the masses; and from poverty and obscurity he suddenly became known to the whole civilized world, and was eulogized, vilified and caricatured in both America and Europe.

XL.

A COMPREHENSIVE PLAN TO SUBJUGATE THE SOUTHERN COLONIES

THE great army which was to subdue New York, Pennsylvania, and New England would not reach America until the late spring or summer of 1776. But meanwhile there seemed to the Ministry a good opportunity to employ a moderate force of regulars and war-vessels in occupying the seaboard of the Carolinas or Georgia. At the same time the loyalist population of the interior, supposed to be overwhelmingly large, was to be encouraged to rise; and the Indian tribes, the Creeks and Cherokees to the westward, were to fall upon the frontier and press eastward as far as possible.[1]

It was a most comprehensive and sweeping plan as originally conceived, and seemed as if it must surely crush the South, and if it were followed by the subjugation of New England, New York, and Pennsylvania, the British empire would remain intact. In any event it seemed as if a foothold, the occupation of at least one or two important posts or centres, would be gained in the South; and at that time the southern colonies were regarded as more commercially valuable than the north, and Virginia was the most populous province in America.[2]

Martin, the banished royal governor of North Carolina, was particularly active in forwarding the plan, and though on board ship seems to have been able to communicate with the loyalists far inland and arrange a plan with them for supporting the British army when it should arrive. The British Government was given to understand that thousands of loyal-

---

[1] Correspondence of Henry Laurens, pp. 25–28; Kirke, "The Rear Guard of the Revolution," p. 106.

[2] "Diary and Letters of Thomas Hutchinson," vol. i, p. 555.

ists were ready to rise and that four thousand were already armed in North Carolina.

The Creeks, Chickasaw and Cherokee Indians were at that time living under their chieftains Oconostota and Dragging Canoe in what is now the eastern end of Tennessee; and among them were two British agents, Stuart and Cameron, who organized them for the invasion, and seem to have remained among them throughout the greater part of the Revolution, keeping them steadily in the English interest. The British Government seems to have had very complete and accurate means of communication throughout all the vast distances in America.[3]

General Howe was instructed to send southward from Boston a force which should wait at the Cape Fear River in North Carolina until joined by a larger force from England. and then act with the loyalists as circumstances should indicate. Howe selected General Clinton, a son of a former governor of New York, and a very capable officer, to take command of the military forces of the expedition.

Clinton left Boston with a few troops in the frigate "Mercury" on the 20th of January, 1776, and as the preparations for his departure became known in the patriot army, Washington supposed that he might intend an attack on New York. General Charles Lee was accordingly sent to New York to take every possible measure for its defence.[4]

Lee, a man by turns brilliant or contemptible, and the most extraordinary and inexplicable character in the Revolution, was an English officer who had served in America in the French War and had been at Braddock's defeat. He was as eccentric in appearance as in character, and is described as tall, gaunt, and extremely thin, with an ugly face and an aquiline nose of enormous proportions. His tone is said to have been very distinguished and impressive; he had seen

---

[3] Correspondence of George III with Lord North, vol. i, p. 276.

[4] *American Archives*, fourth series, vol. iii, pp. 1135, 1400 vol. iv, pp. 604–624, 629, 699, 812, 942, 943, 955, 1145, 1506, 1507; Journals of Congress, vol. i, p. 220; Gordon, "American Revolution," edition 1788, vol. ii, pp. 173, 208, 210.

much of the world, and something of the armies and courts of Europe; he certainly was well read in military science; familiar with light literature and history; and was master of such a clever and sarcastic style of writing that he had been suspected of being the author of the Letters of Junius.

The Indians in the French War gave him the very appropriate name of Boiling Water. After that war he served with considerable distinction under Burgoyne in Portugal; but was in effect dismissed from the army and put on half-pay with the rank of major for writing a pungent essay against the Ministry on the subject of Pontiac's Conspiracy. After that he roamed about Europe serving in Russia and in Poland, where he was given the rank of Major General. He applied for further service in the British army, but was refused; and irritated by this refusal he came to America in 1772 and threw in his lot with the patriot party. He travelled about the country to make the acquaintance of the leaders and wrote a political essay, "Strictures on a Pamphlet Entitled 'A Friendly Address to All Reasonable Americans,' " which had great vogue in its day and went through many editions.

His natural brightness and fervor won the hearts of the patriots; and they forgave him even his bad manners. His most amiable trait was his fondness for dogs; but with that rudeness and indifference which Englishmen were fond of showing toward colonials, he brought the dogs into ladies' drawing-rooms, where with his magnificent airs of a man of the world he appears to have considered himself a privileged character not bound by the usual rules of good breeding or even of decency.[5]

---

[5] New York Historical Society Collections, 1874, vol. iv, p. 322. See a very coarse letter he wrote to Miss Franks, of Philadelphia, for which he had to apologize. *Id.*, 1873, vol. iii, pp. 278–280, 302. Several biographies of Lee are collected in New York Historical Society Collections, 1874. Lee Papers, vol. iv. See Wilkinson, Memoirs, vol. i, p. 65. There is a life of him in Appleton's Cyclopædia of American Biography, reprinted with a few changes in the British Dictionary of National Biography. Stedman, " American War," vol. i, p. 100.

But our people were so impressed by what they believed to be his great military genius and experience, that the Congress readily voted him $30,000 to replace in part his estate in England which would probably be confiscated. Burgoyne had recently carried on a correspondence with him which on Burgoyne's part was intended to draw Lee into a conspiracy and treason to America similar to that into which Clinton afterwards drew Arnold. Lee showed the letters to members of the Congress and appeared to reject Burgoyne's treacherous suggestions, but is believed to have sent a secret letter to Burgoyne not shown to any of the patriot party.[*]

He had, however, no opportunity to defend New York, for Clinton's ship merely touched at Sandy Hook for a few days, for no other purpose it appears than to consult with Governor Tryon in his refuge on a British war-ship; and Clinton as he passed down the coast paid a similar visit to Lord Dunmore in his floating loyalist and negro colony near Norfolk, Virginia.

Early in February some of the loyalists of North Carolina had embodied and armed themselves, and Governor Martin from his retreat on the British war-ship appointed one of their number, Donald McDonald, a brigadier general to command them. Many of them were Scotch highlanders, armed with the famous broad sword, and others were the regulators, so called, who had taken part in the battle of the Alamance a few years before. Their commander, McDonald, though eighty years old, was a most ardent monarchist and loyalist. Some fifteen hundred of them began their march through the country about the 9th of February. But their movement was very premature, for Clinton's force was not yet collected at the Cape Fear River to support them.

The patriot militia rapidly assembled to oppose them and were commanded by General James Moore, ably supported by Colonels Caswell and Lillington. More's force of about a

---

[*] Fonblanque, "Life of Burgoyne," pp. 173, 177; see, also, pp. 160, 161, 174; New York Historical Society Collections, 1874, vol. iv, pp. 414, 415.

thousand finally camped near the loyalists on the north side of Moore's Creek bridge, about twenty miles above Wilmington. Finding his position a weak one, Moore left his fires burning all the night and crossed to the south side of the bridge, entrenching himself after having taken up the planks and greased the sleepers. The loyalists must cross at this point if they wished to reach the coast and effect a junction with Governor Martin and the British. The next morning, the 27th of February, they appeared sixteen hundred strong, flushed with confidence because the patriots seemed to have retreated before their terrible broadswords. But those who attempted to cross on the slippery timbers were shot down and the rest scattered in every direction. The battle lasted only three minutes and the patriot loss was only two wounded. McDonald fled ingloriously, and with about twenty others was taken prisoner.

He had conducted a most ill-judged movement long before there was any force on the coast to help him. Clinton had hardly reached the coast and the main body of the British troops from England under Sir Peter Parker did not arrive until April and May.[7]

About two weeks after the defeat of McDonald, the British sloop-of-war "Otter" and two tenders sailed up Chesapeake Bay, taking some prizes, but doing little or no other damage; and a few British ships lying at Savannah, Georgia, made an unsuccessful attack on the town, which was protected by a few patriot militia.[8] These movements may have been intended to assist in the general plan of securing a foothold in all the southern colonies; but they were so weak and ill-timed that they had no effect, and Clinton was obliged to wait for weeks at the Cape Fear River for the arrival of Sir Peter Parker and the main body of troops from England.

---

[7] *American Archives*, fourth series, vol. v, pp. 61–64, 140, 170, 473, 496; vol. vi, pp. 404, 405; Jones, " New York in the Revolution," vol. i, p. 95; Stedman, " American War," vol. i, pp. 179–183.

[8] *American Archives*, fourth series, vol. v, pp. 119, 143–146.

AMERICAN INDEPENDENCE

The first of Sir Peter Parker's fleet arrived at Cape Fear River on the 17th of April, and between that date and May 3d, some thirty odd sail of transports brought the rest of the troops, numbering about three thousand, which, with the sailors and marines of the seven war-vessels, might be supposed capable of some very serious invasion of the South. But they had arrived in May instead of in February, as was planned; and the whole purpose of the expedition had been learned early in April from a British letter describing its objects and methods, intercepted by a patriot naval captain, James Barron.[9]

General Charles Lee, who after fortifying New York against Clinton's expected attack had been intended for the command in Canada, was now hurried to the South to organize the whole southern militia and ward off the efforts of Clinton and Sir Peter Parker at whatever point they might be directed. It was also hoped that the little patriot fleet under Commodore Hopkins would be able to intercept Sir Peter Parker's transports. That would, indeed, have been a signal patriot victory; but it was never accomplished, and Hopkins was at this time the subject of much censure for want of enterprise and activity.[10]

The Ministry, learning how much the expedition had been delayed, sent the sloop "Ranger" with orders to Clinton not to make any attack unless favored by extraordinary circumstances; but this message was not received. Clinton himself had doubts about proceeding with such a bungling expedition, but was encouraged by some reconnoitering southward, and after wasting the month of May and making a couple of unimportant raids on shore he and Parker left the Cape Fear River and took the whole British force to sea.[11]

[9] Gordon, "American Revolution," edition 1788, vol. ii, pp. 239, 278-280.

[10] *American Archives*, fourth series, vol. v, pp. 50, 51, 52, 106; vol. vi, pp. 885, 886.

[11] "Diary and Letters of Thomas Hutchinson," vol. ii, pp. 92, 95, 96; *American Archives*, fourth series, vol. vi, pp. 432, 712, 713.

DEFENCE OF CHARLESTON

Lee was in great doubt where they intended to strike. The probability was that they had gone to South Carolina; although they might intend to draw all the patriot forces in that direction and then attack Virginia. But on the 4th of June, they appeared at the entrance of Charleston harbor with ten war-vessels and thirty transports, and the patriots under Lee concentrated every effort on the defence of the town.

The patriots, however, need not have been in haste, for from the 4th until the 28th of June the British again remained inactive, making pottering investigations of the depth of the water, getting one of their ships over the bar by removing her guns, and sending out one of the regulation proclamations offering his Majesty's gracious pardon to all who would lay down their arms. They lost their best opportunity of taking the town and permitted the patriots to complete all their preparations for defence. Lord Cornwallis was said to have urged more activity and complained of Sir Peter Parker's tardiness. Sir Peter replied that Cornwallis might attack with the land forces if he choose; but that ships must wait for a favorable wind.

The channel approaching Charleston harbor is protected by Sullivan's Island, and on this island the patriots had erected a fort of those spongy palmetto logs which were very effective in stopping the cannon-shot and musket-bullets of that time. General Lee's efforts had collected about five thousand patriot troops. A few of these were placed on James Island, which also commanded the channel; others were placed along the bay in front of the town; and the streets near the water were heavily barricaded; but the main defence was the fort on Sullivan's Island.

All the troops and also the patriot citizens were animated by a most enthusiastic spirit. Patriot gentlemen of independent fortune labored with hoe and spade; and every one had the highest respect for Lee and full confidence that his European military training would enable them to drive off the enemy. It was the best hour of Lee's life. He made no mistakes; his eccentricities were in the background; and his letters and reports of this period are free from his usual extravagance of statement.

On the 28th of June at eleven o'clock in the morning two British war-ships, having passed inside the bar, began a furious cannonade on Sullivan's Island, which Lee had placed in command of Colonel Moultrie. There was no bridge for retreat from the island and the creek which separated it from the mainland was a mile wide.

Lee always had a poor opinion of American soldiers. He never became an American and was always in awe of his own people. He now believed that the garrison whom he described as raw recruits officered by boys, would never endure the violence of such a cannonade; and he had thoughts of sending word to them to spike their guns as soon as their ammunition ran low, and retreat with as little loss as possible. But first of all, he made an effort to get them more ammunition, and he sent his aid to report on their courage and condition.

The report of the aid was so favorable that Lee crossed the creek in a small boat to animate the garrison to greater exertions.

"But I found," he said, "they had no occasion for such encouragement. They were pleased with my visit, and assured me they never would abandon the post, but with their lives. The cool courage they displayed astonished and enraptured me; for I do assure you, my dear General, I never experienced a hotter fire—twelve hours it was continued without intermission. The noble fellows who were mortally wounded conjured their brethren never to abandon the standard of liberty. Those who lost their limbs deserted not their posts." (*American Archives*, fourth series, vol. vi, p. 1184.)

When the flagstaff was shot away, Sergeant Jasper leaped over the rampart and fastened the flag to a sponge-staff, which he planted in the breastwork during the hottest fire from the ships. For more than an hour at one time the fort was silenced while waiting for a fresh supply of ammunition. At best there were only twelve cannon that could be used and three hundred men with which to withstand the shot and shell from the ten British ships, which were supposed to have fired at least twelve thousand times; and yet the garrison suffered only the comparatively trifling loss of ten killed and twenty-two wounded.

They aimed their guns carefully; and this cool, skilful marksmanship, characteristic of Americans, won the day. On the British ships there were sixty-four killed and one hundred and forty-one wounded. The "Sphinx" had her bow-sprit shot away and fell out of the firing line; the "Bristol" had the spring of her cable shot away and drifted end on to the fort which was able to rake her with shot from stem to stern; the "Acteon" was driven ashore, abandoned and burnt, while the other vessels suffered severely in their hulls and rigging. Lord William Campbell, the royal governor of South Carolina, whom the patriots had deposed and banished the year before, volunteered to fight on one of the ships, and was given charge of some guns on the lower deck, where he received a mortal wound.

The rear of the fort was so unfinished as to afford a very imperfect protection; but the ships failed to get up far enough to take advantage of this weakness. Their cannonade was largely intended as a support to the land attack which Clinton was to make with his regulars from Long Island. It was supposed that he could wade across to the fort at low tide; but several days before he had warned Sir Peter Parker that there was no ford at low tide. He offered to place some of his troops on Parker's ships to be landed on Sullivan's Island; but this was not taken advantage of by Parker, who appears to have been sick part of the time, besides being generally incompetent. When the fort was evacuated for an hour or more, he had a grand opportunity to land and occupy it, especially if he had accepted Clinton's offer of troops to go on board his ships. But Parker was one of those British officers who were a great boon to the patriots, and some years afterwards he materially assisted in bringing the Revolution to a close.[12]

---

[12] Clinton, "Observations on Mr. Stedman's History of the American War," London, 1794, p. 3.

Clinton appears to have made several attempts to cross to Sullivan's Island; but was easily repulsed by Colonel Thompson with the North Carolina and South Carolina rangers. The British land and sea forces being thus separated their attack was a failure; and after keeping up the cannonade until nearly midnight Parker's ships retired to their former station just inside the bar. Soon afterwards the whole expedition, men-of-war and transports, sailed away northward to join General Howe in his attack on New York.

The contemporary criticisms on this attempt at Charleston describe it as a most blundering undertaking; and there must have been gross mismanagement or some misunderstanding between the admiral and the general. Not only was there great delay, which gave the patriots time to prepare; but the mistake was made of stopping to fight Sullivan's Island when the ships might have passed it and successfully attacked the town, which was weakly defended. Four years after, in 1780, the British under Admiral Arbuthnot sailed by Sullivan's Island with comparatively little damage and took possession of the harbor.[18]

The attack by the western Indians in support of Clinton and Sir Peter Parker was better timed than the rising of the loyalists. The Shawnees, Mingoes and Delawares were to attack the Virginia frontiers, some of the Cherokees were given the new settlements in eastern Tennessee, and the rest of the Cherokees, with Creeks and Chickasaws, were to descend upon Georgia. But no movement was to be made until Clinton and Parker had begun their assault on Charleston.

The first attack was made in Tennessee by about seven hundred Cherokees, who divided themselves into two bands, one attacking Fort Henry at the forks of the Holston River, and the other Fort Lee at Watauga, farther south. The defenders of Fort Henry, under the leadership of Isaac Shelby, went out to meet the Indians and defeated them before they reached the fort. Fort Lee, commanded by John Sevier, was

---

[18] Jones, "New York in the Revolution," vol. i, p. 99.

besieged for twenty days, but the Indians were compelled to retire with heavy loss.

These Tennessee settlers had only recently crossed the mountains from North Carolina and were a hardy race of hunters and farmers armed with Deckard rifles, a favorite weapon manufactured at Lancaster, in Pennsylvania. Their numbers were very few and they had been able to assemble only a little over two hundred armed men with whom they had repulsed the seven hundred Indians at Fort Henry and Fort Lee.

These two repulses ended the great Indian raids from which so much had been expected. Raven, the chief who started to attack Virginia, came back without striking a blow when he heard of the ill success in Tennessee. The Indians and loyalists who started to raid South Carolina and Georgia were driven back in August by the patriot settlers and militia of those states. Thirty or forty Indian villages were burned, their cattle killed, and their crops destroyed.[14]

The British plan had aimed to cover distances which would be considered enormous even in modern times, and the whole plan had been defeated by comparatively small bodies of patriot Americans at three or four points. The result revealed certain essential weaknesses on the British side. The loyalists, in spite of their numbers, seemed incapable of either organizing or fighting with any effect; the Indians were equally useless; and there was evident incompetency in the British navy and a lack of coöperation between it and the army. This jealousy or inability to coöperate with the army continued throughout the war and is described by Clinton at various times with bitter resentment.

The whole campaign and plan was an unfortunate fiasco for the British Government. It would have been better left unattempted, for it no doubt, raised the spirits of the patriots, filled them with confidence in their power, and encouraged

---

[14] Kirke, "The Rear Guard of the Revolution," 106, 110, 121, 123, 125, 127. Ramsey, "Annals of Tennessee."

their union. It was the first exhibition to Europeans of the fighting qualities of the Southerner. Lee was universally praised for his rapid organization and his skilful disposition of his forces at every available point, which it was believed would have defeated the British even if they had displayed better generalship and persistence. He had found Charleston a helpless, undefended town, and he had made it a stronghold which repelled a British fleet and army. He was now the American palladium, and still greater success was expected from him.[18]

[18] *American Archives*, fourth series, vol. vi, pp. 720, 721, 948, 1128, 1129, 1183–1192, 1205–1208; fifth series, vol. i, pp. 435–440; Gordon, " American Revolution," edition 1788, vol. ii, pp. 280–288; Niles, " Principles and Acts of the Revolution," edition 1876, p. 393.

XLI.

THE ADOPTION OF THE DECLARATION
OF INDEPENDENCE

THE Continental Congress had, on the 23rd of March, 1776, replied to Parliament's Prohibitory Act by resolutions declaring that the American ports were open to the trade of all nations and countries, except those subject to Great Britain; and that all British commerce was now the lawful prey of American privateers. By a resolution of the 15th of May, they declared that all forms of British authority in the colonies should be totally abolished, and that those colonies which had not yet framed constitutions in place of their old charters or other British form of government should do so without delay.[1]

As the whole country between Canada and Florida was independent and had been independent for a year, the royal governors banished, and the British army driven to Nova Scotia, the question naturally arose whether it was not a suitable time to announce formally to all the world that the colonies were independent, entirely separated from Great Britain, and would from henceforth claim a place among nations, with all the rights and privileges of that position.

The patriots in various parts of the country had begun to instruct their delegates in the Congress to move for an immediate declaration. The comparatively small patriot party of North Carolina had been the first to give these instructions, on the 12th of April, 1776, followed by Virginia on the 22nd of May; and on the 7th of June Richard Henry Lee moved in the Congress the famous resolution "That these United Colonies are and of right ought to be free and independent States; that they are absolved from all allegiance to the British Crown, and

---

[1] Journals of Congress, Ford edition, vol. iv, pp. 159, 229, 357; Gordon, "American Revolution," edition 1788, vol. ii, pp. 271, 272.

that all political connection between them and the State of Great Britain is, and ought to be, totally dissolved."[2]

The resolution, it will be observed, described independence as already existing. The Congress assumed to itself no authority to create independence. All that it undertook to do by the Lee resolution, and the subsequent formal document which it adopted, was to announce to the world an existing state of fact in thirteen of the colonies and give reasons to show that that condition had been brought about rightfully and that it was right that it should be continued.

There was, however, serious disagreement in the Congress as to the advisability of formally announcing independence so soon. The argument against an immediate declaration seems to have been that we had not been sufficiently successful in arms, and nothing but real success in arms would make the declaration respectable and save it from the ridicule of the nations. We must wait till we had secured the alliance of France; or, as Patrick Henry is said to have put it, at least wait until it should be known what course France and Spain would take. England would soon send out a great invading force, and a reverse in battle in our weak state would make the declaration seem contemptible, and destroy the possibility of help from France. We were not yet sufficiently united, and the declaration would alienate many who had not grown accustomed to the thought of complete independence.[3]

At first, when the question was debated, in June, the colonies stood seven in favor of an immediate declaration, namely, the four New England colonies, Virginia, North Carolina, and Georgia. The conservative minority, led by Dickinson, was made up of Pennsylvania, South Carolina, New York, New Jersey, Maryland, and Delaware. It was very important, however, to have a unanimous vote. The question was accordingly postponed until July and meantime great exertions were made to have the patriot party in every prov-

---

[2] *American Archives*, fourth series, vol. vi, 1699, 1728, 1729.
[3] *American Archives*, fifth series, vol. i, pp. 95, 96.

ince instruct its delegates to vote for an immediate declaration.[4]

An attack was organized upon those British ships under Commodore Banks which Howe had left at the entrance of Boston harbor to protect supply-vessels which might arrive without knowing that the town had been evacuated. Commodore Banks had just saved from the patriot privateers seven transports loaded with Highland troops. But so effective was the attack upon him that he was obliged to leave the coast altogether; and a few days after he had gone two British transports loaded with highlanders arrived. They succeeded in beating off four patriot privateers which attacked them outside; but ignorant of the evacuation of Boston they sailed on into the harbor, where they were cut off by the patriots and after some desperate fighting the two hundred and fifty-seven Highlanders surrendered.[5]

It could now be said that another victory in arms had been won. As a matter of fact there was the still more important victory of the repulse of Clinton and Parker at Charleston, although the news of this did not arrive in time to influence opinion as to the advisability of a declaration.

When July came four colonies were still in opposition. Of these, the vote of the Pennsylvania delegation was carried for the Declaration by Dickinson and Robert Morris absenting themselves. Delaware, whose vote had been evenly divided, was brought over by the arrival of Cæsar Rodney; and South Carolina was also persuaded. The New York delegation, being without fresh instruction, declined to vote. But the final vote, on the 2nd of July, was almost unanimous, and on the 4th of July the formal paper prepared by Jefferson and his committee was adopted.

Such men as Dickinson and Robert Morris still held to their opinion that the Declaration was premature. ''It was an

---

[4] *American Archives*, fourth series, vol. vi, pp. 813, 814, 917, 931.
[5] *American Archives*, fourth series, vol. vi, pp. 917, 1035, 1127; Gordon, '' American Revolution,'' edition 1788, vol. ii, pp. 266, 267.

improper time," said Morris, "and it will neither promote the interest nor redound to the honor of America, for it has caused division when we wanted union." Morris was very conservative at this time; and had opposed the plan of encouraging the colonies to form new governments and constitutions for themselves independent of all British authority. But Morris signed the declaration after it had been adopted.[*]

It is highly probable that the adoption of the Declaration alienated many people who were hesitating and increased the number of the loyalists. There was a whole class of loyalists who appear to have been willing to act with the patriots and even to make war upon England; but only for the sake of compromise and reconciliation and not for independence. All these people were, of course, lost to the patriot party by the Declaration of the 4th of July. Men like Morris and Dickinson were also afterwards able to say that terrible military disasters followed the Declaration, and that within six months after its adoption the patriot cause had sunk to its lowest ebb, and that the Declaration did not apparently bring us the alliance of France, which came nearly two years afterwards only as a result of a great patriot victory in the field.

But, on the other hand, the Declaration gave the real patriots a rallying point. It showed their purpose, interested the French King, and was a basis for his action when a victory convinced him of the advisability of an alliance. A foreign power could not very well make a treaty of alliance with mere rebels; or with people who were still the subjects of the King of England. It was probably well to declare independence as soon as possible after what seemed to be our first distinct success, because it was a long time before we had another, and we never had one which at once put all the British troops out of the country.

---

[*] Oberholtzer, " Life of Robert Morris," pp. 20, 22; " Life of George Read," pp. 162–166, 226; " Life of Joseph Reed," by W. B. Reed, vol. i, p. 201; *American Archives*, fourth series, vol. vi, pp. 1212, 1232; W. H. Michael, " Story of the Declaration of Independence."

CELEBRATING INDEPENDENCE

Many patriots were, no doubt, inclined to agree with Carter Braxton, who thought the Declaration had strengthened the patriot party, given the Congress something to stand by, and prevented that body disbanding. The patriot party may have lost certain adherents by the Declaration, but it gained others and gained in animation and vigor.[7]

In New York as soon as the patriots heard of the Declaration they dragged down the gilt statue of the king on the Bowling Green and cut off its head. In Savannah, Georgia, the Declaration is said to have been read to a great concourse of people, followed by a parade of the militia, with platoon firing and cannonading. In the evening there was one of those curious ceremonies which the people of that time were very clever at improvising. They held a funeral over the remains of George III, who was interred before the courthouse in the "sure and certain hope that he will never obtain a resurrection to rule again over these United States of America."

In Boston there was a formal military celebration of the reading. In Philadelphia, Mrs. Deborah Logan, sitting at the window of her house at the corner of Fifth and Library Streets, heard the formal reading before what is now Independence Hall, and records in her diary that few people were present except some of the lower orders.

Wherever there were patriot troops they were paraded and the Declaration read to them by an officer. Captain Graydon, who was with part of the patriot army, tells us that the troops took the announcement very quietly. They regarded it as a wise step, though closing the door to accommodation or compromise.

We also find some of the troops expressing their feelings in words which sum up the whole doctrine of independence.

---

[7] *Pennsylvania Magazine of History*, vol. 27, p. 145; Wells, " Life of Samuel Adams," vol. ii, p. 399; *American Archives*, fourth series, vol. vi, p. 505; fifth series, vol. i, pp. 139, 230.

"Now," they said, "we are a people. We have a name among the states of the world." [8]

After the Declaration had been accepted by the Congress, a committee was appointed to prepare a form of league or general government for the colonies which were now independent, and several years afterwards the efforts of this committee resulted in what became known as the Articles of Confederation. Another committee was appointed to prepare a plan for treaties with foreign nations, with which independent America could now assume to deal as an equal.

The Declaration was a remarkable document. There had been nothing exactly like it in the history of the world. Its opening paragraphs, setting forth the doctrine of political equality, the right of revolution, the right of every naturally separated people to independence, have become so familiar to us that we can hardly appreciate the interest they at first aroused. It is true those doctrines were merely the natural and logical result of the writings of Locke, Burlamaqui. Grotius, Hooker, and others whose principles had been known in Europe ever since the Reformation. But to see those principles set forth in such a bold, striking and practical way by colonial insurgents who were prepared to fight for them was a great surprise to Europeans, and the doctrines themselves have not yet been entirely accepted in Europe.

English Tories and American loyalists became, of course. more than ever denunciatory of what they called American perfidy, ingratitude, and treason. America had been originally settled, they said, by the scum of England,—roundheads, Puritans, Presbyterians, and other rebellious sects; followers of Cromwell, who hated the noble British Constitution, and who took with them to America the seeds of sedition, which they had been "as assiduous in sowing in the hearts of their children as they had been in cultivating their

---

[8] *American Archives*, fifth series, vol. i, p. 882; "Life and Correspondence of President Reed," vol. i, p. 195; *American Archives*, fifth series, vol. i, p. 630; see, also, pp. 230, 810, 972; Hazelton, "The Declaration of Independence," p. 265.

lands." England had been fortunate in being delivered from "their venomous fanatic principles" at home; and now in the colonies they had turned with malevolence and spite to sting her.[9]

To the Tories the principle that all men were politically equal was as absurd as to assert that all men were equal in height, fortune, or talents. They pointed with jeers and sarcasm to the thousands of black slaves held by the very men who had signed this declaration of universal liberty; and to modern Englishmen with an aristocracy to support and 290,000,000 East Indians to hold in profitable subjection, even to English liberals, the doctrines of political equality and self-government of the Declaration are still as unacceptable as ever.[10]

The opening paragraphs of the Declaration, dealing with the doctrines of the rights of man, are very brief. The greater part of the document is taken up with a somewhat detailed description of the specific acts of the King, which had compelled the American patriots to fall back on the principle or right of revolution. Most people in reading the Declaration are interested in the short and rather eloquent passage on the rights of man, but soon become weary of the subsequent dry details referring to matters long since forgotten, and stated in such a brief and general way that they cannot appeal to the present generation. But these dry details were the important part of the Declaration at the time of its adoption, and they involved the whole history of the controversy with Great Britain.

They consisted of twenty-eight charges or reasons for

---

[9] Reflections on the State of Parties," London, 1776, pp. 56, 57; "Remarks on the Different Principles Relative to the American Colonies," London, 1776, p. 11, etc.; " A Letter from an Officer in New York," London, 1777, p. 11 etc. Some Whigs in England like Dr. Richard Price defended the Declaration. Numerous pamphlets attacking him for this defence can be found in the Carter-Brown collection in Providence, Rhode Island.

[10] Goldwin Smith, " The United States," pp. 87, 88.

breaking the allegiance to the King. Each charge described a distinct offence or act which had been committed, and all these acts which are complained of are charged upon the King and not upon Parliament. Even where the laws of Parliament are complained of the word parliament is not used; but the King is charged with combining with others to procure the laws and with "giving his assent to their acts of pretended legislation." Indeed although the whole contest for twelve years had been with Parliament, and the taxation and other acts passed by it, yet one would not infer from reading the Declaration that there had been any contest with Parliament at all.

This method, however, was entirely consistent with the patriot position. They had some time before brought their argument to the point where they not only denied the power of Parliament to tax them, but denied its power to control them or legislate for them in any case whatsoever. They would not, therefore, in their Declaration complain of Parliament. They had held that all its acts with reference to them were void, and of no effect; and Jefferson had always been a strong advocate of this view. They would not declare independence of Parliament because they had held that, under the true view of the English Constitution, they had never been subject to Parliament. They had always been independent of it. The only part of the British Government on which they had acknowledged themselves dependent had been the king; and now that the King had declared war against them, and was sending armies and fleets to subjugate them and bring them under the control of Parliament, they had, they believed, good grounds and cause for breaking their slight allegiance to him and declaring themselves absolutely independent.[11]

Accepting the King as the formal head of the empire, not only representative, but responsible for all acts of government, they included in their indictment of him everything unpleasant

---

[11] See the twenty-eight charges discussed in detail in *Pennsylvania Magazine of History*, vol. 31, p. 257.

or unpopular which Parliament, the Ministry or any department of the home government had done since the present King,
George III, came to the throne in 1760, and the reorganization
of the colonies began. In this way they snapped the only
thread of British allegiance which they recognized.

Their attack had to be directed against the King; but it
was in reality, of course, an arraignment of colonialism, an
attack upon the entire system of outside alien control, as it
appeared to the eyes of the patriots. It was most ably and
well done. The felicity of expression in any one of the twenty-
eight charges seems more and more admirable the more we
study the circumstances it was intended to meet and the point
of view of its signers. This felicity we owe principally to
Jefferson, who was a master of that sort of language which
expresses legal or political principles in the most effective and
popular form.

To consider each one of the twenty-eight charges separately
would be to rewrite the history of the Revolution. They were
separately considered and most exhaustively analyzed in two
political pamphlets which appeared in England. One of these,
"An Answer to the Declaration of the Congress," by an
English barrister, John Lind, was generally regarded as prepared at the request of the Ministry and as an expression of
their views. The other, called "Strictures on the Declaration
of the Congress," was written by Governor Hutchinson, and
though less complete than Lind's, is of .great value and importance. The two together afford one of the most interesting
discussions that can be found of the British point of view.[12]

---

[12] *American Archives*, fifth series, vol. iii, p. 1009 note; Freedenwald,
"The Declaration of Independence," reprinted from the *International
Monthly* for July, 1901; Hazleton, "The Declaration of Independence;"
John Adams, Works, vol. ii, p. 514.

XLII.

MILITARY CONDITIONS AND GENERAL STRATEGY

WHILE the British are preparing a grand army to deliver a crushing blow and regain control of the thirteen independent provinces, it may be well to consider the general military theories on which our army and theirs acted during the war; and this brief view will help to a better understanding of the future military movements.

In conquering the Boer Republics of South Africa in the beginning of the twentieth century, England is said to have had in the field at one time over 250,000 troops. If she had had half that number in 1776 one would suppose that the conquest of America would have been a comparatively easy task. With 125,000 men, a thousand sailing vessels for carrying them with their supplies to America, and sufficient money in the treasury to send their food across the Atlantic for two or three years, there could have been a very complete occupation of the country. Boston could have been taken as the most northern point and the control continued on down the coast by the occupation of every important place, Newport in Rhode Island, New London in Connecticut, the City of New York, New Brunswick in New Jersey, and so on down through Philadelphia, Annapolis, Alexandria, and Charleston, to Savannah in Georgia. Such an occupation, with the addition of a force to hold the valley of the Hudson River up to Lake Champlain, would seem as if it must have overwhelmed the patriot cause; and driven its radical followers to take refuge among the Indians beyond the Allegheny Mountains.

But England had not a hundred and twenty-five thousand troops to send to America. It was with the greatest difficulty that she sent out 60,000, all told, during the first three years of the war. Her population and her army were small in those days; and in all her wars she had been obliged to hire troops from other nations. She expected help from the Indians, but it was comparatively slight. She also expected help from the loyalists, and some thousands of them enlisted in her service. But they did not organize themselves so as to occupy large districts or provinces or control the political government of certain states as was expected.

She applied for troops to the Netherlands and also to Catherine of Russia, "Sister Kitty" as Walpole irreverently called her; but in both instances was refused. Many, however, were obtained from Germany, and in 1777 there were said to have been 23,762 of them in the British army. Of these about 12,000 Hessians and 5,000 Brunswickers were sent out to America.[1]

The largest single army England sent to America was the one of 34,000 given to Howe in 1776; and during his three years of command the total sent to him is said to have been 60,000; with a fleet at his disposal of over fifty large war-ships, twenty-five armed sloops and cutters, and four hundred transports. After the French alliance, in 1778, the British Government was obliged to reduce the number of troops in America. Clinton never had over 20,000 troops in all his positions north and south, and seldom as many as twenty-five war-ships.

Looking back at all the events of the Revolution, it seems as if all these land and sea forces of Great Britain would have been sufficient to conquer the seaboard colonies and drive the desperate patriots into the interior, if the patriots had not been assisted by France, and Spain. The whole question hinged on the aid France might give. It was taken for granted that she would give it, because it was so obviously her best policy. The patriots looked forward to it from the beginning; and the English regarded it with such dread and uneasiness

---

[1] *American Archives*, fourth series, vol. iv, pp. 205, 369; vol. vi, p. 356; Fonblanque, " Life of Burgoyne," pp. 153, 213–217; Duval, Letters of George III, vol. i, pp. 293, 297. Parliamentary Register House of Commons 1779, vol. xi, p. 320. See, also, as to British disadvantages, *American Archives*, fifth series, vol. iii, p. 687.

that they exhausted every method of conciliation. The doubt as to the possibility of conquering America under such circumstances was the underlying motive of many a debate in Parliament. It was one of the foundations of the Whig position that the war was useless, impractical and dangerous, because England in her weak and bankrupt condition would become involved in a European war; and certainly if in trying to save America she should lose her much more valuable interest in India, it would be a great misfortune.

Not being able to occupy our whole sea front and settle the war by an overwhelming force, the British Ministry and generals had to decide upon the best way of using the thirty or forty thousand troops which they could send to America. There was no use in keeping a force in Boston, because it was of no general strategic importance. It might be held for years while the patriots in the rest of the country created an independent nation and became self-sustaining. The important place to seize and occupy was the strategical centre of the country. It was generally admitted that the strategical centre was the town of New York and the line of the Hudson River valley up to Lake Champlain and Canada.

This strategical line had been the bone of contention in the French and Indian Wars and was still looked upon by almost everybody on both sides as the key to America. The town of New York, easily defended, because on an island, had the best harbor on the coast, of comparatively easy entrance from the sea, and could not be equalled as a safe headquarters and base for collecting supplies. The Hudson River stretching northward from it formed with Lake George, Lake Champlain, and the Richelieu River, the only highway of the time to Canada. This highway also had the advantage of cutting the colonies in half. It was an obstacle rather difficult to cross, and separated New England from the middle and southern colonies. If held by troops with the British fleet controlling the ocean, New England, "the hot-bed of sedition," would be completely isolated from intercourse with the other colonies. She would be cut off not only from the interchange of ideas, encourage-

ment and reinforcement of troops, but also from the provisions
and supplies which she drew from the more fertile agricultural regions to the south.

In New England itself it seemed well for the British to hold
only Newport, because it was an easy harbor for sailing
vessels to enter and take shelter. They could easily beat into
it in almost any wind, while at New York in spite of the many
great advantages there was some difficulty in beating in and
the water on the bar, except at very high tides, was rather
shoal for deep draft men-of-war to cross. This shoalness,
however, proved afterwards to be a protection to New York,
for it prevented the large French war-ships from entering to
attack the town.[2]

The next strategic point was Chesapeake Bay, with strong
positions in Virginia and Maryland, as at Annapolis, Alexandria, and Norfolk. The line might be extended northward
along the Susquehanna River, which would separate the middle
from the southern colonies. But this position was never seriously attempted except at Norfolk, because it required a larger
force than England could spare. The important part of it was
at Norfolk, from which as a base great devastation could be
wrought in Virginia, at that time the richest and most populous province and as much a source of patriot ideas and energy
as Massachusetts. Clinton during the last three years of the
war accomplished some of his most effective work from Norfolk, and seriously reduced Virginia's value to the patriot
cause.

As for the Carolinas and Georgia, they offered a comparatively easy conquest because of their sparse and scattered population with a large proportion of loyalists. The natural way
to take them was by occupying their three seaports, Wilmington in North Carolina, Charleston in South Carolina, and
Savannah in Georgia. This could be easily done, and was done
towards the close of the war with a rather small force, which,

[2] "A Short History of Last Session of Parliament," pp. 18, 19,
London, 1780; *Pennsylvania Magazine of History*, vol. 22, p. 151.

with the English having control of the ocean, was readily sent in ships, while the northern patriots in order to help their southern brothers had to send reinforcements by the long expensive and wasteful land route through Virginia.[3]

To hold the main strategic centre at New York and up the Hudson, and occupy the Carolinas and Georgia, with a side post at Newport in Rhode Island, and a raiding base at Norfolk in Virginia, was believed to be about all the British land forces could accomplish; and the navy was expected to complete the work of subjugation. The patriot colonists had considerable confidence in their ability to deal with the British land forces; but they were in despair about the navy; and it is probable that none of them had in their hearts much hope of maintaining themselves unless France or Spain protected them by sea. The Revolution in the end turned out to be altogether a question of sea power, and it would be difficult to find a better instance of the importance of that sort of power, especially to a nation that seeks its profit by controlling subject peoples.

The British navy, the glorious British navy, the hearts of oak, was supposed to furnish the most convincing argument for loyalism. Loyalists would admit the validity of all the patriot arguments and then with calm assurance waive them aside by saying, "But how can you withstand the navy; what will your boasted independence amount to before the wooden walls of England, which now protect your commerce and will utterly destroy you in your disobedience and rebellion?"[4]

For the last hundred years the people of England had been

---

[3] There is a curious article by a German officer on the way to conquer the United States in modern times by holding the principal Atlantic seaport towns. See *Literary Digest*, vol. 30, p. 635.

[4] "The idea of aiming at independence at present affords the most frightful of all prospects, while the mother country has such power on the ocean." (*American Archives*, fourth series, vol. ii, p. 872; Durand, "New Materials for History of American Revolution," pp. iii, 6, 46, 47, 54.)

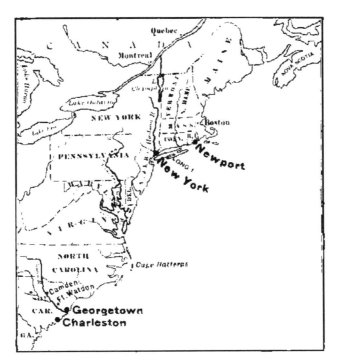

MAP SHOWING THE GENERAL STRATEGY OF THE WAR

in the habit of congratulating themselves that their American settlements, though far away and scattered along twelve hundred miles of coast, had nevertheless in nearly all instances followed the lines of water communication and remained nearer to the mouths than to the sources of rivers. The colonists had settled and remained upon the navigable rivers, natural harbors, bays and sounds which are so numerous and convenient on the Atlantic coast. The Kennebec in Maine, the Merrimac in New Hampshire, the harbor and bays of Massachusetts, the Connecticut, the Hudson, the Delaware, Chesapeake Bay and its tributary rivers, and the tributary rivers of the sounds of the Carolinas and Georgia, were at first the reason and means of settlement and afterwards the support and fountain of existence of all the American colonies. Canada was merely the settlements on the St. Lawrence. New York was merely the people living along the Hudson and Mohawk Rivers, and the vast areas of the province away from the shores of those rivers were unpeopled save by Indians. Most of the Pennsylvanians lived along the Delaware; and nearly every Virginia plantation could be reached from the tributaries of Chesapeake Bay.

The ease with which nearly all the people and property of the colonies could be brought under the guns of men-of-war, or reached by their cutters and small boats, had already been exemplified in the destruction of Portland and Norfolk and the shelling of Bristol. Many families living on navigable waters had alreay moved inland to escape the frightful devastation and slaughter which they thought was sure to come; and it certainly seemed as if America, without a navy of her own, was wide open to attack by such a great maritime power as England.[5]

--- ---- --

[5] Joshua Gee, "Trade and Navigation of Great Britain," sixth edition, p. 71; Gordon, "American Revolution," edition 1788, vol. i, pp. 431, 432; vol. ii, p. 20; Journal of Congress, vol. i, p. 56; American Archives, fourth series, vol. ii, pp. 872, 873; vol. iii, p. 3; "Life of Colonel Hanger," p. 187; Eddis, "Letters from America," pp. 194, 241, 242, 248, 257, 362, 420.

But the expected seldom happens. The sea-power problem
was worked out not quite in the way that was foretold. The
dread of universal devastation proved to be largely a mere
scare, encouraged very likely by the bluster of the captains and
sailors who had long been stationed on the coast and posed as
the typical and terrible British sea-dogs. In the early part of
the war the ministry abstained from devastation in the hope of
encouraging the patriot party to compromise before France
could interfere; and except for the destruction of Portland
and Norfolk, already described, the British navy during the
Revolution was in some respects a very harmless collection of
men, guns, and ships. No where did it keep up a really effective blockade. De Grasse repulsed Graves at the Chesapeake.
In the West Indies the British were inferior to the French
fleets until Rodney took command at the close of the war. Except for his famous victory over De Grasse the British navy
did very little more than convoy transports or the mere privateersman's work of seizing defenceless merchant vessels. It
could be aroused to action at times by extreme hunger for fresh
provisions and under this incentive Bristol was shelled and
some notable raids committed for mutton and beef on the coast
of New England. It fought no great naval battles and won no
victories until Rodney chanced on his in the West Indies in
1782.*

This inefficiency was partly caused by the bad administration of Lord Sandwich, who was at the head of the navy,
and whose profligate character and partisan methods of political
jobbery and corruption demoralized the service. Very inferior officers were sent to the American coast; ships were
badly equipped; and the method of handling fleets in battle
was obsolete and a great hindrance to success. It was fortunate that our Revolution took place during a period of de-

---

*The scurvy was no doubt a somewhat serious matter for the
British war-ships unless they could make raids for fresh provisions.
American Archives, fourth series, vol. v, p. 1330.

pression in the British navy and of improvement in the navy of France.[7]

Our naval attacks on Great Britain were confined almost exclusively to privateering on her commerce. Our small navy created by the Congress was also of some value for this privateering work, but unable as a rule to meet the British war-vessels, which retained complete control of the ocean so far as to make it perfectly safe for England to send troops to America and up and down our coast between New York and the Carolinas. This was England's strong point in the contest. So long as she had unobstructed ocean transportation for troops and their supplies she had a good chance to conquer America. But it was also her weak point; for if the Americans could persuade the two great naval powers, France and Spain, to combine their fleets so as to cut off England's access to our coast, our people could be as independent as they pleased.

Receiving less assistance from their navy than was expected, and prevented by complications between Howe and Burgoyne from taking possession of the Hudson River valley, and Lake Champlain, the British Ministry were much disappointed in the outcome of their general plans. They held the town of New York all through the war as the English headquarters in America. They held Newport for several years; they held Philadelphia for nine months; and met with their greatest success in the South, where they conquered Georgia and South Carolina, and devastated Virginia.

Independently of these strategic positions and theories, the important thing for them was to defeat the American armies in battle, compel them to surrender or scatter and demoralize them, so that they could not be reorganized. The occupation of cities and important points, so effective on the continent of Europe, would have little effect upon Americans so long as they could keep an army in the field; and their army must not be merely out-generaled in two or three battles, but practically annihilated before they would acknowledge the fall of

---

[7] English Dictionary Nat. Biog., vol. 38, pp. 256, 257; vol. 39, p. 83.

the patriot cause. "It is a matter worthy of observation," said General Knox, "that in most countries which have been invaded one or two battles have decided their fate; but America rises after a defeat." [8]

During the first three years of the war General Howe defeated our army under Washington in the only two pitched battles fought, Long Island and Brandywine; but no surrender was forced, and there was no relentless or effective pursuit. Washington, being undisturbed after each battle, was always able to reorganize his defeated army and again take the field.

Besides holding strategic positions and defeating the enemy's army, the third most effective means of warfare is to devastate the country, destroy the food supplies, burn towns and farm-houses, imprison the non-combatant men and the women and children, if they are of the white race, and if they are dark-skinned put large numbers of them to the sword. If during the first three years of the war General Howe had conducted a systematic devastation of the country, backed by devastation by the British fleet, it might have broken up the patriot party and their army. But he refrained from anything of the sort, and it was at first the intention of the Ministry that he should refrain. They intended to begin by conducting a very mild war, to send out to America an olive branch, along with the sword; so that the injury done to the country during Howe's command was merely the ordinary damage and pillage incident to the presence of a hostile army. After the French alliance, when General Clinton took command, the olive branch was withdrawn. But Clinton's force was so small that he could not make the devastation as effective as he wished.

As the Americans were acting on the defensive their strategy largely depended on what the British attempted to do. Our numbers were small. For particular occasions we could sometimes raise a good sized army, as, for example, the 14,000 effectives for the battle of Long Island, the 11,000 for Brandy-

---

[8] Drake, "Life of General Knox," p. 53.

wine, and the 11,000 at Saratoga. But these numbers were largely militia, who could be held together only for the particular occasion and then quickly disappeared. The number that could be steadily maintained in our main army under Washington, was, according to his own statement, hardly 5000.[*]

Our general policy was to follow the British attack from place to place, with such numbers as could be raised. Our main reliance all through the war was to prevent the British from securing control of the line of the Hudson Valley. This was the great contention and controlling motive, and almost every military move in the Revolution, except those in the South, was connected with the control of the Hudson.

In the great line of water communication up the Hudson and through Lake Champlain, there were two strategic points which completely commanded the navigation. The northern one was Ticonderoga, at the southern end of Lake Champlain, where, as already described, the water was narrow and two points jutting out from both sides could be fortified so as to command a long stretch of water in every direction and at the same time be easily protected from the land side. This was the northern gateway of the great strategic line; and the patriots tried to fortify it as strongly as possible, and reinforced it by outlying forts at Crown Point, Chamblee and St. Johns, commanding the approaches from Canada.

The southern gateway was at West Point, forty miles above the town of New York, where there was a similar conformation of two points, which, owing to the mountainous character of the shores of the Hudson, could be made almost impregnable. As Ticonderoga was strengthened by outlying forts so West Point was intended to be strengthened by forts lower down the river, like Montgomery and Stony Point, commanding the approaches from the town of New York.

The patriots were never able to drive the British from the town of New York; or from Charleston, in South Carolina;

---

[*] Writings of Washington, Ford edition, vol. 7, p. 242.

nor could they prevent the British from occupying Canada as a stronghold. But so long as the patriots could hold Ticonderoga and West Point, they felt that the holding of New York and Canada was in one sense useless to the British. The town of New York was valuable largely as a basis from which to take West Point; and Canada was valuable as a basis from which to take Ticonderoga. But with West Point and Ticonderoga untaken, the middle section of the Hudson Valley was in the control of the patriots; the colonies could not be cut in half; and might remain unconquered for an undefinite period.

We have already seen how the patriots in the very beginning saw the importance of Ticonderoga and captured it at the first opportunity; and although it might have been better fortified and protected, yet they managed to hold it all through the war, except for a few weeks during Burgoyne's invasion from Canada in the autumn of 1777. In the same way they saw the importance of West Point. General Schuyler, who was familiar with the whole Hudson Valley, was very anxious for the rapid fortification of the Hudson Highlands, as the region about West Point was called. He urged the importance of it on the Congress in May, 1775, about the same time that Ticonderoga was taken. He feared that the British would see the opportunity and by quickly sending a large force to seize West Point and by establishing a line of vessels to keep up the communication with New York, ruin the patriot cause.[19]

A really enterprising enemy might have made a rush in force for West Point. But the British let the opportunity pass, and the patriots, though moving too slowly to suit Schuyler, began at last to protect this vital spot in the most elaborate manner. West Point and every approach to it soon bristled with fortifications, constructed at enormous expense by the Congress. A great chain, the remains of which are still shown at the Military Academy, was stretched across the river to stop ships. All these constructions were under the direction of two French officers, Du Portail and De Gouvion, supple-

---

[19] *American Archives*, fourth series, vol. iii, pp. 1065, 1108.

mented afterwards by the more practical and effective work of American engineering. It was this position which Arnold intended to surrender to the British so as to end the war at one stroke, retain the colonies for the British empire and prevent their falling into the hands of France.[11]

Galloway, the loyalist, used to complain that the military mistakes of the British in the early part of the Revolution were childish, that their errors could have been corrected by school boys;[12] and it seemed quite extraordinary to many people, when the English had an army of over 30,000 men at New York in 1776, assisted by a large fleet of war-vessels, that they did not mass it on West Point's uncompleted defences and secure a permanent foothold there with an impregnable line of communication over the short water distance to New York harbor.

In the last years of our Revolution, when the British held South Carolina, Georgia and the town of New York, and had no hope of securing the line of the Hudson Valley, they changed their methods, and adopted a plan of conquest which disregarded the strategical position on the Hudson and sought to wear out the patriots by conducting heavy devastating raids at every point that could be reached by sailing vessels from their position in New York. As their vessels could move to almost any point of the coast without interference from a patriot navy these raids were very severe, and finally were on the eve of wearing out the patriot party and compelling the collapse of their cause in spite of their holding the strategical position on the Hudson. This was the most serious period for the patriots and a time of high hope in England; for even with the assistance of France and Spain the American cause seemed lost.

It has accordingly been suggested that perhaps the

---

[11] *American Archives*, fourth series, vol. iii, pp. 735, 1912; vol. vi, pp. 672, 792, and title " Highlands " in index of volumes of *American Archives;* Boynton, " West Point "; Heath, Memoirs, pp. 207, 243.

[12] " Diary and Letters of Thomas Hutchinson," vol. ii, p. 371.

strategical value of West Point and the Hudson Valley was exaggerated. Du Portail, the French engineer, who served with much credit through the war, thought it a mere "cabinet idea" and not of as much practical value as was supposed. But the weight of the contemporary opinion of the time was overwhelmingly the other way; and no one believed in the importance of West Point more thoroughly than Washington. From the summer of 1778 to the summer of 1781 he fought no battle, sought no advantage or distinction in the field; but devoted his whole energy during that gloomy period to holding fast to West Point. He often said that its loss would be fatal, that the cause would never survive the cutting of the communication between New England and the middle states; and the day when he saw how nearly Arnold had turned it over to the British was probably the darkest hour of his life.[18]

[18] Jones, "New York in the Revolution," vol. i, p. 209; *American Archives*, fifth series, vol. iii, pp. 332, 1468; Writings of Washington, Ford edition, vol. v, p. 492; vol. vii, pp. 45, 212; vol. viii, p. 95; G. W. Greene, "Life of General Greene," vol. i, p. 369; Lee, Memoirs, vol. i, p. 11 note; Mahan, "Influence of Sea Power," p. 342.

XLIII.

WHILE the Congress was debating in June the question of announcing independence, several divisions of the great British army of invasion were on the ocean making their way towards New York.

General Howe left Halifax, and on the 25th of June, a week before the final vote on independence, he arrived in the "Greyhound" off Staten Island, opposite New York, followed four days later by one hundred and thirty sail of transports with his Halifax troops, which immediately took possession of Staten Island.

At Sandy Hook he had found Governor Tryon living on a British war-ship, where he had been ever since the patriots expelled him from New York. With the assistance of loyalists and his former officers, he was trying to keep up a continuance of gubernatorial dignity upon the water until the British army should restore him to authority upon the land.[1]

On the 12th of July Admiral Howe reached the coast with war-vessels and transports deep laden with troops and supplies. From the high ground of the Narrows below New York and from Red Hook, the anxious eyes of patriots and loyalists were every day scanning the horizon for new arrivals of this great English Armada that was to establish Anglo-Saxon toryism in America. All through July ships were arriving, twenty or thirty at a time. On the 30th of July Clinton came up from the south with the troops he had used in his fruitless attack on Charleston. On the 12th of August two fleets of transports convoyed by Commodore Hotham, brought a large number of troops, including some 8,000 Hessians, the first of the 12,000

---

[1] *American Archives*, fifth series, vol. i, p. 122; vol. ii, pp. 493, 494.

of these troops which had been hired for service in America.
On the 14th of August, Sir Peter Parker, who had assisted
Clinton at Charleston, arrived with twenty-five sail, bringing
Lord William Campbell, who had been governor of South Caro-
lina, and also Lord Dunmore, with about one hundred of the
sickly black and white troops which he had had on the coast of
Virginia.[2]

Thus every available force was collected, and this great
armament now concentrated on New York had for the last
six months been the talk and wonder of everyone in England.
It was the largest army that up to that time had ever been sent
out of England, far larger than any army Spain had sent to
conquer South America; and was within two thousand of
equalling the army which Wellington had at Waterloo in 1815.
The credit of preparing and sending it appears to have been
due to the activity and persistence of that much-abused member of the Ministry and secretary for the colonies, Lord
George Germain.[3]

The size of the army has been variously stated; but according to the best sources of information, without counting the
sailors and marines in the fleet, General Howe had there before
New York, 34,614 men in good health and perfectly armed
and disciplined. The fleet included fifty-two large war-vessels,
twenty-seven armed sloops and cutters, and four hundred
transports. This vast fleet of nearly five hundred sail must

---

[2] *American Archives*, fifth series, vol. i, pp. 105, 193, 949, 963, 1064,
1077, 1109; W. B. Reed, "Life of Joseph Reed," vol. i, p. 213; vol. iii,
p. 1029; Writings of Washington, vol. iv, p. 325, 326 and note; G. W.
Greene, "Life of Gen. Greene," vol. i, pp. 195, 196, 198, 199, 200, 202;
Gordon, "American Revolution," edition 1788, vol. ii, pp. 301, 304, 305,
1073. The last of the Hessian contingent with 1000 Waldeckers, some
English troops and 2000 baggage animals in 72 transports, did not
arrive in New York until October 15. (Gordon, "American Revolution,"
edition 1788, vol. ii, p. 337.)

[3] "Diary and Letters of Thomas Hutchinson," vol. i, pp. 497, 505, 514;
vol. ii, pp. 11, 16, 40, 41; *American Archives*, fourth series, vol. vi, p.
766; "Reflections on the Present State of the American War," London,
1776, p. 7.

have been an interesting and beautiful sight as it lay off Staten Island disembarking the troops in their scarlet uniforms.[4]

The plan of the Ministry had been to send a force of such overwhelming size that peace would be compelled at the mere sight of it. There would be no necessity for devastation and destruction; and in any event, one or two battles would be enough when accompanied by the very conciliatory proposals, pardon for all who would lay down their arms, and the fullest assurances of the mildest and most liberal sort of colonial government in the future. The olive branch was to be extended to the erring colonists and to make it seem more effective it was twined round a most stupendous sword.

A London pamphlet [5] of the time ridicules the olive branch and all thought of compromise and recommends what, with England's accumulated experience, would undoubtedly now be her policy, namely, to use Howe's great army in the most merciless and destructive manner until every trace of independence or rebellion was blotted out. But Howe would not have used his army in that way, even if he had been ordered to do so. He did not consider it large enough even for the very mild and moderate plan of warfare he adopted. He was continually calling for reinforcements and in his "Narrative" he complains that they were not sent. During the three years of his command in America they sent him, according to Galloway, over 50,000 men, and Lord North told Parliament that it was over 60,000, with which to destroy a ragged patriot

---

[4] Beaston, " Naval and Military Memoirs of Great Britain," vol. vi, pp. 44, 53; Collier, " Naval Chronicle," vol. xxxii, p. 269. The number 34,614 agrees with the statement of a spy, who reported the British force as over 35,000, and also with Howe's letter to his wife, in which he says his army is 35,000. Force, fifth series, vol. i, pp. 1110, 1531, 1532, Jones, " New York in the Revolution," vol. i, p. 602; *American Archives*, fourth series, vol. iv, p. 1127; fifth series, vol. i, p. 27; vol. ii, p. 1318; " Diary and Letters of Thomas Hutchinson, vol. ii, pp. 70, 71, 98.

[5] " Reflections on the Present State of the American War," London, 1776.

army that only once reached 14,000 effectives and usually varied between 4000 and 10,000.[6]

General William Howe, who, for the next two years, had in his hands more power in the great controversy than any other person, was a Whig member of Parliament, and had served in the House of Commons for some fifteen years, representing the town of Nottingham. His father had been Viscount Howe, of the Irish peerage. On the other side he was the first cousin once removed of the King; for his mother was the illegitimate daughter of George I, by his mistress, the Hanoverian Baroness Kilmansegge.

His elder living brother, Lord Richard Howe, was an admiral in the British navy, and commanded the fleet which now lay off Staten Island. There had been a still older brother, George Howe, who had served as an officer in the colonies during the war with France, and was killed at Ticonderoga in 1758. This brother had been one of the few British officers whom the colonists had really liked. The Massachusetts Assembly had erected a monument to him in Westminster Abbey. Wolfe and Bouquet they had admired, but they were particularly fond of George Howe, because he understood them and adopted their mode of life. He dismissed his retinue, equipage, and display of wines and high living, ate the colonists' plain fare, and drank their home brew, their punch, and their whiskey. He carried provisions on his back, went scouting with rangers, and slept on a bearskin and a blanket.[7]

His brother, General William Howe, now in command of the army of invasion, had none of this personal attractiveness. He had served in the colonies in the French War, and knew the people, but they never showed any particular regard or liking for him. He was, however, always popular with his soldiers and subordinate officers. Although continually indulging himself in his passion for gambling, wherever he was,

[6] Cobbett, Parliamentary History, vol. 29, p. 766.
[7] Mrs. Grant's "Memoirs of an American Lady," Munsell edition, 1876, p. 223.

GENERAL HOWE

whether in England or America, he was strong and shrewd enough not to allow himself to be ruined by it, as Charles Fox and so many others were at that time; and he was generally believed to have increased rather than diminished his fortune by the American war.

In the introduction to his "Orderly Book," which has been published, it is said that he and others of his family were sullen, hard, and cruel. But this charge cannot be sustained. The only evidence that might sustain it is that his commissaries allowed American prisoners to be starved and very severely treated. But other commanders, and the British Government itself, allowed this sort of treatment. Galloway, who was by no means his friend, admits that he was a liberal man and not corrupt in money matters, except that he allowed illegitimate opportunities to his subordinates. He was, like the admiral and the rest of the family, quite easy-going and generous. His most conspicuous characteristics were great personal courage, and a certain contemptuous indifference, which enabled him to bear himself with great dignity and defend himself with great adroitness in the storm of criticism which came upon him for his conduct of the war. He is described as a large man, of dark complexion like all his family, with heavy features, and very defective teeth.[8]

His brother, the admiral, was so swarthy that the sailors called him Black Dick. He was, apparently, fond of business and details, never gambled or dissipated, and his face in his portraits is rather refined and scholarly. He, too, was of an extremely liberal and generous disposition. Although he commanded a fleet to put down the American rebellion, he is known in the Revolution chiefly for his peace negotiations.

That General Howe should take command if there was any serious war in America was inevitable. He was of suitable age and had at that time seen more successful service in actual warfare than any other officer of high rank in England, except

[8] Galloway, " A Reply to the Observations of General Howe," p. 111; " Diary and Letters of Thomas Hutchinson," vol. ii, p. 336.

possibly Amherst, the conqueror of Canada, who was growing old and does not seem to have been seriously thought of for the American command. Howe had been a great deal in America and had a most brilliant record of service. He had served as a lieutenant in the regiment of Wolfe, who had spoken highly of him. At the siege of Louisburg he had commanded a regiment. At the attack on Quebec he was again with Wolfe and led in person the forlorn hope up the intrenched path. In the expedition against Montreal the next year he commanded a brigade. He had another large command at the siege of Belle Isle, on the coast of Brittany, and was adjutant-general of the army at the conquest of Havana. For these services at the close of those wars he had been given the honorary position of governor of the Isle of Wight, and he was now a major-general, with a high reputation for efficiency and general knowledge of his profession. He had recently added to British army methods the improvement of light-equipped companies selected from the line regiments and drilled in quick movements.*

He did not at once attack and take New York, as he might possibly have done while the patriot forces were weak and unprepared. He remained quietly on Staten Island for nearly two months waiting for the last of the reinforcements, and hoping, no doubt, that his forbearance and the olive branch proposals which had been sent ashore would have their effect and bring about some sort of peace or compromise.

The Prohibitory Act passed by Parliament in the previous December had mentioned peace commissioners who should be empowered to exempt from the terrors of war and the operation of the Prohibitory Act any colony, district, or even a county or town, which should return to loyalty and obedience. There had been a great deal of discussion in America about

---

* The best biography of Howe is in the " English National Cyclopædia of Biography." His own narrative reveals a great deal; and there is, of course, much to be learned in the accounts and criticisms of his campaigns by Galloway, Van Schaack, Jones, and others.

these commissioners, and many conservative and hesitating patriots had been hopeful that England intended to send out a great peace commission which would hold formal sessions, make a treaty with the Congress, and give a material body and definite proportions to that phantom of many meanings, called reconciliation. But, as John Adams shrewdly suspected, these wonderful commissioners proved to be in the end no more than the regular military and naval commanders, and their powers for peace, when stripped of the cumbersome phrases in which they were concealed, were nothing more than the ordinary power to grant pardons for laying down arms.[10]

Immediately after his arrival, Admiral Howe prepared letters to the governors of all the colonies, accompanied by copies of a proclamation announcing that he and General Howe had been appointed commissioners under the Prohibitory Act, and were ready to issue pardons to the people of any town, county, or colony, who should return to British allegiance.

The British governors having been expelled from all the colonies there were no officials but patriot governors as in Connecticut and Rhode Island, or chairmen of revolutionary conventions or committees, to whom these letters could be delivered. The admiral appears to have been aware of this; but nevertheless expected that his proclamation would be widely circulated through the country.

The packet containing the letters for the colonies south of New York was sent ashore at Amboy, New Jersey, and fell into the hands of General Mercer, who sent it to General Washington, and by him it was sent to the Congress. The packet for the New England colonies was sent by the "Merlin" sloop-of-war, to Newport, Rhode Island. One of her officers landed under a flag and seems to have delivered the packet in person to the patriot governor of the state, who sent back a polite note, saying that he had received the letter and procla-

---

[10] *American Archives*, fourth series, vol. v, pp. 931, 942, 943, 1009.

mation and laid them before the assembly, and that the assembly had ordered them sent to the Congress at Philadelphia.[11]

The loyalists had great expectations from these documents; and doubtless many moderate patriots, who saw the stupendous force assembled with so much pomp and display of power, had hopes that some honorable compromise might be arranged before the impending blow was struck. It was a critical time; and there must have been many a violent or bitter discussion between patriot and loyalist of which no record has reached us.

The documents, however, were a mere repetition of the Prohibitory Act, which was already an old story. The Congress thought that they showed so clearly the warlike and merciless intentions of Great Britain that they ordered them to be published in the newspapers, so that all classes of patriots could see for themselves the futility of any discussion about reconciliation.

But the Admiral evidently intended to effect a settlement outside of the Prohibitory Act and his formal powers of pardon. He immediately began to send out hints that he had other powers in reserve and that if the Americans were willing, he could bring about a compromise. He sent a familiar and very friendly note to Franklin, accompanied by books, letters and parcels which Franklin's friends in England had taken the opportunity of sending out by the admiral, who, to show his general friendly feeling, sent all these packages ashore without the usual military precaution of examining their contents.

The Congress allowed Franklin to reply to the admiral, and Franklin wrote one of his masterful letters, full of excellent feeling, quaint and telling humor and keen satire on Britain's "lust of dominion," which is as applicable to-day at it was in 1776. The letter became very famous, especially the sentence: "Long did I endeavor with unfeigned and unwearied zeal to

---

[11] *American Archives*, fifth series, vol. i, pp. 605, 608, 895, 896.

preserve from breaking that fine and noble porcelain vase—the British empire.'' [12]

On the 17th of July, Admiral Howe addressed a letter to ''George Washington, Esq.,'' and sent it ashore under a flag. When the flag was seen approaching Washington suspected that the letter would be addressed very much as it was, because there had, it seems, been considerable public discussion on this subject, and he consulted with some of his officers as to how such a letter should be received. They were unanimous in their opinion; and General Reed, who was sent to meet the flag, refused to receive the letter. The British officer who brought it expressed great regret, said that the letter was civil rather than military, and that Admiral Howe had been given large powers for negotiation.

Soon afterwards General Howe, having received a letter from General Washington about some transactions in Canada, addressed his reply to ''George Washington, Esq., &c., &c., &c.'' This also was refused; and then General Howe sent one of his officers of high rank, General Patterson, to remonstrate and discuss some questions relative to the treatment and exchange of prisoners. General Patterson took with him the last letter, but did not show it until he got into Washington's presence. Washington received him with great formality and distinction. They had a pleasant but meaningless conversation on general topics of the war and the treatment of prisoners, the British general meanwhile making the most diplomatic efforts to induce Washington to accept the letter; and finally laying it on the table in the hope that Washington would pick it up. [13]

It was a small matter on which to waste so much time; but no doubt the Howes had been instructed by the Ministry

---

[12] See the Admiral's reply to this letter, *American Archives*, fifth series, vol. i, p. 979.

[13] *American Archives*, fifth series, vol. i, pp. 329, 330, 352, 353, 471, 472, 500, 502, 789; vol. iii, pp. 1000, 1001; Writings of Washington, Ford edition, vol. iv, pp. 249, 258, 263, 264, 284–286.

to press as far as possible the point of not recognizing rebel titles. After Patterson's failure the attempt was entirely abandoned. The admiral expressed great regret that he had not arrived before the Declaration of Independence, which had, he said, made his mission of peace more difficult. But he continued his efforts in furtherance of that mission.

The reinforcements had pretty much all arrived by the 12th of August, and it seemed as if he could not delay much longer the taking of New York; but nevertheless, he sent Lord Drummond ashore under a flag on the 17th of August to wait upon Washington with some documents and letters which had passed between Drummond and the admiral. One of these documents was a sketch of propositions for a compromise, in which the colonies of their own free will were to vote supplies for the general welfare of the empire, in return for which "a formal relinquishment shall be made, on the part of Great Britain, of all future claim to taxation over these her colonies." [14]

This was apparently in accordance with instructions the admiral had received to carry out the resolution of Parliament of the 20th of February, 1775, which promised to relieve any colony from parliamentary taxation, except duties for the regulation of commerce, so long as the colony should voluntarily contribute a fund for the common defence of the empire and its own civil government. Lord Drummond's proposition was rather broader than the resolution of Parliament; and this broadening was probably intended to feel the way and see if the Americans were in any humor at all for compromise.

The patriot party had the year before rejected the resolution of Parliament of the 20th of February, 1775, and they were not now deceived by Drummond's broader way of stating it. They questioned the sincerity of his mission and rejected his offer. Was it a mere military stratagem to gain time, or a

---

[14] *American Archives*, fifth series, vol. i, pp. 226, 227, 1135, 1158, 1159, 1179; Writings of Washington, Ford edition, vol. iv, p. 350; vol. v, p. 464 note, 465 note.

device to shake the patriots loose from their devotion to absolute independence, lead them into negotiation and compromise, which would give England a foothold in the country to be afterward improved as opportunity should offer?

"I am exceedingly at a loss," wrote Washington to the Congress, "to know the motives and causes inducing a proceeding of such a nature at this time, and why Lord Howe has not attempted some plan of negotiation before, as he seems so desirous of it. If I may be allowed to conjecture and guess at the cause, it may be that part of the Hessians have not arrived as mentioned in the examination transmitted yesterday; or, that General Burgoyne has not made such progress as was expected to form a junction of their two armies; or (what I think equally probable), they mean to procrastinate their operations for some time, trusting that the Militia who have come to our succour will soon become tired and return home, as is but too usual with them." (*American Archives*, fifth series, vol. i, p. 1026.)

Thus the Drummond mission came to naught; and there was nothing left for the Howe brothers to do but take New York and see what effect that would have in bringing about a satisfactory compromise.

XLIV.

THE BATTLE OF LONG ISLAND

THE town of New York at that time extended from the Battery only to Chatham Street, and the point of land on which it stood was much narrower than at present. Breastworks and redoubts, planned by General Charles Lee and a couple of committees, had been thrown up along the shores of both rivers and cannon planted in them. Two of the lighter British war-ships, the "Phœnix" and the "Rose," sailed by these defences, without receiving any serious damage from a heavy cannonade, and after proceeding as far up as Tarrytown returned with equal safety.

But the Howes had no intention of testing these batteries by attempting to shell New York. It was full of loyalist property; it was part of the empire; why should Englishmen destroy an English town which they intended to make the headquarters of their army in America.[1]

The patriot military forces when General Howe first arrived were only about nine thousand, of whom two thousand were destitute of arms, and the weapons of half the others were in such bad condition that they were scarcely fit to use. What chance was there that such a ragged half-armed force could maintain the newly declared independence or offer the slightest resistance to the superb armament from England? It was a most dispiriting and hopeless condition. "Had I known the true position of affairs," wrote Colonel Reed,[2] "no considera-

---

[1] *American Archives*, fifth series, vol. i, pp. 223, 230, 231, 255, 356, 509, 751, 762, 766, 1029, 1066, 1120, 1143; vol. ii, p. 237; G. W. Greene, " Life of General Greene," vol. i, p. 181; Flick, " Loyalism in New York," pp. 107, 118; Gordon, " American Revolution," edition 1788, vol. ii, p. 304.

[2] *American Archives*, fourth series, vol. vi, p. 1124; Gordon, " American Revolution," edition 1788, vol. ii, pp. 277, 278; Niles, " Principles and Acts of the Revolution," edition 1876, pp. 191, 192.

tion would have tempted me to have taken an active part in this scene; and this sentiment is universal.''

There must have been high confidence and spirit in the patriot party to have rejected without question the admiral's proposals of compromise, which he very naturally supposed would be most acceptable to people in their condition. Washington and his officers never faltered and the Congress never hesitated although as individuals they were evidently very uneasy. They made most earnest efforts and appeals in all the neighboring colonies and as far to the south as Delaware and Maryland to collect every man and every old musket and shot-gun that would resist this attack on New York. It would be the decisive and final campaign of the war; neither side, it was said, could endure a defeat at this vital point; and if our people should be able to stop the British at New York as they had stopped them at Charleston, it surely would be a wonderful victory that would in all probability bring immediate foreign recognition of independence.

During July and August, while General Howe waited for the last of his reinforcements, the strenuous efforts of the patriots to obtain some on their side began to meet with success. Hundreds of pounds of lead were stripped from the windows of the old Dutch houses in New York and molded into bullets. The gilt statue of the king, erected on the Bowling Green after the repeal of the Stamp Act, had been dragged down as soon as independence was proclaimed, and the head cut off. The body now furnished eight hundred pounds of lead, "melted majesty," it was said, to be fired at the king's troops. Enthusiasm and rumors raised the numbers of the patriot troops to 50,000. It had seemed to them as if before long they must surely have that number, and many expected more. These exaggerations were valuable and were no doubt encouraged by the officers to increase confidence and enlistments.[3]

---

[3] "Life of Joseph Reed," vol. i, p. 212; *American Archives*, fifth series, vol. i, pp. 369, 370. The gilt head of the king, said to be a good likeness, was taken to Fort Washington, north of New York, to be

But by the actual returns made by Washington, his forces, all told, were only 20,275. Of these the sick were so numerous that those fit for duty were only about fourteen thousand. The large sick-list was apparently the result of shocking unsanitary conditions, which for long afterwards were characteristic of the patriot camps; and in winter they were always afflicted with the small-pox. Besides disease, which was so prevalent among them, they were a most undisciplined, disorderly rabble, marauding on the inhabitants and committing all kinds of irregularities. Except a few troops, like Smallwood's Marylanders, they were for the most part merely a collection of squads of farmers and militia bringing with them the guns they had had in their houses.[4]

It was no longer exclusively a New England army. It contained numerous troops from the middle and southern colonies, and its size may be said to have indicated the high-water mark of patriotism, under the influence of the Declaration of Independence, and the belief that a great victory had been gained some months before by compelling Howe to evacuate Boston. It was the largest number of patriots that were collected in one army during the whole war. To handle such a disorganized mob so as to offer any respectable resistance to Howe's disciplined troops was a task requiring qualities of mind and character which few men besides Washington

---

erected on a pole, and when the fort was taken it fell into the hands of the British engineer, Montressor, who gave it to Lord Townsend. (Bolton. "Private Soldier under Washington," p. 115; "Life of John Jay," p. 44: "Diary and Letters of Thomas Hutchinson," vol. ii, pp. 167, 168; *American Archives*, fifth series, vol. i, pp. 144, 228, 368, 443.)

[4] DeLancey's note to Jones' "New York in the Revolution," vol. iv. pp. 599–603; Irving, "Life of Washington," edition of 1861, vol. ii, chap. xxx, p. 283; Gordon, "American Revolution," edition 1788, vol. ii, p. 304; *American Archives*, fifth series, vol. i, p. 835. A committee of Congress which visted the army at New York somewhat later reported a total of 25,373, of which 16,905 were fit for duty. This total included 3,649 men taken from the Flying Camp in New Jersey. (*American Archives*, fifth series, vol. ii, p. 1385; Writings of Washington, Ford edition, vol. iv, p. 326 note.)

possessed. John Jay, General Charles Lee, and others believed that no attempt should be made to hold New York. The risk of an overwhelming defeat was too great; and the general patriot plan for that summer of 1776 should be to wear it away with as little loss as possible.

It was a delicate question to decide, and no doubt a great deal could be said in favor of making a present of New York to the British without a battle; allowing them to lock themselves up there, and reserving the patriot force to check their subsequent expeditions. But Washington seems to have been influenced by a principle of conduct on which he frequently acted. He must make some sort of resistance to Howe's entering New York if the patriot cause and its army were to retain any reputation. He also wished to delay Howe so that after settling in New York he could make but few expeditions into the country before winter.

Washington was obliged to use nearly half of his effective force in the fortifications and in guarding various points in the town. The most important place to defend seemed to be Brooklyn Heights, on the Long Island side of the East River directly opposite New York, and commanding it very much as Bunker Hill or Dorchester Heights commanded Boston. If Howe should land on Long Island and take Brooklyn Heights, he could cross the East River and enter New York. Fortifications of fallen trees and trenches on Brooklyn Heights had been suggested by General Lee, and constructed by General Greene. But a bad attack of malarial fever prevented Greene from continuing the command. He was superseded by Sullivan, who in his turn was superseded by Putnam.[5]

Putnam's eight thousand men at Brooklyn Heights were in some respects in a trap, for if Howe attacked them in front, their chance of escaping across the river was doubtful, and he could absolutely prevent it by sending the fleet into the river behind them. Military critics have commented on this risk,

---

[5] G. W. Greene, " Life of General Greene," vol. i, pp. 157, 158; *American Archives*, fifth series, vol. i, pp. 1231, 916.

and the only answer seems to be that, under all the circumstances, Washington thought himself justified in taking the chances rather than abandon New York without a blow.

General Howe proceeded to dispose of the patriots on Brooklyn Heights, and he showed the same thorough knowledge of the ground and of the enemy opposed to him which he afterwards displayed at Brandywine. He also showed his skill in winning easily so far as it suited his purpose to win. He had remained on Staten Island from his arrival on the 30th of June until the 22d of August, when he took across to Long Island about twenty thousand of his men, a force which was certainly ample for defeating the eight thousand Americans on Brooklyn Heights.

Between Brooklyn Heights and the place where Howe had landed on Long Island there was a wooded ridge, and a large part of the patriot force, leaving their breastworks at Brooklyn Heights, were sent out on this ridge by Putnam, to check the advance of Howe's army. Their right was commanded by William Alexander, of New Jersey,—or Lord Stirling, as he was called from a lapsed Scotch title which he had ineffectually claimed,—and their left was commanded by Sullivan, of New Hampshire; while Putnam, after making this disposition, remained in command of the troops which were left within the defences at Brooklyn. This movement in force to the ridge has been criticized as risking too much, because the army was not well organized or officered, and had not the sort of troops necessary for advanced positions.[*]

Several roads led directly from Howe's position to the ridge and to Brooklyn Heights. On the night of the 26th of August, he sent nearly half his force by these roads, under command of Generals Grant and De Heister, with orders to make a direct attack on the Heights. Grant, who had command of the left of these troops, was the same blustering Grant who had delivered the speech in Parliament on American vulgarity and cowardice; and De Heister was one of the Hessian officers.

---

[*] *American Historical Review*, vol. i, p. 650.

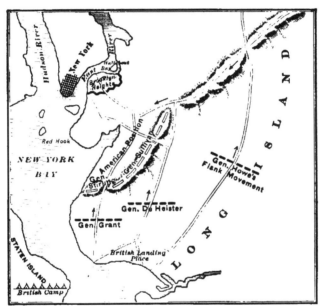

MAP OF THE BATTLE OF LONG ISLAND

HOWE'S FLANK MOVEMENT

The design of this front attack was to conceal the more important movement made by Howe himself, who, taking the rest of his force with Clinton and Cornwallis, went by another road far to the eastward to make a long détour and come upon the American flank and rear just as the battle was beginning with Grant and Heister. Sullivan afterwards said that he had suspected this flanking movement by Howe, but could not convince any one of the importance of guarding against it. He had paid horsemen $50 to patrol in that direction, but they proved of no avail, and this incident is evidence of the disorganized condition of the patriot army.[†]

The Hessians under De Heister began their attack soon after daybreak and had little difficulty in driving back the Americans in front of them. At the same time General Grant, commanding the British left, met with a more stubborn resistance from the Maryland and Delaware troops, which composed the American right. These attacks by Grant and De Heister were, however, mere feints to draw attention from Howe's flanking movement, which had now at daybreak completely circled the American left, and even penetrated to their rear. The timing of this movement, as was usual with Howe's manœuvres, was most exact and successful. Perfect secrecy was observed. The American patrols he met during the night march were all captured; and guided by a loyalist he struck the American flank and rear early in the morning just as the attack by De Heister and Grant began.

Some of the Americans of Sullivan's division, being caught by Howe's forces behind them, were driven to and fro between him and the Hessians and cut to pieces.

"The Hessians and our brave Highlanders gave no quarter; and it was a fine sight to see with what alacrity they dispatched the rebels with their bayonets after we had surrounded them so they could not resist. We took care to tell the Hessians that the rebels had resolved to give no quarter—to them in particular—which made them fight desper-

---

[†] Onderdonk, "Revolutionary Incidents of Long Island," pp. 140, 142; *American Archives*, fourth series, vol. iii, p. 9.

ately, and put to death all who came into their hands." (Onderdonk, "Revolutionary Incidents of Suffolk and Kings Counties," p. 138.)

Sullivan's division, which had Howe on its flank and rear, and the Hessians in front, after fighting for two hours were nearly all killed or taken prisoner; and Sullivan himself was captured while trying to escape through a cornfield. But as Howe's flanking column pressed on to crush the American right, which was attacked by Grant in front, a more obstinate resistance was encountered. The patriots in this part of the field were Lord Stirling's division, composed of Haslett's Delaware troops, Smallwood's Marylanders, Atlee's regiment and Kirkline's Pennsylvania riflemen.

This was the first appearance in the Revolution of these southern troops, some of whom afterwards became so famous for their gallantry, smart appearance, and discipline. Smallwood's regiment had been recruited from the best families in Maryland; and Haslet's Delawares were a similar body. Stirling had placed them on rising ground where they resisted Grant's attack for several hours and held their own even after Howe had begun to gain their rear.

"The Delawares and Marylanders," said Haslet, "stood firm to the last; and after a variety of skirmishing, the Delawares drew up on the side of a hill, and stood upwards of four hours with a firm, determined countenance, in close array, their colors flying, the enemy's artillery playing on them all the while, not daring to advance and attack them, though six times their number and nearly surrounding them." (Onderdonk, "Revolutionary Incidents of Suffolk and Kings Counties," p. 143.)

The British, as Lord Stirling and Smallwood explained, were unwilling to attack because they expected soon to take the Delawares and Marylanders by the movement behind them. Part of Smallwood's men made a spirited attack upon Cornwallis, and under cover of this the Delawares and the rest of Smallwood's command started to cut their way out. They reached Brooklyn Heights by severe fighting, wading, and swimming across a marsh and creek, but with heavy loss in killed and prisoners, and Lord Stirling was captured.

Washington, who was watching these troops cut their way

out, is said to have wrung his hands and exclaimed, "Good God, what brave fellows I must this day lose." One of the Maryland riflemen has left us a description of his experience, and he describes the bad markmanship of the British soldiers.

" The Major, Capt. Ramsay, and Lt. Plunket were foremost and within 100 yards of the enemy's muzzles, when they were fired on by the enemy, who were chiefly under cover of an orchard, save a few that showed themselves and pretended to give up; clubbing their firelocks till we came within forty yards, when they immediately presented, and blazed in our faces. They entirely over-shot us, and killed some men away behind in the rear. I had the satisfaction of dropping one the first fire. I was so near I could not miss. I discharged my rifle seven times that day." (Onderdonk, id., p. 148.)

Washington's estimate of his loss was a thousand in killed, wounded and prisoners. But General Howe's report of his success was totally inconsistent with this estimate, for he said he had taken prisoner over a thousand American privates besides ninety-one commissioned officers, and that, besides these, the Americans lost twenty-two hundred in killed, wounded and drowned, making their total loss over three thousand against Washington's estimate of one thousand. As to his own loss, Howe put it at less than four hundred killed, wounded and prisoners. But the almost universal testimony of the American officers supports Washington's estimate, and some of them put the British loss in killed and wounded higher than the American; or as one of them said: "We killed more of them than they did of us; but they took the most prisoners." [*]

Howe's report of the battle, carried to England by one of his staff officers, filled all London with joy. The great Armada was surely subduing the rebellion, and the Court and Ministry displayed their satisfaction with the utmost ostentation. General Howe was forthwith made a Knight Companion of the

* Memoirs of the Long Island Historical Society, vol. iii, p. 202; American Archives, fifth series, vol. ii, pp. 167, 445; " Life of G. Read," p. 328.

Bath, and instructions were sent out to Admiral Howe to perform at New York the ceremony of investing his brother with the insignia of his new rank. At the same time Lord Mansfield, who had made such strong legal arguments to uphold the supremacy of Parliament over all British colonies, was created an earl.[9]

Our people had a lucky escape back to Brooklyn Heights from what might have been a still more overwhelming disaster if the English had been better marksmen. Clinton, Cornwallis, and Vaughan, all urged Howe to pursue the Americans at once into their intrenchments, and the common soldiers were with difficulty restrained from pressing on. Howe admitted that the intrenchments might be easily taken, but declined to take them in that way. He thanked his officers for their zeal and advice, said enough had been done for one day, and the intrenchments could be taken by regular approaches with less loss.[10]

The battle was a curious one, because its results now largely depended upon the direction of the wind. It had apparently been intended to use the men-of-war and send them into the East River behind Brooklyn Heights. But the wind was northeast, and after beating against it they were compelled to anchor when the tide turned; and only one vessel, the "Roebuck," exchanged shots with Red Hook.

Possibly Howe expected that in making his approaches the next day the fleet would coöperate with him, go round into East River, and entrap the force at Brooklyn. But the wind continued from the northeast, with rain. Washington brought

---

[9] Memoirs of Long Island Historical Society, vol. iii, p. 199; *American Archives*, fifth series, vol. ii, p. 1112.

[10] "Remarks upon General Howe's Account of His Proceedings on Long Island," London, 1778; see, also, Howe's " Narrative; " Stedman, "American War," edition of 1794, vol. i, p. 196, London. Clinton, in his MS. notes to Stedman, p. 196, says that Howe may have had political reasons for not attacking Brooklyn Heights. Clinton's MS. notes are in the Carter-Brown Library, Providence, Rhode Island, and a copy of them is in the library of Harvard University.

reinforcements over to Brooklyn Heights, raising the force there to nearly ten thousand men. He remained there all of the day after the battle, evidently believing that as long as the wind blew northeast he was safe.

The next day, the 29th, the wind and rain continued, but the British were pushing their approaches, and there was constant skirmishing. Washington was unwilling to trust any longer to the northeast wind, because the British trenches were coming nearer and his troops had been standing in the pelting rain for nearly two days, without sleep, not daring to lie down at night, and with nothing to eat but cold bread and raw pork. He had himself been riding along the lines to encourage the men during all that time without leaving his saddle.

He accordingly issued an order during the morning to collect every kind of boat that could be found along the neighboring shores for the ostensible purpose of carrying the sick and wounded to New York and bringing some fresh regiments from New Jersey. At eight o'clock in the evening the embarkation began with much marching and countermarching. As each regiment departed for the shore at Fulton Ferry, another would be moved or extended to fill up the gap, and the fires were kept burning and the outposts at their stations.

At first the northeast wind rendered the movements of the boats to the opposite shore very slow. But before midnight the weather cleared, and the wind changed to southwest, so that Glover's Massachusetts men from Marblehead and Hutchinson's from Salem, most of them seamen, could use sails on the boats. But even with this advantage there were some six regiments still in the works when daylight appeared, and they could hear the pick-axes and shovels of the British in the trenches. Luckily a morning fog arose, and under cover of it, these regiments slipped down to the ferry. The whole army of nearly ten thousand with their prisoners, wounded, baggage and stores got safely across to New York, and it has been counted one of the most skilfully conducted retreats of history.

Word of the movement was sent to Howe, possibly by Mrs. John Rapelje, a loyalist; and according to Stedman, Howe knew of the movement in time to prevent it. But his reconnoitering parties, which cautiously drew near the works, found them empty and silent, and when they rushed to the ferry the last of the Americans had left the shore.[11]

---

[11] Stedman, "American War," edition 1794, vol. i, pp. 197, 198; Parliamentary Register, 1779, vol 13, pp. 55, 315; Onderdonk, "Revolutionary Incidents," p. 130; Memoirs of Long Island Historical Society, vol. iii, pp. 213–224; W. B. Reed, "Life of Joseph Reed," vol. i, p. 225; Gordon, "American Revolution," edition 1788, vol. ii, p. 313.

There are innumerable secondary authorities on the Battle of Long Island, which has been much obscured by explanations. The original reports, letters, and testimony of the officers and eye-witnesses can be found in the *American Archives*, fifth series, vol. i, and they have been collected and well edited in volume iii of the Memoirs of the Long Island Historical Society.

XLV.

MORE PROPOSALS OF PEACE

MILITARY critics have suggested that it might have been better for General Howe to have made a mere feint at Brooklyn Heights on Long Island and sent most of his force up the Hudson to land on Manhattan Island above the town of New York. He could then have drawn his large force across the narrow island from the Hudson to East River and hemmed in Washington in the town where he might be forced to a surrender; or if he attempted to retreat across to Long Island, he would again be isolated; and if he attempted to retreat across to New Jersey, he would have wide water to cross and would have to run the gauntlet of the British fleet.

This criticism presupposes a favorable wind for taking the troops up the Hudson. It may seem to be strengthened when we find that now after the successful Battle of Long Island, Howe still had before him the problem of locking up Washington in New York by crossing over to the part of Manhattan Island above the town. But he was in no hurry to make the movement and astonished everyone by remaining quietly on Long Island for over two weeks without attempting to enter New York. He seemed to the patriots a very slow general, or else he was trying to be their friend.[1]

But this delay was apparently to give time and opportunity for more peace proposals by the Admiral. General Sullivan who had been captured on Long Island was sent ashore on his parole to visit the congress in Philadelphia and deliver a message to the effect that Admiral Howe would be glad to have an informal conference with them. In this new attempt he meant to waive his own rank as well as theirs, and as a mere private gentleman meet some of them as mere private

[1] Drake, " Life of General Knox," p. 31; Jones, " New York in the Revolution," vol. i, p. 119.

gentlemen to talk over the subjects of controversy. Sullivan reduced to writing and submitted to the Congress the verbal message the Admiral had given him, and it certainly had the appearance of a serious attempt at reconciliation.

> " That he, in conjunction with General Howe, had full powers to compromise the dispute between Great Britain and America upon terms advantageous to both; the obtaining of which delayed him nearly two months in England, and prevented his arrival at this place before the declaration of independence took place.
>
> " That he wished a compact might be settled at this time when no decisive blow was struck, and neither party could say, that they were compelled to enter into such agreement:
>
> " That in case Congress were disposed to treat, many things which they had not as yet asked might and ought to be granted them; and that if, upon the conference, they found any probable ground of accommodation, the authority of Congress must be afterwards acknowledged, otherwise the compact would not be complete." (*American Archives*, fifth series, vol. ii, p. 1329.*)

If the Admiral really gave Sullivan such a message as this, hinting at a possible recognition of the authority of the Congress, one would suppose that the Admiral was exceeding his instructions. It is possible to conceive of the Whig party or a Whig politician standing ready to recognize the authority of the Congress, but it is hard to believe that the Tory Ministry of that time were ready for such recognition unless they were much weaker kneed than has been usually supposed.

In his own account of the affair which the Admiral sent to the Ministry, he did not describe his message by Sullivan as going so far as to say that the authority of the congress might be recognized. Sullivan's anxiety as a prisoner, or his natural impetuosity may have led him to see more in the Admiral's words than were intended. The Admiral, however, admitted having told him that it was a mistake to suppose that the peace mission of himself and his brother was confined to granting pardons; that his majesty's paternal desire was

---

* " Life of George Read," p. 174; Works of John Adams, vol. iii, p. 73; *American Archives*, fifth series, vol. ii, p. 105.

to make his American subjects happy and that both the Admiral and the General "were willing to consult any persons of influence, and that reconciliation, union and redress of grievances might be the happy consequence."[3]

In either of its forms the message was a rather curious proceeding, and coupled with the previous similar attempts showed an apparently intense desire on the part of the Admiral and the General to effect some sort of compromise, or reconciliation as it was called.

The Congress were uneasy lest the news of this willingness for peace negotiation might unsettle the timid and moderate patriots, so they resolved to send a regularly appointed and formal committee consisting of Franklin, John Adams and Rutledge to learn from Admiral Howe the exact extent of his powers and the terms he had to offer.[4]

There was great expectation and excitement as to the results of the meeting. Some believed that a full settlement would be reached and the patriot army disbanded, while others were entirely skeptical as to the admiral's professions and intentions. Adams, who has given a most graphic account of this meeting, said that on the way to it he and his colleagues were filled with great anxiety for their cause by the patriot troops they found, both officers and men, straggling and loitering in the taverns of New Jersey; but they were determined not to be disheartened, and with easy, composed countenances, on the 11th of September, took their seats in the admiral's barge, which carried them over to Staten Island. He came down to the shore and received them in the most handsome manner.

"We walked up to the house between lines of guards of grenadiers, looking fierce as ten Furies, and making all the grimaces and gestures and motions of their muskets, with bayonets fixed, which, I suppose, military etiquette requires, but which we neither understood nor regarded. . . . His lordship had prepared a large handsome room, by

---

[3] Parliamentary Register, vol. 8, p. 249.
[4] "Life of George Reed," pp. 189, 190; *American Archives*, fifth series, vol. ii, pp. 178, 192, 272, 1331, 1332.

spreading a carpet of moss and green sprigs, from bushes and shrubs in the neighborhood, till he had made it not only wholesome, but romantically elegant; and he entertained us with good claret, good bread, cold ham, tongues, and mutton." (John Adams, Works, vol. iii, p. 77.)

The greatest good feeling and politeness prevailed. The Admiral was profuse in his expression of gratitude to Massachusetts for erecting a monument in Westminster Abbey to his brother. He said that he felt for America as for a brother, and if America should fall, he should feel and lament it like the loss of a brother. To which Franklin replied, "My lord, we will do our utmost endeavors to save your lordship that mortification."

The committee's report of the interview agreed substantially with that of the Admiral to his Government. The only power he had beyond that of issuing pardons under the Prohibitory Act was to receive any terms the patriots had to offer and transmit them to the Ministry; but first of all the patriots must submit and return to British allegiance. That being done the Admiral had no doubt that certain acts of Parliament would be revised and many grievances removed.[5]

This was, of course, merely beating the Devil round the bush; and the Congress would have nothing more to do with the negotiation. But the Admiral would not cease from his efforts and in a few days he and his brother issued a proclamation in which they announced that the Congress had "disavowed every purpose of reconciliation not consonant with their extravagant and inadmissable claim of independency;" but that, nevertheless, the Admiral and the General were still desirous to restore peace and a permanent union with the British empire; and they further declared that the King was "most graciously disposed to direct a revision of such of his royal instructions as may be construed to lay an improper restraint upon the freedom of legislation in any of his colonies and to concur in the revisal of all acts by which his subjects there may think themselves aggrieved." Wherefore, the patriots

---

[5] *American Archives*, fifth series, vol. ii, pp. 323, 324, 914, 915, 972, 1342, 1343; Writings of Washington, Ford edition, vol. iv, pp. 284, 336.

should abandon their precarious cause and accept the blessings of peace "upon the true principles of the constitution." [6]

The Admiral no doubt thought that the patriot party had been so badly shattered in the recent defeat that the moderates might compel the Congress to offer terms. Lord Percy writing home on the 2nd of September, had said "this business is pretty near over," and very likely that was the general opinion in the British army.[7]

The proclamation of the Howes was published in England and the Whigs immediately seized upon it as valuable material for action in Parliament. On the 6th of November, Lord Cavendish in a sarcastic speech expressed his surprise and delight that the Ministry had authorized their Admiral and General to say to the Americans that the King would concur in the revisal of all acts by which the colonists were aggrieved. He felt, he said, "a dawn of joy break in on his mind." He was ready to coöperate with the Ministers in their noble work, and he, therefore, moved "that this House will resolve itself into a committee, to consider of the revisal of all acts of Parliament, by which his Majesty's subjects in America think themselves aggrieved." [8]

Lord North replying for the Ministry, declared that the proclamation was entirely in accordance with instructions given to the Howes and called attention to the words of their commission which had recently been published in the *Gazette*. The Ministry had always been willing to hear and redress American grievances, and part of the duty of the Howes as peace commissioners, was to transmit an account of those grievances "and to engage on the part of the legislature that redress would be granted, whenever a good cause for redress existed." But the Americans must first give up their notions of sovereignty and independence, acknowledge Britain's right to rule and then the Ministry would "adopt the most efficacious

---

* *American Archives*, fifth series, vol. ii, pp. 565, 1180.
⁷ "Letters of Earl Percy," Bolton, p. 71.
* *American Archives*, fifth series, vol. iii, pp. 1006, 1007.

and speedy measures, not only to remedy real grievances, but even to bend to their prejudices in some instances.''

The motion of Lord Cavendish was lost by a vote of 109 to 47; and the patriots afterwards discovered that the sending by the Congress of a committee to meet Admiral Howe had been used by the Ministry to show the French government that the patriots were inclined to compromise. In consequence France had for a time, withdrawn her aid; for if the Americans were about to compromise or become reconciled to England, it was not for the interest of the French nation to help them. France's only reason for helping them was to enable them to become absolutely independent of England. From this the patriots learned the valuable lesson that their true policy lay in rejecting absolutely and without negotiation or consideration, any compromise proposals of England which, as John Adams said, were mere stratagems to divide and weaken the patriot party, prevent aid from France and encourage the loyalists.[9]

The loyalists, inferred from the effort the Admiral made, especially in the Drummond mission that he had full powers not only to pardon, but to arrange a compromise, and Galloway regrets that he did not use this power to its full extent. But an examination of the secret instructions and orders to the Howes, now accessible in the Record Office in London, shows that they had no power beyond what they themselves and Lord North described.[10]

---

[9] Writings of Washington, Ford edition, vol. v, p. 239 note.

[10] Galloway, "A Letter to the Right Honorable Lord Viscount H—e," London, 1780. I have had a copy made of the original Orders and Instructions to the Howes in the London Record Office and turned it over to the Historical Society of Pennsylvania for preservation.

XLVI.

THE MOTIVES OF THE HOWES

NEITHER the Admiral nor the General made any more peace proposals. The efforts of the Admiral in this direction had been earnest and persistent, beginning two years before in his secret negotiations with Franklin in London. He had possibly tried to obtain from the Ministry larger powers for peace and compromise than were given him and for that purpose had delayed his departure from England. But the Ministry knew better than to trust a Whig politician with any large authority of that kind; and there is a curious letter from Wedderburn in the 9th Report of the Historical Manuscripts Commission which indicates quite clearly the embarrassment of the Ministry in being obliged to entrust to a Whig politician the carrying out of a Tory policy. They were suspicious of the Admiral's intentions and not willing to trust him with peace proposals unless he was closely bound by implicit instructions.[1]

This brings us to the great controversy of the time over the motives of the Howes, a controversy which must be continually referred to during their command in America in the next two years. Their motives were very naturally suspected: They were charged with delaying the war and trying to compromise with the Americans on Whig principles, when they should have been vigorously subduing them on the Tory principles of the Ministry who gave them their commands and sent them out to America.

The Howes, we must remember, were Whigs of the extreme type. George Howe, during his lifetime, had been the family member of Parliament, and had represented Nottingham until

---

[1] Part iii, p. 84; see also *American Archives*, fifth series, vol. i, pp. 272, 273; see also vol. iii, p. 1227.

he fell at Ticonderoga in 1758. As soon as his mother heard the news she issued an address to the electors asking them to choose her youngest son, William, which they promptly did; and he seems to have thought of himself as continuing the existence and principles of his brother. He became a strict party man voting with the Whigs against the Stamp Act and all the other Tory legislation for America; and now he was out in America as the general to carry out the Tory policy against which he had been voting for ten years.

Before he came out as general he had said as a politician that he not only thought it wrong to make war on the Americans, but useless and impractical. A large section of his party, the Rockingham Whigs, and men like the Duke of Richmond and Charles Fox were in favor of allowing the colonies to form, if they could, an independent nation, just as, in the year 1901, a section of the liberal party were in favor of allowing the Boer republics of South Africa to retain their independence.[2]

The rest of the Whigs, represented by such men as Barré, Burke, and Lord Chatham, would not declare themselves for independence. They professed to favor retaining the American communities as colonies; but they would retain them by conciliation instead of by force and conquest. Their position was an impossible one, because conciliation without military force would necessarily result in independence. But they professed to think that if the troops were withdrawn from America, and no invasion or subjugating attempted, the colonies would voluntarily submit or enter into some agreement by which they would remain in the empire.

It was certainly a little peculiar that a Whig member of Parliament holding such opinions as these, should be sent to America to carry out a Tory policy of repression and subjugation. But the Ministry, it is said, were inclined to bestow important employments, military and naval, on those who were

---

[2] Lecky, "England in the Eighteenth Century," edition 1882, vol. iii, p. 544.

in the habit of opposing their measures in order to secure
themselves from attack and carry their measures more easily.
Howe had told his constituents that if the command against
the colonies were offered to him he would not accept it. This
reckless remark was characteristic of him, and when he made
it he must have known that there was every probability that
he would be sent against the Americans in some capacity if
not in chief command.[3]

It is somewhat surprising to a modern American to find
that a politician and a member of Parliament of such long
service as Howe was also at the same time an officer of the
British regular army. Under our national Constitution we
have always avoided conferring conflicting offices and duties
on the same person. But this principle of distinct separation
of the departments of government, which we have carried so
far, was at that time not much regarded in England. Admiral
Howe was also a member of Parliament and so were Generals
Burgoyne, Cornwallis, and Grant. Such a system may have
worked well enough until the soldier or sailor was directed
to carry out what as a politician he had opposed.[4]

After all that Howe had said to his constituents about the
righteousness of the American cause, and that he would not
fight against such people, there was surprise and some indignation among the Whigs in England when his appointment
was announced, and he sailed for Boston. The Congress at
Philadelphia declared that "America was amazed to find the
name of Howe in the catalogue of her enemies. She loved
his brother."

"You should have refused to go against the Americans,"
said his old supporters at Nottingham, "as you said you
would." But Howe, not in the least disconcerted, replied that
his appointment came not as an offer, but as an order from
the King, and he had no choice but to obey. Significant re-

---

[3] Stedman, "American War," vol. i, p. 319.
[4] In Burgoyne's expedition from Canada in 1777 six of his staff
officers were members of Parliament.—Writings of Washington, Ford
edition, vol. 6, p. 150.

marks were made that the war would now after all be conducted on Whig principles in spite of the Tory Ministry.[5]

At first the peace proposals and comparatively gentle
methods of the Howes seem to have been approved by the Ministry, and were in accordance with the Ministry's instructions.
But in the end the Howes kept up the gentle methods too long
and as their careers in America developed, grave suspicions
as to their motives were entertained in England and by
loyalists in America.

Loyalists and Englishmen found the conduct of General
Howe very difficult to understand unless they assumed either
that he was a man of rarest ignorance and incompetence, or
that as a Whig member of Parliament, he was so influenced
by partisan feelings that he was unwilling to conduct the war
in a way which would give the Tory party in Parliament any
advantage. If the Americans had showed a willingness to
come to terms and enter into some engagement by which they
would remain at least nominally a part of the empire with
privileges and liberties satisfactory to themselves, all the
Whig prophecies of Burke, Barré and Chatham would have
been fulfilled, and the Whig program would have been carried out to the letter.

To accomplish such a Whig success it was strongly suspected, that the Howe brothers refrained from subjugation,
and would use the vast military and naval forces committed
to their care only for the purpose of suggesting to the colonists
that sort of voluntary settlement and submission which was
the Whig ideal of colonial relations with the mother country.

Admiral Howe's naval operations during the three years
of his command were certainly conducted on good Whig principles, but were very exasperating to loyalists like Joseph
Galloway and not calculated to extend British dominion. In
1776 he had with him fifty-six war vessels, and in the next

---

[5] "Address to the People of Ireland," p. 8; *American Archives*,
fourth series, vol. iv, p. 311; Galloway, " Reply to the Observations of
Lieutenant-General Sir W. Howe," pp. 112, 138, London, 1780.

year he had eighty-one. He could have placed them within sight of one another along the coast from Boston to Charleston. The original plan had been to station the large vessels at the mouths of the great rivers and bays, the Hudson, the Delaware, and the Chesapeake, and the rest were to cruise up and down the coast three deep, but not in file, so as to render it more difficult to cross them. But Admiral Howe never attempted any such complete blockade; and made only a partial and very weak blockade of Delaware Bay and the Chesapeake.

His war-ships in those waters were easily evaded. American vessels and the privateers which preyed on English merchantmen found a safe entrance at Egg Harbor on the Jersey coast, whence, by way of the Mullica River, goods were hauled in wagons to Philadelphia and other points. His blockade of the Chesapeake was easily avoided in the same way by means of the Machipongo Inlet, twenty-five miles above Cape Charles; and in the Carolina Sounds the Americans did as they pleased. When asked why he did not commission loyalist privateers to destroy American merchantmen, the admiral is said to have replied, "Will you never have done, oppressing these poor people? Will you never give them an opportunity of seeing their error?" He was a most ardent believer in conciliation.[6]

The Ministry had intended the olive branch to be offered along with the sword. But the olive branch was to be withdrawn if not immediately accepted; and before long Lord North, Lord George Germain and the whole Ministry declared

---

[6] Galloway, "Letter to the Right Honorable Lord Viscount Howe," London, 1779; Galloway, "Detail and Conduct of the American War," third edition, p. 26, etc., London, 1780; Stevens, "Fac-similes," vol. xi, p. 1163; Eddis, "Letters from America," p. 345; *American Archives*, fourth series, vol. iv, p. 1127; vol. vi, p. 685; fifth series, vol. i, p. 463; vol. ii, pp. 318, 1319; "Diary and Letters of Thomas Hutchinson," vol. ii, p. 222. Alexander Hamilton is reported to have said, "All that the English need have done was to blockade our ports with twenty-five frigates and ten ships of the line. But thank God they did nothing of the sort." Pontgibaud, "A French Volunteer of the War of Independence," p. 147.

that they were extremely disappointed in the conduct of the Howes. Letters were written to General Howe calling for more severity, and extracts from these letters were afterwards read by Charles Fox in Parliament. But Howe in defending himself denied that the letters contained positive instructions, and his statement is interesting because it shows how strongly he was inclined to refrain from pressing the patriots with the full rigor of war.[1]

> " For, sir, although some persons condemn me for having endeavored to conciliate his Majesty's rebellious subjects, by taking every means to prevent the destruction of the country, instead of irritating them by a contrary mode of proceeding, yet am I, from many reasons, satisfied in my own mind that I acted in that particular for the benefit of the king's service. Ministers themselves, I am persuaded, did at one time entertain a similar doctrine, and from a circumstance not now necessary to dwell upon, it is certain that I should have had little reason to hope for support from them, if I had been disposed to acts of great severity. Had it been afterwards judged good policy to turn the plan of the war into an indiscriminate devastation of that country, and had I been thought the proper instrument for executing such a plan, ministers, I presume, would have openly stood forth, and sent clear, explicit orders. Ambiguous messages, hints, whispers across the Atlantic, to be avowed or disavowed at pleasure, would have been paltry safeguards for the honour and conduct of a commander-in-chief." (Cobbett, " Parliamentary History," vol. xx, pp. 682, 683.)

If the suspicion which seems to be in Howe's mind were correct, the Ministry wished to avoid the responsibility of severe devastating measures, because the cruelty of them would arouse Whig eloquence and perhaps increase the Whig party to a majority. If, however, by means of expressions, the meaning of which was uncertain and could be avowed or disavowed, they could lead Howe, a Whig general, into measures of severity, the blame for cruelty, if the measures failed, could be shifted to a Whig. If, however, the severity succeeded in bringing about a peace or compromise, the cruelty would be of little moment or soon forgotten.

---

[1] Parliamentary Register, House of Commons, 1779, vol. 13, pp. 271, 272, 350, 357, 358, 368; Cobbett, Parliamentary Debates, vol. 19, p. 766; vol. 20, p. 844.

AMBIGUOUS WHISPERS

The instructions or messages which Fox read in Parliament, and which Howe said were ambiguous whispers across the Atlantic, seem to be contained in two or three letters written to Howe by Lord George Germain, the colonial secretary. The first one is dated the 3rd of March, 1777, and was received by Howe on the 8th of May. After regretting the loss of Trenton, enjoining care against similar accidents, and referring to certain inhuman treatment said to have been inflicted by the patriots upon Captain Phillips, the letter closes by saying:

> "And here I must observe that if that impudent people, in contempt of the gracious offers contained in the late proclamation, shall persist in overt acts of rebellion, they will so far aggravate their guilt as to become altogether unworthy of any further instances of his Majesty's compassion; and as they who insolently refuse to accept the mercy of their sovereign cannot, in the eye of impartial reason, have the least room to expect clemency at the hand of his subjects, I fear that you and Lord Howe will find it necessary to adopt such modes of carrying on the war that the rebels may be effectually distressed, so that through a lively experience of losses and sufferings they may be brought as soon as possible to a proper sense of their duty, and in the mean time may be intimidated from oppressing and injuring his Majesty's loyal subjects."
> —Parliamentary Register, House of Commons, 1779, vol. xi, p. 394.

Bancroft quotes a passage from a letter which he says was sent at this time, but follows his custom of giving no authority for it.

> "At the expiration of the period limited in your proclamation, it will be incumbent upon you to use the powers with which you are intrusted in such a manner that those persons who shall have shown themselves undeserving of the royal mercy may not escape that punishment which is due to their crimes, and which it will be expedient to inflict for the sake of example to futurity."—Bancroft, "History of the United States," edition of 1886, vol. v, p. 146.

In another letter, written on the 18th of February, 1778, and received by Howe on the 14th of April, Germain says that the King has accepted Howe's resignation, but he is to remain until his successor arrives; and the letter goes on to describe the serious attempt at peace the Ministry was making by sending out a strong commission for that purpose, and adds that the King has full confidence that while Howe remains in command he "will lay hold of every opportunity of putting an end to the rebellion and inducing a submission to legal government." If the rebel colonists obstinately refuse the offers of the peace commission, " every means will be employed to augment the force . . . in the prosecution of the war." At the close of the letter Howe and his brother, the Admiral, are directed to make such an attack upon the New England coast as will destroy the rebel privateers and incapacitate the people from fitting out others. This expedition against New England Howe declined to make, giving as his reason that it was too hazardous, because of the fogs, "flatness of the coast," together with other very peculiar excuses.[8]

The contents of these letters have been given somewhat at length in order that the reader may judge for himself whether they are ambiguous. They do not contain positive instructions, and yet they show what the Ministry wished the General and the Admiral to do. They are very like numerous other directions and suggestions in the other letters from Germain printed in the Parliamentary Register. Howe was not sent out to America under binding or positive military instructions.[9] He was sent out, as is usual in such cases, with full discretionary power to suppress the rebellion; and at such a great distance the Ministry was obliged to assume that, as a rule, he was the best judge of his surrounding circumstances. As commander-in-chief he could take the responsibility of refusing to carry out a direction or request of the Ministry if he deemed it unwise, impracticable, or too hazardous, unless he had positive instructions that it was to be carried out at all hazards on the responsibility of the Ministry alone. He knew all the political, military, and other conditions of the time, and had assumed responsibility for his actions.

---

[8] Parliamentary Register, 1779, vol. xi, pp. 462, 466. It is necessary to warn the reader that owing to the peculiar way in which the Parliamentary Register is published, there are often two volumes bearing the same number and distinguishable only by their dates.

[9] " View of the Evidence Relative to the Conduct of the War," etc., p. 112.

XLVII.

DURING the delay of two weeks over the Admiral's last peace negotiations Washington and his officers had ample time to consider their best course and even to send on to the Congress at Philadelphia for its opinion. As Howe took no advantage of his possession of Brooklyn Heights to attack New York, he evidently intended to land on Manhattan Island above the town and cut off all retreat from it. Washington's force disheartened by defeat and weakened by companies of militia deliberately returning home, was spread out from the city through the whole length of Manhattan Island, a distance of fourteen miles up to King's Bridge, ready to resist or evade any hemming in movement on the part of Howe.

Washington was at first inclined to defend New York at all hazards, because many of the patriot party expected such a defence and he dreaded the dispiriting effect on the patriot cause of anything like hasty retreat or abandonment of an important point. But he was obliged to admit that his army was demoralized and unfit for such a task, when whole companies and even regiments of militia were deserting and going home.

His officers and general opinion were divided. Some were for retaining New York at all hazards. Others, notably General Greene, were in favor not only of abandoning New York, but of burning it to the ground. Two-thirds of the property in it, they said, belonged to loyalists. The destruction of it would deprive the British of winter quarters and of a general market for supplies; but if they once occupied it with their army, it was so naturally strong and defensible that the Americans could never hope to retake it until they had a naval force equal to that of Britain. John Jay was in favor not only of burning New York, but of desolating all the country below the Hudson Highlands and then retiring with the main body of the army to those Highlands and West Point, which should be made impregnable and the river filled up with stones rolled down from the mountains, so that the British could never get possession of this vital strategic position.[1]

But the Congress and a council of war decided to abandon New York without burning it, and place the army beyond the scope of any attempt by the British to shut them up in the town. On the 15th of September, when Howe finally started to take the city most of the baggage and stores of Washington's army and all the troops except about 4,000 under Putnam, had been removed to Harlem Heights at the upper end of Manhattan Island.[2]

The point selected by Howe for entering New York was on the East River near what is now 33d street, where the patriots had a battery manned by three Connecticut regiments under Colonel Douglas. On Sunday morning, the 15th of September, five British war-ships, which had come into the East River with but little difficulty, opened a heavy cannonade on Douglas's regiments and kept it up for three hours, while at about the same time three other British war-ships came up the Hudson directly opposite to those in the East River, and the combined fire of the two forces reached quite across the island. Douglas's men were driven from their position, and the British force easily landed under cover of the cannonade, and occupied the high ground in the neighborhood of Thirty-fifth street and Fifth avenue, then covered with corn fields.

Douglas's brigade fled in confusion fearing they would be

---

[1] *American Archives*, fifth series, vol. ii, pp. 120, 121; Writings of Washington, Ford edition, vol. iv, pp. 393, 403; "Life of Joseph Reed," vol. i, p. 213.

[2] Memoirs of Long Island Historical Society, vol. iii, pp. 227–230; W. B. Reed, "Life of Joseph Reed," vol. i, pp. 213, 229, 234, 235; *American Archives*, fifth series, vol. ii, pp. 182, 237, 325, 416, 465, 1330; G. W. Greene, "Life of Nathanael Greene," vol. i, p. 212.

intercepted, and the panic was communicated to several bodies of troops which came to reinforce them. Washington riding up at this moment, tried to assist the officers in stopping the flight. His passionate nature was thoroughly aroused, and various traditional accounts have come down to us of his distress and rage at what he considered a disgraceful retreat. He threw his hat on the ground, fired his pistols and in his efforts to renew the fight almost rushed into the British lines.[3]

On the Hudson River side where the war-ships shelled the shore, General Mercer tried to hold his men at their posts, but in vain; and both they and the troops under Douglas retreated to Harlem Heights. The four thousand men under Putnam down close to the city were now in danger of being entrapped and they began to move as best they could towards Harlem Heights. Putnam with his horse covered with foam dashed about to encourage them to the utmost exertions; but the day was so hot that some of them were dropping dead at the springs and brooks, where they drank.[4]

Howe had now crossed the East River, and could have easily cut off Putnam's force if he had merely extended his lines with a little promptness to the westward. But as he had allowed the patriot army plenty of time to make up their minds to evacuate New York, so now he made no real attempt to hem them in on the narrow island. Putnam's division panting and fainting with the heat, passed by unmolested within sight of Howe's right wing, while he and some of his officers were lunching with Mrs. Robert Murray at that part of New York still known as Murray Hill.[5]

Mrs. Murray was a patriot and, as the pretty story goes, invited Howe to lunch for the purpose of delaying him and

---

[3] Writings of Washington, Ford edition, vol. 4, p. 407 note; Jones, "New York in the Revolution," vol. i, p. 604.

[4] Memoirs of Long Island Historical Society, vol. iii, p. 232; Gordon, "American Revolution," edition 1788, vol. ii, p. 327; Jones, "New York in the Revolution, vol. i, p. 607.

[5] Clinton's MS notes to Stedman's "American War," vol. i, p. 208, in Carter-Brown Collection at Providence.

saving Putnam's force; or, at any rate, her offer of lunch and entertainment, as we are solemnly informed by historical writers, is supposed to have had that effect. But that Howe and the officers with him, and all the other officers who were not at the lunch, were deceived in this way seems almost incredible. A suspicion arises that there may have been an intention to move easily and give the patriots every chance. The lunch at the patriot house and the jokes that are said to have passed at the table seem very much like a part of the conciliatory method thus far adopted by the Ministry or by Howe. They appear to have thought that under this method the movement for independence would finally collapse. But under modern British methods Mrs. Murray would have been captured and locked up in a reconcentrado camp.[*]

This was the beginning of the serious suspicions of General Howe's motives; and from this time he seems to have extended the olive branch more than the Ministry intended. The next day to the great delight of the numerous loyalists, he took formal possession of New York, which the British retained as their headquarters to the end of the war. A few days after they entered the town it was set on fire at night in several places, with the intention as some supposed of totally destroying it. But whether this was the act of mere incendiaries, or of patriots who wished to burn out the British army, has never been determined.

A high wind was blowing, the fire soon had consumed one-fourth of the houses; and it required the utmost exertions of the troops to save their future winter quarters. Exciting tales were told. Many of the incendiaries who were caught at their work were said to have been shot down, pitched into the flames or hung up by the heels. Some six hundred, it is said, were

---

[*] Memoirs of Long Island Historical Society, vol. iii, pp. 225–240; *American Archives*, fifth series, vol. ii, pp. 351, 352, 369, 370, 400. The assertion that Mrs. Murray saved the American army may have been originally a joke or humorous remark of Colonel Grayson which historians have taken seriously. Gordon, "American Revolution," edition 1788, vol. ii, p. 329.

CONTEMPORARY FRENCH ENGRAVING OF THE BURNING OF NEW YORK

afterwards imprisoned on suspicion; and many of these, according to patriot accounts, were punished in the most inhuman manner. "They have hanged numbers by the feet," says one report, "and then cut their throats."[7]

The patriot army now collected at Harlem Heights was suffering from the usual demoralization of defeat. They were in want of supplies, tents, blankets, clothes and were indiscriminately robbing patriot and loyalist houses. There was an additional cause of disorganization in the scandal of the panic of the Connecticut troops which Washington had tried to check. Washington himself had reported it to Congress as "disgraceful and dastardly." There were already jealousies between the sections of the country, and the New Englanders were not softened in their resentments when every day they heard themselves called dastards and cowards by the men from New York, Pennsylvania and Maryland. Terms of reproach were so freely used, that it was said that the northern and southern troops would as soon fight each other as the British.

The feeling was intensified by the extreme democratic and levelling principles of the New Englanders and the aristocratic ideas of the officers from the Southern States. Among the New England soldiery the officers were all elected by the privates; and, as Graydon noticed, there were very few officers who belonged to the upper classes of society. South of New England, the officers were appointed instead of elected, usually prided themselves on their rank as gentlemen, and believed that only such men could successfully command armies and secure the obedience of troops. Washington on one occasion urged that only gentlemen should be appointed to military office; and the southerners now thought that the conduct of the Connecticut troops showed the value of such a rule and that

[7] *American Archives*, fifth series, vol. ii, pp. 462, 463, 466, 524, 548, 820; Evidence in Card Catalogue Penna. Historical Society; Gordon, "American Revolution," edition 1788, vol. ii, p. 330; Writings of Washington, Ford edition, vol. iv, p. 430 notes; Jones, "New York in the Revolution," vol. i, p. 611; Stedman, "American War," vol. i, p. 209.

nothing but disaster would result from New England levelling applied to military organization.[8]

The results of this unfortunate quarrel clung to the patriot army for many years. It might, one would suppose, have been checked by the gallant conduct of some Connecticut troops the very next day. For on the morning of the 16th, Washington ordered the Connecticut Rangers, under Colonel Knowlton, to reconnoitre from Harlem Heights southward and discover any new movements of the British. These rangers were a picked body of men, volunteers from New England regiments, and Knowlton was the officer who had fought at the rail fence at Bunker Hill.[9]

With his one hundred and twenty rangers he pushed southward until he found the British light infantry at what is now the northern end of Central Park. He resisted them behind a stone wall until they outflanked him and as he retreated he was followed by fresh reinforcements with their bugles playing a fox hunting tune. They ventured too far, however; for patriot troops attacked them in front while Knowlton's men assailed their flanks. They fled from their fox hunt, with considerable loss, but the gallant Knowlton was killed.

Receiving still more reinforcements the British came on again, and the patriots sallied out from Harlem Heights until there was an appearance of a general engagement. The patriot officers thought it a good opportunity to reanimate their men who were quite dispirited by the disasters of the last few weeks, and they succeeded in again driving the British back to their lines. It was most inspiring for the patriots.

----

[8] Memoirs of Long Island Historical Society, vol. iii, pp. 240–243; W. B. Reed, "Life of Joseph Reed," vol. i, p. 239; Gordon, "American Revolution," edition 1788, pp. 324, 331, 332; "Life of George Read," pp. 192, 193; G. W. Greene, "Life of Nathanael Greene," vol. i, p. 209; *American Archives*, fifth series, vol. ii, p. 1101; vol. iii, pp. 1032, 1498. Gordon represents the northern side in this controversy and Graydon in his memoirs takes the southern side.

[9] *American Archives*, fifth series, vol. ii, p. 465.

"They find," said Knox, "that if they stick to these mighty men they will run as fast as other people."[10]

It was a few days after this engagement that one of those apparently unimportant incidents occurred which sometimes fix themselves forever in the public mind. Anxious for information as to the intentions of the enemy, Washington had sent spies into their camps, and among those who had volunteered their services was a handsome young officer from Connecticut, Captain Nathan Hale of Knowlton's Rangers. He was caught at his work, confessed and was promptly hung, saying upon the gallows that he was sorry he had only one life to give for his country. His case differed in nothing from that of numerous spies who were hung on one side or the other during the war, and were as devoted and heroic as he. But his youth and beauty, his rank above that of an ordinary spy, and his last words brought him an universal sympathy and greatly excited public feeling. The British were denounced in unmeasured terms for this new atrocity of the invader; and for the rest of the war, and even long afterwards, as much feeling could be aroused by the mention of the death of Hale as by the mention of the burning of Norfolk or of Portland.

On the night of the same day on which Hale was hung, the patriots tried to off-set their disasters by achieving a minor success like that of Harlem Heights. Colonel Jackson, with three hundred men in four or five flat boats, attacked the British fort on Montressor's Island in Hell Gate in the East River. The first boat landed and drove back the guard, but the other boats drew off and shamefully deserted their comrades, who were obliged to escape as best they could with the loss of Major Henly killed and Colonel Jackson and about twenty others wounded.[11]

---

[10] W. B. Reed, "Life of General Reed," vol. i, p. 237; *American Archives*, fifth series, vol. ii, pp. 500, 548; Drake, "Life of General Knox," p. 32.

[11] *American Archives*, fifth series, vol. ii, pp. 523, 524; Gordon, "American Revolution," edition 1788, vol. ii, p. 336, and title " Montressor " in index; Heath, Memoirs, p. 56.

XLVIII.

WHITE PLAINS AND FORT WASHINGTON

CONTINUING his plan of allowing long delays, apparently for the purpose of bringing about a compromise, General Howe left Washington undisturbed at Harlem Heights for nearly a month. During that time he wrote the Ministry a very peculiar letter in which he said that the further progress of his army seemed "rather precarious," and that he could do nothing more without great reinforcements. "I have not the smallest prospect," he said, "of finishing the contest this campaign until the Rebels see preparations in the spring that may preclude all thoughts of further resistance."[1]

In other words, in spite of the great army and fleet that had been sent him, he writes that all hope of subduing the patriots must be put off for another year, and even then, apparently, they are not to be attacked or conquered, but are "to see preparations that may preclude all thoughts of further resistance." He was always harping on this idea of compelling a voluntary submission by a great display of force.

With Washington it was now a question of holding the place he was in, and defending it at all hazards, or of abandoning it to avoid being locked up in it. Harlem Heights was a naturally strong position and the patriots had fortified it by redoubts and entrenchments on the high ground. But the map shows that Howe, by occupying the narrow strip of country to the north of it, between the sound and the Hudson, could shut it in and prevent all retreat except possibly across the Hudson to New Jersey, and that might be prevented by the fleet.

This was so obviously Howe's best move that he was ex-

---

[1] *American Archives*, fifth series, vol. ii, pp. 518, 519.

pected to start on it any day. The New York patriot leaders feared that Washington would obstinately remain and allow himself to be entrapped. They wrote letters to one of his staff officers, Colonel Tilghman, and openly expressed the hope that General Mifflin or General Charles Lee, whose reputation since the battle at Charleston had grown prodigiously, would soon arrive, reveal to Washington the true situation and give him some sound advice. Tilghman replied that Washington was ready for any movement of the British; and it is possible there were some who favored remaining at Harlem Heights where, if the British attacked, they would be slaughtered as they were at Bunker Hill.

General Lee soon arrived, was given command of an outlying force, and it appears to have been a commonly accepted opinion at the time of the Revolution that Washington, supported by some of his chief officers, would have remained in the trap had it not been for Lee, who urged them to go out to White Plains from which it was easier to retreat.[2]

Washington, however, was always so exhaustively painstaking in canvassing every aspect of a situation, that it is difficult to suppose that he did not understand this one as well as Lee, or the anxious patriots of New York. He was probably reserving his retreat for the last moment, and wished to keep up a bold front as long as possible. Howe gave him every possible notice and warning of the entrapping movement, and it was scarcely possible for Washington to have been caught in it, even with his very undisciplined and disorganized army.

The patriot army was in such a state that it was a marvel that it held together at all. People expected that Howe would scatter it to the winds; and no enemy could have ridiculed

---

[2] Gordon, Lafayette, Reed and Stedman describe this service of Lee as a fact, of which they appear to have had no doubt. Lafayette, Memoirs, vol. i, p. 49. Stedman, "American War," edition 1794, vol. i, p. 211; W. B. Reed, "Life of Joseph Reed," vol. i, pp. 251, 255; Gordon, "American Revolution," edition 1788, vol. ii, pp. 337, 338.

its condition more than it was ridiculed by its own officers, Washington and General Reed.

> "A spirit of desertion, cowardice, plunder, and shrinking from duty when attended with fatigue or danger, prevailed but too generally through the whole army. And why should I disguise any part of the truth, by concealing that it was more conspicuous in one part of the army than another. The orderly books and concurrent testimony of impartial and sensible officers, even among themselves will prove it." (W. B. Reed, "Life of Joseph Reed," vol. i, p. 240.)

The indiscriminate plundering by the patriot troops had reached such a pass that Washington declared that it would ruin both the army and the country. "I am wearied to death," he wrote, "with the retrograde motion of things, and I solemnly protest that a pecuniary reward of twenty thousand pounds would not induce me to undergo what I do." Reed was so disgusted that he offered to resign, declaring it impossible to introduce discipline in a mob so disorganized and so insane with levelling and democratic ideas that they would endure orders from no one except as mere suggestions to be obeyed or not at their pleasure.

> "It is impossible for any one to have an idea of the complete equality which exists between the officers and men who compose the greater part of our troops. You may form some notion of it when I tell you that yesterday morning a captain of horse, who attends the General, from Connecticut, was seen shaving one of his men on the parade near the house." (W. B. Reed, "Life of Joseph Reed," vol. i, p. 243.)

Great events and great nations may, however, grow out of what seems very inadequate material, and such is the eternal lesson of history; easy to see in the retrospect; but very difficult to foresee.

Washington went through all the forms of disposing these disorganized forces in the best and most soldier-like manner for meeting Howe. While the main army at Harlem Heights watched and waited for Howe's entrapping movement another patriot force of Pennsylvania and Delaware militia called the "flying camp" was placed in New Jersey, opposite Staten

Island to resist any side movement of the British towards Philadelphia.³

At last, however, on the 12th of October, General Howe embarked the greater part of his force on boats, and passing through the East River landed on Throckmorton's or Throg's neck, a point of land which became an island at high tide and lay to the north and east of Washington's position at Harlem Heights. Meanwhile, Lord Percy moved up from the city by land and made a feint attack on the few troops remaining at the Heights. This movement by Howe was apparently the entrapping movement which had been so long expected. But if he had really intended it to be successful he would have pushed on immediately after landing at Throg's Neck, so as to cut off Washington's retreat. Instead of that he waited at Throg's Neck for five days which gave Washington abundant time to call a council of war of his officers and under their decision move deliberately and leisurely out of the trap.⁴

On the 18th of October Howe moved from Throg's Neck, but proceeded eastward as if he wished to give the Americans still greater opportunity to escape into the open country. Washington kept moving out while small bodies of his force, with a goodly number of riflemen kept up constant skirmishing and minor actions with the outskirts of the British army. As he moved in this way his march was by his left flank so as to keep a front towards the enemy. But he had few horses, and the baggage and artillery had to be dragged by hand. The men would drag part of it forward and then go back and drag the rest. He entrenched his men on every hill as soon as he reached it; and thus his movement was a line of detached and entrenched camps which it was hoped could

---

³ "Life of George Read," pp. 192-195, 198, 200-202, 204, 205, 208, 211, 217, 219.

⁴ *American Archives*, fifth series, vol. ii, pp. 1117, 1118; Memoirs of Long Island Historical Society, vol. iii, pp. 265, 266; Heath Memoirs, pp. 59, 62, 64. Throgmorton's Neck was so named from its first settler, and the name was shortened to Throg and sometimes to Frog. (Jones, "New York in the Revolution," vol. i, p. 620.)

be taken by the superior numbers of the British only with heavy loss.

When he arrived near White Plains on the 28th of October, the British were close at hand, and the advance of the patriots in following out the plan of occupying high ground was in possession of Chatterton Hill, on which they had begun intrenchments and which was separated from the rest of Washington's army by the Bronx River. Seeing that the patriots on this hill were isolated by the river, General Howe attacked them with a force of about four thousand men, mostly Hessians. General McDougal who commanded the patriots on the hill had only sixteen hundred, and of these four regiments deserted him. But with the six hundred that remained, he defended the hill for an hour against a combined attack of British and Hessians supported by artillery. The advantage the Americans had in being intrenched on a hill was overcome in this instance by the effective fire of the British artillery.[5]

"Their light parties soon came on, and we fired upon them from the walls and fences, broke and scattered them at once; but they would run from our front and get round upon our wings to flank us; and as soon as our fire discovered where we were, the enemy's artillery would at once begin to play upon us in a most furious manner. We kept the walls till the enemy were just ready to surround us and then we would retreat from one wall and hill to another and maintain our ground there in the same manner till numbers were just ready to surround us. Once the Hessian Grenadiers came up in front of Colonel Douglas's regiment, and we fired a general volley upon them at about twenty rods distance, and scattered them like leaves in a whirlwind; and they ran off so far, that some of the regiments ran out to the ground where they were when we fired upon them, and brought off their arms and accoutrements, and rum, that the men who fell had with them, which we had time to drink round with before they came on again. They formed at a distance, and waited till their artillery and main body came on, when they ad-

<hr>

[5] *American Archives*, fifth series, vol. ii, pp. 991, 1025, 1168, 1188, 1202, 1203, 1205, 1240, 1270; vol. iii, pp. 472, 543, 547, 576, 922, 925; Gordon, " American Revolution," edition 1788, vol. ii, pp. 339–342; Jones, " New York in the Revolution," vol. i, p. 601; Stedman, " American War," vol. i, pp. 210–215; W. B. Reed, " Life of Joseph Reed," vol. i, pp. 246, 247; Memoirs of Long Island Historical Society, vol. iii, chap. 7.

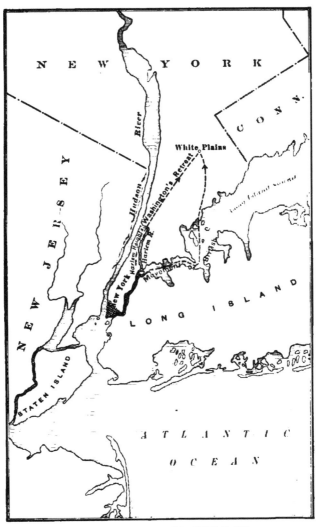

MAP SHOWING MOVEMENTS TO WHITE PLAINS

vanced in solid columns upon us, and were gathering all round us ten to our one. . . . Our loss on the whole may be seventy or eighty, killed and wounded. It is said by all the deserters and captives, who agreed in their stories, that the enemy had about three hundred killed and wounded. The scene was grand and solemn; all the adjacent hills smoked as though on fire, and bellowed and trembled with a perpetual cannonade, and fire of field-pieces, howitzers, and mortars." (*American Archives*, fifth series, vol. iii, p. 473; see also p. 654.)

The taking of this mere outpost on Chatterton Hill satisfied Howe, and he would go no farther. He made no attempt on the weaker parts of Washington's line, although, after taking Chatterton Hill, he received reinforcements and in the opinion of most military men had a chance to inflict irreparable damage. He remained inactive for the next three days, the two armies confronting each other without fighting. During the night of the third day the Americans retired, falling back to almost unassailable heights at North Castle, where Washington took every possible precaution to protect his flanks, and Howe, after waiting five days longer, quietly returned by land to New York.[*]

His extraordinary slowness and laxity again aroused suspicions both in America and England that he had no serious intentions of crushing the rebellion by force; but was working out some ulterior political purpose. This feeling was strengthened when his defence of himself was published. He admitted in his "Narrative" that after taking Chatterton Hill he had intended a further assault on the American lines, but, "for political reasons" refused to explain why that assault was not made.

"An assault upon the enemy's right which was opposed to the Hessian troops, was intended. The committee must give me credit when I assure them that I have political reasons, and no other for declining to explain why that assault was not made." ("The Narrative of Lieutenant-General Sir William Howe," London, 1780, p. 6.)

In further defence of himself he said:

---

[*] Gordon, "American Revolution," edition 1788, vol. ii, p. 343; Writings of Washington, Ford edition, vol. 5, pp. 3, 4, 7.

"By forcing the lines we should, undoubtedly, have gained a more brilliant advantage, some baggage, and some prisoners; but we had no reason to suppose that the rebel army could have been destroyed."

People, however, could not understand why he had not wanted to press the enemy hard, inflict as much damage as possible, come as near as he could to destroying them, and end the war as quickly as possible. But he declared himself as having been entirely content with doing enough to force them to retreat; and said he did not care to risk any more of his men.

In the inquiry into his conduct before Parliament, his confidential officer, General Cornwallis, was asked to give the reasons why more was not done, and he replied:

"From political motives it is impossible for either the General or myself to explain these reasons." (Parliamentay Register, House of Commons, 1779, vol. 13, p. 3.)

These mysterious "political reasons" it was further explained did not refer to politics in England, but to politics in America; and when all this came out in print it is not surprising that a conviction stronger than ever grew up in the public mind, that there was some very strange purpose in Howe's peculiar military manœuvres during the three years of his command. People very naturally inferred that he was trying to bring about a compromise by lack of severity, or that he was determined to stop just short of crushing the rebellion and prove the Whig position that the rebellion was unconquerable.[7]

But the patriot party gave not the slightest sign of a wish to compromise. Washington assumed that Howe's next move would be either up the Hudson to seize the important strategic position at West Point and the Hudson Highlands, or across

---

[7] "Observations on the Conduct of Sir William Howe at the White Plains," London, 1779; "A View of the Evidence Relative to the Conduct of the War under Sir W. Howe;" Galloway, "Letters to a Nobleman on the Conduct of the War" and "A Reply to the Observations of Lieutenant-General Sir W. Howe;" W. B. Reed, "Life of Joseph Reed," vol. i, pp. 244–247; Jones, "New York in the Revolution," vol. i, p. 639.

New Jersey to Philadelphia; and during the next two weeks, after the battle of White Plains, the patriot army was stationed so as to give as much resistance as possible to either of these movements. Lee, with seven thousand men, soon reduced by desertion to four thousand, remained not far from White Plains with instructions to retire towards the Hudson Highlands and fortify himself against any move by Howe in that direction. Heath was sent to strengthen the Highlands themselves; while Washington with a force of about four thousand retired across the Hudson to New Jersey in the hope of checking any movement that might be made against Philadelphia.[8]

But the patriot force was melting away; there were hardly men enough left to offer resistance. News arrived of the defeat of Arnold's fleet on Lake Champlain with the prospect that Ticonderoga might be taken, and then Carleton could march down the Hudson Valley to join Howe's victorious army. Washington's aid, Tench Tilghman, wrote at this time that there was more to be dreaded from Carleton and his army than from Howe.[9]

But Tilghman and the other officers assumed a bold and hopeful front and the disposition of the patriot forces left both Lee's and Washington's troops in such positions that they could finally unite against Howe, whichever course he took. If he went up the Hudson Washington could recross it and join Lee, in an attempt to protect the vital point at the Highlands. If, on the other hand, Howe advanced across New Jersey towards Philadelphia, Lee could cross the Hudson and join Washington in an attempt to protect Philadelphia.

If the line of the Hudson River to Lake Champlain was the controlling strategic position of the country, as every one, including Howe himself, admitted it to be, it is a little re-

---

[8] *American Archives*, fifth series, vol. ii, p. 1094; vol. iii, pp. 555, 557, 560, 620, 630, 639, 657; Writings of Washington, Ford edition, vol. v, pp. 4, 8, 24.

[9] *American Archives*, fifth series, vol. ii, p. 1205.

markable that he did not now take the opportunity to seize it from a defeated and beaten army. He had the largest force commanded by a British general during the war; and at no time during the war, were the Americans so little able to protect West Point and the Highlands. One would suppose that a British general of any energy and serious intentions would have at once occupied the Highlands and secured a thoroughly protected line of navigation down to New York. But Howe, as we shall see, would never do anything to secure the line of the Hudson, nor would he assist any other British officer in securing it.

Two weeks after the battle of White Plains he devoted himself to taking Fort Washington situated at the line of defence Washington had occupied at Harlem Heights. This fort was on the bank of the Hudson and a heavy chain had been stretched across to Fort Lee on the Jersey shore. Old vessels loaded with stone had been fastened to the chain and sunk so that they hung just below the surface of the water; and it was supposed that British war-vessels would be stopped by this obstruction and subjected to a heavy fire from the two forts.[10]

It was an ingenious but futile plan, for the war-ships passed the obstructions without difficulty. Fort Washington itself was utterly useless and should have been abandoned by the patriots when they abandoned Harlem Heights. General Greene, however, was strongly in favor of holding it. He thought it would be an annoyance to the enemy. It was now isolated in the midst of the British; but its garrison, he thought, might at the last moment escape across the Hudson to New Jersey. Other officers were also of this opinion, and

---

[10] Memoirs of Long Island Historical Society, vol. iii, p. 264. Several attempts were made to obstruct the Hudson and also the harbor of Portsmouth, New Hampshire, by means of a chain supported by rafts; but except at West Point the immense weight of water and the rapidity of the current usually parted the chain. (*American Archives*, fifth series, vol. iii, pp. 752, 316, 782, 783, 1031, 1043, 1140; Writings of Washington, Ford edition, vol. v, p. 359 note.)

Washington and a council of war finally consented that it should be retained.

Washington afterwards bitterly regretted the retention of the fort, and at this distance of time, the attempt to hold it seems like a most useless sacrifice of the 3000 patriots who were killed or taken prisoner. But in the minds of Washington and his officers there was the old feeling that Congress and the patriot party might be dispirited if there was too sudden and complete an abandonment of every position before Howe's advancing force. The patriot army was growing smaller from desertions and disasters; and it might become panic-stricken and disappear entirely, never again to be recruited, if its officers and leaders showed that they had no hope.[11]

Fort Washington as Graydon describes it, was scarcely a fort at all; but merely an open earthwork without a ditch or outside obstruction of any consequence, and with high ground in its rear. It had no barracks, casemates, fuel, or water. The troops that were supposed to be holding it found that they could protect themselves better by remaining outside of it; and the New Englanders, Graydon complains, were quite willing to see the southern troops, some three thousand Pennsylvanians and Marylanders, sacrificed in the attempt.

There was desultory fighting round them for many days, and Graydon's descriptions are interesting. There was the patriot lad of eighteen who killed a regular and brought in his shining, beautiful arms, such a contrast to the brown and battered American weapons; and those shining arms were with much ceremony formally presented to the boy at evening parade. There was the sergeant who killed a British officer, stripped him of his uniform, and wore it like a glittering peacock in the patriot camp. Graydon describes the British soldiers as absurdly bad marksmen. They threw up their guns with a jerking motion and pulled the trigger the instant the

[11] Memoirs of Long Island Historical Society, vol. iii, p. 283; W. B. Reed, " Life of Joseph Reed," vol. i, pp. 249, 263.

531

gun reached the shoulder. Ten of them fired at him within forty yards and missed him.

It was an advantage to Howe that one of the garrison deserted to him and revealed all its approaches. He summoned the fort to surrender on the 15th of November, in the old-fashioned way of threatening them with no quarter if they refused. He gave them until the next day to accept his terms, and it has been supposed that he hoped they would retreat across the Hudson during the night and save him the men he might lose in an assault.[12]

Washington watched the attack on the morning of the 16th of November and at first actually had hopes of success. Colonel Magaw, who commanded the fort formed most of his men outside of it on commanding ground and for a time repulsed the British. He was soon, however, driven back, the enemy got behind his lines, and his men began to take refuge in the fort in such a confused and dispirited state that he seems to have been unable to get them to man the works and fight. Washington sent a messenger directing him to hold out until evening when the garrison could be rescued in boats and brought across to New Jersey. But Magaw had surrendered, and there were about three thousand ragged prisoners for the amusement of the British officers.[13]

Graydon, who was one of the prisoners gives most vivid descriptions of the scenes. They were threatened with the butts of guns, reminded that they would be hung, cursed as "damned rebels," and mock orders were given to kill prisoners. The patriots had any sort of clothes and accoutrements they could get, and some of their equipments had once been the property of the British government. Graydon had a belt with the British army marks G.R. stamped upon it; and as soon as this was recognized it was wrenched from him with violence.

---

[12] Gordon, " American Revolution," edition 1788, vol. ii, p. 348.

[13] *American Archives*, fifth series, vol. iii, pp. 707, 856, 1071; Jones, "New York in the Revolution," vol. i, p. 626; Drake, " Life of General Knox," pp. 33, 34; Stedman, " American War," vol. i, p. 217.

TREATMENT OF PRISONERS

The officers surrounded them in crowds, and were as much amused as they had been in Canada at the inferior social condition of the patriot captains and lieutenants. As the names were written down there were shouts of laughter at each tattered farmer who announced that he was a captain, or "keppun," as one of them pronounced it. Young officers, insolent young puppies, anxious to show that they were soldiers, were continually coming up to curse the captives in affected Billingsgate, and to parade them over and over again under the pretence of looking for deserters.

> " On the road, as we approached the city, we were beset by a parcel of soldiers' trulls and others, who came out to meet us. It was obvious, that in the calculation of this assemblage of female loyalty, the war was at an end; and that the whole of the rebel army, Washington and all, were safe in durance. Which is Washington? Which is Washington? proceeded from half a dozen mouths at once; and the guard was obliged to exert itself to keep them off." (Graydon, Memoirs, edition 1846, p. 222.)

The prisoners were afterwards treated with great severity, crowded into stables, and churches, almost starved to death, and the raw pork and maggoty biscuit that they were allowed was thrown into them to be scrambled for as if they were animals. They were obliged to sleep and die in the utmost filth; and the descriptions read like those of Andersonville and Libby during the Civil War. Deaths were numerous every day, and many of those who were exchanged were in such a frail state of health from barbarous usage, that they died on the road before reaching home.[14]

The loss of nearly three thousand troops with all their equipment at Fort Washington, was a terrible disaster and dispirited the patriot party more than anything that had happened. Both Washington and Magaw, were bitterly censured. The New England troops could, however, draw some comfort from it. They had been reviled by the Southerners

---

[14] *American Archives*, fifth series, vol. iii, pp. 1233, 1234, 1429, 1430; Gordon, " American Revolution," edition 1788, vol. ii, pp. 428–430, 459.

for cowardice ever since the retreat of the Connecticut men when Howe took New York. They now declared that they were very glad that it was Southern troops that had surrendered Fort Washington and they were not slow to abuse Magaw and his men for surrendering too soon.

Washington's reputation even among his own friends, sank to the lowest point it reached during his life. He had hesitated and vacillated, they said, until the fatal blow was struck. He felt the misfortune keenly, and tried to put the best face on it.[15]

[15] *American Archives*, fifth series, vol. iii, pp. 762, 763, 766, 889, 1498; Gordon, " American Revolution," edition 1788, vol. ii, p. 350; Writings of Washington, Ford edition, vol. 8, pp. 23, 24.

XLIX.

THE RETREAT ACROSS NEW JERSEY AND THE CAPTURE OF LEE

FORT LEE, on the Jersey shore opposite Fort Washington, was Howe's next object; and on the night after taking Fort Washington, a strong force under Cornwallis, crossed the Hudson and the next morning dragged their cannon up the high bluffs. The patriots abandoned the fort precipitately; and in his report to the Ministry, Howe declared that Cornwallis was within an ace of capturing some two thousand prisoners. As it was, they suffered another huge loss of supplies and artillery, and were obliged to retreat so suddenly, that they left their tents standing and the kettles on the fire.

When Washington crossed the Hudson to New Jersey, he had expected to be reinforced by 5000 troops from that region. But he did not obtain half that number and lost hope of checking the advance of the British to Philadelphia. It was a terrible clearing out and dispersion of the supporters of independence, and would have been far worse if Howe had been more in earnest.[1]

The British force which crossed to take Fort Lee, intended to enclose the patriot troops in the narrow neck of land which lies between the Hudson and the Hackensack Rivers; but Washington escaped in time across the Hackensack. He was now in another narrow neck between the Hackensack and the Passaic, and the land was so level that there was no opportunity for the usual patriot tactics of resistance. Hills were always the great resource of our troops against the superior numbers of their enemy. By entrenching on a hill and retreating just before they were outflanked, they could usually inflict greater loss on the British than they suffered themselves.

[1] *American Archives*, fifth series, vol. iii, p. 1275.

Washington, accordingly left this strongly loyalist country, crossed the Passaic, and passed down towards Newark. If Howe had sent a force from New York by way of Amboy to reach the neighborhood of Newark before Washington arrived, the patriot army might have been cut off, and, in any event, would have been in a serious predicament. The loyalists were surprised that Howe did not take this obvious advantage, and Cornwallis was soundly abused for not pursuing closely after Washington, who lay in Newark nearly a week before Cornwallis moved upon him. Washington fell back to New Brunswick, and having followed him to that town, Cornwallis discontinued the pursuit, leaving Washington to retreat at his ease to Princeton.[2]

From Princeton, Washington on the 2nd of December took the main body of his army to Trenton on the Delaware, having left some twelve hundred men at Princeton to watch the British and report if they again began the pursuit. The British were so slow in coming that Washington after sending his heavy baggage over the Delaware had some thoughts of facing about and moving towards Princeton. The extraordinary slowness of the pursuit, attracted universal attention; and a Hessian officer entered in his diary that Cornwallis had been instructed to follow until the patriots should make a stand, and then not to molest them.[3]

The actual fact was, that Howe had ordered Cornwallis to go no further than New Brunswick; but why this great precaution was taken has never been explained. Inasmuch as Howe had not sent an overwhelming force to seize the Hud-

[2] *American Archives*, fifth series, vol. iii, pp. 765, 789, 790, 925; Gordon, " American Revolution," edition 1788, vol. ii, p. 354; Jones, " New York in the Revolution," vol. i, p. 131; Writings of Washington, Ford edition, vol. v, pp. 41–46.

[3] *Pennsylvania Magazine of History*, vol. xxii, p. 149; " A View of the Evidence Relative to the Conduct of the War," etc., p. 98. Galloway, of course, has much to say on this subject. See, also, Paine's " Crisis," no. 5; Stryker, " Battles of Trenton and Princeton," pp. 16, 327; *American Archives*, fifth series, vol. iii, pp. 1026–1028, 1037.

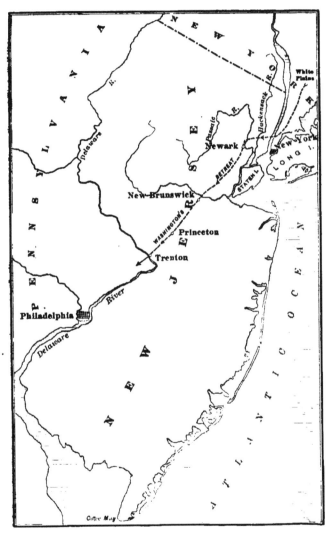

MAP OF WASHINGTON'S RETREAT ACROSS NEW JERSEY

son Highlands and control the water highway up to Lake Champlain and Canada, it might be supposed that he would make a rapid pursuit of Washington's small straggling force of about thirty-five hundred men and capture or scatter it. But instead of that, he was sitting down comfortably in New York and had prohibited Cornwallis and his five thousand troops from pursuing any farther than New Brunswick.

Within three or four days, however, accompanied by reinforcements, Howe joined Cornwallis at New Brunswick, apparently in order to make sure of careful work. He marched his whole pursuing force with the utmost dliberation to Princeton where he rested seventeen hours, and then on the 8th of December took seven hours to march twelve miles to Trenton, where Washington crossed the river at midnight just ahead of him, having first secured all the boats along the shores for a distance of seventy miles.

There never was such an instance of studied and masterly slowness by a disciplined regular force of some six thousand men pursuing a defeated, disorganized band of only thirty-three hundred, which was all Washington had when he crossed the river; and of these, less than three thousand were effectives. All that saved America at this time, said Washington, was "the infatuation of the enemy." "Nothing was more easy to them, with a little enterprise and energy, than to dissipate the remaining force which still kept alive our expiring opposition." [4]

Philadelphia could now easily have been taken by the overwhelming numbers of the British. Washington fully expected that this would be the next event. The patriots were building some frigates there, which could have been destroyed in a few hours. But Howe would not go into Pennsylvania. He said he had no boats with which to cross the Delaware; and after looking along the shores for boats, he gave up the attempt, although the lumber to make flat boats and rafts was

---

[4] Writings of Washington, Ford edition, vol. 8, pp. 394, 503.

lying in piles before his eyes in Trenton, and he could have also brought boats from New Brunswick.[5]

Washington felt sure that Howe would cross the river; he would surely build boats, or bring them from New York; he must beyond all question, intend to take Philadelphia; and the patriot forces were accordingly, spread along the Pennsylvania shore to watch for any movement to effect a crossing. But the precautions were hardly necessary, for, although British scouting parties were seen along the shore as if looking for a good place to cross, yet nothing in the way of crossing was done. Howe was entirely content with the conquest of New Jersey and Washington soon became convinced that Philadelphia had nothing to fear for the present. But he still took for granted that Howe would act the part of a vigorous general, and begin operations again as soon as possible. He had still much to learn about Howe.[6]

The situation expressed in figures is the most extraordinary one ever recorded—a victorious army of thirty-four thousand declining to end an independence movement, represented by only thirty-three hundred wandering half-clothed guerillas. The patriot Congress had fled from Philadelphia to Baltimore; it was a migrating Congress, meeting at Lancaster, York or any place that was safe, for many a day afterwards; and its papers and printing press were carried about in a wagon. Thousands of people in New Jersey and New York were coming in to take the British oath of allegiance and receive their certificates of protection under the "Prohibitory Act." Joseph Galloway and the Allen family of Pennsyl-

---

[5] Stryker, "Battles of Trenton and Princeton," pp. 16, 18, 20, 27, 37: Jones, "History of New York in the Revolution," vol. i, p. 128; Stedman. "American War," edition 1794, vol. i, pp. 220, 223; *American Archives*, fifth series, vol. iii, pp. 1053, 1081, 1094, 1095, 1107, 1108, 1119, 1137, 1138, 1148, 1166, 1275, 1316, 1317; Gordon, "American Revolution." edition of 1788, vol. ii, p. 390; Wilkinson, Memoirs, vol. i, pp. 114–121.

[6] *American Archives*, fifth series, vol. iii, pp. 1201, 1215, 1216, 1217. 1231, 1232, 1233, 1242, 1245, 1246, 1258, 1310, 1340; Writings of Washington, Ford edition, vol. v, pp. 72–84, 89, 100.

vania, now abandoned the patriot cause altogether and came over to New Jersey to make their submission to General Howe.[1]

The general received these loyalists as subjects of the Crown and gave them a written certificate to that effect. A proclamation was issued on the 30th of November ordering all rebels in arms and all rebel political bodies to disband; and a certificate of pardon and protection was promised to all who, within sixty days, should take the oath of allegiance to the king.

Thousands availed themselves of these certificates; and no doubt the Howes had confidence that in time, with a continuation of their moderate and forbearing use of the army and navy, this system would grow into some sort of a general compromise. Many of those who were submitting themselves were patriots who had been in favor of the independence movement if it should succeed; but they could now see no advantage in prolonging such a struggle and sacrificing life and property to the patriotic sentiment that it was better to die than to live political slaves. The defection of such people from the patriot party was ruining it. Elkanah Watson describes an evening he spent in Boston with many devoted patriots at the house of Major Thomas, who had just returned from the retreat through New Jersey.[8]

"We looked upon the contest as near its close, and considered ourselves a vanquished people. The young men present determined to emigrate and seek some spot where liberty dwelt, and where the arm of British tyranny could not reach us." (Memoirs of Elkanah Watson, p. 24.)

It really looked as if the peculiar method of the Howes was succeeding; that there would be a voluntary submission accomplished by a Whig general; that the colonies would accept

---

[1] *American Archives*, fifth series, vol. iii, pp. 1377, 1434; Gordon, "American Revolution," edition 1788, vol. ii, p. 357; Parliamentary Register, vol. 8, p. 252. See also *American Archives*, fifth series, vol. ii, pp. 1074, 1075, 1159, 1164; vol. iii, pp. 927, 1123, 1408.

[8] See also "Diary and Letters of Thomas Hutchinson," vol. ii, pp. 105, 124, 125, 147; "Life of George Reed," p. 224; *American Archives*, fifth series, vol. iii, p. 1275.

the supremacy of Parliament; and that the American idea of self-government and independence for naturally separated peoples would become a mere anacronism.

All that winter the prominent loyalist refugees in London were filled with these hopes. They had been living for several years on pensions from the British Government, visiting country seats, indulging in walking or coaching tours, which was all well enough in its way. But for many of them it was an exile from property, home, old friends and old associations; and now they heard that they could soon return to America with order and good government reëstablished. They prepared for departure. "They began," said one of them, "to count the months of their punishment. A New York gentleman told me if I did not mean to be hurried, it was time to pack up."[9]

It was the universal opinion of the time, that if there had been one vigorous pursuit by Howe, one following up of any one of his advantages; any of the usual methods of war, these loyalists would have realized their expectations, would have returned to their old homes and estates with perhaps additional rewards from the confiscated estates of rebels. Many of the conservative patriots were said to be now ready for any sort of compromise; and the submission of several provinces was daily expected.[10]

The extreme patriots, however, though comparatively few in numbers, nerved themselves to fight to the last. The Congress neither disbanded nor offered a compromise. Dr. Rush afterwards said, that all that saved them from disbanding was the Declaration of Independence. They were ashamed to abandon it.[11] It gave them a rallying point and a tangible ideal. The vast unexplored continent was behind them; and Washington prepared to cross the Alleghanies.

---

[9] "Diary and Letters of Thomas Hutchinson," vol. ii, pp. 147, 153, 172, 173.

[10] *Pennsylvania Magazine of History*, vol. 27, p. 145; Jones, "New York in the Revolution," vol. i, pp. 134, 135; Eddis, "Letters from America," p. 341.

[11] *Pennsylvania Magazine of History*, id. 274–41.

CONFIDENCE IN LEE

"We must then retire to Augusta County in Virginia. Numbers will repair to us for safety, and we will try a predatory war. If overpowered, we must cross the Alleghany Mountains." (Irving, "Washington," vol. ii, chap. xii.)

Thus the romantic retirement of the patriots to live among the Indians and the buffalo, which Burke had so eloquently described, very nearly came to pass. It would have been a migration away from British rule very much like the grand trek of the Boers of South Africa in the next century; and some fierce and free republics might have grown up in the Mississippi Valley.

Washington was in the position of a badly beaten general; and as always happens, under such circumstances, everything he had done seemed to be a fatal mistake; and some other general, Lee for example, could have done a great deal better. Washington's habit of consulting others so industriously, and reserving his final decision until the last moment, was denounced as his hopeless weakness and indecision which had caused the whole train of disasters. His laborious consultations with others over every minute detail, brought him, it was said, under the influence of incompetent minds. His intimate friend, General Reed, lost all confidence in him; and wrote to Lee imploring that general to unite the scattered army, reorganize it, and supply that judgment, experience and decision of character which were, he said, so notoriously lacking in Washington.

"Oh, General, an indecisive mind is one of the greatest misfortunes that can befall an army, how often have I lamented it this campaign. . . . you have decision, a quality often wanted in minds otherwise valuable, and I ascribe to this our escape from York Island, from King's bridge, and the Plains, and have no doubt had you been here the garrison of Mount Washington would now have composed part of this army. . . . Every gentleman of the family, the officers and soldiers generally, have confidence in you—the enemy constantly inquire where you are, and seem to be less confident when you are present." (W. B. Reed, "Life of Joseph Reed," vol. i, p. 255.)

This unquestioning confidence in Lee was now at its height. He was much elated by it and intimated in no doubtful terms that he was quite ready to take the supreme command in place of the officer from Virginia, whose indecision of mind was, he said, ''a much greater disqualification than stupidity or even want of personal courage; accident may put a decisive blunder in the right, but eternal defeat and miscarriage must attend the man of the best parts if cursed with indecision.'' [12]

Plausible phrases like these are to be found in most of Lee's writings, which can be read in the archives side by side with the sanity and equipoise of the letters of Washington. When Washington had been driven across New Jersey he had written to Lee to join him with such forces as he had left. But Lee delayed, thinking he had an opportunity to cut off an exposed division of the British. After he crossed into New Jersey he still delayed, possibly in the hope that he could fall upon the rear of the British who were pursuing Washington, cut their communications and distinguish himself. Finally on the 13th of December, he negligently passed the night at White's Tavern, near Baskingridge, several miles outside of his own lines.

Colonel Harcourt, commanding a British scouting party in that neighborhood, was told by a loyalist of the exposed position of the ''American Palladium,'' and the next morning he surrounded the tavern. It was a curious coincidence, that Harcourt's party was composed of a company of light dragoons which Lee had himself commanded in 1762 in Spain at the taking of Villa Velha.

Harcourt ordered Cornet Banistre Tarleton, afterwards famous in the south, to begin the attack on the tavern; and according to some accounts Lee begged for his life and claimed the benefit of the proclamation of pardon under the Prohibitory Act. But it seems best to follow the account by Wilkinson, who was an eye witness, and said that Lee behaved with great coolness and asked what had become of his guard. Wilkinson went to the other end of the house where he had last seen them, but they were flying in every direction pursued by the

---

[12] W. B. Reed, " Life of Joseph Reed," vol. i, pp. 257-262.

dragoons. Believing it a mere marauding party Wilkinson placed himself against the wall with a pistol in each hand. But all the British wanted was Lee. They demanded his surrender and when he gave himself up they mounted him on Wilkinson's horse which stood ready at the door and hurried him off bareheaded and in his slippers.[12]

Both Washington and Congress made every effort to secure the exchange of Lee, and the Congress sent him a sum of money for his necessities, while in captivity. The British, however, were at first inclined to treat him as a deserter to be sent to England to be hung or shot. But at the time he joined the American army, he had resigned his half pay in the British service, and this saved him from a trial under the military law as a deserter.

Severe retaliation was threatened by the patriots if Lee was in any way ill-treated. For this reason, Howe would not send him to England for fear retaliation might be inflicted on the Hessian officers who had been taken prisoners and cause mutiny and discontent among his foreign troops. Lee was, therefore, extremely well treated; lived luxuriously in the rooms of the New York assembly; had the full liberty of the city and its limits; horses were furnished him; he was allowed to have his dogs and invite friends to dinner; and was finally exchanged in May, 1778.

Some months after he became a prisoner he is said to have announced to General Howe that he did not approve of the Declaration of Independence, but favored a compromise and believed that some compromise could be effected. As this was exactly in the line of Howe's policy, Lee was given leave to communicate with the Congress and wrote that body a letter,

---

[12] Wilkinson, Memoirs, vol. i, pp. 105, 108; "Diary and Letters of Thomas Hutchinson," vol. ii, p. 136; Stryker, "The Battles of Trenton and Princeton," pp. 55–59; *American Archives*, fifth series, vol. iii, pp. 1041, 1121, 1122, 1153, 1202, 1203, 1204, 1239, 1262, 1265, 1365, 1377; Jones, "New York in the Revolution," vol. i, p. 672; Fonblanque, "Life of Burgoyne," p. 50 note; New York Historical Society, collections 1874, vol. iv, pp. 387–391.

on the 9th of February, 1777, asking for the appointment of a committee to communicate with him on matters of great importance to himself and to the country. Washington, Robert Morris and some others were in favor of sending this committee. But after much discussion and hesitation, the Congress refused. There had already been too much negotiation, and the previous communications with the Howes had injured our cause in France by making it appear that we were willing to accept a compromise instead of absolute independence.

A year afterwards in January, 1778, Elias Boudinot, had a private conversation with Lee, then still a prisoner in New York, and Lee told him that his object in asking for the committee from Congress had been to disclose to them the plan of the British campaign for the following summer, which he had accidentally discovered.

We now know that about the time Lee's request for the committee failed, he had prepared a written plan professing to show that the best way for the British to conquer America would be by occupying positions at Alexandria and Annapolis on Chesapeake Bay. His having prepared such a plan was not generally known until nearly a century after the Revolution, when the plan in his handwriting was discovered among the papers of Howe's private secretary. The plan from a military point of view was not a good one; and what were Lee's purposes in this plan and in telling Boudinot that he would have disclosed the British plan of campaign would be difficult to fathom.[14]

---

[14] *American Archives*, fifth series, vol. iii, pp. 1369, 1374, 1428, 1607; Writings of Washington, Ford edition, vol. v, p. 168 note; 431 note, vol. vi, p. 299 note, 463, 491; Fonblanque, "Life of Burgoyne," p. 161 note; Appleton's Cyclopaedia of National Biography, title "Lee;" New York Historical Society Collections, 1874 vol. iv, pp. 404, 416–424; Boudinot's Journal, p. 74, 1894; J. J. Boudinot, "Life of Boudinot," vol. i, p. 140.

L.

ARNOLD DEFEATED ON LAKE CHAMPLAIN

WHEN the patriot army was driven out of Canada in the end of June of this year 1776, it will be remembered, that Burgoyne stopped the pursuit of it at Isle aux Noix. But the island was so damp and unhealthy that another retreat was made to Crown Point. Soon Schuyler and Gates, who were now in command, began another retreat to Ticonderoga which brought indignant protests from Washington, and many of the field officers under Schuyler and Gates signed a written protest. This continual retreating, they said, when no enemy pursued was too humiliating, was abandoning too much, and sacrificing at once the naval supremacy of the lake, which could be better maintained with Crown Point as a base. But Schuyler and Gates were unmoved in their opinion, defended with vigorous arguments the reasonableness of the move, and, being on the ground, claimed the right to use their own discretion. They began building a navy which was put under the command of Arnold. They made most strenuous efforts to restore the health of their men and gather recruits; and they fortified the high ground on both sides of the narrow stretch of water at Ticonderoga.[1]

The summer of 1776 passed away while Arnold on one side and Carleton on the other were preparing armed gondolas, barges, sloops and schooners to fight for the supremacy of the lake. Arnold, meantime, had displayed the weak side of his nature in two violent quarrels, one with Colonel Hazen and the other with Colonel Brown.[2]

General Schuyler, also at this time became indignant at

---

[1] *American Archives*, fourth series, vol. vi, pp. 1071, 1074, 1101, 1107, 1108, 1200–1203.

[2] Gordon, "American Revolution," edition 1788, vol. ii, pp. 379, 380; *American Archives*, fifth series, vol. iii, p. 1158.

the attacks on his character, fomented by the New Englanders, as well as by neglect and slights, which he thought he had received from Congress. He resolved to resign and publish a vindication revealing all the details of insubordination, confusion and mismanagement of inferior officers in the northern army. It may, perhaps, be said that constantly sick with ague, and worn out with anxiety and work he was irritable, and over sensitive; and yet, in spite of this consideration, it cannot be denied that there was much ground for the indignation he felt.

He was finally persuaded by Washington, and other leaders, and also by the Congress, not to resign, and above all not to publish a vindication which would dispirit the patriot cause by revealing the shocking conditions of disease and insubordination in the northern army. Congress, and also the Connecticut assembly, gave him a vote of confidence and important persons combined to soothe and pacify him. But the hatred of the New Englanders pursued him for the rest of his life. He despised the New England officers, because they were not from the upper ranks of life. He refused to ask any of them to dine or drink with him, and on almost every occasion he treated them with studied rudeness and contempt. The New Englanders were proud of their levelling and democratic principles, and they deeply resented Schuyler's insolence. Whole generations of them, long after the Revolution, were brought up to believe all manner of evil of the Albany aristocrat, and the prejudice against him was so strong and deep rooted, that Daniel Webster confessed that with him it was almost ineradicable.[3]

Gates had instructed Arnold to run no wanton risk and not to cruise too far down Lake Champlain. On the 16th of September, Arnold learned from one of his spies that Carleton would soon be greatly superior to him in ships, men and guns. Not believing this information, or as some have supposed not wanting to believe it, Arnold sent the

---

[3] *American Archives*, fifth series, vol. ii, pp. 440, 709, 846, 1206, 1384; Lossing, " Life of Schuyler; " G. W. Greene, " Life of Nathanael Greene," vol. i, pp. 435, 436.

spy in irons to General Gates and accepted a different and more agreeable story from two other spies who proved to be impostors.[4]

On the 7th of October, Arnold had pressed far down the Lake below Crown Point, and was wondering why the enemy did not come. He had three schooners, a sloop, eight gondolas, and four galleys, with guns and swivels manned by about eighty men. Carleton's force was a ship, two schooners, a radeau, a gondola, 20 gunboats, and some long boats manned by 700 sailors with a very large number of heavy guns, 24 pounders, 9 pounders, and 6 pounders, handled by a detachment from the royal artillery.

To meet this overwhelming odds, Arnold anchored his little fleet between an island and the main land in Valcour Bay. On the 11th of October, having been warned of the approach of the British fleet under a press of sail before the northwest wind, he got his vessels under way and stood out to meet them. But on discovering their superior force he returned to his position between the island and the main land, and there the enemy attacked him late in the morning, having run a little by him and then beat up against the wind to his position.

Arnold was advised by General Waterbury to make sail and fight them on a retreat in the main lake; but he insisted on fighting where he was at anchor. This gave the British the advantage of surrounding him with their small boats and of putting Indians in the woods on shore to annoy him with the fire of small arms. But the fire from these Indians had little or no effect; and if we admit that it was proper for Arnold to stop and fight such a superior force, instead of retreating and reserving his fleet to fight near Ticonderoga, we must also acknowledge that his position, in the opinion of military men, was well chosen. His flanks were protected, his force condensed, and his fire concentrated.

The two fleets fought each other all the afternoon, with

<hr />

[4] Wilkinson, Memoirs, vol. i, pp. 81, 87; *American Archives*, fifth series, vol. ii, pp. 885, 999, 1080, 1186.

serious loss in ships and men for the Americans, who, nevertheless, held their own with wonderful courage against the enormous odds of the British. If it be true that Arnold had purposely risked this unequal contest, and the loss of his men and ships, merely to gain personal distinction for himself, he accomplished his purpose.

An American schooner and a gondola were destroyed, and the rest badly shattered; while the British lost three gondolas, two sunk and one blown up with sixty men. Arnold fought with such conspicuous heroism as to attract the admiration and surprise of the British. Being in great want of gunners, he was obliged to point with his own eyes and hands most of the guns on the Congress.

At night fall the British ships ceased firing and fell back over 600 yards to the southward. The Americans having used nearly all their ammunition, Arnold decided to escape during the darkness directly through the British fleet, and he accomplished this by one of those devices at which our people were always so skilful, and the British always so slow to detect.

"The Trumbull galley commanded by a Colonel Wigglesworth of the Massachusetts militia, led the retreat with barely sail enough set to give her steerage way, and a lanthorn under her stern, so masked as not to be seen except by those directly in her wake, and the rest of the squadron followed in succession equipped in the same manner with lanthorns, at intervals of two or three hundred yards; General Waterbury of Connecticut, and General Arnold, in the Congress and Washington gallies, bringing up the rear. The night was profoundly dark, and the atmosphere was charged with a heavy fog; strict silence and stillness was enjoined, and we passed the enemy's line, without seeing one of his vessels or being ourselves perceived." (Wilkinson, Memoirs, vol. i, p. 90.)

The next day the British pursued with Arnold fifteen miles ahead. But the wind soon sprang up from the southwest and blew a light gale against which Arnold's vessels in their crippled condition could not beat and several of the smaller ones were run ashore and abandoned. The next morning the pursuit continued with the wind from the northwest. The British drew near enough to renew the fight, and captured

General Waterbury and his ship. Arnold soon afterwards found the remains of his fleet in a sinking condition. He ran them ashore, set them afire with colors flying, while his men posted themselves on the bank and protected the colors from the enemy until all were consumed.[5]

Arnold's craving for distinction was always passionate and overwhelming. He had conducted the expedition through the Maine wilderness to Quebec brilliantly and heroically; but with no valuable result; and some have gone so far as to say that he had now sacrificed his fleet in a rash defence, in which victory was impossible, and no end could be gained, but the enhancement of his reputation for courage.

During the last year he had become very abusive, inconsiderate and quarrelsome with his fellow officers; and under the plea of military necessity, he was believed to have enriched himself by seizing and selling for his own advantage, the goods of merchants in Montreal.

The American fleet of Lake Champlain was now wiped out of existence. Arnold and the remains of his crews escaped overland to Ticonderoga. It was expected that Carleton would attack Ticonderoga and attempt to press southward to Albany and the Hudson River Valley to join General Howe, who had taken New York and inflicted severe defeat on Washington's army. Schuyler, Gates and Arnold redoubled their exertions to defend Ticonderoga; and if Carleton should succeed in taking it they hoped to check his march to Albany.

More than two weeks passed without any sign of an enemy; for the wind was against them. But on the morning of the 28th of October they appeared in sight and landed regulars,

---

[5] *American Archives*, fifth series, vol. ii, pp. 933, 982, 1028, 1038, 1079, 1116, 1117, 1040, 1069, 1143, 1224; "Diary and Letters of Thomas Hutchinson," vol. ii, p. 116; Gordon, "American Revolution," edition 1788, vol. ii, p. 583; Wilkinson, Memoirs, vol. i, pp. 88, 93, 47, 49, 58, 70, 75; Cooper, "History of the Navy of the United States;" "American Historical Record," vol. iii, p. 438; Sparks, "Correspondence of American Revolution," vol. i, appendix; "American Historical Record," vol. iii, pp. 438, 501.

Indians, and Canadian troops on the west side of the lake as if intending to attack at that point. All day their boats were moving and reconnoitering from one side of the lake to the other; but in the evening they all reëmbarked and sailed away northward to Crown Point. A few days afterwards the American scouts who followed them, reported that the whole British force had returned to Canada and the beautiful water highway of Lake Champlain was once more a silent wilderness.

Carleton seems to have decided that an assault on Ticonderoga would be a useless waste of life. A long siege during the winter was, he thought, equally impractical. He would have to open trenches in ground that in a few days might be frozen, and at the same time keep open his long line of communications, back to Canada. He was much criticised in England, and by his own officers; for the general belief was that he could have taken Ticonderoga and pressed on southward to Albany where he might have been met by Howe with his victorious army, coming up from New York. This with the recent disasters to the patriots in New York and New Jersey would be so overwhelming a triumph of the British arms that the war, it was said, would have been ended.

But Carleton may have been wiser than they supposed. Subsequent events showed that Howe was not to be relied upon for any movement of that sort; and Carleton was hardly prepared for pressing down to Albany and keeping open his communications with Canada. It seems probable, however, from what happened the following year, that he could have taken Ticonderoga much more easily than he supposed. Its garrison under Gates consisted, it is true, of 9000 effective men; but a neighboring height, called Sugar Hill, commanded all the fortifications, and if Carleton had taken this hill the garrison would have been at his mercy.[e]

---

[e] *American Archives*, fourth series, vol. vi, p. 1263; fifth series, vol. ii, pp. 885, 999, 1080, 1186, 1125, 1131, 1132, 1138, 1142, 1144, 1170, 1172, 1192, 1205, 1257, 1287, 1297, 1299, 1314, 1315; vol. iii, pp. 501, 511, 526, 605, 607, 621, 641; Fonblanque, " Life of Burgoyne," pp. 218, 220, 224, 225; Wilkinson, Memoirs, vol. i, pp. 90–94.

CARLETON AND HOWE

The gossip of London described Carleton as a man of strong resentment. He disliked Germain and was supposed to have been deeply mortified that Howe, his junior in rank, had been given the important command in America, while he had been confined to Canada. He was, therefore, resolved, it was said, to do no more than keep Canada clear of the Americans, and he would make no expedition down the Hudson Valley to assist his rival and increase that rival's reputation.[7]

Howe, on the other hand, was said to be equally jealous of Carleton, and would make no expedition up the Hudson to join an expedition from Canada, for fear that Carleton would reap the benefit of it. He wished, it is supposed, to avoid bringing Carleton down into the rebellious colonies, where he would assert his superior rank and claim the chief command.

Carleton had saved one province for the British empire, and he was the only one of the British officers in the Revolution who accomplished what he was sent out to do. He has been described as possessed of greater and more masterful qualities than any general that the British had in America during the war. Bourinot gives him high praise as the saviour of Canada, and compares him with Frontenac as a soldier and with Lord Elgin as a statesman.[8] Indeed, he impresses one as possessed of rather more effective character and energy than any of the other English officers, except perhaps Clinton, who was energetic but with the luck and odds against him.

---

[7] "Diary and Letters of Thomas Hutchinson," vol. i, p. 505; vol. ii, p. 117.

[8] Bourinot, "Story of Canada," p. 281 Heath, Memoirs, p. 316.

LI.

In that long campaign of the summer and autumn of 1776 the patriots had been defeated at every point. They had been driven out of Canada, deprived of the naval supremacy of Lake Champlain, defeated at the battle of Long Island, New York taken, Fort Washington taken, Washington's army scattered, and the remnant of it under his personal command driven across New Jersey; and yet Howe stopped short, took no more active measures, followed up none of his advantages.

His successes, as he afterwards put it in his Narrative, "had very nearly induced a general submission." He seemed to be waiting for the "general submission" to be voluntarily offered by the patriots. He apparently expected from them some compromise plan which would show that the colonies could be retained without subjugation as the Whigs under Burke and Chatham supposed was possible.

But, as loyalists like Galloway pointed out, this stopping just short of complete subjugation and waiting for a voluntary submission merely brought into the British lines the timid patriots to get certificates of protection for the time being, while it gave the determined and courageous nucleus of the patriot party time to recuperate, collect a new army and make another stand for independence.

When the Congress departed so hurriedly from Philadelphia on the 12th of December, they left Robert Morris in charge of their affairs and General Putnam as military commander to keep down the loyalists and make as good a defence as possible. The town was a scene of distress and confusion, the streets filled with beds, furniture and baggage and scarcely

552

anybody willing to remain but the Quakers and the sick soldiers in the hospital.[1]

Morris's willingness to become the solitary representative of the infant government of the United States at a time when it was abandoned and very near extinction, was his first conspicuous service in the Revolution. He was a merchant, an owner of ships, cargoes and privateersmen after the manner of the times, bold and confident in commercial speculation or privateering venture, a whole-souled, humorous, broadminded sort of man. Two other members of the Congress, when it fled to Baltimore, had been appointed to act with him as a committee of executive affairs in Philadelphia; but they went home and left all to him.

For the next few months he conducted the executive business of the patriot government, borrowed money, gave directions to the captains of the continental war-vessels, superintended the sale of prizes they brought in, bought ammunition and supplies for the remains of Washington's army, hastened the work on the new frigates, and, in short, kept the practical work of the government alive almost under Howe's nose.[2]

It seemed as if Howe purposely refused to move again until Washington had a sufficient number of men to meet him. Months passed away before Washington was able to collect ten thousand men, and nearly a year after, in September, 1777, he had only eleven thousand with which to fight the battle of the Brandywine. He never again got together as many as he had had at New York.

Settled down in New York for the winter with Mrs. Loring and cards for his entertainment, Howe made no effort to wear out the scattered patriot commands or to complete and make permanent his conquest. He never did anything in

---

[1] Oberholtzer, " Life of Robert Morris," p. 24; Stryker, " The Battles of Trenton and Princeton," p. 34; *American Archives*, fifth series, vol. iii, pp. 1198, 1199; Stedman, " American War," vol. 2, p. 230.

[2] Oberholtzer, " Life of Robert Morris," pp. 24–30. See, also, *American Archives*, fifth series, vol. iii, pp. 1371, 1373, and title " Robert Morris " in index of *Archives*.

winter. The three winters he spent in repressing the rebellion were passed in great luxury in the three principal cities, Boston, New York and Philadelphia, waiting for a voluntary submission. His great army of thirty thousand was larger than the population of New York, and filled the houses, churches, and public buildings, crowding out alike both the loyalist and the patriot, spreading out into the suburbs and cutting down the woodlands for miles in every direction to supply fuel.

At the time Howe pursued Washington across New Jersey he sent a force of some six thousand troops under Clinton, to occupy Newport, Rhode Island, because its easy access from the sea rendered it a convenient place of call for British war-vessels. Clinton, it is said, would have preferred to go to Philadelphia, the taking of which would have been a much more serious loss to the patriots. He, of course, had no difficulty in taking Newport which was defenceless, and he compelled Commodore Hopkins with his small patriot fleet to retire up Narragansett Bay to Providence, where he remained for some time inactive.[a]

It also seemed necessary that Howe should do something to retain control of New Jersey, which he had passed through with his army in pursuit of Washington; and, accordingly, he placed cantonments of troops at different points in a line from Staten Island to Trenton. One was at Amboy, near Staten Island, one at New Brunswick, another at Princeton, and two cantonments of fifteen hundred Hessians each at Trenton and Bordentown on the Delaware. The cantonments at Trenton and Bordentown were six miles apart. Trenton was twelve miles from the force at Princeton, and New Brunswick eighteen miles from Princeton.

The forces at Trenton and Bordentown were small and

---

[a] *American Archives*, fifth series, vol. iii, pp. 1112, 1114, 1115, 1130, 1131, 1142, 1145, 1146, 1162, 1176, 1222, 1315, 1316, 1389, 1390, 1423; G. W. Greene, "Life of Nathanael Greene," vol. i, p. 300; Jones, "New York in the Revolution," vol. i, p. 639; Gordon, "American Revolution," edition, 1788, vol. ii, p. 359; Stedman, "American War" vol. i, p. 221.

MAP SHOWING THE POSITION OF THE BRITISH ARMY IN NEW YORK IN DECEM-
BER, 1776, WITH ITS CANTONMENTS FOR HOLDING NEW JERSEY

the placing of them in such an exposed position was a fatal error which has been universally condemned by all persons of military knowledge.[4] Considering the enormous army Howe had in New York, he might easily have made his outposts larger and arranged them within supporting distance. Indeed that a general of so much ability as Howe should make such a great blunder has always seemed to every one who has studied the subject most extraordinary and inexplicable. Cornwallis, who is said to have advised the placing of these outposts, said that they were large enough and that no misfortune would have happened to the one at Trenton if Colonel Rall, who commanded the Hessians there, had fortified and protected his post in accordance with the orders that had been given to him. As it was, however, these two isolated posts, Trenton and Bordentown, so far from support, were tempting objects of attack. Washington saw his opportunity to make a turning point in the war and prepared to destroy them.

Trenton was then a small village of only about one hundred houses. Colonel Rall, its Hessian commander, had distinguished himself by gallant conduct at White Plains and at the taking of Fort Washington; but at Trenton, he appears to have spent his time in gay confidence of security, talked lightly of going to Philadelphia when the river was frozen and had visions of capturing Washington in some of the raiding parties of patriots that constantly hung round his pickets and outposts. When his officers complained that his men needed warmer clothing, he laughed at them. He would soon, he said, run barefoot over the ice and take the city of Philadelphia; and if his officers did not care to share his honors they might retire from the post. He placed no fortifications round the town and allowed his men to plunder and disaffect the inhabitants. The fifteen hundred Hessians lower down the Delaware at Bordentown, were under Count Donop, and

---

[4] Clinton said that Howe admitted that they were too far away. Clinton's MS. notes to Stedman's "American War," vol. i, p. 224, in Carter-Brown Collection; Stryker, *id.*, pp. 224, 225; *American Archives*, fifth series, vol. iii, p. 1317.

seem to have been intended to cover the neighboring town of Burlington.[5]

Washington collected the remains of Lee's forces, which, together with his own and some sent down from Lake Champlain, gave him six thousand effectives, which represented all there was left of fighting enthusiasm in the patriot population. There was still something to fight for before retreating to the western wilderness. The Congress had not disbanded, and Robert Morris was carrying on an executive government at Philadelphia which Howe had fortunately abstained from attacking. But everything hung on a thread, and Washington was urged to make some capital stroke and make it quickly, "or" as Reed said, "give up the cause."

So many were taking advantage of the offer of pardon, that in a little time the American army would be dissolved; and Reed thought that a great number of the militia officers would soon take the benefit of that offer of pardon and go over to the British.[6]

There was also another reason for attacking the post at Trenton. Although Howe had not attacked Philadelphia, it was, nevertheless, inconceivable that he would not soon go there, especially if the upper part of the river froze over; and Washington had what he believed to be secret, and sure information that the British would cross the Delaware as soon as the ice was strong.[7] If, therefore, the patriots should make a successful attack upon Trenton, it would presumably delay

---

[5] Parliamentary Register, vol. 13, pp. 4, 95; Stedman, "American War," vol. i, p. 224; Stryker, "Battles of Trenton and Princeton," pp. 99, 105; "Observations on the Conduct of Sir William Howe at the White Plains," p. 19, London, 1779. See, also, *Pennsylvania Magazine of History*, vol. xxii, p. 462.

[6] The rolls gave Washington's numbers as 10,804; but as so often happened, nearly half of these were sick or absent. (Stryker, "Battles of Trenton and Princeton," p. 85; Wilkinson, Memoirs, vol. i, p. 124; W. B. Reed, "Life of Joseph Reed," vol. i, pp. 270, 272.) A New Jersey militia colonel had already, it seems, accepted one of these pardons. (Stryker, "Battles of Trenton and Princeton," p. 78.)

[7] *American Archives*, fifth series, vol. iii, p. 1420.

any British movement to Philadelphia, save the patriot frigates there, and the headquarters for raising money and supplies which Robert Morris was conducting.

These preparations of the patriots to rehabilitate themselves, show what a fatal mistake Howe had made in not following up his opportunities. He had left the patriots just enough to rebuild upon, and so long as he had left them this chance the resolute nucleus of the party would never come to that voluntary submission which he appeared to be expecting.

The Congress finding itself safe at Baltimore immediately set about the work of rehabilitation without the slightest thought of submission. They adopted a resolution increasing Washington's authority, giving him power to raise recruits and appoint and dismiss officers in his own way; to take property whenever and wherever he wanted it, allowing a reasonable price; and to arrest and confine loyalists and those who would not take the continental money. These dictatorial powers were given him for a period of six months, and full confidence was expressed that he would not misuse them.[8]

But he did not receive these powers until the end of December, and, meantime, it was only by the greatest persuasion that he kept together his small force of six thousand men. That peculiar character, General Gates, had gone to the Congress at Baltimore to persuade them that Washington was making a mistake, that while he was watching the enemy at Trenton they would cross the river lower down and reach Philadelphia, and that Washington should retire south of the Susquehanna and there form a new army.[9]

Artists and sculptors have represented Washington's troops as dressed in handsome uniforms. But those who saw them agree in describing them as dressed in ragged summer clothes, with their shoes so worn that the frozen roads cut their bare feet. Their camps along the Delaware were filled with loyal-

---

[8] This resolution was adopted December 27, before the Congress had heard of the battle of Trenton on the 25th. (Stryker, *id.*, pp. 243, 244; *American Archives*, fifth series, vol. iii, p. 1613.

[9] Wilkinson, Memoirs, vol. i, p. 127.

ists and spies, for the most of the people in that region were lukewarm or hostile, had given up the war as hopeless, and thought that the best plan was to make some sort of peace with Howe.

Washington was well informed of the condition and numbers of the Hessian troops at Trenton and Bordentown, largely, it is said, through the fidelity of a half idiot youth who acted as a spy. He was so deficient that the enemy allowed him to wander about everywhere; but he had sufficient intelligence to return to Washington with very accurate reports of what he saw. He was afterwards suspected by the British, and confined in prison where he starved to death.[10]

Having finally made up his mind what to do Washington divided his force into three divisions, which were to cross the Delaware through the floating ice at about the same time. One under Cadwalader with eighteen hundred men was to go against Donop at Bordentown; another with about eleven hundred, under Ewing, was to cross almost in front of Trenton and station itself on the other side of Assunpink Creek directly south of the village to cut off escape and prevent any reinforcements from Donop; and the third, of about twenty-five hundred of the best troops under Washington himself, was to cross considerably above Trenton and come down to make the main attack upon the village. If Cadwalader was successful at Bordentown and Ewing and Washington successful at Trenton, all the divisions would unite and push on against Princeton and New Brunswick.[11]

For some time small squads of patriots had been in the habit of crossing the river almost every day and skirmishing with the Hessians guards and outposts. Whether this was intended as a preparation for the main attack, so that when the Hessians should see its advance guard, they would think it only another skirmishing party, is not clear; but it was well calculated to have that effect.

---

[10] Gordon, "American Revolution," edition 1788, vol. ii, p. 391.
[11] Stryker, *id.*, pp. 81, 82, 113, 344-347.

Galloway said that there was a division arranged to draw off Donop's attention and prevent him going up to the relief of Trenton. For this purpose an irregular band of some four hundred, many of them boys, were sent up from Philadelphia along the Jersey side of the Delaware towards Bordentown with orders not to fight, but to encourage Donop to pursue them down the river and as far away from Trenton as possible. This part of the plan is said to have succeeded; and Donop pursued this party until most of his men were twelve miles from Bordentown and eighteen miles from Trenton. But Gordon says, and apparently with truth, that this diversion was accidental, and of no particular effect, for Donop had returned to Bordentown before Trenton was attacked.[12]

Washington felt the greatest uneasiness at hazarding an attack on which so much depended. If he failed, if he was beaten back what would become of the patriot cause! At the last moment he found that his effective troops were far fewer than he had any conception of; and yet he felt that he must go on. "Necessity," he said, "dire necessity, will, nay must justify my attack." He wrote to Reed to arrange minor attacks on as many of their posts as possible, for the "more we can attack at the same instant, the more confusion we shall spread, and greater good will result from it."[13]

The two divisions under Cadwalader and Ewing met with serious difficulties in crossing the Delaware. To cross through the ice was cold and difficult, but not dangerous work. If the ice was floating loosely the passage could be made, but if the pieces were closely packed together by the tide, boats could not be forced through them.

Where Washington himself crossed, above the influence of the tide, the ice appears to have been floating loosely. It was Christmas night, cold, and at eleven o'clock a northeast snow-

[12] Galloway, "Letters to a Nobleman on the Conduct of the War," p. 159; W. B. Reed, "Life of Joseph Reed," vol. i, p. 273; Stryker, "The Battles of Trenton and Princeton," pp. 74, 200; Gordon, "American Revolution," edition 1788, vol. ii, p. 393.

[13] *American Archives*, fifth series, vol. iii, p. 1376, 1377, 1400.

storm began, which became sleet before morning. It was severe exposure for patriots with ragged summer clothes and worn-out shoes. They labored hard with boats and artillery, most efficiently assisted by Glover's Marblehead sailors, and encouraged by some of the best officers that the Revolution had thus far developed, Greene, Sullivan, Knox, Lord Stirling, St. Clair, and Stark. But with their utmost exertions far more time was spent in crossing than they expected. It was three in the morning before Knox had all his artillery over, and nearly four when they took up their line of march. The timing of the combined movements had evidently failed, and Washington saw that he could not reach the Hessian camp before dawn, and that his chance of surprising them in the darkness was gone. It was a serious moment in the American cause, while he hesitated what to do. It was a momentous decision when he resolved to take all chances and press on to the straggling village of one hundred houses, where Rall and his fifteen hundred men had been celebrating Christmas night.

It has been supposed that Washington had resolved to stake his life on the issue, and not survive defeat. The patriot cause, he believed, was to be rehabilitated or extinguished that night. Circumstances, however, favored him; for although daylight was coming the enemy had no entrenchments and were protected only by pickets and sentinels. Rall spent the whole night with wine and cards. A loyalist sent him a note warning him of Washington's movements, but he thrust it into his pocket without reading it. He had previously been warned by numerous loyalists and spies that the Americans were preparing for some sort of attack; but he would not believe it and spoke contemptuously of his enemies.[14]

Early in the evening a roving band of about fifty patriots who had been scouting for three days in New Jersey, and knew nothing of the intended attack on Trenton, moved up near Rall's picket on the Pennington road and exchanged a few shots. This is supposed to have led the Hessians to believe

<hr />

[14] Stryker, " Battles of Trenton and Princeton," p. 125.

that no other attack was intended and they immediately relaxed their vigilance.

It was broad daylight and exactly eight o'clock in the morning when Washington's force reached the first pickets and drove them in on the village. In spite of the daylight, the Americans accomplished a complete surprise, which, in addition to their greater numbers, gave them an overwhelming advantage. They were in the streets and Knox was using his artillery before the Hessians, hurrying from the houses, could fully make up their minds what to do. The Hessians, says Knox, "endeavored to form in streets the heads of which we had previously the possession of with cannon and howitzers; these in the twinkling of an eye cleared the street. The backs of the houses were resorted to for shelter. These proved ineffectual. The musketry soon dislodged them." Some started to escape towards Princeton, but Washington, seeing the movement, sent a force which cut them off. A few escaped by the way which Ewing was intended to have obstructed if he had succeeded in crossing the river. The rest carried on a hopeless and confused fight in the streets, which is supposed to have lasted thirty-five or forty minutes, at the end of which time Rall had been mortally wounded, and most of his men had surrendered.[15]

Poor Rall, while trying to rally his men, had been struck in the side by two balls. He was assisted into the Methodist church at Queen and Fourth Streets, and thence carried on one of the benches of the church to his own headquarters, where Washington and General Greene visited him, took his parole, and through an interpreter exchanged some kindly words before he died.

The completeness of the surprise and the utter inability of the Hessians to get together and defend themselves, is shown by the casualties. The Hessians lost twenty-two killed and

---

[15] Stryker, *id.*, pp. 218, 220; Drake, " Life of General Knox," p. 36; Stedman, "American War," vol. i, pp. 230–234; Wilkinson, Memoirs, vol. i, p. 128.

eighty-four wounded, while Washington had only two officers and two privates wounded.[16]

The other two divisions which intended to support Washington, seem to have found the ice jammed by the tide, for they failed to cross that night. But the next day Cadwalader crossed at Burlington, to find that Donop had retreated.[17]

The Hessian prisoners were sent to Philadelphia to be paraded in triumph for the sake of animating the patriots and depressing the loyalists. It was a curious scene as they marched up Chestnut Street by Independence Hall, patriot women screaming at them and threatening to choke them, and others trying to give them bread. They were warmly clad in good uniforms; but the patriots troops who guarded them had on summer clothes and some of them were marching barefooted on that cold winter's day.[18]

Four handsome Hessian battle flags had been captured; and one of these, a beautiful silken standard with a lion rampant, and the motto *Nescit Pericula*, was sent to Baltimore to the Congress. They needed all the comfort that could be given to them. They had nearly gone out of existence; and it is curious to reflect that what is now the most powerful government in the world was in January, 1777, hiding itself in a little room in Baltimore and taking a homely and pathetic delight in decorating the wall with a Hessian battle flag.[19]

It was a wonderful success for the patriots; it continued the war when it had almost ceased and the patriot cause was about to expire; it reanimated the whole patriot party; it convinced Europeans of the ability of Washington to seize an opportunity; it was a momentous turning point in the Revolution; and a typical instance of American promptness, energy and good luck.

---

[16] Stryker, *id.*, pp. 194, 195.

[17] Niles, "Principles and Acts of the Revolution," edition 1876, p. 249; Stryker, "Battles of Trenton and Princeton," p. 218.

[18] Stryker, "Battles of Trenton and Princeton," pp. 213, 214; *American Archives*, fifth series, vol. iii, pp. 1429, 1441–1448.

[19] *American Archives*, fifth series, vol. iii, pp. 1507, 1509, 1510.

SUCCESS REANIMATES THE PATRIOTS

It has even been said that the failure of Ewing to cross the river directly in front of Trenton was an advantage; and some have called it a most providential circumstance; for if he had succeeded in crossing during the night, as was intended, he might have found it impossible to conceal his force until Washington's delayed force arrived long after daylight. Ewing had no orders to attack, and his eleven hundred militia were hardly competent to make a successful attack on the Hessians. He might have been seen in crossing, as there was a picket and an outpost close to the shore; and if he had crossed unseen and carried out his orders of stationing himself on the other side of the creek on the south of Trenton, to cut off the escape of the Hessians, they would probably have seen him and have been well prepared long before Washington arrived with the main body. In fact, it has been thought that Washington may not have intended that the movements of Ewing and Cadwalader should be anything more than mere feints on the other side of the river.[20]

---

[20] Stryker, *id.*, pp. 231, 233; "Diary and Letters of Thomas Hutchinson," vol. ii, pp. 139, 140.

LII.

PRINCETON

IMMEDIATELY after the affair at Trenton, Washington returned to the Pennsylvania side of the river, with his prisoners, captured artillery and other spoil. But these being secured and finding no vigorous movement made from New York, he recrossed and again occupied Trenton. It was a very hazardous movement, military men have thought, to thus put his little force between the barrier of the river and the overwhelming force Howe might send to avenge Trenton.

Cornwallis with eight thousand men set out from New York and Washington crossed Assunpink Creek immediately south of Trenton, and entrenched himself along a ridge on the bank of that stream, where he was joined by Cadwalader's force and all the recruits that the greatest exertions of the patriots could send to him. He and his officers were borrowing money on their private credit in order to offer a bounty of ten dollars to all the men who would re-enlist when their term expired on the first of January. Robert Morris sent him $50,000 which he had raised on his own credit from friends of the cause in Philadelphia.[1]

But even with the assistance, Washington was likely to lose half his force on the first of January. He made earnest appeals to them to remain. General Knox addressed them. General Mifflin used all his eloquence. He was famous for his skill in addressing troops and encouraging enlistments; and he now promised that if they would remain six weeks longer they would receive a share of captured property, besides the

---

[1] *American Archives*, fifth series, vol. iii, p. 1514; Stryker, "Battles of Trenton and Princeton," p. 256; Oberholtzer, "Life of Morris," p. 32; Wilkinson, Memoirs, vol. i, pp. 133-135.

ten dollars bounty. At the close of his stirring appeal, fourteen hundred of the ragged bare-footed veterans poised their muskets in token of their assent.

Thus the patriot force was dragged over another crisis, and counting old and new troops, Washington had scraped together about five thousand men. But they were in a somewhat dangerous position, which Washington seemed again determined to fight out or perish in the attempt. How was he to meet Cornwallis, who had left New York with eight thousand men? Cornwallis had reinforced the cantonments on his way, and marched from Princeton on the 2nd of January, 1777, with about fifty-five hundred men to retake Trenton.

Washington had the day before, sent several strong detachments composed largely of Hand's riflemen to harass the enemy on their march from Princeton and dispute every inch of the way. The weather had become milder, and on the night of the 1st of January, it rained heavily, so that on the next day roads deep in mud assisted the riflemen to delay the British march.

Rendered cautious by the vigor of the resistance in front of them from every clump of woods and fence row, Cornwallis consumed the whole day on the march of twelve miles and entered Trenton just before sunset, where the two forces exchanged cannon shots across Assunpink Creek.

It was impossible for Washington to retreat across the Delaware in the presence of the British. To retreat southward along the Jersey shore and take the chances of an opportunity to cross to Pennsylvania was possible, but it would be defeat, would invite pursuit, and possibly the breaking up of the army. To attack the superior disciplined British the next day or allow them to attack, would also be defeat. All the success at Trenton would be undone and the patriot cause would sink back into hopelessness and the old questions of voluntary submission or retreat to the western wilderness would again arise. Any form of retreat must be avoided; and here the delay of the British, and their late arrival in Trenton made an opportunity.

Drawn up along the Assunpink Creek with his left on the

Delaware and facing the British in Trenton, Washington was
in a position to have his right flank turned and be hemmed
into the triangle formed by the creek and the Delaware. The
British officers saw this weakness and discussed the question
of proceeding at once to hem in Washington that night. The
quartermaster-general, Sir William Erskine, said, "If Washington is the general I take him to be he will not be found
there in the morning." But the others agreed with Cornwallis that there was plenty of time, that Washington had
no means of retreat and that they could, without much difficulty, "bag him" in the morning. So sure of this did Cornwallis feel, that he sent no scouts round Washington's right
to give warning of any attempt to retreat.[1]

Washington's headquarters had become untenable from
the fire of the enemy and he called a council of his officers to
meet at the quarters of General St. Clair and consult as to
what should be done in the serious predicament in which they
found themselves. Washington was inclined to hazard an
engagement; but St. Clair, who had had occasion to examine
the roads on the right flank during the day suggested, it is
said, a bold and brilliant solution of their difficulties, which
was at once accepted by Washington and the other officers
and carried out with great promptness.[2]

At midnight they left their camp fires burning, and men
working noisily on entrenchments, and with the rest of the
force, passing out through the way Cornwallis had left un-
guarded, performed the brilliant manœuvre of marching to

---

[1] Cornwallis was, of course, severely criticised in England for this
piece of carelessness. (Stryker, *id.*, pp. 268, 461, 464; Clinton's MS.
notes to Stedman's " American War," vol. i, p. 236.)

[2] The credit of suggesting this successful movement was claimed
by St. Clair, and there is no evidence that Washington ever directly
denied it. (Wilkinson, Memoirs, vol. i, p. 140; St. Clair Papers, vol. i,
pp. 35, 36; G. W. Greene, " Life of Nathanael Greene," vol. i, p. 303;
Stryker, *id.*, p. 273.) In his report of the battle Washington's language
does not necessarily imply that he originated the movement. (Writings
of Washington, Ford edition, vol. v, p. 148.)

the rear of that general and striking his line of communications toward Princeton and New York. In boldness and originality of conception it was worthy of Napoleon.

The weather had changed and grown cold. The mud which had delayed the British advance from Princeton, was frozen hard. The patriots passed over it rapidly, marking it with blood from their naked feet and dragging some light artillery with the wheels wrapped in old cloths to keep the rumbling from being heard.[4]

They reached Princeton about daybreak when three regiments of British reinforcements were starting out to join Cornwallis at Trenton. One of them under Colonel Mawhood, followed by part of another regiment, passed out of Princeton on Washington's left as he entered by another road. Mawhood was riding a brown pony with his two favorite spaniels frisking about him. Seeing the Americans entering the village, he turned back and attempted to seize a good position along a hedge-row. A patriot brigade under Mercer reached it first and fired at the close range of only about thirty yards. The British then performed their favorite movement of instantly charging before the patriots could reload, and they drove them back with the bayonet, killing Colonel Haslet of the famous Delaware regiment, and mortally wounding Mercer, who fought with his sword and refused to surrender because they called him a rebel.

Having few bayonets, Mercer's men were driven back to the top of a ridge where Washington rallied them in person, within thirty yards of the enemy. Mifflin's and Cadwalader's troops and Hand's riflemen, rushed to the rescue and there was a hot fight for some minutes. The British charged with courage and precision; but they were effective only with the bayonet. Their marksmanship was ridiculous. They could scarcely, as some one has said, hit a barn when they were inside of it. Their artillery fired over the heads of· their

---

[4] *Pennsylvania Magazine of History*, vol. 20, p. 515; Lee, Memoirs, vol. i, p. 273 note.

en'emy; while almost every shot from the American guns was true, and the fire of the riflemen was so deadly, that "the British screamed as if so many devils had got hold of them." Their charges were all repulsed with heavy loss; and Mawhood was only too glad to draw off his men, abandon his artillery and continue his march to join Cornwallis at Trenton, pursued for several miles by the patriots who in this "fox chase" as Washington called it captured fifty of his men.[5]

The other regiment and a half of British, which were left in Princeton, fought for awhile in the college buildings, and the light battery commanded by young Alexander Hamilton, sent some shots into Nassau Hall which retains the marks of them to this day. These British also made a stand outside of Princeton; but the superior numbers of the Americans soon sent them in full retreat to New York.

The battle, from the modern point of view, was a small affair. The engagement with Mawhood is said to have lasted hardly twenty minutes; and the troops engaged in that affair and in the fighting in the streets of Princeton were only about four thousand or five thousand Americans against some two thousand British. But coupled with Trenton as part of a sudden success in the midst of overwhelming defeat, it aroused great rejoicing among the patriots, and deserves all that has been said of it.

The artist Trumbull, who served as a patriot officer in the Revolution, regarded the moment when Washington saw how he could escape from before Cornwallis, and attack Princeton as the acme of his career; and in the perhaps over-idealized

---

[5] The American loss was about forty killed and wounded and the British loss has been variously estimated at from 400 to 600 killed, wounded, and prisoners. (Stryker, *id.*, p. 292; Writings of Washington, Ford edition, vol. v, pp. 148, 151; "Life of George Read," pp. 328, 250; Wilkinson, Memoirs, vol. i, pp. 141–150.) See as to the bayonet *American Archives*, fifth series, vol. i, pp. 887, 1065. The British soldiers aimed so badly that they had to shoot cattle, it is said, by platoon fire. ("Correspondence of Henry Laurens," p. 25.)

but, in many ways, valuable portrait which Trumbull painted, he represented Washington at the supreme instant of the first thought of this manœuvre.[6]

When Cornwallis awoke in the morning and found that his enemy had eluded him and had gone to the rear by a movement of such originality as to be entirely outside of the scope of the British military mind, he was greatly alarmed about his communications, the valuable stores and the £70,000 in the military chest at Brunswick. He started at once with his whole force to save them, and "in a most infernal sweat," as his enemies delighted to relate, and indulging in not a little profanity, hastened to catch up with the patriots.

Less than a month before Howe had spent over two days in pursuing Washington from New Brunswick to Trenton; but now Cornwallis, with the fear of losing the £70,000 before his eyes, made the march from Trenton to New Brunswick in exactly one day. He was close on the heels of Washington, who was destroying bridges and throwing every obstacle in his way. General Lee was supposed to be imprisoned at New Brunswick; and if the patriots could capture the money chest and also rescue Lee, it would be such a success that Washington thought it might put an end to the war.

But there was a limit to human endurance. The ragged and barefooted patriot troops had been marching and fighting for nearly forty-eight hours, and were falling asleep in the intense cold by the roadside. Washington hesitated. He did not wish to lose the superb advantage he had already gained by aiming at too much. He called a council of his officers, and some were inclined to take the shortest safe road to the Delaware and cross back into Pennsylvania. But an officer suggested turning northward into the heart of New Jersey, and taking up a very strong position on high ground which he

---

[6] Stryker, *id.*, p. 263. Frederick the Great said that Washington's achievements in those ten days, from the 25th of December to the 4th of January were the most brilliant recorded in military annals (Stryker, *id.*, p. 464.).

knew of at Morristown, west of New York, and half way between New York and the Delaware.[7]

Cornwallis was intent only on saving the money and supplies. If the patriots had reached new Brunswick ahead of him and captured the money chest he would have been the most outwitted and disgraced general in history. Having reached New Brunswick he was content to secure that place and Amboy. All the rest of New Jersey was abandoned, and Putnam came from Philadelphia with a few patriot militia and occupied Princeton without molestation for the rest of the winter and spring. During the same time Washington remained quietly at Morristown. He had destroyed three British outposts, nearly captured a fourth; and Howe made no attempt to restore them. For the next five months Washington, with only about six thousand men, which at times sank to only three thousand, held two widely separated posts in New Jersey, while Howe remained totally inactive with twenty-eight thousand men at New York, Amboy and New Brunswick. So quiet and secure was it at Morristown, that Mrs. Washington and other wives of patriot officers came to the camp to join their husbands. The Congress also left Baltimore and returned to Philadelphia, where, as sometimes happens in a revolution, there was a scene of gaiety, speculation and extravagance strangely inconsistent with the poverty and rags of the patriot army.[8]

That "these wonderful days in New Jersey" were a bitter disappointment to loyalists and Englishmen, goes without saying. But there was one person who seems to have been supremely indifferent and undisturbed and that was General Howe. Washington had now taken his measure and under-

---

[7] It is disputed whether the officer who made this suggestion was Greene, Knox, or St. Clair. Stryker, *id.*, p. 300; Gordon, "American Revolution," edition 1788, vol. ii, p. 402; St. Clair Papers, vol. i, p. 42; Drake, "Life of Knox," pp. 38, 40.

[8] G. W. Greene, "Life of Nathanael Greene," vol. i, pp. 309, 356; Jones, "New York in the Revolution," vol. i, p. 170; Stedman, "American War," vol. i, pp. 239–241.

stood his methods. For the rest of the British general's year and a half in America, the patriot general, no matter how low his force dwindled, always remained encamped within a few miles of the vast host of his Whig antagonist undisturbed and unpursued. There was no need of retreating among the Indians and the buffalo of the West.

That was a marvellous winter in New York with a gorgeously caparisoned army far outnumbering the population of the town in time of peace. Thousands of loyalists crowded into the town as a city of refuge, and their newspapers constantly assured them of the impossibility of American independence and the absurdity of American self-government by mob rule and tar and feathers. They had their concerts, plays, balls and charades, their coffee houses and their taverns with a band of music playing God Save the King.*

But the poor loyalists outside the town, as a British officer informs us, were not so fortunate.

> "Several good families whom their armies have ruined come daily shivering for our protection, and meet with such a reception, according to their stations, as can only be obtained from clemency guided by order and economy. Many of the poor ladies have scarce a petticoat to cover them, being stripped of furniture, apparel, and everything that could make a Yankee soldier either a shirt or a pair of breeches." ("A Letter from an Officer in New York," London, 1777, p. 2.)

Judge Jones, who spent that winter in New York, has left us a graphic and indignant description of the opportunities for money making which were allowed in the British army. The commissaries, quartermasters, barrack masters, engineers, and their assistants and followers, were making prodigious fortunes by the most wholesale fraud. The loyalists about New York had supplied the invading army with horses and wagons in the campaign of 1776, and were cheated out of their payment. In the campaign of 1777 they again supplied the horses and wagons, and were again defrauded. The quartermaster,

---

*Van Tyne, "Loyalists of the American Revolution," pp. 251–265.

571

Judge Jones says, netted for himself £150,000 out of that campaign and retired to England a rich man. His successor made another fortune. During the seven years of the war, four quartermasters in succession returned with fortunes varying from £150,000 to £200,000. These were enormous sums in those times, fully the equivalent of three million dollars in our day. The fifth quartermaster was stopped halfway on his road to a fortune by the arrival of Sir Guy Carleton to take command in 1782.

Howe's favorite engineer received for merely levelling the patriot fortifications about New York a fortune, with which he retired and bought a town house and a country seat. His successor was given greater opportunities. The barrack-masters seized private houses, public buildings, and churches, for which, of course, they paid nothing, and rented them to the army. They cut down the oak and hickory forests all round New York and for sixty miles along the Sound, selling two-thirds of a cord to the army at the price of a cord, sixteen to twenty-eight shillings, and selling the fraudulently reserved third to the loyalists at £4 and £5 for two-thirds of a cord. Like the quartermasters and engineers, they too became nabobs of the West. And then there were commissaries of forage, commissaries of cattle, and commissaries of artillery, not to mention the commissaries of prisoners, together with all their dependents, male and female, who enjoyed a perfect carnival of plunder and wealth.[20]

Meantime, light and hope for the patriots began to appear in France, although few besides the secret committee of the Congress knew of the favorable turn of affairs. That committee had sent Silas Deane to France. The French court would not enter into a war with England; but they would assist the Americans by sending from Holland £200,000 worth of arms and ammunition to St. Eustatius, or other ports in the

---

[20] Jones, " New York in the Revolution," vol. i, chap. xvi; " Thoughts on the Present War," etc., p. 51, 1783; Stedman, " American War," vol. i, p. 311, London, 1794; Stevens, " Fac-similes of MSS.," vol. vii, p. 707.

West Indies, and from the governors of these places the Americans could obtain them by asking for Monsieur Hortalez.[11]

Hortalez and Company was the firm name Beaumarchais had assumed; and under this name he carried on in appearance a peaceful mercantile business in Paris. But the money was furnished him by the French Government and his cargoes went to the Americans. He was a strange character, watchmaker, speculator, adventurer, the author of "The Barber of Seville" and "The Marriage of Figaro," still a distinguished light of French literature, and filled at that time with the most devoted enthusiasm for the patriots under Washington.

But the Congress wanted more important assistance from France than supplies of arms and clothing. They wanted the French King to make a treaty of alliance with America and declare war against England. The Congress, accordingly voted on the 30th of December, just before the battle of Princeton, that the European powers might rest assured that the Congress would maintain American independence and not compromise with Great Britain, that if France would assist with her army and fleet in capturing the fishing banks and the islands of New Foundland and Cape Breton, those valuable fisheries should henceforth be held in common by the United States and France to the exclusion of all other nations, and half the island of New Foundland should be ceded to France. All the West India islands that should be taken from England should also belong to France. At the same time the Congress voted that if Spain would declare war against Great Britain the United States would assist in securing for Spain the town of Pensacola in Florida, and would also, under certain circumstances, assist Spain in a war against Portugal.[12]

In September the Congress had appointed Franklin and Jefferson to go to France as commissioners and join Silas Deane in the work of negotiating with the French Court. The

[11] *American Archives*, fifth series, vol. ii, pp. 818–822, and title " Silas Deane " in index of *Archives*.

[12] Journals of the Congress, Ford edition, vol. vi, pp. 1054–1058.

ill-health of Jefferson's wife compelled him to decline, and Arthur Lee, who was already acting as agent for the Congress in Europe, was elected in his place. On the 26th of October, 1776, Franklin left Philadelphia and with his two grandsons drove some fifteen miles down the Delaware to Marcus Hook, where the "Reprisal" a swift war-ship of the Congress, awaited him.[13]

The "Reprisal" and Wicks, her captain, afterwards became famous in the Revolution for their numerous prizes and persistent good luck. Franklin, too, was a lucky man and with him on board the fleet "Reprisal" outsailed all the British cruisers, made the voyage to Quiberon Bay on the coast of France in thirty-three days, and as she entered the bay captured two British vessels loaded with lumber, wine, brandy and flaxseed, which when sold, together with a small cargo of indigo carried in the "Reprisal," would go to pay the expenses of the mission to France.

Franklin already famous in that country as a man of science and a philosopher, was now arriving in the midst of that excitable people in the most unexpected and romantic manner; fresh from the American wilderness and the rebellion; and coming in with two great merchantmen as prizes, which were to pay his way in the world of European diplomacy. It was like a scene from the Arabian Knights, and the French received him with an outburst of enthusiasm which never abated during the nine years of his residence among them.[14]

---

[13] *American Archives*, fifth series, vol. ii, pp. 1198, 1212–1216, 1237.
[14] *American Archives*, fifth series, vol. iii, pp. 1117, 1118, 1197.